William Shenstone

Facsimile of the Frontispiece to Volume I. of his
"Works in Verse and Prose," 1764.

The Letters of
William Shenstone

*Arranged and Edited with Introduction,
Notes and Index*

by MARJORIE WILLIAMS

BASIL BLACKWELL
OXFORD
1939

Printed in Great Britain for BASIL BLACKWELL & MOTT LTD.
by the KEMP HALL PRESS LTD. in the City of Oxford

PREFACE

In editing this volume which contains the Letters of William
Shenstone, I have been confronted with various difficulties.
Something more than a third of the letters have never been
published before. Manuscripts have been carefully copied and
Shenstone's peculiarities, of which there are many, fully preserved, underlining of words and parts of words being shown
by italics. The letters to Thomas Percy in the British Museum
were published by D^r. Hans Hecht but have been newly
copied by me in their entirety. Many letters have come from
private collections and some from collections such as those in the
Assay Office Library in Birmingham and in the Library of the
Society of Antiquaries; many have come from American
Libraries. The source of each at the time when it was copied
has been indicated at the head of the letter and to all who have
been kind enough to help me in discovering them I express my
thanks. Two printed collections are represented, that of
Thomas Hull, printed in two volumes in 1778, under the title
*Select Letters between the late Duchess of Somerset, Lady Lux-
borough, Miss Dolman, Mr. Whistler, Mr. R. Dodsley, William
Shenstone Esq. and others*, and that of Dodsley, which formed
the third volume of Shenstone's collected *Works* and was first
published by J. Dodsley in 1769. The editors of these volumes
had their own peculiarities and I have carefully preserved these.
In showing W.S.'s habit of underlining, they have both
indicated that the whole word has been underlined. Manuscript letters prove that this was seldom Shenstone's method,
if the word 'method' can be applied at all to his underlining. As
the plate giving an example of his handwriting shows, he
underlined words quite erratically, emphasising a letter or two,
or an indefinite part of the word, without rhyme or reason.
However, as he intended nothing complicated, I have adopted
italics for the whole word, in all cases.

Moreover, the first editors obviously printed from a second
draft of a letter, on occasion, nor were their editorial methods
as scrupulous as those demanded of a twentieth century editor.

That the letters printed by Dodsley and Hull are tampered with is an indisputable fact. Writing to Dodsley, November 17, 1767, Richard Jago said, "Mr. Graves & I have exchanged some letters on the subject I mentioned to you. He says he has about 150 of Mr. Shenstone's Letters, some of which he has lately shown to the Bp. of G. who in a cover in which they were enclosed wrote 'Letters like these cannot fail to please.' " Mr. Graves adds however that he 'believes that these were some of the most interesting of the whole Number, & expresses many Fears, and Difficulties concerning their Appearance; some grounded on a Point of Delicacy relating to the printing of private Correspondence; and others relating to the Privacy of Mr. S— situation, and the Want of great Variety, and uncommon Events in the Subject of the Letters themselves. These Objections I have in a good Measure encountered, but as he has a very great Charge upon his hands & but little Leisure, and as I told him that the whole of the Correspondence must not only be carefully revised by us, but also transcribed for reasons wch I have given, he will not think of undertaking without having some assurance beforehand of reaping some Benefit from it, and he has enquired of me what Terms we may expect.'

I have sometimes given two manuscript versions of a letter to prove that W.S. did make copies of his letters—and these with airs and variations. I have, moreover, sometimes given Dodsley's version beside Hull's and both beside the manuscript version, to amuse the curious in editorial method. After a good many years' search, I have not found the originals of a large number of letters and it may be that I shall be confronted with one of the greatest disappointments an editor of letters experiences—the volume being published, the originals may turn up.

Shenstone himself, and his first editors in a greater degree, used dashes to indicate names which for some reason or other they wished to suppress. I have usually been successful in elucidating political or literary references, though I have seen little possibility of deciding in all cases the name of the person mentioned; especially is this true in connection with the letters dealing with a visit to Cheltenham in 1743. For instance we

find mention of a certain Mrs. A . . . and in the circle there was
a Mrs. Aubrey and the wife of one Mr. Arnold. The reference
to Miss C. . . . is baffling and I see no likelihood of deciding
whether the lady in question is Miss Carter or Miss Carrington. Mr. M . . . may be either Mr. Marriett or Mr. Meredith.
Mr. D . . . may be, as far as the context shows, Mr. Dean or
Mr. Davenport. At Whitchurch Shenstone dined at 'Mr.
W . . .'s and once at Mr. W . . .'s.' It is impossible to decide at
what point he is referring to Mr. Whistler and at what point
to Mr. Walker, the former's step-father. Lady Luxborough
was puzzled by a letter from W.S. on one occasion and he
wrote 'The person whose name I wrote with a Dash was not
Mr. Meredyth but Mr. Miller.' Moreover in such cases, I
have come to the conclusion that the matter is worth no long
search.

The reader will see that I have modified Dodsley's dating of
the letters as the date he gives is often manifestly wrong. In
this I have been much helped by the work of two American
scholars, J. E. Wells and J. F. Fullington, and I here acknowledge my debts, with gratitude. Usually notes make my reason
for placing the letter quite clear.

Sometimes letters contain no definite date and no historical or literary allusions to help in fixing it. In these instances
I have placed letters where they seem by their contents best to
fit. For example the reader will hear a definitely summer tone
in some letters and an equally definite winter tone in others.
The weather and solitude affected W.S. Sequence however
matters curiously little in the letters Shenstone wrote. Thomas
Hull noted in 1778, 'The accurate Reader will discover some
Letters erroneously placed in Point of Date, owing principally
to some Copies not being received early enough for their proper
Situations; but as no Chain of Events is interrupted, it is
hoped the Error may easily be excused.'

Wherever possible, I have kept Dodsley's sub-titles, as they
are most picturesque.

Finally I should like to thank especially Professor Morley
for the unstinted help she has always given to me. I also desire
to express my gratitude to Professor Dewar for his kind
interest; to Mr. Havelock Ellis; Mr. A. C. Coldicott of

Beaudesert, who knows everything there is to be known about the neighbourhood of Barrels; Mr. Watkin-Jones for handing on to me information he had collected in American Libraries: Mr. Arthur Westwood of the Assay Office Library, Birmingham, and to my sister, Miss W. R. Williams, who helped with my index and has patiently assisted me on every possible occasion. Mr. Dudley Wright's work—checking of proof sheets and arrangement of index—has been invaluable.

Without substantial grants from the University of London Publication Fund and from the Royal Society of Literature, the printing of Shenstone's letters would have been impossible and I here record my very grateful thanks to these two bodies.

Guildford, December 1938.   M.W.

CONTENTS

LIST OF PLATES

INTRODUCTION

WE who live in the heat and bustle of the twentieth century cannot help envying the leisure of a period when time was found to make more than one copy of a letter and to execute little drawings to illustrate the text. Such things give a unique flavour to letters like those of William Shenstone and the present editor hopes that readers will savour that taste and find it palatable. W.S. was a prince of letter writers and with justification looked upon his letters as some of his chefs-d'œuvre, being considerably angered when he learned that those to his friend Whistler had been destroyed at the latter's death. Writing to Graves he said, 'I confess to you that I am considerably mortified by Mr. W——'s conduct in regard to those Letters; and, rather than they should have been so unnecessarily destroyed, would have given more money than it is allowable for me to mention with decency. I look upon my Letters as some of my chef-d'œuvres; and could I be supposed to have the smallest pretensions to propriety of style or sentiment, I should imagine it must appear principally in my Letters to his brother, and one or two more friends. I consider them as the records of a friendship that will be always dear to me, and as the history of my mind for these twenty years past.'

It is well in introducing a correspondence to mention the chief events in the life of its author, though, in Shenstone's case, they were about as important, so he told Jago, as the tinsel on his (Jago's) little boy's hobby horse.

He was born at The Leasowes, Halesowen, near Birmingham, the elder of the two sons of Thomas Shenstone. His mother was Anne Penn of Harborough, and she came of a family of some note in the neighbourhood. Johnson attributes W.S.'s melancholy to the fact that he lived in retirement near the scenes of the former magnificence of his family. He went to school at Solihull and met Richard Jago of Beaudesert, with whom he struck up a life-long friendship. About the same time he came to know William Somervile of Edstone, on the Stratford road. He went up to Pembroke College, Oxford, and a close friendship began with Richard Graves, author of *The Spiritual Quixote*, and with Anthony Whistler, a gentleman of some wealth, who later dabbled in poetry but irritated Shenstone by his dilettante attitude towards 'that thing called taste.'

He made no mark while he was at Pembroke, the 'nest of singing birds,' which sheltered Samuel Johnson and, among others of scarcely less note, George Whitefield and William Blackstone. He left the university without academic honours and retired to 'solitude & the country,' having inherited The Leasowes on the death of his father in 1724. From Oxford however he took the warm affection of his friends and in the letters which he wrote to them he reveals himself fully. The events of his life, I have said, were few, but he tells of these in such an engaging manner that we lose ourselves in the tranquil recital of the daily happenings in the life of a gentleman of taste in the mid eighteenth century.

After he had settled at The Leasowes he seldom left it save to visit Lady Luxborough at Barrels, to spend a few days 'in an agreeable loiter' at the home of one or other of his closest friends, or to go to London, to lodge with Mr. Wintle, Mr. Shuckburgh or Mr. Gosling, yet wishing to be considered 'as a man of the world, & endeavouring to elicit that pleasure from gaiety, which my reason tells me I shall never find.' While he was young, he snatched at joy and was worried because he had only '4 or 5 whimsical years left.' Charming as are his letters describing the delights to be found in London, in its theatres, coffee-houses and streets, we feel that the gay metropolis was not really his milieu. He complained at The Leasowes that he was 'forced to die in a rage, like a poisoned rat in a hole' and said 'my soul is no more suited to the figure I make . . . than a cable rope to a cambric needle.' But he was never truly happy except when pottering in his garden, feeding his wild ducks, watering his carnations, supervising his labourers, or spending a leisurely hour in polishing his verse, in writing of this reading or that to one of his friends, looking over his collection of prints or coins, painting flowers, designing cuts, enjoying a new book with his brother Joseph who lived with him, visiting a friend who resided at an easy distance, or receiving some fashionable callers. For after he set his hand to beautify his paternal home, to make a fine landscape garden which should show some of the beauties of the Italian landscape painters on the face of nature, the number and magnificence of his visitors increased daily.

His first poems were printed while he was still at Oxford in 1737, and the volume contained the first draft of *The Schoolmistress* which was printed in an enlarged version in 1742. The letters tell the story of his literary output and give a minute account of at any rate two great ventures of the age in which he lived—Dodsley's *Collection of Poems by Several Hands* and Percy's *Reliques of Ancient English Poetry*. They tell too of those literary friendships which meant so much to him and contain a considerable amount of criticism of the writings of his contemporaries and of that of older tried writers, which shows a keenness of insight rare at the time at which he wrote. Indeed his contribution to the history of criticism is by no means negligible.

From 1745 onwards gardening was the most absorbing of his occupations. He was encouraged by visits from his neighbours at Hagley and more especially by the interest of William Pitt. By the men of his own generation Shenstone was accepted as the best exponent of the methods of picturesque gardening which had caught the imagination of all who had any pretensions to refinement and his advice was sought by many who desired to figure as men of cultured pursuits and hobbies. Robert Dodsley thus described the achievement at The Leasowes: 'Far from violating its natural beauties, Mr. Shenstone's only study was to give them their full effect. And although the form in which things now appear be indeed the consequence of much thought and labour, yet the hand of art is no way visible either in the shape of the ground, the disposition of trees, or (which are here so numerous and striking) the romantic fall of his cascades.'

So he filled his days, pointing his prospects, winding his waters, or with the help of his ever faithful servant Tom, building a root-house to be dedicated to my Lord Stamford or a gothic bench to bear the name of a departed friend, beautifying the Lover's Walk by a judiciously placed urn or supervising the erection of the 'ruinated Priory' for no garden was complete in the eighteenth century without the ruin, which was to give to the scene a pleasant air of the antique.

By his work as a landscape gardener Shenstone became famous and the taste shown by the owner of The Leasowes was accepted as the most refined example of the age. 'England has produced many greater poets than Shenstone,' wrote Hugh Miller, 'but she never produced a greater landscape gardener.' The lords, his neighbours, courted him as his estate became fashionable and he spent much time going from great house to great house to give advice on the laying out of grounds. His letters, as time passes, become more contented in tone and fuller of a quiet pride in his growing intercourse with the aristocracy. He had just paid a visit to Lord Stamford at Enville when he was seized with 'the putrid fever' which ended his life in 1763, at the moment when a pension was about to confer on him the public recognition for which he longed.

He wrote letters, so he tells us, to please himself, and like all good letters, they fully reveal the man, the manner ever being more important than the matter. He was dull when his friends left him—'I have ruined my happiness by conversing with you (i.e. Graves) & a few more friends; as Falstaff says to Hal, "Company, *witty* company, has been the ruin of me".'—he changed his 'Pleasure' to 'Amusement' when left without a kindred soul to whom he could talk, and so he sat down, pen in hand, to open his heart in no casual outpouring. In spite of the apparent spontaneity of his letters, he was a most self-conscious letter-writer. 'I seriously approve of egotism in letters,' he said and 'I love letters written at different Periods *myself*.' So he 'soothed' himself as his epistles grew, those for transport to Barrels being sent finally to Mr. Williams, 'painter in Birmingham.' Mr. Williams was, according to Emme, the Halesowen postwoman, 'the pleasantest spoken man in all the Waurld.' In return she brought W.S. 'a good sizeable Packet.' Writing to Graves he said, 'I beg you will write me a long letter ... & contrive, if you can, to make it look like a packet, as your last did, for the sight thereof is exceedingly comfortable.' Shenstone's was an artistic temperament that was never secure in its own happiness. Tranquil as were his days in his own home, he fretted because his means were small and, because he could not indulge a somewhat extravagant taste, he longed for a chat with one of his near friends for he found his neighbours uninteresting. 'I *do* hate all hereabouts already, except one or two.' 'The human goose is neither fit to be heard nor eaten.' Yet we love best to think of Shenstone among his neighbours, doing a small kindness to this man or that, his plain face lighting up the while with benevolence, as we are told it did, interested in the affairs of the parish in which he lived, exchanging a visit with young John Scott Hylton of Lepall, when the talk was all of trifles dear to the heart of the virtuoso, a standish, some new shoe-buckles, a snuff box, Birmingham 'toys,' or the tobacco-stopper made from Shakespeare's mulberry tree. We feel most fully the peculiar charm of Shenstone when we see him against the background of The Leasowes, receiving Lord Dudley with 'his upper servants' who went round the walks 'en famille,' uplifted because Lady Luxborough came with a small retinue to stay with him for some days. He felt some pride at the sight of a coach with a coronet at his door and duly recorded the warmth of his feelings in letters to Graves and Jago. A call from the Lytteltons and their aristocratic guests who gave suggestions anent the laying out of his 'environs,' engaged Shenstone's thoughts pleasurably for some time.

The letters to his most considerable correspondent, Lady Luxborough, Lord Bolingbroke's half-sister and a 'lady of quality' reveal the man more fully than do any others. We see him in his 'refined solitude'—'refinement is an endless thing' —writing of all the things that interested him with a simplicity often lacking in letters to more scholarly friends—Lady Luxborough had no use for a Latin quotation—'I remember y^t you never own'd yourself acquainted with ye Pedantry of Latin Phrases, or ye antique turn of expressions in *that Language*.' Rather she preferred the chit-chat he poured out without order or arrangement. 'I beg Pardon for grouping the particulars of this Page.' The details grouped included enquiries after her ladyship's health,—he hoped she was 'on the mending hand,'—a few words about quill pens and their use, comments on the dinner he had had with the aldermen of

Halesowen, advice on urns and their disposition, remarks on 'the abele that imitates the waterfall' and the writers in Lord Orford's ministry. His letters gave both the recipient and the writer infinite pleasure and after he had written with evident enjoyment of improvements which might be carried out in the gardens at Barrels, he would conclude with pardonable pride with a list of his own fashionable visitors and 'I will release you from this unpleasing scrawl . . . though I mean to write again soon.' Even then he found it necessary to add a postscript.

Shenstone really longed for human society, though he prided himself on his 'finical taste' and sought to develop a philosophy which should make him rise superior to loneliness. 'Indolence will, in a thousand instances, give one all the advantages of philosophy.' He liked the companionship of his fellows, and in spite of virtuoso leanings felt that 'all attachments to inanimate beauties, to curiosities and ornaments, satiate us presently.' This desire for intercourse makes his letters what they are. He was alone and shared his thoughts with an absent friend in the letter he wrote. 'Now I am come home from a visit —every little uneasiness is sufficient to introduce my whole train of melancholy considerations, & to make me utterly dissatisfied with the life I now lead, & the life which I foresee I shall lead. I am angry, & envious, & dejected, & frantic, & disregard all present things, just as becomes a madman to do. . . . I cannot bear to see the advantages alienated, which I think I could deserve & relish so much more than those that have them—Nothing can give me patience but the soothing sympathy of a friend, & *that* will only turn my rage into simple melancholy—I believe soon I shall bear to see nobody. . . . As Mr. G— complained to me (and, I think, you too, both unjustly), "I am no character"—I have in my temper some rakishness, but it is checked by want of spirits; some solidity, but it is broke in upon by laziness, imagination, & want of memory, &c—I could reckon up twenty things throughout my whole circumstances wherein I am thus tantalized—Your fancy will present them—Not that all I say here will signify to *you:* I am only under a fit of dissatisfaction, and to grumble does me good—only excuse me, that I cure myself at your expence.' So we get to know him and the little world in which he moved, the world of the hopes and aspirations of an egotist perhaps, but of one who always had time to give a helping hand and a friendly word to others less fortunate than himself, and one who reveals himself as a singularly charming person. Undoubtedly his reputation should rest finally on his letters for while few appreciate him as a poet and some only enjoy the flavour of his pensées in *Men and Manners*, many will muster an affection for the man who shows himself in his correspondence and learn to love the letters as they learn to love the author. As Dodsley said in his preface to the first published edition of the letters, 'They will not fail . . . to afford an agreeable entertainment to such as can relish an animated display of the various efforts of a fine Imagination for a length of years, whether amusing itself with rural embellishments, or occupied in other pleasures of learned retirement, and a warm disinterested friendship.' The original editor thought the public would be pleased 'to be furnished with such genuine examples of the Author's style and sentiments, together with an authentic history of his mind, for so long a space of time. The talents of this Author, on whatever subject they were exercised, were so uncommon, & the fame of his little Ferme ornée under the conduct of a taste entirely original, was become so considerable, that every specimen of the one, and every anecdote relative to the improvement of the other, seemed too interesting to be buried in oblivion.'

In a style which is entirely adequate, the letters record the passing moods of an eighteenth century man of taste, we get to know intimately the inner circle of his friends and enjoy the account of the activities of a small literary coterie living in Warwickshire or on its borders; we follow the fortunes of men moving in the larger world of literature or fashion, Robert Dodsley, the Duchess of Somerset, Joseph Spence, Thomas Percy, Thomas Hull; we take more than a fleeting interest in those to whom Sir George Lyttelton introduced him, James Thomson, 'that sweet-sould bard,' the Pitts and Admiral Smith.

Shenstone's letters were certainly written with an eye to possible publication yet they have all the art which conceals art, and as examples of 'propriety of style & sentiment,' enter-

taining as well as psychologically revealing, are of unusual
interest. He laid no claim to fine writing, 'generally the effect
of spontaneous thoughts & a laboured style.' 'The style of
letters should not rise higher than the style of refined conversation.' 'I hate a style as I do a garden, that is wholly flat &
regular.' His letters tell of the sweets to be found in rustic
surroundings, simple homes and country things and extol
friendship and virtue, they tell of the latest addition to the
ferme ornée or of the stuccoing and decoration of his rooms.
Few have crystallized the vivid impression of the passing
moment more truly than William Shenstone and all he wrote is
the more attractive in that there is an element of the unex-
pected about the man who insisted on wearing his own hair
long before such a thing was considered possible in polite
society. In retirement at The Leasowes he followed the advice
he once gave to Jago, 'I would have you cultivate your garden;
plant flowers, have a bird or two in the hall (they will at least
amuse your children); write now & then a song; buy now &
then a book; write now & then a letter.' The estimate of Lady
Luxborough, written with partiality no doubt, justly sums up
the achievement of W.S. 'You give innocent pleasure to yourself and instruction as well as pleasure to others by the amusements you follow. Your pen, your pencil, your taste & your
sincere unartful conduct in life (things which make you appear
idle) give such an example as it were to be wished might be
more generally followed—few have the capacity, fewer have
the honesty to spend their time so usefully as well as un-
blameably.'

ABBREVIATIONS, ETC., USED IN THIS VOLUME

W.S.: William Shenstone.

Works: *The Works in Verse and Prose of William Shenstone Esq.* Two vols. R. and J. Dodsley, 1764. Vol. III. *Letters.* J. Dodsley. 1769.

Recollection: Richard Graves. *Recollection of Some Particulars in the Life of the late William Shenstone Esq.* Dodsley. 1788.

Hull: Thomas Hull. *Select Letters between the late Duchess of Somerset, Lady Luxborough, Miss Dolman, Mr. Whistler, Mr. R. Dodsley, William Shenstone, Esq. and others.* Two vols. Dodsley. 1778.

Luxborough, Letters: Lady Luxborough. *Letters written by the late Right Honourable Lady Luxborough to William Shenstone, Esq.* J. Dodsley. 1775.

Hecht: Dr. Hans Hecht. *Thomas Percy und William Shenstone.* Strassbourg. 1909.

Courtney: W. P. Courtney. *Dodsley's Collection of Poetry. Its contents and contributors. A chapter in the history of English literature in the eighteenth century.* 1910.

Wyndham: Maud Wyndham. *Chronicles of the Eighteenth Century.* Two vols. 1924.

Anglia, 1911–12: J. E. Wells. *The Dating of Shenstone's Letters.* Anglia, 1911–12, pp. 429–452.

Williams: Marjorie Williams. *William Shenstone—a Chapter in Eighteenth Century Taste.* 1935.

Any editorial addition to the text as it appears in the MS. or, where no MS. has been discovered, as it appears in the work of the first editor, is enclosed in square brackets. If doubtful, the addition is accompanied by a ?.

LIST OF LETTERS

An asterisk denotes that the letter has not been printed before
in any form.

APPENDIX I

APPENDIX II

Hull, I, 1.

To Mr. D[EAN].

Oct. 19, 1736.

I am sorry to put you to an Expence for a trifling Letter at this Distance. It seems too, to give you leave to expect something extraordinary, or uncommon. Whatever is so in my Letters, I am sure, must be on the bad Side. I may however have the greater Power to convince you, that Distance is incapable to separate you from my Thoughts.

I am, at present, in a very refined State of Indolence and Inactivity. Indeed I make little more Use of a Country Life, than to live over again the Pleasures of *Oxford*[1] and your Company. You might convey me a Letter full, would you be so exceedingly good as your Promise. I am vastly self-interested, for I write only to beg a Letter from you, with very small Hopes of your receiving much Pleasure from mine.

I should here give you an Account of the Pleasures we had at M[ickleton][2] but my Paper won't contain it. There was only one wanting, *pour le comble*—you'll be the last to find it out—your Company. I aim at rendering my Letters as odd and fantastical as possible; but when I write to a Person of your elegant character, my Compliments degenerate into downright Truths, just (I was going to say) as the Sun burns bad Wine to Vinegar; but downright Truths are sometimes valuable, though a Person of your Taste might reasonably expect more refined— at least less obvious ones. Sometimes, however, Vinegar has also its Use, though to treat a Gentleman with it entirely may well create a *Nausea*. I fancy my poignant Simile grows stale by this Time. I write to an Intimate and a Man of Sense, whose Good-nature will forgive what his Judgment may find fault with.

I hope your Ring gives you all imaginable Happiness, however fatal it may prove to female Ken. I suspect to hear of you as the finest Performer on the Spinnet in the World. Were I a Poet, I should be highly pleased to celebrate the admirable Conduct of your little Finger—'*Tui Pollices Ictum*,'[3] says *Horace*; vile Pedant that I am! who shall deliver me from the Influence of Formality?

I heard at *Oxford* of the Addition of the Side-Diamonds; I guessed, lest the Splendour should be extinguished by a greater, *où vous sçavez*. I want to see you exceedingly; you are, I assure you, a vast Part of my Pleasure at *Oxford*, as Pope is in the Country; indeed, you might share that Effect with Mr. Pope, would you write. It is a Favour, for which I must grow importunate; notwithstanding which, the Favours I have already received, would make me uneasy, were I not conscious who bestows them.

Of all the moral Virtues, Gratitude is sure the most beautiful; so far from betraying any Thing mean or ignoble in her Behaviour, she has an Air which naturally discovers her Quality—I can't stay to describe her now—It is sufficient that I pay some Sort of Tribute to her, when I call myself Mr. D[ean]'s

Obedient, humble Servant,

W.S.

My humble Service to your Parents—Direct to *Harborough*.[4]

NOTES

[1] W.S. entered Pembroke College, Oxford, as a gentleman commoner, in 1732, and his name remained in the College books for ten years, but after 1736 he seldom resided in Oxford. Graves, *Recollection*, 36. From this biography much of our knowledge of Shenstone is gained.

[2] In Gloucestershire, the home of the Graves family. Richard Graves (1715–1804), author of *The Spiritual Quixote, Columella*, etc., was a lifelong friend of W.S. who was a frequent visitor at Mickleton. Graves, *op. cit.*, 40 and 48.

[3] Cf. Horace, *Odes IV*, 6, 35. Apparently W.S. is quoting from memory, or deliberately adapting the words of Horace. This adaptation is characteristic of much of his quotation, as will be seen throughout the letters.

[4] Near Halesowen, Shropshire. W.S. lived here for a time after he came of age. His mother was Anne Penn, of Harborough, and in after life the poet retained a romantic veneration for the place, commemorated in his *Elegy XV*. Dr. Johnson suggested that Shenstone's melancholy was due to the fact that he lived in retirement near scenes of the former magnificence of his family.

II

Hull, I, 5.

To Miss G[RAVES].[1]

Sent *Oct.* 30, 1736.

I have sent the Patterns, though with far less Expedition than you might expect from one so entirely yours. The truth is, I was sensible how insupportable the Transition must be from your Company to none at all, so contrived to pay several Visits immediately after I had left M[ickleton]. You'll guess how sufficient a Mortification I found even thus. To pass from yours to the Company of dull Aunts and Cousins must needs prove tedious, as the Reverse would be agreeable.

As to the Draughts, I am satisfied in what a ridiculous Light they must appear; it was a Task I was very much unused to, and solicited rather out of an officious Fondness to be employed for you, than any Skill I was conscious of in myself. I must beg Mr. G[raves]'s Pardon for engaging in a Work, wherein he is far my Superior. Such as they are, I beg you would believe they are the best I am capable of. I would rather have my Judgment than Care censured, in any Thing I am employed in for you. You'll be surprized to find them joined with a Paper scrawl'd over with dull Poetry: however, I must confess, as I wrote it to please myself, I sent it, not without Hopes that it might, in an inferior Manner, please you. One may sometimes amuse one's-self with what one can't entirely approve. As I can't flatter myself, your Judgment can excuse, so I can't apprehend your Good-nature will expose me. To vindicate my Character to you, as a Poet, I shall only join these alleviating Circumstances; First, that nothing makes so awkward a Figure in Verse (as well as in some other Respects) as Sincerity. Secondly, that these Lines were wrote when I had no great Flow of Spirits, namely, when I had just left M[ickleton], and you; but I shall want your Patience elsewhere, so will say no more about 'em—only this—that I should not have mentioned Miss L[owe?], were I not persuaded that, as you are entirely free from the other Faults of your Sex, so you are from that of not bearing to hear another commended. It is a Sign of a great Want of Accomplishments, when a Person is continually suspicious of being rivalled; and, for that Part, you may give every One many more than their Due, without the least Danger of being so.

I could not help envying Whistler's[2] Happiness, when I came away; I fancy your Lives have been a constant Round of Delights; I don't know any Neighbourhood more likely to produce 'em. I could reconcile myself, however, pretty well to

Harborough's melancholy Scenes,[3] were I not conscious of such superior Pleasures, *où vous sçavez*. You might convey me a Letter full of them, but you'll, perhaps, think it an impertinent Request. I could set what Value you please on the Favour, though the Pleasure I can't pretend to limit.

I must now break my Letter in as aukwark [sic] a Manner as I take my Leave, which is likewise usually most aukward, where I have most Respect. I'll e'en lay aside further Ceremony in this, as in the other Case, and say no more than that I am,

Madam,

Your humble Servant,

(In the most obsolete Sense)

W.S.

NOTES

[1] Sister of Morgan and Richard Graves. W.S. was, for a time, in love with her. *Recollection*, 46, 47.

[2] Anthony Whistler of Whitchurch, Oxon, a college friend of W.S., author of a mock-heroic poem, *The Shuttlecock*, and of four other poems which appeared in Dodsley's *Collection*, IV, 320–2; V, 60–1. He was, to quote Richard Graves (*Recollection*, 18), 'a young man of great delicacy of sentiment; and though, with every assistance at Eton, he had such a dislike to learning languages, that he could not read the Classics in the original, no one formed a better judgment of them.' Hull prints several letters from Whistler to W.S., which are quite unstudied, and show a spontaneity lacking in the latter's careful replies. Most of W.S.'s letters to Whistler were destroyed at Whistler's death.

Courtney, 141, gives some account of Whistler.

[3] Graves describes Harborough (*Recollection*, 33), as 'situated by the side of a large pond, shaded by venerable oaks and elms; and rendered more solemn by a colony of rooks, who seemed to have been coeval with the worthy family that gave them protection.'

III

Bodleian Library MS. Montagu d. 18.

Hull, II, 63.

[*To* Miss LOWE].[1]

Mad^m.

I fancy I've been condemn'd a thousand times on account of not sending the tunes.—One of 'em was Lent out, & I had not an Opportunity of Fetching it till last week—I don't know whether this Reason will prove sufficient but I assure you 'twas ye Real one. I tore 'em out of my Book & on y^t

Account you have some others with them. I was willing you shou'd have 'em in yᵉ best shape possible, & dare say you'll Improve as much upon 'em as I have degenerated from 'em.— I want exceedingly to hear from you. but you'll scarce think it consistent with a rural reputation to write your self. 'Tis indeed scarce worth while to hazard it to give me ever so great a Pleasure but I cou'd wish you'd here remember the Character of a Town-Lady. Lord! how does Miss Uty.[2] I didn't wonder you shou'd mutually envy each other since you are both so great objects of Envy. More Particularly as Modesty has taught you to think yʳ own Merit small in Comparison with yᵗ. of others. Voilà la seule source de toute envie! I'm surely vastly Impertinent for I'm not Positive you understand French. But I guess'd yᵗ a Lady so Accomplish'd in all other Particulars, might. I fancy you've enjoy'd a vast deal of Agreeable gayety since I left you, whilst I have been wandring about Harboroughs Gloomy walks & Pools like a Shepherd 'Despairing beside a clear stream—Oh I want to know whether, or no, for yᵉ. common good of our Society in particular, as of our Country in general it is & may be Lawfull to admit, without yᵉ usual Number of members being Present at yᵉ solemnity. For I judge it better to lay aside some Part of yᵉ Ceremony yⁿ yᵗ any one shou'd Dye un-initiated. Whether or no as in Baptism[3] I was truly going too Far. I am safe enough let me go wᵗ lengths I will in subscribing my self

The humblest of yʳ Humble Servᵗˢ
W. SHENSTONE.

NOTES

[1]The letter has been placed here as its tone and contents connect it with the previous letter to Miss Graves.

[2]Is this Miss Utrecia Smith of Mickleton, in whom both W.S. and Graves were keenly interested? She died young and an urn to her memory, with an inscription, was placed by Graves in Mickleton Church, while W.S. wrote *Elegy IV*, *Ophelia's Urn. To Mr. G——. Recollection*, and Williams, op. cit.

[3]Several words are struck out here in the MS. and are not legible.

IV   *Works* III, 1.

To Mr. JAGO,[1] *with a Song, and the Author's Sentiments on Musical Composition.*[2]

1739.

Dear Sir,

As my head is considerably more confused than usual, by reason of a bad cold, I shall aim no higher in this letter than at bare *recitative*, reserving all my *airs* for a season when my mind is more in *tune*. Such, I hope, will be the time which you set apart to attend the *chief musician*, at Birmingham. I thoroughly design to lend an *ear* to *his* performance, on condition he will not refuse one to a proposal I intend to make, of having, one day or other, a merry strain at The Leasows. But if you have any *penchant* to see the face of your humble servant at Birmingham, your most effectual way will be to inform him when these solemn nuptials betwixt Tweedle-dum and Tweedle-dee are to be consummated. I will, *certes*, not be absent at the throwing of the stocking, any more than Parson Evans in Shakespeare would be 'absence at the grace.'[3] I have sent a song, not that I am sure I have not sent it before; but that, if you can see any joke that it containeth, the fore-mentioned gentleman may be asked to translate it into music. When I use this expression, you will, peradventure, look upon it as my opinion, that in musical compositions, sound ought as much to answer sense as one language does another, insomuch, that such and such thoughts ought to bring into our heads such and such sounds, and *vice versa*. But in case there is no sense, and no thought, the more languages a sentence is translated into, the more 'tis exposed. And in case it be the misfortune of my little piece to have neither, I beg that Mr. Marriett[4] may not inform any body what it signifies in music. As a farther proof of the confused state of my intellects, you see, almost at the end of my letter, my thanks for the packet, &c. which ought to have been placed in the very front of it, in order to express, in some degree, the sense I have of your favours. I long to see you; and am, dear Sir,

Your most obedient
and faithful servant,
W. SHENSTONE.

SONG

'When bright Ophelia treads the green[5]
'In all the pride of dress and mien;
'Averse to freedom, mirth, and play,
'The lofty rival of the day;
'Methinks to my enchanted eye,
'The lilies droop, the roses die.

'But when, disdaining art, the fair
'Assumes a soft, engaging air:
'Mild as the op'ning morn of May,
'And as the feather'd warblers gay:
'The scene improves where'er she goes,
'More sweetly smile the pink and rose.

'O lovely maid! propitious hear,
'Nor think thy Damon insincere.
'Pity my wild delusive flame:
'For tho' the flowers are still the same,
'To me they languish, or improve,
'And plainly tell me that I love.'

NOTES

[1]Richard Jago (1715–1781), author of *Edge-Hill*, life-long friend of W.S. from his school-days at Solihull. *Recollection*, 27.

[2]W.S. was known to his friends as a lover of music. *Recollection*, 175, 176. 'On the harpsichord, and with his voice (for he played and sung tolerably) he gave everything the most affecting expression.'

[3]*Merry Wives of Windsor*, I, 1.

[4]Possibly Richard Marriett of Alscot, Preston-on-Stour, who died unmarried March 8, 1744. See J. H. Bloom's *Walks round Stratford*, p. 25. According to Bloom the Marrietts had some interest in music for Richard's father left to his daughter Mrs. Lowe a harpsichord. Did Miss Lowe (see ante p. 4) belong to the same family?

[5]'When bright Ophelia treads the green,' was first published, *Works* I, 1764, 157, 'When bright Roxana treads the green.' The version differs from this one at several points.

V

Works III, 24.

To Mr. REYNOLDS.[1]   LEASOWS,[2] 1740.

Dear Sir,—

Wonderful were the dangers and difficulties through which I went, the night I left you at Barels;[3] which I looked upon as ordained by fate for the temporal punishment of obstinacy. It was very kind, and in character, for you to endeavour to deter me from the ways of darkness; but having a sort of *penchant* for needless difficulties, I have an undoubted right to indulge myself in them, so long as I do not insist upon any one's pity. It is true, these ought not to exceed a certain degree; they should be *lenia tormenta;*[4] and I must own the labours I underwent that night, did not come within the bounds which my imagination had prescribed. I cannot forbear mentioning one imminent danger. I rode along a considerable piece of water, covered so close with trees, that it was as probable I might have pursued the channel, which was dangerous, as my way out of it. Or, to put my case in a more poetical light, having by night intruded upon an amour betwixt a Wood-nymph and a River-god, I owed my escape to Fortune, who conveyed me from the vengeance which they might have taken. I put up finally at a little alehouse about ten o'clock, and lay all night awake, counting the cords which supported me, which I could more safely swear to than to either bed or blanket. For farther particulars, see my epistle to the Pastor Fido of Lapworth.[5]—Mr. Graves says, he should be glad to shew you any civilities in his power, upon his own acquaintance; and will serve you as far as his vote goes, upon my recommendation; but is afraid, without the concurrence of some more considerable friends, your chance will be but small *this* year, &c. If the former part of this news gives you any pleasure, I assure you it gives me no less to communicate it; and this pleasure proceeds from a principle which would induce me to serve you myself, if it should ever be in my power.—I saw Mr. Lyttelton last week: he is a candidate for the county of Worcester,[6] together with Lord Deerhust;[7] I hope Mr. Somerville[8] will do him the honour to appear as his friend, which he must at least think second to that of succeeding.

I hear you are commenced chaplain since I saw you. I wish you joy of it. The chaplain's title is infinitely more agreeable than his office; and I hope the scarf, which is expressive of it, will be no diminutive thing, no four-penny-halfpenny piece of ribboning; but that it will

'High o'er the neck its rustling folds display,
'Disdain all usual bounds, extend its sway,
'Usurp the head, and push the wig away.'

I hope it will prove ominous, that my first letter is a congratulatory one; and if I were to have opportunities of sending all such, it would entirely quadrate with the sincere wishes of
Your faithful humble servant,
W. SHENSTONE.
I beg my compliments to Mr. Somerville, Mrs. Knight,[9] and your family.
Leasows, *Aug.* 1740.

NOTES

[1]Probably the Jackie Reynolds of Lady Luxborough's *Letters*, who was chaplain to Lord Somervile, of Somervile's Aston. A John Reynalds (sic) was vicar of Wootton Wawen near Henley-in-Arden during Lady Luxborough's time.

[2]The Leasowes, Halesowen, Shropshire, the small grazing farm belonging to his father, which W.S. converted into a fine landscape garden. *Recollection*, 7.

[3]The home of Lady Luxborough, near Henley-in-Arden, Warwickshire. Here she lived in retirement after her separation from her husband.

[4]Horace, *Odes III*, XXI, 13.

[5]On the road between Birmingham and Henley-in-Arden. According to Robert Hudson's *Memorials of a Warwickshire Parish, Lapworth* (1904), in 1690 Edward Welchman became Rector of Lapworth and died in 1739. In 1736 he left Lapworth for Solihull, but continued Rector of Lapworth till May 19, 1739. William Darby held the living of Lapworth from 1739 to 1757, but he probably never took up his residence there. In 1744, at any rate, Richard Jago was curate in charge, for one of his children was privately baptized. Assuming that he went to Lapworth after Edward Welchman's death, W.S.'s reference is to his friend.

[6]George Lyttelton. See Wyndham, I, 82, and Nash's *History of Worcestershire*. See also *Recollection*, 80: 'In 1740 Mr. Lyttelton stood for the county of Worcester, whose interest Mr. Shenstone warmly espoused; and, I believe, did him more services than might have been expected from a man of his limited fortune and retired way of life. But Mr. Lyttelton's and his father's (Sir Thomas's) political connexions, made a majority of the country gentlemen, both Whigs and Tories (who were united against Sir Robert Walpole), against him; and his Persian Letters, which were written with a freedom to which we were then less accustomed, disgusted the clergy, and made them his adversaries; so that Mr. Lyttelton's not succeeding was not matter of much surprise.'

[7]Son of Lord Coventry—Thomas Henry Coventry, styled Viscount Deerhurst.

[8]William Somervile (1692–1742), poet, author of *The Chace*, of Edstone, between Henley-in-Arden and Stratford-on-Avon.

[9]Henrietta Knight, wife of Robert Knight (son of the cashier of the South Sea Company), and half-sister of Henry St. John, the celebrated Viscount Bolingbroke. Robert Knight was created Baron Luxborough in 1745, and later Earl of Catherlough. For details of Lady Luxborough's life see W. Sichel, *Bolingbroke and his Times*. Vol. II contains a memoir of Lady Luxborough and Bolingbroke's correspondence with her. She was a firm friend of W.S. as their letters show.

VI

Works III, 6.

To a Friend [Rev. R. JAGO], *too ceremoniously declining to purchase a Horse for him*

1739. [*After Sept.* 1740.]

Sir,

I cannot avoid imagining the first part of your letter was mere raillery. I am sure it gave me a good deal of pleasure (for I can bear very well to hear my foibles exposed, though not my faults), and on that account must needs make grateful mention of it. I acknowledge the goodness of the letter which occasioned it, and could not expect that such an ill-formed application could have produced an answer so very oratorical. In the first place, you lay open the subject, or indeed, what you call the offices in which I am pleased to employ you. In the next, you alledge your own inability to enter upon matters of such great concernment. That this is rhetorical, nay, pure rhetoric, I gather from the exordiums of all the declamations that I ever heard in my life. 'Tis, moreover, not uncommon with declaimers to give some reasons why they should not absolutely decline the subject, though they are sensible of their insufficiency (otherwise they might be expected to sit down, and hold their tongues). And this is what you have done, by saying that you are unwilling to dissent from the world in regard to the subjects you are engaged in. That you, therefore, chose to steer a middle course, by that means avoiding the imputation of presumption on the one hand, and indifference on the other. When this is done, you enter gravely upon the subject, and, to give it a greater perspicuity, divide it into two parts. The first part happens to be 'concerning the purchase of *an* horse.' On this occasion, you inform me, that I am in a good country for horses; and secondly, that I have a number of acquaintance round about me, who are very well skilled in the nature of them. Now each of these informations seems, at first sight, to mean no more than what I have better opportunities of knowing than the person who informs me, and, on this account, to err in point of superfluity. But, upon second thoughts, they have *this force* (to speak like a grammarian); namely, that I am entirely negligent of my own affairs; and, secondly, that I care not whom I give trouble to, if I can but avoid it myself; so that the sentences have really a beauty, when one searches beneath their superficies. After you have said this and more, which includes all that can be said upon the subject, you descend to the second division, in relation to which I am too grateful to be otherwise than *serious* in my acknowledgments.

I had not expatiated thus far but to shew, that I am not insensible of a sneer; nor should I expatiate any farther but to prove, that I am equally sensible of a favour.

I desire you would believe, that I absolutely assent to your critique. That some of your sentiments were my own before I communicated the verses; and others, as soon as you had favoured me with the discovery of them. That I would, *per præsentes*, return my thanks for them; which you might justly have claimed, whether I had approved them or not. One exception to this approbation my modesty bids me mention, on account of your too great partiality in my favour. My gratitude you are entitled to without exception or limitation.

It will, perhaps, gratify your curiosity to know, that Mr. G[raves] has a copy of verses in the last magazine, entitled, 'The little Cur.' There are several strokes that are picturesque and humourous; I believe it was done in haste. The motto is exquisite, and much more properly applied by Mr. G. than the Emperor Adrian,[1] in my opinion, notwithstanding all that Pope says. Tell me your judgement of Mr. L[yttelto]n's in the same paper.[2] The epigram 'To one who refused to walk in the Park, &c.'[3] is a good one.

I have waved sending the verses to Mr. Somervile at present because I hope to see you soon either at The Leasows or at Birmingham. I can't tell whether I shall have time to inclose in this letter my ballad.[4] If I do, consider it only as some words that I chuse to make use of to some notes of which I am more than ordinarily fond.[5] It is as much designed for my own singing (in private I mean) as ever was a bottle of cherry-brandy for an old woman's drinking. Now I think of it, I really believe that I every day approach nearer and nearer to the capacity, the way, the insignificancy, of an old woman. Mrs. Arnold[6] has certainly, by her *charms*, her incantations, and her conversations together, contributed a good deal to this transformation. Pray come over if you can, and try to reinstate me in my right mind, in proportion to the soundness of which I shall be more and more

Your friend and servant,

W.S.

NOTES

[1]*Gentleman's Magazine*, Sept. 1740.

On a favourite Little Cur,

Animula! vagula, blandula,

Hospes, comesque—

(Evidently this letter was written after the issue of the September number of *The Gentleman's Magazine*. We must therefore question its date—1739.)

[2]The editor of *The Gentleman's Magazine*, Sept. 1740, wrote, 'We are greatly obliged to our Correspondent who sent us the following beautiful poem. Tho' he wrote not a syllable in the cover to it, we hope we did not misinterpret his Intentions, by immediately consigning it to our Magazine.

Mr. Lyttelton to Mr. Poyntz.

Oh thou, whose friendship is my joy and pride,

Whose virtues warm me and whose precepts guide.' etc.

[3]'An epigram upon a young gentleman's refusing to walk with the Author in the Park, because he was not dressed well.

Friend Col and I, both full of whim,

To shun each other oft agree;

For I'm not beau enough for him,

And he's too much a beau for me.

Then let us from each other fly,

And arm in arm no more appear;

That I may ne'er offend your eye,

And you may ne'er offend my ear.'

[4]*The Princess Elizabeth, a Ballad alluding to a story recorded of her, when she was prisoner at Woodstock*, 1554, *Works* I, 120. The poem was first published in Dodsley's *Collection*, Vol. IV.

[5]In *Works* III, 10, the following note is added: 'The tune "Come, and listen to my ditty, &c." The words founded upon a true history of Queen Elizabeth, who, looking from a castle wherein she was a prisoner, and seeing a country milk-maid singing, expressed great envy at the girl's condition, and dissatisfaction with regard to her own.'

[6]Dodsley notes: 'His house-keeper, of whom very respectful mention is made in the course of this correspondence.' W.S. arranged for the maintenance of Mrs. Arnold in his will. 'I give to my servant Mary Cuttler one annuity or yearly Rent Charge of Thirty Pounds Clear of all Taxes & all other Outgoings. . . . I also Order & Direct that my old servant Mary Arnold shall be removed to the care of the said Mary Cuttler & for her Maintenance for Life the said Mary Cuttler shall also be Entitled to a further annuity of six pounds half yearly from my Death. . . .'

Unfortunately when one studies the Chancery Suit of 1765—Cutler vs. Graves—one comes to the conclusion that W.S.'s treatment of his servants was not as generous as it appears to be. About 1749, when Mary Cutler had been in W.S.'s employment some six years she spoke of leaving him. He wanted a housekeeper and repeatedly assured her that he would make the office remunerative. In addition to a salary of £10 per annum, he promised occasional gratuities. He was constantly in need of money, and owed wages to Mary Cutler from 1744 to 1749. Moreover he frequently borrowed sums from her. He made promises of substantial payment in the event of his death, and made provision in his will. The Chancery Suit also reveals the fact that his servant Tom

(Thomas) Jackson, died and cancelled a debt of £89. Finally Mary Cutler charged W.S.'s executors with having received money from the estates without paying anything to her. It is not too much to suppose that the devoted Mrs. Arnold also worked for little money and so established a claim upon W.S. The whole question is dealt with in my *William Shenstone*.

Whistler, in a letter to W.S., described Mrs. Arnold as 'an Example of the simple Force of moral Beauty.' Hull, II, 30.

VII

Works III, 31.

To [Mr. REYNOLDS].

1740.

Sir,

Your last letter gave me a good deal of uneasiness in regard to Mr. Somervile's indisposition. I hope, if he is better, you will omit no opportunity of gratifying me with the news of it. I shall be glad to employ you and Mr. Jago in my little rivulet before winter comes, when one must bid adieu to rural beauties. Those charming scenes, which the poets, in order to render them more compleat, have furnished with ladies, must be stript of all their ornaments. These incomparable nymphs, the Dryads and the Nereids, which have been my constant companions this short summer, will vanish to more pleasing climes; and I must be left to seek my assistance in real beauties, instead of imaginary ones. In short, I am thinking to live part of this winter in Worcester, or some other town. I was at a concert there, a very full one, lately. I observed Dr. Mackenzie[1] talking to Mr. Lyttelton; and I hope, on that account, he is in his interest; otherwise Mr. Somervile would do Mr. Lyttelton great service by engaging him.—Mr. Lyttelton took occasion to mention to me, the obligation he lay under to Mr. Somervile for his letter, as well as his other designs in his favour—that he had long received great pleasure from that gentleman's pen, and wished for the honour of his acquaintance. I told him, I believed the satisfaction would be mutual, or to that purpose. He added, that The Chace was an *extremely* beautiful poem,[2] the best by far ever written on the subject. But now the fiddles squeaked, the harpsichord jingled, and the performers began to feel the divine enthusiasm. The god of music invaded them as he did the Sibyll of old:

'Deus, ecce Deus! cui talia santi
'Ante fores, subito non vultus, non color unus,
'Non comptæ mansere comæ; sed pectus anhelum.
'Et rabie fera corda tument, majorque videri,
'Nec mortale sonans.'[3]

I am, Sir, with all due compliments to Mr. Somervile,

Yours sincerely,

W. SHENSTONE.

NOTES

[1] James Mackenzie (1680?–1761), Worcester physician of repute. Dr. Mackenzie was apparently on terms of intimacy with Somervile. See Somervile's *Epistle to Dr. Mackenzie.*

[2] The poem appeared in 1735. Most critics agree, even to-day, with Lyttelton's opinion of *The Chace.*

[3] Virgil, *Aen.* VI, 46.

VIII

Works III, 27.

To [MR. REYNOLDS].

*From Mr. Wintle's Perfumer,
at the* KING'S ARMS, *by* TEMPLE-BAR,
FLEET STREET, 1740.

[*January*, 1741.]

SIR,

I am heartily obliged to Mr. Somervile, that he will make use of any means to serve me; more especially that he will take the trouble of consulting which may be most effectual to that end; and I desire you would represent these sentiments to him in the most expressive manner.

I have, since I arrived here (which was last Saturday night), heard Lowe[1] sing, and seen Cibber act. The laureat spoke an epilogue made *upon*, and, I suppose, *by* himself, in which he does not only make a bare confession, but an *ostentation* of all his follies:

'Of *such* (says he) whoe'er demands a bill of fare
'May look into my life—he'll find 'em there;'[2]

or some such lines, I cannot accurately recollect them. I do not wonder he pleased extremely; but to a considering man there is something strangely disagreeable, to hear a scandalous life recommended by one of his age, and as much satisfaction shewn in the review of it, as if it had been a perfect galaxy of virtues. An Athenian audience would have shewn their different sentiments on this occasion. But I am acting the part of Jeremy Collier,[3] and indeed in some degree of an hypocrite, for I confess I was highly pleased with him myself. I have nothing to add, but a fine close, if I had it; as I have not, you must be content with the vulgar one, that I am

Yours sincerely,
W. SHENSTONE.

NOTES

[1]Thomas Lowe (d. 1783), vocalist and actor, first appeared at Drury Lane Sept. 11, 1740, and during the next two years he became famous in a variety of parts. The *D.N.B.* says that Lowe sang Arne's songs in *Twelfth Night*, on January 15, 1741.

[2]Colley Cibber (1671–1757), actor and dramatist, became Poet Laureate Sept. 27, 1730. He retired from the stage at the close of 1733, but he reappeared on several occasions. The *Epilogue upon Himself* is given in *The Egotist*. W.S. misquotes:

'If for my Folly's largest List you call,
My life has lump'd 'em! There you'll read 'em all.'

Robert W. Lowe in his edition of Cibber's *Apology for his Life*, says that on January 12, 13 and 14, 1741, Cibber acted Fondlewife. Hence, following the argument of the article in *Anglia*, 1911–12, I modify Dodsley's dating of this letter.

[3]Jeremy Collier (1650–1726), wrote numerous pamphlets on the stage.

IX

Works III, 33.

To MR. JAGO, *from London, with Observations on the Stage, etc.*
Jan. 21, 1741.

Sir,

You see I am *extremely expeditious* in answering your letter; the reason of which is a very powerful one, namely, the information which I received last night, that it would be agreeable to you I should do so. Please, therefore, to set aside the sum of eighteen pence, or thereabouts, for letters which you will receive whilst I am in London; and, to make it seem the less profusely squandered, consider it amongst any other casual expences which you carelessly submit to, merely to gratify your curiosity.

I went the other night, with the greatest expectations, to see 'The Merry Wives of Windsor' performed at Covent-Garden. It is impossible to express how much every thing fell below my ideas. But I have *considered since*; and I find that my expectations were really more unjust than their manner of acting. *Persons*, in order to act well, should have something of the author's fire, as well as a polite education. And what makes this the clearer to me is, that you hear ten plays well read by gentlemen in company, to one that you find well performed upon the stage.——Nothing can be more ignorant or affected than the scornful airs which some people give themselves at a country play; because, forsooth, they have seen plays in town. The truth is, the chief advantage of plays in town lies entirely in the scenery. You seldom observe a set of strollers without one or two actors who are quite equal to their parts; and I really know of no good one at either of the two Theatres Royal, except Cibber, who rarely acts, and Mrs. Clive.[1] I will add one more, in *compliance* with my *own* taste *merely*; and that is Mr. Neal,[2] a fellow who, by *playing the fool*, has gained my particular *esteem*.

After the play, we had an *entertainment*; falsely so called! It was that of Orpheus and Eurydice, the most *un-musical* thing I ever heard, and which lasted, I believe, three hours, with some intermixtures of Harlequin;[3] both so dull, and yet heard with patience, that I was amazed, astonished, confounded: but really a *man* of *sense* ought not to be so; because they were not calculated for *him*.

I want you here extremely: pray come up for a week. I suppose you will not, so I will not argue superfluously. However, write soon; and believe that your letters are the most agreeable things in the world to, Sir,

Yours most faithfully,

W.S.

NOTES

[1] Kitty Clive (1711–1785), friend of Horace Walpole, a famous actress who appeared with Garrick. She was considered to be better in comedy, than in serious plays.

[2] Thomas Davies mentions Neale as a good comic actor. 'Neale was a sort of grotesque actor, whose particular talent was suited only to some very peculiar characters, in which he was sure to excel everybody else. Mr. Garrick, when he was under some difficulty to distribute a part, used to say, "Come, I will give it to Neale; for, I am sure, he will make more of it than anybody can." He excelled in Shakespeare's Lancelot in the *Merchant*

of Venice, Slender in *The Merry Wives of Windsor,* and Sir Joseph Wittol in *The Old Bachelor.' Memoirs of the Life of David Garrick, Esq.,* I, 35.
   [3]*Biographia Dramatica,* 1812, IV, 108. Henry Sommer's *Orpheus and Euridice with the Pantomime Entertainment* was first acted in 1740.

X

Works, III, 13.
To a Friend [R. JAGO], *from London, describing his Temper, and Manner of Living there*
From Mr. Wintle's, *Perfumer, near* TEMPLE-BAR, *&c.*
6*th Feb.* 1740. [*New style. Feb.* 6, 1741].

Dear Sir,

I am now with regard to the *town* pretty much in the same state in which I expect to be always with regard to the *world;* sometimes exclaiming and railing against it; sometimes giving it a good word, and even admiring it. A sun-shiny day, a tavern-supper after a play well acted, and now and then an invigorating breath of air in the Mall, never fail of producing a chearful effect. I don't know whether I gave you any account of Quin's[1] acting Falstaff in my former letter; I really imagined that I saw you tittering on one side me, shaking your sides, and sometimes scarce containing yourself. You will pardon the attitude in which I placed you, since it was what seemed *natural* at that circumstance of time.—Comus[2] I have once been at, for the sake of the songs, though I detest it in any *light:* but as a *dramatic* piece, the *taking* of it seems a *prodigy;* yet indeed *such-a-one,* as was pretty tolerably accounted for by a gentleman who sate by me in the *boxes.* This learned sage, being asked how he liked the play, made answer, 'He could not tell— pretty well, he thought—or indeed as well as any other play— he always took it, that people only came there to see and to be seen—for as for what was said, he owned, he never understood anything of the matter.' I told him, I thought a great many of its admirers were in his case, if they would but own it.

On the other hand, it is amazing to consider to what an universality of learning people make pretensions here. There's

c

not a drawer, a chair or hackney-coachman, but is politician, poet, and judge of polite literature. Chimney-sweepers damn the Convention, and black-shoe-boys cry up the genius of Shakespeare. 'The Danger of writing Verse'[3] is a very good thing; if you have not read it, I would recommend it to you as poetical. But now I talk of learning, I must not omit an interview which I accidentally had the other night in company with Lord D[udley][4] and one Mr. C——. We were taken to sup at a private house, where I found a person whom I had never seen before. The man behaved exceedingly modestly and well; till, growing a little merry over a bottle (and being a little countenanced by the subject we were upon), he pulls out of his pocket about half a dozen ballads, and distributes them amongst the company. I (not finding at first they were of his own composition) read one over, and, finding it a dull piece of stuff, contented myself with observing that it was exceedingly well *printed*. But to see the man's face on this occasion would make you pity the circumstance of an author as long as you live. His jollity ceased (as a flame would do, should you pour water upon it); and, I believe, for about five minutes, he spoke not a syllable. At length, recovering himself, he began to talk about his country-seat, about Houghton-Hall, and soon after desired a health, imagining (as I found afterwards) that Lord D[udley] would have given Sir Robert's. But he did not, naming Sir T[homas] L[yttelton]:[5] mine, which followed, was that of Mr. L[yttelton].[6] Now, who do you think this should be, but honest Ralph Freeman (at least, the writer of the paper so subscribed), your father's old friend and intimate, Sir Robert's right-hand, a person that lives elegantly, drives six of the best horses in town, and plays on St. John's organ: (you know Mr. L[yttelton] is not only Sir Robert's greatest enemy, but the Gazetteer's proper antagonist.) We were invited to see him very civilly, and indeed the man behaved with the utmost good humour, without arrogance, or any attempts at wit, which, probably, would not have been very successful.—Ask your father what he would say to me, if I should join in the cause with his old friend, and take a good annuity under Sir Robert, which, I believe, I might have; and little encouragement, God knows, have I met with on the other side of the question. I say,

I believe I *might have*, because I know a certain person gives pensions of three pound a week to porters and the most illiterate stupid fellows you can imagine, to talk in his behalf at ale-houses: where they sit so long a time, and are as regularly relieved as one centry relieves another.—At least tell him that I expect in his answer to my letter (which I shall not allow him to assign to you), he write something to confirm me in my integrity, and to make me prefer him, and you, and honesty, to lace, brocade, and the smiles of the ladies,

'Et Veneri, & cunis, & plumis Sardanapali.'[7]

But I hope to keep my Hercules in view, whether in print or manuscript; and though I am as fond of pleasure as most people, yet I shall observe the rule,

'Positam sic tangere noli.'[8]

I desire I may hear from you next post: I have a line or two, which I intend for the *sons of utter darkness* (as you call them) next magazine: I would send them to you, for your advice; but cannot readily find them. I like everything in Mr. Somervile's, but the running of the last line. I think to insert them. Should be glad to have a line or two of *yours*, that one may make a bold attack. I look on it as *fun*, without the least emotion, I assure you.[9]

I am, dear Sir,
Your faithful scribbling slave,
W. SHENSTONE.

NOTES

[1]James Quin (1693–1766), accepted representative at Covent Garden after 1732 of various Shakespearian parts and among them Falstaff, who seems to have been W.S.'s favourite Shakespearian character.

[2]*Comus* was several times adapted during the eighteenth century, the adaptation, 1738, by John Dalton (1709–1763) being the most famous. Dalton is interesting in connection with the Shenstone circle as he was tutor to Lord Beauchamp, son of the Duchess of Somerset, and Horace Walpole (*Letters*, (Cunningham) VI, 233), accused Lady Luxborough, W.S.'s friend and correspondent, of too great an interest in him. It has been suggested that this was the cause of her banishment to Barrels.

[3]An extract from *On the danger of Writing in Verse* by Mr. W. Whitehead of Cambridge appeared in *The Gentleman's Magazine*, January 1741. The poem is included in Chalmers, *English Poets*, XVII, p. 119. William Whitehead (1715–1785), became Poet Laureate in 1757.

[4]Of The Grange, Halesowen.

Ferdinando Dudley Lea, nephew of the former Lord, succeeded to the Barony, failing heirs male in the direct line, in 1740. He died unmarried October 21, 1759, when the Barony of Dudley fell into abeyance. W.S. was executor to his will. *A Study of The Family of Shenstone the Poet*, S. Grazebrook, reveals the fact that Lord Dudley was a relation of the poet. This accounts for the intimacy between the two. See *Times Literary Supplement*, September 1, 1927, and *Recollection*, 96.

⁵Sir Thomas Lyttelton of Hagley Hall.

⁶George Lyttelton.

⁷*Juvenal* X, 363. The quotation is inaccurate.

⁸Horace, *Satires I*, 2, 106.

⁹W.S. evidently refers to the riddle controversy. See post, pp. 21 and 22.

XI

Works III, 11.

To the [Rev. RICHARD GRAVES ?], *from Town.*
1739. [*After February* 13, 1741.]

Dear Sir,

I return you my thanks, most heartily, for the poetical resentment which you have shewn against my censurers, the Riddle-masters.[1] I have sent Mr. Somervile's verses[2] and yours to Cave;[3] though I am ashamed to own I neglected it so long, that, I fear, he will have no room for them this month. If you can extirpate false wit in a manner, you will do no small service to the true: you do no small *honour* to it, whether you extirpate the other or not.

You have heard of the motion; have heard, probably, all that I can tell you of it. That it was ill-concerted; that it has done the opposition great disservice; that the King is now confirmed in the opinion of Sir Robert's honesty; that the younger Mr. Pitt's speech was the most admired on the opposite side,[4] and Sir R[ober]t's on the court side; that they did not leave the House till five in the morning; that Sir R[ober]t and P[ultene]y[5] are so violent, that the Sp[eake]r is continually calling them to order; finally, that the affair has occasioned this print, which I address to your curiosity merely, though the lines upon the Bishop are humourous enough.[6]—Now I mention curiosity; do you take notice of the many quaint contrivances made use of to catch people's natural inquisitiveness in the pamphlets, viz. 'Are these things so?'—'Yes, they are'—'What, then?'—'The devil of a story.'—

'Hoy, boys.'—'Up go we.'—And a thousand others.—What do you think must be my expence, who love to pry into every thing of this kind? Why, truly, one shilling. My company goes to George's Coffee-house,[7] where, for that small subscription, I read all pamphlets under a three-shilling dimensions; and, indeed, any larger ones would not be fit for coffee-house perusal.—Lord Dudley lent me two sermons, given him at the House of Lords, which I read last night. In the first, there are a great many animadversions delivered in a style that is tolerable; in the other, there is as great a want of common English as there is plenty of common observations.— Have you seen the sermons on the Martyrdom and on the Fast-day? If you read either send for the first—You'll find me degenerate from a gentle bard into a snarling critic, if my poem[8] does not please (you'll say I am no very candid one at present): but let its fate be what it will, I shall lay no small stress upon the opinion of some that have approved it. As it is at present *in keeping*, it discovers no uncommon impudence, and runs no very great risque; but who can answer for it, when it has the gracelessness to *come upon the town?—Ora pro nobis*, must soon be my motto. Its virtues and faults will then be incapable of addition or diminution, and the pious assistance of friends must—but I am no Roman Catholic.—The intrinsic merit of a book when it is printed, as well as the past life and conversation of a man that is departed, must damn, or give it immortality—I mean, to a certain degree. I scribble what comes uppermost, and desire you would do the same.—

Yours,
W.S.

NOTES

[1]W.S., among others, had contributed riddles to *The Gentleman's Magazine* and in October 1740 there was a poem, by one S.S. censuring the frequency of such insertions, and a laboured apology by the Editor. In December 1740, there appeared *An Encomium on Enigmas, shewing their great and universal use: In answer to S.S.* During the following months various poems appeared, the writers taking one side or the other.

Graves, *Recollection*, 98: 'I do not know whether it is worth mentioning, that about this time (i.e. 1742), or a year before, Mr. Shenstone was engaged in a poetical contest with some writers in the *Gentleman's Magazine*, against enigmas or riddles; in which controversy, as he was rather serious in the affair, he called in the assistance of Mr. Whistler, myself, and one or two more of his friends. He insisted on it that as obscurity was the reverse of good writing, and concealing their meaning was the profest intention of an enigma, it ought to be banished from the commonwealth of learning. . . . As I find the squib, which I let off on this occasion, in a MS. letter to Mr. Shenstone—as it has something of a thought, though far fetched in the conclusion, and is one of my earliest attempts at rhyming, I will transcribe it for you.

As the ladies were a powerful party against us, it is addressed

TO A LADY, ON HER FONDNESS FOR ENIGMAS

1

Fie Chloe, scorn this affectation,
    Plain common sense, for once, endure!
Those sops should raise your indignation,
    Whom you think deep, because obscure.

2

Their subtle meaning to explain,
    Your thoughts you puzzle night and day;
Believe me, girl, you seek in vain,
    A needle in a load of hay.

3

With labouring throes their songs commence;
    The mountain bellows in our ears;
We look for prodigies of sense—
    When, lo! a starveling mouse appears.

etc.

March 7, 1741.'

[2]Graves, Somervile, Shenstone and Whistler were all engaged in the riddle contest and the " verses " referred to are probably some of those which appeared, on the Shenstone side of the controversy, in *The Gentleman's Magazine* for February and March, 1741.

[3]Edward Cave (1691–1754), printer, began *The Gentleman's Magazine*, 1731. *The London Magazine* (1732–1781) was its most successful rival.

[4]William Pitt, first Earl of Chatham, first showed his great powers of oratory when, on March 8, 1739, he attacked the convention with Spain, and again on February 13, 1741, when he supported the motion for the removal of Walpole, because of the turmoil raised by his determined peace policy. Apparently it is to this 'motion' that W.S. refers, so that the date of the letter in the *Works*—1739—must be modified.

[5]William Pulteney, Earl of Bath.

[6]In *Anglia*, 1911–12, p. 431, the writer of the article quotes verses on the Bishop of Lichfield:

'Next the Prelate comes in Fashion,
Who of Swine has robb'd the Nation
Tho' against all Approbation.'

[7]'The acknowledged region of gallantry, wit, and criticism' where the 'polite scholar and wit' were to be found. *Connoisseur*, I, January 31, 1754.

[8]W.S. refers to his poem, *The Judgment of Hercules*, advertised in *The Gentleman's Magazine*, April 1741: 'Judgement of Hercules. A Poem printed by R. Dodsley. Price 1. S.' An extract was quoted in the same magazine, 'which we believe will shew the Author has been no less happy in the execution of his Design than in the Choice of Patron.' (i.e. George Lyttelton, Esq.). Then follows a passage from *The Judgment of Hercules*, and 'Virtue's Answer is very beautiful; but we are oblig'd to shorten this article.'

XII

Works III, 18.

To the [Rev. RICHARD GRAVES?] *at Bath, on his* [*W.S.'s*]
publishing his Poem of the Judgment of HERCULES.
From Mr. Wintle's.
April 30, 1740[1]
[*April* 30, 1741].

My good friend!

I heartily thank you for the service your letter did me. And
a considerable service, no doubt, it *is*, to raise the spirits of a
person so habitually dispirited as I have been for some time.
For this, and all former favours, as the sullen fellow says in
Shakespeare, 'I thank you; I am not of many words, but I
thank you.'[2]

I beg you would cease to apologize for your letters: In the
first place, it will lay *me* under a necessity of doing *so;* and, in
the next place, you may be assured, that no friendly letter of
yours will ever be otherwise than infinitely agreeable to me.

I sent a letter to Mr. Marriett at Bath, to be left with you at
your former place of residence; you will be so kind as to give
it to him.

If I wish for a *large* fortune, it is rather for the sake of my
friends than myself: or, to compromise the matter with those
moralists who argue for the universality of *self-interest*, it is
to gratify myself in the company, and in the gratifications, of
my friends.

Dr. Ratcliff[3] has sent me a letter, which gives me much
satisfaction in respect of my poem; notwithstanding, he cannot
forbear adding, that he expects to hear, since my pen has so
well adorned the fable, that my conduct will, with equal propriety and elegance, illustrate the moral. However, the simple
approbation of a *sincere* man affects one more, than Pliny's
panegyric could do, from a more courtly one.

There are several errors of the press, which neither sagacity
nor vigilance itself, I now see, can prevent, and which I beg
you to correct with your pen, in a copy which I must get you
to present to C[harles] L[yttelton][4] together with the inclosed

letter. Please to be at the expence of having it stitched in purple paper, and gilt at the edges; and I will re-pay you.

I was loitering yesterday in the coffee-room, when two persons came in, well dressed, and called for my poem; read a page or two, and commended the four lines upon Mr. L[yttelton] extremely, ('Lov'd by that Prince, &c.')[5] repeated them forty times, and, in the end, got them by heart, mentioned them to a *third* person, who said he knew of no virtue that the prince *was* fired with, and then endeavoured to mimic the prince's way of talking; but, says he, *I'll* shew *the four best lines in the poem, and then proceeded to* "Twas youth's perplexing stage, &c.' which are flat enough, God knows—but to my first heroes; one of them reads, 'When great Alcides to a grove retir'd.' *Ay, ay, you know Mr. L[yttelton] did retire, he was in the secession; read on: you'll find he mentions Delia anon. Don't you remember Mr. L[yttelton] wrote a song upon Delia? but proceed—you'll find he is going to give a description of two ladies, of different characters, that were in love with Mr. L[yttelton].* One was (here he named two names, which I have forgot). *Upon my word, it is fine: I believe it is Pope's; but how comes Pope to praise himself there?* ('Lov'd by that Bard, &c.')   *No doubt, however, it was written by Mr. Pope or Mr. D[odsley]*[6]

My critics proceeded to the reading of the last simile *immediately, without* the lines preceding it, and, agreeing that it was a very good thing, called out for, 'The Oeconomy of Love.'[7] So you see, Laudant *illa,* sed *ista* legunt,'[8] is the case. A person cannot be supposed vain from the approbation of such critics, or else I would not have inserted such a *commendatory* paragraph. I never enquire how my poem takes, and am *afraid* to do so. However, I find *some do* allow it to be *Mallet's*[9]—I am impatient till I hear from you: I shall be here till this day fortnight; afterwards at The Leasows—I must add this, 'Ne, studio nostri, *pecces*';[10] but at the same time also

—————————————'O defend,
'Against your judgment, your most faithful friend.'[11]

W.S.

These *opposite* petitions delineate my state of mind: it is well for me that I have you at Bath.

NOTES

[1]The fact that *The Judgment of Hercules* was published April, 1741, proves Dodsley's dating of this letter to be wrong.

[2]*Much Ado About Nothing*, I, 1.

[3]Probably Dr. John Ratcliff, Master of Pembroke College, Oxford, from 1738 till his death in 1775. Boswell tells us that Johnson, in 1754, 'waited on the Master, Dr. Radcliffe, who received him very coldly. Johnson at least expected that the Master would order a copy of his Dictionary, now near publication: but the Master did not choose to talk on the subject, never asked Johnson to dine, nor even visit him, while he stayed at Oxford. After we had left the lodgings, Johnson said to me, "There lives a man, who lives by the revenues of literature, and will not move a finger to support it."' Both Johnson and W.S. were educated at Pembroke College, but the latter's relations with the Master seem to have been more fortunate than Johnson's.

[4]Charles Lyttelton, created Dean of Exeter in 1748, brother of George Lyttelton, and son of Sir Thomas Lyttelton of Hagley. W.S. did not care for 'the antiquarian dean' of Lady Luxborough's *Letters*.

[5]*Works I*, 245.

> 'Lov'd by that prince whom ev'ry virtue fires:
> Prais'd by that bard whom ev'ry muse inspires:
> Blest in the tuneful art the social flame;
> In all that wins, in all that merits fame!'

These lines were written in praise of George Lyttelton.

[6]Mr. Robert Dodsley. *Recollection*, 93, 'Mr. Shenstone had the satisfaction at a coffee-house, to hear the judicious remarks of some young people on his poem; who came to a resolution, that it must certainly be either Pope's or Mr. R. Dodsley's.' Robert Dodsley (1703–1764), publisher and playwright, was fairly well known to the public by the time this letter was written for he had produced *The Toy Shop*, *The King and the Miller of Mansfield* and *Sir John Cockle at Court*.

[7]By Dr. John Armstrong (1709–1779).

[8]Martial, *Epigrams* IV, XLIX.

[9]David Mallet or Malloch (1705–1765), poet and miscellaneous writer.

[10]Horace, *Epist.*, I, 13, 4.

[11]Dryden, *Epistle to Congreve*, I, 72.

XIII

Works III, 38.

To MR. [GRAVES][1], *on his taking Orders in the Church.*

LEASOWS, *June* 1, 1741.

Dear Sir,

I write to you out of the abundant inclination I have to hear from you; imagining that, as you gave me a direction, you might possibly expect to receive a previous letter from me. I want to be informed of the impressions you receive from your *new* circumstances. The chief aversion which some people have to orders is, what I fancy you will remove in such as you converse with. I take it to be owing partly to dress, and partly to the *avowed profession* of religion. A young clergyman, that has distinguished his genius by a composition or two of a polite nature, and is capable of dressing *himself*, and his *religion*, in a different manner from the generality of his profession, that is, without formality, is certainly a genteel character. I speak this not with any sly design to advise, but to intimate, that I think you very capable of *shining* in a dark-coloured coat.—You must consider me yet as a man of the world, and endeavouring to elicit that pleasure from gaiety, which my reason tells me I shall never find.—It is impossible to express how stupid I have been ever since I came home, insomuch that I cannot write a common letter without six repetitions. This is the third time I have begun yours, and you see what stuff it is made up of. I must e'en hasten to matter of fact, which is the comfortable resource of dull people, though, even as to that, I have nothing to *communicate*. But I would be glad to know, whether you are under a necessity of residing on week-days; and, if not, why I may not expect you a day or two at The Leasows very soon.—Did you make any enquiry concerning the number of my poems sold at Oxford? or did you hear anything concerning it that concerns me to hear?—Will S[aunders][2] (for that is his true name) is the excess of simplicity and good-nature. He seems to have all the industry imaginable to divert and amuse people, without any ambitious ends to serve, or almost any concern whether he has so much as a laugh allowed to his stories, any farther than as a laugh is an indication that people are delighted. This, joined with his turn of thought, renders him quite agreeable. I wish it were in my power to conciliate acquaintance with half his ease.—Pray do not delay writing to me. Adieu!

W. SHENSTONE.

NOTES

[1]Probably this letter is addressed to Richard Graves, who, according to a letter from Miss Graves to W.S., dated May 12, 1740 (Hull, I, 8), 'determined to leave the Study of Physic, and turn Friar.' He returned to Oxford in 1740, took his M.A. degree, and was then ordained and given a living at Tissington, Derbyshire, by William Fitzherbert, friend of Dr. Johnson. Graves was family chaplain at Tissington Hall for three years, and it was during that time that he came to know the country described in *The Spiritual Quixote*.

[2]Graves's copy of Shenstone's *Works*, containing notes by the owner, supplies this information. The volume is the subject of an article by Hans Hecht, *Anglia*, 1934, 131. Probably William Saunders is W.S.'s cousin, mentioned in his will. 'I give to my cousins, John Sanders and William Sanders, of Tardebigge, one Hundred Pounds each.'

XIV

Works III, 48.

To Mr. [GRAVES], *from the Leasows.*

THE LEASOWS, *June* 17*th*, 1741.

Dear Sir,

If a friend of yours who lived in the farthest part of China were to send you a pinch of snuff wrapt up in a sheet of writing-paper, I conceive the snuff would improve in value as it travelled, and gratify your curiosity extremely by the time it reached your fingers ends.—Very true—you will say— why then, *that very consideration* was my inducement to write to you at this time; and that sort of progressional value is what you are to place upon my letter. For, be assured, I am not ignorant how much this my letter doth resemble a pinch of snuff in point of significancy, and that both the one and the other are what you may as well do without.—My letter is as follows.

You must know, in rainy weather, I always soothe my melancholy with the remembrance of *distant* friends only: you cannot easily conceive the high value I place upon their good qualities at such a time; so that at this very instant I am *impatient* to see you. To-morrow, if the sun shines bright, I shall only *wish* for your company as for a *very great good*. If you are unemployed when you leave Bath, I should think, you might stay some time with me this summer. Refined sense is what one is apt to value one's self upon; but really, unless one has a refined soul or two to converse with, it is an inconvenience. I have ruined my happiness by conversing with you and a few more friends: as Falstaff says to Hal, 'Company, *witty* company, has been the ruin of me!'[1] Before I knew that pleasure, I was contented as could be in my solitude; and *now*, the *absence* of *entertainment* is a *positive* pain to me. London has amused me a while with diversions; but now they are past, and I have neither any one about me that *has* the least *delicatesse*, or that I can inspire with the *ambition of having any*. W—— W—— comes in a dirty *shirt*, and an old coat, without a stock, to pay me a visit. He pulled out a pair of scissars, and, giving them an intricate turn over his two thumbs, said, that *he* could do that, and *I* could make a poem; some for *one* thing, some for another:

'Hic nigri succus loliginis, hæc est
'Ærugo mera.'[2]

It was *splenetic* weather *too*.—The man is curst who writes verses, and lives in the country.—If his *celestial* part inspires him to converse with Juno, his *terrestrial* one necessitates him to stoop to his landlady; so that he is in as disagreeable a situation, as if one person were to pull him upwards by the *head*, and another downwards by the *tail*.—Do you never find anything of this?—I mean, that your *pride* and your *social* qualities torture you with their *different* attractions? Indeed one would always give way to the last, but that few are familiarity-proof, few but whom it teaches to despise one. Albeit I am conscious of the bad influence of freedom myself; yet, whilst it tends to discover wit, humour, and sense, it only renders me more and more

Your most obedient friend and servant,

W. SHENSTONE.

NOTES

[1]'Company, villainous company, hath been the spoil of me.' *Henry IV*, Pt. I, iii, 3.
[2]Horace, *Sermonum*, I, 4, 100. Hic nigrae, etc.

XV

Works III, 4.

To the [REV. RICHARD JAGO], *in the Manner of* PAMELA.[1]

1739. [*July* 22, 1741.]

WELL! and so I sate me down in my room, and was reading *Pamela*—one might furnish this book with several pretty decorations, thought I to myself; and then I began to design cuts for it, in particular places.[2] For instance, one, where Pamela is forced to fall upon her knees in the arbor: a second, where she is in bed, and Mrs. Jewkes holds one hand, and Mr. B. the other: a third, where Pamela sits sewing in the summer-house, &c. So I just sketched them out, and sent my little hints, such as they were, to Mr. R[ichardso]n. As soon as I had sealed my letter, in comes Mrs. Arnold—'Well, Mrs. Arnold, says I, this Mr. Jago never comes—what can one do? I'm as dull as a beetle for want of company.' 'Sir, says she, the hen—' 'What makes you out of breath, says I, Mrs. Arnold, what's the matter?' 'Why, Sir, says she, the hen that I set last-sabbath-day-was-three-weeks has just hatched, and has brought all her eggs to good.' 'That's brave indeed, says I.' 'Ay, that it is, says she, so be and't please G—d an how that they liven, there'll be a glorious parcel of 'em. Shall I bring 'em up for you to see?' says she. 'No, thank ye, Mrs. Arnold, says I; but aren't ye in some apprehensions from the kite, Mrs. Arnold?'—'No, Sir, says she, I hope there's no danger; I *takes* pretty good care of 'em.' 'I don't question your care, says I; for you're seldom without a duck or a chicken about you.'—'Poor pretty *creters*, says she; look here, Master, this has gotten a speck of black upon her tail,'—'Ay, I thought you wern't without one about you, says I—I don't think, says I, Mrs. Arnold, but your soul was design'd for a hen originally.' 'Why, and if I *had* been a hen, says she, I believe I should have done as much for my chickens as yonder great black-and-white hen does, tho' I say't that shou'd not say't, says she.' Aye, that you would, thought I. 'Well, but now when Mr. Jago comes, have you got e'er a chicken that's *fit to kill?*' 'No, says she, I doubt there is ne'er-a-one.' 'Well, says I, Mrs. Arnold, you and your chicken may go down; I am going to write a letter.' So I sat down, and wrote thus far: scrattle, scrattle, goes the pen—why how now? says I—what's the matter with the pen? So I thought I would make an end of my letter, because my pen went scrattle, scrattle. Well, I warrant I shall have little pleasure when Mr. Jago *comes*; for I never fixed my heart much upon anything in my life, but some misfortune happened to balance my pleasure. —After all, thought I, it must be some very ill accident that outweighs the pleasure I shall take in seeing him.

W. Shenstone.

Leasows, *July* 22.

NOTES

[1]Richardson's *Pamela* was written between November 10, 1739, and January 10, 1740, and the generally accepted date of publication is November, 1740. Hence Dodsley's dating of this letter, 'in the manner of Pamela,' is manifestly wrong.
[2]W.S.'s power with his pencil was known to his friends. *Recollection*, 176.

XVI

Works III, 22.

To Mr. JAGO, *on the Death of his Father.*[1]

LEASOWS, *Aug.* 28, 1740.

[*Aug.* 28, 1741].

Dear Mr. Jago,

I find some difficulty in writing to you on this melancholy occasion. No one can be more unfit to attempt to lessen your grief than myself, because no one has a deeper sense of the *cause* of your affliction. Though I would by no means be numbered by you amongst the common herd of your acquaintance, that tell you they are sorry, yet it were impertinent in me to mention a mere friend's concern to a person interested by so many more tender regards. Besides, I should be glad to alleviate your sorrow, and such sort of condolence tends but little to promote that end. I do not chuse to flatter you; neither could I, more especially at this time; but though I could perhaps find enough to say to persons of less sense than you, I know of nothing but what your own reason must have suggested. Concern indeed may have suspended the power of that faculty; and upon that pretence, I have a few things that I would suggest to you. After all, it is time alone that *can* and *will* cure *all* afflictions, but such as are the consequence of vice; and yours, I am sure, proceeds from a *contrary* principle.

I heard accidentally of this sorrowful event, and accompanied you to London with the utmost concern. I wished it was in my power to mitigate your griefs by sharing them, as I have often found it in yours to augment my pleasures by so doing.

All that I can recommend to you is, not to confine your eye to any single event in life, but to take in your whole circumstances before you repine.

When you reflect that you have lost one of the best of men in a father, you ought to comfort yourself that you had such a father; to whom I cannot forbear applying these lines from Milton:

—————'Since to part!

'Go, heav'nly guest, ethereal messenger!

'Sent by whose sovereign goodness we adore!
'Gentle to me and affable has been
'Thy condescension, and shall be honour'd ever
'With grateful'st memory——'
End of Book VIII, Par. Lost.

I would have you by all means, come over hither as soon as you can. I will endeavour to render the time you spend *here* as satisfactory as it is in my power; and I hope you will ever look upon me as your hearty friend, through all the vicissitudes of life.

Pray give my humble service to Mrs. Jago[2] and your brother.[3]

I am, with the utmost affection,
Yours sincerely,
W. SHENSTONE.

NOTES

[1]Richard Jago's father was Rev. Richard Jago of Beaudesert, Warwickshire, where he held the living from 1709–1740. On an outside wall of the church is a tablet to his memory, which runs thus:

In Memory of

The Revd. Mr. Jago
A native of St. Mawes in Cornwall
and many years Rector of this Church
He died in the 62nd Year of his Age
On the 29th of July A.D. 1741

The Registers record his burial July 31, 1741. The inscription on the monument is now almost illegible. It is obvious from the above details, that the letter of sympathy which Shenstone wrote to Jago, should be dated a year later.

[2] Jago's mother.
[3] John Jago.

XVII

Works III, 40.

To MR. GRAVES, *on similar Taste and Manners.*

THE LEASOWS, *Sept.* 23, 1741.

Dear Sir,

I was very agreeably entertained by your last letter, as indeed I am by every one of yours. It were affectation to except a paragraph or two on account of partiality, where, to say the truth, the partiality itself pleases one. This I am very positive of, that to have a friend of your temper and taste will always give me pleasure, whether I please the world or no; but to please ever so much, without some such friendship, would, in all probability, signify but little. I shall, therefore, value any means that tend to confirm my opinion of your esteem for me, preferably to any that shew me I am merely deserving of it. After all, though a very limited number of *friends* may be sufficient, an idle person should have a large *acquaintance*; and I believe I have the least of any one that ever rambled about so much as I have done. I do not know how it is, but I absolutely despair of ever being introduced into the world. It may be objected by some (but you will not object it), that I may be acquainted with a sufficient number of people that are my *equals*, if I *will*. They may be my *equals* and *superiors*, whom they mean, for aught I care; but their conversation gives me no more pleasure than the *canking* of a goose, or the quacking of a duck, in affluent circumstances: rather *less* indeed of the two, because the idea of the fat goose flatters one's appetite; but the *human goose* is neither fit to be heard nor eaten. I wish indeed to be *shewn into* good company; but, if I can at all distinguish the nature of my inclinations, it is more in hopes of meeting with a refined conversation than anything else. I do not at all insist that my genius is *better* than that of my vociferous neighbours; if it is *different*, it is a sufficient reason why I should seek such companions as suit it; and whether they are found in high or low life, is little to the purpose. But you will perhaps discern the operations of *vanity* in all my endeavours; I will not disagree with you, provided you will allow *amusement* an equal share in them. It is the vanity to be intimate with men of distinguished sense, not of distinguished fortune. And this is a vanity which you should not disapprove, because it will bind me a lasting friend to you and your family.

I have been over at Shiffnall,[1] and, in order to make myself agreeable, rode a-hunting with Mr. Pitt. I confess I was somewhat diverted; and my horse was so much an enthusiast, as to be very near running headlong into a deep water. I believe, if I were to turn sportsman, I should soon break my neck, for fear the huntsman should despise me.

I will certainly endeavour to see you at Birmingham; but beg you would write me a long letter in the meantime; and contrive, if you can, to make it look like a packet, as your last did, for the sight thereof is exceedingly comfortable.

Though my wishes will not suffer me to believe that your eyes are in the danger you represent; yet, supposing them to be only very weak, I would recommend some musical instrument, that is most agreeable to you. I have often looked upon music as my dernier resort,[2] if I should ever discard the world, and turn eremite entirely. Consider what other amusement can make an equal impression in old age.

I have filled my paper, not without difficulty, through the barrennness of my brain and situation: my heart ever flows with the most warm streams of gratitude and affection for you. Adieu!   W.S.

NOTES

[1]Shifnall in Shropshire, the home of Humphrey Pitt, friend of Thomas Percy. It was at Pitt's house that Percy found the old folio manuscript of ballads, 'lying dirty on the floor under a bureau in the parlour, being used by the maids to light the fire.' These formed the nucleus of Percy's *Reliques of Ancient English Poetry*, 1765.

[2]*Recollection*, 175, and ante, 6.

XVIII

Works III, 43.

To a Friend [Rev. RICHARD JAGO], *expressing his Dissatisfaction at the Manner of Life in which he is engaged.*

1741.

Dear Sir,

I wonder I have not heard *from* you lately—*of* you indeed I have, from Mr. W[histler]. If you could come over, probably, I might go back with you for a day or two; for my horse, I think, gets rather better, and may, with indulgence, perform such a journey. I want to advise with you about several matters:— to have your opinion about a *building* that I *have built*, and about a journey which I design to Bath; and about numberless things, which, as they are numberless, cannot be comprehended in this paper. I am,

Your most affectionate friend,

W. SHENSTONE.

D

Now I am come home from a visit—every little uneasiness is sufficient to introduce my whole train of melancholy considerations, and to make me utterly dissatisfied with the life I now lead, and the life which I foresee I shall lead. I am angry, and envious, and dejected, and frantic, and disregard all present things, just as becomes a madman to do. I am infinitely pleased (though it is a gloomy joy) with the application of Dr. Swift's complaint, 'that he is forced to die in a rage, like a poisoned rat in a hole.'[1] My soul is no more suited to the figure I make, than a cable rope to a cambric needle:—I cannot bear to see the advantages alienated, which I think I could deserve and relish so much more than those that have them.—Nothing can give me patience but the soothing sympathy of a friend, and *that* will only turn my rage into simple melancholy.—I believe soon I shall bear to see nobody. I *do* hate all hereabouts already, except one or two. I will have my *dinner* brought upon my table in my absence, and the plates fetched away in my absence; and nobody shall see me: for I can never bear to appear in the same stupid mediocrity for years together, and gain no ground. As Mr. G[raves] complained to me (and, I think, you too, both unjustly), 'I am no character.'—I have in my temper some rakishness, but it is checked by want of spirits: some solidity, but it is softened by vanity: some esteem of learning, but it is broken in upon by laziness, imagination, and want of memory, &c.—I could reckon up twenty things throughout my whole circumstances wherein I am thus tantalized. Your fancy will present them.—Not that all I say here will signify to *you:* I am only under a fit of dissatisfaction, and to grumble does me good—only excuse me, that I cure myself at your expence. Adieu!

NOTE

[1] Swift's letter to Bolingbroke, March 21, 1729: 'not die here in a rage, like a poisoned rat in a hole.'

XIX

Works III, 51.

To the [Rev. RICHARD JAGO], *with an Invitation to accompany him to Town*

THE LEASOWS, *Nov.* 25, 1741.

Dear Sir,

The reason why I write to you so suddenly is, that I have a proposal to make to you. If you could contrive to be in London for about a month from the end of December, I imagine you would spend it agreeably enough along with me, Mr. Outing,[1] and Mr. Whistler. According to my calculations, we should be a very happy party at a play, coffee-house, or tavern. Do not let your supercilious friends come in upon you with their prudential maxims. Consider, you are now of the proper age for pleasure, and have not above four or five whimsical years left. You have not struck one bold stroke yet, that I know of. Saddle your mule, and let us be jogging to the great city. I will be answerable for amusement.—Let me have the pleasure of seeing you in the pit, in a laughter as cordial and singular as your friendship. Come—let us go forth into the opera-house; let us hear how the eunuch-folk sing. Turn your eye upon the lillies and roses, diamonds and rubies; the Belindas and the Sylvias of gay life! Think upon Mrs. Clive's inexpressible comicalness; not to mention Hippesley's joke-abounding physiognomy![2] Think, I say, *now;* for the time cometh when you shall say, 'I have no pleasure in them.'

I am conscious of much merit in bringing about the interview betwixt Mr. L[yttelton] and Mr. S[omervile]; but merit, as Sir John Falstaff says, is not regarded in these costermonger days.[3]

Pray now do not write me word that your *business* will not allow you *ten minutes* in a fortnight to write to me; an excuse fit for none but a cobbler, who has ten children dependent upon a waxen thread. Adieu!

W.S.

NOTES

[1]Captain Outing, secretary and factotum to Lady Luxborough. There are numerous references to this amiable man in the letters of the Shenstone circle.

[2]John Hippisley (d. 1748), comic actor. He was in the original cast of *The Beggar's*

Opera, 1728, as Peachum. His curious appearance excited laughter. 'A comedian of lively humour and droll pleasantry.' Davies, *Life of Garrick*, I, 32.
    ³*Hen. IV*. Pt. II, I, 2.

XX

Works III, 62.

To the [Rev. RICHARD JAGO?], *with some Observations on*
SPENSER.

Leasows [1741]
The Day before Christmas.

Dear Sir,

Though your last letter seemed to put my correspondence upon an ostentatious footing, namely, an inclination to be witty, yet I assure you it was not any punctilious consideration of that kind that has kept me so long silent. Indeed with some people one would stand upon the nicest punctilios; for though ceremony be altogether lighter than vanity itself, yet it surely weighs as much as the acquaintance of the undeserving. But this is trifling, because it can have no reference to a person for whom I have the greatest affection.

In regard to my Oxford affairs, you did all I could expect. I have wrote since to Mr. M[arriett], who, either for your sake or mine, will, I dare say, settle them to my satisfaction.

I wish your journey and head-ach would have permitted you to have been a little more particular concerning the seat of the Muses; but I suppose nothing material distinguished your fortnight.

Mr. Whistler has relapsed at Whitchurch;¹ but purposed, when I last heard from him, to go to London before this time. I do not entirely understand his schemes, but should have been sincerely glad of his company with me this winter; and, he says, he is not fond of London.—For my part, I designed to go thither the next month, but the fever (which is chiefly violent in towns) discourages me.

Some time ago, I read Spenser's Fairy Queen; and, when I had finished, thought it a proper time to make some additions and corrections in my trifling imitation of him, the School-mistress.²—His subject is certainly bad, and his action inexpressibly confused; but there are some particulars in him that charm one. Those which afford the greatest scope for a ludicrous imitation are, his simplicity and obsolete phrase; and yet these are what give one a very singular pleasure in the perusal. The burlesque which they occasion is of quite a different kind to that of Philips's Shilling,[3] Cotton's Travestie,[4] Hudibras,[5] or Swift's works; but I need not tell *you* this. I inclose a copy, for your amusement and opinion; which, if franks are plentiful, you may return, and save me the *tedious* trouble of writing it over again. The other paper was, *bona fide*, written to divert my thoughts from pain, for the same reason that I smoaked; actions equally reputable.

Mr. Somervile's poem upon hawking, called 'Field Sports,'[6] I suppose, is out by this time. It was sent to Mr. Lyttelton, to be read to the Prince, to whom it was inscribed. It seems, he is fond of hawking.[7]

I have often thought those to be the most enviable people whom one least envies—I believe, married men are the happiest that are; but I cannot say I envy them, because they lose all their merit in the eyes of other ladies.

I beg sincerely that you would write in a week's time at furthest, that I may receive your letter *here*, if I should go from home this winter. I will never use anything by way of conclusion, but your old Roman

Farewell!

W. Shenstone.

NOTES

[1]Whistler's mother, who appears to have been an invalid, also lived at Whitchurch, Oxon, having married the Rev. S. Walker, rector of Whitchurch. 'Mr. Whistler having a mother alive, who was married to a clergyman of fortune, they lived in the manor-house; but had fitted up a very small box for him in the same village, where he lived in an elegant style, and was visited by all the genteel families in the neighbourhood.' *Recollection*, 149.

[2]*The School-Mistress, a Poem. By the Author of The Judgment of Hercules. (Price Six Pence)* was published by Robert Dodsley in May, 1742. The version, expanded from the poem of twelve stanzas which appeared in W.S.'s *Poems upon Various Occasions*, published at Oxford in 1737, consisted of twenty-eight stanzas, with the Advertisement and Index, and the Latin mottoes which appear on the half-title and the title pages. See Clarendon Press facsimile of 1742 edition, 1924.

[3]Besides his poem *Cyder*, 1708 (cf. post, p. 61), John Philips (1676–1709), wrote also *The Splendid Shilling*, 1705, a mock-heroic in imitation of Milton.

[4]Charles Cotton (1630–1687), poet, friend of Isaac Walton, in 1664 issued anonymously *Scarronides or the First Book of Virgil Travestie.*

⁵Samuel Butler (1612–1680) wrote *Hudibras* in 1663 and the following years. It was still very popular in the eighteenth century.

⁶William Somervile's *Field Sports*, humbly addressed to his Royal Highness, the Prince, a supplement to *The Chace*, was published in folio, 1742, and was advertised in *The Gentleman's Magazine* and *The London Magazine* of January, 1742. It is probable then that the date of this letter should be 1741 and not 1742.

⁷See *Field Sports*, l. 1.

> 'Once more, Great Prince, permit an humble bard
> Prostrate to pay his homage at your feet;
> Then, like the morning lark from the low ground
> Towering aloft, sublime to soar, and sing;
> Sing the heart-cheering pleasure of the fields,
> The choice delight of heroes and of kings.'

XXI

Works III, 58.

To MR. GRAVES, *on Benevolence and Friendship.*

THE LEASOWS,

Jan. 19, 1741–2.

Dear Mr. Graves,

I cannot forbear immediately writing to you: the pleasure your last letter gave me puts it out of my power to restrain the overflowings of my benevolence. I can easily conceive that, upon some extraordinary instances of friendship, my heart might be *si fort attendri*, that I could bear any restraint upon my ability to shew my gratitude. It is an observation I made upon reading to-day's paper, which contains an account of C. Khevenhuller's success in favour of the Queen of Hungary.¹ To think what sublime affection must influence that poor unfortunate Queen, should a faithful and zealous General revenge her upon her enemies, and restore her ruined affairs!

Had a person shewn an esteem and affection for *me*, joined with any elegance, or without any elegance in the expression of it, I should have been in acute pain till I had given some sign of my willingness to serve him.—From *all* this, I conclude that I have more humanity than some others.

Probably enough I shall never meet with a larger share of happiness than I feel at present. If not, I am thoroughly convinced, my pain is greatly superior to my pleasure. That pleasure is not absolutely dependent upon the mind, I know from this, that I have enjoyed happier scenes in the company

of some friends, than I can possibly at present;—but alas!
all the time you and I shall enjoy together, abstracted from the
rest of our lives, and lumped, will not perhaps amount to a
solid year and a half. How small a proportion!

People will say to one that talks thus, 'Would you die?'
To set the case upon a right footing, they must take away the
hopes of greater happiness in *this* life, the fears of greater
misery hereafter, together with the bodily *pain* of dying, and
address me in a disposition betwixt mirth and melancholy; and
I could easily resolve them.

I do not know how I am launched out so far into this complaint: it is, perhaps, a strain of constitutional whining; the
effect of the wind—did it come from the winds? to the winds
will I deliver it:

'Tradam protervis in mare Creticum,
'Portare ventis—'[2]

I will be as happy as my fortune will permit, and make
others so:

'Pone me pigris ubi *nulla campis*
'*Arbor* æstiva recreatur aura—'[3]

I will be so. The joke is, that the description which you
gave of that country was, that you had few trees about you;
so that I should *trick* Fortune if she should grant my petition
implicitly. But in earnest, I intend to come and stay a day or
two with you next summer.

Mr. Whistler is at Mr. Gosling's, bookseller, at the Mitre
and Crown, in Fleet-street, and enquired much after you in his
last letter to me. He writes to me; but I believe his affection
for one weighs less with him, while the town is in the other
scale. Though he is very obliging. I do not know whether I do
right, when I say I believe we three, that is, in solitary circumstances, have an equal idea of, and affection for, each
other. I say, supposing each to be alone, or in the country,
which is nearly the same; for scenes alter minds as much as the
air influences bodies. For instance, when Mr. Whistler is in
town, I suppose we love him better than he does us; and when
we are in town, I suppose the same may be said in regard to him.

The true burlesque of Spenser (whose characteristic is
simplicity) seems to consist in a *simple* representation of such
things as one laughs to *see* or to *observe* one's self, rather than
in any monstrous contrast betwixt the thoughts and words.[4]
I cannot help thinking that my added stanzas have more of his
manner than what you saw before, which you are not a judge
of, till you have read him.   W.S.   ·

NOTES

[1]See *The Gentleman's Magazine*, January 1742. The same magazine for March 1742,
under 'Foreign Affairs,' contains an account of the plight of the Queen of Hungary
and of Count Khevenhuller's efforts on her behalf. It also contains Maria Theresa's
letter to the Count.

[2]Hor., *Carminum*, I, 26, 2, 3.

[3]Hor., *Carminum*, I, 22, 17, 18.

[4]The Advertisement to the 1742 edition of *The School-Mistress* runs thus: 'What
Particulars in Spenser were imagin'd most proper for the Author's Imitation on this
Occasion, are, his Language, his Simplicity, his manner of Description, and a peculiar
Tenderness of sentiment, visible throughout his Works.'

XXII

Works III, 29.

To the [Rev. RICHARD JAGO?].

March [1742].

Dear Sir,
  I thank you for the favour of your last letter, particularly
your readiness in transmitting to me any thing of Mr. Somervile's. It so fell out, that Mr. Outing delivered to me the verses,
and I had the pleasure of reading them, about a moment before
he gave me your epistle.
  The town expected something of importance, namely, a
motion for a committee of enquiry into late measures, would be
moved for to-day. If any thing of this nature has been carrying
on, I will add an account of it before I close my letter. In the
mean time it is, I believe, very credible, that Lord Orford[1]
has a continued influence over the King; and that the Duke of
Argyle[2] is sufficiently disgusted, to have talked of the resignation of his posts again.
  An odd story enough the following, and I believe true!
Somebody, that has just learnt that Hor[ace] W[alpole]'s
gentleman's name was Jackson, writes a letter to Mr. Flover,

keeper of the Tower, intimating his master's desire to speak with him. Floyer dresses the next morning, and waits upon H[orac]e, comes into his room—'Sir, says Horace, I really don't know you.—' 'Sir, my name is Floyer,—' 'Ay, by G–d, that may be; but, by G–d, I don't know you for all that—' 'Sir, says he, I am keeper of the Tower—' 'G–d d—n your blood, says H[orac]e, produce your warrant damn you, produce your warrant; or, by G–d, I'll kick ye downstairs—'

Frighted at these threats, the gentleman retired; and on his way home had leisure to consider the joke that was put upon him, and more particularly turned upon the person to whom he was sent.

If you direct a line to Mr. Shuckburgh's, bookseller, in Fleet-street, it will arrive agreeable to

Your humble servant,
W. Shenstone.

March,
Tuesday night,
My compliments to your patron.

NOTES

[1]Sir Robert Walpole, 1st Earl of Orford, (1676–1745), received the title on February 9, 1742. Hence this letter probably belongs to March, 1742.

[2]John Campbell (1678–1743), second Duke of Argyll. Both *The London Magazine* and *The Gentleman's Magazine*, of March 1742, comment on the Duke of Argyll's 'resignation of his posts.'

XXIII

Works III, 73.

To the [Rev. RICHARD GRAVES] *from Town; with a Specimen of Plays and Politics.*

> From Mr. Shuckburgh's, Bookseller,
> in Fleet street, your Brother's
> Lodgings, about 1743.
>
> [*March* 1742.]

Dear Mr. Graves,

I have just been spending my evening at a coffee-house; and, notwithstanding the confused effect of liquor, am sitting down to write to a person of the clearest head I know. The *truth* is, I write to please *myself*, which I can do no other way so effectually; upon which account, you are not obliged to me for the *advances* I make in correspondence. Extraordinary things will be expected from my *situation;* but extraordinary things ought never to be expected from *me*. I keep no political company, nor *desire* any, as, I believe, you know. If you enquire after the stage,—I have not seen Garrick; but, more fortunately for *you*, your brother *has*. Me nothing has so much transported as young Cibber's[1] *exhibition* of Parolles, in Shakespear's '*All's well that ends well*.' The character is admirably written by the author; and, I fancy, I can discover a great number of hints which it has afforded to Congreve in his Bluff.[2] I am apt to think a person, after he is twelve years old, laughs annually less and less: less heartily, however; which is much the same. I think Cibber elicited from me as sincere a laugh as I can ever recollect. Nothing, sure, can be comparable to his representation of Parolles in his bully-character; except the figure he makes as a shabby gentleman. In his first dress he is tawdry, as you may imagine; in the last, he wears a rusty black coat, a black stock, a black wig with a Ramillie, a pair of black gloves; and a face!—which causes five minutes laughter. —Instead of politics, I have transcribed these epigrams from the Evening Post[3]—though I hate transcribing:

'THE CHOICE, to Sir ROBERT——

'When opposition against power prevail'd;
'When artful eloquence and bribery fail'd;
'Timely you quit the ship you could not steer,
'Disdain the commons, and ascend a peer:
'Conscious that you deserve to *bleed* or *swing*,
'You chuse the axe as nobler than the string.'

The OPPOSITION.

'With huge Antæus as Alcides strove,
'The Son of Neptune one, and one of Jove,
'Oft as he threw the giant on the ground,
'His strength redoubled by the fall he found.

'Th' unwieldy monster, sprung of mother Earth,
'From *her* had vigour, as from her he'd birth:
'Enrag'd, the hero a new method tries;
'High lifts in air, and, as he mounts, he dies.'

I think the last a good thought; the first not a bad one, and
what I have had in my head a thousand times.   I saw Mr.
Fitzherbert at Nando's, but chose not to reconnoitre him
there, though to ask after *you*. I purpose waiting on him at his
lodgings, for the same end. Pray write soon to me. I wish I
could say more to deserve it from you—I would fain deviate
from the common road in every letter I send you; but am so
very uniformly your friend, that I cannot vary my manner of
expressing how *much* I am so, which is all my letters aim at.
Adieu!

W. Shenstone.

NOTES

[1]Theophilus Cibber (1703–1758), actor and playwright, a son of Colley Cibber,
made his first appearance on the stage in 1721.

[2]Captain Bluffe, in whom the influence of Ben Jonson is strong, is a character in
The Old Batchelor, by Congreve.

[3]*London Evening Post*, Tuesday, March 2—Thursday, March 4, 1742: 'The CHOICE,
address'd to a late Great Man.' W.S. quotes very inaccurately. The fact that the epigram
is to be found in the *Evening Post* of March 4, 1742, makes necessary the correction of
Dodsley's dating of this letter, 'about 1743.'

XXIV

Works III, 35.

To the [Rev. RICHARD JAGO].

1741. [*March,* 1742.]

Dear Sir,

As I have no sort of library in town, I find several minutes
upon my hands, for which, if I employ them in scribbling to
my friends, they are but *slenderly obliged* to me. I hope no friend
of mine will ever be induced by my *example*, to do any thing
but avoid it; I believe no one breathing can say, with more
truth, 'Video meliora, &c.'[1] It is not from a spirit of jealousy
that I would advise my acquaintance to seek happiness in the
regular path of a fixed life. But, though I very highly approve
it, and envy it, my particular turn of mind would be as little

satisfied with it, as it is like to be in a *different* one. Yet, however I *complain*, I must own, I have a good deal reconciled myself to this mixture of gratification and disappointment, which must be my lot till the last totally prevails.

Yet, after all, to tell you the truth, I am not pleased with being advised to retire. I was saying the other day to Mr. Outing, that I *had* been ambitious more than I was at present, and that I grew less so every day. Upon this he chimed in with me, and approved my despondency; saying, 'that *he* also had been ambitious, but found it would not do.' Do you think I liked him much for this?—no—I wheeled about, and said, 'I did not think with him; for I should always find myself whetted by disappointments, and more violent in proportion to the intricacy of the game.' I spent a night with him and Mr. Meredith,[2] and with him and Mr. Dean: in the latter party he had laid his hand upon his sword six times, and *threatened to put a dozen men to death*, one of which was Broughton the prize-fighter.[3]—Mr. Whistler's company seldom *relieves* me on an evening; and I go to plays but *seldom*, because I intend no more to *give countenance* to the *pit*.—I have got a belt!!! which distinguishes me as much as a *garter*—it captivates the eyes of all beholders, and binds their understandings in golden bandage.—I heard a pedant punning upon the word βέλτιςος and a wag whispering that I was related to *Beltishazzar*. In short I may say, from the Dragon of Wantley,[4]

'No girdle, nor belt, e'er excell'd it;
'It frightens the men in a minute:
'No maiden yet ever beheld it,
'But wish'd herself tied to me in it.'

The Dunciad[5] is, doubtless, Mr. Pope's dotage, τᾶ Διὸς ἐνύπνια ; flat in the whole, and including, with several tolerable lines, a *number* of weak, obscure, and even punning ones. What is now read by the *whole world*, and the *whole world's wife*, is, Mr. Hervey's Letter to Sir T. Hanmer.[6] I own my *taste* is gratified in it, as well as that *unluckiness*, natural to every one; though people say (I think idly) he is mad. For this *long* letter I shall expect *two*, soon after you have received it. Adieu!

Did you see a poem called 'Woman in Miniature,' written with spirit, but incorrect?[7] The people that were carrying Lord Orford in effigy, to behead him on Tower Hill, came into the box where he was, accidentally, at George's, to beg money of him, amongst others.

NOTES

[1] Ovid, *Metamorphoses*, VII, 20.

[2] A MS. note in the B.M. copy of Lady Luxborough's *Letters* tells us something of the Meredith family. 'Mrs. Meredith was daughter to Mr. Cholmondely of Vale Royal (by an Aunt of Lady Luxborough) and wife to Amos, son of Sir Wm. Meredith, who died in his father's life-time. Henrietta married the Honble Frederick Vane, second son of the Earl of Darlington.' Mrs. Meredith, her son, who succeeded to the family estates and title in 1752 on the death of his grandfather, Sir William Meredith, and her two daughters, find frequent mention in letters of W.S. to Lady Luxborough.

[3] Davies, *Life of Garrick*, I, 63, referring to Thomas Fleetwood, patentee of Drury Lane, wrote: 'This man of genteel address and polite manners conceived a peculiar fondness for the professors of the art of boxing; his company was divided between sturdy athletics and ridiculous buffoons; between Broughton, James and Taylor the most eminent of our boxers, and the tumblers of Sadler's Wells; the heroic combatants of Hockley in the Hole and the Bear Garden graced the patentee's levy almost every morning.'

[4] Henry Carey (d. 1743), poet and musician, author of *Sally in our Alley*, wrote *The Dragon of Wantley*, a burlesque opera, produced October 26, 1737.

[5] The *Dunciad* was first published May 1728. *The Gentleman's Magazine*, March 1742, advertises "'The New Dunciad'; as it was found in the Year 1741, pr. 1s. 6d. Cooper."

[6] Thomas Hervey (1698–1775), pamphleteer, eloped with Sir Thomas Hanmer's wife, and henceforward made Sir Thomas (1677–1746, speaker of the House of Commons), a constant subject of attack. The letter referred to here—*A Letter to Sir Thomas Hanmer Bart.*—contained a complaint of the baronet's sale of the wood on the estate in Wales vested in him in reversion. See the long discussion concerning the date of this letter of W.S. in the article in *Anglia*.

[7] *London Magazine*, March 1742. 'Woman in Miniature. Printed for J. Huggonson, price 6d.'

XXV

Works III, 53.

To the [Rev. RICHARD JAGO], *on occasion of Printing the School-mistress.*

1741. [1742—May?]

Dear Sir,

I trust you do not pay double postage for my levity in inclosing these decorations. If I find you do, I will not send you the *thatch'd house* and the birch-tree, with the sun setting and gilding the scene[1]—I expect a cargo of franks; and then for the beautiful picture of Lady Gainsborough, and the deformed portrait of my old school-dame Sarah Lloyd![2] whose house is to be seen as thou travellest towards the native home of thy faithful servant.—But she sleeps with her fathers; and is buried with her fathers; and—Thomas her son *reigneth* in her stead!—I have the first sheet to correct upon the table. I have laid aside the thoughts of fame a good deal in this *unpromising* scheme; and fix them upon the landskip which is engraving, the red letter which I purpose, and the fruit piece which you see,[3] being the most seemly ornaments of the first sixpenny pamphlet that was ever so highly honoured. I shall incur the same reflection with Ogilby, of having nothing good but my decorations.[4]

I have been walking in the Mall to-night.—The *Duke* was there, and was highly delighted with two dogs; and stared at me more enormously than ever Duke did before. I do not know for what reason; unless for the same which made him admire the *other* puppy-dogs, because they were large ones.

I expect that in your neighbourhood, and in Warwickshire, there should be about twenty of my poems sold. I print it myself. I am not yet satisfied about mottoes. That printed is this, 'O, quà sol habitabiles illustrat oras, maxime principum!'[5] It must be short, on account of the plate. I do not know but I may adhere to a very insignificant one:

'En erit ergo
'Ille dies, mihi cum liceat *tua* dicere facta!'[6]

I am pleased with Mynde's engravings; and I can speak without affectation, that . . . is not *equally* in my thoughts— One caution I gave Mr. W[histler], and it is what I would give to all my friends with whom I wish my intimacy may continue so much as I wish it may with you. Though I could bear the *disregard* of the town, I could not bear to see my friends alter their opinion, which they say they have, of what I write, though millions contradict them. It is an obstinacy which *I* can boast of, and they that have more sense may surely insist on the liberty of judging for themselves. If *you* should faulter, I should say you did not deserve your *capacity* to judge for yourself. Write soon—you never are at a fault—'tantummodo *incepto* opus est, cætera res expediet.' Adieu!

W.S.

NOTES

[1]An engraving of the thatched house and the birch tree is on the title-page of the 1742 edition, which displays 'the red letter' of which W.S. writes. Unfortunately, as D'Israeli pointed out, *Curiosities of Literature, II, Shenstone's School-Mistress,* 'What is placed in the landskip over the thatched-house, and the birch-tree, is like a falling monster rather than a setting sun.'

[2]*Works*, I, 335.

> 'The noises intermix'd, which thence resound,
> Do Learning's little tenement betray:
> Where sits the dame, disguis'd in look profound,
> And eyes her fairy throng, and turns her wheel around.
>
> Her cap, far whiter than the driven snow,
> Emblem right meet of decency does yield:
> Her apron dy'd in grain, as blue, I trowe,
> As is the hare-bell that adorns the field:
> And in her hand, for scepter, she does wield
> Tway birchen sprays.'

[3]D'Israeli, *op. cit.*: 'The fruit-piece at the end, the grapes, the plums, the melon, and the Catharine pears, Mr. Mynde has made sufficiently tempting.' James Mynde was an engraver, particularly of birds. Two collections of his are in the British Museum. His signature—J. Mynde Sc—is seen below the engraving on the title-page, 1742 edition *The School-Mistress*.

[4]John Ogilby (1600–1676), miscellaneous writer and printer of many splendid books, was ridiculed as a bad poet by Dryden in *MacFlecknoe* and by Pope, in *The Dunciad*. It was said that admiration of the lovely plates in Ogilby's editions first turned Pope as a boy to the study of the classics.

[5]The motto appears on the title-page, 1742 edition. See Horace, *Carminum* IV, 14, 5.

[6]Virgil, *Eclogues*, VIII, 7, 8.

XXVI

Works III, 68.

To the [Rev. RICHARD GRAVES], *on the Publication of The School-mistress.*[1]

[*May* 1742].

Dear Mr. Graves!

I depended a good deal on an immediate answer from you, and am greatly fearful you never received a packet of little things, which I sent you to Oxford, inclosed in a frank; though, if it arrived at all, it must have arrived several days before you left it. I beseech you to send me a line upon the receipt of these, which will free me from much perplexity; though it is doubtful whether I can defer my schemes so as to make your criticisms of service. I would have you send them notwithstanding.

I cannot help considering myself as a sportsman (though God knows how poor a one in every sense!) and the company as my game. They *fly up* for a little time; and then *settle* again. My cue is, to discharge my *piece* when I observe a number together. This week, they are straggling round about their pasture, the town: the next, they will flock into it with violent appetites; and then I discharge my little piece amongst them. —I assure you, I shall be very easy about the acquisition of any fame by this thing; all I much wish is, to lose none: and indeed I have so little to lose, that this consideration scarcely affects me.

I dare say it must be very incorrect; for I have added eight or ten stanzas within this fortnight. But inaccuracy is more excusable in ludicrous poetry than in any other. If it strikes *any*, it must be merely people of *taste;* for people of *wit* without taste (which comprehends the larger part of the critical tribe) will unavoidably despise it. I have been at some pains to secure myself from A. Philips's[2] misfortune, of mere *childishness*, 'little charm of placid mien, &c.'[3] I have added a ludicrous index, purely to shew (fools) that I am in jest:[4] and my motto, 'O quà sol habitabiles illustrat oras, maxime principum,' is calculated for the same purpose. You cannot conceive how large the number is of those that mistake burlesque for the very foolishness it exposes (which observation I made once at the Rehearsal,[5] at Tom Thumb,[6] at Chrononhotonthologos[7] all which are pieces of elegant humour). I have some mind to pursue this caution further; and advertize it, 'The Schoolmistress, &c.' A very *childish* performance every body knows (*novorum morè*). But if a person seriously calls this, or rather, burlesque, a childish or low species of poetry, he says wrong. For the most regular and formal poetry may be called trifling, folly, and weakness, in comparison of what is written with a more *manly* spirit in ridicule of it.—I have been plagued to death about the ill execution of my designs.—Nothing is certain in London but expence, which I can ill bear. Believe me, *till death*,

Yours, sincerely and particularly,

W. SHENSTONE.

NOTES

[1]As *The School-Mistress* was advertised in the *London Magazine* and *Gentleman's Magazine* of May 1742, the probable date of this letter is May 1742.

[2]Ambrose Philips (1671–1749), wrote his *Pastorals* mainly in imitation of Spenser.

[3]Cf. Chalmers, *English Poets*, XIII, p. 125: 'To Miss Georgiana, youngest daughter to Lord Carteret, August 10, 1725.'

[4]See Clarendon Press reprint 1742 edition. D'Israeli *op. cit.* thoroughly appreciated the 'exquisitely ludicrous turn' of *The School-Mistress*, and much regretted its inclusion later by Dodsley, in *Works*, 1764, among the *Moral Pieces*. Dodsley also omitted the 'ludicrous index.'

[5]*The Rehearsal* by George Villiers, 2nd Duke of Buckingham (1628–1687), was first performed December 1671. It was long popular on the stage, and was imitated by Fielding, in *Tom Thumb*, and by Sheridan, in *The Critic*. Evelyn, December 14, 1671, 'went to see the Duke of Buckingham's ridiculous farce and rhapsody called the Recital, buffooning all plays, yet profane enough.'

[6]*The Tragedy of Tragedies*, 1731, by Henry Fielding, appeared at the Haymarket Theatre in 1730 as *Tom Thumb—A Tragedy*.

[7]Henry Carey's *Chrononhotonthologos, the most tragical tragedy ever tragedised*—an amusing burlesque, was first performed at The Haymarket, February 22, 1734.

XXVII

Hull, I, 45.

To the Honourable MRS. KNIGHT[1]

THE LEASOWES. [*Early* 1742?]

Dear Madam,

As it has hitherto seemed good to you to expatiate pretty largely on so diminutive a Subject as a Thimble, I flatter myself that you may read with Patience an Account of the Life and Conversation of your most trifling humble Servant. Otherwise, I should not have told you, that I am extremely unhappy in my present Situation; that, when you left the Country, I had recourse to another Kind of natural Beauties, namely, that which is to be found in 'Groves, Meads, and murmuring Streams,' and so long as Summer was pleased to continue his Favours, I looked upon your Departure as what only changed my Pleasure to Amusement. Now, indeed, Summer has forsaken me likewise; the Trees and Groves are stripped of their Covering, and I am left without any Fence

E

against Spleen, Vapours, Megrim, Discontent, and a numerous Train of such Sort of Beings, which plague me to Death, whenever I offer to recollect your Absence; and how often that happens, I leave any one to guess but yourself, because any one else is better acquainted with the numerous Ways and Means you have of rendering your Company agreeable. I appeal also to the same Persons to guess how provoking you are, when you mention the Possibility there was that I might have seen you at the *Leasowes* some Time ago. What need you tell one of it, since it could not be effected? Why will you put me upon cursing Fortune upon more Accounts than I have already Occasion to do? Pray let me endeavour to conform myself to my real Circumstances, rather than give me a Glimpse of the Pleasure which you was about to do me, and yet had not the Goodness to go through with. I want no Inducements to come to *Worcester*, since I discovered that you lived there, and that being all that was necessary, tho' you have mentioned others that are attractive.

I beg you would make my Compliments agreeable to Mrs. WINSMORE, which you are best capable of doing, for two Reasons; first, because you know the Sincerity of my Esteem, and, secondly, because I have no Idea how any Thing you say can be disagreeable. The Consideration that she remembers me, and that she spoke of me in the same Breath with Mrs. KNIGHT (as my Vanity interprets your Letter) makes me so vain, that I, with the utmost Assurance, take the Liberty of subscribing myself,

Madam,

Your most obedient, humble Servant,

W. SHENSTONE.

P.S. I believe I shall go to L[ondo]n the End of next Week. If I were to receive a Letter from you, as I put my Foot into the Stirup, I should bid Mrs. ARNOLD take in her Bottle, for I had no Occasion for a Cordial. Your Affair (*où vous sçavez*) diverts me highly.

NOTE

[1] This letter appears to precede XXVIII where mention is made of the 'Piping Faunus at Rackstrows' which W.S. purchased for Mrs. Knight and which she acknowledged May 29, 1742.

XXVIII

Yale University Library
and Hull, I, 48.

To The Hon. Mrs. KNIGHT.

Madam,

A Lady whose conversation is ever discovering somewhat new & agreeable, may possibly find some Amusement in a subject that is new, tho' with no other Recommendation. Tis upon this Account that I beg your Acceptance of this grotesque Poem.

I took great Pleasure in seeing ye Piping Faunus at Rackstrow's,[1] because, as it is certainly a genteel Design, it must needs prove agreeable to Mrs. Knight. Connoiseurs wou'd chuse to have his Musical Intention express'd as it is at present by the Posture merely; if the Pipe was added 't'would be more obviously agreeable. If I might presume to advise, it shou'd be to calculate it in some Degree for Tastes less refin'd y^n your own, because there are millions of the former Species to perhaps one or two of the latter, & I know you take a superior Pleasure in ye satisfaction of others.

Trifles light as Air, or as ye Poem I am sending, acquire a fresh weight with me, as often as they give me an ccasion of assuring you that I am, Madam,

Your most oblig'd
and obedient h^{ble.} Servant
W. SHENSTONE.

Nando's Coffee-House,
    near Temple-Bar. *May.* [1742?]

[The following footnote is upside down on the top of the first page in the original.]

The share I had of y^r con: in Town was very $\frac{\text{agreeable}}{\text{fortunate}}$ to me & fortunate in it's consequences, as it gives some Pre-$\frac{\text{y}^e \text{ freedom of}}{}$ tence for presenting you wth this little Poem, & of assuring you y^t I am

[At top of second page in original].

I don't know whether I am right or no w^hn I wou'd excuse [?]

If there be any part of this Poem y^t be truly picturesque, & in y^t Light affords you y^e least Amus

NOTE

[1]Rackstrow (d. 1772). His museum was at 197 Fleet Street, and contained natural curiosities and anatomical figures. In *Newspapers thirty-five years ago* Lamb tells us, 'From the office of the *Morning Post* . . . we were transferred, mortifying exchange! to the office of the Albion Newspaper, late Rackstrow's Museum, in Fleet-street.'

XXIX

Works III, 46.

To the [REV. RICHARD JAGO].

1741. [*June* 1742.]

Dear Sir,

You must give me leave to complain of your last letter, three parts of which is filled with mere apology: I thought we had some time agreed, for our mutual emolument, to lay aside ceremonies of this species, till I was made Poet-laureat, and you Bishop of Winchester.—Why Bishop of Winchester, for God's sake? Why—because—he is Prelate of the Garter—an order, in all kinds of ceremony so greatly abounding.—Here am I still, trifling away my time, my money, and, I think, my health, which I fancy greatly inferior to what it would be in the country. Truth is, I do make shift to vary my days a little here; and, calling to mind the many irksome hours, the stupid identity of which I have been so often sick in the country, I conclude that I am less *unhappy* than I shall find myself at home.—However, next month I hope to see The Leasows with an appetite.—Walks in the park are now delightfully pleasant: the company stays in the Mall till ten every night.—Mrs. Clive, Mrs. Woffington,[1] Barbarini,[2] and Mr. Garrick (happy man!) are gone over to Ireland,[3] to act there for two months.— Mr. Outing, the last time I saw him, told me of how Dr. Mackenzie cured him of ever fighting with scrubs, &c. "I was just going, says he, to kick a fellow downstairs, when the

Doctor cries out, 'Mr. Outing! hear our Scotch proverb before you proceed any farther;—He that wrestles with a t—d, whether he get or lose the victory, is sure to be b—s—t.' I had great difficulty (continued he) to contain myself till he had finished his story, but I found it so pat that it saved the fellow's neck." I wish *I* could *cure* him as easily of these Quixotical narrations.—I know no soul in town that *has* any taste, which occasions me the spleen frequently. I remember W[histler?] and I were observing, that no creatures, though ever so loathsome (as toads, serpents, adders &c.), would be half so hated as ourselves, if we were to give vent to our spleen, and censure affections so bluntly as some people do. I would not venture this hint, if I did not believe you experience the same. For my part, people contradict me in things I have *studied*, and am *certain* of; and I keep silence even from *good words* (*bons mots*), though it is pain and grief to me. I must give up my *knowledge* to *pretence*, or vent it with *diffidence* to fools, or there is no peace. *These*, *these* are *justifiable* motives to wish for some degree of fame; that blind people may not bully a man that has his eyesight into their opinion that green is red, &c. Deference from fools, is no *invidious* ambition: I dare own to you that I *have* this; and I will contend that I have no more *haughty* one.—This subject I could expatiate upon with pleasure; but I stop: a tasteless fellow has spoiled my Mall-walk to-night, and occasioned you some trouble in these dull observations.—I am

Yours affectionately,
W. SHENSTONE.

NOTES

[1]Margaret 'Peg' Woffington, (1714?-1760), was a very popular eighteenth-century actress. Cf. Austin Dobson, *Side Walk Studies*. The D.N.B. places Mrs. Woffington's return to Dublin in the summer of 1742. Hence we must question the date of this letter.

[2]Signora Barberini, a dancer. . . . 'in the first week in June was in his chaise with Margaret Woffington and Signora Barberini—a dancer—posting down to Park Gate.' Fitzgerald, *Life of David Garrick*, 59.

[3]David Garrick (1717-1779). 'His success at Dublin exceeded all imagination, though much was expected from him; he was caressed by all ranks of people, as a prodigy of theatrical accomplishment. During the hottest days of the year, the playhouse was crowded with persons of fashion and rank, who were never tired of seeing and applauding the various essays of his skill.

The excessive heats became prejudicial to the frequenters of the theatre, and the epidemical distemper which seized, and carried off great numbers, was nicknamed the Garrick fever,' Davies, *Memoirs of the Life of David Garrick, Esq.*, I, 51.

XXX

Works III, 65.

To the [REV. RICHARD GRAVES], *with a Continuation of the same Subject* [*i.e. Observations on Spenser*].

June, 1742.

Dear Mr. Graves!

I am glad the stay you make in Herefordshire amuses you, even though it puts you upon preferring the place you reside at to my own place of residence. I do not know whether it be from the prejudice of being born at The Leasows, or from any real beauty in the situation; but I would wish no other, would some one, by an addition of two hundred pounds a year, put it in my power to exhibit my own designs. It is what I can now do in no other method than on paper. I lived in such an un-œconomical manner, that I must not indulge myself in the plantation of a tree for the future. I have glutted myself with the extremity of solitude, and must adapt my expences more to sociable life. It is on this account that it seems more prudent for me to buy a chair while I am in town, than to carry down twelve guineas for the model of the tomb of Virgil, an urn, and a scheme or two more of like nature.—I long to have my picture, *distantly* approaching to a profile (the best manner I can think of to express myself), drawn by Davison.[1] I have seen your sister's, and think the *face* well done in every respect; —but am greatly indignant with other things of a less fixed nature. The cap, though a good cap enough, has a vile effect; the formality of stays, etc. not agreeable.—I do not know if you saw the picture of a Scotch girl there at full length! Miss Graves has the advantage of her's, or any picture there, in her person; but certainly this girl's hair is inexpressibly charming![2] There is the genteelest negligence in it I ever saw in any picture:—what follows, but that I wish your sister would give orders to pull off her cap, and have hair after the manner of this picture—? To speak abruptly; as it *is*, I dis-approve it: were it altered, I should like it beyond any I ever saw.—I am glad you are reading Spenser: though his plan is detestable, and his *invention* less wonderful than most people

imagine, who do not much consider the obviousness of allegory; yet, I think, a person of your disposition must take great
delight in his *simplicity*, his good-nature, &c. Did you observe
a stanza that begins a canto somewhere,

> 'Nought is there under heav'n's wide hollowness
> 'That breeds,' &c.[3]

When I bought him first, I read a page or two of the Fairy
Queen, and cared not to proceed. After that, Pope's Alley[4]
made me consider him ludicrously; and in that light, I think,
one may read him with pleasure. I am now (as Ch[al]mley
with [Utrecia Smith]),[5] from trifling and laughing at him,
really in love with him. I think even the metre pretty (though
I shall never use it in earnest); and that the last Alexandrine
has an extreme majesty.—Does not this line strike you (I do
not justly remember what canto it is in);

> 'Brave thoughts and noble deeds did *evermore* inspire.'[6]

Perhaps it is my fancy only that is enchanted with the running
of it. Adieu!

W.S.

NOTES

[1]Jeremiah Davison (1695(?)–1750(?)), Scottish portrait painter. See Walpole'
Anecdotes of Painting (1849), II, 702.
[2]Cf. Letter XXXII, 59.
[3]*Faerie Queene*, I, 3.
[4]1764 ed. Pope's *Works* II, 4. *Imitations of English Poets*, II. *Of Spenser. The Alley.*
[5]The note in Graves's copy of W.S.'s *Letters* supplies this information.
[6]*Faerie Queene*, IV, canto X, verse XXVI.

XXXI

Works III, 55.

To [Rev. R. JAGO], *from Town, on the Death of Mr. Somervile,*[1] *&c.*
1741. [*July* 1742.]

My good friend,
    Our old friend Somervile is dead! I did not imagine I could
have been so sorry as I find myself on this occasion. 'Sublatum
quærimus.'[1a] I can now excuse all his foibles; impute them to

age, and to distress of circumstances: the last of these considerations wrings my very soul to think on. For a man of high spirit, conscious of having (at least in one production) generally pleased the world, to be plagued and threatened by wretches that are low in every sense; to be forced to drink himself into pains of the body in order to get rid of the pains of the mind, is a misery which I can well conceive, because I may, without vanity, esteem myself his equal in point of oeconomy, and consequently *ought* to have an eye on his misfortunes. (As you kindly hinted to me about twelve o'clock at the Feathers)[2] I should retrench;—I will; but you shall not see me;—I will not let you know that I took your hint in good part. I will do it at solitary times, as I may: and yet there will be some difficulty in it; for whatever the *world* might esteem in poor Somervile, I really find, upon critical enquiry, that *I* loved him for nothing so much as his flocci-nauci-nihili-pili-fication of money.[3]

Mr. A[nnesley] was honorably acquitted: Lord A[ltham], who was present, and behaved very insolently they say, was hissed out of court. They proved his application to the carpenter's son, to get him to swear against Mr. A[nnesley], though the boy was proved to have said in several companies (*before* he had been kept at Lord A[ltham]'s house) that he was sure the thing was accidental. Finally, it is believed he will recover the title of A[ngels]ea.[4]

The apprehension of the whores, and the suffocation of four in the round-house by the *stupidity* of the keeper, engrosses the talk of the town.[5] The said house is re-building every day (for the mob on Sunday night demolished it), and re-demolished every night. The Duke of M[arlborou]gh, J[ohn] S[pencer] his brother, Lord C—— G——, were taken into the round-house, and confined from eleven at night till eleven next day: I am not positive of the Duke of M[arlborou]gh; the others are certain: and that a large number of people of the first fashion went from the round-house to De Veil's, to give in informations of their usage. The justice himself seems greatly scared; the prosecution will be carried on with violence, so as probably to hang the keeper, and there is an end.

Lord Bath's coachman got drunk and tumbled from his box,

and he was forced to borrow Lord Orford's. Wits say, that it was but gratitude for my Lord Orford's *coachman* to drive my Lord Bath, as my Lord Bath *himself* had driven my Lord Orford. Thus they.[6]

I have ten million things to tell you; though they all amount to no more than that I wish to please you, and that I am

Your sincere friend

and humble servant.

I am pleased that I can say I knew Mr. Somervile, which I am to thank you for.[7]

NOTES

[1]Cf. the obituary notice in *The Gentleman's Magazine*, under the date July 19, 1742: 'Wm. Somerville, Esq. author of *The Chace*, a Poem. His Estates both in Gloucester and Warwickshire, are fallen to the Lord Somerville one of the 16 Scots Peers.'
A similar notice appeared in *The London Evening Post*, July 20–22. Shenstone's *Elegy XVIII* mourned the death of Somerville.
The letter is evidently written to Jago, as the concluding remark shows. Dodsley's dating of this letter is clearly wrong.

[1a]Horace, *Carm.*, 3, 24, 32.

[2]An inn at Halesowen, 'The Plume of Feathers,' to which Hugh Miller resorted after visiting The Leasowes. *First Impressions of England and its People*, 155.

[3]W.S. seems to have been pleased with this remark for in *Men and Manners*, 155, he wrote: 'I loved Mr. Somervile, because he knew so perfectly what belonged to the flocci-nauci-nihili-pilification of money.'
The expression appears to have interested later writers. Hazlitt—*On reading new books*, 'Writers who are set down as drivellers at home shoot up great authors on the other side of the water; and a work, of which the flocci-nauci-nihili-pilification, in Shenstone's phrase, is well known to every competent judge, is placarded into eminence.'
Lamb, *Letters*, 1935 ed., Vol. I, p. 7: 'Well may the "ragged followers of the Nine" set up for flocci-nauci-what-do-you-call-'em-ists.'
Scott, diary, March 8, 1826, says: 'I have arrived at a flocci-pauci-nihili-pilification of misery, and I thank whoever invented that long word!'
And again, on March 18, 1829, he speaks of 'a flocci-pauci-nihili-pilification of all that can gratify the outward man.'
It would be interesting to discover if the word was Shenstone's invention.

[4]The paragraph is apparently a reference to the trial of James Annesley for murder, July 15, 1742. In *The Gentleman's Magazine*, 1743, the story is told under the title *Memoirs of a Young Nobleman*.

[5]See *The London Evening Post*, Saturday, July 17, 1742–Tuesday, July 20, 1742: 'The late Misfortune, which befel four innocent and unhappy Persons in St. Martin's Round-house, engrossing the Conversation of almost the whole Town at present, it is thought not improper to give the following short Account of it.' The account follows of the giving by Colonel de Veil and John Bromfield, Justices of the Peace for the City of London, of an order to search for undesirables. About twenty women were brutally thrust into a small prison and some died by suffocation. The affair was hushed up by those concerned. The story throws vivid light on the treatment of prisoners. As long as the women could pay for drink, they were not thrust into the 'stinking Whole' and they were offered beds for a considerable sum. Those who had no money suffered most.

[6]Walpole, in a letter to Horace Mann (ed. Cunningham, I, 189–192) tells the story of the drunken coachman.

⁷Somervile was known to Jago in the latter's boyhood when Jago lived at Beaudesert quite near to Edstone, the home of Somervile.

'O Beaudesert . . .
Haunt of my youthful steps! Where I was wont
To range, chanting my rude notes to the wind,
While Somervile disdained not to regard,
With candid ear, and regulate the strain.'—*Edge-Hill.*

W.S. and Jago were together at Solihull Grammar School, and probably the former became known to Somervile at that period.

XXXII

Works III, 80.

To the [Rev. RICHARD GRAVES].

1743. [*August,* 1742.]

Dear Mr. Graves,

Dr. Swift would not have scrupled to print your parody, with his name to it. Why should you, *without* your name? I had a violent inclination to print it in large folio, four leaves, price fourpence: but I dare not do it, for fear you should think it of evil importance with regard to the clergy. You excell me infinitely in a way in which I take most pleasure; odd picturesque description. Send me word whether I shall print it or no—and that right soon.—I have lingered in town till now, and did not receive your letter till this morning.—I do not know whether I shall send you with this letter a little thing which I wrote in an afternoon, and, with proper *demands* of being concealed as the author, sold for two guineas. Next time I am in town, I will get money like a haberdasher. I will amuse myself with finding out the peoples weak side, and so furnish them with *suitable nonsense.*—I would have you do the same.—Make your wit bear your charges. Indeed, as to the little parody you send, it would fix your reputation with men of sense as much as (greatly more than) the whole tedious character of Parson Adams.¹ I read it half a year ago; the week after I came to town: but made Mr. Shuckburgh take it again, imagining it altogether a very mean performance.—I liked a tenth part pretty well; but, as Dryden says of Horace, (unjustly), he shews his teeth without laughing:² the greater part is *unnatural* and *unhumourous.* It has some advocates; but I observe, those not such as I ever esteemed tasters. Finally, what makes *you endeavour* to like it?

My printer was preparing his bill for the School-mistress, when I stopped him short, with a hint to go to Dodsley, who has not yet reckoned with me for Hercules. Let *the dead* bury their *dead*. Dr. Young's Complaint[3] is the best thing that has come out this season (these *twenty years*, Pope says) except mine, for so *thinks* every author, who does think proper to say so: poor Pope's history, in Cibber's Letter,[4] and the print of him upon the Mount of Love (the *coarsest* is most *humourous*), must surely mortify him. Your sister does me great honour to think my hint any thing; but I am quite zealous in my approbation of that Scotch lady's hair. I will *ever* aim at *oddness* for the future; it is cheaper to follow taste than fashion, and whoever he be that devotes himself to *taste* will be *odd* of course. —You send me the verses on Lord Ilay: they were hacked about town three months ago, and I saw them. The town is certainly the scene for a man of curiosity. I do not purpose to be long away; but I must think of retrenching.—I have ten thousand things to tell you, but I have not room. Such people as *we* should meet as regularly to compare notes as tradesmen do to settle accounts, but oftener; there is no good comes of long reckonings;—I shall forget half—I think it should be four days in a fortnight—it would not do; it would make one *mindful* of, and consequently more uneasy on account of, absence. Every one gets posts, preferments, but myself.— Nothing but my ambition can set me on a footing with them, and make me easy. Come then, lordly pride! &c. The devil thought with me in Milton,

'*All* is not lost, th' unconquerable will,[5]
'And study never to submit or yield.'

I have been in new companies; but I see no reason to contradict my assertion, that I find none I like *equally* with *you*. Adieu!

W. SHENSTONE.

NOTES

[1]A character in Fielding's *Joseph Andrews*, the prototype being William Young who at one time collaborated with Fielding.

²Dedication to Translations from Juvenal.

³Edward Young (1683–1765). *The Complaint, or Night Thoughts on Life, Death, and Immortality*, began to appear June 1742; the first 'Night' was followed by later 'Nights' at various dates.

⁴*A Letter from Mr. Cibber to Mr. Pope*, 1742, was advertised in The *Gentleman's Magazine*, July 1742. This fact, together with Shenstone's remark about Young's *Complaint* proves that the date of this letter was after July 1742. Various causes contributed to inflame the anger of Cibber and Pope, and the quarrel led to the substitution of Cibber for Theobald as the hero of *The Dunciad*. The feud is discussed at length by Isaac D'Israeli, in *Quarrels of Authors*.

⁵*Paradise Lost*, I, 105.

XXXIII

Works III, 70.

To the [REV. R. GRAVES]; *with a humourous Description of his Conduct in regard to Form and Equipage.*

THE LEASOWS, *Nov.* 1742.

Dear Sir,

Presuming you may be at Tissington by this time, I write to solicit a description of the several adventures, accidents, and phœnomena, that have amused you in your travels; and will *equally* affect me, as they relate to you. Above all things, be particular in regard to your calculations respecting Mickleton. I would have certainly met you there, as you desired me: there is no company I am fonder of than yours, and your sisters; and no place at which I have spent more agreeable hours than Mickleton. But your brother has lost one of his recommendations in my eye; that is, his *irregularity* of house-keeping. He has several left which are sufficient to preserve my utmost esteem; but that was a jewel indeed! I love to go where there is nothing much more in form than myself. I have no objection to visit *young*, *unsettled people*, with a mountebank's inconsistency in my equipage. But where a considerable family keeps up its forms (as marriage requires), I should not care to appear with an hired horse, and a *Sancho* for my valet. The case is, I *could* live in a way genteel enough, and uniformly so; but then, I must forego megrims, whims, toys, and so forth. Now, though it gives me pain, *sometimes*, not to appear of a piece; yet that *infrequent* pain is not a balance for the substantial happiness which I find in an urn, a seal, a snuff-box, an engraving, or a bust. Ambition, too, as it puts me upon wishing to make a figure, makes me very indifferent as to making a common every-day-gentlemanly figure; and saves me from appearing solicitous about the 'res *mediocriter* splendidæ,' by raising my imagination *higher*. I pour out my vanity to you in cataracts; but I hope you will rather consider it as a mark of my *confidence*, and, consequently, my sincere esteem and affection: for, I take it, the former seldom subsists without the latter. And as to what I said about my love of flattery, I hope, you will not construe it as any *hint*; neither, if I am right, would you be so ungenerous as to comply with me. I sincerely think, that flattery amongst foes is absolutely desirable; amongst one's *common acquaintance*, a behaviour *rather inclining* to it: but amongst *friends*, its consequences are of too dangerous a nature.

I am so unhappy in my wintery, unvisited state, that I can almost say with Dido, 'tædet cœli convexa tueri.'[1] I am miserable, to think that I have not thought enough to amuse me. I walk a day together; and have no idea, but what comes in at my eyes. I long for some subject about the size of Philips's Cyder, to settle heartily about; something that I could enrich by episodes drawn from the English history: *Stonehenge*[2] has some of the advantages I like; but seems a dead, lifeless title. If you chance to think of a subject which you do not chuse to *adorn* yourself, send it me to *write upon*.

I shall be vastly desirous to see you here in spring; and am in hopes Whistler will stay a month with me. I have sent an imperious letter about his dilatory correspondence.—He mentioned you in his last letter; was going to Oxford; thence to London: where, if he stays till February, I may see him. I hope you will write the very next post: you cannot oblige me or please me more than by so doing; if you think I deserve to be pleased, or am worth obliging. Adieu!

W.S.

NOTES

[1]Virgil, *Aeneid*, IV, 451.

[2]Dr. Charleton, friend of Dryden, had written on the subject of Stonehenge. Dryden wrote a set of verses, 'To my honoured Friend, Dr. Charleton, on his learned and useful Works, but more particularly his Treatise of Stonehenge, by him restored to the true Founder.'

XXXIV

Works III, 76.

To the [REV. RICHARD GRAVES], *with various Schemes of Composition.*

Feb. 1743.

Dear Mr. Graves,

You say it is no way unpleasing to you to receive my letters; if you say the thing that is not, the fault, like others, produces its own punishment.—You are now my only correspondent. I do not know what reason Whistler has for not caring to write, unless he thinks that we ought not to trouble ourselves about one another, but bend our whole endeavours to mend our fortunes; though I do not *know* his imaginations. I was afraid, after what I had said concerning *sameness* in my last, that you would interpret it to your own disadvantage; but was too lazy to write my letter again, trusting that I could deny the extent of my complaint to any one besides myself in some future letter. There is as much variety in your genius, as fortune can introduce into your circumstances.

Some time next week, do I purpose to set out for London. The reasons for my going at all do *barely* preponderate. I cannot, *conscientiously*, print any thing. I have two or three little matters in hand: none that I am greatly fond of, much less that are at all mature. One is, what you have seen, though in its mortal state, 'Flattery, or the fatal Exotic;'[1] so very quotidian and copious a subject, that I dislike it entirely. Another 'Elegies in Hammond's Metre,'[2] but upon *real* and natural subjects:[3] this I have objections to. A third, 'An Essay on Reserve,'[4] the subject genteel, I think, but scarce ten lines finished. A fourth, 'An Essay, in blank Verse, on Oeconomy, with Advice to Poets on that Head, concluding with a ludicrous Description of a Poet's Apartment.'[5] I think it were better to *annex* that poem thus, to prevent its clashing, like an earthen pot, against Philips's silver vase, though his humour lies chiefly in the language. My favourite scheme is a poem, in blank verse, upon Rural *Elegance*,[6] including cascades, temples, grottos, hermitages, green-houses, which introduces my favourite episode of the Spanish lady (you will wonder

how, but I think *well*) to close the first book. The next,
running upon planting, &c. will end with a vista terminated by
an old abbey, which introduces an episode concerning the effects
of Romish power, interdicts,[7] &c. in imitation of Lucretius's
'Plague of Athens,' taken from Thucydides, Virgil's Murrain,
and Ovid's Pestilence, &c. The two episodes in great forwardness;—but, alas! I do not like formal didactic poetry, and
shall never be able to finish aught *but* the episodes, I doubt:
unless I allow myself to treat the rest in *my own* manner,
transiently—as Camilla skimmed over the wheat-stubble.[8]

I have altered this ballad, you see; I doubt, not to your mind:
but send your criticisms, and I will be all obedience. From
London I will send you mine on your more important poem;
your critique will be important upon my silly affair; mine
silly, I am afraid, upon your momentous one—but you do not
think it momentous, as you ought. Direct to Nando's. I am
Your most sincere and affectionate friend
and humble servant,
W.S.

I question whether I should be more unhappy in any mere
mechanical employment; for instance, making nails[9] (which
seems to deal as much in *repetition* as any trade), than I am in
great part of my time when my head is unfit for study.—My
neighbour is gone to London, and has left me a legacy of
franks, so I shall be able to return your poem, &c. at least by
parcels. I strenuously purpose to be there (or to set out) next
week; but, as I *am* here at present, I think you ought to pay
some deference to the *vis inertiæ*, at least to the centripetal
force of matter, and direct to The Leasows one more letter,
with your opinion concerning the various readings in the trifle I
inclose, writing the first post that you well can. Once more adieu!

Feb. 16, 1743.

NOTES

[1]*Flattery or the Fatal Exotic* was never published, but the MS. is preserved in the
Bodleian.

FLATTERY, OR Yᴇ FATAL EXOTICK,

A SATIRICAL RHAPSODY

'Tertius e cælo cecidit *Cato*,' sed tamen.

From *Persia's* Throne to Earth's remotest Ends
The *Syren* Flattery's banefull Art extends.

Where Nature teems with animated clay;
Or gives yᵉ Limbs to move, yᵉ Lungs to play,
Some flatter Heroes; others *flatt*er E*lve*s;
Some all they meet; and all we meet, themselves.
   And yet wise Nature's equal Hand is known
To give each clime *some* produce *all it's own.*
Some varying shrub, or Flow'r, or Cast of Mind,
And, who transplants it, { debilitates } yᵉ *Kind*
                        { must debase, }
Will *Lapland's* Boors their futile Toils bestow,
To see fair Lemons burnish Hills of Snow?
Or will *Hibernia* ways and means explore,
To settle Poison on her hostile Shore?
Whence then arose this toilsom waste of time,
To tempt mean Falshood from the native Clime?
Flatt'rys coy weed, in foreign Realms so fair,
That shews } an alien scorn of *English* Air.
Betrays }
Slow and uncouth yᵉ shrivel'd Branches rise;
Crampt by yᵉ Impulse of ungenial Skies.
Yet on our Plains, with fruitless fond desire,
We nurse this *awkward stranger,* and admire,
Fondly yᵉ *British* Tongue essays to feign;
Denoyer bends our nervous Limbs in vain;
Each hardy Fibre nauseates *French* controul;
And rebel virtue vindicates yᵉ Soul.
See wayward Truth yᵉ fraudfull Aim defeat;
And break yᵉ flowing current of Deceit!
See { restive Faith her utmost
    { native *Honour* all his efforts try;
To }
And } cramp yₑ fair proportion of a Lye!
Yet with strange cringes cours yᵉ courtly slave,
And quits yᵉ Form erect, which Nature gave,
And Nature's God—who bade him trace on high
The lofty wonders of yᵉ spangled Sky;
Not yₑ Dim stars yᵗ on *some* Bosoms shine;
What Kings can *grant,* and Broiderers *design;*
Proceed, but ah let x x x uncensur'd live;
And, whom so much you mimick, ah forgive.

---

²James Hammond (1710–1742), wrote 'Love Elegies by Mr. H–nd written in the year 1732. With Preface by E. of C–d. 1743.' Johnson said these elegies had 'neither passion, nature, nor manner,' nothing 'but frigid pedantry.' W.S. particularly admired Hammond's metre. In *A Prefatory Essay on Elegy, Works I,* 7, he writes, 'Heroic metre, with alternate rhime, seems well enough adapted to this species of poetry; . . . The world has an admirable example of its beauty in a collection of elegies not long since published; the product of a gentleman of most exact taste, and whose untimely death merits all the tears that elegy can shed.'

³*Ibid.,* 10: 'The author of the following elegies entered on his subjects occasionally, as particular incidents in life suggested, or dispositions of mind recommended them to his choice. If he describes a rural landskip, or unfolds the train of sentiments it inspired, he fairly drew his picture from the spot; and felt very sensibly the affection he communicates. If he speaks of his humble shed, his flocks and his fleeces, he does not counterfeit the scene; who having (whether through choice or necessity, is not material) retired betimes to country solitudes, and sought his happiness in rural employments, has a right to consider himself as a real shepherd.'

⁴Never published. The ideas for the poem appear *Men and Manners, On Reserve, A*

Fragment, Works II, 49. 'These were no other than a collection of hints, when I proposed to write a poetical essay on Reserve.'

[5]*Œconomy, a rhapsody addressed to young poets. Works,* I, 285.

[6]*Rural Elegance; an ode to the late Duchess of Somerset, written* 1750. *Works* I, 105.

[7]The reference is apparently to *The Ruin'd Abby; or, The Effects of Superstition. Works* I, 308.

[8]Cf. Pope, *Essay on Criticism,* Part II, l. 126.
> 'Not so when swift Camilla scours the plain,
> Flies o'er the unbending corn and skims along the main.'

[9]Nail making was the trade of Halesowen. See Hugh Miller's description, *First Impressions of England and its People,* 132, 133.

XXXV

Works III, 98.

To MR. GRAVES, *written in Hay-Harvest.*

July 3, 1743.

Dear Mr. Graves,

I did not part from you without a *great deal* of melancholy. To think of the *short* duration of those interviews which are the objects of one's *continual* wishes, has been a reflection that has plagued me of old! I am sure I returned home with it then, more aggravated as I foresaw myself returning to the same series of melancholy hours from which you had a while relieved me, and which I had *particularly* suffered under all this last spring! I wish to God, you might happen to be settled not far from me: a day's journey distance, however; I mean an *easy* one. But the odds are infinitely against me. I must only *rely* for my happiness on the hopes of a never-ceasing correspondence!

Soon after you were gone, I received my packet. The history of Worcestershire is mere stuff. T—— I am so fond of, that, I believe, I shall have his part of the collection bound over again, neatly and separately. But sure Hammond has no right to the least *inventive* merit, as the preface-writer would insinuate. I do not think there is a single thought, of any eminence, that is not literally translated. I am astonished he could content himself with being so little an original.[1]

Mr. Lyttelton and his lady[2] are at Hagley. A malignant caterpillar has demolished the beauty of all our *large* oaks. Mine are secured by their littleness. But, I guess, the park suffers; a large wood near me being a mere winter piece for nakedness.

F

At present, I give myself up to riding and thoughtlessness; being resolved to make trial of *their* efficacy towards a tolerable degree of health and spirits. I wish I had you for my director. I should proceed with great confidence of success; though I am brought very low by two or three fits of a fever since I saw you. Had I written to you in the midst of my dispirited condition, as I was going, you would have had a more tender and unaffected letter than I *can* write at another time: what I think, perhaps, at all times; but what sickness can alone elicit from a temper fearful of whining.

Surely the 'nunc formosissimus annus'[2a] is to be limited to hay-harvest. I could give my reasons: but you will imagine them to be, the activity of country people in a pleasing employment; the full verdure of the summer; the prime of pinks, woodbines, jasmines, &c. I am old; very old; for few things give me so much mechanical pleasure as lolling on a bank in the very heat of the sun,

'When the old come forth to play
'On a sun-shine holiday—'[3]

And yet it is as much as I can do to keep Mrs. Arnold from going to neighbouring houses in her smock, in despite of decency and my known disapprobation.

I find myself more of a patriot than I ever thought I was. Upon reading the account of the battle,[4] I found a very sensible pleasure, or, as the Methodists term it, perceived my heart *enlarged*, &c. The map you sent me is a pretty kind of *toy*, but does not enough particularize the scenes of the war, &c. which was the end I had in view when I sent for it.

'O dura messorum ilia!'[5] About half the appetite, digestion, strength, spirits, &c. of a mower, would make me the happiest of mortals! I would be understood literally, and precisely.

Adieu!

W.S.

NOTES

[1] Most of Hammond's elegies were very near translations of Tibullus.

[2] Lucy Fortescue, first wife of George Lyttelton. Everyone concurred in praising her amiable character. See Letter XXXVII.

[2a] Ovid, *Ars. Amat.*, Book 2, 315.

[3] Cf. *L'Allegro*, l. 97.

[4] The Battle of Dettingen, June 27, 1743.

[5] Horace, *Epod.*, 3, 4.

XXXVI

Works III, 94.

To Mr. JAGO [*describing his Situation, & State of Health*].

The Leasows, *Saturday,*
July the 9*th,* 1743.

Dear Mr. Jago,

It is not a contrived apology, or an excuse, which I am going to offer for the disappointments I have given you. I have actually been so much out of order ever since I wrote to you, nay, ever since I *formed a design* of a Sunday expedition to L[apworth], that it never has been in my *power* to execute my intentions. My vertigo has not *yet* taken away my senses: God knows how soon it may do; but my nerves are in such a condition, that I can scarce get a wink of even *disordered* rest for whole nights together. May you never know the misery of such involuntary vigils! I ride every day almost to fatigue; which only tends to make my want of sleep more *sensible*, and not in the least to remove it. I have *spirits* all day, good ones; though my head is dizzy, and I never enterprize any study of greater subtlety than a news-paper. I cannot say the journey to L[apworth] would be at all *formidable* to me; for I ride about fifteen miles, as I compute it, every day before dinner. But the nights from home would be insupportable to me. I have fatigued Mrs. Arnold's assiduity, to the injury of her health; by occasioning her to sit in my room a'nights, light my candle, put it out again, make me perspiratory wheys, and slops; and am amused by the most silly animadversions she is capable of making. I never knew her usefulness till now; but I *now* prefer her to *all* of *her station*. If I get over this disorder, concerning which I have bad apprehensions, you may depend upon seeing me the first Sunday I dare venture forth. I hope *you* continue mending. The benefit of *riding* is not only universal, and would cure *me* too, could I but make one previous advance towards health. Have you tried cold-bathing? Perhaps it may not suit your case. I wish I had not dropt it. I take my fluctuation of nerves to be caused, as that of the sea is, by wind; which I am continually pumping up, and yet find it still renewed. When I am just sinking to sleep, a sudden twitch of my nerves calls me back again—to watchfulness and vexation! I consider myself as in the state of the philosopher, who held a bullet betwixt his finger and thumb, which, whenever he was about to nod, was ordered so as to fall into a large brass pan, and wake him—that he might pursue his lucubrations.

I will mention one circumstance regarding the weakness of my nerves;—and not my spirits, for I told you those were tolerable:—the least noise that is, even the falling of a fire-shovel upon the floor, if it happen unexpectedly, shocks my whole frame; and I actually believe that a gun fired behind my back, unawares, amidst the stillness of the night, would go near to kill me with its noise.

I am just going to bed; and dare not be any more attentive, as I hope to close my eyes for a minute. So fare you well!

It is now six o'clock in the morning, and I have had about five hours middling sleep; which encourages me greatly: so I will *hope* to be able to see you next Sunday sevennight.

What think you of the battle? Are not you so much in love with our King that you could find in your heart to serve him in any profitable post he might assign you?[1]

Capt. L[yttelton] is wounded in the thigh.[2]

When I ride in my chair round my neighbourhood, I am as much stared and wondered at, as a giant would be that should walk through Pall-mall. My vehicle is at *least as* uncommon hereabouts as a blazing comet. My chief pleasure lies in finding out a thousand roads, and delightful little haunts near home, which I never dreamt of: egregious solitudes, and most incomparable bye-lanes! where I can as effectually lose myself within a mile of home, as if I were benighted in the desarts of Arabia. Adieu!

NOTES

[1]King George took over the command of the army at Aschaffenberg, June 19.

[2]In June, Captain Richard Lyttelton received a 'musquett shott' in the thigh at Aschaffenberg, where a small engagement took place ten days before the battle of Dettingen. The despatch announced that 'the ball only grazed and caused a slight contusion; he continued in the field till the affair was over, and then at the desire of Lord Stair, who said "For God's sake, Lyttelton, go home, I give you my word of honour there will be nothing more; I will have you go home:" he went home, and as soon as he found the ball was not ledged in the thigh, he got a horseback again.' Wyndham, I, 123.

XXXVII

Works III, 89.

To Mr. GRAVES, *describing his Situation, and State of Health, &c.*

THE LEASOWS.
[*July,* 1743.]

Dear Mr. Graves,

To-morrow morning I set out for Cheltenham, to make trial of the waters there. I shall, perhaps, add to this letter at several stages, and conclude it at the place to which I am going; so that, like those springs, you may, perhaps, find it impregnated with the nature of all those places through which it passes; perhaps quite the contrary.

—, if I mistake not the man, is an encourager of works of taste, &c. though I am going to instance this oddly: he was a hearty stickler for my poem upon Hercules at Bath, as D. Jago sent me word. Perhaps it was complaisance to Mr. Lyttelton, with whom, Charles, &c. he is intimate, if, as I said before, I do not mistake the person. I flatter myself, I do not; and I hope that we two shall ever find the same persons, or the same kind of persons, our friends, and also our enemies.

If I get over this ill habit of body, depend upon it, I *will* have a *reverend* care of my health, as Sir John Falstaff advises the Chief Justice,[1] I solve all the tempests that disturb my constitution into *wind*: it plagues me, first, in the shape of a bad appetite, then indigestion, then lowness of spirits and a flux of pale water, and at night by watchings, restlessness, twitchings of my nerves, or a sleep more distracted than the most active state of watchfulness. But I think purging lessens all these symptoms, and I trust my scheme that I am entering upon is right.

I was on Monday at Hagley, to wait on Mr. Lyttelton, who was going to Sir John Astley's,[2] to see his grand edifice.—As to Mrs. Lyttelton, if her affability is not artificial, I mean, if it does not owe its original (as it *ought to do* its *management*) to art, I cannot conceive a person more amiable;—but *sense* and *elegance* cannot be feigned: to *exhibit* them, is to *have* them.

How is my song set? Miss Carrington[3] procured it that

favour; but I have never seen a copy, nor knew of its being to be printed. Howard has set another of mine,[4] which I received last post; but my harpsichord is out of order, and I have found no one yet to explain the hieroglyphics which convey it. You may probably find it in some future number of the British Orpheus. 'By the side of a stream, &c.'

I am in as good spirits this instant as ever I was in my life: only 'Mens turbidum lætatur.'[5] My head is a little confused; but I often think seriously, that I ought to have the most ardent and *practical* gratitude (as the Methodists[6] chuse to express themselves) for the advantages that I have: which, though not eminently shining, are such, to speak the truth, as suit my particular humour, and, consequently, deserve all kind of acknowledgement. If a poet should address himself to God Almighty, with the most earnest thanks for his goodness in allotting him an estate that was over-run with shrubs, thickets, and coppices, variegated with barren rocks and precipices, or floated three parts in four with lakes and marshes, rather than such an equal and fertile spot as the 'sons of men' delight in; to my apprehension, he would be guilty of no absurdity.— But of this I have composed a kind of prayer, and intend to write a little speculation on the subject; this kind of gratitude I assuredly ought to have, and have. For my health, if one reflects, a country-fellow's stock of it would be unfit for solitude; would dispose one rather to bodily feats, and, what Falstaff calls in Poins, *gambol* faculties,[7] than mental contemplations, and would give one that kind of pain which springs from *impatience*. My constitution was given me originally good; and with regard to it now (as G. Barnwell[8] says) 'What am I?— What I *have made myself*.' Or, to speak with Milton,

> 'Him after all disputes
> 'Forc'd I absolve: all my evasions vain,
> 'And reasonings, tho' thro' mazes, only lead
> 'But to my own conviction. First and last
> 'On me, me only, as the source and spring
> 'Of all corruption, all the blame lights due.'[9]

Though this is but vulgarly expressed in Milton neither.

Jago has been here this last week, and I drove him to Dudley

Castle,[10] which I long to shew you: I never saw it (since I was
the size of my pen) before: it has great romantic beauty, though
perhaps Derbyshire may render it of small note in your eye.

One is tempted to address the K[ing] as Harry the Eighth
does his wife, *mutatis mutandis:*

> 'Go thy ways, George!
> 'Whoe'er he be that shall assert he has
> 'A *bolder* king, let him in nought be trusted
> 'For saying false in that——'[11]

I have a mind to write an ode in praise of him, and in rivalship of Cibber.[12]—Mine should be of the ballad style and
familiarity, as expressing the sentiments of a person returning
from a dislike to a thorough approbation of him, which seems,
at present, the sense of the nation.—But herein I am not in
earnest.——

My pen has run on a whole page at random. It amuses me
to encourage it, and so I will try to get a frank.

I am at this moment arrived at Cheltenham, after an expensive and fatiguing journey. I called yesterday at Mickleton;
saw the portico, and snapped up a bit of mutton at your
brother's;[13] drank a dish of tea with Miss S——; and, in
opposition to the strongest remonstrances, persisted in an
endeavour to reach Cheltenham after five o'clock. The consequence was, that, about ten, I found myself travelling back
again towards Stowe;[14] and had undoubtedly wandered all
night in the dark, had I not been fortunately met by a wag-
goner's servant, who brought me back to the worst inn but
one I ever lay at, being his master's.—Here I am: which is all I
shall say in this letter.

Adieu!

W.S.

NOTES

[1]*Hen. IV*, Pt. II, Act I, Sc. 2.

[2]Sir John Astley Bart. of Patshull, Co. Stafford.

[3]Was this lady, Miss C——, with whom Shenstone fell in love at Cheltenham? Cf.
Recollection, 103.

[4]Samuel Howard (1710–1782), organist and composer. A collection of his called
The Musical Companion (1775?) contains about fifty of his cantatas, solos and duets, with
accompaniments for harpsichord and violin. The words of *Florellio and Daphne* are by
W.S., some of whose songs are in *The British Orpheus*, IV, and *The Vocal Musical Mask*.
Miss A. Hazeltine in her account of *William Shenstone and his Critics* says that the MS.

in the hands of Professor George Herbert Palmer of Harvard University has this note at the foot of *The Scholar's Relapse* (*Works* I, p. 164, 'By the side of a grove'): 'Set by Howard and printed vilely in his British Orpheus.' *The Rose-bud* (*Works* I, p. 165. 'See, Daphne, see, Florelio cry'd,') has this: 'Set by Galliard.' The latter is however given in the *British Orpheus* as 'set by Mr. Howard' while the former finds no place in the collection.

I have traced several of Shenstone's songs with their accompaniments in the song-books of the time. *English Songs*, printed by J. Johnson, 1783, contains (1) 'I told my nymph, I told her true' (*Works* I, p. 149) 'set by Mr. Joseph Harris' (d. 1814).

(²) 'The western sky was purpled o'er' (*Works* I, p. 125) 'set by Mr. Dibdin' (1745–1814, dramatist and song writer).

Vocal Music (1770?), Vol. II, contains 'Shepherd, would'st thou here obtain' (*Works* II, 346), the tune being by Samuel Arnold (1740–1802).

⁵Horace, *Odes* II, xix, 6.

⁶W.S. seems to have been little interested in the Methodists, though George White-field was a contemporary of his at Pembroke College, Oxford. Graves, as *The Spiritual Quixote* shows, was much interested.

⁷*Henry IV*, Pt. II, Act II, Sc. IV.

⁸*The London Merchant* (1731) or *The History of George Barnwell* by George Lillo (1693–1739), became a stock piece, and was acted at Christmas and Easter for the London Apprentices.

⁹*Paradise Lost*, X, 827.

¹⁰The seat of the ancestors of Lord Dudley.

¹¹*Henry VIII*, Act. II, Sc. 4. This letter was evidently written soon after the Battle of Dettingen, during July, 1743.

¹²Colley Cibber was made Poet Laureate, September 27, 1730.

¹³W.S. was keenly interested in all the improvements which Morgan Graves intro-duced at Mickleton, and it was probably while staying with the Graves family that he first dabbled in landscape-gardening. 'This had encouraged Mr. G—— to do something in the same way at M–kl–ton; which, though in an indifferent country, has many natural beauties; of surrounding hills, and hanging woods; a spacious lawn, and one natural cascade; capable of great improvement, though, from various circum-stances, the place is to this day in a very unfinished state. This, however, was sufficient to engage the attention and excite the active imagination of Mr. Shenstone.' *Recollection*, 49.

¹⁴ Cf. *Recollection*, 119, and Shenstone's *Elegy VII*, *Works* I, 27.

'On distant heaths, beneath autumnal skies,
Pensive I saw the circling shade descend;
Weary and faint I heard the storm arise,
While the sun vanish'd like a faithless friend.'

XXXVIII

To the [Rev. R. JAGO].

Works III, 85.

1743. [*July.*]

Dear Sir,

I long heartily to talk over affairs with you *tête à tête;* but am an utter enemy to the fatigue of transcribing what might pass well enough in conversation.—I shall say nothing more con-cerning my departure from L[apworth], than that it was necessary, and therefore excusable.—I have been since with a gentleman upon the borders of Wales, Bishop's Castle, from whence I made a digression one day beyond Offa's Dyke: saw mountains which converted all that I *had* seen into mole-hills; and houses which changed the Leasows into Hampton Court: where they talk of a glazed window as a piece of magnificence; and where their highest idea of his Majesty is, that he can ride in such a coach as 'Squire Jones or 'Squire Pryce's. The woman of the inn, at one place, said, 'Glass (in windows) was very genteel, that it was; but she could not afford such finery.'

You agree with the rest of the married world in a propensity to make proselytes. This inclination in some people gives one a kind of dread of the matter. They are ill-natured, and can only wish one in their own state because they are unhappy; like persons that have the plague, who, they say, are ever desirous to propagate the infection. I make a contrary conclusion when *you* commend marriage, as you seem to do, when you wish Miss—may reconcile me to more than the *name* of wife. I know not what you have heard of my amour:[1] probably *more* than I can thoroughly confirm to you. And what if I should say to you, that marriage was not once the subject of our conversation?

> —'Nec conjugis unquam[2]
> 'Prætendi tædas, aut hæc in fœdera veni.'

Do not you think every thing in nature strangely improved since you were married, from the tea-table to the *warming-pan?*[3]

I want to see Mrs. Jago's hand-writing, that I may judge of her temper; but she must write something in my praise. Pray see you to it, in your next letter.

I could parodize my Lord Carteret's letter from Dettingen,[4] if I had it by me. 'Mrs. Arnold (thanks be praised!) has this day gained a very considerable victory. The scold lasted two hours. Mrs. S—e was posted in the hall, and Mrs. Arnold upon the stair-case; which superiority of ground was no small service to her in the engagement. The fire lasted the whole space, without intermission; at the close of which, the enemy was routed, and Mrs. Arnold kept the field.'

Did you hear the song to the tune of 'The Cuckow?'

> 'The Baron stood behind a tree,
> 'In woeful plight, for nought heard he
> 'But Cannon, Cannon, &c.
> 'O word of fear!
> 'Unpleasing to a German ear.'

The notes that fall upon the word 'Cannon,' express the sound with its echo admirably.

I send you my pastoral elegy[5] (or ballad, if you think that name more proper), on condition that you return it with ample remarks in your next letter: I say 'return it,' because I have no other copy, and am too indolent to take one, Adieu!

W.S.

NOTES

[1]*Recollection*, 103: 'I believe, on parting from Miss G—— on some occasion, Mr. Shenstone first sketched out his "Pastoral Ballad" in that style which I saw two or three years before he went to Cheltenham in the summer of 1743. But meeting there and becoming very intimate with Miss C——, who is still living, he became so far enamoured, as to feel himself unhappy on leaving Cheltenham, and the object of his passion. On this occasion he enlarged, and divided it into the four distinct parts, under the titles of "Absence," "Hope," "Solicitude" and "Disappointment."

[2]Virgil, *Aeneid* IV, 338–9.

[3]Jago's first wife was Dorothea Susanna Fancourt, daughter of the rector of Kimcote, whom Jago had known long.

[4]Lord Carteret, as Secretary of State, accompanied the King when he went to take over the charge of the Army, and Carteret's letter to the Duke of Newcastle was published in *The Gentleman's Magazine*. 'My Lord, His Majesty (God be prais'd) has this day gained a very considerable Battle, etc.'

[5]*The Pastoral Ballad.*

XXXIX

Hull, II, 15.

To MR. WHISTLER.

[*Nov.* 1743.][1]

Dear Mr. Whistler,

THIS is the first Evening I have had to myself since I left *Cheltenham;* and as one wants some very favourite Subject to engross one's Thoughts a little, after a long Dissipation, I could think of nothing more effectual than a Letter to one who has so large a Share in them; beside, they have given me your

Letter from *Bradfield*, and I am in Pain till I have acknowledged so affectionate and so polite a Present. People, whose
very Foibles are so many Elegancies, can scarce write any
Thing more agreeable than a plain unaffected Account of
them. I remember, I used to think this a Kind of Distinction
between Mr. GRAVES and you; that the one had the Knack of
making his Virtues unenvied, and the other of rendering
(what I perhaps unjustly termed) his Weaknesses enviable. I
am almost afraid of inserting this, lest it should seem to injure
the superlative Esteem I have of you: but I must add, that I
consider a Mixture of Weaknesses, and an ingenuous Confession of them, as the most engaging and sociable Part of any
Character; if I did not, I could not allot them you, whose
Manner is so distinguishedly amiable.

Since I left *Cheltenham*, I have been at Mr. B[rown]'s,
in *Bishop's-Castle*. I rode one Morning with him about three
Miles, that I might say, I had been in *Wales*, and seen *Brecon*,
Caderidris, and *Plinlimmon*, with an extensive Chain of other
Mountains. I called at a small Ale-house, where the People
lived all the Winter without any Glass in their Windows. I was
wondering how they could live so, in a more cold Country
than you have, perhaps, experienced. The Wife said, 'True it
was, she could like Glass very well.' 'Yes,' says the Husband,
'Glass is very genteel, that it is.' 'Nay, says the Wife, 'not for
the Genteelness neither, though it is very genteel, that's the
Truth on't.' This Circumstance struck me a good deal, that
they should discover the genteelness of Glazing, and never
once think of its *Expediency*. Mr. B[rown] is a Man you would
like upon Acquaintance, though, as I remember, you had
some Objection to the Superfluity of his Wit. We shall, in all
Probability, have frequent Interviews with him at *Bath*,
London, &c. He would fain have seduced me to have travelled
into *Portugal*, &c. with himself, and one Mr. MOORE, his
Neighbour; an agreeable, modest Man, and late Member for
Bishop's-Castle. I declined it for two Reasons; first, on Account
of the Expence, and secondly, that I could not think of spend-
ing two Years in *this* Part of my Life abroad; dead to one's own
Country, and procuring, at best, very perishable, and useless
Friendships in another. If I could have staid, I was to have

gone with him to a *Welsh* Sessions, fraught with Irascibility. He is a Justice of Peace there.

As to good Acquaintance, though I much desire it, I have as literally a Genius for avoiding, as any one ever had for procuring it. I cannot approach within fifty Yards of Servility for fear of it.

I want sadly to talk to you about a thousand Things, I have some Notion of spending a Week at Mr. D——'s. Act sublimely, and give me the Meeting then, notwithstanding.

Though I was enamoured with the Politeness of Mr. W——'s Conversation, I should not, perhaps, have been very forward to express my Sentiments, if you had not intimated, that he made favourable mention of me. I begin to grow a little pleased with Prudence, and I think it a Debt one owes her, to reserve one's Encomiums till one knows one's mutual Sentiments; for certainly, he that happens to commend an Enemy, happens to condemn himself. I beg my Compliments.

I believe poor J. D[olman] is alive—Farther I cannot learn.

I did not think it possible, I could have been so much engaged by love as I have been of late.—Poor Miss C——!

It must necessarily be an Honour to a Girl, to have pleased a Man of Sense, (I know not but I am vain in supposing myself of that Number) let his Station be how low soever. Now it must be a Disgrace to captivate a Fool, however high it be; the former is the strongest Evidence of Merit, the latter of the Want of it.

Now I talk of Vanity, I beseech you never check yourself in your Letters—I don't purpose it; and I think it makes as pretty a Figure in the Letters of a Man of Taste, as it does in the Embroidery of a Beau. I am as much yours, as human Nature will admit of.

Adieu!

W. Shenstone.

NOTE

[1]The date of this letter can be nearly ascertained as the death of Jack Dolman is mentioned as having taken place on November 9, 1743.

XL

Works III, 101.

To the [Rev. R. GRAVES], *after the Disappointment of a Visit,*

1743.

Dear Sir,

I am tempted to begin my letter as Memmius does his harangue. 'Multa me dehortantur à vobis, ni studium virtutis vestræ omnia exsuperet.'[1]—You contrive interviews of about a minute's duration; and you make appointments in order to disappoint one; and yet, at the same time that your proceedings are thus vexatious, force one to bear testimony to the inestimable value of your friendship! I do insist upon it, that you ought to compound for the disappointment you have caused me, by a little letter every post you stay in town. I shall now scarce see you till next summer, or spring at soonest; and then I may probably take occasion to visit you, under pretence of seeing Derbyshire. Truth is, your prints have given me *some* curiosity to see the original places. I am grateful for your intentions with regard to giving me part of them, and impertinent in desiring you to convey them to me as soon as you can well spare them. Let me know if they are sold separately at the print-shops. I think to recommend them to my new acquaintance, Mr. Lyttelton Brown. I like the humour of the ballad you mention, but am more obliged for your partial opinion of me. The notes that fall upon the word 'Cannon, Cannon,' are admirably expressive of the sound, I dare say: I mean, jointly with its echo; and so, I suppose, you will think, if you ever attended to the Tower-guns. I find I cannot afford to go to Bath previously to my London-journey; though I look upon it as a proper method to make my residence in town more agreeable. I shall, probably, be there about the first of December; or before, if I can accelerate my friend Whistler's journey. The pen I write with is the most disagreeable of pens! But I have little else to say; only this,—that our good friend Jack Dolman is dead at Aldridge; his father's benefice.

I beg, if you have leisure, you would inclose me in a frank the following songs, with the notes: 'Stella and Flavia,' 'Gentle

Jessy,' 'Sylvia, wilt thou waste thy prime?'[2] and any other that is new. I should be glad of that number of the British Orpheus which has my song in it, if it does not cost above six-pence. Make my compliments to your brother and sister; and believe me, in the common forms, but in no common degree,

Dear Mr. Graves's
Most affectionate friend and servant.
W. SHENSTONE.

The Leasows,
    Nov. 9th, 1743.
Do write out the whole ballad of 'The Baron stood behind a tree.'

NOTES

[1]Sallust, *Jugurtha*, 31.
[2]'Stella and Flavia' appears among the songs of Samuel Howard, the words being by Mrs. Pilkington.

> 'Stella and Flavia ev'ry Hour
> Do various Hearts surprize:
> In Stella's soul is all her Pow'r,
> And Flavia's in her Eyes.' etc.

'Gentle Jessy' and 'Sylvia, wilt thou waste thy prime?' I have been unable to trace.

XLI

Works III, 104.

To the [REV. RICHARD GRAVES], *on the Receipt of a Present of Prints.*

THE LEASOWS, *Dec.* 23, 1743.

Dear Sir,
    You may reasonably have expected a letter before now, either as an acknowledgement for your genteel present, or, at least, by way of information that I had received it. The prints have given me a pleasure, which, however considerable, would soon have languished, if I had bought them at a shop; but which is now built upon the esteem I have for the giver, and cannot have a more durable foundation.—As for the rest, I am most pleased with the view of Matlock, and shall have no peace of

mind till I have seen the original. I have been gilding the frames, and wishing all the while for your company.

I will alter the ballad according to your advice; dividing it into three parts, and adding a stanza or two to the shortest, some time or other. I have had no opportunity of trying the tunes. 'Arno's vale' has pretty words, and recommends itself to one's imagination by the probability that it was written on a real occasion. The similitude of rhimes in the close inexcusable.[1] For all that has been the subject of my letter hitherto, as the country people say, I can but thank you, and I do very sincerely; though as to the songs I will re-pay you.

I have your poem by me, which I have read often with the greatest pleasure. I have many observations to make; and only defer the communication till I know whether you have a copy at Tissington to turn to. I think, the most *polite* and *suitable* title to it would run thus: 'The Villa, a Poem; containing a Sketch of the present Taste in Rural Embellishments, written in 1740.'[2] Your preface has a pretty thought towards the close; otherwise is on no account to be admitted. Pardon my freedom; but, I think, there is no manner of occasion for a preface; and those strokes, which I *know* to be real modesty in *you*, the world will undoubtedly impute to affectation.—If you give me encouragement, I will be very minute in my criticisms, allowing you to reject ten to one that you admit of.

Whistler has gone to Bristol, and has bilked me.—I said, he is gone; but, I believe, he is only upon going—I linger at home, in hopes of gleaning up a little health; and through a dread of being ill in a place where I can be less attended on.— I can continually *find out* something in my preceding diet that, I *think*, disorders me; so that I am constantly in hopes of growing well:—but, perhaps, I never shall:

'Optima quæque dies miseris mortalibus ævi
'*Prima* fugit, subeunt morbi——'[3]

When I was a school-boy, I never knew there *was any such thing* as perspiration; and now, half my time is taken up in considering the immediate connexion betwixt that and health, and endeavouring to promote it.

Mr. Lyttelton has built a kind of alcove in his park, inscribed, 'Sedes contemplationis,' near his hermitage. Under the aforesaid inscription is 'Omnia vanitas:'—the sides ornamented with sheeps-bones, jaws, sculls, &c. festoon-wise. In a nitch over it, an owl.

As to schemes, I have none with regard to the world, women, or books. And I hate, and have deferred writing to you (for some days) for that reason. I am sick of exhibiting so much sameness:—I am constantly poring over some Classic, which I consider as one of Idleness's better shapes. But I am impatient to be doing something that may tend to better my situation in some respect or other. It is *encouragement* can alone inspire one.

> ——'Multa & præclare minantem
> 'Vivere nec *recte*, nec *suaviter*——'[4]

expresses the whole of me. Thus my epistles persevere in the plaintive style; and I question whether the sight of them does not, ere now, give you the vapours. I have an old aunt that visits me sometimes, whose conversation is the perfect counterpart of them. She shall fetch a long-winded sigh with Dr. Young for a wager; though I see *his* Suspiria are not yet finished. He has *relapsed* into 'Night the Fifth.'[5] I take his case to be wind in a great measure, and would advise him to take rhubarb in powder, with a little nutmeg grated amongst it, as I do.

Dear Mr. G[raves], write down to me; and believe me to be, invariably,

Your most sincere
and obliged friend, &c.

W. SHENSTONE.

NOTES

[1]'Arno's Vale.—set by Mr. Holcombe'(Henry Holcombe 1690–1750), is to be found in the same volume of *The British Orpheus* as 'Stella and Flavia.'

> When here Lucinda first we came
> Where Arno rolls his Silver Stream,
> How brisk the Nymphs, the Swains how gay,
> Content inspir'd each rural Lay.
> The Birds in livelier Concert sung,
> The Grapes in thicker clusters hung:
> All look'd as Joy could never fail,
> Among the sweets of Arno's Vale. etc.

The words of this poem by Charles Sackville, afterwards Earl of Dorset, were written at Florence in 1737, on the death of John Gaston the last Duke of Tuscany of the house of Medici, and addressed to Signora Muscovita, a singer, a favourite of the author's.

²The performance alluded to may be the one to which Graves gave the title—'To Morgan Graves, Esq. on the Improvements at Mickleton, 1740,' *Euphrosyne* I, 122.

³Virgil, *Georgic* III, 66–7.

⁴Horace, *Epistles* I, 8, 3.

⁵*The Gentleman's Magazine* of December 1743 advertised 'Night Thoughts. Night 5th. The Relapse. pr. 1s. 6d. Dodsley.'

XLII

Works III, 108.

To the [REV. RICHARD GRAVES], *with Observations on Hypocrisy, &c.*

1743.

Dear Sir,

You must know, my last letter to you was written before I received yours from Tissington; and I should take shame upon myself for not answering it, were I not furnished with this excuse—that I waited for a frank for you.—There are but few things I have to say to you, and such as are not worth transcribing; yet, as our distance from one another requires it, I will scrawl them over as negligently as I can, to let you see I lay no stress upon them. A good excuse for laziness! you will say: and lazy enough I am, God knows! I believe, any one who knows me thoroughly will think, that there never was so great an inconsistence as there is betwixt my words (in my poem) and my actions.—This is what the world calls hypocrisy, and is determined to look upon with *peculiar* aversion. But, I think, the hypocrite is a *half*-good character. A man certainly, considering the force of precedent, deserves some praise who keeps up appearances; and is, no doubt, as much to be commended for talking better than he acts, as he is to be blamed for acting worse than he talks. So much for casuistry. I would seem, you must know, to have some meritorious views in talking *virtuously;* but who does not know that every one who writes poetry looks directly with his face towards praise, and whatever else his eye takes in is viewed obliquely? Praise, as I said to foible-confessing W[histler?], is the desired, the noted, and the adequate reward of poetry; in which sort he that rewards me, Heaven reward him, as Sir John Falstaff says.¹ There is something very vain in repeating my own

G

sayings; but I could not conscientiously use a joke to you which I had used in another letter, without owning it.—In short, it is necessary to have some *earthly* aim in view; the next world, whether it be in reality near or far off, is always *seen* at a distance. All that the generality of young people can do is, to act *consistently with* their expectations there. Now, though fame, &c. be obviously enough in the eye of reason dissatisfactory; yet it is proper enough to suffer one's self to be deluded with the hopes of it, that is, it is proper to cherish some worldly hopes, that one may avoid impatience, spleen, and one sort of *despair*: I mean that of having no *hopes* here, because one sees nothing here that deserves them. If I were in your case, I would make all the efforts I was able towards being a Bishop. That should be my earthly aim: not but I would act with so much indifference as to bear all disappointment unconcernedly —as, I dare say, you will.—There is but one passion that I put upon an equally sprightly footing with ambition, and that is love; which, as it *regularly tends* to matrimony, requires certain favours from fortune and circumstance to render it proper to indulge in.—By this time you think me crazed— as it often happens to me to doubt, *seriously*, whether I am not: but if it be the 'mentis gratissimus error,'[2] I do not mind. You are very obliging to endeavour to continue my madness and vanity.—I should be as glad to see Mr. Graves, your brother, as any one I know: I live in a manner wherein he would find many things to exercise his good-nature.

Pamela would have made one good volume:[3] I wonder the author, who has some *nice* natural strokes, should not have sense enough to see that.—I beg you will collect all the hints, &c. of your own, or others, that you think may tend to the improvement of my poem against winter; that you would mention any flat lines, &c. Write me word some time ere you come over; but write to me immediately. I am

Yours faithfully,
W. SHENSTONE.

Once more adieu!

NOTES

[1]*Henry IV*, Pt. I, Act V, Sc. 4.
[2]Horace, *Epistles* II, 2, 140.
[3]Cf. p. 262.

XLIII

To Mrs. A——.

Hull, II, 65.

(1743?)[1]

Dear Madam,

I Promised to give you some Account what became of *Cheltenham*, after Mr. A—— had pillaged it of all that was most valuable. Possibly before this Time, you may have forgot both my Promise and me, and it may not be extremely political to renew your Remembrance of a Person who has been so long seemingly neglectful. The Truth is, I can no more bear to be forgot by those I esteem, than I can be censured of Forgetfulness with Regard to them, and I know no Way but Writing, by which I can evade both.

Some Sort of Apology I ought to make, that I did not write before; you will therefore please to observe, that I am but just arrived at Home, though I left *Cheltenham* the Day after you. I stayed, indeed, to hear Mr. B—— preach a Morning Sermon; for which I find Mrs. C—— has allotted him the Hat, preferably to Mr. C——. Perhaps you may not remember, nor did I hear till very lately, that there is a Hat given annually at *Cheltenham*, for the Use of the best foreign Preacher, of which the Disposal is assigned to Mrs. C——, to her and her Heirs for ever. I remember (tho' I knew nothing of this whilst I was upon the Place) I used to be a little misdeemful, that all who preached there had some such Premium in their Eye. This Hat, 'tis true, is not quite so valuable as that of a *Cardinal*, but while it is made a Retribution for Excellence in so (if properly considered) sublime a Function, it is an object for a Preacher in any Degree. I am sorry, at the same Time, to say, that as a *common Hat*, merely for its *Uses* it would be an Object to too many *Country Curates*, whose Situations and slender Incomes too often excite our Blushes, as well as Compassion. There should be no such Thing as a *Journeyman Parson*; it is beneath the Dignity of the Profession. If we had fewer *Pluralities* in the Church, this Indecorum might, in a great Measure, be abolished.

Mr. N—— (*Squire N*——) I hear is fitting up his Castle at L—— for the Reception of the little Widow; and the Mercer at *Cheltenham* has completed his great Arcade, for the better, Disposition of his Crapes and Callimancos.

I am an ill Relater of Matters of Fact, and as I said before, did not continue above four and twenty Hours and some odd Minutes upon the Place longer than you that enquire after it: but I survived long enough to hear very frequent Mention of Mrs. A——, Miss CARTER, &c. and such Mention, as has confirmed me in an Opinion, that Persons of real Merit, without any Expence of Airs, &c. will by Degrees engross the Admiration of any Place they come into. But this is a Kind of Language you would never indulge me in; you might very securely; for I should never be able to express half the sincere Esteem and Respect with which I am,

Madam,
your most obedient, humble Servant,
W. SHENSTONE.

NOTE

[1] This and the following letter probably belong to 1743 when W.S. paid a long visit to Cheltenham.

XLIV

Hull, II, 68.

To MISS CARTER.[1]

[1743?]

Dear Miss Carter,

PERHAPS you may remember to have seen an odd Kind of Fellow when you were at *Cheltenham*, who threatened you with a Letter, and who is now endeavouring to be as *bad* as his Word; however he hopes for some little Partiality on his Behalf, having delayed the Execution of his Menaces for a considerable Time, and even now promising to say as few Things in your Favour as the real Sentiments of his Heart will admit of.

But Peace to Buffoonery.——After I parted from you, Mr. M——N, with great Simplicity, endeavoured to keep up my Spirits, by speaking in Praise of the Family we had left, as though that was not the ready Method to aggravate the Sense of one's Loss; and yet to aggravate it was utterly impossible in the Opinion of a Person already so sensible of it. But he mentioned one Article which was more successful, and that was a Proposal to accompany me to *Stoke*, and to let me know when it suited his Convenience.

When I came to *Cheltenham*, I was not unmindful of that solemn Vow that I had made, not to survive your Family there a single Hour: but I found it near five o'Clock, and my Conscience said, that as I had made it so late, by my Attendance upon you, though I did stay another Night, I hoped I might be excused.

I have been, since leaving this Town, at Mr. BROWN's who lives upon the Borders of *Wales*.—Poor Man! He has been the most obliging Person in the World to the most stupid of Companions. 'Tis hardly possible to determine which was greater, the Zeal with which he shewed me his Fossils, Plants, Poetry, &c. or the stupid Inattention with which I observed them. He commends you and Mrs. AUBREY highly; so, indeed, do all I know, or I would soon forget that I had ever seen their Faces. He had found out a Method at last of seducing me to talk, by frequent Mention of your Merits, and it was a good While before I discovered his Artifice; and even when I had discovered it, I was ill able to elude the Force of it.

I am now just returned Home, which is my Apology for not writing to you about *Cheltenham* as I promised. I really scarce recollect any Circumstance belonging to it, except that you and Mrs. AUBREY were there the most favourable, agreeable, and praise-worthy.

What, does Mr. M—— boast of the glorious Absurdity he committed at parting, in mistaking my Horse for his? When I see him next, I will produce a Hundred I have been lately guilty of, to no one of which his is able to compare. His, you know, commenced in the very Moment of parting, and consequently was little wonderful, in Comparison of those I have since committed; besides, his Horse had a Spot or two of Brown on him, and was therefore easily mistaken at such a Time for one that was a Sorrel all over.

After all, you are a very wicked Lady—you defrauded me

of the Croslet you promised me, putting me off with a single Bead; but it was yours, and that's enough. The most trivial Donation from a Person we esteem, has a large Value. I acknowledge to have a great *Penchant* for what the Vulgar call *Keep-Sakes*. The *French* are notably practised in these little Elegancies; we are not so much so, as, I think, a polished People ought to be.

I am, dear Miss CARTER,
Your most sincere Admirer, and humble Servant,
W. SHENSTONE.

Don't expose the Nonsense-Verses I gave you, I entreat you.

NOTE

[1]Is this the lady with whom Shenstone fell in love? See Williams, *op. cit.*, 29.

XLV

Works III, 111.

To a Friend [REV. R. JAGO], *with a Parody.*

THE LEASOWS,
March 1, 1743–4.

Dear Sir,

You are upon very *good* terms with me, and *have* been all along. I guessed the causes of your silence, and have been sincerely sorry for them; not however that I did not believe you were more happy than any one in the world who is neither a lover nor a poet, though not able to turn himself for money-bags.——I am really going to London; and am about the purchase of an elegant pair of pistols from Birmingham. I indulge myself in this expence, because they shall serve in two capacities; one while to garnish my chair, another while my horse. And some time next week you will probably see your old friend on horse-back, armed *at all points*, and as very a knight to all *appearance* as any body.

——'*Well! they say the Owl was a Quaker's Daughter*—*one knows what one* IS, *but one does not know what one* SHALL *be.*' Ophelia in Hamlet.[1]

But I digress. If I just call to see you, God forbid that I should be burthensome to you. I will send my horses to H——,[2] and lodge there, or somewhere. But I am perfectly impatient to unbosom my soul to you, and to see Mrs. Jago, whom I should have mentioned first. Wednesday or Tuesday indeed seems the most likely day.—Though I am not sure; nor do you confine yourself.

Poor Mariett! *I* too am emaciated; but I hope, by means of some warm weather, to acquire *plus d'embonpoint*. I design to call upon him, and keep him in countenance.

My ballad, in the midst of your hurry, must appear as ridiculous as Cinna the poet does, when he swears nothing but death shall restrain him from addressing Brutus and Cassius (and that the night before the battle) with two doggrel verses— and those the worst I have ever read;[3] and that makes the simile the more just. It is now a good deal metamorphosed. Your parody is prodigiously droll: the first line delights me! I think I could furnish Mrs. K[night] with as good mottoes, and as cheap, though I say it, as any-body; but, alas!—Did I send you the following parody or no, before?[4] I believe not. *Le voila!*

'When first, Philander, first I came
'Where Avon rolls his winding stream,
'The nymphs—how brisk! the swains—how gay!
'To see *Asteria*,[5] Queen of May!—
'The parsons round, her praises sung!—
'The steeples, with her praises rung!—
'I thought—no sight, that e'er was seen,
'Could match the sight of Barel's-green!——[6]

'But *now*, since old *Eugenio* dy'd—
'The chief of poets, and the pride—
'Now meaner bards in vain aspire
'To raise their voice, to tune their lyre!
'Their lovely season, now, is o'er!
'Thy notes, Florelio, please no more!—
'No more Asteria's smiles are seen!—
'Adieu!—the sweets of Barel's-green!—'

It is a kind of extempore, so please excuse it.—You have seen the song of Arno's Vale.

I am taking part of my farm upon my hands, to see if I can succeed as a farmer;—but I am afraid I am under the sentence, 'And, behold, whatsoever he taketh in hand, it shall *not* prosper.'

My good friend, I sincerely confide, that, however we may be separated, no time shall extenuate our mutual friendship. I am

Your zealous, unserviceable friend,
W. SHENSTONE.

NOTES

[1]*Hamlet*, IV, 5.
[2]Possibly Harbury near Edgehill. Lord Willoughby de Broke appointed Jago to the livings of Harbury and Chesterton in 1746 and he remained at Harbury till 1754 when he moved to Snitterfield.
[3]*Julius Caesar*, IV, 3.
[4]The parody is of *Arno's Vale*.
[5]The name under which W.S. addressed Lady Luxborough in his poems.
[6]Barrels.

XLVI

Works III, 83.

To Mr. JAGO, *from London.*

1743. [*May* 30, 1744.]

Dear friend,

I SHALL send you but a very few lines, being so much indisposed with a cold, that I can scarce tell how to connect a sentence. I am just got into lodgings at a gold-smith's—a dangerous situation, you will say, for *me*; 'Actum est, ilicet, periisti!'[1] Not so;—for of late I have not so violent a taste for toys as I have had; and I can look even on snuff-boxes 'oculo irretorto.'[2]

London is really dangerous at this time; the pick-pockets, formerly content with mere *filching*, make no scruple to knock people down with bludgeons in *Fleet-street* and the *Strand*, and that at no later hour than eight o'clock at night: but in the Piazzas, Covent-garden, they come in large bodies, armed with couteaus, and attack whole parties, so that the danger of coming out of the play-houses is of some weight in the opposite

scale, when I am disposed to go to them oftener than I ought.
—There is a poem of this season, called 'The Pleasures of
Imagination,'[3] worth your reading; but it is an expensive
quarto; if it comes out in a less size, I will bring it home with
me. Mr. Pope (as Mr. Outing, who has been with Lord
Bolingbroke, informs me) is at the point of death.[4]—My Lord
Carteret[5] said yesterday in the house, 'That the French and
Spaniards had actually *said*, they would attempt a second
invasion.' There is a new play acted at Drury-Lane, 'Mahomet,' translated from the French of Voltaire;[6] but I have no
great opinion of the subject, or the original author as a poet;
and my diffidence is rather improved by the testimony of those
who have seen it.—I lodge between the two coffee-houses,
George's and Nando's, so that I partake of the expensiveness
of both, as heretofore. I have no acquaintance in town, and
but slender inducement to stay; and yet, probably, I shall
loiter here for a month.

T[homas] H[ead] was knighted against his will,[7] and had a
demand made upon him for an hundred pounds before he
could get out of St. James's; so soon are felt the inconveniences of grandeur!—He came out of the court in a violent
rage, 'G—d! Jack, what dost think?—I am knighted!—the
devil of a knight, e'faith!' I believe he was sincere in his disgust; for there had been two barge-masters knighted in his
neighbourhood some time before.

I saw, coming up, Lady Fane's grotto,[8] which, they say,
cost her five thousand pounds; about three times as much as
her *house* is worth. It is a very beautiful disposition of the finest
collection of shells I ever saw—Mr. Powis's[9] woods, which are
finer.—Mean time, if I had three hundred pounds to lay out
about The Leasows, I could bring my ambition to peaceable
terms. I am, dear Sir, with all affection, yours and Mrs.
Jago's.

W. Shenstone.

Write soon. It is this moment reported that Pope is dead.[10]

NOTES

[1]Plautus, *Cist.*, IV, 2, 17.
[2]Horace, *Carm.*, II, 2, 23.

[3]By Mark Akenside (1721–1770), poet and physician, published by Dodsley in January, 1744.

[4]Joseph Spence in his *Anecdotes*, records the last visit of Bolingbroke to Pope.

[5]John Carteret (1690–1763), Secretary of State.

[6]*Mahomet*, a tragedy by Voltaire, 1742, translated by James Miller & J. Hoadly, 1744, and performed at Drury Lane, April 25, 1744.

[7]'1743–4. March 5. Thomas Head, Sheriff of Berks (at S. James's on presenting an address from the Sheriff, Justices of the peace, grand jury, etc. etc. of Berks, on the threatened invasion of the Pretender's son).' Shaw, *Knights of England*.

[8]Mary, sister of James, 1st Earl Stanhope, wife of Charles, Viscount Fane of Basildon, Berks. Dodsley's *Collection*, V, 62. *To Lady Fane, on her Grotto at Basildon*. 1746. By Mr. Graves.

[9]Of Harleyford, Bucks.

[10]May 30, 1744. This necessitates the alteration of Dodsley's dating of this letter, 1743.

XLVII

Messrs. Maggs & Hull, II, 8.

[*To* Rev. R. GRAVES.]

[*Nov.* 1744.]

Dear Sir,

I did indeed give you up for lost, as a Correspondent, & find by your Letter y^t I am to expect but very few future ones. I will endeavour all I can to avoid any suspicion of your Indifference for my own Satisfaction. But I don't know for certain y^t I shall be able, unless you assist my Endeavours, like my good Genius, by a course of suitable Epistles at certain distances—I myself correspond but very little now, so you will meet with the more Indulgence—I don't find by your Letter y^t you have much more Philosophy y^n me. I cant tell indeed what ye situation of y^r House is, I own mine gives me offence on no other consideration y^n that it does not receive a sufficient Number of polite Friends, or y^t it is not fit to receive 'em, were they so dispos'd. I wou'd else cultivate an Acquaintance with about Three or Four in my Neighbourhood, y^t are of a Degree of Elegance, & station superior [last word above in another hand] to ye common Run. But I make it a certain Rule Arcere profanu vulgus.[1] Persons of vulgar *minds*, who will despise you for ye want of a good set of Chairs, or an uncouth Fire-shovel at ye same Time y^t they can't taste any Excellence in a mind that overlooks those things; or, (To make a *conceit* of this Sentiment) with whom tis in vain that y^r Mind is furnish'd if y^r walls are naked—Indeed one loses much of one's Acquisitions in virtue by an Hours converse with such as Judge of merit by Money. Yet I am now & then impell'd by ye social Passion to sit half an Hour in my Kitchen.

I was all along an Admirer of Sr Thomas Head's Humour & wit, And I beg you wou'd represent me in y^t Light if occasion happons. [sic] Tis not impossible y^t I may penetrate this winter as far as y^t neighbourhood, connecting a set of visits which I have in my Eye—Tell Mr. Whistler when you see him that if he must have *some* Distemper, I cannot but but [sic] be pleas'd y^t it is one which is a Forerunner of Longevity. Don't tell him so neither for ye compliment is trite. From ye Birmingham Gazette—'We hear that on Thursday last was married at Hales-owen in Shropshire Mr Jorden an eminent Gunsmith of this Town to a sister of ye Rt hon^{ble} Ferdinando Ld Dudley.[2] I was yesterday at ye Grange, where his old Father (wth a number of People) was celebrating ye nuptials of his son; when in the midst of his Feasting, and high Jollity & and [sic] grand Alliance the old Fellow bethought him of a Piece of Timber in ye neighbourhood y^t was convertible into good Gunsticks, & had some of it sent for into ye Room by way of Specimen! Animae nil magnae Laudis egentes—! Pray is your sister at Smethwick? for I have not heard. You said you wou'd give me y^t Picture which I long earnestly for cou'dn't you contrive to have it sent me directly? I am quite in y^r Debt with regard to downright goods and moveables & what is ye proper subject of an Inventory—neque tu pessima muneru ferres diviti me scilicet artium quas aut Parrhasius protulit aut scopas—Sed non hæc mihi vis![3] I will however endeavour to be more upon a Par with you wth regard to presents, tho I never can with regard to ye Pleasures I have received frō y^r conversation—I make People wonder at my Exploits in pulling down walls, Hovels, Cow-houses etc. and my Place is not ye same. I am that is, wth Regard to you a Faithfull Friend, & h^{ble} serv^t·

W.S.

M^r. Whistler & you & I & Sr T. Head, (whō I shou'd

name first, speaking after ye manner of Men) have just variety
enough & not too much, in our Charact: to make an Interview
whenever it happens Entertaining—I mean that we were not
old Friends & Acquaintance.

NOTES

[1]Horace, *Odes* III, 1.
[2]Lord Dudley had five sisters. Catherine, the fourth, married November 16, 1744,
Thomas Jorden of Birmingham, gunsmith.
[3]Horace, *Carm.*, 4, 8, 4.

XLVIII

Works III, 140.

To [Rev. R. JAGO], *from The Leasows.*

1747. [1744.?][1]

Dear Sir,

It is not much above two hours since I received your
obliging letter, and I am already set down to answer it.—To
speak the truth, I had almost given you over: I imagined you
had taken umbrage at some expression or circumstance in my
epistle, and were determined to make me sensible you did so,
by your silence. I hope, this error of mine will serve to establish one rule on *both* sides.—It is what ought, I am sure, always
to take place, where people wish a perpetuity of friendship.
I mean, never, upon circumstances of disrespect, to admit of
circumstantial evidence.

I am very grave, so you may depend on the sincerity of all
I shall say. I saw several beauties in your former elegy; but,
though it was 'formosa,' it did not appear to me 'ipsa forma.'
I like this that you have now sent *very* much. It has a simplicity
which your last a little wanted, and has thought *enough*. I
begin to be seldom pleased with the compositions of others,
or my own; but I could be really *fond* of this, with a few
alterations, that I could propose:—but you must know, at the
same time, that these are such as no one would approve beside
myself.—I know it.—However, there are some seeming *faults*
in it.

I have been greatly mortified in my correspondents of late.—

I even said in my haste, All friends are faithless.—G[raves], after a month's expectation, which he had confirmed to me, of seeing him here, let me know a fortnight since, that I had more leisure than him; and, since it did not suit his convenience to come, I ought to take the opportunity of visiting him, and seeing Derbyshire while he continues in it—— W[histler] has not wrote to me these six weeks.—Outing has been, moreover, dumb for the same space of time; and I purpose in my heart to behave with some distance towards both, for this neglect (see my rule of circumstantial evidence).

It is a pity you cannot spare a day or two to come and see me. My wood grows excessively pleasant, and its pleasantness vexes me; because nobody will come that can taste it.

Your health, according to your description, is much the same with mine; but from the gaiety of your style and *designs*, I collect that it is greatly better.

I have an alcove, six elegies, a seat, two epitaphs (one upon myself) three ballads, four songs, and a serpentine river, to shew you when you come. Will the compositions come safe to you, if I send my book, which contains the *only* copies of several things (which I could not remember if they were lost)? —but I will not send them. If my horse gets well, I may essay a visit for two days, and bring them with me, that I may make comments while you read them, as beseemeth a genuine author to do.

I am raising a green-house from the excrescences of Lord Dudley's; but I do not find that 'vient l'appetit en mangeant,' that I grow fonder of my collection proportionably as it increases.

I should think myself fortunate enough at present, if, like you, I could only find that I had been mentioned for a vacant post; but I have withdrawn all my views from court-preferment, and fixed them on finding a pot of money, which I determine to be the far more probable scheme.

I have little health and frequent mortification, so that no one need envy me; and yet, I believe, there *are* that do. Is any enviable but such as are unambitious? I never shall be able to reckon myself of that tribe, which have engrossed all *happiness* to themselves, and left the rest of the world nothing but hopes and possessions. Yet I do not much feel the pains of ambition while I am conversing with ingenious friends of my own level: but in *other* company it hurts me. Let me advise you, now I think of it, to dread the company of silly people, out-of-the-way people, and, in one word, what men of genius *call the vulgar*. You run ten times the risque of being mortified, voluntarily or unknowingly, amongst the latter of these, to what you do amongst men of sense and politeness, be they ever so malicious;—but my paper is filled.

Do write soon.

NOTE

[1]Graves left Tissington, Derbyshire, in 1744. Hence Dodsley's dating of this letter, which suggests a visit to him there, is obviously wrong.

XLIX

Works III, 114.

To Mr. GRAVES, *on Social Happiness.*

About 1745.

Dear Mr. Graves,

There is not a syllable you tell me concerning yourself in your last letter, but what applied to *me* is most literally true. I am sensible of the daily progress I make towards insignificancy, and it will not be many years before you see me arrived at the *ne plus ultra*. I believe it is absolutely impossible for me to acquire a considerable degree of knowledge, though I can understand things well enough at the time I read them. I remember a preacher at St. Mary's (I think it was Mr. E——) made a notable distinction betwixt *apprehension* and *comprehension*. If there be a real difference, probably it may find a place in the explication of my genius. I envy you a good *general* insight into the writings of the learned. I must aim at nothing higher than a well-concealed ignorance.—I was thinking, upon reading your letter, *when* it was that you and Mr. Whistler and I went out of the road of happiness. It certainly was where we first deviated from the turnpike-road of life. Wives, children, alliances, visits, &c. are necessary objects of our social passions; and whether or no we can, through particular circumstances, be happy *with*, I think it plain enough that it is not possible to be happy *without* them. All attachments to inanimate beauties, to curiosities, and ornaments, satiate us presently.—The fanciful tribe has the disadvantage to be naturally prone to err in the choice of *lasting* pleasures: and when our passions have habitually wandered, it is too difficult to reduce them into their proper channels. When this is the case, nothing but the change or variety of amusements stands any chance to make us easy, and it is not long ere the whole species is exhausted. I agree with you entirely in the necessity of a *sociable* life in order to be happy: I do not think it much a paradox, that any company is better than *none*. I think it obvious enough as to the present hour, and as to any future influence, solitude has exceeding savage effects on our dispositions.—I have wrote out my elegy: I lay no manner of stress but upon the piety of it.—Would it not be a good kind of motto, applied to a person you know, that might be taken from what is said of *Ophelia* in *Hamlet*,

> 'I tell thee, faithless priest!
> 'A ministring angel shall Ophelia be
> 'When thou art howling.'[1]

I have amused myself often with this species of writing since you saw me; partly to divert my present *impatience*, and partly as it will be a picture of most that passes in my mind; a portrait which *friends* may value.—I should be glad of your profile: if you have objections, I drop my request.—I should be heartily glad if you would come and live with me, for any space of time that you could find convenient. But I will depend on your coming over with Mr. Whistler in the spring. I may possibly take a jaunt towards you ere long: the road would furnish me out some visits; and, by the time I reached you, perhaps. afford me a kind of climax of happiness. If I do not, I shall perhaps be a little time at Bath. I do not speak of this last as a scheme from which I entertain great expectations of pleasure. It is long since I have considered myself as *undone*. The *world* will not perhaps consider me in that light entirely, till I have married my maid![2] Adieu!

NOTES

[1]*Hamlet*, Act V, Sc. 1.

[2]W.S. died a bachelor, but one can well imagine that he might have married his maid as does the hero of Graves's *Columella*, an obvious study of the poet's life. Cf. Isaac D'Israeli, *Curiosities of Literature. Shenstone vindicated*.

L

Works III, 117.

To the [Rev. RICHARD GRAVES], *with Observations on the Rebellion, and its probable Consequences.*

THE LEASOWS,
Nov. 22, 1745.

Dear Mr. Graves,

My life, for aught I see, will pass away just as it *has* done, without introducing sufficient improvement into my circumstances to give a chearful cast to my correspondence. In *one* respect, in regard to my inviolable friendship for *you*, I hope you will hear with some satisfaction that I continue still the same. And this kind of *identity*, I think, I could promise you, though every circumstance in my fortune, every particle of my body, were changed; and others, ever so heterogeneous, substituted in their place. After this, it would be no compliment to say, that the *pretended* heir to these kingdoms could not alter it, were he to subvert the British constitution; which must, out of all doubt, be the consequence of his success. The rebellion, you may guess, is the subject of all conversation. Every individual nailer here takes in a news-paper (a more *pregnant* one by far than any of the London ones), and talks as familiarly of *kings* and *princes* as ever Master Shallow did of John of Gaunt.[1] Indeed it is no bad thing that they do so; for I cannot conceive that the people want so much to be convinced by *sermons*, of the absurdities of *popery*, as they do by *news-papers*, that *it* may *possibly* prevail. The reasons and arguments too in favour of the present Government are so *strong* and *obvious*, that even I, and every country 'squire, and every country clerk, and Sam Shaw the taylor, seem to be as much masters of them as the Bishops themselves. I must not say we could express them so politely.—I like Secker's[2] the best of any sermon on this occasion. He gives his audience a view of such evil consequences from a *change*, as no man of sense can possibly doubt of, when fairly stated: and, I own, I cannot see one single *good* it could produce, in compensation for its inevitable and abundant *mischiefs*.—I have read Dr. Sherlock's[3] sermon on this occasion: and I have read Mr. Warburton's;[4] and, at your request, I will read his Legation.

I have often thoughts of a jaunt as far as your country this winter. Some kind of pilgrimage I must make, to avoid a lethargy.—Public places I want to visit a little; to peep at and renew my idea of the *world's* vanity; but either Bath or London would steep me so far in poverty, that I should not probably emerge before the middle of next summer. I have spent this last summer agreeably enough with some of my young relations, Mr. Dolman's children.—They have an excellent taste for their years.—I have been upon several jaunts with the son to Litchfield, Worcester, Mr. Fletcher's, &c. amusing him, what I could, under the loss of his father.[5] Miss W[inny] F[letcher] asked very earnestly after you. Two of the sisters have been with me at The Leasows, and upon several parties of pleasure in my chair.—Broom is disposed of—I do not understand upon what inducement.—After all, I am miserable;—conscious to myself that I am too little selfish: that I ought now or never to aim at some addition to my fortune; and that I make large advances towards the common catastrophe of *better* poets, poverty.—I never can attend enough to some twelve-penny matter, on which a great deal depends.— My amour, so far as I indulge it, gives me some pleasure, and no pain in the world.—I have read Spenser once again: and I have added full as much more to my *School-mistress*, in regard to *number of lines; something* in point of *matter* (or *manner* rather) *which* does not displease me. I would be glad if Mr.— were, upon your request, to give his opinion of particulars, for two reasons; as you say he has some taste for this kind of writing, and as he is my enemy, and would, therefore, find out its deficiencies.

I have a reason, of a most whimsical kind, why I would wish

H

you to preserve this letter. Pray write soon, and believe me most affectionately

Your friend and humble servant,

W. SHENSTONE.

NOTES

[1]*Henry IV*, 2, Act III, 2.

[2]Thomas Secker (1693–1768), Archbishop of Canterbury, a typical orthodox eighteenth-century prelate.

[3]Thomas Sherlock (1698–1761), Bishop of London.

[4]William Warburton (1698–1779), Bishop of Gloucester, married the favourite niece of Ralph Allen, Esq., of Prior Park, and so was later connected with the circle of Richard Graves.

[5]Rev. Thomas Dolman of Broome married Mary Penn, W.S.'s maternal aunt at Churchill, near Kidderminster, February 17, 1725–26. She died April 2, 1733, and her husband was buried at Broome on May 9, 1745. They had three children: Thomas, born January 23, 1726, Nathaniel, who died in infancy and Mary, born December 6, 1730. This relationship accounts for the lengthy law proceedings in which Shenstone was involved with 'Young Dolman'—the only living relation he had on his mother's side—concerning their respective shares in the Harborough estates.

LI

Bodleian Library, MS, Montagu, d. 18,
and Hull, I, 14.

To MISS WINNY FLETCHER, *at Acleton.*

THE LEASOWS, *Nov*[r]. 28—1745.

Dear Miss Winny.

On a Time, as tis reported, the Mountains were in Labour; when after a long Course of Pains & Inquietudes they made a shift to produce that puny Animal a Mouse. Now that very individual Mouse, according to the mysterious & Figurative Import of Types & Shadows was the perfect Image & Representative of this mine Epistle. A groveling, starvling insignificant Production, conceiv'd wth much difficulty, & transmitted to you wth Confusion of Face. In short, you may look upon it as y[e] noble Booty you have taken, by baiting your *Trap*, so artfully with Praise & Compliment about two or three Months ago—True it is, that considering y[e] Politeness & Complaisance of your Obliging Letter, My Behaviour since must appear the most *unknightly* of all Proceedings. But your Packet did not arrive till three weeks after it was sent—so you will Excuse my silence 'till the Day after I receivd it, & whatever was *more* than that, I freely acknowledge, came of sin. However you will, upon Confession, pardon me, as you expect Pardon from your Confessor shou'd ye Benedictines & Friars get a Footing in this Island—which I find, your Brother is endeavouring to prevent.

I can be no longer ludicrous on this last Article. I am too seriously concern'd for his safety. Yet I don't fear but the Rebels will be defeated, & may be, all Danger over in less than a Fortnight. But General Wade's Behaviour, loitering so long at Newcastle, astonishes me.[1] I was at Birm: on Tuesday morning from whence I saw ye Remains of Ligonier's Horse march with vast Spirits & Alacrity. They wish to have What they *call*, the Refusal of the Highlanders. They are men of experienc'd Bravery, & fought like Furies at ye Battle of Fontenoy. May they do so now, & with better success!

Binnel[2] told me your Brother wou'd borrow my Pistols. At that Time supposing him in Jest, I sent no very *serious* Answer. I now think it incumbent on me to say that I wou'd lend them him with all my Heart, but that one of them is broke in ye stock, & cannot be fir'd with safety 'till it is stock'd afresh. Perhaps he might recollect it was so, when I was at Acleton.

We have been best Part of a Week at Lichfield, where we liv'd like Chickens in a Pen, confind & cramm'd, & where we serv'd God After the Manner of Popes & Cardinals—I only allude to Cathedral-Service. Mr. and Mrs Dolman seem'd quite disposd to entertain us agreeably. The Son & Daughter, to say the least, appeard much more indifferent in that Particular. These, as Shakespear says, are certainly better X^tians or else worse than we.[3]

You have escap'd me at Birmingham by concealing ye Time of y^r Visit. Surely you will come over to Broom e'er it be long & give me my Revenge.

Tell Mrs Anne my Ears make great Shoots, & such as may tempt her Hand egregiously. But If I *am* metamorphosed into an Ass entirely, I will come & serenade her in a Morning when she has been up late ye Night before.

I beg my Compliments to all Friends. I must not make my

Letter much longer—The Mouse will grow to y.ᵉ size of a Rat—I beg you to accept this Idle Billet in Part of an Answer to y.ʳ Elegant Letter, & in Lieu of a Thousand Professions of the Friendship & Esteem w.ᵗʰ w.ᶜʰ I am Dear Miss Winny Your most obedient & faithfull H.ᵇˡᵉ Serv.ᵗ

W. SHENSTONE.

NOTES

[1]George Wade (1673–1748), field-marshal, concentrated his army on Newcastle in September 1745. Meanwhile the Highland army outwitted him and captured Carlisle, and Charles Edward Stuart marched south to Derby, and escaped again north between the armies of Wade and Cumberland.

[2]Probably Rev. Robert Binnel, nephew of Mr. Pitt of Shifnal and a contemporary of W.S. at Pembroke College, where he became a commoner, May 10, 1733, and whence he took his M.A. in 1739. (Nash, *History of Worcestershire* I, 529.) He became minister of Newport in Shropshire. He was responsible for notes in Grainger's *Tibullus*, printed some sermons, and 'has a very high and just character given of him in the preface to a New Version of Solomon's Song, printed for Dodsley in 1764, 8vo.'

[3]Is W.S. thinking of Shylock's exclamation, *The Merchant of Venice*, I, 3, line 149?

LII

Works III, 125.

To the [REV. RICHARD GRAVES], *with a Theory of Political Principles.*[1]

Dear Mr. Graves,

I have lately received a letter from Mr. Whistler, which conveys your compliments to me, and, by so doing, prompts me to acknowledge the receipt of your last kind letter. I observe you adhere strictly to the apostolical precept of being 'swift to *hear*, slow to *speak*;' the latter part of which I would fain conclude you understand too literally.

Your neighbour, I see, is not a little embarrassed with his mills at Whitchurch. I have long had an eye upon his advertisement in the London Evening Post, and been not a little scandalized thereat.[2] What has the name of a poet to do with the publication of lands and tenements? or the idea of harmony with the noise of a water-mill? yet has he extracted music from the subject, and mirth from his misfortunes; having sent me a ballad upon the miller, written with much ease and some drollery.

As to the light in which you place your present fortunes, I can only say, that you have not that situation I could wish you for your *own sake*: for as far as I am concerned in your elevation, I can assure you very faithfully, that no circumstances in the world could more endear you to my affection, or recommend you to my respect, than the present. My *affection*, you will easily observe, from the very *nature* of affection in general, would stand no chance to be increased by your promotion; and as for respect, if I knew the degree you desired, I would acquit myself of it to your satisfaction *now;* and were you settled at *Lambeth*, I should expect that you would require no *more* from me upon that account; at least in private: so that, so far as either *deference* or *friendship* is concerned, you are an Archbishop to *me* to all intents and purposes.—As to figure in the world, it depends much, I know, upon advancement; and yet even here you will be ever *sure* of that kind of weight which ingenuity gives; discernible to the *smaller* indeed, but undoubtedly the more *valuable* part of the world;—but this is improper, as it is *philosophy*, and as it is *advice;* neither of which is it suitable for me to suggest to you—'Alcinoo Poma, &c.'[3] As to the long series of *my* lamentations, I will not now enter upon the reasonableness of them. It is a subject, to tell you the truth, on which you cannot reply without some danger of hurting me.—As for politics (you will blame this letter for dwelling so much upon the subject of yours); but as for politics, I think *poets* are *tories* by nature, supposing them to be by nature poets.—The love of an individual person or family, that has worn a crown for many successions, is an inclination greatly adapted to the fanciful tribe. On the other hand, mathematicians, abstract-reasoners, of no manner of attachment to persons, at least to the *visible* part of them, but prodigiously devoted to the ideas of virtue, liberty, interest, and so forth, are generally *whigs*. It happens agreeably enough to this maxim, that the whigs are friends to that wise, plodding, un-poetical people the Dutch.—The tories, on the other hand, are taken mightily with that shewy, ostentatious nation the French. Fox-hunters, that reside amongst the beauties of nature, and bid defiance to art, in short, that have intellects of a poetical *turn*, are frequently tories;—citizens, merchants, &c.

that scarce see what nature is, and consequently have no pretensions to a poetical taste, are, I think, generally argumentative and whiggish;—but perhaps I carry this too far.—Something there is in it however, you will see: not that I would apply what I here say to particular revolutions, &c. I would only advance something general and speculative. Nor would I approve or condemn by this any one set of people now existing. Nor would I have you pretend to fish out my party from any thing I have said; for I am of none —The letter I sent you last was *occasional*, and when I see you I will tell you the occasion. I absolutely agree with you in every tittle of your political observations.—I am glad I do; for I know the poisonous nature of party: and though we are *neither* violent, yet I should fear it. My schemes are *doubtful* at present, but my face is set towards Bath—I am confident of the service those waters would do me.—I hope you will exhilarate me with a letter soon.—I would fain have furnished out a letter to amuse you after so long a silence, but I find myself unable; even *as* unable as I am to express the regard with which I am

Yours

W. Shenstone.

The Leasows,
April 6, 1746.

NOTES

[1]'In politics, I am convinced, he would have made no inconsiderable figure, if he had had a sufficient motive for applying his mind to political studies; as, I think, might appear from the letter written during the rebellion of 1745, and from others which I received about the year 1762, on the state of public affairs at that critical period.' *Recollection*, 181.

[2]*The London Evening Post.* Thursday, January 16, 1746: 'To be Lett, and enter'd upon at Lady-day next, or immediately if requir'd,

'Whitchurch Mills, lately in the Occupation of Thomas Antrum, consisting of three Water Corn-Mills, situate on the River Thames, at Whitchurch in Oxfordshire; well accustome'd for Country Business, and very convenient for the London Trade; with the Eyotts and Fishing thereunto belonging, and a Dwelling-House adjoining.

'Note. The Mills are forthwith to be rebuilt, or repair'd in whatever Manner the Tenant shall chuse. Enquire of John Peareth, Esq., at his Chambers, No. 7. in King's Bench Walks in the Temple, London; Mr. Whistler, at Whitchurch aforesaid; Mr. John Brooker, at Thatcham, Berks; or Mr. Blandy, at Henley-on-Thames.'

[3]Equivalent to 'Coals to Newcastle.'

LIII

Works III, 129.

[*To the* REV. R. GRAVES]. *Continuation of the same.*

THE LEASOWS, *May* 11, 1746.

Dear Mr. Graves,

Though I feel an irresistible propensity to write to you this very post, yet I cannot say that I am able to advance any thing tending either to your own or my satisfaction.—What is worst of all is, I cannot fix the time of seeing you with so much precision as I would always endeavour where my pleasure is so much concerned—I will tell you the whole affair.—I have for a long season purposed to drink the Bath waters this spring; and *did* think of setting out in a week's time, when I received your letter, purposing to stay there a month; and from thence take a circuit which should indulge me in a sight of you, Mr. Whistler, and some few others in my way home. The latter part of this scheme (though far the more agreeable to me) was rather doubtful and precarious; depending (as you express it) on the state of my finances after a month's continuance at Bath; which I considered, and *do* consider, as a very probable means of bettering my constitution.—Now I covet to see you so much, that I would bring nothing but health in competition.—What I wish is, that you could, with convenience, either *hasten* or *delay* your journey, that you might find me before mine, or after my return, though I should infinitely, and for many reasons, prefer the former. I long to talk with you particularly now. I have much to say in regard to our friend's amour, to which you alluded in your last. I request it as a favour of you, that you would conjure him, by the friendship I have ever born him, and by any esteem which he has ever professed for me, that he would do nothing very *material* in the affair till I have talked it over, and given him my faithful sentiments, 'quod censet amiculus.'[1]

I am not willing the balance should turn entirely on the whig side: I would give it a greater equilibrium, if the following suggestion might effect it. Tories, I said, have great, and sometimes partial affections for the *person* of a king.—We will suppose the kings are alternately good and bad: their loyalty to the good one is commendable; their partiality to the bad one not to be vindicated. Whigs have *no* passion, *no* gratitude, towards the good prince: there they are wrong. They are severe upon the bad one, in which they are justifiable. I wish I had not begun these wholesale distinctions, this miserable specimen of my politics. I protest against all epistolary disputes. I am now embarrassed in one, on much such another score, which fills up all my letter; for I love the last word, like a scold or a child.——I thank you for your little anecdotes from time to time: you may depend upon it, that I have never heard anything *before;* for I never *do* hear any thing.——I am one very thankful letter in debt to your neighbour Whistler. I have at present nothing but the *propensity* of a good correspondent; but I will write soon. In the mean time, if you see him, ask him if he goes to Bath or Bristol this season.——I beg you would write to me directly *when* you can come, and how I may regulate my motions so as to be best assured of seeing you.—— Pray do not neglect a post. I am

Yours most entirely,

W.S.

NOTE

[1]Horace, *Epistles* I, xvii, 3.

LIV

Works III, 121.

To the [Rev. R. GRAVES], *with Remarks on the Execution and Behaviour of Lords Kilmarnock and Balmerino.*[1]

1746, ineunte anno.

Dear Mr. Graves,

I believe it is impossible for me to disagree with you on any other score, than the scanty pittances you allot me of your company; and, if I have disclosed any symptoms of resentment on that account, you will, perhaps, overlook them, out of regard to the motive from which they proceeded.——I thank you for your persual of that trivial poem. If I were going to print it,

I should give way to your remarks *implicitly*, and would not *dare* to do otherwise. But as long as I keep it in manuscript, you will pardon my silly prejudices, if I chuse to read and shew it with the addition of most of my new stanzas. I own, I have a fondness for several, imagining them to be *more* in Spenser's way, yet more independent on the antique phrase, than any part of the poem; and, on that account, I cannot yet prevail on myself to banish *them* entirely; but were I to print, I should (with *some* reluctance) give way to your sentiments (which I know are just), namely, that they render the work too diffuse and flimzy, and seem rather excrescences than essential parts of it.

But of these things I say no more now. I purpose staying a month with Mr. Whistler, in December, if it suits him; and then I hope I shall have a great deal of your company. Let me hear something in your next of your *domestic affairs*. I beg you would not make any grand decision, without giving me some previous information. I esteem this as due to the friendship I have so long professed for you, and from the friendship you have so long professed for me.

I look upon the death of the two Lords as equally decent upon their respective principles. Lord Kilmarnock, I suppose, joined the rebels through a view of bettering his circumstances, conscious to himself that he was guilty of a crime the moment he did so. This is agreeable to his speech before the Lords, and to that melancholy which he discovered upon the scaffold. Death, aggravated by guilt, would sit heavier upon him than upon the other, even supposing him to have had the same resolution. Balmerino's life was quite *unie*, and his death equal to the character he aimed at. We are to observe, that he meant to suffer as a Friend to the Stewarts, a Soldier, and a Scotsman. The first he manifested when he came out of the Tower, by his reply of 'God save King J[ame]s;' the second, by his dress, and numberless ostentations of intrepidity; the last, by his plaid night cap. Did you hear the story of his sending a message to Lord Kilmarnock? 'That he had been practising how to lye upon the block; and had found out, the easiest way of receiving the blow was, to bite his tongue hard: or even if he bit it off, it was no matter, they should have no further use for it.' His behaviour seems to have wanted coolness, or else to equal that of Adrian,[2] Cato,[3] Sir T. More,[4] &c. or any of those heroes who had spirit enough to make an ostentation of their uncon-cern. I had, from the printed accounts of their behaviour, an idea of their persons, exactly conformable to the description I read afterwards in your paper;—but enough—you send me sterling matters of fact, and I return you tinsel observations.— I thank you for accenting Crŏmĕrtie and Balmĕrĭno; I learnt Cullōden from you *before*.

I have had little company since I saw you.—One day indeed I was surprized by a visit from Mr. Thomson, Author of the Seasons.[5]—Mr. Lyttelton introduced him.[6] I have not room to tell you all that passed.—They praised my place extrava-gantly;—proposed alterations, &c. Thomson was very face-tious, and very complaisant; invited me to his house at Rich-mond.[7] There were many things said worth *telling*, but not *writing* to you.—This has been a summer that I have spent more *socially* than any one these three years. I expect a good deal more company this week, the next, and the week after.— Lady Luxborough talks of coming, and I believe *will*.—The visit would bring my little walks into repute.—When will the time come, that I shall enjoy your company here a month uninterrupted?

Dear Sir,

Yours most faithfully,

W. SHENSTONE.

NOTES

[1]The Lords Kilmarnock and Balmĕrino were executed, August, 1746, because of the part which they took in the 1745 rebellion.

[2]The lines of the dying emperor to his soul are often quoted as an instance of the 'ostentation' of his 'unconcern.'

'Animula, vagula, blandula,
Hospes, comesque corporis,
Quae nunc abibis in loca
Pallidula, rigida, nudula;
Nec ut soles, dabis jocos.'
(Aelius Spartianus, *Hadriani Vita*).

[3]Marcius Porcius Cato (95–46 B.C.), when he had news at Utica of Caesar's decisive victory over Scipio and Juba, resolved to die rather than surrender, and committed suicide after spending the night in reading Plato's *Phædo*. The closing events of his life were dramatised by Addison in *Cato*.

[4]Sir Thomas More, before he was executed on July 7, 1535, exclaimed to one who stood by, 'Friend, help me up; when I come down again, I can shift for myself.' He bade the executioner put aside his beard, 'for it never committed treason.'

[5]James Thomson (1700–1748). *Winter* appeared 1726; *Summer*, 1727; *Spring*, 1728; *The Seasons*, 1730.

[6]Thomson was a friend of George, Lord Lyttelton, and frequently visited at Hagley Hall. Wyndham, *op. cit.*

[7]He had a cottage with a pretty garden in Kew Foot Lane.

LV

B.M. Add. MSS. 28958.
and Hull, I, 60.

[*To* LADY LUXBOROUGH].

Madam,

I am quite asham'd that it has not been in my Power to make a speedier Inquiry into the Event of your Ladyship's Journey. It wou'd give me the utmost uneasiness to find you underwent any Inconvenience from a visit which was calculated to give me so much Pleasure, and yourself so little.

I am somewhat apprehensive that one ought to guard not only against *Ambition* but even too much *Admiration*, if one wou'd prepare to live as it beseems a poor *Hermit* to do. Your Ladyship will observe therefore how dangerous a visitant you are, & how much you must have retarded my Progress towr'ds an eremitical Temper of Mind; having diffus'd an Air of Dignity thro' my solitary Paths which will not fail to present itself as often as I resume them. Perhaps Politeness, Elegance, and Taste may be some of those amiable Accomplishments which it may be allowable for a *Hermit* to admire under certain Limitations; If not, I can only say that I must remain a very *imperfect one*, so long as I remember y[e] Honour you have done me; And if I am not likely to succeed *that Way*, I may as well indulge my Ambition to the full, which I never fail to do as oft as I am permitted to subscribe myself

Your Ladyship's most oblig'd
& most obedient humble Servant,
WILL SHENSTONE.

I hope to have an opportunity of waiting on your Ladyship at Barels very soon. In the mean Time I wou'd beg leave to borrow Mr. Whitehead's[1] & Mr. Mallets Poems.[2]

Miss Dolman³ desires her Duty to your Ladyship. I am now at her Brother's at

Broom, *August* the 10ᵗʰ 1747.

NOTES

¹William Whitehead had written at this time *The Danger of Writing Verse*, 1741, *Atys and Adrastus*, 1743, *Anne Boleyn to Henry the Eighth*, 1743, *On Ridicule*, 1743.

²David Mallet's *Poems on Several Occasions*, belongs to 1743.

³W.S. had a very great regard for Maria Dolman, his cousin, and there are several letters from her to him in Hull. She died of smallpox (see *post*, p. 396 and seq.) and W.S. raised an urn to her memory in the garden at The Leasowes. Dodsley wrote *A Description of The Leasowes*, Shenstone, *Works* II, 356: 'This very soft and pensive scene, very properly stiled the Lovers' Walk, is terminated with an ornamental urn, inscribed to Miss Dolman, a beautiful and amiable relation of Mr. Shenstone's, who died of the small-pox, about twenty-one years of age.'

LVI (A)

Hull, I, 41.

To the REV. MR. JAGO, *at Bishop's Itchington, near Kineton, in Warwickshire.*¹

THE LEASOWES,
Sept. 17, 1747.

Dear Mr. Jago,

I think I have out-corresponded all my Correspondents; whether you are the last that is to be subdued, I cannot say; but the Rest are so fatigued, that they are not able to achieve a Line. Apprized of this and being by Nature disposed to have Mercy on the Vanquished, '*Parcere subjectis,* & *debellare superbos,*'² I seldom write a Syllable more than is requisite to further some Scheme, or ascertain some Interview; the latter being the Purpose of this mine Epistle. I am in great Hopes I shall be at Liberty to see you, ere many Weeks be past, and would beg of you to let me know by a Line, when I am most likely, or when very unlikely, to meet with you at Home. The Reason why I can fix no week, at present, is, that I am in daily Expectations of Mr. LYTTELTON, and the HAGLEY Family. I dined there some time since with Mr. PITT,³ Mr. BOUHOURS, Mr. CAMPION, and all the World. Mr. THOMSON, that right friendly Bard, was expected, and I fancy may be there now.

Mr. LYTTELTON offered me the Visit, and I own I am pleased with the Prospect of shewing him something at the *Leasowes* beyond his Expectations. I have made a great Improvement in VIRGILS Grove,[4] since you were here, and have finished a new Path from it to the House, after the Manner you approved. They are going to build a Rotund to terminate the Visto at *Hagley*;[5] I think there is a little Hill joining the Park, that would suit one better, tho' it will be very pretty where it is.

If I come to your House, I won't go to Mr. M[ILLE]R's.[6] He has been twice, as near me as the *Grange*, with CHARLES LYTTELTON, but never deemed my Situation worth seeing. I doubt you are a little too modest in praising it, wherever you go. Why don't you applaud with both Hands?'—

'*Parcentes ego Dexteras odi-*
Sparge Rosas'——[7]

I am so very much enamoured, that is, so very partial to my native Place, that it seems a Miracle to me how it comes not to be famous. But to be serious—How my Lord DUDLEY is tumbled about the World! He was overturned in going to Town, and now again in coming back. Is not this falling up Stairs and down Stairs?—Nevertheless, he is safe and sound, and able to sit up with you and me till twelve or one at Night, as I know by last *Monday's* Experience.

I have somewhere about a thousand Things to say to you——not now tho'—Mrs. KNIGHT's Visit I reserve till I see you. A Coach with a Coronet is a pretty Kind of Phænomenon at my Door;—few Things prettier—except the Face of such a Friend as you; for I do not want the Grace to prefer a spirituous and generous Friendship to all the Gewgaws that Ambition can contrive.

I have wrote out my Elegies, and heartily wish you had them to look over, before I come, but I know not how to send them. I shall bring and leave much Poetry with you—'*Thus &*
Odores!'—or rather a Covering *Thuri & Odoribus*—[8]

Yet, I pray you,
If you shall e'er my foolish Lines repeat,
Speak of me, as I am—nothing extenuate,
Nor set down aught in Malice—then

Must you speak

Of one who—

Is, Sir,

Your most affectionate and faithful Servant,

W. SHENSTONE.

NOTES

[1]Hull, I, 41, adds a note to the letter given here: 'In Dodsley's Collection of Mr. Shenstone's letters, the 47th, addressed to a Friend, begins, and contains some Passages, exactly similar to this, but as the Editor's Copy (Mr. Shenstone's own Transcript) specifies the particular Correspondent, to whom it is addressed, and contains more subject, it was judged not improper to be inserted in this Collection.' The letters, *Works*, III, 144, is dated thus: 'It is somewhere about the 20th of Sept. 1747; and I write from The Leasowes.' The Hull and Dodsley letters are very similar, and I have given in addition a third MS. version, which at the time of copying was in the possession of Messrs. Alwin J. Scheuer of New York. The editorial methods of Hull and Dodsley can be to some extent compared and contrasted, but I suspect that the Dodsley version was copied from a later copy of the letter, probably made by Shenstone himself. We know that he was in the habit of making copies. The Dodsley version speaks of the projected visit of Thomson to the Lytteltons as then taking place. I think it very possible that Shenstone made a copy of the letter of September 17, a few days later, altered parts of it to fit in with the facts and added a certain amount of quotation by way of ornament.

[2]Virgil, *Aeneid*, VI, 852.

[3]Probably William Pitt, afterwards Earl of Chatham. He had been a contemporary of George Lyttelton at Eton, and Thomas Pitt, the elder brother of William married Christian Lyttelton. William Pitt assisted with landscape gardening at Hagley. See Wyndham, *op. cit.*, I, 178–81. Graves, *Recollection*, 81, records that Pitt was much interested in W.S.'s gardening at The Leasowes. 'Mr. William Pitt (afterwards Lord Chatham) was particularly charmed with the place; and once observed to Mr. Shenstone, that Nature had done every thing for him, to which Mr. Shenstone replied, that he hoped he had done something for Nature too, by displaying her beauties to the best advantage. Mr. William Pitt afterwards, though a younger brother, and his fortune then not large—with a noble contempt for money, any further than a means of doing good, or conferring favours—as he saw several possible improvements which Mr. Shenstone could not afford to execute, gave him a hint, by means of Mr. Miller of Radway, that, with his permission, Mr. Pitt would please himself by laying out two hundred pounds at the Leasowes. This, however, Mr. Shenstone considered as a species of dalliance with his mistress, to which he could not submit.' See also *A Pastoral Ode to the Honourable Sir Richard Lyttelton*, Shenstone, *Works* I, 179.

> 'Ev'n Pitt, whose fervent periods roll
> Resistless, thro' the kindling soul
> Of Senates, councils, Kings,
> Tho' form'd for courts, vouchsaf'd to rove
> Inglorious thro' the shepherd's grove
> And ope his bashful springs.'

[4]Dodsley in his *Description of the Leasowes*, Shenstone, *Works* II, p. 363, says, 'We descend now to a beautiful gloomy scene, called Virgil's Grove, where on the entrance we passed by a small obelisk on the right hand with this inscription:

> P. Virgilio Maroni
> Lapis iste cum luco sacer esto

. . . It is not very easy either to paint or describe this delightful grove; . . . Be it, therefore, first observed, that the whole scene is opake and gloomy, consisting of a small deep valley or dingle; the sides of which are inclosed with irregular tufts of hazel and other underwood; and the whole over-shadowed with lofty trees rising out of the bottom of the dingle, through which a copious stream makes its way through mossy banks, enamelled with primroses, and variety of wild wood flowers,' etc.

[5]W.S. was keenly interested in every detail of Hagley improvements, which were in the hands of Sir Thomas Lyttelton's eldest son George. G. Lyttelton wrote to Molly West, the cousin who almost lived at Hagley, from Argyle Street, March 29, 1748: 'It vexes me that you can't find fencing enough from all my father's woods to enclose the plantation that Pitt marked out for the cottage. He will be much disappointed not to see it done, and so indeed shall I; much more so than at the delay of the Rotunda . . .' Wyndham, I, 179–180. The Rotunda, imitated from the Temple of Vesta at Rome, is still to be seen through a 'visto.'

Hugh Miller, *First Impressions of England and its People*, Ch. VI, gives an excellent description of Hagley, as it was early in the nineteenth century.

[6]Sanderson Miller of Radway, near Edgehill, pioneer Gothic Architect, friend of Jago, who was a near neighbour of his. See Hutton, *Highways and Byways in Shakespeare's Country*, 31, 32, 33. Radway Grange, a mixture of all styles, is a curious monument of eighteenth-century architectural taste. Miller designed for Sir George Lyttelton the new Hagley Hall, mention of which is several times made in W.S.'s letters. Most people prefer Miller's classical designs, the most notable of which is Warwick County Hall. Jago, in *Edge-Hill*, praises Miller's achievement:

> 'Thanks, Miller! to thy paths,
> That ease our winding steps! Thanks to the fount,
> The trees, the flow'rs, imparting to the sense
> Fragrance or dulcet sound of murm'ring rill,
> And stilling ev'ry tumult in the breast!
> And oft the stately tow'rs, that overtop
> The rising wood, and oft the broken arch,
> Or mould'ring wall, well taught to counterfeit
> The waste of time, to solemn thought excite,
> And crown with graceful pomp and shaggy hill.'

Many agreed in admiring Sanderson Miller's amiable character, but W.S. seems to have regarded him with a certain amount of jealousy. See Dickins and Stanton, *An Eighteenth Century Correspondence*.

[7]Horace, *Carminum*, III, 19, 22.

[8]Horace, *Epistles*, II, 1, 269–270.

LVI (B)

Works III, 144.

It is somewhere about the
20th of Sept. 1747,
and I write from The
LEASOWS.

Dear Sir,

I think I have lived to out-correspond almost all my correspondents; whether you are the last that is to be subdued, I will not say; the rest are so fatigued, that they are not able to atchieve a line. Apprized of this, and being by nature disposed to have mercy on the vanquished, 'parcere subjectis,' I seldom write a syllable more than is requisite to further some scheme, or ascertain some interview, the latter of these being the purpose of *this* mine epistle. I am in great hopes I shall be at liberty to see you ere many weeks be past; and would beg of you, in the mean time, to inform me, by a letter, when I am likely, or when very *unlikely*, to meet with you at home. I am detained, just at present, by continual expectations of the Hagley family.

As I was returning home from church on Sunday last, whom should I meet in a chaise, with two horses length-ways, but that right friendly bard, Mr. Thomson? I complimented him upon his arrival in this country, and asked him to accompany Mr. Lyttelton to The Leasows, which he said he would with abundance of pleasure; and so we parted. You will observe, that the more stress I lay upon this visit, and the more I *discover* to you, the more substantial is my apology for deferring mine into Warwickshire. I own, I am pleased with the prospect of showing them something at The Leasows beyond what they expect. I have begun my terras on the high hill I shewed you, made some considerable improvements in Virgil's grove, and finished a walk from it to the house, after a manner which you will approve. They are going to build a castle in the park round the lodge, which, if well executed, must have a good effect; and they are going likewise to build a rotund to terminate the visto. The fault is, that they anticipate every thing which I propose to do when I become *rich*; but as that is never likely to be, perhaps it is not of any importance; but what I term *rich*, implies no great deal; I believe, you are a witness to the moderation of my desires; and I flatter myself that you will believe your friend in *that* respect something above the vulgar.

> 'Crede non illum tibi de scelesta
> 'Plebe dilectum, neque sic fidelem,
> 'Sic lucro aversum, potuisse nasci
>   'Patre pudendo.'[1]

If I come to your house, positively I will not go to see Mr. M[iller]. He has been twice as near me as The Grange, with C[harles] L[yttelton], and never deemed my place worth seeing. I doubt, you are a little too modest in praising it wherever you go.—Why don't you applaud it with both hands, 'utroque pollice?'—'Parcentes ego dexteras odi, sparge rosas.' —I am so very *partial* to my native place, that it seems a miracle to me that it is not more famous. But I complain unjustly of you; for, as you have always contributed to my happiness, you have taken every opportunity to contribute to my figure. I wish I could say the same of some who have it *more* in their *power*.

I have yet about a thousand things to say to you—not now, though.—Lady L[uxboroug]h's visit I reserve till I see you. A coach with a coronet is a pretty kind of phænomenon at my door—few prettier, except the face of such a friend as you; for I do not want the grace to prefer a generous and spirited friendship to all the gewgaws that ambition can *contrive*. I have wrote out my elegies, and heartily wish you had them to look over before I come.—I know not how to send them.— I shall bring and leave some poetry with you.—'Thus & odores!' or rather a proper covering for 'Thus & odores, & piper, & quicquid chartis amicitur ineptis.'

Adieu! dear Sir.

Believe me ever yours,
W. SHENSTONE.

NOTE

¹Horace, *Carm.*, 2, 4, 17.

LVI (c)

Messrs. Alwin T. Scheuer. New York.

THE LEASOWS *Septr* 17 1747.

Dear Mr. Jago

I think I've out-corresponded all my Correspondents; whether you are the last that is to be subdu'd I will not say; but the rest are so fatigu'd that they are not able to atchieve a Line. Appriz'd of this, & being by Nature dispos'd to have Mercy on ye vanquish'd, parcere subjectis & debellare super-

I

bos, I seldom write a syllable more than is requisite to further some scheme, or ascertain some Interview; The latter being ye Purpose of this mine Epistle. I am in great Hopes I shall be at Liberty to see you e'er many weeks be past, & wou'd beg of you to let me know by a Line when I am most likely, or when very unlikely, to meet with you at Home. The Reason why I can fix no week at present, is, that I am in daily expectations of Mr. Lyttelton & ye Hagley Family. I din'd there sometime since with Mr. Pitt, Mr. Bouhours, Mr. Campion & all ye world. Mr. Thomson, that right Friendly Bard was expected, & I fancy may be there now. Mr. Lyttelton offer'd me ye visit, & I own I am pleas'd with the prospect of shewing him something at ye Leasows beyond his Expectations—I've made a great Improvement in Virgils Grove since you were here, & have finished a new Path from it to ye House, after ye manner you approvd—They are going to build a Rotund to terminate ye visto at Hagley—I think there is a little Hill joining ye Park y't wou'd suit one better; tho 'twill be very pretty where they design to plan it—If I come to your House, I wont go to see Mr. Miller's. He has been twice as near me as the Grange with Charles Lyttelton; but never deem'd my situation worth seeing. I doubt you're a little too modest in praising it, wherever you go. Why don't you applaud it with both Hands? Parcentes ego dexteras odi—sparge rosas. I am so very much enamour'd, that is, so very partial to my native Place, that it seems a miracle to me how it comes not to be famous—But to be serious—How my L'd Dudley is tumbled about ye world!—He was overturned in going to Town, & now again coming back—Is not this falling upstairs & downstairs? Nevertheless he is safe & sound & able to sit up with you & me till 12 or one at Night, as I know by last Monday's Experience—I've somewhere about a Thousand things to say to you—Not now tho—Lady Luxborough's visit I reserve till I see you. A Coach w'h a Coronet is a pretty kind of Phœnomenon at my Door—Few things prettier—except ye Face of such a Freind as you—For I do not want y't Grace to prefer a spirituous & generous Friendship to all ye Gewgaws that Ambition can contrive—I have wrote out my Elegies, & heartily wish you had 'em to look over before I come; but I

know not how to send 'em. I shall bring & leave much Poetry
with you—Thus & odores or rather a proper covering Thuri
& odoribus

                    —yet I pray you
If you shall e'er my foolish Lines repeat
Speak of me as I am—nothing extenuate
Nor set down ought in Malice—then must you speak
Of one that—

                    is Sir your most affectionate &
                                    faithfull
                        Serv't W. SHENSTONE.

LVII

Works III, 136.

To the [REV. R. GRAVES], *with Thoughts on Advice.*

THE LEASOWS,
Sept. 21, 1747.

Dear Mr. Graves,

   I am under some apprehension that you dread the sight of
a letter from me, as it seems to lay claim to the compliment of
an answer. I will therefore write you one that shall wave its
privilege, at least till such time as your leisure encourages, or
your present dissipation does not forbid, you to send one.—I
dare now no longer expatiate upon the affair you have in hand;
it is enough for me, if you will excuse the freedom I *have* taken.
I have often known *delay* produce good effects in some
cases which even sagacity itself could not surmount; and, if I
thought I did not go too far, would presume to recommend it
now.—You know I have very little of the temper of an alder-
man. I almost hate the *idea* of wealthiness as much as the *word*.
It seems to me to carry a notion of fulness, stagnation, and
insignificancy. It is this disposition of mine that can *alone*
give any weight to the advice I send you, as it proves me not
to give it through any partiality to fortune. As to what remains,
you are, I hope, assured of the value I must ever have for you
in *any* circumstances, and the regard I shall always shew for
any that belongs to you. I cannot like you *less* or *more*.—I now

drop into other matters. Bergen, I see, is taken at last;[1] pray what are the sentiments of your political companions? I dined some time ago with Mr. Lyttelton and Mr. Pitt, who both agreed it was worth twenty thousand men to the French; which is a light in which I never used to consider it. Any little intimation that you please to *confer* upon me, enables me to seem *wise* in this country for a month; particularly if I take care to adjust my face accordingly.—As I was returning last Sunday from Church, whom should I meet in my way, but that *sweet-souled* bard Mr. James Thomson, in a chaise drawn by two horses lengthways.—I welcomed him into the country, and asked him to accompany Mr. Lyttelton to the Leasows (who had offered me a visit), which he promised to do. So I am in daily expectation of them and all the world this week. I fancy they will lavish all their praises upon *nature*, reserving none for poor *art* and *me*. But if I ever live, and am able to perfect my schemes, I shall not despair of pleasing the few I first began with; *the few friends prejudiced in my favour*; and then 'Fico por los malignatores.' Censures will not effect me; for I am armed so strong in *vanity*,[2] that they will pass by me as the idle wind which I regard not.—I think it pretty near equal, in a country place, whether you gain the small number of tasters, or the *large crowd* of the vulgar. The latter are more frequently met with, and *gape*, *stupent*, and *stare* much more. But one would chuse to please a few *friends* of taste before mob or gentry, the great vulgar or the small; because therein one gratifies both one's social passions and one's pride, that is, one's *self*-love. Above all things, I would wish to please *you*; and if I have a wish that projects or is prominent beyond the rest, it is to see you placed to your satisfaction near me; but Fortune must vary from her usual treatment before she favours me so far.—And yet there *was* a time, when one might probably have prevailed on her. I knew not what to do.—The affair was so intricately circumstanced—your surprizing silence after the hint I gave.—Mr. D[olman] offering to serve any friend of mine; nay, pressing me to use the opportunity.—His other relations, his guardians, teizing him with sure symptoms of a rupture in case of a refusal on *their* side.—Mr. P—— soliciting me if the place were *sold*, which it could not legally be.

Friendship, propriety, impartiality, self-interest (which I *little* regarded), endeavouring to distract me; I think I never spent so disagreeable an half year since I was born. To close the whole, I could not *foresee* the event, which is almost foretold in your last letter, and I knew I could not serve you; but I must render it a *necessary* one. In short, when I can tell you the whole affair at leisure, you will own it to be of such a nature, that I must be ever in suspence concerning my behaviour, and of course shall never reflect on it with pleasure. Believe me, with the truest affection, yours,

W. SHENSTONE.

NOTES

[1] Bergen-op-Zoom fell into the hands of the French, September 16, 1747, after the Duke of Cumberland was defeated at Lauffeld.

[2] Cf. *Julius Caesar*, IV, 3.

> 'For I am arm'd so strong in honesty
> That they pass by me as the idle wind
> Which I respect not.'

LVIII

Works III, 147.

To the [REV. RICHARD JAGO], *with a Song.*

1747.

Dear Sir,

Being just returned from a small excursion, it was with the utmost pleasure that I read over your letter; and, though it abounds both in wit and waggery, I sit down incontinently to answer it, with *none*.

The agreeableness of your letters is now heightened by the surprize they give me. I must own, I have thought you in a manner lost to the amusements in which you once delighted, correspondences, works of taste and fancy, &c. If you think the opinion worth removing, you need only favour me with such a letter now and then, and I will place you (in my imagination) where you shall see all the favourites of fortune cringing at your feet.

I think I could add about half a dozen hints to your observations on electricity,[1] which might at *least* disguise the facts; and then why will you not put it into some news-paper, or monthly pamphlet? you might discover yourself to whom you have a mind. It would give more than ordinary pleasure at this time.—— Some other will take the hint.—Pity your piece should not have the advantage of novelty as well as of wit!

I dined and stayed a night with Dr. E——; he was extremely obliging, and I am glad of such a friend to visit at B. He asked much after you.—He shewed me his Ovid—I advised him to finish some one epistle *highly*, that he might shew it.—The whole will *not take*, though it goes against me to tell him so. I should be glad he could succeed at B.; and could I serve him, it would be with a safe conscience; for I take him to excel the rest of B. physicians far in point of speculation and diligence, &c.

I send you the song you asked for, and request of you to write me out your new edition of the election verses; and, at your *leisure*, a copy of the poem which we altered.

THE LARK

'Go, tuneful bird, that gladd'st the skies,
'To Daphne's window speed thy way,
'And there on quiv'ring pinions rise,
'And there thy vocal art display.

'And if she deign thy notes to hear,
'And if she praise thy matin song;
'Tell her, the sounds that sooth her ear,
'To simple British birds belong.

'Tell her, in livelier plumes array'd,
'The bird from Indian groves may shine:
'But ask the lovely, partial maid,
'What are his notes compar'd to thine?

'Then bid her treat that witless beau
'And all his motley race with scorn;
'And heal deserving Damon's woe,
'Who sings her praise, and sings forlorn.'[2]

I am, Sir,

Your most faithful friend and servant,

W. SHENSTONE.

Have you read Watson,[3] Martyn,[4] and Freke,[5] on electricity? I accidentally met with the two former, by which my head is rendered almost giddy—electrics, non-electrics, electrics *per se*, and bodies that are only conductors of electricity, have a plaguy bad effect on so vortical a brain as mine.

I will infallibly spend a week with you, perhaps about February, if it suits you; though I think too it must be later.

I have been painting in water colours, during a visit I made, flowers.[6] I would recommend the amusement to you, if you can allow it the time that is expedient.

I trust you will give me one entire week in the spring, when my late alterations may exhibit themselves to advantage.

NOTES

[1] Jago's Essay on Electricity was never published. A letter from Dodsley to W.S. (B.M. Add. MSS. 28959), dated October 8, 1747, contains the following: I suppose you know by this that ye Museum is dropt, but I think your Essay* too good to be lost, if therefore you have no objection I will endeavour to get it inserted in some other of ye Public Papers. . . .

*My good Friend Mr. Jago's prose essay on electricity, an exquisite piece of Humour; and never yet printed.

May 12, 1759.   W.S.

[2] *The Skylark*, *Works* I, 152, shows several verbal changes.

[3] William Watson (1715–1787), physician, naturalist, electrician.

[4] John Martyn (1699–1768), botanist, practised as an apothecary.

[5] John Freke (1688–1756), surgeon, experimented with electricity.

[6] Graves, *Recollection*, 176, writes: 'In painting flowers (which he performed with some skill), by the management of his lights and shades, he produced the strongest claro-obscuro, and gave them a very striking and beautiful appearance.' Shenstone, *Works* I, 142: 'Written in a flower book of my own colouring, designed for Lady Plymouth. 1753–4.'

LIX

B.M. Add. MSS. 28958.

[*To* Lady LUXBOROUGH.]

Dec. 26, 1747.

My Lady,

I have heard from several of my Friends, who are glad to gratify me upon any *good Foundation*, how favourably you are pleas'd to speak both with regard to the Leasows & myself. A *Reflection* so interesting as this, is what I never can esteem a meagre Diet. It is a *Dissert* indeed but such as my Ambition can very well subsist on; as it had done for a considerable Time.

when *it* receiv'd a fresh supply in the Paragraph with which you lately honour'd me.

I have been long confin'd at Home by many *real* Impediments, & if there were any imaginary ones, your Ladyships Postscript was sufficient to remove them. Amidst a thousand of y^r brightest Qualifications your Ladyship may consider yourself as no small Heroine; for you have at one stroke demolish'd ye most furious Lion upon Earth. You will be a little surpriz'd at the Atchievement I assign you, but all I mean is that *visionary Lion*, which *Indolence* had station'd in ye way to Barels, as she does in ye way of all that is aimiable. I assure your Ladyship this Lion was delineated by her in ye most lively Manner, and yet perhaps not half so naturally as the stag which Mr. Outing, by your direction, sent me. *She* express'd not only the Teeth, the Paws, & the Voice of y^t terrible Animal, but whisper'd likewise at the same Time ye great Probability that I shou'd find your Ladyship to be in *Cheshire*, even supposing I cou'd 'scape his Fury. I approve of her *Artifice* in *one* Respect, as well as her Justice: She never durst presume to depreciate that infinite Pleasure I shou'd receive from your Ladyship's conversation, provided I *cou'd* surmount all Difficulties, & find you at Barrels. Had she proceeded *so* far, I shou'd have seen thro' her Delusions at once, as I now do. Perhaps she was desirous to revenge that little Abuse I bestow'd on her, long ago, in a printed Madrigal;[1] tho a Revenge of this kind (had her Plot succeeded) cou'd not fail to appear very cruel and inadequate. Your ladyship has dissolv'd the charm in a moment; & I am now amaz'd, (considering how far ye Hearths of Barrels exceed ye scenery of stowe,[2] whenever y^r Ladyship *draws near* 'em) y^t I have not *already* embrac'd the Pleasure I design to do myself *some day next Week*. I will then return your Pamphlets, tho I have only to say in regard to my Opinions of them, what is indeed it's highest Panegyrick, that it is entirely similar to your own. I am

Your Ladyship's most oblig'd

& most obedient Servt

WILL: SHENSTONE.

The Leasows, *Dec^r*. 26
1747

NOTES

¹Possibly the reference is to *Sloth*, 'Hither, dear Boy, direct thy wandering Eyes,' *Poems upon Various Occasions*, Oxford, 1737. The poem was not again printed.

²At Stowe Lord Cobham continued the work of his father, Sir Richard Temple, and the gardens were constantly being added to until 1755. Stowe was regarded as the height of perfection by early landscape gardeners. Bridgeman, Kent, and Vanbrugh all had a hand in its designing. Pope's lines in praise of it, *Moral Essays*, Ep. IV, 65, are well known.

> 'Still follow sense, of ev'ry art the soul
> Parts answ'ring parts shall slide into a whole;
> Spontaneous beauties all around advance,
> Start even from difficulty, strike from chance,
> Nature shall join you; time shall make it avow
> A work to wonder at—perhaps a Stow.'

LX

Works III, 151.

To the [Rev. RICHARD JAGO], *after a Visit.*

Sunday,
Feb. 14, 1747–8.

Dear Mr. Jago,

I am tempted once more to apologize for the unseasonable visit I paid you, though I feel myself entirely innocent in that respect, even as much so as the post-boy was guilty; for had my previous letter arrived in due time, you had then been furnished with an opportunity of waving my company till a more convenient season. I was *only*, or, at least *chiefly* uneasy upon *your* account. I spent my time very agreeably, and only less so than I might, had I not been conscious to myself that I was intruding upon domestic tendernesses.

I spent the Sunday night and the next day at Mr. Wren's;¹ and am now just returned from Mr. Dolman's, who has made me a genteel present of Spence's Polymetis.² I have not yet *read* many dialogues in it, but I have *dipped* in several; and have reason to be well enough satisfied with the simple and uninvidious manner in which he has introduced Mr. Lowth's poem.³ I have long known of this intended *introduction* (which I accidentally found to have been settled betwixt them before I published *mine* on the same subject), and a little dreaded the *form* of it. I have long ago made considerable improvements in mine, and have a mind one day to publish it once more; after which, let it sleep in peace. I have sometimes thought of printing my next title-page thus, viz. 'Poems: consisting of Songs, Odes, and Elegies, with an improved edition of The Judgement of Hercules, and of The School-mistress.' But I have but very few critical acquaintance, and I live at a great distance from those I have; stationed amongst the *makers* and the *wearers* of hobnails,

'Far from the joys that with my soul agree,
'From *wit*, from *learning*—very far from thee.'
PARNELL.[4]

I know I have thrown a great number of careless things into your hands, I know to *whom* I intrusted my follies; but I know *not* what they *are*:—I believe, in general, that they consist of mis-begotten embryos and abortive births, which it had been merely decent to have buried in—some part of my garden; but I was morally assured, that you would expose nothing of mine to my disadvantage. As to some that are *less imperfect*, you promised your observations, and I desire you would make them with the utmost freedom. I can bear any censure which you shall pass by way of letter, and I beg once more that you would not be sparing. It will be esteemed as great a favour as you can do me. When they have gone through your hands, and those of one or two more friends, I shall, perhaps, think of publishing them; though as to that, much depends upon the advice I receive, and previously on the opportunity I have of receiving. I am in hopes that you will be pretty full in discovering to me, *which you dislike the least*, *what faults you find*, and *what improvements they are capable of*. I set you a tedious task; but I will return the favour as far as I am able, either in *the same way* or any other. This brings me to say, that, if there be any compositions of yours that you would have me correct (and there are several of which I want a copy), I would beg you to send them. Your Blackbird[5] excels any singing-bird I ever heard, and I beseech you to convey it to The Leasowes by the next opportunity, that he may acquire fame near other rills, and in other valleys, than those in which he was produced.

I have many compliments to make in your country; to Mr.
H[ardy], Mrs. N——, Mrs. J[ago], Mr. F[ancourt],[6] Mr.
T——, and your brother. If I go over to Mr. W[ren]'s, I will
assuredly call and spend a night with you.—*That* is precarious.
—But whether I do or not, I would willingly hope to see you
this spring and summer more than once; as a *critic*, and as a
friend: nor do I forget the promise of Mr. H[ardy] and Mr.
F[ancourt];—but of these things more when I send for the
papers, which I purpose to do to-morrow fortnight, that is, the
twenty-ninth of February.

I have suffered greatly by railing at the black button on a
parson's great coat. Had Mr. Hall's[7] been thus distinguished,
he could not have mistaken mine for his own; which latter I
sent in order to be commuted at Birmingham, and was almost
starved to death before I could accomplish the exchange.
There is no trifling with any *part* of orthodoxy with impunity.
—That is the moral.

I have received a very obliging letter from Lady Luxborough, wherein she tells me that Lady Hartford admires my
place in her description.[8] Mr. Thomson is intimate at Lady
Hartford's, and I suppose Lady Hartford may have been
informed by L[ady] L[uxborough] that Mr. Thomson has
been here; so I conclude, in mere vanity, that my farm is
advancing in reputation. What think you of Mr. Carte's
History?[9] or what of his narrative concerning the Pretender's
touching for the King's evil? I think one is not, however, to
give up his book entirely; because, with *all his superstition*, he
may have several anecdotes that one would like to read.

I have had great expectations from the beautiful veins of a
piece of oak of which I have had a table made; but, upon a
thorough survey of it, it is so like nothing in the world as old
B's callimanco night-gown.

I have nothing to add worth beginning upon another page;
but I happened not to make a regular conclusion in my preceding one.

You must give me some time to colour you a collection of
flowers (that octavo edition I shewed you here); and then I
will make Mrs. Jago a present of it. I believe I can engage Mr.
Dolman to assist me, who is much my superior in point of

accuracy; and the inscription at the beginning is to run some-
how thus:

'ELEGANTISSIMAE PUELLAE

'DOROTHEAE FANCOURT,

'QUAE PERDILECTI SUI CONDISCIPULI

'RICHARDI JAGO

'AMORES MERVIT.

'D. D.

'GULIELMUS SHENSTON;

'DEBITAE NYMPHIS OPIFEX CORONAE.'

That is, by trade a garland-maker; but this inscription I may
alter, if I think of any thing more expressive of the regard
which I have ever born and still bear you.

Lord Dudley is gone, and franks are no more. I have nothing to wish you but health and preferment;—'det vitam, det
opes;'[10] with these you will easily compound that cordial
happiness, having every other ingredient that is requisite at
hand.

I am, most affectionately,

Your very faithful friend, &c.

W. SHENSTONE.

NOTES

[1]W.S. visited Christopher Wren (1675–1747), son of Sir Christopher Wren, architect,
of Wroxhall Abbey, friend of Somervile and of the Warwickshire coterie generally, a
numismatist of some repute, who published, 1708, *Numismatum Antiquorum Sylloge*.
He compiled memoirs of his family, *Parentalia*, which were published by his son
Stephen. W.S.'s visit to Wroxhall continued after the death of Christopher Wren the
elder and we find him still visiting the son, another Christopher Wren.

[2]Joseph Spence (1699–1768), author of *Polymetis*, 1747, and *Anecdotes of Books and
Men*, much admired by W.S. when he came to know him later. At Byfleet, Spence
carried out experiments in landscape gardening similar to those at The Leasowes.

[3]Robert Lowth (1710–1787), bishop of London, Joseph Spence's close personal
friend and executor. *The Choice of Hercules* appears in Roach's *Collection*, VI, as well as
in *Polymetis*.

[4]Quoted inaccurately from the *Lines to Mr. Pope*, Chalmers, *English Poets*, IX, 361.

[5]Jago's elegy, *The Blackbirds*, originally appeared in Hawkesworth's *Adventurer*,
37, March 13, 1753, but, with other poems, was afterwards inserted in Dodsley's
Collection, IV.

[6]Mr. Hardy was a son of Admiral Sir Thomas Hardy and Mr. Fancourt, Jago's
father-in-law.

[7]Parson Hall, one of the many friends of Lady Luxborough, became rector of
Beaudesert, Henley-in-Arden in 1741 and perpetual curate at Henley.

[8]Frances Thynne, Lady Hertford, afterwards Duchess of Somerset, friend of Lady
Luxborough and a letter writer of charm. See Hull, and *Correspondence between Frances,
Countess of Hertford and Henrietta Louisa, Countess of Pomfret, between the years*

1738–1741. Lady Luxborough writes (*Letters*, 9): 'Lady Hertford writes me word, she is charmed with your retreat; as she has only had the description of it from me, judge what she'd be if she saw it, at least if Mr. Thompson described it to her.'
(Lady Hertford was the patroness of James Thomson who dedicated his *Spring* to her.)
[9]Thomas Carte (1686–1754). His history appeared December 1747, and was advertised in *The Gentleman's Magazine*, January 1748.
[10]Horace, *Ep.* I, 18, 112.

LXI

B.M. Add. MSS. 28958.

[*To* LADY LUXBOROUGH].

1747[8] *Fast Day.* [*Feb.?*]

Madam.

I am asham'd to think that I have suffer'd your Ladyship to make any Apology for my Reception at Barrels, when I ought immediately, upon my arrival at Home; to have obviated every thing of that kind by an Acknowledgment y[t] I was never in my Life more agreeably entertain'd. I am ambitious enough to be pleas'd with y[e] Honour of your Ladyship's Company, tho' I had no Taste; & I have Taste enough, to be pleas'd with the Politeness of it, tho' I had no Ambition. If I found any uneasiness, it was to reflect how little I cou'd contribute towards your Amusement in return, & in that Respect *only* was my Ambition disappointed.

I was in Hopes your Ladyship wou'd have weigh'd those trifling verses[1] rather in the scale of *Sincerity* than that of *Poetry*. I meant them as a real expression of the satisfaction I found by your Fireside, & as an Intimation of my Thanks; which, (if I had attempted to return them by word of mouth) I might have express'd with all the awkward Hesitation of a *Clown in earn*est; & yet if my Tongue had hesitated upon *that occasion*, I am sure it must have prov'd very unfaithfull to my Sentiments.

Your Ladyship's notion of solitude & of Company is extremely just. A polite & friendly Neighbourhood *in y[e] Country*, or, (in Lieu of that) agreeable visitants from *any* Distance, give a Person all y[e] Society he can extract from a Crowd; & then he has the *rural Scenery*, which is all *clear*

*Gain*s. For I fancy no one will prefer ye Beauty of a *street* to ye Beauty of a Lawn or Grove; & indeed the Poets wou'd have form'd no very tempting an *Elysium*, had they made a *Town* of it.

Your Ladyship also mentions ye checker'd scenes of Life. I believe I am as void of superstition as any person in the world, & yet I have accustom'd myself *so much* to consider Life in the same light, that I find almost every Pleasure lessen'd by that very consideration. I expect a Pain to ballance it. May Fate prevent my receiving any Pain to ballance the Pleasure which your Letter gave me! I'm sure it must be excessive. But as I had been plagu'd with a very dispiriting Affair before, I hope I am quit; & that your obliging Letter was to make me amends, as it did sufficiently. However this *Habit* of mind in *general* gives me some Evenness of temper; as my *uneasiness* is thus mitigated by *Hope*, & my Pleasure chequ'd by Fear— But not to trouble y^r Ladyship with my Pains or Pleasures of *Mind*, I will tell you my *bodily* sufferings, for ridiculing *formerly* the black Button & button-hole on a Parson's great Coat. Surely no one may laugh at ye most *extrinsick* circumstance of Orthodoxy, but a Punishment attends him. I mention this because Mr. Hall's mistake must needs be owing to the want of this necessary distinction, & having sent *his* very regularly back to Birmingham, I was almost starv'd to Death before I cou'd compleat the Exchange.

I am very much oblig'd to your Ladyship for y^r Receipt to make sealing wax.² I could very conscientiously sign & seal my Respect for your Ladyship under every colour'd wax that you can direct me to make. I have not yet had an opportunity of experimenting in any of the colours. I think I shou'd be most pleas'd with a beautifull *yellow*; but I might perhaps be thought to discover a *Party*-spirit on y^e *outside* of my Letters, which I shall never do *within*.

Lady Hartford's Character I have the greatest veneration for; pursuant to those Features of it, which your Ladyship describ'd to me, & also to a Letter of hers which you shew'd me concerning Ld Beauchamp's³ Death. If she shou'd happen to speak of my Place to Mr. Thomson he *seemd* here to be enough pleas'd with it, to countenance your Ladyship's kind Partiality.

I *did think* to have accompany'd this Letter with some little Pieces of Poetry that might amuse your Ladyship for the Space of ten Minutes; but it grows very late, & my Spirits have been dissipated all this day; so I beg leave to perform my Promise a short time hence, which I will not fail to do. Nevertheless I send a trifle, that was written *last* winter;[4] a winter, that was not exhilarated by any visit at Barels. I send your Ladyship *Winter-songs*, little considering y^t your own (for Miss Nanny Knight)[5] puts all mine out of Countenance, & has all ye advantages of Simplicity and Imagery. I will positively write no more of that kind I have now tir'd your Ladyship with my Impertinence & ought to hasten towards a Conclusion. If you please sometime to honour me with a Line, it will be a Favour I can no way deserve, but by the *Value* I shall *place* on it: But if that sort of Merit be admitted, I will no more allow any one a superiority in it, than in that Respect & deference with which I am, Mad^m.

Your Ladyship's most oblig'd
& most faithfull Servant,
WILL: SHENSTONE.

The Leasows. Fast Day, 1747–8.
I will one day beg ye Favour of y^r
Ladyship to lend me those Designs of Inigo Jones &c: I have a mind to have a small Hand-candlestick executed by y^t urn at ye beginning, which I will draw out upon Paper & return ye Book wth Care.

NOTES

[1]*Upon a visit to the Same in Winter*, 1748, 'On fair Asteria's blissful plains.' *Works* I, 135. Lady Luxborough describes her reception of the trifle which W.S. left behind after a visit to Barrels, *Letters*, 7 and 8.

[2]The Bolingbroke family appears to have been famous for receipts, and Lady Luxborough (*Letters*, 27) tells how 'the late King George' ate two of her mother's brandied peaches every night all the year round.

W.S.'s taste in sealing wax is shown in his MS. letters, various colours—though not a yellow—and various beautiful seals having been used.

[3]Lady Hertford's son, who died of small-pox at Bologna, September 11, 1744.

[4]Possibly the 'winter-song' mentioned here is *Song XV. Winter* 1746, *Works* I, 166.

[5]Apparently W.S. is referring to the second of Lady Luxborough's four poems published Dodsley's *Collection*, IV. 1. *The Bulfinch in Town*. 2. *Song written in Winter*, 1745. 3. *Written in a Tempestuous Night*. 4. *Written at a Ferme Ornee*. I suppose Miss Nanny Knight to be Lady Luxborough's daughter Henrietta. There is, however, nothing in the *Song written in Winter*, 1745, to suggest that Miss Nanny Knight was the one for whom it was written.

LXII

Works III, 157.

To Mr. JAGO.

The Leasows,
Mar. 23, 1747–8.

Dear Sir,

I have sent Tom over for the papers which I left under your inspection; having nothing to add upon this head, but that the more *freely* and *particularly* you give me your opinion, the greater will be the obligation which I shall have to acknowledge.

I shall be very glad, if I happen to receive a good large bundle of your own compositions; in regard to which, I will observe any commands which you shall please to lay upon me.

I am favoured with a certain correspondence, by way of letter, which I told you I should be glad to cultivate; and I find it very entertaining.

Pray did you receive my answer to your last letter, sent by way of London? I should be extremely sorry to be debarred the pleasure of writing to you by the post, as often as I feel a violent propensity to describe the notable incidents of my life: which amount to about as much as the tinsel of your little boy's hobby-horse.

I am on the point of purchasing a couple of busts for the nitches in my hall; and believe me, my good friend, I never proceed one step in ornamenting my little farm, but I enjoy the hopes of rendering it more agreeable to you, and the small circle of acquaintance which sometimes favour me with their company.

I shall be extremely glad to see you and Mr. Fancourt when the trees are green; that is, in May; but I would not have you content yourself with a single visit this summer. If Mr. Hardy (to whom you will make my compliments) inclines to favour me so far, you must calculate so as to wait on him whenever he finds it convenient; though I have *better hopes* of making his reception here agreeable to him when my Lord Dudley comes down.—I wonder how he would like the scheme I am upon, of exchanging a large tankard for a silver standish.

I have had a couple of paintings given me since you were here. One of them is a Madona, valued, as it is said, at ten guineas in Italy, but which you would hardly purchase at the price of five shillings. However, I am endeavouring to make it out to be one of Carlo Maratt's,[1] who was a first hand, and famous for Madonas; even so as to be nick-named 'Cartuccio delle Madonne' by Salvator Rosa.[2] Two letters of the cypher (C M) agree; what shall I do with regard to the third? It is a small piece, and sadly blackened. It is about the size (though not quite the shape) of the Bacchus over the parlour door, and has much such a frame.

A person may amuse himself almost as cheaply as he pleases. I find no small delight in rearing all sorts of poultry; geese, turkeys, pullets, ducks, &c. I am also somewhat smitten with a blackbird which I have purchased: a very fine one; brother by father, but not by mother, to the unfortunate bird you so beautifully describe, a copy of which description you must not fail to send me;—but, as I said before, one may easily habituate one's self to cheap amusements; that is, *rural* ones (for all town amusements are horridly expensive);—I would have you cultivate your garden; plant flowers, have a bird or two in the hall (they will at *least* amuse your children); write now and then a song; buy now and then a book; write now and then a letter to

Your most sincere friend,

and affectionate servant,

W. Shenstone.

P. S. I hope you have exhausted all your spirit of criticism upon my verses, that you may have none left to cavil at this letter; for I am ashamed to think, that *you*, in particular, should receive the dullest I ever wrote in my life. Make my compliments to Mrs. Jago.—She can go a little abroad, you say.—Tell her, I should be proud to shew her The Leasows. Adieu!

NOTES

[1]Carlo Maratta or Maratti (1625–1713), historical and portrait painter.
[2]Salvator Rosa (1615–1673), Italian landscape painter, whose work had much influence in forming the English taste in landscape gardening. See Manwaring, *Italian Landscape in the 18th Century*.

K

LXIII

B.M. Add. MSS. 28958
& Hull, I, 53.[1]

[*To* LADY LUXBOROUGH].

THE LEASOWS, Lady-Day,
1748.

Madam.

After having own'd that the Fear your Ladyship has been under is in reality to be imputed to *me*, I am at a loss to express my *concern*, or to alleviate my *Fault*. I will not in the least disallow that the Book[2] came to Hand regularly, and much sooner than I cou'd reasonably expect it, or that the Letter inclos'd in it gave me uncommon Pleasure, as your Ladyship's never fail to do. I have nothing to say in my Behalf, but that I have never of late had such Health or Spirits as might encourage me to think I cou'd return ye Answer I *ought*: And even *to-night*, my Spirits are so bad, & my Head so confus'd, that I have no reason to hope these lines can do any thing more than free you from your present uncertainty. But, if I am honour'd with a Line from your Ladyship hereafter, I will *immediately acknowledge it* as well as I am able, be my capacity what it will. I do not know how far your Ladyship's Name may be distinguish'd by a Post-woman's Ear; but *this* I know, that if I had been Mr. Holyoak,[3] you shou'd have never known from *me*, that there was any woman in the World who cou'd express herself concerning you with the Disrespect you mention.[4] I am astonish'd no less at her Forgetfulness. There seems to me to be no surer method of conveyance to be found, than this by the *Farmer*; by whom I sent my Letter to the Post-office at Henley, & by whom, I suppose, your Ladyship convey'd your Parcell. An old-woman goes from my Neighbourhood three Times a week to Birmingham, with a single Exception, all the year round: Her business is, to bring hither from the Post Office every thing that is directed to this Part of the Country. And, as she calls me her *best Master*, & knows how gladly I receive a Letter &c. she siezes what is directed to me, with eagerness and rapidity. However, in obedience to your Ladyships Commands, I have sent this Letter to Master Holyoak[5]

& shall have an additional Pressure on my Spirits 'till I hear
you have been pleas'd to forgive my Neglect—I know extremely well that *want of Leisure*, & some *other* Excuses
which are often made for not writing, can be of weight from
no one but a Cobler, that has ten or twelve children dependent
on a Tatchin-end. But I know *as* well, that your Ladyship's
is no ordinary correspondence; & that a Person ought to have
his Head clear & his Imagination unembarass'd when he sits
down to answer any Letter of yours. For my part I can hardly
look upon this as any Letter at all, and will infallibly write
again as soon as I can recover my natural state of Mind. I
have as little Reason to consider yᵉ Inclos'd as *Poetry*. But as
they were *short* compositions, I had been writing them out
yesterday with a design to send them to the Post-office to-
morrow morning. (I mean yᵉ Henley Post-office.) I must
own to your Ladyship, that they were written long ago. I am
afraid I have tir'd you with madrigal & Roundelay. I hope
when yᵉ weather becomes finer, (with which my Spirits *generally* sympathize,) to vary my Style for your Ladyship's Amusement. In the mean Time I have sent you a Poem written by a
Gentleman of my Acquaintance, & shewn up in *Print* for a
College-Exercise.[6] As it was never *publish'd*, you can scarce
have seen it *before*. You will soon discover a *juvenile* want of
Judgment in some Places; but I believe, the Elegance &
variety of his Fancy, you will admire. He sometimes comes and
stays a Month with me at the Leasows in yᵉ Summer; the
next Time he does so, I will be oblig'd to your Ladyship for
Leave to introduce him at Barrels, where, if I am not mistaken,
he will be pleas'd almost to a Degree of Enthusiasm.

As to *Dodsley's Collection*[7] I find it is approv'd on all
Hands; tho' *I* should have been much better pleas'd with him,
if he had giv'n me previous notice e'er he publish'd my
Schoolmistress; that I might have *spruc'd her up* a little before
she appeared in so much Company. They tell me he purposes
a *second* Edition[8] concerning wᶜʰ I have wrote to him; &,
with a view to which, I have declin'd yᵉ Purchase of it in yᵉ
First: so that I have not seen it. Fitzosborne's Letters[9] I
bought & read upon your Recommendation. I think they are
written with Judgment, Elegance, & Fancy; but rather too

much with an *Eye to the Press*. They wou'd *read* much better
with *real* Names; however, I have been inform'd y^t he abuses
Dr. King under ye character of *Mezentius*; that Dr. King
was his wife's Father,[10] & had spent her Fortune &c. Lord
Bolingbroke's Tracts[11] I will buy and read, when I can attend
& think; which is but very little during ye Winter-Season.

As to your Ladyship's Lameness, tho' it comes *last* in this
irregular Letter, I assure you, it gave me real concern to hear
it was *bad*, & very sensible Pleasure to hear it was abated. I
as sincerely wish your Health & Happiness as you do yourself;
& as I always experience this disposition of Mind, I *will* hope
to be forgiven if I shou'd at any time fall short in my means of
expressing it.

I am, Madam,

Your Ladyship's most oblig'd & most

obed^t. Servant

W. SHENSTONE.

I beg my Compliments to Mr. and Mrs. Holyoak [upside
down at head of letter].

NOTES

[1]The letter in Hull differs verbally from the B.M. MS. The whole of the interesting
paragraph dealing with the 1st edition of the first three volumes of Dodsley's *Collection*
is omitted, as is the account of what W.S. has been reading.

[2]A book of Inigo Jones's designs, mentioned p. 127.

[3]Rev. William Holyoak of Oldberrow, on the border of the Barrels estate. He and his
wife were firm friends of Lady Luxborough. At the end of Lady Luxborough's *Letters*
(414) is the letter sent by Mr. Holyoak, telling W.S. of Lady Luxborough's death.

[4]For the account of the incivility of the post-woman see Luxborough, *Letters*, 10.
The question of the safe and speedy delivery of letters caused eighteenth-century
correspondents much anxiety and W.S. and Lady Luxborough frequently discussed
the matter. The latter felt that 'our servants had better be a little fatigued with journies
between the Leasowes and Barrells, than be molested with impertinent Post-people,
indolent or careless chance-messengers, or idle drunken farmers, who undertake to
carry letters they never think of afterwards.' (*Letters*, 366.) Occasionally no servant or
horse could brave the weather and letters had to be sent via London. (*Letters*, 365.)

[5]'Franky' Holyoak had some sort of post in the warehouse of Matthew Boulton,
Snow-hill, Birmingham. Lady Luxborough (*Letters*, 10) asks Shenstone to send a letter
to 'Master Franky Holyoake, at Mr. Bolton's, Wholesale Toymaker, upon Snow-hill,
in Birmingham.'

[6]Whistler's *Shuttlecock*. Cf. Luxborough, *Letters*, 13.

[7]The first three volumes were published in January 1748.

[8]This letter, and that of June 1, 1748, are interesting in calling attention to the
extraordinary popularity of Dodsley's venture. By March of the year of publication a
second edition was proposed, and by June 1 of the same year was actually being printed.

[9]By William Melmoth (1710–1799). Cf. Luxborough, *Letters*, 14.

[10]William King (1685–1763), principal of St. Mary Hall.

[11]*A Collection of Political Tracts by the Author of the Dissertation on Parties*, 1748.

LXIV

Works III, 199.

To a Friend [REV. RICHARD JAGO?] *on various Subjects.*

1750. [*Early months,* 1748.]

Dear [Mr. Jago?],

With the utmost gratitude for the observations which you sent me, and with the highest opinion of their propriety in general, do I sit down to answer your obliging letter. You will not take it amiss, I know, if I scribble broken hints, and trace out little sketches of my mind, just as I should go near to explain it if I were upon the spot, as often as I think of you, which I beg leave to assure you happens many times in a day. They say, 'A word to the wise is enough;' a word, therefore, to a friend of understanding may be supposed to be something more than enough, because it is probable he is acquainted with three parts of one's mind before.—The censure you have passed upon Milton's Lycidas, so far as it regards the metre which he has chosen, is unexceptionably just; and one would imagine, if that argument concerning the distance of the rhimes were pressed home in a public essay, it should be sufficient to extirpate that kind of verse for ever. As to my opinion concerning the choice of English metre, I dare not touch upon the subject, and I will give you my reason: I began upon it in a letter which I intended for you about a month ago; and I soon found that I had filled a sheet of paper with my dissertation, and left no room for other things which I had more mind to communicate. Beside, I found it so blotted that I did not chuse to send it; and as the subject is so extremely copious, I shall decline it entirely, till *talking* may prove as effectual as *writing.* —As to your advice, with regard to my publications, I believe it to be just, and shall, in all probability, pursue it.—I am afraid, by your account, that Dodsley has published my name to the School-mistress. I was a good deal displeased at his publishing that poem without my knowledge, when he had so many opportunities of giving me some previous information; but, as he would probably disregard my resentment, I chose to stifle it, and wrote to him directly upon the receipt of yours, that I would be glad to furnish him with an improved copy of the School-mistress. &c. for his second edition.[1] He accepts it with some complaisance, desires it soon; and I am at a fault to have the opinion of my friends, what alterations or additions it will be proper to insert. I have scribbled a copy, which I send this day to Mr. Graves and Mr. Whistler; but I am greatly fearful I shall not receive their criticisms time enough, and I shall have the same longing for yours. A journey to Whitchurch, which I have long proposed, might unite all these advantages; and I heartily wish I may be able to effect it without inconvenience. If I go thither, I call on you.

I am,

ever and entirely yours,

W. SHENSTONE.

NOTE

[1]This letter was evidently written during the early months of 1748 when the first and second editions of Vol. I, Dodsley's *Collection*, were printed.

LXV

B.M. Add. MSS. 28958.

[*To* LADY LUXBOROUGH.]

THE LEASOWS, *April* yᵉ 18ᵗʰ 1748.

Madam.

Your Ladyship's obliging correspondence is the greatest Honour that was ever done me. I am sufficiently asur'd that a Profession of this sort cannot properly bear yᵉ *Appearance* of a Compliment; for tho' I have a Few Intimates whose *Genius* & *Merit* I very greatly esteem, I was never very assiduous in cultivating The Friendships of my *Superiors*, & (whether thro *that Omission*, or any *other* Deficiency) certain it is, that I have acquir'd but Few of them. Be that as it will, I am never to be humbled by *Neglect*, whatever I might by *Favour* & *Prosperity*. In *this* latter Case, I believe, the *Contraste* betwixt my *good-Fortune* & my *Desert* might exhibit me to my own Eyes in a very mortifying Shape. I have some kind of reason to draw this Conclusion, because I am never more

humble than at the Time I sit down to acknowledge, according
to my small Abilities, the particular satisfaction I receive from
your Letters. I am extremely glad to find that your *Gout*
has entirely disappear'd from the Face of them. I hope it is
also vanish'd in reality. And yet tho' I was really concerned
for your Pain, I was delighted wth y^e *Expressions* it drew from
you concerning Riches, so exactly agreeable to *my Conduct*.
But whether or no I am to be *steep'd in Poverty to the very
Lips*'[1] (by which I suppose Othello means ye want of a Glass of
Wine) I have ventur'd to write an Essay in verse entitled 'The
Œconomists,'[2] address'd to Poets. Of this I will shortly beg
your opinion. My Friends seem to think it is wrote with some
Spirit, but a Friendly *Ear* (tho' from a nobler *Motive*) is very
near as partial as a Flatterer's *tongue*. However, welcome!
ever welcome to *me* be an Error of this kind! I had rather be
somewhat deluded by ye kind partiality of Friends, than
acquire the greatest Fame, with no *genuine* Friendships at all.
Your Ladyship will however observe, (what may be seen thro
all my trifling compositions) some Picture of *myself* in this;
my Pleasures & Pains; wch circumstance may render it something more amusing; as This, tho' no very *agreeable* Portrait, is
ye Resemblance of a person y^t has your Ladyship in ye highest
veneration. I cannot transcribe this or any other Poem *now*,
but I shall beg Leave to trouble you with it, upon ye Arrival
of the first fair weather.

Your Ladyship's Sentiments concerning Mr. Whistler's
Genius are extremely interesting to *me*, & must give *him* y^e
most rational Pleasure: He does not indeed *want* to be inform'd of your Ladyship's Taste. If he *did*, the *Manner* in
which you bestow your commendations, wou'd sufficiently
prove ye Genuis of ye Person that bestows them, & of consequence give them all the Weight he can desire.

Poor Dick Graves (of whom you may have chanc'd to hear
me speak) has sent his Farmer's Daughter to a Boarding-
School in London.[3] He says she was lately much admir'd at a
Play, which she went to see for her Dancing-Masters Benefit.
He indited ye Sonnet I enclose upon leaving her there, and if
Love *alone* can make a marriage happy, he can hardly fail of
Happiness to the Degree I wish it him.

My Lady Lyttelton was snatch'd away suddenly;[4] her ill-ness, as far as I can find, being little else beside a common Cold; and, as I ever experienc'd from her the most *Friendly* complaisance, I ought to mix a Tear with that stream which will not fail to be shed by all her poor neighbours.

When I began to write this Letter I did intend to have return'd, with Thanks, your Ladyship's Book of Inigo Jones's Designs; for I am afraid you want it; but As I have a mind to sketch out a chimney-piece or two, I *will* hope to be forgiven if I keep it till next Thursday at which Time I will be sure to send it.

I cannot prevail on myself to send you the Size &c. of my Niches because I built them at random, whereas it will be expected from your Ladyship that you should build by ye rules of Art; which may be done altogether as cheaply. Besides, I have some Doubts whether ye middle Nich shou'd not exceed ye others in Heigth & Breadth; & if your Ladyship will give me Leave, I will take a little Time to consider of ye most proper ornament I can contrive for y^t place, to answer ye End you propose—As to y^r Lady's *Atchievements in Lead*, I have not ye highest Relish for any thing wch I esteem so *frail*: And if your Ladyship chuses to go to the expence of wood-carving, I shou'd think ye most proper ornaments on each side the stucco wou'd be 'Lyres, Laurels, Fistulas,' Pipes, Masks, &c. united by a kind of Bandage falling easily down the Wainscott. These wou'd bear an obvious Relation either to the Busto or the Library. I am going to have something like ye Group I have enclos'd, engravd upon ye lid of a standish, for wch I shall exchange some old Plate in London by Mr. Outing's Assistance—I have but little Room to express ye unlimited Respect with wch I wou'd subscribe myself your Ladyship's most dutifull & obedient Servant

WILL SHENSTONE.

NOTES

[1]*Othello*, Act. IV, Sc. 2.

[2]*Œconomy, a Rhapsody addressed to Young Poets. Works* I, 285.

[3]Graves married Lucy Bartholomew, daughter of a gentleman farmer with whom he lodged when curate at Aldworth, Berks. The story of the courtship and marriage is told in the history of Mr. Rivers in *The Spiritual Quixote*. Future letters of W.S. and Lady Luxborough contain many references to the amiable Mrs. Graves. By his marriage

Graves lost his fellowship at All Souls and brought on himself the displeasure of his relations.

⁴Christian Lyttelton, wife of Sir Thomas Lyttelton, a daughter of Sir Richard Temple of Stowe.

LXVI

B.M. Add. MSS. 28958.

[*To* LADY LUXBOROUGH.]

May 5th 1748.

Madam.

I have wasted half this Afternoon with a Tenant whom I've been endeavouring to seduce into an agreement to pay me half a year's rent; & yᵉ Result of our conference, (little more agreeable to *me* than *him*) was, that he *wou'd* pay me half a years rent (at a Time that he owes me for *two* year's) but that he could not fix any *time* because he was unwilling to *break his Promise*. This Circumstance together with that of rainy weather, render it a Point of self-*Interest* in me to engage in some Amusement which may engross my whole Attention; so that heavy solemn unvary'd Rains, & heavy illiterate worldly conversation may leave behind 'em no bad Impression. And all this Advantage I am in hopes to reap from an *Acknowledgment* of yᵉ satisfaction your last Letter afforded me; nor have I the least reason to doubt of success. if I can find but half as much relief in answering, as I did Pleasure in receiving it— Your Ladyship's verses to Mr. Outing entirely convince me yᵗ both your Pow'r & *Will* to confer Honour, where you do not entirely disapprove, are as great as I can desire. But in gratitude for The Honour you do *me* on that Epistle, I must be so free as to inform your Ladyship yᵗ if you wou'd shun yᵉ Character of a *Poetess* (wᶜʰ as you well observe can make no addition to your Character) you must never write in Heroic verse with half the Elegance you *do*. The Consequence *will* be, that your *Logicians* & scholastick People will reasonably enough conclude yᵗ you are at least a Poetess *potentially*, if not *actually*; & that it is entirely owing to your own perverseness, that you do not acquire a Reputation in *this*, as well as in every other sort of writing in which you have hitherto

engag'd. For *my* part I am apt to agree wth ye Stoicks that a
Person of an universal Genius is *ev'ry* Thing; a King, a Mathematician, a Poet, a Statesman &c. &c. for y^t very Reason,
because, wth proper contingencies, he has all these things in his
Pow'r. So I give y^r Ladyship warning, that you may look to
it. Nevertheless, I wou'd not have you Endeavour to conceal
your Skill in Poetry from those that you are pleas'd to honour
with your *Acquaintance*. That were *now* too late; They know
too well already y^t you *only despise* those qualifications for
which you are not admir'd, & for which they know you might
be admird if you chose to be so—I like your Ladyship's last
Sonnet extremely; & ye more, as I have ye same aversion with
you to all affected Birds that quit their native notes.[1] I purchas'd a charming Blackbird of one of my poor neighbours;
which is now in my Hall, & has a variety of Notes that are
both masculine & musical. If it were not for ye Faults, wth
wch I'm going to upbraid him, I wou'd compare his voice to
your Lasp's Handwriting; which has all y^e *Firmness* of a
man's Hand, with all the Delicacy of a Female's.[2] But as poor
People *admire* art, tho' they love Nature they have taught y^e
Bird by their foolish Pedantry to demean himself extremely:
And when I've been admiring his Notes for ye Space of ten
Minutes he sinks all of a sudden into calling out *Toby* &
whistling y^e *Horses*. Somewhat like ye Tinker in Shakespeare
who forgetting his present Dignity is every now and then
requesting a Pot of Beer.[3] I like a Decoration in Spence, where
there is an Ass in ye Roman Toga instructing two harmless
Pupils[4]—I ought not here to mention ye Jersey-man who
taught me French; But tho' I can scarce *pronounce* it at all,
I think I can understand it tolerably well, & wou'd beg y^e
Favour of your Ladyship's Fr: Play for a Fort-night, if you
please. I have suffer'd enough from the Character you describe,
to relish ye Pleasure of seeing it expos'd[5]—Your Lady'p
made me laugh concerning My Friend Outing's Ear—May y^e
Powr of Musick preserve *his* refined Taste for Operas and
oratorios! But rather may Heav'n preserve his hearing, that
he may not only hear what the *Multitude*, but what your Lady-
ship says 'then I believe he need not *regret* so much as *despise*
what y^e *Opera-Folk* sing:— —Now I mention Mr. Outing,

I must say a word of ye Amusements he has been so kind as to negotiate for me. The *Bust* arriv'd wth your Ladyship's Letter. I fancy it to be a good Taste, in all stucco Rooms or wherever ye Wainscott is painted like Stone, to have all carv'd work whether Bustos, Festoons, Frames &c: of ye same colour with ye Room itself. Where that is not practicable, & where one has few visitants of y^e *most* refin'd Taste, I think *White* is unexceptionably ye best Colour for most of ye same Ornaments. I shou'd prefer ye native colour of ye Alabaster in a Bust to that *shining* which is given it by Paint; but as frequent Brushing wears away ye Features Paint or varnish becomes *necessary.* I know very well y^t ye antient Statues, as Spence observes, were made to Shine so much as to dazle ye eyes of ye Spectators; but I think ye Spectators eyes ought *not* to be dazled when they are to examine ye Limbs & Features. On ye whole, I approve Rackstrow's Marbling (which is only varnish or white paint *varnished*) considering w^t I said before, & where the Room is not of stone-colour—As for my Standish, I was in Hopes my old Plate of about 40 oz^s. would have paid for it entirely: but ye Man has risen in his Demands, proposing 40 oz. for ye Standish, & reckoning by the Ounce (8^s per ounce) which you will observe may induce him to add to its weight. I shou'd be glad to know y^r Ladyship's Opinion of his Terms, tho I believe I must (If I pretend to Œconomy) at least *postpone* ye Affair at present—Now I mention Œconomy I must acknowledge y^t ye Notion y^r Ladyship has of *mine* is as entirely just, as the Compliment you draw from it in regard to my Genius is properly to be imputed to your Ladyship's Kindness. I assure you I have had no more Œconomy than a Butterdish with a Spout at both ends or y^n ye Sluice of a Pond which lets out twice as much as comes in. But I have been taught some *speculative* Knowledge by a Reflection, how sufficient my Fortune might have been for all my *present* wishes, had I nurs'd it ever so little from the time I receiv'd it. My Comfort is grounded upon a maxim y^t is most indisputably true, that a Person cannot *eat* his Cake and *have* it, & if the Cake *be* to be eaten he takes ye most seasonable Time who eats it when he's most a-hunger'd. Pray my Lady, don't examine this Doctrine too closely—I like Gay's *Motive* to

Œconomy best; Independence; & yet I believe his Œconomy went no further than to superintend the Finances of his green-silk Purse.[6] For my part, (&, I am *as* sure, for your *Ladyship's* part), I can, no more than Brutus 'wring from the Hard Hands of Peasants their vile Trash by any *Indirection*'[7] or even by *all* the methods that are strictly *legal*; & as for Expence I am chiefly faulty wth regard to little sums. I have experience enough to know ye Danger of Pounds and tens of Pounds; but I never yet had a due veneration for Sixpence or a shilling, wch somebody says is a serious Affair. My whole *secret* is, when I've receiv'd a little Money, to *pay* away where I owe, without deliberating. You know Addison says tho' on another occasion 'The Person that deliberates is lost!' Company, Nay, *superior* Company, in Affliction, *lessens* one's grievances, & Mr. Dennis[8] *has* said that if Homer himself was not in Debt, it was—because nobody wou'd trust him. And thus much for *Œconomy*, till I have Leisure to send your Ladyship my *Aldermanly* Treatise on that important subject—It will be no bad digression here to speak a word of my Friend Graves's Proceedings. Your Ladysp's Sentiment is very *ingenious*; but we will suppose that, however he prefer his Lucy to ye good Opinion of the wise world, yet he doesn't so *entirely* despise that Opinion as not to wish to *compromise* Matters (I must beg leave to finish on the Cover) and to render his Conduct something *less* absurd, by rendering her Behaviour something less exceptionable. And who knows but as a *Lover*, he may hope to make them cry out as the Old Trojans do upon seeing Helen on ye Walls, in the third Iliad. Graves looks upon London as a fiery Tryal —If he find her *false*, he is at Liberty to decline; if *true*, as he *sincerely* wishes, She is all Gold thrice purify'd &c. &c. I wish to God there may be no Room to doubt of that Sincerity in *her* which I am pretty sure he cannot easily disbelieve.

I receiv'd a Letter from him yesterday, dated at London, wherein he tells me y^t the most extraordinary Instance of modern Politeness is the Pantin[9]—a sort of Scaramouch made with Card, wch the Ladies bring into Company & the Play-house—he makes their Compliments for Them & serves them for Amusement—The D. of Newcastle[10] brought one into the Privy Council, as the Report goes. I suppose your Ladyship

may have seen them—Has your Ladyship seen Hervey's
Meditations.[11] I don't know how to give my opinion of them.
He admires Dr. Yong & is sometimes affected, but I think
some *Part* of his *Thoughts* & *Style* no way contemptible. It
may perhaps amuse you. It is now printed with two Frontispieces, I see; design'd by Dr. Wall of Worcester,[12] I wrote
this little Trifle on my Kid [13] one Afternoon, thro a Propensity
to write something on whatever has delighted me. I hardly
know whether 'tis *pretty*, or *ugly*; but I am horribly afraid 'tis
middlin—I have also transcrib'd a most woefull Ballad, founded
on a Paragraph in ye Newspapers;[14] & written to supply
words for a melancholy Tune wch some young Girls (on a
visit at the Leasows) seem'd to admire. Tis a good deal extemporaneous (as you will observe by ye neglect to make y^e
first & third Lines in each stanza *rhim*e.) But I beg it may
never be shewn *as mine*. Zealous people wou'd call me dis-
affected,& zealous People may do me a mischief; but, whether
they did or not, wou'd assuredly burlesque mine inoffensive
Madrigal: Tho' I think I cou'd utterly despise ye understanding of such as cou'd elicit Treason from this idle Song.

Has your Ladyship seen Mrs. Pilkington's Memoirs of
Dr. Swift?[15] They gave me great entertainment, but I suppose
what we see in ye last Magazine are only Part of a larger
work.

Having now sufficiently reliev'd *myself*, I ought to be very
fearfull of fatiguing your Ladyship.

I am, Madam,

Your Ladyships most faithfull

and most oblig'd humble serv^t.

WILL: SHENSTONE.

The greatest part of this Letter was written May ye 5th
1748.—that is, on ye very *first opportunity* I had of acknowledging your last Favour; but being call'd aside to Mr. Dolman's at Broom I had not Conveniency of transmitting it
before.

I *had* & *have* some Thoughts of having my *Ballad* printed
by Butler at Birmingham[16] on ye same Paper & in ye same
Form wth common Ballads. To be call'd 'James Dawson's

Garland.' but lest this *shou'd* happen I beseech y^r Ladyship to make a secret of it's Author.

If Williams[17] executes your Decorations &c. well, I shall approve them as much as tho' carv'd for your Room. I have thoughts of employing him to do ye same for my Busto of Mr. Pope.

NOTES

[1]*The Bulfinch in Town.*

[2]Lady Luxborough probably took great pains over her letters to W.S. in her capacity of Egeria to a man of some merit. One very beautiful letter of hers to him is in the possession of a Warwickshire gentleman. On a double sheet of note-paper, she writes in French to the poet—A Shenstone a la Ferme Ornèe. The edge of the note-paper is pale blue, the figures of elegant eighteenth-century beaux and belles, beautifully painted by hand, the flower decoration likewise, the colour is delicate but bright, and the whole effect charming. The handwriting has 'all ye Firmness of a man's Hand, with all the Delicacy of a Female's.'

The envelope—for the owner assures me that the wrapping was intact as an envelope when the letter first came into his possession—seems to be a woodcut, the figures being put in by hand, though much less carefully than those of the letter.

[3]*The Taming of the Shrew*, Induction. Sc. II.

[4]*Polymetis* was illustrated by numerous 'antiques,' 'the decorations' to which Shenstone refers. See 1747 Edition, 291.

[5]Lady Luxborough, *Letters*, 23, tells us that the play is *Le Méchant* by Jean-Baptiste-Louis-Gresset, acted in 1747.

[6]Possibly W.S. is straying in the regions of gossip. Gay was notoriously extravagant with the money he received and may at some time have suggested reform on the lines of 'Independent Oeconomy.' The same idea occurs in *Oeconomy—A Rhapsody, addressed to Young Poets. Works* I, 285.

Of belated patronage he writes:
> . . . the careless bard
> Quits your worn threshold, and like honest Gay
> Contemns the niggard boon ye time so ill.

> Ye tow'ring minds! ye sublimated souls!
> Who careless of your fortunes, seal and sign,
> Set, let, contract, acquit, with easier mien,
> Than fops take snuff! whose oeconomic care
> Your green-silk purse engrosses!

[7]*Julius Caesar*, Act IV, Sc. iii.

[8]John Dennis (1657–1734), critic, general enemy of the wits, the famous Appius of Pope's lines.

[9]See *The Gentleman's Magazine*, 1748, 225.

[10]Thomas Pelham Holles, Duke of Newcastle (1693–1768).

[11]Rev. James Hervey (1714–1758), author of *Meditations among the Tombs, and Reflections on a Flower Garden*, a melancholy religious work very popular in the mid-eighteenth century. It ran into several editions and was much admired by Lady Hertford (Hull, I, 69) and was imitated by W.S.'s kinsman, Pearsall.

[12]John Wall (1706–1776), eminent Worcester physician, wrote *Experiments and Observations on the Malvern Waters*, 1756, which reached a third edition in 1763.

Lady Luxborough, as well as W.S., had little opinion of Wall as an artist, though they consulted him as a physician. Luxborough, *Letters*, 253: 'I never saw anything of Dr. Wall's drawings but his Frontispiece to Hervey's Meditations, which I did not like, and now this to the Scribleriad: but Captain Robinson says that the Doctor's Rooms are adorned with his own Works: but he did not say a great deal in commenda-

tion of them. Mais le dessin n'est pas son metier; il faut donc lui laisser ses ouvrages en
ce genre pour son propre amusement.'

[13]*The Dying Kid*, *Works* I, 147.

[14]*Works* I, 185. The end of this letter makes it clear that the reference is to *Jemmy
Dawson, a Ballad written about the time of his Execution in the Year* 1745. There,
contrary to W.S.'s usual custom, the first and third lines do not rhyme.

Captain James Dawson was one of eight officers belonging to the Manchester Regiment of volunteers, in the service of The Young Chevalier, who were hanged on
Kennington Common in 1746.

[15]Laetitia Pilkington (1712–1750), friend of Swift. *The Memoirs of Mrs. Laetitia
Pilkington, wife to the Rev. Matthew Pilkington, written by herself, wherein are occasionally interspersed all her Poems, with Anecdotes of several eminent persons, living and
dead,* appeared in 1748.

[16]Probably Henry Butler, bookseller of New Street, Birmingham, one of the early
Birmingham printers.

[17]Letters were left with 'Mr. Williams, painter in Birmingham,' the 'my friend, Williams
in New Street, Birmingham' of Lady Luxborough's *Letters,* 22.

LXVII

B.M. Add. MSS. 28958.

[*To* LADY LUXBOROUGH.]

THE LEASOWS, *June y*[e] 1st 1748.

Almost Night.

Madam.

I return my Lady Hartford's Letter by the very first opportunity I meet with; & herein I but discharge my conscience;
as I am in Duty bound to obey your Ladyship's Commands; &
also, to be no way instrumental in delaying your Answer
to a Letter which has afforded me the highest satisfaction.

As to the Choice or Preference of any Trifle of mine which
may be thought most proper to send her Ladyship, it wou'd
be most prudent in me to be guided by your own Opinion; as
the Person best acquainted with Lady Hartford's Taste, &
who, I am apt enough to flatter myself, wishes well to my
Reputation. The Esteem I share at Percy-Lodge[1] is entirely
of your own *creation*; & as you have almost literally *produc'd*
it out of *nothing*, I daresay you *understand* & will *use* the most
proper means to keep it alive. Otherwise, it were much better
for me it had never existed, as a Fall from the greatest Happiness compleats our Idea of the most consummate Misery.
Sure I am y[t] for *my* Part, I am utterly unable to preserve my

Lady Hartford's good Opinion, unless your Ladyship pleases to collogue with me so as to keep her in constant Hopes of something better than I have yet produc'd. I have written a pretty large collection of Elegies on almost every melancholy subject y^t I cou'd recollect; & I had some Thoughts of sending them to ye Press next winter, but I have now dropt y^t Design, as my Friends advise me to publish something else y^t may be of more *general* acceptation. I own they are in some Degree fav'rites with me, & if your Ladyship will please to read them in a copy, which I have now no *Leisure* to transcribe, I will send them very soon. They are written rather wth ye Spirit of *Melancholy* y^n that of *Poetry*; if Melancholy may be said to be fraught with any Spirit at all, as I believe it *may;* for I believe a *Spirit* may be distill'd from *Tears*. This last conceit is almost worthy Dr Yong; which brings it into my Head to say a word more concerning Hervey's Meditations. I must own I do think it doubtfull whether y^r Ladyship will approve them; (tho' I read but *one* volume) & yet my Lady Hartford's opinion is most *literally just*. They are undoubtedly *poetical* & *pious*, & so is Dr. Yong's Collection of Nightthoughts; but surely as remote from true *simplicity* as y^e *arctic* is to the *antarctic* Pole.

The Essay upon Delicacy[2] recommends itself; since one is apt to imagine the author a Man of Taste from his choice of a subject. Mr. Dolman sent for it upon sight of ye Advertisement, and as there is a mutual intercourse betwixt his Library & mine, I shall in a few Days have an opportunity of giving your Ladyship my humble opinion of its merit.

Lady H. is a Patroness to *two* Mr. Thomsons. Has your Ladsp seen A Poem upon Sickness? in ye latter End of wch the Author introduces my Lord Beachamp's Death,[3] which is ye most Poetical Part of ye Poem, as far as I have *read*; for I have only ye First Number. If you would chuse to see it I will take care to send it—As to ye Castle of Indolence[4] I find one Fault wth it already which is that it is printed in an odious *Quarto* & I never cou'd approve such *unbindable* Editions. At least if it *may* be *bound*, it makes but an ordinary *Person of a Book*. I am always in Hopes y^t whenever an Author is either a tall or even a middle-siz'd man, he will never print a Book but in Folio, octavo, or duodecimo; & on the other Hand, when he is short & squab, I collect y^t his partiality to a Figure of y^t kind, will induce him, to my great discomfort, to publish in *Quarto*. But Mr. Thomson, who is certainly of y^e *middle* Size, must be self-convicted. However I long to see his Book. My Schoolmistress, I suppose, is much more in Spenser's way than any one wou'd chuse to write in that writes quite *gravely*; in which Case The Dialect & stanza of Spenser is hardly preferable to modern Heroic. I look upon my Poem as somewhat more grave than Pope's Alley,[5] & a good deal less y^n Mr. Thomson's Castle etc: At least I meant it so, or rather I meant to skreen ye ridicule wch might fall on so *low* a subject (tho' perhaps a *picturesque* one) by *pretending* to *simper* all ye time I was writing. And now I am come to give an excuse, wch will, with y^r Lordship's *Candour*, apologise for this blotted Letter, I have 'the Schoolmistress to write over for Dodsley before I go to Bed to-night; consisting *now* of 350 Lines, in which I expect to make 350 blunders. His miscellanies are gone he says a 2^d time to the Press, & I have reason to doubt whether my Improvements will even now come *time enough*. However, I ought not to take a final leave of you, 'till I have express'd the Pleasure I find in ye last Paragraph of Lady H's Letter; for I am by no means so selfish as to suffer ye satisfaction I take in what she says of my trivial Productions, to smother that I feel upon hearing of any News that must prove agreeable to your Ladyship. I am very faithfully,

Your Ladyship's most oblig'd
& most obedient Servant,
WILL: SHENSTONE.

I will
undoubtedly
wait upon y^r
Ladyship this Summer—
—I fancy I shall admire y^e
French Play—The Pantin
made the Peace, no *doubt*—

NOTES

[1]Percy Lodge, on the Bath Road, near Colnbrooke (the home of Lady Hertford). By the terms of separation from her husband, Lady Luxborough was forbidden to go

on the Bath Road where Percy Lodge was situated. W. Sichel, *Bolingbroke and his Times.*

²*An Essay upon Delicacy* by Nath. Lancaster, Ll.D. (1701–1775), pr. 2s. 3d. Dodsley. *Gentleman's Magazine*, 1748, 240. Hull, I, 70, writes a lengthy note on Lancaster, the 'Rector of Stanford Rivers, near Ongar, in Essex, Uncle to the Editor of these Letters.'

'The Essay on Delicacy, here mentioned, was the Production of Dr. Nathaniel Lancaster many years Rector of Stanford Rivers, near Ongar, in Essex, Uncle to the Editor of these Letters. He was a Man of strong natural Parts, great Erudition, refined Taste, and master of a serious, and at the same Time, elegant Stile, as is very obvious to everyone who has had the Happiness to read the Essay here spoken of. His Writings were fewer in Number than their Author's Genius seemed to promise to his Friends, and his Publications less known than their intrinsic Excellence deserved. Had he been as solicitous, as he was capable, to instruct and please the World, few Prose-Writers would have surpassed him; but in his later years he lived a Recluse, and whatever he composed in the Hours of retired Leisure, he (unhappily for the Public) ordered to be burned, which was religiously (I had almost said irreligiously) performed.

He was a native of Cheshire, and, in his earlier years, under the Patronage and Friendship of the late Earl of Cholmondeley, mixed in all the more exalted Scenes of polished Life, where his lively Spirit, and brilliant Conversation rendered him universally distinguished and esteemed; and even, till within a few Months of his Decease (near seventy-five Years of Age) these Faculties could scarce be said to be impaired.

The Essay on Delicacy (of which we are now speaking) the only material Work of his, which the Editor knows to have survived him, was first printed in the Year 1748, and has been very judiciously and meritoriously preserved by the late Mr. Dodsley, in his Fugitive Pieces, published in two Volumes.'

³William Thompson (1712–1766–?) wrote *Sickness—a poem in five Books*, in 1745, in imitation of Spenser. In Book II the poet calls upon Lady Hertford:

'Come, Hertford! with the Muse, awhile, vouchsafe,
(The softer virtues melting in thy breast,
The tender graces flowing in thy form)
Vouchsafe, in all the beauty of distress,
To take a silent walk among the tombs;
Then lend a charm to Sorrow, smooth her brow,
And sparkle through her tears in shining woe.
As when the dove, (thy emblem, matchless dame!
For beauty, innocence and truth are thine)
Spread all its colours o'er the boundless deep,
(Empyreal radiance quivering round the gloom)
Chaos reform'd, and bade distraction smile!'

After writing of the terrors of small-pox, he continues:

'And, O, our recent grief!
Shall Beauchamp die, forgotten by the Muse,
Or are the Muses with their Hertford dumb!
His op'ning flow'r of beauty softly smil'd,
And, sparkling in the liquid dews of youth,
Adorn'd the blessed light, with blossoms fair,
Untainted; in the rank Italian soil
From blemish pure. The virgins stole a sigh,
The matrons lifted up their wond'ring eyes,
And blest the English angel as he pass'd,
Rejoicing in his rays.'

A note to the poem in Chalmers, *English Poets*, Vol. XV, tells us that Lady Hertford's son was known in Bologna as 'L'Angelo Inglese.'

⁴*The Castle of Indolence*, 1748, by James Thomson, was the most considerable Spenserian imitation of the first half of the eighteenth century.

⁵1764 edition Pope's *Works* II, 4. *Imitations of English Poets*, II. *Of Spenser, The Alley.*

LXVIII

B.M. Add. MSS. 28958.

[*To* LADY LUXBOROUGH.]

THE LEASOWS, *June y^e* 16th 1748.

Madam,

Since I wrote last to your Ladyship I have been unable to, proceed in the Perusal of your Play, partly on Account of Company, and partly through a very dangerous Illness of my Brother's.[1] Mr. Hardy (a son of ye Admiral's) did me the Favour to stay a week with me, but he is now gone & my Brother is recover'd; so having finish'd the Play called Le Mechant now acting at Paris, with Pleasure, I return it with Thanks. The Author, I suppose must be a Man of Delicacy, if one may judge from the character he has chosen to expose; which, tho' too common in real Life, is I think in a Manner new to the *Stage*. There is but little in it y^t can raise a Laugh or even a Smile, but the Solidity of ye critical remarkable Scene betwixt Ariste & Valere, and the fine Moral of the whole, has an admirable Tendency to *open ye Eyes*, & *reform* the *Heart*s of the Audience. Finally I conclude the Writer to be an honest Man; otherwise he cou'd hardly have bore to have expos'd Dishonesty, wⁿ connected with Genius; inasmuch as it must have been ye same as exposing himself.

Tomorrow I expect some Company that will probably enough engage me for this Week. But the time will not be long now, before I change my native Haunts, for a Scene y^t abounds with far superior Pleasures. The next time I have ye Honour to write to your Ladyship, I will take ye Freedom of fixing some Day when I would wait upon you at Barrels. I have often talk'd about it to Miss Dolman, and, if she happen to be with her Brother at ye Time, we shall hope for Leave to pay our Respects, staying with y^r Ladyship one whole Day, & part of ye two in which we travel.

Mr. Lyttelton has near finish'd one side of his Castle. It consists of one entire Tow'r, & three Stumps of Towers, with a ruin'd Wall betwixt them.[2] Perhaps my Pen may better describe it thus. [Picture next page.]

There is no great Art or Variety in yᵉ Ruin, but the Situaion gives it a charming Effect; The chief Tow'r is allowedly about 10 Feet too low. If your Ladyship shou'd ever have an Inclination to see yᵉ Present Face of yᵉ Park, Miss Dolman lives within two miles of admirable Road, where you will find as good a Reception & a far more friendly welcome yⁿ from yᵉ most self-interested Host. 'Tis also within a Mile of yᵉ Bromsgrove Road.

I find this Moment yᵉ Meditations of Mr. Hervey on my Table, wᶜʰ my Brother I see has purchas'd. I remember my Lord Shaftsbury, speaking of *many* that are vulgarly stil'd *good Books*, says, they *may be* so in yᵉ *Main*, but he is sure the *Writer*s of them are a sorry Race.[3] Dr. Wall's *Design*s are pious too, but (To Speak in yᵉ way of *Taste*) about two thirds as Good as the worst of Quarles's Emblems.[4] Nevertheless as *Designing* is not his Profession, I do not mean to reflect on his Ingenuity in yᵉ least. I don't believe that a *twentieth* part of mankind can draw a human Figure that is a whit more like a *Man* than an *Elephant*; And I must say farther in Dr. W's Behalf, yᵗ he seems not have Justice done him by the Engraver —In yᵉ First Volume, a huge tun-bellied Parson with a sleek simpering Face & leaning very indolently against yᵉ Pillar of a Church, is pointing to our Saviour wᵗʰ a Cross. He is drest in his Canonicals, wᶜʰ to be sure is inconsistent wᵗʰ yᵉ Roman Dress of the Person that stands by him.[5] There is, I think, a further Impropriety in yᵉ *Mottos*, but I will not enter on yᵉ subject now.

Mr. Smith, yᵉ Designer of yᵉ Prints of Hagley Park Lᵈ Tyrconnels etc.[6] call'd here last week, & behav'd wᵗʰ a Complaisance yᵗ made us wish to serve him. He shew'd us one *Painting* of a scene at Hagley. He took a Draught of wᵗ your Ladyship may remember *I* call *Virgil's Grove, here*. This he purposes to insert in a smaller Collection; a Kind of drawing-Book, wᶜʰ, if judge aright, will please me much beyond his larger Prints. He wou'd insist on making me a Present of 5

Charming Ruins y^t he has publish'd; &, if one is to believe all Persons of Business *interested* (wch nevertheless I am loth to do) He must needs imagine me to be a Person of greater Influence than I really am. Be that as it will, I am with the highest Respect

Your Ladyship's most obedient
humble Servt.

W. SHENSTONE.

NOTES

[1]Joseph Shenstone who lived with his brother at The Leasowes in pleasant intimacy until the death of the former. Williams, *op. cit*.

[2]George Lyttelton, as a friend of Sanderson Miller, was much interested in building in the Gothic taste. The 'castle' was a sham ruin, still to be seen in the grounds of Hagley. The framework of the windows came from the ruined Halesowen Abbey, so that the castle might have a genuine air. Horace Walpole said, 'It has the true rust of the baron's wars.' Wyndham, I, 178–180.

[3]Anthony Ashley Cooper, Lord Shaftesbury (1671–1713), author of *Characteristics of Men, Manners, Opinions, Times*. The book left its impression on W.S., as we see from *Men and Manners*. The reference here is to *Characteristics*, I, 165 (1732 Ed.).

[4]Francis Quarles (1592–1644), published his *Emblems* in 1635. They were quaintly illustrated by William Marshall and others.

[5]I have been unable to obtain a copy of Hervey's *Meditations* with Dr. Wall's designs.

[6]Thomas Smith of Derby, whose designs were of sufficient merit to be engraved by Vivares, and such engravings in Sale Rooms now have a moderate value. There is in the B.M. a *Catalogue of the Collection of Mr. Smith, late of Derby, Painter, deceased*, sold in 1769. Among the entries appears a View of Newstead Park, Lord Byron's seat, the water-works at Belton, Lord Tyrconnel's seat, a view of Exton Park, Lord Gainsborough's seat, a view of Hagley Park, Lord Lyttelton's seat, and other views, all engraved by Vivares. There is no record in this catalogue of a view of The Leasowes.

LXIX

Hull, I, 72.

To the REV. MR. GRAVES, *at Whitchurch, near Reading, Berks.*

THE LEASOWES, *June*, 1748.

Dear Mr. Graves,

I find a very strong Impulse, prompting me to write to you this Evening. I don't know whether I ever let you into the Secret, that I receive an inward Satisfaction at the Time that I am sending you a Letter, and that this Action partakes of the Nature of all virtuous ones, in being its own Reward. However we are taught to hope for *other* and more *ample*

Rewards attending Virtue, as I am inclined to expect a more considerable Pleasure, when I receive your Answer. My Soul now leans entirely on the Friendship of a few private Acquaintance, and if they drop me, I shall be a wretched Misanthrope. Is it a great Fatigue to you to sit down some vacant Half-Hour, and scribble me a few Lines, relating to the State of your Mind, and your Affairs?——DICK JAGO, who called accidentally at a Public-house, at *Mickleton*, told me, they heard ——; mentioning, at the same Time, his thorough Conviction, that *whatever* might prove the Event of this Affair, as *you* were a Principal, it would be as it *ought*. Mr. SMITH, (the Designer) who knew you too, was here at the Time, and many civil Things, very agreeable to me, were said in your Behalf; '*Immo, Omnes ommnia bona dixere.*' As to—— ——

I thank you for your little Strictures on the *School-Mistress*. I have sacrificed my Partiality to your unbiassed Judgment; *Multa gemens*, have I sacrificed it. The Truth is, I am not quite convinced (tho' I have acted as if I were) that one should give up any Part, that appears droll in itself, and makes the Poem, on the whole, more agreeable, for the Sake of rendering it a more perfect Imitation of SPENCER. But when you have more Leisure, and I collect my Pieces, I don't despair of furnishing a more compleat Edition yet.

Mr. SMITH (whom I mentioned just now) has taken two Views of *Hagley-Park*, which, with two from other Places, compleat a Set; the Subscription-Price, half a Guinea; but he takes other little Views of the closer Scenes, and of particular Beauties, which will form a Drawing-Book, and which I shall like beyond those I have subscribed for. Would you not be surprized to see a Draught of my VIRGIL'S *Grove* inserted among the latter?——He took one, and promised to have it engraved, and inserted somewhere; but I had rather he should stay a Week, and take about four Views, and that you were here, and would give him some Instructions, and it should make a little Drawing-Book to sell for a Shilling. But, 'Ah, me! —I fondly dream'[1]—The Days of Fancy and dear Enthusiasm will never more return! Such as those that flew over our Heads when you were *here*, and at *Harborough*, on your first Visit; when the *merum Rus* of the *Leasowes* could furnish you with pleasanter Ideas, than the noblest Scenes that ever Painter copied.

I am impatient to see you, and resolve to do so when I *can*; and I beg you will *project* some Means of coming to the *Leasowes* without Inconvenience to yourself.

I am,

Your truly affectionate

W. SHENSTONE.

I beg my Compliments to Mr. WHISTLER. I don't know whether I am more *ashamed* or *vexed*, that I cannot set out— to-morrow—for *Whitchurch;* but my Mind will not be easy till I have seen both him and you.

NOTE

[1]Milton, *Lycidas*, l. 56.

LXX

Works III, 132.

To the [REV. RICHARD GRAVES], *on the Mixture of Pleasure and Pain.*

THE LEASOWS,

June the last, 1747 [1748.][1]

Dear Mr. Graves,

It is now, I believe, near half a year since I had the favour of a letter from you. When I wrote last, I discovered a more than ordinary solicitude for *one* immediate answer. It puzzles me to account for your unusual silence, otherwise than upon supposition of some offence you have taken: and it puzzles me as much to guess by what behaviour of mine I have been so unhappy as to give you that offence.

I am vain enough to imagine that the little merit I have, deserves somewhat more regard than I have met with from the world. Be that as it will, the disappointment I must undergo, by any *appearance* of neglect from the friends I value, would more effectually dispirit me than any other whatsoever.

I have published my design of visiting you, and Mr. Whistler in Oxfordshire, to all the world. A thousand incidents have hitherto interfered with it, which I will not now recount. But when I look back upon the regular succession of them, it looks as if Destiny had some hand in detaining me. The most *vigorous* of my *hopes* dwell upon seeing you next winter, though I am not a little indulgent to *those* that tell me I may see you long before.

I have brought my place here to greater perfection than it has ever yet appeared in; and, with the *mob*, it is in some vogue. Nevertheless, I do not know that I ever relished it less in my life than I have done this summer. Bad health, bad spirits, no company to my mind, and no correspondences, are enough to blast the sweetest shades, and to poison the purest fountains. Some of these misfortunes I can impute to my own misconduct, and it embitters them. The two last I can less account for, having at all times done all I was able to recommend myself to my *friends*, behaving at the same time with courtesy to the rest of the world. The fact is not true; otherwise I might resolve it into this that I alone am idle, and all the world is *busy*.

I fancy you will imagine I lay too much stress upon Mr. Thomson's visit, when I mention the following inscription upon a seat in Virgil's grove.

'CELEB'MO POETÆ
'JACOBO THOMSON, S.
'PROPE FONTES ILLI NON FASTIDITOS
G. S.
'SEDEM HANC ORNAVIT.

'Quæ tibi, quæ tali reddam pro carmine dona?
'Nam neque me tantum *venientis*[2] *sibilus* Austri,
'Nec percussa juvant fluctu tam litora, nec quæ
'Saxosas inter decurrunt flumina valles.'

VIRG.

I want your opinion of it, and whether it were not better thus,

'———THOMSON,
'QUI CUM QUICQUID UBIQUE RURIS EST
'AUT AMOENUM AUT VARIUM
'MIRE DEPINXERAT,
'HOS ETIAM FONTES NON FASTIDIVIT.'[3]

But you will discover at first glance an impropriety in both. Now I am upon inscriptions, I send you one from a coin[4] dug up very near me a few weeks ago:

Round the head,

'IMP——U AUG GER DAC M'

On the reverse,

'SPQR OPTIMO PRINCIPI COS VI'

Within which is a human figure sitting, with one hand reclined upon a wand; the other, as I take it, holding forth an olive.—I have given my opinion, it is one of Trajan's; and my virtuoso character will rest upon the truth of it. It is a silver coin, but very obscure. There appears a large mass of ruins, rough stone, very strongly cemented, where they found it.— If you were here, it might amuse you.

Heaviness may endure for a night, but joy cometh in the morning.—I have so settled a notion of the proportionate mixture of pleasure and pain in this life, that I expect one to succeed the other as naturally as day and night. I own, this is owing to the soul as much as to outward incidents. Sorrow prepares it for mirth, and *vice versa*.—The durations of both differ.—Last summer I spent agreeably; this quite otherwise. —To-day I have been quite melancholy; I expect happiness to-morrow, from either an aptitude of mind, or some incident sufficient to overcome its inaptitude.—Perhaps that incident may be a letter from you; I wish it may, and am most truly

Yours,

W.S.

I had a coin of Vespasian given me to-day, and I begin a collection: if you have any duplicates, you will please to oblige me.—I want to correct my elegies, by your assistance.—I will begin no more.

NOTES

[1]The date of this letter should probably be later than that of September 17, 1747, which suggests that James Thomson has, as yet, paid no visit to the Leasowes.

[2]Note, *Works* III, 134, 'The verse whispers here.'

[3]The first inscription was adopted by W.S., *Works* II, 364.

[4]Graves was a keen collector of coins and medals, as was his father, the original of Mr. Townsend, the antiquary of *The Spiritual Quixote*. Williams, 49.

LXXI

*

Hull, I, 76.

To LADY LUXBOROUGH.

THE LEASOWES,
Sunday, July 25, 1748.

Madam,

When I received your Ladyship's Letter on *Friday*, I was just upon the Point of setting out for *Broom;* I therefore declined answering it, till I had spoke with Miss DOLMAN. It is now with the greatest Thankfulness for your obliging Invitation, and the most pleasing Idea of the Visit we propose, that I am to inform your Ladyship, we intend waiting on you upon *Tuesday* or *Wednesday* sev'nnight. If you should have *much* Company at that Time, or the Visit should be otherwise unseasonable, your Ladyship will be so good as to let us know; if not, I will not fail to shew Miss DOLMAN the Way to the most agreeable Entertainment, and the most engaging Conversation, I have met with any where. Your Ladyship will not imagine that I understand *Entertainment* in the vulgar Sense; (tho' what I say is true enough in *that*) my chief Pleasures, I flatter myself, are Pleasures of the *Mind*; and I can say, with great Truth, that my Mind was never more *disposed* to be pleased any where *else*, or found equal Opportunities to gratify that Disposition.

Miss DOLMAN, tho' she has not seen much of the World, has done great Things, or, in other Words, has made good Use of the Opportunities she *has* had, if she can deserve any Part of that favourable Mention you make of her. All I know is, that she has *Taste* enough to put the Pleasure I have promised her at *Barrels* out of all Dispute.

I now proceed to other Things. I have sent your Ladyship the *first Number* of *Sickness*, a Poem, which is all I have. I *send* it as indeed I *offered* it, because it bears some Relation to Lady HERTFORD, on Account of the Panegyrick of Lord BEAUCHAMP, which I believe is just.

I have of late read the Life of Colonel GARDINER,[1] being induced to do so by a Vision, which is described there, and which I hear Mr. LYTTELTON countenances. I will give your Ladyship my Opinion of the Story, when I come to *Barrels*.

Pray don't buy the Books I talked of; you will hardly read them twice; and I can lend you HERVEY's *Meditations*, the *Life of Colonel* GARDINER, and, in a short Time, *Memoirs of Mrs.* PILKINGTON, either of my own, or my Brother's. I beseech your Ladyship, that I may have leave to save you six Shillings, and three Shillings, and three Shillings; that is according to the old Maxim, (*viz. a Penny Sav'd*, &c.) put into the Power of my Gratitude, to be of about twelve Shillings significancy. By so doing, I shall not only talk, but proceed to one *ouvert Act* in the Cause of Oeconomy.—I wish it be not the only one.

In regard to Mr. OUTING, I will only say, that I please myself with the full Assurance of meeting him at *Barrels*. It is out of my Power this Day to send you an *amusing* Letter, whether it be so at other Times or not. There is not a single Cloud or Dimness in the Sky, but has its exact Image or Counterpart in my Imagination; but one's Sincerity does not suffer by Weather, tho' one's Vivacity may; and it is with the greatest Truth that I shall always remain

Your Ladyship's
Most obliged, and most obedient Servant,
W. SHENSTONE.

NOTE

[1]Philip Doddridge, D.D. (1702–1751), nonconformist divine, published in 1747, *Some Remarkable Passages in the Life of the honourable Colonel James Gardiner* . . . with an appendix relating to the antient family of the Munros of Fowlis. James Gardiner (1688–1745), colonel of dragoons, was killed at the Battle of Prestonpans. A poem on his death was advertised in the 1746 May number of *The Gentleman's Magazine*— *On the death of Col. Gardiner.*

LXXII

Works III, 160.

To MR [GRAVES], *on his Marriage.*

This was written August
21, 1748; but not sent
till the 28*th.*

Dear Sir,

How little soever I am inclined to write at this time, I cannot bear that you should censure me of unkindness in seeming to overlook the late change in your situation. It will, I *hope*, be esteemed superfluous in *me* to send you my most cordial wishes that you may be happy; but it will, perhaps, be *something* more significant to say, that I believe you *will:* building my opinion on the knowledge I have long had of your own temper, and the account you give me of the person's whom you have made choice of, to whom I desire you to pay my sincere and most affectionate compliments.

I shall always be glad to find you *præsentibus æquum*, though I should always be pleased when I saw you *tentantem majora*.[1] I think you should neglect no *opportunity* at this time of life to push your fortune so far as an *elegant* competency, that you be not embarrassed with those kind of solicitudes towards the evening of your day;

'Ne te semper inops agitet vexatque cupido,[1a]
'Ne pavor, & rerum *mediocriter utilium* spes!'

I would have you acquire, if possible, what the world calls with some *propriety*, an *easy* fortune; and what I interpret, such a fortune as allows of some inaccuracy and inattention, that one may not be continually in suspence about the laying out a *shilling*;—this kind of advice may seem extremely dogmatical in *me*; but, if it carries any haughty air, I will obviate it by owning that I never *acted* as I say. I have lost *my* road to happiness, I confess; and instead of pursuing the way to the fine lawns, and venerable oaks, which distinguish the region of it, I am got into the pitiful parterre-garden of amusement, and view the nobler scenes at a *distance*. I think I can see the *road* too that *leads* the better way, and can shew it others; but I have many miles to measure back before I can get into it myself, and no kind of resolution to take a single step. My chief amusements at present are the same they have long been, and lie scattered about my farm. The French have what they call a *parque-ornée*; I suppose, approaching about as near to a garden as the park at Hagley. I give my place the title of a *ferme ornée*;[2] though, if I had money, I should hardly confine myself to such decorations as that name requires. I have made great improvements; and the *consequence* is, that I long to have you see them.

I have not heard whether Miss [Graves?]'s match proceeded.—I suppose your objections were grounded on the person's *age* and *temper*; and that they had the less weight, as they supposed you acted indiscreetly yourself: I can say but little on the occasion. You know—better than I do. Only this I must add, that I have so great an esteem for your sister, that it will be necessary to my *ease*, that whoever marries her she should be happy.

I have little hopes that I shall now you see [sic] often in this country; though it would be *you*, in all probability, as soon as *any*, that would take a journey of fifty miles,

> 'To see the *poorest* of the sons of men.'

The truth is, my affairs are miserably embroiled, by my own negligence, and the non-payment of tenants. I believe I shall be forced to seize on one next week for three years and a half's rent, due last Lady-day; an affair to which I am greatly averse, both through *indolence* and *compassion*. I hope, however, I shall be always able (as I am sure I shall be desirous) to entertain a friend of a *philosophical regimen*, such as you and Mr. Whistler; and that will be all I can do.

Hagley park is considerably improved since you were here, and they have built a castle by way of ruin on the highest part of it, which is *just* seen from my *wood*; but by the removal of a tree or two (growing in a wood that joins to the park, and which, fortunately enough, belongs to Mr. Dolman and me), I believe it may be rendered a considerable object here.

I purpose to write to Mr. Whistler either this post or the next. The fears you seemed in upon my account are very kind, but have no grounds. I am, dear Mr. [Graves], habitually and sincerely,

Your most affectionate
W. Shenstone.

My humble service to your neighbours.—Smith (whom you knew at Derby) will publish a print of my grove in a small collection.

NOTES

[1] Horace, *Epist.*, I, 17, 24.

[1a] Horace, *Epist.*, I, 18, 98–9.

[2] Thomas Wheatley, *Observations on Modern Gardening*, 162, gives the origin of the term 'ferme ornée.' 'The ideas of pastoral poetry seem now to be the standard of that simplicity; and a place conformable to them is deemed a farm in its utmost purity.

An allusion to them evidently enters into the design of The Leasowes, where they appear so lovely as to endear the memory of their author; . . . A sense of the propriety of such improvements about a seat, joined to a taste for the more simple delights of the country, probably suggested the idea of an ornamented farm, as the means of bringing every rural circumstance within the verge of a garden.'

LXXIII

B.M. Add. MSS. 28958.

[*To* LADY LUXBOROUGH.]

Madam,

I'm sure I ought to neglect no opportunity of returning our Joint Acknowledgments for yᵉ extreme Civility you shew'd us at Barrels. I am at yᵉ same time to inform your Ladyship, that our *Delay* at Mr. Loggin's was attended with no great Inconvenience in our Return Home: And this I ought more particularly to mention, as your Ladyship may accuse yourself of being instrumental in *it;* since we were tempted insensibly by the Pleasure of your Company to stay there somewhat longer than our Time wou'd well allow. We did indeed encounter certain Gate-posts in passing thro' some Neighbour's Grounds, but we arriv'd at Broom about Eleven of Clock at Night, entirely safe and perfectly well-pleas'd. Miss Dolman & my Brother were extremely delighted with their Journey, & having seen little Company since have scarce talk'd of anything besides. Indeed the Ideas they must have receiv'd at Barels cannot be suppos'd to be easily eras'd, where the greatest Politeness was made use of to recommend yᵉ greatest Variety of Amusements.

I long to hear what is become of Mr. Outing; but 'till I *do*, I shall conclude he has marry'd yᵉ rich Widow with the Farm in her own Hands, & yᵗ he is busy in the Manufacture of Syllabubs for yᵉ Regalement of his Friends. I mean this as Panegyrick, & yᵗ I cannot conceive his Sphere so alter'd, but that his Benevolence will appear in some shape or other.

To jumble some very different Spots of News together, after yᵉ Manner of a Gazette. Mrs. Lyttelton's Monument is arriv'd & put up at Hagley.[1] A Locust has dropt at Birmingham which is shewn as a *Curiosity*, & 'tis to be wish'd it may continue so. The clergyman who saw it told me it's head &

wings resembled those of ye Dragon-Fly, & y^t it look'd very formidable. I suppose ye common People will conclude from ye Death of ye Cattle & ye Arrival of this Insect, y^t ye Plagues of Egypt are coming. If they cou'd convince my Friend Whistler y^t the Frogs wou'd come next, he would expire at ye Thought & never wait for ye Event.

Your Ladyship's Camera obscura is at present with Mr. Dolman who purposes to try it upon his Machine, which he has near compleated. Some Means of excluding ye Light seems obviously requisite. A Coach *may* be darken'd & so it may be us'd upon ye Road; but I shou'd think not conveniently.

The Paper-Book left in y^r Ladyship's Hands was what I intended to shew you, y^t I might not seem forgetfull of what I formerly propos'd. But your Ladyship is convinc'd by this Time how incompleat it is, & Will I dare say return me this Copy y^t I may do myself y^e *Justice* & y^e *Honour* of presenting you with an *improv'd* one. I purpos'd to insert some Things you have *not* seen, & to furnish you wth a something better $Edit^n$ of those you *have*.

I am going to procure a Convex Glass to see Landskips with, & to have it fitted up by a Joiner in my Neighbourhood. I fancy some of Smith's *designs* well colour'd will appear to great Advantage thro these Machines, but it wou'd be Pity to injure them by careless or unskilfull colouring.

If your Ladyship's Niches are Compleated you will give me ye satisfaction of telling me how you like them; & thus I finish my *Rhapsody*; which I think is not unlike a Beggar's Garment, consisting of mere Rags & Trumpery ill-tack'd together. Albeit, your Ladyship will see, thro it, ye Real Poverty of my Imagination & be induc'd to excuse it on y^t score, & then I will pray as heartily for your Ladyship as any Beggar y^t subsists by your Bounty.

I am, Madam
Your most oblig'd
and most obedient Servant,
WILL: SHENSTONE.

The Leasows, *August*, Monday morning.
1748.

NOTE

[1]Lucy, beloved wife of George Lyttelton died January 19, 1747.

LXXIV

B.M. Add. MSS. 28958.

[*To* LADY LUXBOROUGH.]

Broom, *August* y*ᵉ* 24*ᵗʰ* 1748.

Madam,

I date this from Broom, where I happen to be upon an Affair alike disagreeable to my *Compassion* & my *Indolence*; & yet at yᵉ same time extremely *necessary* & for yᵗ reason very *proper*, to apologize for yᵉ short Answer I am oblig'd to give to your Ladyship's most agreeable Letter. The Affair I allude to is yᵉ Distreining on a Tenant concerning which I was in deep consultation when I was told of your Servant's arrival. Pleasure & Pain continue to interfere! and I cou'd be well enough content if they wou'd come *separate*: for I wou'd have my Pleasure untainted; & then when Pain was to arrive, wou'd prepare myself for it by giving myself up to no other Expectation. Sweet & Acid join'd together I believe recommend a *syllabub*, of which Mr. Outing (to my great grief) disallows himself a Manufacturer; but I think 'tis otherwise in *Life*, & yᵗ one wou'd wish to have them, *there*, by no means intermingled: In other Words, I wou'd be willing yᵗ *Pleasure* shou'd make Incroachments upon *Pain*, but *Pain* shou'd never revenge itself upon Pleasure—To put an End to this formal Casuistry, I do fully believe that when We see your Ladyship at Broom, we shall be *compleatly* happy, & I am extremely glad to hear yᵗ your Postilion gives a favourable verdict in Regard to the Roads. The Business I mentioned in yᵉ first Part of my Letter took up yᵉ Forenoon, & your Servant I fancy thinks it Time he shou'd be going. I must beg your Ladyship's Interest wᵗʰ Mr. Outing to obtain a Pardon for not answering his Letter *now*; for I really am not able. I hope you will command him to believe that I was ever in Spirits when I met him, & that I shall be now so as much as ever, *notwithstanding*.

I am,
Madam,
Your Ladyship's most oblig'd
& most obedient Servant
WILL: SHENSTONE.

There are now at Hagley, Mr. Lyttelton, Mr. Pitt, Mr. Miller yᵉ Projector &c. &c.

I beg your Ladyship wou'd excuse yᵉ Blunders I have *committed*, & yᵗ Mr. Outing wou'd forgive me yᵉ Letter I have omitted. I would have avoided *both* these Faults, but that I have compassion on your Footman who waits, & who has been so kind as to speak *smoothe* Things of yᵉ Way yᵗ leads you hither.

Mr. Dolman desires his compliments to Mr. Outing & will be very glad to wait on him.

My Brother desires his Compliments to your Ladyship.

LXXV

Works III, 164.

To Mr. JAGO, *with an Invitation to The Leasows.*

Sep. 3. *Saturday night,*
1748.

Dear Mr. Jago,

I hardly know whether it will be prudent in me to own, that I wrote you a *long letter* upon the receipt of your last, which I now have upon my table. I condemn this habit in *myself* entirely, and should, I am sure, be very unhappy, if my friends, by my example, should be induced to contract the same. The truth is, I had not expressed myself in it to my mind, and it was full of blots, and blunders, and interlinings; yet, such as it was, it had wearied my attention, and given me a disinclination to begin it afresh. I am now impatient to remove any scruple you may have concerning my grateful sense of all your favours, and the invariable continuance of my affection and esteem.—I find by your last obliging letter, that my machinations and devices are not entirely private.—You knew of my draught of Hagley Castle about the bigness of a barley-corn; you knew of our intended visit to Lady Luxborough's; and I must add, Mr. Thomas Hall knew of my contrivance for the embellishment of Mr. Hardy's house. Nothing is there hid that shall not be revealed.—Our visit to Barrels is now over

M

and past.—Lady Luxborough has seen Hagley Castle in the original:—and as to my desire that my draught might be shewn to no *Christian* soul, you surely did but ill comply with it, when you shewed that *drawing* to a *Clergyman*. However, you may have acted up to my *real* meaning, if you have taken care not to shew it to any connoisseur. I meant chiefly to guard against any one that knows the rules, in whose eyes, I am sure, it could not turn to my credit.—Pray how do you like the festoons dangling over the oval windows?—It is the chief advantage in repairing an old house, that one may deviate from the rules without any extraordinary censure.

I will not trouble you *now* with many particulars. The intent of Tom's coming is, to desire your company and Mrs. Jago's this week.—I should be extremely glad if your convenience would allow you to come on Monday or Tuesday; but, if it is *entirely* impracticable, I would beseech you not to put off the visit longer than the Monday following, for the leaves of my groves begin to fall a great pace.—I beg once more, you would let no small inconvenience prevent your being here on Monday.—As to my visit at Icheneton,[1] you may depend upon it soon after; and I hope you will not stand upon punctilio, when I mention my inclination that you may all take a walk through my coppices before their beauty is much impaired. Were I in a sprightly vein, I would aim at saying something genteel by way of *answer* to Mrs. Jago's compliment.—As it is, I can only thank her for the *substance*, and applaud the *politeness* of it.—I postpone all other matters till I see you. I am, habitually and sincerely,

Your most affectionate friend,
W. SHENSTONE.

I beg my compliments to Mr. Hardy.

P. S. I am not accustomed, my dear friend, to send you a *blank* page; nor can I be content to do so now.

I thank you very *sensibly* for the verses with which you honour me. I think them good lines, and so do others that have seen them; but you will give me leave, when I see you, to propose some little alteration. As to an epistle, it would be executed with *difficulty*, and I would have it turn to your credit as well as my own. But you have certainly of late acquired an *ase* in writing; and I am tempted to think, that what you write henceforth will be universally good. Persons that have seen your elegies like *The Blackbirds* best, as it is most assuredly the most *correct;* but I, who pretend to great penetration, can foresee that 'The Linnets'[2] *will* be made to excel.—More of this when I see you. Poor Miss G[raves] J[ackie] R[eynolds] says, is married; and poor Mr. Thomson, Mr. Pitt tells me, is *dead.*[3]—He was to have been at Hagley this week, and then I should probably have seen him *here.*—As it is, I will erect an urn in Virgil's Grove to his memory.[4]—I was really as much shocked to hear of his death, as if I had known and loved him for a number of years:—God knows, I lean on a very few friends; and if they drop me, I become a wretched misanthrope.

NOTES

[1]Probably the home of Hardy and presumably Bishop's Itchington of Letter LVI (a), which is 'beyond Warwick.'

[2]*The Goldfinches. An Elegy to William Shenstone, Esq.* 'To you, whose groves protect the feather'd choirs', etc., Dodsley's *Collection* IV, 311.

[3]Thomson died August 27, 1748.

[4]Dodsley makes no mention of this urn in his description of The Leasowes, though (Shenstone, *Works* II, 364) he writes of a seat inscribed to Thomson.

LXXVI

Works III, 168.

To the [Rev. RICHARD JAGO].

Sunday night,
Sept. 11, 1748.

Dear Mr. Jago,

I take this opportunity of acknowledging the justice of your excuses. Mrs. Jago's present circumstances render her visit quite impracticable, and yours I have the same kind of reason to dispense with; as I guess, that she could as soon take the journey *herself* at this time, as bear that *you* should.—But to say I was not greatly mortified, would be doing myself the greatest injustice. *Disappointed* I was, you may be sure, to hear excuses; even as much as Sir John Falstaff, when Mr. Dombledon put him in mind of *security,* instead of sending him *two* and *thirty yards* of sattin to make him a *short* cloak.[1] And on the whole, I began to accuse you and Mrs. Jago of *colloguing* together, to fix your visit at a time when you were well assured you should have an *apology* to send me instead. Now, if I should press this accusation, pray how would you evade the force of it?—The next thing I am to speak to, is your verses. I have made you my acknowledgments *before*; and as you are so good as to accept them, I will not trouble you with additional professions, or repetitions of the past. I will depend upon your good-sense for an excuse, if I only add what I think proper as to any *alteration;* wherein I have a view to *your* credit, as well as my *own*. I confess, it requires some nicety to inscribe such an elegy as The Gold-finches without the danger you foresaw. But I think it *may* be done (and *is* pretty nearly) in such manner that no man of *taste* will be tempted to ridicule it; and as for the vulgar, of whatever *rank* they be, it is absolutely necessary many times to *give them up. Taste* and *tenderness* are absolutely connected; and you may very readily call to mind some charming things, that must excite the laughter of your men of *fire* and *banter*, but are by no means thought the worse of by men of *true genius*. I will only mention Andrew Marvel's *Fawn*² in Dryden's Miscellanies. I inclose the elegy with some few proposed alterations, so I will not risque the *filling* my *letter* with criticism. I also inclose the other verses you sent me, which I think good ones, and to stand in need of little alteration, beside that of the inglorious name at the head of them; to which, notwithstanding, I will never submit. Pray who is the young gentleman that translates your elegy into Latin?—The new dress will give you some amusement; and, if these lines *be* the product of the genius of a boy of that age, he will in a year's time be able to extend the fame of your compositions. I shall then be glad to see The Gold-finches under his hand; though I have no extraordinary fondness for the Latin of a modern; at least, till your eldest son begins to translate our madrigals.

I have not yet seen Mr. Thomson's Castle of Indolence.—I waited for a smaller edition; but am now too impatient not to send for it on Thursday next.—I am fully bent on raising a neat urn to him in my lower grove, if Mr. Lyttelton does not inscribe one at Hagley *before* me.³ But I should be extremely glad of your advice whereabouts to place it.—You speak of my dwelling in a Castle of Indolence, and I verily believe I *do*. There is something like enchantment in my present inactivity; for, without any kind of lett or impediment to the correction of my trifles that I see, I am in no wise able to make the least advances. I think within myself I could proceed if you were here; and yet I have reason to believe if you *were* here, we should only ramble round the groves, and chat away the time; and perhaps *that*, upon the *whole*, is of full as much importance. —I do not know but I do myself some little injustice here, for I *have* wrote out my *levities* and my *sonnets*, good and bad, with many ornaments from the pencil; and the next thing I do will be to transcribe my elegies. The fault is, I take no pains to *improve* what I transcribe, and consequently am only able to exhibit my nonsense in a fairer dress.—You must give me leave, ere it be long, to insert two or three lines (I think in *verse*) before Mrs. Jago's flower-piece.—I am sure, I am obliged to her for a fruit I greatly love.—It was not entirely ripe; but it was the only one I have tasted since I was last in London.—Yesterday dined here Lady Luxborough, Mr. Outing and Mr. Hall, Lord Dudley, Miss Lea, Counsellor Corbet and Mr. Saunders, Mr. Perry, Mrs. Perry and Miss Dolman,[4] and half a dozen foot-men beside my own servants and labourers; so you may guess we had no small fracas. I now sit down amid solitude and silence, and can hear little else beside the pendulum of my clock;—yet my spirits are no way sunk, but afford me just such a temperature of mind as inclines me to write to some familiar friend: albeit I have a thousand things to *talk* of to you, which I do not care to *write*. I hope to be able to spend a few days with Mr. Hardy, before his melons are all gone; and yet I would not have him keep one a *moment* longer upon *my* account. I desire he would accept of my compliments, as I trust he will.—Franks at present run low with me; but I send you *one*, which you cannot use so soon but I shall be able to send you others immediately. I wish I could send you any thing more than the means of obliging.

Sir,

Your most affectionate friend,

W.S.

NOTES

[1]II, *Henry IV*, i, 2.

[2]*The Nymph complaining for the Death of her Fawn.*

[3]At Hagley, in Thomson's Hollow, was a semi-octagonal temple dedicated to Thomson, 'a sublime poet and a good man.'

[4]The visitors contained in Shenstone's list are most of them by this time well known to the reader. Miss Lea was Lord Dudley's youngest sister, the only one at this time unmarried. Mr. Saunders is evidently not the cousin of Shenstone living at Tardebigge. He may be Thomas Saunders, a surgeon, who was patronized by Lord Lyttelton. Mr. Perry is the 'Parson Perry' frequently mentioned in the later correspondence. 'Counsellor Corbet' is possibly a member of the well-known Shropshire family.

LXXVII

B.M. Add. MSS. 28958.

[*To* LADY LUXBOROUGH.]

Septr 1748.

Madam,

I have not time to say anything more than that I am extremely sensible of ye Honour you intend me, & y^t I shall be happy in waiting on y^r Lasp, Mr. Outing & Mr. Hall. Were I to prolong ye Time by expressing myself more fully, I might justly risque the giving offence to your Servant; which it wou'd be as imprudent to do, as to irritate one's Jury. As it is, I have no Fault to find with him; He allows ye Road to be *practicable*, tho' not altogether so smoothe & easy as *my* Friend Johnson[1] represents it. I think coal-carriers are transform'd into Angels of Light; at least *I* shall never esteem 'em to be Ministers of Darkness, whilst they give Representations so favourable to my Wishes.—'Tis very natural for me to fix on y^e *former* of ye Days you propose, & accordingly I build upon ye Hopes of seeing your Ladyship on *Saturday*. But as I send to Broome to-Night, I will presume upon your Ladyship's Goodness for Leave to *alter* that Day in Case I find anything in Mr. Dolman's Answer that requires it. If so, I will send my Servant to Barrels on Thursday; Otherwise I will by no means think of deferring my Happiness, for a moment longer y^n the time it is offer'd me. I am,

Your Ladyship's

most oblig'd & most obed

Servant.

WILL. SHENSTONE.

Miss Dolman talk'd
of sending a Servant
the Beginning of this
week. I beg my
Compliments to Mr. Outing
& Mr. Hall.

NOTE

[1] The 'my friend Johnson, who serves me with coals and lives at Northfield' of Lady Luxborough's *Letters*.

LXXVIII

B.M. Add. MSS. 28958.

[*To* LADY LUXBOROUGH.]

THE LEASOWS, *Sept^r* 11th 1748.

Madam,

I cannot content myself even with the Pleasure I receiv'd from your Ladyship's Company, 'till I have had the additional satisfaction of hearing that you got safe Home. I hope you suffer today as little as *possible* from your Fatigue, by which *I* only was a Gainer. I was extremely sorry that I was not able to alleviate it by *suitable* Accommodations in Point of Lodging; I took care to state ye Case twice over to Mr. Outing, & if your Ladyship had thought proper to accept of such a Bed as we cou'd furnish, it wou'd have been attended with no kind of Inconvenience to me, but on the contrary with the greatest Pleasure. Twas moreover a mortification to me to see you leave ye Company just as you had begun to brighten up the Conversation; when I knew what a Change wou'd be wrought by your Departure—I ought to inform your Ladyship y^t

the Company, farther than Lord Dudley & his Sister, was accidental; only Parson Perry,[1] who din'd wth me on a Paltry Dinner ye Day before, was told, y^t if he came *following* Day, he wou'd partake of a better, as well as of your Ladyship's Company, which was far superior to any Dinner in the World. In Consequence of this He brought his Wife with Him—Mr. Sanders is an Apothecary of Stourbridge, eminent in his *Way*; a good-natur'd generous Man, that loves, (like me) to have his Schemes & Machinations admir'd. He has distinguish'd himself by keeping Polypus's. I never saw him here before—Mr. Corbett I never saw before. He is Son of Serjeant Corbett & is a young Barrister that has gone ye Circuit about twice; perhaps *not*, *hitherto*, very eminent in *his* Way. Things were in some Confusion when these People came, & I had not an opportunity of introducing Lord Dudley properly. Your Ladyship will not take amiss the Manner of his Address; He has no ill or sinister Meaning, & I think, at Table, endeavour'd more to please, than I have often seen Him. I'm sure I've great Reason to claim a like Indulgence, but I trust (as my Lord Stair said at ye End of his Declaration to ye States) y^t your Ladyship *on account of ye sincerity of our Purpose, & ye Uprightness of our Heart*, will *pardon all* our *Failings*—I do accuse myself however of some Rudeness in Regard to Parson Hall; & not the less so, for his good-Nature in seeming to disregard it; I have an extreme good opinion of Mr. Hall; & I think there were some Freedoms taken w^{ch} (tho' trifling amongst *Friends*) as there were *strangers* by, were *wrong*. I hope your Ladyship also feels some Compunctions of this kind, wch may induce you the more readily to say something on my Behalf—After you went, the Company walk'd once more round my Walks, & gave them great Encomiums; which however made but faint Impression on me, after your Ladyship's Approbation—For want of proper Contingencies, how many Noble Schemes have prov'd abortive! My Lord Dudley shou'd have met your Ladyship in ye Morning, & attended you thro' my Walks with extraordinary Complaisance & *Sprightliness*; Your Ladyship shou'd have been *unfatigu'd* y^e *Moment* you got out of y^r Chaise; notwithstanding y^e *Length & Roughness* of your Journey; & as you came to the

Seat which commands yᵉ Water in Virgil's Grove, I shou'd have come behind & dropt these Verses into your Lap, scribbled *extempore* no doubt with a blacklead-Pencil.

> Here *Dudley* deigns to spend a social Hour:
> Spring fast ye Greens! the favour'd Haunt embow'r!
> Here *Luxb'rough sate*; Ye streams yᵗ gently glide,
> Whene'er you chance to meet a *richer* Tide,
> Ah! warn it not to slight your little Store;
> Say, Luxb'rough prais'd you, & you ask no more.

I believe I must beg yᵗ my Servant may stay till Morning at Barrels, as He will arrive late, & I can, on no *other* Terms expect a Line from your Ladyship. I am your Ladyship's most oblig'd &

> most obedient humble servant,
> WILL: SHENSTONE.

My Brother and Miss Dolman desire your Ladyship may accept of their Compliments.

NOTE

[1] A neighbouring clergyman and a frequent visitor at The Leasowes. He was a small poet, and his *Malvern Spa*, 1757, appeared in Dodsley's *Collection* V, 84. One is reminded of Gray's remark to Nicholls, June 24, 1769, that W.S.'s correspondence was 'about nothing else but his place and his own writings, with two or three neighbouring clergymen who wrote verses too.' Courtney, *op. cit.*, 118, gives a short account of Rev. John Perry.

LXXIX

B.M. Add. MSS. 28958.

[*To* LADY LUXBOROUGH.]

Sunday night, Sept. 25. 1748.

Madam,

As your Ladyship confers *obligations* wᵗʰ a Grace superiour to any one I know, so I cannot but observe that your *Menaces* afford me greater Pleasure than I cou'd receive from any Courtier's *Promises.*—I hope to be doing some little erroneous Matter, ev'ry year, about my Farm, sufficient to call down upon

me what you call the *Punishment* of a visit, as often as your
Ladyship is at Leisure to inflict it. I am going incontinently to
raise an Urn to Mr. Thomson in my *lower* Grove; & have this
Ev'ning requested a very ingenious Builder from Birmingham
to call upon me. So your Ladyship may *threaten* as much as
you please, & I assure you I will provoke your Threat'nings
as far as I am able. Now I mention Mr. Thomson, I receiv'd
yesterday y^e 'Castle of Indolence.' I waited, I believe three
Months, to buy it in a smaller Edition; & ye same Moment
y^t I receiv'd y^e *large* one, I saw ye octavo *Edit*: advertis'd in
ye Papers. It is I think a very pretty Poem, & also a good
Imitation of *Spenser*; which latter Circumstance is ye more
remarkable, as Mr. Thomson's Diction was not reckon'd y^e
most *simple*. I own I read it wth partiality of y^e *Author*, as I
had seen & lik'd y^e *Man*; as his Merit was but *inequally*
recompenc'd; and as he is now *dead*. This last Article adds a
Tenderness, tho' I must have read it wth ye Partiality of a
Friend, had he been yet alive. There is a Compliment *again* to
Mr. Lyttelton.[1] *That Gentleman* call'd on me last Saturday
sen'night, together with one Mr. *Mitchell*, whom I know not;
yet I think I have seen his *Name* somewhere in Print. They
found me just as I had din'd, and as they were obliged to go
back to Hagley to dinner did little more than walk around y^e
House & approve my laying Things *open*. I remember'd my
Disappointment *last* year, & being somewhat mortify'd at y^e
Shortness of the visit, I wish my Expostulations were not a
little too *brusque*. However he gave me Hopes of seeing him
again before he left ye Country, which nevertheless I do not
much *expect*. Those Lines in ye Castle of Indolence are pretty,

> I care not, Fortune, what Thou canst deny;
> > Thou canst not rob me of Free Nature's grace;
> Thou canst not shut ye Windows of ye Sky,
> > From whence *Aurora* shews her radiant Face.
> Thou canst not &c. . . .[2]

I know Mr. Outing will be more delighted wth ye description of

> 'A little, round, fat, oily Man of God' &c.[3]

which I own is very drole; & puts one in Mind of Dr. Shaw—

I hear my Lord Gower[4] went to London *immediately* after yᵉ Races at Lichfield; extremely dissatisfy'd that yᵉ Tories had *out-shone* Him. I have some Notion too, that he has not perform'd yᵉ visit he promis'd at Hagley: There *was* a Report yᵗ he had been there, which prov'd a false one.

I heard, too, yᵗ Mr. Lyttelton open'd a Letter at Hagley, & cry'd, 'So! There's an End of yᵉ Peace'. But of *No* Report will I assure yᵉ Truth. I scribbled yesterday a little Autumn Song,[5] wᶜʰ if your Ladyship desires, you shall see in my next. A few lines are added after 'approaching Pain' which spoil it for a Song,

I have not seen Lord Dudley since your Ladyship was here. We chose to drop our visit yᵉ next Day, for particular Reasons— If Mr. *Sanders* knew you call'd Him an *ingenious* Man, he wou'd ride precipitately to Barels with his Convex-Glass &c. behind him, & perhaps break it by the way. I have not yet receiv'd yᵉ Glass he is to procure me, but I was thinking of a *small* Improvement of my own; which consists in pasting all yᵉ Pictures on a long scroll of Canvas, like a welch Pedigree; & so having a Roller behind & before, turning on an Axis, by which means one may by turning round yᵉ *latter*, shew yᵉ Pictures with all yᵉ Ease imaginable—It was *not* thro' a *consciousness* of sneering that I desir'd some Apology to be made to Mr. Hall; for I meant nothing like it; But Mr. Perry happen'd to say yᵗ He thought I went too far; & I now *sincerely believe* yᵗ Perry was nettled *himself* at wᵗ I said about his Preaching for Mr. Hall at Henley, & so took that method of endeavouring to mortify me.—September yᵉ 28ᵗʰ. Thus far was written in order to have been sent last Monday, but yᵉ Post-woman calling *prematurely*, I was oblig'd to wait for yᵉ *present* opportunity: and by that means am able to add a few things which your Ladyship will please to accept upon yᵉ Cover—For such do I design this to be—I have ventur'd to transcribe the Trifle I before mention'd as a mark of my *Simplicity*, tho' none, of my *Genius*. I mean, that as I wou'd be understood *literally* when I call what I write a *Trifle*, so it shews my confidence in yᵉ *Person's goodness*, to whomsoever that Trifle is communicated.—*More* Interest for yᵉ green Book!—But why talk I of yᵉ *green*-Book? who am now writing out my lamentable Elegies in a Book as red as

Blood—Your Ladyship knows that Red is sometimes us'd for second *Mourning*—& *Art* for ought I know may be fondest of *that* Colour, tho' *Nature* out of doubt deals far more frequently in Green—I saw my Builder this afternoon & we have fix'd upon the Model your Ladyship approv'd without any Alteration. Twill be erected in about a Fortnight, as soon as He can compleat ye Pediment. I also gave Him a Model for an Urn to Mr. Thomson, which I will sketch out for your Ladyship's opinion ye next Time I write. These two will be compleated, I believe before Winter—And if I *live*, & can *content myself wth white-brick* for a building in ye Center of my upper Grove, I may, very possibly, execute *that* in ye Spring; And then I think my Place will not be so unpleasant y^t any one need studiously avoid ye Sight of it—If your Ladyship have Dodsley's Miscellany, (tho' I do not remember to have seen it at Barrels) I shoud be oblig'd if you wou'd lend it me— I have waited *long* for a second Edition wch Dodsley propos'd in great *Haste*, but I do not see it advertis'd *yet*. I desire my Compliments to Mr. Outing & Mr. Hall. I am

Your Ladyship's most oblig'd
& most obedient servant
WILL SHENSTONE.

If I do not see Mr. Outing soon,
I will take care to acknowledge ye Favour
of his Last Letter. I am at present under ye Dominion
of *Indolence*, & It is evry whit as certain y^t my
House is ye individual *Castle* wch Thomson describes,
as y^t ye Chapel of Loretto traveld from Jerusalem into
Italy.⁶

To the Right Honble Lady Luxborough
at Barrels;
To be left with Mr. Williams Painter
in Birmingham.

NOTES

¹*Castle of Indolence*, canto I, 65:

'Another guest there was, of sense refin'd
Who felt each worth, for every worth he had;
Serene, yet warm, humane, yet firm his mind,
As little touch'd as any man's with bad.'

There is a description of Hagley in *The Seasons*, *Spring*.
    [2]*Ibid.*, canto II, 3.
    [3]*Ibid.*, canto I, 69. In this character of his friend Dr. Murdoch, Thomson repro-
duces the same characteristics which he describes earlier in his correspondence. The
description of the 'little, round, fat, oily man of God' appealed to the whole Shenstone
circle. In Luxborough, *Letters*, 58, the description is applied to Parson Hall.
    [4]John, Viscount Trentham, co. Stafford, and Earl Gower.
    [5]W.S.'s note, 'a few lines are added after "approaching Pain" which spoil it for a
Song' makes it clear that the 'little Autumn Song' alluded to is the poem entitled
Verses written towards the close of the Year, 1748, *to William Lyttelton, Esq.*, *Works*,
I, 181.
    [6]There was a legend concerning the Holy House at Loretto that the home where the
Virgin Mary had been brought up was converted into a church by the Apostles, and
that, when threatened with destruction by the Turks, angels removed it by successive
stages to Loretto.

LXXX

B.M. Add. MSS. 28958.

[*To* LADY LUXBOROUGH.]

THE LEASOWS, *Novr 9th* 1748.

Madam,

The Prospect I had of conveying your Ladyship a Letter
by the Return of Mr. Outing and Mr. Hall has kept me silent
till *now*, & will, I hope prove my Apology. But I shou'd be
inexcusable if I defer'd a Moment longer to acknowledge y^e
repeated Pleasure & satisfaction I receive from your Ladyship's Letters: I may add, the Happiness I have enjoy'd, &
may yet *hope* from your conversation; & I think I ought not to
omit, ye opportunity I have by means of your Acquaintance to
shew ye Trifles I write to a Person of so unexceptionable a
Taste, as to render her Approbation very interesting; & at y^e
same Time of such a friendly Partiality, as not entirely to
refuse that Approbation.

I ask your Ladyship's Pardon for any Freedom's I have
taken with your favourite Season. It is not *Youth*, God knows,
but a kind of premature Old-Age y^t makes me bid Autumn
less welcome y^n I shou'd otherwise do. I am *afraid* now of
what I have hitherto sought opportunities of indulging; I
mean, that pleasing melancholy wch suits my Temper *too
well*. This your Ladyship will discover by some very *solemn*

Elegies wch I shall shortly put into your Hands. I cannot but consider Autumn as y^e *Follower* of Summer, & y^e *Harbinger* of a Season which your Ladyship yourself dislikes. And as it reminds one of past Pleasure for y^t reason, & also of approaching Pain, It seems to centre in itself rather too *much* of ye douce Melancholie; a *little* whereof is ye most refin'd Pleasure we know—Your Ladyship will say, why do I raise an Urn to Thomson? The Pleasure that can afford must be of ye melancholy kind—Tis very true—But I can retire to Thomson's urn when I think *proper* (at least I cou'd if it was erected as at present it is *not*.) But Autumn obtrudes its pensive Look in every nook & Corner. If it paints my Grove with ever so many colours, Those Colours are so many symptoms of *Decay;* For however *Nature* may carry on her *Scheme* alike in *all* seasons, The several *Parts* of of [sic] her Dominion, the *Trees* & *vegetables* do no doubt flourish & decay by Turns. If It *strip* those Leaves & throw them into my Brook, 'tis all *right* & *natural*, but yet I had rather see my Brook uninterrupted & running transparently over it's Pebbles.—After all—I find myself wonderfully *inclin'd* to think wth your Ladyship. I read in your Ladyship's Letter all y^t cou'd possibly be said *for* Autumn: There was a fine day or two succeeded, &, betwixt both, I was convinc'd y^t I ought to write a Recantation so far as concerns *Autumn at Barels*, & so far as concerns y^e *former Part of it* & with the Limitation, y^t I may give my Madrigal ye Title of 'A *fine Day* in Autumn.' But I laid aside ye Scheme in Hopes y^t your *Ladys'p* whose *peculiar* favrite ye Season is, & who are capable of adorning ye subject in a better Manner yⁿ myself, wou'd please to throw into verse ye best things y^t can be said in it's Favour: And then even *Spring* shall give it Place.

I desire to subscribe to yours and Lady Hartford's Sentiment in regard to Thomson's Poem. It has several pretty Parts, & several pretty Paintings. I don't know how I came to express myself otherwise, for I did not entirely approve ye Plan at first. I think he shou'd by no means anticipate ye Diseases & Inconveniences of Indolence at ye End of his *first* Canto. You know there is a large Display of them in y^e *second*, where they wou'd have appear'd more strikingly had he not touch'd upon

'em before. I valu'd Mr. Thomson as he was ye only Person
of Figure y^t ever ye Hag[le]y-Family introduc'd me to; Tho'
I once had hopes—but *they* are wither'd whether my Flowers
(according to your Ladyship's Beautifull Quotation) are or no.
In ye next Place he wou'd have prov'd a good Critick in regard
to any little Thing I had intended to publish, & as he was in
years, & his Reputation settled, cou'd have had none of those
little Jealousies y^t often attend such kind of connections.
Finally he wou'd have prov'd a very agreeable Friend &
Acquaintance—but he is gone & his Death is of a Piece wth
my Fortunes. However I will raise an Urn to him, & remember
him wth Pleasure. Had he liv'd, he might have found *some*
satisfaction here notwithstanding ye vicinity and ye Table of
H[agley].

For an Acquiescence in seeing every Thing as he finds 'em,
I know no one y^t I envy so much as my Lord Dudley. He does
not only bring himself to *acquiesce* in what he *finds*, but it is a
Reason with him y^t Things *shou'd* be so because they *have*
been. And this even when Expence is not ye least concern'd.
He will not remove some Pictures out of a Parlour when they
are a kind of blemishes, to another Room where he knows they
wou'd prove Beauties. He lets two giant yew-trees hide y^e
Pillars of his Gates, & spoil a good walk by ye side of them, at
ye same time y^t he will very readily allow of their Impropriety.
But this Insensibility *has* it's Convenience, for which, once
more, I envy Him—

I own I took ye Hint of a Roller for y^t Shew glass from y^e
London Cries—I have had mine fitted up, (But shall not have
ye Roller, till I have a better stock of Pictures.) In ye mean
time I have painted a Couple of *Smith's Views*, & I believe
that no Pictures in ye world can prove more striking. I send
y^r Ladyship my Plan for ye Wood-work of these glasses, &
therefore will say no more concerning them at present.

If y^r Ladyship's *Eolian* Harp shall please me (and I intend
to be within hearing of it soon) I promise to give up my Harpsichord immediately& suffer my right Hand to forget it's little
share of Cunning, with all ye Content imaginable—Moreover
I will frame every Madrigal I write to be sung to y^t Instrument
only.

I have sent yᵉ Shuttlecock for Mr. Allen's[1] Perusal & have added a Translation from Horace wᶜʰ I received some time this Summer.

I can add no more at present; only I beg & entreat that this *random* Letter may be never brought to evidence against that invariable *Respect* wᵗʰ which I am your Ladyship's most oblig'd and most obedient Servant W.S.

NOTE

[1]Parson Allen, of Spernall, a neighbour of Lady Luxborough.

LXXXI

Works III, 173.

To [Rev. R. JAGO].

Sunday, Nov. 13 (1748).

Dear Sir,

I must fairly own, that I have not sate down till now to return my acknowledgments for your last most obliging favour; and yet I have been doing so in *imagination* almost every day since I received it. I have only to desire that you would not think me *stupid*; and then you must of course conclude me highly delighted, to find the verses which had so greatly pleased me, made so *particularly interesting* to me. In testimony hereof, I have caused these my letters to be made *patent*, &c. Furthermore, I am glad to see you dissent from some alterations I proposed; for which, generally speaking, I think I can see your reasons. As to any little matter which I have to mention farther, I chuse to defer it till I wait on Mr. Hardy; which I purpose to do before this month is out. It may possibly *happen* the beginning of the next week; but I dare not lay such stress upon a future *event*, as to give you a commission to say so much to *him*. Instead thereof, please to make him my compliments, and tell him I talk of coming *very soon*.

I borrowed Dodsley's Miscellany of Lady Luxborough, in which are many good things. I long to be making a mark on the head of every copy (as I would do were the books my *own*). Here a cypher; there an asterism of five points, and there one of eight.[1]—If you, and Mr. W[histler], and Mr. G[raves], and I, were together for a fortnight, to correct and revise, might not we make a miscellany of *originals* that would sell?—My fingers itch to be at it;—but I fear it cannot be.—Thomson's poem amused me greatly.[2]—I think his plan has faults; particularly, that he should have said nothing of the diseases attending laziness in his *first* canto, but reserved them to strike us *more affectingly* in the last; but, on the whole, who would have thought that Thomson could have so well imitated a person remarkable for simplicity both of sentiment and phrase?

I study no connections in a letter; and so I proceed to tell you, that I have got a machine to exhibit landscapes, &c. to advantage. It costs about fourteen shillings, and I recommend one to you or Mr. Hardy—Smith's Views (with a little colouring) appear ravishingly;—but if you are not content with *amusement*, and want *fame* (which differs about as much as *fox*-hunting from *hare*-hunting), you must *print*.—However, if you can acquiesce in a *limited reputation*, to give you a proper weight at all your visiting-places (which I think enough for all reasonable ends and purposes), take the following receipt.

'A Receipt to make Fame.

'Take a shoe-maker into your parlour (that is reputed a good workman), and bid him procure a piece of red or blue Morocco leather; let him shape this into the size of a quarter of a sheet of paper, or it may be something larger. Let him double it in such a manner as to leave some part to wrap over; then stitch it neatly at the ends, lining it either with silk or the best yellow leather he can meet with. Then must you bespeak a silver clasp, which you *may* have gilded; but be sure it be neatly *chased*, and properly annexed to the aforesaid Morocco leather. Make a present of this to the prettiest girl you know, but filled with half a dozen of your best compositions; take care that one be in praise of *her* ingenuity. For modesty sake, desire her not to shew them to any living soul; but, at the same time, be careful that your clasp be splendid, and your letter-case made according to the fore-going directions.'

Adieu! seriously yours,

W.S.

N

NOTES

[1] W.S. was in the habit of marking his books in the way he describes here. Writing to Percy, October 1, 1760, he says: 'I have us'd myself to these three marks of approbation, † for the least, ++ for the next, and ⧺ for the highest.' Through the courtesy of Messrs. Quaritch I was able to examine a copy of Prior's *Poems* with MS. notes by Shenstone. On page 1 he writes: 'November y 26th, 1739. Read over all Prior's Works a 2ᵈ. Time, marking the Pieces I most admir'd with a proportionate Number of Crosses.' Numerous marks are made throughout the book, *The Nut Brown Maid* and *Henry and Emma* being among those poems most highly commended.

On Page 2 is the Inscription:

Des Livres
Du Guill: Shenstone
du Coll. du Pem:
a Oxon. 1735.

This method of inscription appears to have appealed to W.S. at this period for in the B.M. (Add. MSS. 28964) is a note book of his containing 'Remarks on Paradise Lost.' It is inscribed thus:

Guillaume Shenstone
a la mode de Paris.
Pem: Coll: 1735.

A design of a flower in a pot follows and sundry printings of his name. On the next page is another conventional design; and on the third a remark by Hull to the effect that the book, the 'ingenious labour' of my well esteemed friend' was given to him by Shenstone's 'niece, Mrs. Mary Wiggin.'

[2] *The Castle of Indolence.*

LXXXII

B.M. Add. MSS. 28958.

[*To* LADY LUXBOROUGH.]

THE LEASOWS, *December the* 18th
1748.

Madam,

I have had such frequent Reason to be convinc'd of your Ladyship's great Penetration, that I have been assur'd for some Days past, you *must* impute my Silence to the real cause. But upon the Receipt of yʳ polite Reproof, my Crime begins to shew itself in very different Colours; & I am no sooner taught to think as I *shou'd* do, than I find it impossible for all the Sagacity in yᵉ world to have known anything of my Situation. 'Twere adding to my Offence to *despair* of your Forgiveness, wherefore I will presume to hope it may be punish'd rather according to the Light in which I *previously* consider'd it, than the Shape in which it *now* appears. At least I will flatter myself, that yᵉ Sentence may be compromis'd, or be adjusted by a Medium of *both*; inasmuch as Faults appear to us, I fancy, as much too excessive *after* they are committed, as they often *before-hand*, appear, too inconsiderable—Your Ladyship will please to remember, that at ye Time I had the Honour of your two last Letters, there remain'd but one entire Day before you set out for Somerville's—Aston.[1] That Day indeed, (as my *only* Servant was extremely busy, & I knew your Journey was fix'd at all Events) I did, I own, neglect to make a proper use of; thoroughly resolving to wait upon your Ladyship either at *Aston*; or if that might not be, upon your Return, at *Barels*. In that Case I was in Hopes you wou'd have pardon'd my Neglect, & admitted of my Apology for declining a visit, which upon *all* Accounts must have been agreeable to my *Inclination*. The Truth is, I had some *secular* affairs to adjust with Mr. Dolman, (with whom I have a small Estate in Partnership) before I cou'd with Prudence move from Home; & in these I found myself engag'd till about Nine Days ago. *Since* that Time I have been setting out for Barrels Daily; and indeed from the *Beginning* have only defer'd writing, because I said within myself To-morrow or in a Few Days, I will make my Apology to my Lady in Person, and return the Books she was so good to lend me. Many Days the weather has discouraged me, & I think this last week has not afforded a good one; so that finding myself detain'd within Doors, I employ'd a Mason & Carpenter to proceed in modeling my Parlour, or rather converting a Kitchen into one. *When* they will finish, is beyond my Power of Conjecture; but until they *do*, I am oblig'd to give *Directions*. The most that I shall gain, will be, a Room 17 Feet long, $\frac{F}{12}$ & $\frac{1}{2}$ Broad, and ten Feet two Inches high; the walls plain stucco with a Cornish; a Leaden Pipe conveying water into a Bason at one end, over a slobb: At the other End a Door leading into a Room, that, (whenever I can afford to finish it) will be my Favourite. As you enter into this last, the *Point* of Clent-Hill appears visto-Fashion thro' ye Door & one of ye windows. The same will be reflected in a Peer-glass at ye End of the former Room. This last Room I purpose to cover wth Stucco-Paper, to place my Niche-chimney Piece from my Summer house at one End of it, over that Mr. Pope's Busto, &, on each side, my Books. The Windows open into my principal Prospect—I wish I was as certain you wou'd be *satisfy'd* with my Apology, as I am that you must be *fatigu'd*. And yet the mortifying Turn you gave to my late Silence (too severe if not meant in Raillery) requir'd this particularity. It grieves me to look Back how much of my Paper is already employ'd, when I have more Acknowledgments to make to you, & to another Lady (by *your Means*) than ye whole extent of my Paper wou'd be able to convey. Were I not so much oblig'd to *you* on the *Dutchess's*[2] *Account* as I am, and cou'd therefore speak with Freedom, I shou'd be tempted to reproach your Ladyship bitterly for suffering her at any Time to complain of your Silence. Sure I am she writes with all the *symptoms* of Sincerity, & *Proofs* of Ingenuity; & that a Correspondence so polite as your Ladyship's must afford ye most sensible Pleasure to a Person of so good a Taste. I am afraid the Partiality she discovers for a muse so very humble as mine, must *appear* no small objection to *that Ta*ste, as also to my Testimony; but I believe the b*est* of Tastes may be prejudic'd by *Friendship*, & then it is a thorough vindication of her Grace, that she is influenc'd by *yours*—I am oblig'd by ye subscription to Mr. Smiths views greatly. I hope your Ladyship will represent me in that Light, when you write to Percy-Lodge. It will be enough y^t I have Leave to transmit her Grace's Name to Mr. Smith; The Prints will no doubt be punctually deliver'd, & I hope afford some Amusement. I guess by ye Letter you enclos'd, y^t you consulted Mr. Smith's Interest further than a Subscription: These continu'd marks of your Regard to my Applications, deserve much more of me y^n mere verbal Expressions of my gratitude; and yet even those are more than I can deliver as I ought. I will not say, (for the Heart of Man is deceitfull above all Things) how far Rank may find a Place in recommending ye Favours you confer, or the Genius you discover; But I shall hardly be persuaded y^t Persons so accomplish'd as your Ladyship or The Dutchess wou'd not excell all I know, as the Mathematicians say, in any *given* station.

I have not seen my Lord Dudley, I think, this Month but intend to do so soon. The last Time he was here he din'd upon a Turkey, with a quill *of which* I am this Moment writing: And if there was one Grain of *Wit* in yᵉ Letter I am sending, I shou'd think I had made a good use both of the Turkey, & his Quill—He generally goes to Town on the Back of Christmas, so that I am doubtfull whether you must expect him before next Summer.

As to Mr. Allen, I desire my Compliments: As to Mr. Outing, He & I must *compromise* yᵉ Affair: As to Mr. Reynalds, I will propose Terms of Accomodation & expect He will insist yᵗ I shou'd propose them a [sic] Somerville's—Aston.

I have not so much as seen yᵉ Peruvian Letters[3] advertis'd. I believe I shall send for Them, & will be carefull you shall see them as soon as they arrive.

I thank your Ladyship for yᵉ Use of Dodsley's Miscell: They have afforded me much Pleasure. The Variety of Styles is an advantage to such Collections. I think, had he reduc'd them to *two* volumes, even tho' he had omitted *my* sublime Piece, the Garland had been more beautifull; But it is as good a Collection as one often meets with. Did your Ladyship ever see The *Flower*-piece. I bought it at Leak's in Bath by way of a Temporary Amusement, many years ago. There are *some* pretty things, which do not occurr elsewhere, at least not often.

These Elegies I beg Leave to place in your Hands till I come to Barrels. The outside of yᵉ Book seems to promise more Perfection than will be found within. I know them to be very imperfect, several Things want to be accommodated to yᵉ present Time, &c.: yet with a thorough Confidence that you will not *expose* them, I venture to send them for your Ladyship's Perusal.

With all their Imperfections on their Head.[4] And I beg your Ladyship to make some kind of Mark on such as (with proper Alterations) you shou'd least dislike. The Seventh in yᵉ order they now stand was partly design'd to commemorate my Lord Beauchamp,[5] but I am convinc'd it would be a cruel office to the Dutchess instead of a kind one.

I hope you will be pleased to acquaint me whether Mr. and Mrs. Reynalds come to Barrels this Xmas. I shou'd be glad to model my journey so as to give them the Meeting.

Mrs. and Miss Dolman desir'd their compliments when I

saw them last, presuming I shou'd see your Ladyship in a Day or two's Time. Miss D. is now at Litchfield. To their compliments I must add those of my Brother.

I suppose, Madam, you may by this time be abundantly weary of y^e *longest* & *dullest* of Letters! Had I any gilt Paper I might have been properly *stinted*, but being forc'd to make use of this, I hope you will hereby discover y^t I take a *Particular Pleasure* in writing to Barrels till such time as I meet with Lett or Impediment, thro' the scantiness of earthly Paper. As I now do, & must therefore subscribe myself your Ladyship's most oblig'd & most constant

humble Servant WILL. SHENSTONE.

NOTES

[1]In Gloucestershire. William Somervile, author of *The Chace*, came of an ancient family long settled at Aston-Somervile. His cousin, Lord Somervile, by arrangement in 1730, obtained the reversion of William Somervile's estates in Gloucestershire, which he inherited on the latter's death in 1742.

[2]The Duchess of Somerset. Lady Hertford became Duchess of Somerset, December 2, 1748.

[3]*Letters wrote by a Peruvian Lady from the French.* Pr. 2s. 6d. Brindley. *Gentleman's Magazine*, 1748, p. 240.

[4]*Hamlet*, I, 2.

[5]It is difficult to decide whether this remark applies to any of the Elegies printed in Shenstone's *Works*. The hints given by Lady Luxborough (*Letters*, 81), do not assist greatly.

LXXXIII

B.M. Add. MSS. 28958.

[*To* LADY LUXBOROUGH.]

Decem: 30th 1748.

THE LEASOWS.

Madam,

I think y^t either Indolent or Irresolute People shou'd not ever delay *writing* thro' an Intention of *coming*; For this Reason, tho' I design to wait upon your Ladyship in a very short Time, I look upon it as expedient to express my Thanks for your last Favour by some more early opportunity.

If I may give any Credit to w^t, I *think*, they call ye Doctrine of *Sympathy*, which has been enforc'd to me by my old Housekeeper for these many years past, I will give you my Sentiments concerning ye Application of *Quills*. In ye first

Place however I must premise y^t Crows shall never be esteem'd inauspicious Birds by Me, since they convey me Intelligence of Your Ladyship's Health & Welfare; & I think I may extend my Indulgence also to Ravens, with whose Quills, I presume, you wou'd be able to write more sprightly Things, than any other Person with ye Quill of a *Mockaw*. As to ye Quills of Turkeys, (tho' Indeed, I, who am no Hero made use of one) I think they are singularly proper for your Military Men; & that whether you regard ye Nature of y^e *Bird*, or ye Temper of his Feathers. The Bird you know is remarkable for empty Noise and Ostentation, & then as to ye Quill it may suit a person very well who has been accustom'd to write his meaning with ye Point of a Sword. I believe he will not find much *difference*, were he to try them both alternately upon Paper. To your Ladyship I wou'd recommend ye Quill of a *Black-bird*; a Bird that has both *spirit* & *Elegance* in his Notes; but as he seems to want *variety*, I must own I know no English Bird expect ye Throstle that unites those three Qualities of all you write & say: And then a *Wood-lark* or a *Nightingale* may be reckon'd to *excell* him; (whereas your Ladyship is *not* excell'd) & these last Birds (& perhaps ye former) have no *writeable* Feathers. I must therefore leave you to make use of whatever Quill you please; well knowing that you cou'd not write disagreeably even with the Quill of a *Bittern*—For *me* the Goose, ye Emblem of Stupidity, will still retain a Feather; And, against ye Time I write in verse, I nourish a very fine Peacock whose harmonious Voice agrees to a tittle with my Versification; as I fear your Ladyship has too plainly experienc'd.

I think you, Madam, are a very good judge of ye most learned Elegy I am capable of writing; But if you are fearfull of leading me into any Scrape by your Decision (which I own will have great weight with me) I must acknowledge myself very much *oblig'd* by your concern, tho' at ye same Time I endeavour to remove it, by owning y^t these Compositions will probably go thro many other Hands. I hope this will be an Inducement to your Ladyship to give me your Opinion which of ye Elegies are least to be dislik'd; The Preface will be either *partly* or entirely omitted.[1] If amidst ye many trifles which I trust (with entire Confidence) into your Hands, there be any

Thing which you guess may be agreeable to the Dutchess, I shall be more & more oblig'd if you please to convey it. I can only say in general that the Hope of acquiring ye least share in her Grace's Esteem gives me ye greatest Pleasure, & I must leave your Ladyship to manage *for* me. I receiv'd yesterday from Mr. Smith ye Letter I enclose. I send it amongst other Reasons y^t I may not hereafter seeme to have *conceal'd* any *Self-interest*, when you find that for ye Service I have done him, he obliges me wth a couple of Views, taken from ye Leasows. I have said nothing in his Favour wch I do not think he deserves; & he was so kind to take a Draught without any kind of stipulation with me, or, for ought I cou'd see, *expectation*.

I know ye Want of gilt Paper is of little Moment to Persons who, like your Ladyship, can make their Letters shine by Dint of Genius merely; but 'tis otherwise with *Me*. I love to have my Scrip of Paper well ornamented *without*, for fear it shou'd have no Merit *within*. I love to have ye Impression of a Seal well taken off; & I am not entirely satisfy'd unless ye Sealing-Wax itself be of a lively Orange-scarlet.—My Room wants now little else than stuccoing & I am daily enquiring after a Person to do it—Since I wrote last, I have been carousing with ye Lord Mayor & Aldermen of Hales-owen; in other Terms, at ye Bailiff's Feast; from whence I escap'd without much Damage to my Constitution—I do not *much* recommend ye Flower-piece. There are some of ye best things I have seen written by y^e *ministerial* writers in Lord *Orford's Ministry*. I am extremely glad to hear y^t your Health is so much improv'd by a *Milk-diet:* It affords me a Prospect of your Longevity. I always approv'd it, but never had Resolution to make use of such other Regimen as was consistent with it—The Abele will imitate ye Noise of a Water-fall, very Luckily near y^r Ladyship's Hermitage—You judge extremely right with Regard to ye Urns—*That* your Ladysp approves, was fix'd on, but ye top was not esteem'd unexceptionable. Perhaps at Barels I may find out a better—I beg Pardon for *grouping* the particulars of this Page, but you will see my Paper oblig'd me—I am, Madam,

Your Ladyship's most Oblig'd & most obedient
Servt W. SHENSTONE.

NOTE

¹Lady Luxborough (*Letters*, 80) was not pleased with W.S.'s *Prefatory Essay on Elegy* (*Works* I) and thought it took away from the interest of the poems. Whether the Preface is inserted in the form in which W.S. originally wrote it I cannot tell, but one would not entirely agree with Lady Luxborough with regard to the relative merits of the Poems and Preface.

LXXXIV

B.M. Add. MSS. 28958.

[*To* LADY LUXBOROUGH.]

THE LEASOWS *April yᵉ 7ᵗʰ* 1749.

Madam,

I have sin'd in detaining your Ladyship's Books so long, & am sensible enough to my offence to avoid yᵉ like, I hope, on any future occasion. But Mr. Dolman having read yᵉ two former volumes, I was under a temptation of saving him yᵉ Price of yᵉ whole by lending him yᵉ subsequent ones. My Brother & I read them almost at yᵉ *same* Time; & *He* might in three more Days have done yᵉ same; & *then* I cou'd something more reasonably have depended on your usual goodness for my Excuse. But when once one deviates from what is strictly right, one is often involv'd in such Degrees of wrong as we never dream't of. Mr. Dolman was interrupted in his Perusal of yᵉ Books by Company, & yᵉ consequence is that I have witheld your Books 'till now, tho' I was sensible your Ladsp has not read yᵉ two last volumes—I think as you do yᵗ that [sic] yᵉ Plan is by no means easy, but must own at the same time yᵗ several *Parts* have afforded me much Amusement. There is a good deal of wit dispers'd thro'out, or rather ty'd up in Bundles at yᵉ beginning of every *Book*. You will conclude my Taste to be not extremely *delicate*, when I say I am cheifly pleas'd with yᵉ striking Lines of Mr. *Western's* Character.¹ It is I fancy a natural Picture of thousands of his majesty's rural subjects; at least it has been *my* Fortune to see yᵉ original pretty frequently. Tis perhaps a Likeness yᵗ is easily taken & moreover he seems to apply it too indiscrimin-

ately to Country-gentlemen in general. But it is ye only
Character y^t made me *laugh*; and y^t is a great Point gain'd,
when one is in danger of losing y^t *Faculty* thro' Disuse. Tis
moreover a Character better worth exposing that his Land-
lords and Landladys wth which he seems so delighted—his
Serjeants and his Abigails &c. Your Book of Gardening is
now at my Booksellers by way of Pattern: I will return it as
soon as I've an opportunity—And the mention of this Book
serves well enough to bring once more upon ye Carpet what I
was saying about ye Alteration in your Garden. My Mistake
lay in calling those Trees *Limes* which I find are *Service*-trees,
In every other Respect you understand my scheme, such as it
is. I dont remember whereabouts the Foot-path runs y^t
leads to Henley. *That* may perhaps be an unanswerable objection: For I am afraid, to ye best of my Memory, it crosses your
Service-walk. Otherwise The Advantage y^t wou'd follow from
my Alteration would consist, in joining your Shrubbery to
your grove by one continu'd walk of ye same kind; enlarging &
greatly improving your Labyrinth of Shrubbs which is I think
rightly situated; avoiding both y^e *Tongue* & y^e *Ear* of y^e
scolding old-woman by filling up ye gravel walk in some
measure with Shrubbs, & perhaps having a serpentine sand-
walk return a little part of ye Way from your Gate; & having
y^e *back Part* of y^r Summerhouse conceald by Plantations of
Trees in ye corner that leads into your Pheasantry. When this
was done wou'd there not be an opportunity of making some
pretty open seat on a small mount at ye very lower end of y^r
Grove just by ye Gate, which shou'd command (by lowering y^e
Hedgerow) the *Walk of Trees* on ye Hill ye Temple & y^e
Country towards Henley &c? But all this may be liable to great
Exceptions. As to your Ladyships Pavilion, I fear I should be
as ill able as can be, to direct your Mason; Else would I
gladly come over at any Time. My chief use wou'd be in laying
out ye Ground, & here I think there is one Rule to be certainly
observ'd, y^t your furthermost Trees shoud not *seem* to join y^e
Front of ye Building by a Foot of a side at least, *when view'd
from your Hall Door;* That being ye most distant Point from
which it is meant to be seen. This may be effected by y^e
Distance at wch you place it from ye Trees. As for any thing else,

provided that Elm Walk is to continue, The situation you chuse for it, is, I think, unexceptionable—If Mr. Hall persists in wishing me to assist him in ye Inscription he speaks of,[2] I will be of what service I am able. At the same Time I shou'd be oblig'd to your Ladyship if you wou'd convince him y^t tho' his Father's Character might be *better* & more *usefull* than many of theirs who are puffd away upon monuments, yet it will not well admit of Flourishes; & y^t it ought to be as plain as possible. This your Ladyship knows, & this he has too much sense to afford you any difficulty in demonstrating—My Lord Dudley has I find been tumbled out of his vehicle in his way to London, for y^e *third successive* Time. If he can but *overturn* my Lord Ward[3] there (with whom he has a suit in Chancery) It will make him some Amends. I have been busy in paving a small serpentine stream & planting Flowers by ye side, but I am afraid I shall find it impossible to preserve them. I would gladly enough compound ye matter wth ye Mob if they wou'd leave me about *Half*, particularly those you were so kind to give me. But I fear they wont, For tho there are Primroses to be gather'd in ye Fields in Plenty yet if they can discover one that is apparently planted, they are sure to crop it. But tis chiefly done by Children & such as can't read, were I to publish my *Placard* as they have done at Hagley-Park.

I take off my sealing wax by a Lamp instead of a Candle. I *do* not nor *will* I forget ye green Book.... [Upside down at head of letter.]

NOTES

[1]From Fielding's *Tom Jones*, published 1749.

[2]Cf. Luxborough, *Letters*, 92–4. W.S.'s skill as a writer of epitaphs was recognised by his friends. Good judges, such as Landor (*Works* III, 518, 1876 Ed.), have described his Latin inscriptions as 'most beautiful.'

[3]Lord Ward of Himley. Visits to and from him are frequently mentioned in letters of W.S. who assisted him in garden design. Graves, *Recollection*, 144.
William (Ward) Lord Dudley, and Baron Ward of Birmingham, d. unm. May 21, 1740; and was succeeded in the Barony of Dudley by Ferdinando Dudley Lea, son of Frances, the former lord's only sister. The Barony of Ward devolved on the heir male, John (Ward) cousin, son of William Ward of Sedgley Park, co. Stafford, by Mary, daughter of Hon. John Grey of Enville. This division of titles probably accounts for the lawsuits which, according to W.S.'s *Letters*, were a feature of the relationship between Lords Dudley and Ward.

LXXXV

Hull, I, 57.

To the Right Hon. LADY LUXBOROUGH, *at Barrels.*[1]

I have sent your Ladyship a Book of Gardening, which I borrowed, about five Years ago, of a Neighbour. If it will be of any Service to you, in modelling the crooked Walks in your Shrubbery, I shall be glad; and you may return it at your Leisure, as I do. It is written by a poor illiterate Fellow, notwithstanding its Dedication to His Majesty, *who is delighted with Enquiries into vegetable Nature.* You will see something of his Ignorance, perhaps, in every Page; more especially Page 204, first Part, where he talks of MINERVA *and* PALLAS for Statues, with many Blunders of like Nature. It was written, seemingly, when the present *natural* Taste began to dawn, and which I wish, rather than hope, may last as long as Nature.

Mr. L[yttelto]n, you may perhaps hear, has been afforded, and has refused the Place of Treasurer of the Navy, in Mr. D[odingto]n's Room.[2]—What a Tide of Success!

May your Ladyship be as happy as Success ever made any Body! and that it is more in the Mind than Externals is to me a Demonstration. I'm sure I shall never be so happy, with with [sic] all my Philosophy and *Success,* as an old Fellow who works for me: but I think your Ladyship has not only a right and philosophical Understanding, but good animal Spirits, which are half in half; so that you may be much Happier than even *him,* which, I assure you is to be greatly so.

I am now a little maudlin after Dinner, and if my Groups are inconsistent and queer, you must excuse me. I hope Mr. ALLEN is, by this Time, well. I have written a Line to Mr. OUTING, at the Head of his Regiment. I am now to take my formal Leave, as I do after a long Visit; that is, with about half a Bow, and the Expression of about half I think; but I include as much as any Body, when I say,

I am,

Your Ladyship's

Most obliged, and most devoted Servant,

W. SHENSTONE.

If your Ladyship could spare me about three Eggs of your *Guinea* Fowl, I should be much obliged.

NOTES

[1]The letter belongs to the early part of 1749 as that was the time when Lady Luxborough was 'modelling' her shrubbery. Moreover W.S. mentions on April 23 a
gardening book by Langley, which he 'sent a week ago.'

[2]George Bubb Dodington, Baron Melcombe (1691–1762), politician and writer of
occasional verses. He was made Treasurer of the Navy under Pelham, December
1744, and resigned his office March 1749.

LXXXVI

B.M. Add. MSS. 28958.

To LADY LUXBOROUGH.]

[Upside down] My Br. desires his Compliments to Your
Ladyship. I am planting Flowers in Abundance. I hope to rise
to Shrubs in
    Time.

THE LEA: *Apr* 23 1749.

Madam,

I shou'd have prepar'd a Letter for last Thursday, but y^t
I did not receive yours before that Time & the present opportunity, upon one account or other is the First I have of obeying
your Ladyship's commands—'Tis nothing new to me to find
you extract *Beauties* out of my *Blunders*: You are capable of
doing ye same by those of Nature; at least if she may be
suppos'd capable of making any such, which indeed she is not.
Blemishes however she must have to ye Eye of such *limited*
Beings as can only comprehend a *Part* of her works; & those
it is ye Province of common Tastes to render tolerable; & of
such as *yours* to convert into Beauties. I cannot avoid pursuing
this Thought a little farther. It is, I think, owing to ye limited
Faculties of Men y^t there is any *need* of Taste to make alterations in our *Environs*. Suppose ye human Eye were capable of
comprehending y^e *Universe*, it wou'd be as absurd for him to
design even such a garden as Lord Cobham's, as it wou'd in
his *present* circumstances, to make a Baby's Garden of half-an-
Ell square. If this be a true state of ye Case, then Taste in
Gardens &c: has little more to do than to *collect* ye Beauties of

Nature into a compass proper for it's own observation. But
you'll say, whence then is ye necessity of making Alterations
Why in order to maintain a due Proportion betwixt ye Objects
you introduce; y^t you may not have so much *Lawn*, as to have
none of the Beauty of *Plantations*; so much *Wood* as to have no
Flower-work, & so on. The necessity of smoothing or brushing
ye Robe of Nature may proceed entirely from ye same Cause
Were one's Eye calculated to *take in* a *larger extent*, in other
words, her whole Person, we shou'd not then discover y^r
Dust or ye *Rumples*—I beg Pardon for this long Digression
My Purpose was to proceed immediately to speak of your
Ladyship's Proposal of filling up your Lime-walk with Shrubs,
which I entirely *approve;* & of causing one of your Shrubbery-
walks to wind across it into y^r Abele Plantat^n which I as much
admire. I am in Hopes Mr. Langley's Book,[1] (which I sent a
week ago) may be of some little Service; as He has a variety of
Plans for Labyrinths; tho' I suppose it will not be proper to
give into ye tenth Part of y^e *Intricacy* y^t He does. The man is
something illiterate, but his Notions are not amiss in *many*
Respects, I think. The quere is, where-abouts y^r continu'd
serpentine shou'd enter ye Coppice, which I must Leave
undetermin'd. Shou'd you think it agreeable to burst into light
before you approach ye Hermitage, I fancy ye proper Place
would be opposite to y^r deep Precipice when you have planted
some few Quince-trees. That Precipice to be ha–ha'd[2] by
a rough wall of about a yard at ye bottom, & ye rest to be
thrown open to ye Field which I spoke of once before. If you
think it more eligible to preserve y^e *retir'd Idea*, 'till you enter
ye Coppice, & not let ye Spectator know ye Limits of ye wood-
work on each Side him, then you will chuse to make it enter
at some greater Distance; I mean somewhat nearer ye corner
of ye Coppice. I cannot determine which I shou'd prefer
myself. But your Ladyship, upon ye spot, will very easily
determine justly. The Scheme of making y^r Serpentine walk
thro' ye Abeles will prove not only cheaper, but I think, more
eligible. I suppose it will be proper to run it as much tow'rds
y^e *Left* as you can, by which means you will very soon have it
perfectly retir'd. And then I see no Reason why you shou'd
not direct *another* crooked walk in your Shrubbery to end at

ye Gate y^t opens to ye Service Trees & let ye Gate continue. It will make a variety; The Bank & the Turf of y^e *service-walk* is Charming. I woud then wish *that* entirely shut up at ye end next ye Hermitage, by which means your Shrubbery wou'd lead by different Windings to two very distinct Beauties. I would have ye winding walks not too narrow, but I fancy those you have already made are of a proper Breadth. You will I suppose plant some kind of Shrubs amongst ye Abeles, by ye sides of y^r new walk. Thus I think I have said all y^t occurs to me concerning *this* propos'd alteration, which I greatly approve. I am glad to hear y^t you are putting up ye Pavilion, or at least doing something tow'rds it. What you *have* done is, I suppose, extremely *right*. I don't know whether I did not speak too *precisely* concerning y^e *Apparent* distance betwixt ye Building & ye Trees; But if you calculate by putting up a Couple of Poles (to represent ye breadth of ye intended Building) & view them from y^r Hall-door, you will be able to adjust this *distance* to your Mind. The Flooring of y^r Pavilion shou'd I think be black & white stone in Lozenges—I believe you will find ye Alteration you are making before your Door a very great Improvement in Point of Beauty & Convenience. Quere, whether white Lead, or a very deep Lead-colour will least interfere with your view of ye Pavilion. I mean for your Palisades; Quere also, whether ye Dial Placed in ye centre of y^r Sweep will not also interfere with it? I don't know y^e *Propriety* of Ld Archer's *Globe* in regard to his Obelisk,[3] but his *Cross* I am *sure* can have none—I can by no means expect any Guinea-Fowl from y^r Ladyship, as your Stock is reduc'd so low; I am thankfull for your obliging offer—I will examine ye Epitaph before I write again by your Ladyship's Permission. I told Mr. Hall at *first*, & have now Room to be convinc'd y^t if you woud vouchsafe to take ye Trouble upon you, you would be by far ye more proper Person. Sr Philip Sidney, I think usd to say y^t a Line of Chevy-Chase affected him like ye Sound of a Trumpet.[4] I shou'd imagine y^e *last* Trumpet could hardly produce a more awful Respect y^n ye first Line of y^r Inscription is fitted to inspire. It introduces ye next Part 'Here lie' very elegantly no doubt; What room there may be for y^r Ladyship's Exceptions to it I cannot easily determine.

Warmth of sentiment is ye most capable of being ridicul'd; bu^t in my *present* way of thinking, I am for retaining it.

I have written your Ladyship a strange unceremonious Letter: But you are kindly pleas'd to indulge me in this Freedom, & I am aiming here *principally* to be of some little *Service*. I hope you will favour me with a Line as you proceed. I am ever with ye greatest *internal* Respect your Ladyship's most oblig'd, & most obedient Servt

WILL: SHENSTONE.

Since I wrote ye foregoing, where I give a Hint of making your Service-walk quite detach'd from ye Coppice, I think you will find it a necessary consequence, not to let your Abele-Serpentine open into a Prospect at all. So y^t what I said of it's opning opposite to ye Quince trees need pass for nothing. The Walk should enter ye Coppice *beyond* it. *That* spot may be either part of y^r Coppice or Part of y^r Service walk wch you chuse—The Reason of this Opinion is, y^t you may either go into your Service walk & enjoy y^e *open view* or into y^r Abele one, & carry y^e *retir'd Idea* with you into ye Hermitage. I will draw a small Sketch, merely to explain my Meaning.

NOTES

[1] Batty Langley (1696–1751), wrote many books on architecture and gardening. He tried to remodel Gothic architecture by the invention of five orders for that style, in imitation of classical architecture. 'Batty Langley's Gothic' was a by-word.

[2] Bridgeman, says Horace Walpole (*Essay on Modern Gardening*), evolved the Ha! ha! 'the destruction of walls for boundaries, and the invention of fosses—an attempt then deemed so astonishing that the common people called them Ha! Has! to express their surprises at finding a sudden and unperceived check to their walk.' One can still see at Barrels a fine example of the ha! ha!

[3] Andrew, Lord Archer of Umberslade, was Lady Luxborough's most considerable neighbour, and her friend and frequent visitor. The 'obelisk,' to be seen from the windows of the 'saloon,' is frequently mentioned in letters to W.S. See Luxborough, *Letters*, 101, 107, and Hutton, *Highways and Byways in Shakespeare's Country*, 291–3. Jago celebrated the beauties of Umberslade in *Edge-Hill*, Book I.

> Such too thy flow'ry pride,
> O Hewel! by thy Master's lib'ral hand
> Advanc'd to rural fame! Such Umberslade!
> In the sweet labour join'd, with culture fair,
> And splendid arts, from Arden's woodland shades
> The pois'nous damps and savage gloom to chase,
> What happy lot attends your calm retreats,
> By no scant bound'ry, nor obstructing fence,
> Immur'd or circumscrib'd; but spread at large
> In open day.

[4] Sidney's *Defence of Poetry*.

LXXXVII

B.M. Add. MSS. 28958.

[*To* LADY LUXBOROUGH.]

THE LEASOWS. *May ye 14th 1749.*

Madam,

Your Ladyship is extremely kind in giving me a Sketch of your Improvements; & I heartily wish you may find as much *Pleasure* in them, as I do, *Propriety*. The Removal of your Pillars was *necessary*, the joining of your Grass-Plats is *right*; & ye continuation you propose betwixt ye Shrubbery & ye Hermitage will, I fancy, add to ye Beauty of *both*. I am sensible how impertinent it is for me to propose Alterations, unless I were upon ye Spot; which I will contrive to *be* about ye Time you alter ye Shrubbery. I don't know what you will think of Mr. Langley's Book; It afforded me some *Amuse-ment*, as I had never seen any Book y^t treated of *modern Designs* in gardening *before*; but ye Reason I sent it was merely y^t you might see his Plans for crooked walks; & if it furnish you with one *Nook* or *Angle* y^t you approve, I shall gain my Point. I have been embroidering my Grove with Flowers, till I almost begin to fear it looks too like a *garden*; If there arrive a Flowering-*Shrub*, it is a Day of rejoicing with me; or (to use a term in *methodism* now so much in fashion) a *Day of fat Things*. (For you must know, I plant in all seasons.) I began to complain of my Neighbours for pilaging ye Flowers,[1] rather too soon. Since ye Publication of my *Edicts*, they have behav'd tolerably well. Half a dozen Flowers were cropt on May-morning, but the offenders have been detected, and brought to open Shame. And this, considering ye Numbers, y^t pay their Compliments to ye Place on Sunday-Ev'nings, is a *small* In-fringement, scarce worth mentioning. I have bought Miller's book of gardening[2] very elegantly bound; so you may expect me e'er long to talk like Solomon of all manner of Plants; from ye Cedars upon mount Lebanon, to the Hyssop y^t groweth against ye wall:[3] But to speak seriously, I shall only dip into it, as your Ladyship does, *occasionally*—I hope ye Painting over ye chimney-piece in your Library is alter'd for ye better.

o

I forgot to mention one thing, wch is, y^t if any shades appear *at all*, now ye whole ground is darken'd, they shou'd be altogether on ye farther side from ye Window, y^t the Light coming in *y^t way* may seem to produce them from Bas-reliefs—I have attempted several Times to make *some* Corrections in Mr. Hall's Epitaph, but find myself so utterly unable to proceed, y^t It seems a Judgment on me for presuming to alter what you write. If I make any more *unsuccessfull* Attempts, I shall be quite convinc'd of it, & then I will only hint at a Line or two which I wou'd have your *Ladyship* alter, & ask for your Pardon for detaining it so long. If I shou'd fancy myself to *succeed* & communicate any alterations, I hope you will do Mr. Hall so much *Justice* as to prefer your own opinion to mine, wherever you happen to dissent from ye latter; assur'd y^t your opinion will infallibly *be* mine, ye very first opportunity y^t offers, to discourse about it—I think this kind of writing extremely difficult, less difficult perhaps in verse yⁿ Prose; tho' ye former c^d hardly be well executed in y^e *present* Case; nor wou'd I attempt it upon any account whatever. Mr. Dolman often talks of waiting on your Ladyship this Summer; If he continues able to perform ye Journey, I wou'd chuse it shoud be some time while your Shrubs are in Blossom; which I think I haven't yet seen *with y^t advantage*. Indeed, I ought, as ye Representative of my poor *Dryads*, to return your visit in ye season you visit *mine*; Instead of that you do Honour to *my* Place when it is in its perfection, & I see yours when at ye worst. 'Tis true I do it ye Justice to admire it *then* & give it it's vernal Beauty as far as I can by Imagination; But my Imagination is not half so lively as your Shrubs are beautifull, & If your Ladyships permits we wou'd do y^m ye Justice to take a view of them in all their glory—I return your Book with thanks. My Bookseller has swerv'd entirely from his Pattern, yet at ye same Time has bound my Books so elegantly y^t I am hardly inclined to condemn his Deviation. He has brib'd me by an *old Fashion* reviv'd of marbling ye Edges of ye Paper which I think extreme pretty. Do not accuse this finical Taste of mine. Is it not happy y^t a Person of small Fortune can be pleas'd wth Trifles? And I assure y^r Ladyship at ye same time I have as great a value for solid *Merit*, genius and gener-

osity, as any one alive; consequently am as much as any one
alive

y^r Ladyships most devoted Servt
W.S.

NOTES

[1]In the Advertisement to James Woodhouse's *Poems on Sundry Occasions*, we learn
something more of the 'pillaging' of the flowers. 'The liberty Mr. Shenstone's good
nature granted was soon turned into licentiousness; the people destroying the shrubs,
picking the flowers, breaking down the hedges, and doing him other damage, produced
a prohibition to everyone without application to himself or principal servants. This was
originally the cause of our poet's being known to Mr. Shenstone, he sending him, on
that occasion, the first poem in this book: which not only gave him the liberty of passing
many leisure hours in those charming walks, but introduced him to Mr. Shenstone
himself.'

[2]Philip Miller (1691–1771), wrote several books on gardening, the best known being
The Gardener's Dictionary, which, from 1731 onwards, was many times reprinted,
enlarged, abridged, translated.

[3]The same idea, and the same form of words, occur on more than one occasion. Gray,
in a similar way, passed on an idea to more than one of his correspondents.

LXXXVIII

B.M. Add. MSS. 28958.
Hull, I, 91.[1]

[*To* Lady LUXBOROUGH.]

The Leasows *June y^e* 3rd 1749.

Madam,

Tho' I may seem to have been extremely lazy, I have really
taken no small Pains in endeavouring to obey your Ladyship's
commands. I wish when you peruse my Packet you may not
rather think me to have been extremely *officious*. Tho' I
should imagine even *that* a Crime by no means equal to *Negligence*, in any Affair wherein you are pleas'd to employ me.
How far I've err'd in *that* Respect, I am utterly unable to
determine; as your Directions to me were not very explicit;
and as I have not been favour'd with a single *syllable* from Mr.
Hall, to inform me, whether, or how far, he approv'd of
Alterations. But I will not call them *Alterations* which I send;
which are indeed only a small cargo of different Expressions,
which you may reject or apply, entirely as you think proper.

Nor shall it give me ye least offence if you reject y^e *whole*, so long as you will acquit me of Presumption in interfering. If I may speak my present Thoughts, I wou'd have the Epitaph be *short* & *general*; which is chiefly what I aim'd at in ye First & Second Numbers. In the third, I have been more explicit; not with any View to have *ye whole inscrib'd* upon ye Monum.^t but y^t I may by that means happen to send *something*, in one Part or another which you may chuse to appropriate. If Mr. Hall approves of an *Epitaph* short & general, & which conveys a meaning pompous enough under a simplicity of expression, He may have a more *particular Account* of his Father taken off by Aris^2 upon a single Sheet, & distribute half a score Copies amongst his Friends. This I think will be doing as much as ye greatest Filial Piety can desire. I am by no means languid in my wishes to perpetuate his Father's Character. I believe he might deserve as *good* a one, as any Person in a publick station. But you remember those Lines of Mr. Pope;

> 'Tis from high *Life*, high Characters are drawn;
> A Saint in crape is twice a Saint in Lawn.
> A Judge is just; a Chanc'lor juster still:
> A Gowns-man learn'd; a Bishop what you will:
> Wise if a Minister; but if a King,
> More wise, more learn'd, more just, more evry-thing.^3

Where, by ye way, ye Second & Fourth Line dwell alike upon the Bishops. But ye whole Paragraph is extremely beautifull. What there is of *weight* in them, is y^t the Character of a person in private Life must not be *express'd* too pompously. I am persuaded your Ladyship will manage it for the best, so I will now take leave of ye Subject. Is it to be executed soon, or may it be postpon'd till I have ye Honour of seeing you?—I lead here ye unhappy Life of seeing nothing in ye Creation half so idle as myself. Mischievous People will think and act ten times as much in a Day, as I shou'd in a Century. I am however pretty frequently pidling in little matters about my Farm. What do you think, Madam, of my publishing verses once a week upon my Skreens or Garden-Seats, for ye Amusement of my good Friends ye Vulgar? The Verses for ye present week are publish'd in Virgil's Grove, Rue de Virgile, & run thus:

Here, in cool grott, & mossy Cell,
We Fauns & playfull Fairies dwell,
Tho' rarely seen by mortal Eye,
When y[e] pale Moon, ascended high,
Darts thro' yon Limes her quiv'ring beam,
We frisk it near this crystal stream.

Then fear to spoil these sacred Bow'rs;
Nor wound y[e] shrubs, nor crop y[e] Flowers,
So may y[r] Path wth Sweets abound!
So may y[r] Couch wth Rest be crown'd!
But ill-betide or Nymph or swain
Who dares these hallow'd Haunts profane![4]

OBERON.

N.B. We have some people here y[t] believe in Fairies; but then such People do not understand verses. My Method is a very cheap one. I paste some writing Paper on a strip of Deal, & so print with a Pen. This serves in Root-houses & under Cover. Your Ladyship has been so unkind as not to let me know, since I wrote last, how your Pavilion proceeds, whether you are happy in Planning, or in beholding your Plans executed. May I hope to hear soon? Two hundred Pounds expended in a Rotund at Hagley, on Ionic Pillars! The Dome of Stone, with a thin Lead-Cover under to keep out wet. Whilst *I* propose, or *fancy* I propose, to build a Piece of *Gothic* Architecture, at sight of which all the Pitts & the Miller's Castles in y[e] world shall bow their Heads abash'd—! like y[e] other Sheaves to Josephs—I send you y[e] Plan. Tis for a Hermits Seat on a Bank above my Hermitage; which Hermitage I do not give up, notwithstanding y[e] Remonstrance of Mr. L. himself. This said Hermit's Seat will amount, on a moderate computation, to y[e] sum of fifteen Shillings & Six pence three Farthings—Pray my Lady what is become of Mr. Outing. Does he quit y[e] barbarous Trade of War, for y[e] Pleasures of repose, this Summer? Or does your Ladyship expect him at Barrels? I have not weight enough wth him to obtain an answer to my Letter dated Feb — I long to see what it is my L[d] Bolingbroke has publish'd, & what he has atchiev'd to ye discomfort of all Grub street.[5] I am, very constantly.

your Ladyship's most oblig'd Servant,
W. SHENSTONE.

Thursday, *June* ye 6th.

I did think to have sent ye former sheet this morning; which having neglected to do, I will endeavour to make some Amends for my Delay by adding another; as an Author now & then throws you in a dull appendix *gratis* in order to attone for his dilatory Publication of a duller Piece.

What an immense deal must it have cost to fit up an House in ye Manner you have done Barrels. Surely ye Inside expences of a House shou'd always be reckon'd at as much as the Shell. In regard to my *own* Habitation who *aim* at nothing y^t is extraordinary *there*, I am frighted at ye expence of common *Decencies*; nay almost, *necessaries*. I never walk beneath my Roof, but one Room cries out, 'Pray why am not I paper'd,'? On which another takes ye Alarm directly, and answers, 'why am not I stucco'd?' a third, 'why have not I a chimney-piece'? a Fourth, 'why not I, a new Floor'? to which two of them rejoin at once, 'And pray why have not we any Floor at *all*'? These are not a quarter of the Complaints; My Beds grown old and decrepit desire to resign their office in favour of others more alert & able. My Chairs suggest that they want *companions*; that being divided one in a Room they are not able to perform ye Ceremonies of it. Nay ye very Pictures I lately purchas'd have caught ye Infection—They also are malecontents; calling out upon the Windows to afford them more Light, to which ye testy old windows reply with a Sarcasm, 'Plague not us with your continual teizings; we transmit Light enough for all *ordinary* occasions; & peradventure, if we transmit more, it will be only to discover ye Cracks & the Imperfections y^t are in y^e. Midst all this Hellish uproar, I walk contemplative; seldom uttering a syllable beside these 'Have *Patience* good People! Peradventure were I to satisfy all your Demands at *once*, I might ill afford to satisfy the Demands of Nature. Let your betters be serv'd first; you *also* in your turn shall find in me your most obsequious humble Servant & vassal.

Amidst all y^t has pass'd betwixt y^r Lasp and myself concerning Urns, I think you have never told me in direct terms y^t you like y^e *Execution* & y^e *situation* of y^{rs} I wou'd fain seduce you to say thus much.

I want also to be resolv'd whether it is your Opinion y^t I may appear at Barrels with an unembarass'd countenance, without ye green Book. What a deal of trouble has my foolish Vanity occasion'd you? for whether you esteem it a Piece of charitable complaisance to an idle writer to sollicit his performances, or whether you really *wish* to see them, in either Case my Proposal has occasion'd you more trouble than the trifles are worth. But my Promise I suppose I must perform; for shou'd *Complaisance* be your only motive in asking for them, I doubt I shall hardly persuade you to own so much. As for ye rest, I have almost *wrote* ye Book thro', but have neither Pencil, Colours nor Leisure, just at present, to add the little Sketches. When I say I have not Leisure, you will please to consider, I make it a point to be an Eye-witness of ev'ry alteration y^t is going forwards; & tho' it wou'd be more *agreeable* to me to be labouring for your Ladyship's Amusement I must attend my workmen whilst I have them; and I must have them if I wou'd be soon shut of them. I have said too much upon such a trifling matter. I fear you think so. Most sincerely do I lament ye Loss of ev'ry Flower that perishes unseen by you. I have two or three Peonies in my grove, y^t I have planted amongst Fern and brambles in a gloomy Place by ye Water's side. You will not easily conceive how good an Effect they produce, & how great a stress I lay upon them. I wou'd advise your Ladyship to plant many of them about *your* Grove, where, if I am not deceiv'd they wou'd appear surprizingly beautiful—Thus has my Pen run on 'till It has cover'd another Sheet; too carelessly I must own, for the Respect with which I shall ever remain, your Ladyship's most oblig'd & faithfull Servant,

W. SHENSTONE.

NOTES

[1]The letter as printed by Hull differs from the B.M. MS. verbally and in details. It ends at 'I send you the Plan: 'tis for a seat on the Bank above my Hermitage and will amount on a moderate Computation to the sum of fifteen Shillings.' The whole of the delightful postscript is omitted by Hull.

[2]Thomas Aris of Birmingham, bookseller, founded the first permanent Birmingham

newspaper, on November 6, 1741.—*The Birmingham Gazette, or the General Correspondent*.

³*Moral Essays*. Ep. I, Pt. II.

⁴In Dodsley's *Collection* IV, 345, and *A Description of The Leasowes*, Shenstone, *Works* II, 335, the poem consists of four verses, and shows verbal changes. Nor is either reading (i.e., the Dodsley versions mentioned above and the one sent to Lady Luxborough) quite like that given to Jago in the letter, p. 202.

⁵W.S. here glances at the posthumous quarrel between Bolingbroke and Pope, because the latter had caused to be printed *The Patriot King* without the former's knowledge. Lady Luxborough's comment on the affair is found in *Letters*, 104, 105. The year 1749 saw the issue of a flood of pamphlets from Bolingbroke and his supporters and from the supporters of Pope. The situation is described by I. D'Israeli, *Quarrels of Authors, Warburton, and his Quarrels, and Bolingbroke and Mallet's Posthumous Quarrels with Pope*.

Lord Bolingbroke's *Letters*: 1. *On the Spirit of Patriotism*, 2. *On the Idea of a Patriot King*, 3. *On the State of Parties at the Accession of George I*, were published in 1749.

LXXXIX

Works III, 176.

To a Friend [Rev. R. JAGO?], *disappointing him of a Visit*.

June, 1749.

Fie on Mr. N——! he has disappointed me of the most seasonable visit that heart could wish or desire.—My flowers in blossom, my walks newly cleaned, my neighbours invited, and I languishing for lack of your company! Mean time you are going to dance attendance on a courtier.—Would to God! he may disappoint *you*, according to the usual practice of those gentlemen;—I mean, by giving you a far better living than you ever expected.

I have no sooner *made* than I am ready to *recall* that wish, in order to substitute another in its place; which is, that you may rather squat yourself down upon a fat-goose living in Warwickshire, or one in Staffordshire, or perhaps Worcestershire, of the *same denomination*. I do not mention Shropshire, because I think I am more remote from the main body of that county than I am from either of the others. But, nevertheless, by all means wait on Mr. N——; shew him all respect, yet so as not to lay out any of the profits of your *contingent* living in a black velvet waistcoat and breeches to appear before him. True merit needeth nought of this. Besides, peradventure, you may not receive the first quarter's income of it this half year. He will probably do something for you one time or other; but you shall never go into Ireland, that is certain, for less than a deanry; not for less than the deanry of St. Patrick's,[1] if you take my advice. Lower your hopes only to advance your surprize; 'grata supervenient quae non sperabimus.'[2] Come to me *as you may*. A week is elapsed since you *began* to be detained; you may surely come over in a fortnight now at farthest;—I will be at home.—However, write directly; you know our letters are long upon their journey;—I expected you the beginning of every week, till I received your last letter, *impatiently*.

For my part, I begin to wean myself from all hopes and expectations whatever.—I feed my wild-ducks, and I water my carnations! Happy enough, if I could extinguish my ambition *quite*, or *indulge* (what I hope I feel in an equal degree) the desire of being something more beneficial in my sphere.— Perhaps some few other circumstances would want also to be adjusted.

I have just read Lord Bolingbroke's three letters, which I like as much as most pieces of politics I ever read. I admire, especially, the spirit of the style. I as much admire *at* the editor's unpopular preface.[3]—I know the family hitherto *seemed* to make it a point to conceal Pope's affair; and now, the editor, under Lord B's inspection, not only relates, but invites people to think the worst of it.—What *collateral* reasons my Lord may have for thinking ill of Mr. Pope, I cannot say; but surely it is not *political* to lessen a person's character that had done one so much honour.

I am, dear Sir,

Your affectionate

W. SHENSTONE.

I have this moment received a long letter from Lady Luxborough; and you are to look on all I said concerning both Lord Bolingbroke's affair and her resentment as premature. My Lady's daughter and son-in-law visit her next week.[4]

NOTES

[1]The reference is to the doubtful preferment which Swift got as Dean of St. Patrick's.
[2]Horace, *Epist*. I, 4, 14.
[3]Bolingbroke's 'three letters' were edited by David Mallet with a preface, and were

thought to have been written by him. In the preface he attacked the memory of Pope for having secretly printed the *Idea of the Patriot King* in 1738.

⁴Henrietta Knight, married Charles Wymondsold, May 7, 1748. She deserted her husband and married secondly the Hon. Josiah Child, second son of Lord Tylney, May 2, 1754. See *Gentleman's Magazine.* According to the tablet on the south wall of Wootton Wawen Church, Warwickshire, she married a third time, Count Duroure.

XC

Works III, 179.

To MR. JAGO.

From THE LEASOWS, *as it appears on a rainy Evening, June,* 1749.

Dear Sir,

It would probably be so long before you can receive this letter by the post, that I cannot think of subjecting my *thanks for your last*, or my *hopes of seeing you soon*, to *such* an *uncertainty.* —I shall not now have it in my power to meet you at Mr. Wren's *immediately*, so would lose no time in requesting your company here *next week*, if you please. I hope Mrs. Jago also will accompany you, and that you will set out the first day of the week, even Monday; that you may not leave me in less than six days time, under a pretence of necessity. As to the verses you were so kind to convey, I will take occasion when you come

—'To find out, like a friend,
'Something to blame, and mickle to commend.'

So I say no more at *present* on that head.

I love to *read* verses, but I *write* none, 'Petti, nihil me sicut ante juvat scribere!'¹ᵃ—I will not say *none;* for I wrote the following at breakfast yesterday, and they are all I have wrote since I saw you. They are now in one of the root-houses of Virgil's Grove, for the admonition of my good friends the vulgar; of whom I have multitudes every Sunday evening, and who very fortunately believe in fairies, and are no judges of poetry:

'Here in cool grot, and mossy cell,
'We tripping fawns and fairies dwell.

'Tho' rarely seen by mortal eye,
'Oft as the moon, ascended high,
'Darts thro' yon limes her quiv'ring beam,
'We frisk it near this crystal stream.

'Then fear to spoil these sacred bow'rs;
'Nor wound the shrubs, nor crop the flow'rs;
'So may your path with sweets abound!
'So may your couch with rest be crown'd!
'But ill-betide or nymph or swain,
'Who dares these hallow'd haunts profane.'

OBERON.

I suppose the rotund at Hagley is compleated, but I have not seen it hitherto; neither do I often journey or visit *any where*, except when a shrub or flower is upon the point of blossoming near my walks.—I forget one visit I lately made in my neighbourhood, to a young clergyman of taste and ingenuity. His name is Pixell,[1] he plays *finely* upon the violin, and very well upon the harpsichord: has set many things to music, some in the *soft* way, with which I was much delighted. He is young, and has time to improve himself. He gave me an opportunity of being acquainted with him by frequently visiting, and introducing company to, my walks.—I met him one morning with an Italian in my grove, and our acquaintance has been growing ever since.—He has a share in an estate that is near me, and lives there at present; but I doubt will not do so long;—when you come, I will send for him.—Have you read my Lord Bolingbroke's Essays on Patriotism, &c.? and have you read Merope?[2] and do you take in the *Magazin des Londres*?[3] and pray how does your garden flourish? I warrant, you do not yet know the difference betwixt a ranunculus and an anemone.—God help ye!—Come, to me, and be informed of the nature of all plants, 'from the cedar on Mount Lebanon to the hyssop that springeth out of the wall.'—Pray do not fail to decorate your new garden, whence you may transplant all kinds of flowers into your verses. If by chance you make a visit at I[cheneton] fifty years hence, from some distant part of England, shall you forget this little angle where you used to muse and sing?

'En unquam, &c.
'Post aliquot, tua regna videns mirabere, aristas.'[4]

I expect by the return of Tom to receive a trifle that will amuse you. It is a small seal of Vida's[5] head, given by Vertue[6] to a relation of mine, who published Vida, and introduced Vertue into business.—Perhaps you remember Mr. Tristram of Hampton, and the day we spent there from school; it was his.

I am, very cordially,
Yours,
W. SHENSTONE.

NOTES

[1a] Horace, *Epod.*, II.

[1] In Dodsley's *Collection* V, 83–4, a poem is headed, 'transcribed from the Rev. Mr. Pixell's parsonage garden near Birmingham, 1757.' '*A Collection of Songs with their Recitatives and Symphonies for the German Flute, Violins, etc. with a Thorough bass for the Harpsichord set to Music by Mr. Pixell*,' was published by Baskerville, 1759. Courtney, 119, gives a short account of the Rev. John Pixell.

[2] *Mérope*, a tragedy by Voltaire, appeared 1743. It was translated by John Theobald, 1744, and acted at Drury Lane, 1749.

[3] *The London Magazine*, or *Gentleman's Monthly Intelligencer* ran from April 1732 to December 1779.

[4] Virgil, *Eclogues* I, 70.

[5] Marcus Hieronymus Vida (c. 1485–1566), Bishop of Alba. His *Art of Poetry*, poem on Silk-worms, and *Game of Chess* were many times translated into English.

Johnson, in his life of Christopher Pitt, records, 'He probably about this time (i.e. 1725) translated "Vida's Art of Poetry," which Tristram's splendid edition had then made popular.' T. Tristram whose edition was published at Oxford in 1722 was a relation of Shenstone on his mother's side, for his maternal grandmother was Maria, daughter of William Tristram of Old Swinford. She died on July 21, 1729, and there is a monument to her memory in Hagley Church.

[6] George Vertue (1684–1756), engraver and antiquary. He had a less famous brother, an artist of Bath.

XCI

Works III, 183.

To the [REV. RICHARD JAGO].

1749.

Dear Sir,

It is now Sunday evening, and I have been exhibiting myself in my walks to no less than a hundred and fifty people, and that with no less state and vanity than a Turk in his seraglio.— I have *some* hopes of seeing you *this* week; but if these should happen to be frustrated, I shall find them revive with double ardour and vivacity the next. Did not you tell me of a treatise that your Mr. Miller had, where the author endeavours to vindicate and establish Gothic architecture? and does not the same man explain it also by draughts on copper plates? That very book, or rather the title and the author's name, I want.—— I shall never, I believe, be entirely partial to Goths or Vandals either; but I think, by the assistance of some such treatise, I could sketch out some charming Gothic temples and Gothic benches for garden-seats.——I do also esteem it extremely ridiculous to permit another person to design *for* you, when by sketching out your own plans you *appropriate* the merit of all you build, and feel a double pleasure from any praises which it receives.——I had here last Wednesday Dean Lyttelton, Mr. William Lyttelton,[1] Commodore West, Miss Lyttelton,[2] and Miss West.[3] They drank tea, and went round my walks, where they seemed astonished they had been so long ignorant of the beauties of the place; said, in general, every thing that was *complaisant* or *friendly*; and left me highly delighted with *their* visit, and with room to hope for many more. Mean time, why do not *you* come? I *do* say, you are not Pylades.[4]——What! you think, because you have an agreeable wife and five fine children, that you must employ all your time in caressing them at home, or laying schemes for their emolument abroad? Is this public spirit? is this virtue? or, if it be virtue, dost thou think because thou art *vartuous*, there must be no cakes and ale? is it not your duty to partake of them with a *friend* sometimes; easing and relieving him under what Boileau calls,

'Le penible fardeau de n'avoir rien a faire;'[5]

And what Pope (*stealing* from the former) denominates,

'The pains and penalties of idleness.'[6]

Pray come the first day of the week, and let Mr. Fancourt accompany you.——I have not much to add by way of news. The Duke of Somerset is going to lay out thirty thousand pounds upon Northumerland-house; nine houses to be purchased and pulled down on the other side the Strand for stables; the Strand there to be widened: I cannot tell you half; but one thing more I will, which is, that there will be a chapel on one side of the quadrangle, with a Gothic wainscot and cieling, and painted glass; and ☞ in it a Dutch stove, contrived so as to look like a tomb with an urn upon it.[7]

What need I *write* all this? am I not to see you in a few days? —Not a word more positively; saving what may serve to assure you that I am, dear Sir,

Inviolably yours,

W. Shenstone.

The Leasows,
    July 9, 1749.

NOTES

[1]Fifth son of Sir Thomas Lyttelton, afterwards Governor of South Carolina.

[2]Hester Lyttelton, youngest child of Sir Thomas, who spent most of her time at Hagley.

[3]The Wests, Gilbert, Molly and Temple, were cousins of the Lytteltons. See Wyndham, and Dickins and Stanton, *An Eighteenth Century Correspondence.*

[4]Orestes, son of Agamemnon and Clytæmnestra, fled to the court of Strophius after the murder of his father by his mother and Aegisthus. There he formed a romantic attachment for Pylades, and he and his friend returned to his former home where they slew his mother and Aegisthus.

[5]Boileau, *Epître* XI, 86.

[6]*The Dunciad* IV, 342.

[7]Lady Luxborough (*Letters*, 104) mentions the fact that she is sending to W.S. the letter from the Duchess of Somerset giving details of the improvements to Northumberland House. The letter is printed in Hull, I, 96: 'My Lord will do a good deal to the Front of the House, in order to make it appear less like a Prison; he builds a new Wing on the Right-hand Side of the Garden, which will contain a Library, Bed-Chamber, Dressing-Room, and a Waiting-Room. I think I told you, that all the Sashes, Doors, and Ceilings, in both Apartments, must be entirely new, and the Floors in my Lord's; the Stair-case is very noble, but will require as large a Lanthorn to light it, as that at Houghton, so much celebrated in the News-papers. The Chimney-Pieces in both Apartments are to be all new, and some of them very expensive; the Draughts are mighty pretty. My Lord's Bed on the Ground-Floor is crimson Damask, with Tapestry Hangings; the next Room is furnished with green Damask, on purpose to set off his Pictures; the next with a Set of very fine old Hangings of the Duke of Newcastle's Horsemanship, with his own Picture, on Horseback, as big as Life; and, now they are clean, looking neat, as when new. The Parlour to be hung with some very good Pictures; above Stairs, the great waiting Room, with Saxon green Cloth Chairs, with gilt Nails, and green Jute-string Window Curtains, marble Table, and large Glass between the Windows; first Drawing-Room, new crimson Damask, with Jute-string Window Curtains, two very fine Japan Tables and Glasses between the Windows, with carv'd and gilt Frames; inner Drawing-Room, Tapestry Hangings, with small Figures very pretty, and as fresh as new. He lays two Rooms together in the right Wing of the Court, on the ground Floor, in order to make a Chapel, with a Gothic Wainscot, Ceiling, and painted Windows; there is to be a Dutch Stove in it, which is so contrived, as to represent a Tomb with an Urn upon it. The Court is to be paved, and the Foot-Way altered; and my Lord is in Treaty for nine Houses on the other Side the Way, in order to pull them down and build Stables, (for there are none belonging to the House) whose Gates are intended to open directly over against those of the Court; if he can agree for this Purchase, he will widen the Street in that Part about eight Feet.'

XCII

B.M. Add. MSS. 28958.

[*To* Lady LUXBOROUGH.]

July ye 30*^{th}*, 1749.

THE LEASOWS.

Madam,

I will not interrupt your Ladyship's Amusement with a long Epistle at present: you are as I have some Reason to suppose, far more agreeably employ'd. Your improvements around Barrels are at this time giving a double satisfaction to a Person of your generous Sentiments, by pleasing *Those* whom you wou'd most desire they shou'd. Mr. Williams, who is a benevolent Man, & (as ye Scripture phrases it) *bringeth good Tidings*, made very honourable mention of your Appearance at Birmingham, with Mr. and Mrs. Wymondsold. What Pity it is, you did not surprize me then with a Coach & Six, fluster me for about two Hours, exhibit my little Ferme ornee & return? I do not mean by way of discharging ye visit which you are so kind to honour me with Periodically, about this time of ye year; but merely en passant & as a visit *par dessus*—My Gothick Building is now compleated; at least exhibits it's full effect; The Ground about it is turf'd but wants Rain; a new Path is made to it, I think, much for ye better; by ye Side of this Path is a little rock with a tree, y^t I think is picturesque. The Floor of it is pav'd Carpet-Fashion, with black and white Pebbles; &, considering how hastily I collected & dispos'd them, has a pretty good Effect. Pray, Madam, is ye Duchess's Carpet-Pavement famous? I mention it, because, having had a second Visit from ye Hagley-Family (Mrs. Pitt, Mrs. Granville, Miss Lytt: Com^{der} West. Mr. Lyttelton &c.)[1] at this very Place they us'd the words '*it is a perfect Somerset*. Now Miss Lyttelton had just before had a violent Fall; & I want sadly to know whether they alluded to y^t Fall or to ye Floor. I rather imagine it was ye Fall, for it happen'd to be a pretty extraordinary one. I shall now I fancy have many visits from y^t Family to *see* or to *shew* my little Improvements if I behave orderly and well. But I do not forget that it was your Ladyship commended *first*, & gave very liberal

Encomiums to my humble Territories, when as yet they had none given them—I am but just recover'd from a most violent Fit of ye Cholick; which was not tolerably subdu'd under many Days. It grew at last into an Inflammation, & I am even now taking Drops & Draughts in order to reduce the remaining Fever. But I now consider myself as *well*; & I now am impatient to see Barrels. Mr. and Miss Dolman tell me they are ready, & ask me to go with them.

> 'Accurs'd be he, Earl Douglas said,
> 'By whom this is deny'd—
>
> Chevy Chace.

Tom comes now merely to mention this and to enquire when it will be suitable to your Ladyship to receive us. The moment it is, we all set out, for about a couple of Days. I believe my Brother too intends it; so y^t if y^r Conflux of visitants be not yet over I *hope* & *beg* y^r Ladyship will make so free as to mention it. I said I wou'd not interrupt you by a long Letter, but I fear I have. I am therefore, in very *few*, but *sincere* Words, your Ladyship's most oblig'd & most obedient humble Servant.

WILL SHENSTONE.

Pray, my Lady, who is y^t *Warwickshire clergyman* that supplants me in my Province of *Elegy*, & addresses y^r Ladyship?[2]

NOTES

[1]The relationships of the group of men known as the 'Cobham Cousinhood' cannot be understood without reference to the family trees of the Grenvilles and the Lytteltons. See Dickins and Stanton, *An Eighteenth Century Correspondence*, 145–147. Hester Temple married Richard Grenville of Stowe, and became Viscountess Cobham. Her daughter Hester married William Pitt, Lord Chatham. Christian Temple, sister of the first Hester, married Sir Thomas Lyttelton of Hagley and had a large family of whom Mrs. Pitt (Christian Lyttelton, who married Thomas, elder brother of William Pitt, Earl of Chatham, at this time unmarried) and Mr. Lyttelton (probably William Lyttelton), were members. Mary, third daughter of Sir Richard Temple, married Dr. West. Between the Lytteltons, Grenvilles and Wests there was great intimacy.

[2]Lady Luxborough, *Letters*, 40, says 'the clergyman who has troubled the press with his Lamentations over Polyanthos's . . . is one Mr. Perks of Coughton.' She goes on to say that Parson Allen made a 'Dedication in imitation of the other.' *A Dedication of a Pastoral Elegy humbly imitated*, (*Mr. Perks's Dedication to Lady Luxborough, corrected by Parson Allen*), is included in Luxborough, *Letters*, 41. Her Ladyship admits that Parson Allen 'does not pretend to be a poet!'

XCIII

B.M. Add. MSS. 28958.

To LADY LUXBOROUGH.]

August ye 9th 1749.

Madam,

I believe I shall write very *incoherently*, but I flatter myself
it will be *some* satisfaction to your Ladyship to find I can write
at *all*; especially after an Illness which was sufficient to confine
me to my Bed when you was, amongst Strangers, in my
Dining-Room—My Disorder began on Sunday morning after
green tea, & as it continu'd ye whole Day & longer I was
advis'd towrds Night to put off ye visit by sending Tom on
Monday morning early; but having momentary Hopes of
it's *ceasing*, & imagining I cou'd not have Mr. Meredyth's
company upon any *other* Day, I chose to *take my Chance* of
being tolerably well ye next. Those Hopes, as it happen'd, were
not well grounded; but I have too much *conviction* of your
Ladyship's good sense, to imagine you will require an *Apology*
for Events y^t I cou'd not foresee; & for whatever might happen amiss in y^r Reception, that might be imputed *to such
Events* by a Person of Candour. I will then save myself & your
Ladyship ye trouble of *making* and of *reading One*; But I will
by no means forget to assure your Ladyship y^t I enjoy y^e
Honour of y^r Visit, *notwithstanding* what happen'd; & as to
the *Pleasure* & *satisfaction*, I find your Conversation, *that* I
shall always partake of with gratitude, whenever it is *allotted*
me; but must also submit to be depriv'd of, sometimes, as well
as to other Misfortunes—I am concern'd to hear of what you
suffer'd at Birmingham nor did I ever once dream of y^e
water's being ris'n. You had great good Fortune y^t you did not
take Cold, & indeed so had *I*; for it wou'd have given me
uneasiness, (tho' I were not faulty) in being accessary to a
Journey, the Pleasure of which to you wou'd have been so ill
able to ballance such an Inconvenience—I am greatly oblig'd
to your Ladyship for ye Verses you design'd me.[1] I am unable
at present to tell you my Sense of them in Poetry, but if I
may entertain your Ladyship with Honesty & Prose, y^e

P

unleaven'd Bread of Sincerity & Truth, I can conscienciously say, that I think them *good Lines*; & whether I am not like to be greatly affected by y^r *Compliments*, I leave your Ladyship to guess—*Mr.* Dolman came here yesterday; *Miss* Dolman was confin'd by her Servant—Maid's having ye Cholick; but will both of them wait upon you soon—And now let me speak to this Point—Immediately after you were gone my Disorder turn'd to ye Jaundice, which I find *they* make light off; but which I most earnestly long to see remov'd, being conscious y^t, upon its removal, I shou'd be perfectly well—But I fear it will not be so easily effected—However I feed myself with Hopes y^t we may all come to Barrels next week; I wou'd not have them go *without* me, for more Reasons y^n one; as I wou'd not lose the Pleasure of pointing out w^t I think Beauties there, & as I think they wou'd be apt, alone, to be too much upon ye Reserve. But I will write to your Ladyship again on Saturday— Your Ladyship did not see, it seems, my little Serpentine stream, that is pebbled—No great Beauty perhaps, but what introduces a variety into ye Walks—I shall, perhaps, if I get well & wait on you at Barrels, be tempted to beg ye Favour of a visit to repair my Loss of y^r Last—I long to know ye Particulars of y^r Introduction of ye Shrine for Venus, into y^r Pavilion—Is it a Semicircle in ye Middle of ye Back-wall— I beg my compliments to Mr. Hall, I hope he mentioned to y^r Ladyship y^t I press'd your stay as much as I thought consistent wth y^r *Freedom* of *Choice*; for it requires a particular Temper to be quite easy in a Sick House & if you cou'd not wave ye Fear of giving Trouble—at y^t Time (as you in justice might) I knew you wou'd not be easy—I can by no means think ye Living worth Mr. Hall's Acceptance—My Brother & Mr. Dolman desire their Compliments—They are just going to drink Tea at Ld Dudley's.

I am your Ladyship's most entirely oblig'd W.S.

NOTE

[1] The lines *Written at a Ferme Ornee, near Birmingham; August 7th,* 1749. Dodsley's *Collection* IV, 310.

XCIV

B.M. Add. MSS. 28958.

[*To* Lady LUXBOROUGH.]

THE LEASOWS, *August ye 13th* 1749.

Madam,

I defer'd writing 'till to-day, hopeing I might by this means be able to fix 'some time for our Visit on a less *precarious Footing*, than I cou'd *before*. But I cannot acquaint your Ladyship that my Health is yet confirm'd. Far from it. It is indeed tolerable; & *has* been since I wrote last; but there is not a Day passes in which I do not experience three or Four Returns of my former Complaint; short ones indeed, & not extremely painfull; but such as I cou'd not undergo without much *Regret* while I shou'd be enjoying your Company & your Improvements at Barrels. *This* I will promise your Ladyship that I will endeavour the more sollicitously to be well soon, that I may perform this Journey; but in ye mean Time having made that Resolution, it will be prudent for me not to think too much upon ye Subject; For y^t would render my intermediate confinement extremely tedious. . . . I have taken some Walks about my Farm and am not at all conscious y^t I have taken any Cold; but ye Disorder has not been yet thoroughly remov'd by Med'cines. If this proves a good week with me, I tell Mr. & Miss Dolman we will all set out to-morrow—that is monday—Sennight. In ye meantime if it prove less suitable to your Ladyship y^t we shou'd come then, we will depend upon your waving ye Visit with all Freedom.

I have had many messages to enquire after my Health; *Theirs*, who, I guessed, might really wish it, (amongst which I am convinc'd I may reckon your Ladyship's) I took extreme kindly. Poor Ambrose seem'd to be concern'd himself, & deliver'd his Message in a manner that became him. . . . Lord Dudley I believe wishes me very well, & has sent often. Sr Tho: Lyttelton sent his Gardener to-day on ye same Errand. Your Ladyship knows ye Fellow; my Brother has been taking him round my Walks, & ye poor Soul is extremely afflicted that he had not had ye disposal or laying out of every individual Place; He cou'd have done it to so much greater

Advantage! Is not this provoking? To have Lady Luxborough commend in *general*, to have her write very elegant Lines upon my Contrivances, and then to have them all aspers'd by a mere *watering*-pan! mangled by a mere Pruning-knife! Does not this exceed all Patience? Surely I shou'd think I did that Gardener Honour, if I suffer'd him to mark out yᵉ Figure of a sallad-Bed. But ever since he has been able to raise Orange-Gourds, fit to be tipt with silver & to make Punch-Ladles, he has been so vain there is no endureing him. Yet a Wind *may* come & destroy his Gourd, as it did yᵉ Prophet Jonah's very suddenly, & then witherewithall shall he pride himself?— This is mere Raillery, for I do not hate, I only laugh at him— He talks of getting Leave to come over to Barrels soon—I will now take my Leave, & write again to your Ladyship on Thursday next or Saturday.

I am your Ladyship's most oblig'd
& most obedient Servant,
W. SHENSTONE.

I fancy yᵉ new Mrs. Lyttelton[1] plays finely on yᵉ Harpsichord; They borrow mine in order to be ready for her, as soon as she comes down.

NOTE

[1]George Lyttelton married secondly, August 10, 1749, Elizabeth, eldest daughter of Sir Robert Rich, Bart. The marriage was unhappy. Elizabeth Rich was a great friend of Lucy Fortescue, George Lyttelton's first wife.

XCV

B.M. Add. MSS. 28958.

[*To* LADY LUXBOROUGH.]

THE LEASOWS, *Aug.* 20ᵗʰ 1749.

Madam,

I can say with a safe conscience that No one was ever more impatient to make a visit, than I am to wait upon your Ladyship at Barrels: At this time particularly, as I long to make my Acknowledgments for your *last* obliging condescension, to see yʳ various Improvements, & to shew Mr. Dolman the several Beauties and curiosities of yᵉ Place. But I am in yᵉ

Condition of a *Spring* y^t is push'd back, & ye more it is so, presses forward with ye greater Energy. I am this moment risen from my Bed, where I have lain down to remove a Fit of my Cholick with ye Assistance of White-wine Whey & Blankets. And this is ye means I've been forc'd to have recourse to every Day this week. For, if I escape a Fit all *other* Times of ye Day, I'm sure to be troubled with it about half an hour after Dinner. And yet ye Disorder is pretty soon over, & ye Pain not extremely violent. But what can I do? I dare not risque having a Return upon y^e *Road*, where I cannot apply to my usual Remedies. I must beg Leave to put off our Visit for a week longer, hoping I may by extraordinary Care be able to master my Complaint before that Time. And as this is ye real state of ye Case I will submit my Apology to your Ladyship upon this Issue.

I am at this instant as free from Pain as I hope *you* are; & if I had any Circumstance y^t I cou'd foresee wou'd amuse your Ladyship in a Letter. I cou'd write them down with Pleasure.

I am upon ye Search for a Motto to my Gothick Building, which I would have consist of a Stanza or two of old English Verse; & which I wou'd cause to be inscrib'd in old English Letters. I've been looking over Spenser, but cannot yet fix upon one to my Mind. Perhaps your Ladyship may chance to find one. I begin to prefer English Mottoes in general. There is scarce one Gentleman or Clergyman in Fifty y^t remembers anything of Classick Authors. But above all things, I long to have ye fine Compliment you pay me written by yourself upon one of my Skreens; You know it must be written by no *other* Hand; & if it might be, I'm sure I shou'd not chuse it shou'd.

I will not conclude without inculcating this necessary Assertion; That we all desire y^r Ladyship will not defer ye Reception of any Company you may expect, on our Accounts; I doubt our Propos'd visit, may have caus'd you to decline some Company already. I beg it may do so no more. We will come on any Day you fix when my Disorder leaves me. My Cholick has been very capricious, but *I* am, Madam,

> Your Ladyship's most constant &
> most oblig'd, W. SHENSTONE.

I hope you will please to excuse ye Liberty I take in permitting Tom to stay all Night at Barrels; I c^d not send him earlier *to-day*, & *to-morrow* he will be employ'd in Harvestwork—My Service to Mr. Hall.

XCVI

B.M. Add. MSS. 28958.

[*To* LADY LUXBOROUGH.]

August ye 30th 1749.

Madam,

Tho' I am always extremely delighted with an opportunity of hearing from Barrels, yet *now*, at ye Sight of your Ladyship's servant my Conscience flew in my Face, and reminded me of a neglect in writing which I know not how to excuse—you were pleas'd in your last Letter to allow me some Time for ye Payment of my visit, 'till my Health shou'd be confirm'd. This I thought a Liberty which in my present situation I ought not to disregard, & accordingly determin'd with what Patience I well cou'd, to defer my Journey, to another week. I shou'd have certainly inform'd you of this *to-morrow*, but have very little to say for not doing so on monday *last*. I have been now, many Days, without any considerable Pain. What I feel is generally about half an hour after dinner; some slight symptoms, which rather alarm than hurt me; and I believe I might next week be able to travel to Persia, with a provisionary Box of Pills, & with Liberty to eat & drink what I've a Mind: That is, I might eat *Rice*, I fancy, very safely, but I must beg to be excus'd as to drinking *Sherbett*.—When I said 'Liberty to eat what I've a Mind, I should rather have said 'Liberty to eat what I've *not* a Mind. I must give up Sauces & every thing that relishes; excepting only your Ladyship's Conversation, which being a Pleasure of ye Mind only, I may enjoy without Regret or Measure. And indeed as for eating, the Breast of a Partridge or a Barn-door Fowl are very pleasant Food, & neither of *these* is in ye least degree formidable—So that, on the whole, I cou'd with great Alacrity set forward on Monday for my *own* Part, but Mr. Dolman it seems goes then to Lichfield Races; & his Servant is now in the House in order to borrow my Horse. He has waited for me this Month, & wou'd hardly forgive me if I went to Barrels without him. The Delay however cannot be of long continuance, when Persons propose themselves so much Pleasure as we do from this Journey.

I take little Rides almost every Day & visit my next Neighbours. Yesterday I din'd with Lord Dudley by Invitation at a third Person's House; & the afternoon *before* I was at ye Grange. My Lord ask'd very kindly after your Health; & *wonder'd* you did not take a Bed at his House; upon which I took Care to deliver your Compliments.

I am oblig'd to your Ladyship for ye Eggs you sent me. I wou'd not eat one for the World; as I fancy I have some little Chance of raising a Breed from them. They shall be put under a Hen directly, who is to exert her Influence upon them, under ye Protection & *Auspices* of ye fortunate Mrs. Arnold.

I am glad to hear of every contrivance near y^r Hermitage that seems likely to tend to ye Hermitess's *Repose*.—I had just fix'd up ye Lines I enclose in my Gothick Building, when who shou'd arrive but Mr. Lyttelton, Mr. Pitt, & Mr. Miller. Twas impossible for me to conceal these, as I was oblig'd to accompany my Visitants all round my Walks. They happen'd to be much commended; all, except ye two first Lines of ye last Stanza; which I knew were flimzy, but which as I thought the auntient Guise might possibly excuse.[1] The Building itself escap'd full as well as I cou'd reasonably expect; & indeed *better*. Many Parts of my Farm were extravagantly commended, but the Grove especially. The poor Summer-House was, as it were ye Scape-Goat, which suffer'd for all the Blunders I had committed else-where. I believe y^r Ladyship is my witness that I thought it bad, & talk'd of pulling it down long ago— but many things may be said in behalf of *me* tho' not of *it*. I built it merely as a *Study*, without regarding it as an *object*; & at ye Time I built it had no Thoughts of laying out my Environs; that's one thing. another is, that I built it upon my *own* Land, & did not foresee a kind of Exchange (since made)

by means of wch I might have situated it better. The Road
now coming behind it, renders it intolerable—They spend an
afternoon here, with Mrs. Miller[2] & whom besides I know not,
perhaps tomorrow. But I will detain y^r Ladyship no longer
now; I will write again on Saturday. I have kept your Servant
long, & must conclude. I am whether in Haste or at Leisure,
invariably

your

your [sic] Ladyship's most oblig'd hum: Servt

W.S.

NOTES

[1]From Luxborough, *Letters* 119, 120, we learn that the version of 'Here in cool grot'
sent with this letter was the longer four-stanza version finally set up in the root-house, for
Lady Luxborough mentions 'Beechen-bowl' as occurring in the first line of the last
stanza (the portion of the poem to which George Lyttelton objected). Hence we gather
that the verses again underwent an alteration, for these words occur in none of the
published versions.

[2]Sanderson Miller of Radway married in 1746 Susannah, only daughter of Samuel
Trotman, Esq., of Shelswell, Oxfordshire. The marriage was ideally happy, and letters
to Miller from his friends the Lytteltons, and others, often make mention of 'your
sweet little woman.' Dickins and Stanton, *An Eighteenth Century Correspondence.*

XCVII

B.M. Add. MSS. 28958.

[*To* Lady LUXBOROUGH.]

Sunday,

The Leasows, *Septem; y^e* 10^*th* 1749.

Madam,

Being very uncertain whether this Letter will arrive before
it becomes *superfluous,* I will say nothing more than that Mr.
Dolman &c. are just gone from hence in their Return from
Lichfield Races; will Employ monday & tuesday in preparing
their Linnen; & will, with me, wait upon your Ladyship on
Wednesday next, some-time in ye Afternoon. I beg my
Compliments to any Friend to whom you have an *easy* oppor-

tunity of delivering them and am with sincere Respect your
Ladyship's

most oblig'd humble Servant,
WILL: SHENSTONE.

To
    The Right Honourable
       Lady Luxborough,
   at Barrels. To be left
wth Mr. Williams, & sent as soon
    as possible.

XCVIII

B.M. Add. MSS. 28958.

[*To* LADY LUXBOROUGH.]

THE LEASOWS, *Septr y^e* 12th 1749.

Madam,
    If my Letter had been sent yesterday by Mr. Williams, as
I hop'd it wou'd, I shou'd not have had altogether so much
Reason to accuse myself of Neglect, as I seem to have at present. *That* Letter your Servant has now in his Pocket, & I
chuse he shou'd take it if peradventure it may prove any kind
of Justification—Mr. Dolmans *Continuance* at Lichfield is
to be plac'd to ye Account of some near Relations which he has
there, & not of the Races only. But I hasten to repeat my
Promise that if there be no violent Rain we will be at Barrels
to-morrow in the Afternoon. I was by *Agreement* to be at
Broom to-night, and to set out from thence with them in y^e
morning, but I believe now I shall perform it all in one Day—
I will not trouble y^r Servant with Instructions concerning the
Turf-Seat.—If you have Roots enough, & will give Tom leave
when he comes with me to build himself such a *trophy* or two
at Barrels, he will do it with great *inward* Satisfaction. He is
my only Architect for this kind of work, & I think as *good*
and *safe* a one as I can discover else-where—Pray if you please,
detain Mr. Outing—but now I remember he doesn't propose

going 'till Thursday next—Since I wrote last I have din'd one
day at Hagley where I found Mr. Lyt. Mr. Pitt, & Mr.
Miller flown; The first of these being calld up to London on
Business. Mrs. Lyttelton I saw—Sr Thomas askd whether you
had seen ye Park this year, & I conceive, they wish you *had*.
Since that I took a Ride thither wth a neighb'ring Clergyman to see some things wch I never *had* seen before: The Cottage
for one. But chiefly an Adjacent Wood of theirs called Wich-
bury, which as much exceeds ye Park for Views, as Hare-
court Pump does the Streams of Aganippe—We were out for
about seven hours, dinnerless; & I came Home and eat too
much—Doesn't y^r Ladyship remember that my summer-
house *is* rendered of a Stone-colour & ye Roof like Slates? It
is. I am your Ladyship's

most oblig'd & obedient Servant,
WILL: SHENSTONE.

XCIX

B.M. Add. MSS. 28958.

[*To* LADY LUXBOROUGH.]

[*Early Oct.* 1749?]

Madam,[1]

A Person y^t has so little *Claim* to Ceremony as myself, may
well be suppos'd willing to lay but little Stress upon it; And
yet if it was any way instrumental in procuring me a more
speedy Letter from your Ladyship, I cannot say but it is an
Article to which I am greatly oblig'd. I convey'd ye Message
you were so good to send to Miss Dolman, yesterday, & will
make use of ye first opportunity she gives me to return her
Acknowledgments. We arriv'd safe at the Leasows something
after eight o'clock; having call'd to refresh ourselves at Shirley-
street,[2] and also deviated from our Road in order to take a view
of my Ld Archer's Obelisk. As to ye Deficiency of *Balls* I
believe I must give it up, *there*; because they cou'd not have
been distinguish'd from his Salon, in Case he had chose them.
Yet ye Obelisk continues to appear small to me, & I shou'd

think must do so, at ye Place from which it shou'd be seen. It has a good effect from some Lanes adjoining to ye Park, and it is no doubt capable of being made good use of, from ye Woods on each side his House. The Park itself seems as improveable as any Place I ever saw, & yields to Sr Thos Lyttelton's only in regard to ye Country round it, for I scarce remember any where such a Length of *even* Country as there is from Henley to my House. My Lord has a delightfull Valley, y^t runs crosswise, betwixt his House & his Obelisk with Water enough to be thrown into what shape he pleases. After observing thus much we proceeded forward, as I mean my Letter shall do. While I was enjoying your Ladyship's Improvements, I find my own were undermin'd at Home. I was oblig'd, you must know, to a Neighbour for a Path which led thro' another Coppice to mine. This I have often been within a guinea or two of agreeing to purchase, & as often promis'd y^t no Step shou'd be taken in regard to it without my knowledge. But ye Proprietor happening to live servant wth y^e *Parson of our Parish*, was advis'd, in my *Absence*, to stock up every Inch of it, & his Commands were obey'd so precisely when I came home, y^t ye Path was cover'd wth Roots & ye communication entirely obstructed. I believe I shall acquire a Path upon my own ground as good as that *was*, but nothing equal to what that might have been made at ye least expence imaginable. Had I been here when ye Fellow began, I cou'd have manifested it to be, and indeed have *made* it his Interest, to let ye Underwood remain. As it is, the Parson has renew'd his quarrel wth me which will probably last for Life; I am meditating Revenge on ye Persons y^t are engag'd in it; I have lost ye finest Opportunity of Improvement y^t ever Person had; & I shall never walk y^t way without ye disagreeable sense of Indignation[3]—You must not think I wou'd hereby intimate y^t I repent my Journey, for it was every way agreeable—& this had been done, I suppose, ye very first time I was absent— Mr. Outing let me into ye Secret concerning your intended Urn & I approve y^r Design extremely. The chief difficulty will be where to place it. The shape of ye Pedestal must be according to one of ye orders, Those must be chosen by ye Size of your Urn, & ye Size of your Urn adjusted by y^e

Place from whence it shou'd be view'd. I wou'd not have it
calculated to be seen from your Summer-house, & I wish you
may not hereafter imagine y^t Arbor too close a situation. I
raised two Pedestals for urns in my wood in much such Places,
but I afterwards dislik'd, & remov'd them. I will think about
it, & your Ladyship who thinks *better*, will consider of a
situation in ye mean Time—I *knew* y^t lowering your *walk*
to ye Pavilion w^d have ye Effect propos'd; but I wou'd willingly
have produc'd the same by a more sudden slope at ye End
y^t you might not seem to *descend*, so far as y^r walk continu'd;
but as your Ladyship says ye farther End is higher, you have
acted rightly. I wou'd have ye Instructions to y^r Joiner to be,
y^t he shou'd make ye Pediment as low as they ever *are* made,
in other terms, not different from what is practis'd. Quere as
to ye use of three neat urns in wood upon y^r Pediment. I have
no particular fondness for them but they wou'd *heighten*; &
please *most* Eyes. The Alteration at this End of your Shrubbery can be no otherwise than Right. If you have a mind to
have a small Passage there into your Garden you may crooken
a Path thro' ye Shrubs & so hide ye Gate. I shou'd be oblig'd
to your Ladyship if you cou'd learn what Books are useful for
young Beginners in Architecture. I have receiv'd Gibbs,[4]
which consists entirely of Plans, & supposes some previous
knowledge—I met my Lord Dudley yesterday going round my
Walks with his upper Servants, en famille, & I deliver'd him
your Compliments. He enquir'd, and was glad to hear of your
Health, Wou'd be glad of an opportunity to wait on you, but
could fix no Time.—I enclose to your Ladyship ye Product of
one Morning, & which may be rather call'd ye Sketch or Plan
of an Ode y^n an Ode itself. But if it expresses about a tenth
Part of what I think, & has any thing you do not disapprove in
y^e *Design* or *Manner*, I give it up as to Brilliancies; & may
correct it another Time, But till it *be* corrected you must give
no Copy. I hope as I know it will give you Pleasure, y^t Mrs.
Meredyth is arriv'd. Miss Meredyth will find out some large
Oak, in some retir'd corner where your Urn shou'd be Plac'd.
She will also sketch out upon Paper ye Effect it will produce.
But I wou'd caution your Ladyship to take Particular Care y^t
it be not done so agreeably as to make you like upon Paper

what you should not approve in ye Execution. You may jogg
her Hand (but don't say that I advis'd you) as she is drawing,
& by that means stand a better Chance of not being impos'd
upon *by* ye Delicacy of her Pencil—This Letter is already a
mere Rhapsody, and I can hardly render it less coherent let
me write how I will, & therefore What if you were to plant
here & there a Yew-tree in your Shrubbery to look wild & to
continue about ye size of your other Shrubs. Moreover as you
continue ye Terras on ye Side of y^r Shrubbery Wou'd not here
& there such a wild yew tree all along ye Side have a good
effect from y^r Bowling-green &c: One thing I believe you will
allow, that there shou'd be particular Care taken to vary y^e
Shrubs on y^t side so as to produce as strong a Contraste as
you can betwixt them; (Have you any Birch?) & I think y^e
Shrubbery in general shou'd be permitted to grow thicker—
You have this Advantage from ye Futility of my proposals y^t
you may entirely neglect them, & I not be displeas'd, which
your Ladyship knows is a greater Priviledge y^n *my* Criticks are
likely to allow me—

We were all extremely pleas'd & oblig'd by our Reception
at Barrels, & Miss Dolmans Scrawl appears to me too little
to contain a quarter of what she feels on y^t occasion—But my
own Letter is at least as much too long, especially as it has
expatiated on other subjects to ye neglect of that on which it
shou'd be most particular; I mean the sincerity with which I
am your Ladyship's most oblig'd & most obedient Servant,

W. SHENSTONE.

Upon revisal I am asham'd to send this stupid Letter; but
to write another, I must have waited 'till saturday. I beg my
compliments to Mr. Hall.

NOTES

[1]In the B.M. collection, this letter and the two following ones are placed at the end
because undated. Internal evidence connects the first two with the letter of October 18,
1749, where occurs the joke about Emme setting Birmingham on fire. The letters begin
with 'Madam,' and use 'cou'd' and 'wou'd,' all signs of early letters. Lady Luxborough's
letter of October 10, 1749, is a reply to this one.

[2]Apparently the Saracen's Head at Shirley-street was a usual stopping place on the
road to Barrels. Cf. Luxborough, *Letters*, 5. A Warwickshire friend writes: 'The word
"street" applied to non-Roman roads is very common about here. All the old people
call Ullenhall Village "Ownhall Street" to this day. Shirley is on the road between here
(i.e., Henley-in-Arden), and Birmingham. By "Shirley-street" Shenstone was indicating
Shirley Village as it was in his day: now it is really a suburb of Birmingham.'

[3]Shenstone's dislike for the 'parson of our Parish' seems to have been based on a certain amount of reason when we remember the story of him told post, 287.

Dr. Pynson Wilmot was appointed vicar of Halesowen, 1731.

[4]James Gibbs (1682–1754), architect, published several books on architecture. He designed the Radcliffe Library at Oxford, as well as other well-known places.

C

B.M. Add. MSS. 28958.

[*To* LADY LUXBOROUGH.]

THE LEASOWS. *October y^e* 18th 1749.

Madam,

Your Ladyship cant imagine how I scold at old Emme[1] for permitting Mr. Williams to say he has no Letter for me: And on Saturday Morning last, in case she did not succeed, I gave her positive orders to set fire to the Town of Birmingham. At last I *did* condescend to moderate my Injunctions, & consented that she shou'd only pull down *new*-street, the Square, & part of Temple-Row. As far as I can discover, she has not hitherto done it; so that it is in your Ladyship's Power to make ye Town appear worth saveing, if you will but throw half a Dozen Lines into it, of your own Hand-writing. It is not, I think, ye first Time that Cities have been spar'd, for the sake of some valuable manuscripts they contain'd. I forget the particular Instances, but I am sure there are *some*; especially when mighty Heroes, like me, have been concern'd. And why shou'd not I set as great a value upon what you write, which without a Compliment affords me more *interesting* Pleasure than the works of Homer or of Aristotle.

Now tho' I'm well enough convinc'd that *one* single Letter of your Ladyship's outweighs more than fifty of mine, yet I cannot avoid requesting that if ever hereafter you find me in ye least dilatory you woud admit, as Evidence in my Favour, this my present work of supererogation. And yet what shall it avail me, to have my *negligence* at one time contrasted with my over-*officiousness* at another. The truth is, I can neither deserve ye Favour of your Letters by *writing* or by *silence*; so, I am to impute it altogether to y^e *activity* of your Benevolence.

But as Sir John Falstaff says, 'he is not only witty in *himself*, but the cause that wit is in *other Men*;'[2] so your Ladyship is not only thus obliging *yourself*, but instrumental in causing your Friends & ye Persons I esteem, to make favourable mention of me. I here think of Mrs. Weymondsold; I must not forget Mrs. Davis.[3] Tis too obvious to mention the Duchess & I am indebted to you lately for an Instance of civility from my Lord Archer. I cannot repay you but in Proportion to a very limited sphere, & so far as that extends, I shall never be wanting.

I hope your Ladyship is now planting furiously; I do not mean *rashly* and indiscreetly, but diligently and judiciously. I applaud myself for ye little Hint I gave for ye Encrease of your Shrubbery, & The Sweep for ye Coach. I can see no Reason to doubt, of it's *Propriety*, or that it will afford you satisfaction, both which indeed are synonimous Expressions. I am sure you will acquaint me when your Urn & Pediment are compleated. Shall you have a glimpse of either while there is a yellow ling'ring Leaf upon ye Trees? For *my* Part, I cannot yet place Autumn upon a Footing with Spring; & I think ye Duchess of Somerset betray'd the cause she seem'd to defend by num-bering the melancholy objects that season introduces. At least fifty Persons to one wou'd reckon *that* a disadvantage. And yet certain it is, that Melancholy has and ever had its charms for Persons of y^e *finest Taste*. Shakespear observes it[4]—I wish you don't say that *I* too, by this last Sentence, have betray'd the cause I was seemingly defending; Be that as it will, I believe I shall venture to print my Madrigal[5] on that occasion in some future Magazine of *this year*; least by appearing *afterwards* it shou'd grow *many* degrees inferiour to a last year's Almanack.

I enclose a Letter from Mr. Whistler, ye only one I've receiv'd from him for above this half year.[6] I began indeed to grow a little jealous that his Affection was going 'to sicken & decay'[7] but I find I have no Reason, if I may judge by his Letter; wherein he treats me with abundant partiality accord-ing to Custom. Your Ladyship I hope will excuse my com-munication of it.

I am, as often as my servants have Leisure, employ'd in extending my Path, so that it will now in a short time lead round my whole Farm, &, if I be not mistaken, furnish out a *variety* of scene in Proportion to its Length.

I think yᵉ Welchmen usd to drink Sir Watkin's⁸ Health, 'for *ever and two-Dey:*' I wish your Ladyship's as long, and am with like Attachment.

Your Ladyship's most oblig'd,
& most obedient Servant
WILL. SHENSTONE.

Is it contrary to yᵉ
Rules, pray to desire my
Compliments to Mrs. and Miss
Meredyths, if they are
with you? If so, I submit.

NOTES

[1]Emma Scudamore, 'Postwoman' at Halesowen, as a note at the bottom of MS. says.

[2]*II Henry IV*, Act I, Sc. 2.

[3]Mrs. Davies of Stratford-on-Avon, a friend of Lady Luxborough and a constant visitor at her house. In the Victoria and Albert Museum (Forster Collection, No. 5012) is a copy of *The School-Mistress*, 1742, and *The Judgment of Hercules*, 1741. The inscription is as follows : 'To the aimiable [sic] Mrs. Davies, from her ever faithfull votary Will Shenstone. The Leasows, Sept. 2nd, 1752.'

[4]W.S. was probably thinking of Jaques, who liked melancholy 'better than laughing.'

[5]Lady Luxborough's Letter XXXV, and the letter which follows this one, make it clear that the madrigal here mentioned is *An Irregular Ode after Sickness*, 1749. *Works* I, 137.

[6]Probably that of October 7, 1749. Hull, I, 102.

[7]*Julius Caesar*, III, 2.
'When love begins to sicken and decay,
It useth an enforced ceremony.'

[8]See 242 and 245 note 2.

CI

B.M. Add. MSS. 28958.

[*To* LADY LUXBOROUGH.]

Friday Morning 5 o'clock.
[*Late Oct.*, 1749?]

Madam,
Yesterday prov'd so extremely fortunate on Account of Amusements sent me, Compliments paid me, Friendship

shewn me, & Honours done me, y^t I think I ought to give it a red Letter in y^e *Calendar* of my *Life*. Your Ladyship's Packet wanted nothing to compleat my happiness, when presently arrives old Emme with a Cargo of new Books & Pamphletts; sufficient of *themselves* to support my Spirits many Days. In short I was so *glad*, and so eager to write, that I cou'd not write *at all*. Accordingly I ordered some *Tinder* & *Matches* to my Bedside & resolv'd to wake early & write this morning, And this is what I am now doing. Your Ladyships obliging Letter, which shews y^t you have remember'd me at so many distinct Periods,[1] has made me ample Amends for ye Doubts I have undergone by reason of y^r Silence. At last indeed comparing all circumstances, I began to take Heart, & by ye Assistance of a strong Belief persuaded myself you were gone into Cheshire. This I had no sooner done y^n Emme confirm'd me in the Opinion, by saying Mr. W.[2] did not know whether you were yet come Home. And now what Mischiefs may arise from a dilatory Conveyance of Letters! Miss Meredyth's *first* agreeable Sketch[3] did not arrive 'till last Night, when it ought to have done so on *Saturday*. On Saturday Emme had issu'd forth tow'rds Birmingham full Fraught with Tinder-box, Matches, & Indignation! Desperate indeed had been ye Case of y^t poor devoted Town, had not Mr. Williams by his mild Demeanour & and [sic] affable Deportment first cheated her of Resentment, & then of her Combustibles! Telling her an idle Story as how her *Eyes* would be *sufficient* in case she kept her Resolution; But alas! she had no more *Inclination*, than her Eyes had *Power*, to destroy a Town where her Friend Williams resided, whom she calls ye pleasantest Spoken man in all the Waurld. So, in short, ye Town has held out, till now; and now seduc'd by y^r Ladyship & Miss Meredyth I have no more Inclination to fire it, y^n ye Person I employ. I shou'd express my Concern for y^r Ladyship's late Illness but y^t I feel it so much more agreeable to forget it, in order to enjoy ye Pleasure of your Recovery—As to those trifling Verses you commend, I do not intend to alter above half a dozen words: For Instance *Rage* instead of *wrath* in ye last stanza, then *blame* instead of *Rage*. Bewail *for ever* instead of *incessant*, as giving a better *flow* & so forth; and then to *add* about 4 lines in regard

Q

to this very Urn you are erecting[4]—Mr. Whistler is a sincer
and generous Hearted Man—He will not come here till I'v
been at Whitchurch; but when He does, his greatest Pleasur
will be to wait on your Ladyship—I am oblig'd to your Ladys
for ye Book of Architecture;[5] shall pry a little into it, but sha
be glad to hear of some modern Book or Book more generall
us'd in ye same Way.—I hope to manage it so y^t you may no
regret My Parson's Barbarity, especially as you never saw w
that Coppice *might* have produc'd—I *never* wa*n*t Inducement
to come over to Barrels, I'm sure I see *Abundance* at *present*
If I have ye Happiness (as I am not without some Hopes
shall) to come while those Ladies are there, I must either giv
up my Dislike to Autumn, or you must allow me a Distinctio
betwixt Autumn at Barrels, & Autumn at ye Leasows. Thi:
you very well may, & in Return I will proclaim *your Lady
ship's* Autumn to be Finest of all Seasons. Indeed my Verdic
is only *special* in regard to my *own* Country. I only say 'tis
melancholy season. There is Room for much *Debate* upon y
Pains or Pleasures of melancholy, *afterwards*. I remember y
Sketch in Watteau. Tis no disadvantage to Miss Meredyth:
Copy y^t 'tisn't finish'd. Tis perfect in its *kind*. I mean as a
Sketch. Tis what all must allow to be natural and affecting.
I am highly oblig'd to ye Ladies for their Compliments, as
these give me an opportunity of presenting Mine, and wishing
them a Series of Fine Weather at Barrels—They will want
nothing else—My Brother is from Home—I caus'd your
Servant to see Ld Dudley's Green-house & to present y^r
Compliments. He *saw* ye Pine-apples too, I suppose. Mr.
Hall's Sermon[6] I will carefully return.

Addend. . . .

I believe *sacred* Things are often usd as a cover for Pro-
faneness; Mr. Hall will excuse me, if, for once, I make mention of *secular* or *profane* Things, upon a Cover for *sacred*.

The Book you lent me treats of ye very Points I want to
know; & *may* be very *accurate*, but ye Figures in ye Divisions
are so small, & ye Style in some Places so obscure, y^t I cannot
help wishing for a better—Nevertheless wth y^r Ladyship's
Leave I will keep this something longer.

I am in y^r Ladyship's Mind concerning Gibb's. One time or other I will *change* y^t Book. I like but few Things in't. The Front of Prior's House is *one*. Colstone's Monument *another*; an Urn or two, a Garden Building or two, & some Pedestals for Busts, that's all[7]—An *Altar* had formd a *disproportionate* Pedestal. Otherwise y^r Ladsp's Scheme of an altar to *Friendship*, wth Mr. Somervile's Urn upon it had been genteel.

To the Rt. Honourable
Lady Luxborough.

NOTES

[1]Luxborough, *Letters*, XXXV.

[2]Probably Mr. W(illiams), painter, of Birmingham, where letters for The Leasowes were left.

[3]Miss Patty Meredith had sketched an urn, which Lady Luxborough (*Letters*, XXXV), enclosed for W.S. to see. Her ladyship proposed to raise an urn at Barrels to the memory of William Somervile.

[4]The poem, *Works* I, 137, shows the alterations suggested here, but apparently the lines dealing with the urn were never added.

[5]Lady Luxborough (*Letters*, 130) had sent W.S. a book on Architecture, 'the only one I have that teaches the rudiments of that science. Worse print or worse paper you never saw! It cost me five shillings at one of Osborne's sales, thirteen years ago.'

[6]Mr. Hall's Assize sermon. Luxborough, *Letters*, 136.

[7]The reference is to James Gibbs's *Book of Architecture, containing Designs of Buildings and Ornaments*, 1728.

CII

B.M. Add. MSS. 28958.

[*To* LADY LUXBOROUGH.]

[*Oct.* 1749?]

Madam,

Your Ladyship will please to observe y^t ye remaining Part of my Letter will relate solely to ye Improvements you propose; & that if I seem to express my self *authoritatively*, I do it merely for ye sake of Brevity & not thro' any Presumption y^t my Opinions are *conclusive*. *Apruptly* therefore, *Balls* will suit ye Simplicity of your Dorick Building better than *Urns*, & will come five times Cheaper—As to ye Urn you intend to Mr. Somerville, I have a great deal to say. The shape of ye antique one you propose is not amiss, the *Antiquity* is certainly an

Advantageous Circumstance;[1] Nevertheless My Eye seems t
require y^t The lower Part of ye Urn shou'd be some thin
fuller. However, I send your Ladsp (what they send *me* fo
'Gibbs Book of Architecture' where you may find a Number c
Urns which may either tend to alter your Choice, or to confirn
you in it. There are few pretty ones. The first of Page ye 14
seems to me as good as *any*. How can Mr. Hands[2] dream c
twenty Inches for ye Height of your Pedestal? 'Twill be
mere *Daading*: Mr. Holyoak will not fail to call it a Child'
Play-gawd. It must be at least as big as the Lesser ones a
Hagley in ye whole; and as to proportioning ye height of y
Pedestal you may have either ye taller *Corinthian* Pedestal, o
ye lower *Ionick*. *That* will depend upon ye Place from whenc
tis to be view'd. One thing I believe is certain, that to loo
down much upon Urn or Pedestal will produce a bad Effec
—Wood is I find as dear as Stone; Stone in this Case is greatl
preferable—I beg Leave to hesitate as to an *Altar*-Pedestal. I
it *proper*, considering y^e *different* $\frac{\text{Intent}}{\text{use}}$ of Altars and Urns
Is it ever *done*? If you are satisfy'd in the *Affirmative*, yet un
doubtedly Mr. Williams's Notion is just, y^t y^e Altar shou'
be square; and that, for y^e Reason he gives. *His* Altar is
think genteel—but it must have *Authority*; for if it be not
true *antient* Altar, it is *nothing*; As Altars are *particular* Kin
of Things, & we have no *modern* Originals. As to his Manage
ment of ye Lyre and Wreath, I don't admire it; much less Mr
Hands's Scheme, to have *Four* Lyres, which wou'd introduc
much *Formality* & *sameness*, at as large an expence as migh
introduce *variety*—I wou'd by all means chuse to have tw
Festoons, join'd together by flourish'd Knotts, surround y
Body of ye Urn. *From* these Knotts should depend, on *on*
side a Lyre, *obliquely*; & on y^e *other*, the old Roman Reeds
I wou'd not have *more* Instruments y^n one in a Place. Th
Garland pendent betwixt these Knotts &c: will be ornamen
enough for ye two remaining Sides—I will venture to add m
Thoughts here as to ye Inscription. There shou'd be one I thinl
on *one* side ye Pedestal, expressive of his Character by a few
Epithets; and as short as possible. After wch what if you were
to put 'HIS SALTEM! which I shou'd imagine, wou'd suggest

ough to any *classical* Reader. On some *other* side of ye edestal I wou'd have a chosen Motto. Such as This—

> Postquam *Te* Fata tulerunt,
> Ipse Pales agros, atque Ipse reliquit Apollo![3]

or I think it a *prime* good one, & what I wou'd use myself pon Occasion—And now am I come by slow Degrees to peak to ye Article of a *Place* for this Urn; of which I can say othing, unless I were upon ye Spot. Tis ye nicest Thing in ye orld to place an Urn judiciously, so y^t it may have as solemn n Effect as possible; be seen at a proper distance; & have just cenery enough around it to make ye whole picturesque. And et as difficult as it is, if your Ladyship will accept of my *im- licit* approbation, I will very readily give it you in Favour of e Place Miss Meredyth proposes; only ye Urn must *not* ppear in a *direct Line* with ye Tree, if you please. I thought I vas well acquainted with all your Environs but I am surpriz- ngly at a Loss in regard to y^r Sketch. I forget ye Steps, The Villows, the Tree &c. I believe I shall entirely approve of *lopeing* ye Precipice—only leaving a small Part perpendicular t Bottom by way of *Fence*, & no where *visible*—I can say othing more particular on this occasion—only y^t ye Place for r Urn is certainly *thereabouts*—Let Mr. Williams finish his Piece; give his Urn a little-bolder Relievo; try ye Effect of a yre & Festoons *as above*; bring a little Water before ye Urn from left to Right, which then may turn & lose itself mongst ye Trees. Then insert ye Inscription & Motto legibly —I fancy this wou'd render it no unaimiable Picture. I am our

Ladyship's most oblig'd

W. SHENSTONE.

NOTES

[1] The urn which Lady Luxborough proposed, she 'drew from a little pair the Duchess of Somerset turned for me in wood, from an Antique urn the Countess of Pomfret brought her from Italy.' Luxborough, *Letters*, 131.

[2] A joiner at Warwick. Luxborough, *Letters*, 130.

[3] Virgil. *Eclogues* V, 34, 35.

CIII

B.M. Add. MSS. 28958.

[*To* LADY LUXBOROUGH.]

THE LEASOWS, *Nov.* *y.* 13^{*th*} 1749.

Madam,

I can assure your Ladyship that Emme (Skudamore) receives *her* share of ye Pleasure you give by your Letters; All the Difference is, that she is never *more* happy, & I am never so *much* so as when she brings me a good Sizeable Packet from her Friend, Mr. Williams. This Pleasure of her's is not vulgar; since I pay her irregularly and in the Lump; at what Intervals I think proper. Nor was it in ye least *her* Fault, that I did not receive your last Letter 'till late on saturday; whereas your Ladyship expected I shou'd have answer'd it that very Day. What then remain'd for me but to fulfill your Commands as punctually as I *cou'd*, tho' not as I cou'd *wish*. In order thereto, I sent a Carpenter this Morning to take ye Dimensions of the Urns &c. at Hagley; and these you will find amongst the Draughts I send (No. 11) The lesser I suppose will be sufficient for your *Area*, and the *Distance* from whence you are to view ye Urn. I like y^e *Ionick* best of any Pedestal; & shou'd do so, even if it were to seen from *level* ground; but if you place your Pedestal *below* the Eye, I think it will be out of all *Doubt* that you shou'd chuse *no lower order*.

I have no other quere to make as to ye situation you propose, than *this*; viz. whether you shall have Area enough round ye bottom of your Pedestal for y^e *situation* to seem *natural* & *easy*. If so, I believe it will be a *good* one, tho' I hope to see it before your Urn is erected.

Soon after I wrote last, I was endeavouring to make y^e *Lyre* depend from ye Knott in a tolerable easy Manner; but was not able to please *myself* in y^t respect. Miss Meredyth I'm sure has candour enough to pardon me, when I own I am not entirely satisfy'd with ye Manner in which *she* has connected it. At the same Time, I am somewhat doubtfull, whether a *profest* Carver cou'd adjust this matter gracefully. At *best*, here is a Difficulty which your Ladyship mentions, & which was in some measure aware of *before*, & this concerns the *projection* of the lower Part of the Lyre. All I can say is this, that if it *does* project, it must project so much (your Urn being small *downwards*) that it will injure ye Appearance of ye Urn from two remaining sides; And if it *bends with* the *Urn*, it will be strangely unnatural. Perhaps your Ladyship will ask the Carver's opinion here. This Consideration occasion'd me (while the Man was measuring ye Urns at Hagley) to *try Fancies;* in order to discover whether you cou'd not introduce some of y^e *Poetical Attributes* to advantage on the *Pedestal.* The Result of which, I send your Ladyship in these three or four Sketches. You will please to observe that the *Ionick* Proportion is not observ'd very accurately in any of the Pedestals except Number V. And *even there*, not so in regard to y^e *smaller members* of *Base* & *Capital.* And yet I believe the Plinth, ye Base, the Shaft, & the Capital are each of a Proper Height, so y^t you see the Figure of ye Ionick Pedestal in *general.* I will now speak a word concerning each Number.

No. I. I think the Oval wreath, manag'd in this manner, has a good effect within y^e *oblong square;* and furnishes out an agreeable ornament for *one* side of your Pedestal. If you think so too, the Quere then will be whether you like some such Festoon as this on ye same side of Urn, over it, or whether you wou'd not prefer ye antient

Pipe & Fistula

as being properly exhibited together or at ye same time with ye wreath below, & yet affording more variety y^n ye Festoon here express'd.

No. II. If your Ladyship shou'd be inclin'd to give up the *surrounding Festoon* upon ye Urn & take ye Pipe &c: you will want something by way of Ballance on ye opposite side, for wch Reason I have sketch'd out another sort of one upon ye Urn, & have shewn you the Effect of a Lyre upon the Pedestal. At ye same Time I own y^t the Lyre on ye Pedestal *here* gives it too *considerable* an Air in proportion to the Urn; wch ought certainly to appear as principal.

No. III. If the Lyre was too considerable *alone* on ye former Pedestal, you will have more just objections to this; so I say no more about it. As to the Festoons *round* the Urns, I speak *once for all*, that I prefer *natural Flowers*, & did not mean anything else, even in No. I. tho I scrawled over those others for Quickness.

No. IV. This may only serve to add to your choice; and y^t but little truly.

No. V. I believe you will like ye Proportion of this Pedestal; which, as I said before, may be right in *general*, (unless your Author deceives me.) The *Neck* or Part y^t comes betwixt y^e *Plinth* & the *Urn* is at *best*, I suppose, a *modernism*, and must not be allow'd you. I sketch'd it for variety. The Ornament upon ye Urn here I like a good deal; only it shou'd be somewhat *higher* on ye Body of it. Quere, whether this Ornament on ye Urn & a Lyre on ye Pedestal (of but low *Relieve*) woud not furnish out one handsome Side? And then ye Laurel wreath on ye Pedestal of No. I. and the slight Festoon on ye Urn of No. II, to decorate ye Pedestal and the Urn for another View. N.B. This supposes your Views to be opposite.

As to what I call y^e *Necks* (for want of a better word) I can only wish you not to have them too *thick*; & I suppose both the *Urns* and *they* may be shap'd at Discretion. You lose some *relative* Beauty by receding occasionally from ye Antients, but you often gain some *absolute* Beauty by so doing. Thus have I finish'd a tedious *Comment* on a very stupid *Performance*; enough to make you all wish me hanging by the string on which I said the *Harp* shoud Hang; but if your Ladyship can glean any thing from w^t Ive been *saying* or *drawing*, I beg you wou'd apply it as you please. Compound, separate, transform the particular Parts & decorations as you think fit. I have no Fame in Building, at *present* to lose; And I wou'd give all I shall ever *acquire* to see this Urn both plan'd & situated so as to appear very *solemn* & venerable; infusing an agreeable Melancholy into all Bosoms y^t respected Mr. Somerville.

I hope Tom will arrive before Mrs. Meredyth's Departure from Barrels. I imagin'd their stay at Barrels had been longer,

& then I propos'd to myself ye Pleasure of seeing them. I am
not *contented* in this Disappointment; & yet I believe I *ought*;
For I have an *Inklin* yt your Ladyship has set me in a better
Light, than my Conversation can ever answer. However if
your Ladyship be so kind as to inform me when they come *next*,
I will most eagerly risque any Disadvantage of *that* kind, to
enjoy a Pleasure which will so amply ballance it. Methinks
this last Sentence looks some how faint & languid, & to express but half my sentiments Your Ladyship however will
witness for me, yt I esteem no one but on account of *Taste*
& *Generosity* of Temper, & will on yt account vindicate my
Sincerity when I desire my *best Respects* to Mrs. & Miss
Meredyths. I am to thank Miss Harriet for demolishing ye
Precipice by ye Pitt side, & converting it into a Slope, which,
(as I *conceive* it,) is ye very thing Ive been labouring at ever
since I knew Barrels. I am to thank Miss Patty for ye little
Boy from *Watteau*; who, this minute, peeps at me over my
Chimney-Glass, and looks exceeding archly—Please, my Lady,
to give my Service to Mr. Outing if he comes, & tell him he
neither visits me, nor gives me his Reasons—I'm oblig'd to
your Ladyship for ye sight of Mr. Hall's Sermon: He applies
many scripture Phrases very spirituously—Lord Dudley is
gone this Day to London; call'd up I believe very suddenly;
but on what Account, I cannot penetrate;[1] tho' I sate up with
him on Friday night last to an Hour wn many Hearts are open
—I conceive the Mechanick Part of Architecture to be a
science easily acquir'd; & that a tolerable good *native* Taste is
generally what gives ye *Distinction*—Old Pedley[2] is hewing
me two small Gothick Turrets for my building—He desires
me to mention him to your Ladyship; says he has workd you
some Urns formerly & shou'd be glad to serve you hereafter.
He is an honest man, will be *glad* to work *cheap*, & as to ye
manual operation, I fancy works very well—I have made two
little Islands in ye stream that runs thro Virgil's Grove; The
stream appears considerably larger, & ye *ground* is mended. I
will not give my Opinion of these Alterations *yet*—I have
procur'd some charming Sans-pareille, with a Cargo of
exquisite Havannah from London. As Cibber says *moderate
matters* in ye Country, serve for one's Amusement![3]

I have taken you too long from ye conversation of your
Visitants, when every minute is valuable.

I desire to be always esteemed

Your Ladyship's most oblig'd

& most obedient humble Servt

I sent a servant,   W. SHENSTONE.
because you desir'd to
have ye dimensions of y^e
Urns before Mrs. Meredyth left
Barrels.

Before I receiv'd your Ladyship's last Letter I had been
scrawling upon Paper those small draughts that are marked
No. I. II. III.

No. I. I have some little Fondness for ye surrounding wreath
with 4 Knotts—as I think the Urn shou'd have *some* Decoration where ye Pedestal has any; And this wreath with 4 Knotts,
instead of two, produces as little Irregularity as any thing—
But after all, you like a plain Urn best; and a plain one no
doubt will have ye best effect at a distance.

No. II. A Whim merely! And yet I think A French Horn
wreath'd with Laurel (in Allusion to ye Chace) wou'd be y^e
properest decoration in ye World for Mr. Somerville. But As I
cou'd not manage it so as to *look well* I dropt *that*, & give up
this.

No. III. I doubt this decoration upon ye Urn wou'd project
so much as to be disagreeable on y^e *other* sides; even tho' you
shou'd like it on *this*. I have also drawn it much too large.
Quere whether the Tibia &c: are ever carv'd wth out any *support*; but I believe they are—not to represent ye things themselves, but ye carving of an Urn.

After I receiv'd y^r Letter I drew

No. IV. & No. V.

No. IV. is I think a neat Urn, & I am much mistaken if you
do not approve of that ornament on ye Pedestal. I added
Flutes *here*, for a Reason before mention'd, (viz.) y^t ye Eye
seems to require some ornament on ye Urn where there is some
on ye Pedestal. And the ornaments here will happen at proper
distances.

No. V. As I rather concluded from y^r Letter y^t you wou'd chuse this very kind of Urn, I drew it with some w^t more Attention y^n ye rest. The Urn itself is I think well proportion'd and ye Pedestal *pretty* exact according to your Friend Scammozi.[4] Yet perhaps ye modern Practice may somewhat vary, & ye Pedestal may very safely, (& usually is) left to ye Workman. If Mr. Hands supervises it, it will be right. His Calculation is so, & what makes ye difference at Hagley is ye superior Height of a *Strawberry* to y^e *Ball* wch we propose: and tis better—Y^r Ladyship must yourself determine whether you like y^e *double* Plinth above ye Pedestal wch raises y^r Urn about two Inches & half. I us'd it on *mine*, & am glad I did; tho it is not so at Hagley. It must be considered y^t my situation is extremely low, & y^{rs} will be upon ground y^t rises gradually— I believe I shall like it *there too*, but you may take Mr. Hands's Opinion when he comes—Most of y^e Bodies of y^e Urns I draw are *seven* Parts at broadest an eight Parts in Height. This, (No. V.) for Instance is meant to be 21 Inches broad, & 24 high.

Theirs are as No^s II. & III.

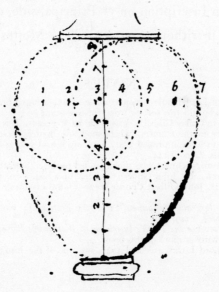

I am oblig'd to you for y^e sight of y^r Urn, wch with y^r Alteration of a proportionably thicker Foot & Cap will be pretty near alike to this (No. V.) I fancy. I took y^e Liberty to set a *good* Joyner to copy it which he has done, very indifferently. Two of them make me top-ornaments for a triflingly small cabinet wch you may remember in my Room—I lead an extreme dull Life this Time of ye Year, & am forc'd to indulge myself with continual Amusements from ye Bookseller. If I live to grow very old (wch I know I shant) I will have no other Bill. The Books I have *now* sent for are 'The Life of Socrates,[5] and The Theory of agreeable Sensations lately publish'd;[6] together wth Langley's Book with ye quaint Title of 'Y^e Builder's Jewell'[7]—Has your Ladyship ever seen or do you care to see the genuine tryal of my Lord Lovat[8]—In my opinion tis well worth reading. Poor old Lovat seems to represent Sr John Falstaff as well as Quin ever did. Tis a pamphlett, but an half guinea one—& I can lend it you as well as not.— I desire my Compliments to Mr. Allen and Mr. Hall hope to see y^r Ladyship at Barrels this Xmas entreat y^t you wou'd excuse this Scrawl, & am once more, your Ladyship's most

oblig'd &c:

N.B. a plain Inscription on y^e Principal side, only. Perhaps more in taste if without even $\frac{\text{Esq:}}{\text{Armigero.}}$ Mottos on the other sides.

NOTES

[1]For the reason of Lord Dudley's departure, see Luxborough, *Letters*, 167.

[2]A stonemason who did this sort of work for Shenstone.

[3]The Dedication to Colley Cibber's *Apology for his life*, reads, 'It is true I took advantage of your leisure in the country, where moderate matters serve for amusement.' The remark seems to have impressed Lady Luxborough as well as Shenstone, for she too quotes the words. *Letters*, 144.

[4]Vincenza Scammozi, architect, was much lauded in the eighteenth century.

[5]*The Life of Socrates.* By John Gilbert Cooper, Jun., Esq. 8 vo. 3s. 6d. *Gentleman's Magazine*, 1749, 528. John Gilbert Cooper (1723–1769), was a poet and miscellaneous writer.

[6]*The Theory of Agreeable Sensations.* From the French, 12 mo., 28s. 6d. Owen. *Gentleman's Magazine*, 1749, 528.

[7]*The Builder's Jewel or the Youth's Instructor & Workman's Remembrancer*. London 1741. There were many editions of this book.

[8]Simon Fraser, Lord Lovat, executed 1747, was one of the instigators of the 1745 Rebellion.

CIV

B.M. Add. MSS. 28958.

[*To* LADY LUXBOROUGH.]

THE LEASOWS *Novr* 26. 1749.

Madam,

I have been of late so conversant with *Lists* & *Astragals;* *Plinths* & *Cymatia;* yt your Ladyship will have good Fortune if I entertain you with any thing besides. Yet of all ye Urns & Pedestals I have drawn within this Fortnight, I like none so well as ye sort you seem to prefer. The principal Debate I have with myself, is, how much or how little they shou'd be ornamented, & herein, (as different Tastes may be good in their kind) I think all persons yt build, shou'd allow something to their own natural Relish.

I like ye *situation* you propose for ye Urn extremely; at least I *remember* none so proper. The idea of *yt Place* has constantly occurr'd to me, as often as your urn was mention'd; and tho' I durst not be positive yt your Ladyship and your *ingenious visitants* might not possibly discover some one scene yt was preferable, yet I fancy most of my Letters of late must have glanc'd obliquely towards that very corner. I own I have also some partiality for this double Oak,[1] as the First time I saw Mr. Somerville at Barrels, I sate with him upon ye Bench yt is at ye Foot of it. How far this Partiality may depreciate my Decision, I must leave your Ladyship to determine. As to the management of this situation, ye secreteing ye Urn, ye distance it shou'd stand from ye Foot of ye Oak, & ye Breadth of ye Area that shou'd [sic] left around it, I will offer my futile opinion when I wait upon you at Barrels, which I trust will be, sometime, before your Urn can be compleated. Mean-time, I can see no Reason why it shou'd not produce a good Effect from *several* Points of View. For Instance, 'From ye Bottom of yr Service-walk & all along it, appearing hence in an open area slightly surrounded with a few trees & thickets:' From ye Coppice 'From ye Place where your Chairs are and where you propose a Root-house:' From some Part of ye tall Elm walk as one approaches ye House; And perhaps also, 'from some part of yr Shrubbery. All these, besides the near view, en passant, of yᵉ Front which you intend to ornament. Of these, the View from yᵉ Bottom of yᵉ Service-walk or Corner of your Garden, as far as I can recollect, will be by no means inferior to any of yᵉ Rest. Perhaps your Ladyship may be well *acquainted* with all these advantages, but I chose to enumerate them, because if your Urn is to be calculated for all these Points, it ought out of doubt to have no *considerable* irregularity. I am of opinion your Ladyship need not fear yᵉ *Laurel wreath* upon this Account; unless the *Relieve* be very high indeed, it will hardly be discover'd from any Part but where you wish it *shou'd*. My Reason is, that you effectually lose sight of yᵉ sides of a *square*, when you stand in Front of it; And tho a greater Projection may appear on them at some *considerable distance*, yet even *there* such a *slight* projection will scarce be seen at all. (The Case is otherwise with a Round of which you see one half.) If your Ladyship think so too, you may carve this wreath on yᵉ Pedestal very safely; If you think otherwise, you must either omit yᵉ Laurel wreath, or add some slight Festoon to ballance it. Or something

of this nature

(Mantling, I think they call it) may serve, which I shoud imagine must cost but a trifle. So much for yᵉ Pedestal. Only I must add yᵗ I blundered in respect of yᵉ Ionick order. The *Shaft* of *that* is nearly square. Tis yᵉ *Composit* you will find to answer your *Idea*; & if you direct yᵉ Workman to let yᵉ 60 *minutes* of his *model* stand for *Quarters-of-Inches*, it will produce you a Pedestal exactly similar to their smaller one at Hagley.

As to yᵉ Inscription, if your Ladyship prefer an *English* one, and cou'd find a Motto in Mr. Somerville's own Writings yᵗ was both good in *itself* and *applicable* to this Purpose (as you know Shakespeare's Pedestal is thus supply'd)² it wou'd have a double Beauty. If otherwise you make use of the *Latin* ones, The Inscription must also be in Latin *betwixt the Wreath*; The Motto 'His saltem' on yᵉ Plinth above it, and (to avoid an

improper Jumble) that of Postquam &c on yᵉ side of yᵉ
Pedestal yᵗ Fronts yᵉ Service Walk on yᵉ upper part of the
Shaft. It will also add something to yᵉ Beauty of this side—
And now for yᵉ Urn itself properly so call'd. Since I wrote
last I have discover'd a method of suspending yᵉ Fistula which
I believe your Ladyship will approve. And as you have no
Fondness for yᵉ *surrounding* wreath, you will probably think
this itself to be ornament sufficient. Tis better *not* to add yᵉ
Lyre here because the Carving of these alone may be so much
yᵉ bolder; whereas if you adjoin yᵉ Lyre, the multiplicity of
Parts, in so small a compass, will occasion a confusion; & there
will be no one instrument distinguishable. If this single Trophy
be not carv'd in very *high* Relieve (and I think it need not as
you are to view this Front-side *near*) you will have no occasion
for any more carving to ballance this in Profile, I believe. But
if your Carver be of a different opinion he may add this kind
of Festoon

or this mantling

On yᵉ 3 remaining Sides—

This Ornament

                                             Cap
(something like a Strawberry) is upon yᵉ top of yᵉ smaller Urn at
Hagley.

If your Ladyship remember, I *said*, yᵉ Foliage on yᵉ Foot
of yᵉ Urn cou'd not be *allowd* you, even tho' you *had* a *Fondness* for it. I do now most explicitely & unconditionally give
up the *Foliage*, not there, but al   yᵉ *neck*; and if you please yᵉ
[Impression lso in   [Impression Places; And if you shou'd
  of seal]   insist   of seal]   Laurell on yᵉ Foot of yᵉ
Pedestal. Your Urn will be in yᵉ *higher* taste, if you have no
other carv'd work yⁿ the Tibia & Fistula suspended; but in

this Case I cannot advise, because I cannot discover what I shoud do myself.

Old Pedley is now at Work for me—The Devil take all Gothicism! I was told, (& by an *experienc'd* Judge) that I might have two Pinnacles hewn in stone for my Gothick Building, for a *trifle*. They are now done, & have taken more stone than wou'd have built me an Urn; & cost me *within* a Trifle as much as ye Building. I am as full of Cholers as Parsons Hugh Evans was;[3] but 'tis done! the Building *is* improv'd by them & I have gaind *Experience*.

This last Week they have hewn me also an Urn, almost big enough for y^e 'Bacco-stopper of an Inhabitant of *Brobdignag*.' And yet, small as it is, It has I think a charming Effect, from ye situation I have given it in Virgil's Grove. The Inscription I design for it has supply'd me with a Hint for a *Device* and *Motto* on a Seal. Tis I think a tolerably genteel one. This.

1.   2.

[Seal]   [Seal]

The second is added by way of *companion*; an Altar ornamented & highly blazing with an Inscription to ye Goddess *Friendship*. But tis ye first y^t is y^e *galante* one, viz; An Urn upon it's Pedestal—the Motto 'To remember you, than to *converse* with others.' But this by way of deviation. To return to old Pedley. He desires his Duty to your Ladyship & offers to undertake ye Urn (at Barrels) & find Stone, (your own Teem drawing it Home) for Four Pounds. He means, *exclusive* of Carving. At this Rate he will work it in *Cobberton* or *Commerton*-stone (some such Name) which he says is better y^n Warwick stone, But I fancy this is not material. He says ye Warwick-People *may* afford to do it cheaper (as he lives at a distance & must have some *previous* Trouble) but He questions whether they *will*. After all I *think* I can agree with him on terms more advantageous to your Ladyship. In ye mean time, you will please to learn what they will do it for, at *Warwick*. The *Terms* propos'd for one 21 Inches high, seem'd to be exorbitant; I hope they do not mean to *raise them* in proportion to this larger Size.

The Pamphletts & Books I receiv'd were, I thought, such as your Ladyship woud not regard. Of y^e first Sort were, a

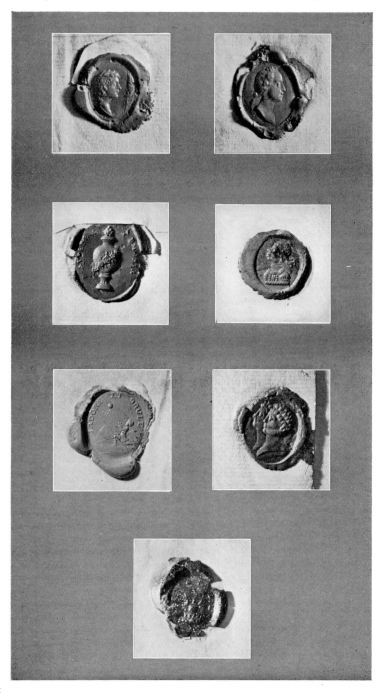

Specimens of seals used by Shenstone.

To face page 240

Sale-work Performance entitled y^e Life of Charles Duke of Somerset;[4] and a Letter from Dr. Addington of Reading on his refusing to consult wth a licens'd Physician[5]—The *Books* were, Dr. Grey's Edition of Hudibras,[6] Sandby's new Horace wth antiques,[7] & a little History of England wch I buy as a memorandum-Book.[8]

Mr. Wintle, of whom I buy my Sans-pareille, is a Perfumer next Door to Temple-Bar. I think his Sans-pareille is good— but his Havannah, & Lavender water are, I *know extremely* in Vogue. He seems to me to have most things y^t he deals in good of their kind; and is a very obliging Man. I lodg'd there 3 months one year, & have dealt with him for Lavender Water, Wash-Balls & Havannah ever since.

I have been so tedious (as you must needs think me) in explaining my insignificant opinions wth regard to ye Urn, that I have but little Paper, left to make my proper Acknowledgments, for ye latter & very obliging Part of your Letter. No Entertainment can engage me more y^n what you give me a glimpse of in Miss Meredyths *Acting* Plays. I am particularly glad y^t She excells in ye charming Part of *Ophelia*—The Green Book *shall* be presented to you, with ye Addition of ye Ode your Ladyship mentions, and every other Improvement I am *capable* of making—My Summer-house must not come down as *yet*, for I cannot give up my good Friends y^e *Mob*, 'till my Place has a *larger* share of *polite* Admirers. I beg my Compliments to Mr. Allen and Mr. Hall, and am your Ladyship's most oblig'd and most obedient

Servt. WILL SHENSTONE.

NOTES

[1]The double oak stands at Barrels and retains much of its former glory. The urn is no longer to be seen.

[2]The statue of Shakespeare on the North wall of the Town Hall at Stratford, bears on the pedestal the lines from Hamlet—
> '. . . take him for all in all
> We shall not look upon his like again.'

[3]*The Merry Wives of Windsor.*

[4]*Memoirs of the late Duke of Somerset.* I. S. Carpenter. *Gentleman's Magazine,* 1749, 480.

[5]Anthony Addington, M.D. (1713–1790), father of Henry Addington, 1st Viscount Sidmouth. The action of Dr. Addington aroused a good deal of discussion, notably *A Letter to Dr. A. of Reading on his refusal to join in consultation with a physician who had taken his degree abroad and was approved and licensed by the College of Physicians in London,* by Richard Russel, M.D.

R

[6]Zachary Grey (1688–1766), published 1744, *Hudibras in three parts, written in the time of the late Civil Wars, corrected and amended with large annotations and a preface, adorned with a new sett of cuts.*

[7]*Q. Horatii Flacci Opera (with engravings from ancient sculptures and gems).* 2 vols. Gul. Sandby. Londine 1749.

[8]Possibly that advertised in *The Gentleman's Magazine*, 1749, 576: *A brief History of England, by way of question and answer*, by J. Lindsay. 6s. Owen.

CV

B.M. Add. MSS. 28958.

[*To* LADY LUXBOROUGH.]

THE LEASOWS *December* ye 5th 1749.

Madam,

I remember, when I was of Oxford, the *Moderator* us'd to put an End to our Disputations-in-Form by ye Latin Word, 'sufficit'; a word of altogether ye same Import with your Ladyship's 'cela suffit. And indeed considering ye Futility of those Exercises in general, a very *slender* Portion of them might be said to be sufficient. But as every syllable of yours, is, without a *Compliment*, of greater Importance, you will never be able to produce ye Idea of Satiety, any more y^n you will to occasion an expression, of it. Your Ladyship has indeed of late been mighty good; & I too, tho' not altogether so good, *did* write a Letter, and send a Packet, which you might *possibly* have receiv'd before you wrote your last. 'Twas an extreme dull Letter; all, as I remember upon ye subject of Urns; concerning which I must also introduce a Word or two in *this*; tho not just at present, least I scrawl my Paper over with nothing but *Circles* & *Elipticks*. I have interested myself in ye Westminster Election ever since ye Poll began; & shou'd be glad to find that Ld Trentham had exchang'd his seat in ye House of Commons for a Seat in ye French Play-house—as ye News-writer well expresses it. Is not y^t a droll application. 'Sr George he is for England' &c:? I think wth your Lordship entirely in Regard to ye Execution of Penlez.[1] I admire with you, the King's Speech to ye Duke of New-castle; and think ye Circumstance might be made good use of on Sr Watkyn's Monument.[2] It might also have been a striking Part of Mr.

Cowley's Epitaph, y^t King Charles ye second said 'He had not left a better Man behind him in England.'[3] The sayings of Princes will have an additional Weight; & this of his present Majesty, y^e *more* so, as it was spoken of a Person y^t he esteem'd his Enemy. Nevertheless there is a grand objection to my Scheme, which your Ladyship's Penetration has already discoverd, & which I need not therefore mention. You have sent me such a Deal of fashionable Intelligence,[4] y^t I might *appear* polite at once, were I situated in a Country where my Politeness wou'd be *visible*. A Fashionable Word is certainly of equal Importance wth a New fashiond Sleeve or Skirt of ones Coat. I have sometimes known a poor Country Parson (when he has caught one at his Patron's Table) as glad of it as one y^t findeth great spoils; You tell me of y^e *Epigrammatical* Turn of ye very fashionable World. I can only say y^t I have remark'd *inexpressible* Folly in y^t Sphere ever since I can remember. Acrosticks! Riddles! Puns! Connundrums! Ideal Vomits! Selling of Bargains! Rebuss &c. &c. What a Catalogue! As to Miss Hamilton's Ballad[5] if I cou'd possibly tolerate *Puns* (on wch ye whole depends) I shou'd call it a good one; For it is easy and genteel. As it is, it will be of great use to me to shew about; since I have try'd it upon two or three common Capacities in my Neighbourhood, & it pleases them to ye Life— Ought not one to envy ye Gentleman his *Lady* much more y^n his *Play*;[6] which I think as dull as most I have read, always excepting Dr. Hoadley's[7]—I remember there is a Dedication of Erasmus's Praise of Folly to Sr Thomas More, & in it a very far-fetch'd Pun upon his name.[8] Mōros you must know is greek for a Fool. The author tells him, that he was influenced in the Choice of his Patron by his Sur-name of *More* which was as nearly similar to y^t or his Subject, (Moria or Folly) as he himself was distant from the Thing—The Planting in Lines *where you mention* is undoubtedly right; So are ye Vistas you propose; & I wish your Ladyship better Luck among Ecclesiasticks y^n it has been my Lot to experience. I fear ye Mischief *he* has begun in y^t Coppice will be of much greater Extent y^n I at first apprehended. I wish the King wou'd make him Bishop of Nova-Scotia, where he might display his Talent of extirpating Trees to ye Benefit of ye Country. *Here* his Advice has been prejudicial both to *me*, and to yᵉ *Owner*—I have had a Mind to surprize your Ladyship next Spring with an Urn (not yᵗ before-mentioned) in a retired Part of my Farm wᶜʰ you have not seen; But I can contain yᵉ secret, no longer— Old Pedley then and his Son have almost finish'd me a Plain Urn, wᶜʰ is to be set up on Friday next. I have gain'd some experience herein wᶜʰ may be of use to your Ladyship—First then yᵉ Stone itself will cost you about half a Guinea for yᵉ Urn & Pedestal, exclusive of Carriage. As far as I can gather, it is somewhat more yⁿ a Month's Work for *one* Man this Winter Time; & less in proportion for two. But herein I cannot be exact—As for yᵉ Stone it will cost you three-pence or three pence half-penny a Foot, & about 35 Foot will be sufficient. On yᵉ Whole I shou'd imagine a Plain Urn of this Size shou'd not exceed 3 Pounds, including stone and tho' you pay *full Wage*s, wᶜʰ, I own *I* do *not*. I took Advantage of old Pedley's Vacation, and *must* have done so, or dropt my Urn. I shall inscribe it on yᵉ Body of yᵉ Urn itself with only two Words & one Letter. I had a violent Hankering after yᵉ *surrounding Wreath* but found yᵗ yᵉ small *size* of yᵉ Urn (yᵉ same you propose) & yᵉ *softness* of yᵉ *stone*, & yᵉ *Dearness* of *Carving*, deterrd me; the two former Circumstances I would have your Ladyship weigh deliberately. I *believe* Warwick stone is soft. I hope to hear from your Ladyship & am with all yᵉ Affection my *Respect* will permit me to express, Madᵐ

Your Ladyship's. W.S.

[Upside down at head of letter.]

Don't my Lady, speak of it; but Mr. M[iller] tells it about yᵗ my Grove exceeds any thing at Hagley of yᵉ kind; but *yᵗ yᵉ Buildings at Hagley are better!* Is not this drole?⁹

NOTES

¹See Luxborough *Letters*, 142. The case of Pen Lez, who was condemned to death for rioting, excited a good deal of interest at the time of his execution, for, it was alleged, he had only fallen in with the rioters by accident. See *The Gentleman's Magazine*, 1749, 528, 512.—*The case of the unfortunate Bosavern Pen Lez.* Pr. 1s. Clement.

(The author of the piece doubts, as the proclamation was not read, whether the demolishing dwelling houses, and burning the furniture, by several hundred disorderly fellows, can legally be called a riot? Mr. Fielding therefore takes no notice of it.)— Henry Fielding was at this time 'Justice of the Peace for the County of Middlesex and for the City and Liberty of Westminster,' and in the same issue of *The Gentleman's Magazine* mentioned above was advertised his reply to his attacker—*A true state of the case of Bosavern Pen Lez.* By H. Fielding Esq. 1s.

2Sir Watkin Williams Wynn (1692–1749), had incurred the resentment of the government by complicity in the 1745 rebellion. King George's generous estimate of his
character—'He was a worthy man and an open enemy'—(Luxborough *Letters*, 142)
—is borne out by the obituary notice in *The Gentleman's Magazine*, September 1749.

3During his life, Cowley had lived in expectation of reward from Charles I and
Charles II, but his services were requited only by the words of Charles II spoken after
the poet's death.

4Luxborough *Letters*, 143, 144.

5Miss Hamilton's *Ballad* is inscribed in the B.M. copy of Luxborough, *Letters*,
the notes in that volume being by Edward Gulston. 'The intimate friend' in the Country to whom the Ballad was sent was Miss Duck, daughter of Stephen Duck, the poet.

> Would you think it my Duck (for the fault I must own)
> Your Jenny at last is quite covetous grown
> For millions, if fortune would lavishly pour
> Yet I should be wretched if I had not *Moore*.
>
> As gay as I am, could I spend half my days
> In dances & Operas, Ridottos & plays
> Hard fate your poor Jenny with tears would implore
> For alas! my dear girl, What are these without *Moore*.
>
> 'Tis the same thing with pleasure, with money, with men,
> And I think I shall never be happy again,
> I have lovers, and danglers and—good store
> And yet like true woman, I still sigh for *Moore*.
>
> Mama she cries Jenny why all this ado
> You may have a husband you know child or two
> But I pouted & whimpered, & fretted & swore
> That I would have none, if I could not have *Moore*.
>
> The Giant poor Devil! has just now been here
> And has offered to settle eight hundred a year
> But I answered the fellow, as I once did before
> You know it wont do Sir, for I must have *Moore*.
>
> Tho' the fools I despise should censure my name
> Yet I am as wise as some folks I could name
> I but worship that Idol which others adore,
> For those that have thousands would gladly have *Moore*.
>
> Now in spite of this craving I vow & protest
> That avarice ne'er had a place in my breast
> For I swore I'd not envy the miser his store
> If I had enough for myself and one *Moore*.
>
> Yet will my girl wonder who this dear one can be
> Whose merit can boast such a conquest as me
> But you shan't know his name tho' I told you before
> It begins with an M. I dare not say *Moore*.

Gulston adds a note to this effect:—Miss Jenny Hamilton was daughter of Charles
Hamilton and Granddaughter of James, 6th Earl of Abercorn. They married May 17,
1750. She was made necessary woman at S. James's where I have often been in her
society, & a most charming woman she was.

6Moore's comedy, *The Foundling*, was produced at Drury Lane, February 13, 1747–8,
and met with no success.

7Benjamin Hoadley, M.D. (1706–1757), was the author of *The Suspicious Husband*, a
successful comedy played at Covent Garden, February 12, 1747.

[8]When Erasmus came to England he lodged with More and wrote within a week *Encomium Moriae*, or *The Praise of Folly*, which became very popular.

[9]Lady Luxborough (*Letters*, 173), was very angry at the comparison drawn between Hagley and The Leasowes, and stirred up W.S.'s jealousy.

CVI

B.M. Add. MSS. 28958.

[*To* LADY LUXBOROUGH.]

Saturday-Night
THE LEASOWS, *December y* 7th 1749.

Madam,

I have Reason to think yt I am *now* trespassing upon your Ladyship's Patience; but my Motive for running some small Risque in this Respect, is as follows. Mr. Pedley has today, finish'd, & set-me-up a plain neat Urn & Pedestal; which, to say ye truth, I wou'd hardly exchange for either of their ornamented Urns at Hagley. He lives at some Distance Northward from hence, & will be now going Home, unless your Ladyship chuses to employ him. I told your Ladyship the Result of my Experience in my last Letter, as to ye quantity of Stone, ye Time it takes up &c: I told you likewise that I took some Advantage of their Necessities in ye Price *I* gave them—but, as the 'Pothecary says in Shakespear,

'My *Poverty* & not my *will* consented.'—[1]

So, in Short, I now take ye Liberty of sending you the old Man's Son, with such *general* Proposals as they have this Moment made me 'That they will either *agree* with your Ladyship by ye *Day*, or they will agree wth you by the *whole*; & find, or *not* find the Stone, as your Ladyship pleases: And in either of these Cases will finish your Urn cheaper yn you will procure it done at Warwick, leaving ye Determination to your Ladyship's own Breast. In other words they will compleat ye Urn & leave their Recompence to your Ladyship without farther Limitation; A Method wch I fancy you will hardly pursue.—

I have nothing to *add* on this Head; I wou'd only do *them*
y^e *Justice* of *repeating*, that I think they have both *behav'd*
& *done* their *Work, well.* Pedley is an inoffensive old man, &
seems to discover, notwithstanding his Infirmities, y^t He has
seen a good deal of ye World—And if *ye World* be taken in a
Scripture-Sense, he has seen too *much* of it. He has been a
great Sufferer by Undertaking Birmingham new-Church; w^ch
was, I think, a *Design* of ye late Groom-Porters.[2] Certain it is,
y^t he has been a great sufferer by the Groom-porter himself;
concerning wch he relates a Story not much to ye Groom-
porter's Honour. So y^t if your Ladyship happen to employ him,
The Act of Charity with regard to *him*, will occasion a Satisfaction to a Bosom like yours, as well as ye Act of *Piety* in
Regard to Mr. Somerville. Also, if you can supply them w^th
Lodging w^thout Inconvenience, it will be *some* Amusement to
you to see how they proceed—upon reviewing what I have
wrote, I seem to *press* ye Affair; which I do not *mean* to *do*.
I wou'd have your Ladyship consult only your *own* opinion.
I am not in ye least interested.

I mentioned, in a former Letter your Ladyships *returning*
those Urns I sketch'd out; but I meant nothing more y^n
what you might effect by committing them to the *Flames.*
If you please to fix what Ornament you chuse, I can sketch it
out as well as if you sent them.—Perhaps tho' they may be of
some Use to your Ladyship in explaining your meaning to a
Carver. I am asham'd of y^e *Fluctuation* of my Opinion in
regard to ye Ornaments. I am now afraid the *Fistula* &c. will
render ye Side-Form of y^r Urn vastly irregular. However, y^r
Determination before this Time is *deliberate*, and 'tis no wide
conclusion, to add that it is *right*—N.B. *Fluting* is now, in my
Opinion, Abominable: Worst of all on y^e *Body* of an Urn; as it
shews itself on ye lesser urn at Hagley.

I have thoughts of inscribing *my* Urn to Mr. Somerville;
and if so, I hope your Ladyship will assist here (in crowning it
with an anniversary Chaplet, and makeing such Libations as I
can afford of Port-wine—Whilst we sit in a Circle round it.
But this the Spring, y^t produces every thing thats agreeable
must also produce. And I do hereby promise to be a very
faithful Pilgrim & Votary at ye Urn your Ladyship shall

erect. You know there were Devotions paid to our Lady of Walsingham &c; as well as to our Lady of Loretto;[3] And tho' yours probably may be esteem'd Mr. Somerville's primary & peculiar Urn, yet there may not be wanting those, who, in ye Blindness of their Superstition, may to mine attribute equal Merit.

Poor Mr. Somerville! what wou'd he say now—as a Separate Spirit—to see how we are employ'd? I leave it to y^r Ladyship to pursue this Thought—I *turn'd* much of ye Urn (properly so call'd) wth my own Hands; wch your Ladyship may also do & *add* to ye Honour you do him, unless you think it too laborious. I hope to wait upon you e'er 'tis done, & am in y^e *mean* time, and shall be *then*, & at *all* times,

> Your Ladyship's most oblig'd
> and most obedient Servant,
> WILL: SHENSTONE.

Mr. Outing's Laziness first affected his *Riding*; next his *Writing*; what can it influence next?—I am afraid when I meet him I shall find him *dumb*.

Your Ladyship will permit this young Fellow to stay till Morning.

NOTES

[1]*Romeo and Juliet*, V, 1.

[2]Although the date of this letter is 1749 the evidence that Birmingham New Church is St. Philip's is fairly convincing in spite of the fact that it was consecrated in 1715. The Church seems to have been constantly referred to as the New Church throughout the century. The building began in 1709 and among the Commissioners to carry out the scheme was Thomas Archer, who was selected as Architect. 'He was a person of some consideration being appointed groom-porter to Queen Anne, George I and George II. He was a pupil of Vanbrugh and in addition to his work at St. Philip's was architect at Heythorpe Hall in Oxfordshire, of the well-known church of St. John's, Westminster, & of the house to which he retired at Umberslade in Warwickshire. . . .'

On September 9th, 1709, we find a minute with regard to the stone to be used, as follows:—'Mr. Pedley undertook to go to Mr. Archer's quarry, & to Rowington Quarry, to enquire about the price of stone there and the carriage of it to Birmingham for the use of the said Church.' *Two Centuries of Church Life*. 1715–1915. *S. Philip's, Birmingham*. A. H. Baynes.

[3]Walsingham Priory in Norfolk was formerly much resorted to by pilgrims and was regarded as the rival of our Lady of Loretto.

CVII

B.M. Add. MSS. 28958.

[*To* LADY LUXBOROUGH.]

THE LEASOWS, *Decr. y^e. 20th* 1749.

Madam,

I am really concern'd for Mrs Davis's Loss,[1] not only as it
affects your Ladyship, but as she is a Person whom I thought
extremely agreeable during the time I had an opportunity of
seeing her at Barrels; & whom I have not ceas'd to esteem
ever since—Now I mention *those Day*s, I cannot avoid acknowledging that I never recollect them, but with a great *deal* of y^t
melancholy satisfaction which Pleasures *past* afford one. Since
that Time what a Number of Deaths, what a Number of
changes! And yet your Ladyship supports the Genius of the
Place, & we find no kind of Deficiency while we converse with
you at Barrels. Yet your *Ladyship* must suffer on these Accounts, & we are all *born* to suffer. It wou'd for ought I know
bear some Dispute whether our Griefs (which are always
heighten'd by a Delicacy of Imagination) *are* best reliev'd by
downright *Philosophy*, or by y^e *Diversion* one may effect by
means of *Amusement*. But I think it not improbable, y^t,
wherever the Power of *Imagination* prevails, it will be most
readily reliev'd by affording it a *Diversion*. And perhaps it may
be *Philosophy* likewise so to do. I have my Share of Misfortunes, & I feel them very sensibly; & if I were to fill my Letter
with *these alone*, (as I cou'd *easily do*) what wou'd it avail?
Evils there *are* in ye world which affect individuals, & also
societies; but which are, no doubt, connected with ye good of
the *Whole*, and must remain as long as that *whole* continues.
At least, if those *evils* are not connected with universal good,
The *Principles* are *from* which they often flow. For instance,
moral Evil, (which wou'd be easily prov'd ye greatest) flows
from ye Nature of Free-will itself. This occasions variety of
Passions in ye World, & these, very often, malice and *mutual*
Mischief. I ask Pardon for this Pedantry, & will hurry out of
it as fast as I can—Mr. Outing is gone, I find, before this
Time. He is a very sincere Friend, but a very indolent Acquaintance; a Fault of which it ill becomes me to complain—I

am pleas'd with your Ladyship's Project concerning Pigeons;[2] But we must not *practice* it. Old Emme woud inevitably fire her Musquet at them, tho' I believe at ye same time she hardly knows a *Gun* from a *Beesom*. There is a Person in this Parish, who, she thinks, will hereafter be her successor, & she hates him most inordinately And I am sure y^e *innocence* of *Doves*, in *this Case*, wou'd not protect them—As to ye Designs for seals, (tho I laid ye chief stress on ye former) your Ladyship chose right. The Altar makes a better *impression*, & ye Inscription is more in y^e *simple antique* taste. The former is ye more artfull & after ye manner of ye French.—See what comes of Art and Disguise! The Person whose name I wrote with a Dash was not Mr. Meredyth, but Mr. *Miller*—I wonder'd he shoud speak of my Buildings as *any* thing; which are—*nothing*. My very Roothouses have as much Pretence to Architecture, as any Building I have; unless I may except this last Urn. And now the subject of Urns is fairly introduc'd. I think the Price they ask at Warwick is not unreasonable. I very much question whether Pedley (if one reckons his Board) wou'd have done it for ye same. Indeed he said (as I mention'd before) y^t ye Warwick-people *might* afford to do it cheaper y^n He. He told me, before he went from hence, y^t he durst by no means venture to undertake it at a Distance from Barels; because, he thought, there wou'd be ye utmost Danger of breaking ye Mouldings in ye Carriage. My Charity tempted me to say more y^n I needed in his Behalf, but I own I shall be very well satisfy'd with your having it done at Warwick; provided there can be any method found of conveying it safe to Barrels—Your objection to y^e *season* of ye year is a very good Reproof of my *Precipitancy* But *my* Work does not depend upon *Mortar*. The distinct Parts of ye Pedestal &c: are of one entire stone; except ye lower Plinth, (which had better have been so too) but was in Parts on acc^t of Carriage. I wou'd then recommend it to y^r Ladyship, to have y^e 'lower-Plinth', 'the Base, 'the Shaft, and y^e 'Capital of ye Pedestal' of one entire stone, a-piece; The 'Plinth or Plinths the' Foot, the 'Body, & y^e 'Top of Urn, ye same. The Workman will not object to it, as it saves in work, what it wastes in stone, & *more*.—I have sent your Ladyship a few more Draughts, of which I will speak a word on a separate Paper. I am well assur'd your answer was for ye best, when my Lord did me ye Favour to enquire after my Place. If I have ye further Honour of waiting on Ld Archer in ye Spring, I shall probably mention ye Leasows as an easy distance from Sr Harry Gough.³ if my Lord shou'd be inclin'd to take an Afternoon's Ride. The Honour he woud do me wou'd be very *certain*; the satisfaction he wou'd find here wou'd be more precarious. I am very zealously your Lady-ship's most oblig'd W. SHENSTONE.

NOTES

¹The death of her husband—Luxborough, *Letters*, 149.

²Lady Luxborough, *Letters*, 151, suggested the introduction of pigeons to carry missives from The Leasowes to Barrels.

³Sir Henry Gough of Edgbaston. Jago in *Edge-Hill*, Book III, mentions the seat of Sir Harry Gough as affording a quiet spot near Birmingham:

> 'Queen of the sounding anvil! Aston thee,
> And Edgbaston with hospitable shade,
> And rural pomp invest. O! warn thy sons;
> When for a time their labours they forget,
> Not to molest these peaceful solitudes.
> So may the Masters of the beauteous scene,
> Protect thy commerce and their toil reward.'

CVIII

B.M. Add. MSS. 28958.

[*To* LADY LUXBOROUGH.]

THE LEASOWS, *Jan^ry y^e* 28^*th* 1749–50.

Madam,

When I own that I have been return'd to the Leasows almost these nine days, you will scarce imagine me to have been so impatient, as I really *have*, to make my proper Acknow-ledgments for your obliging Reception at Barrels, & to enquire after ye Progress of ye Schemes you then took in Hand. But a kind of *tumultuary unsettled* spirits after what *I* call a pretty *long excursion*, indispos'd me for writing; & I cou'd never write with any degree of satisfaction to myself, till now. *Now* indeed, I return to ye correspondence with which you are pleas'd to honour me, with my usual Pleasure; no Places I have seen, & no Conversations I have heard, being capable of

extinguishing the Relish I have for your Ladyship's Company
and Barrels. My Principal jaunt in yᵉ way of curiosity was a
Ride to Mr. Miller's, of whom your Ladyship has formerly
heard me speak. He happend to be from home, but we saw
his *Place*,[1] and his Improvements round it. He lives at yᵉ
Bottom of a Hill wᶜʰ communicates with Edge-Hill. There is
nothing beautifull in yᵉ outside of his *house* but a couple of
Bow-windows, built in yᵉ Gothick Taste; which are really
delightfull. His Farm lies betwixt his House & yᵉ Hill. He
has therefore, rightly enough, taken yᵉ advantage of some
double Hedges which surround his Farm to make a shady
Path betwixt yᵗ conveys you to his Hill. This Path very *fortunately* begins as soon as you come out of his Library or Parlour
an advantage, (I mean this of getting immediately into Shade.)
which *I* can never obtain for *my* situation. In this Path you
have some Views over yᵗ flat Country, *something* variegated,
but not *much;* Before I go further, let me mention that his
Trees are detestable, viz: old *Ashes* stunted & crop'd & newly
sprouting out again: such as ought by all means be destroyd for
yᵉ sake of Trees of a more agreeable *Form*; more early *vegeta-
tion*, & more lasting *verdure*. Before we ascend the wood we
are taken to an artificial Piece of ground & waterwork. Tis a
detach'd thing; utterly unlike, & I think inconsistent with yᵉ
genius of his Land in general. At yᵉ Top of this is a Reservoir
(which as Lord Bolingbroke well observes may spurt forth a
little frothy water on some gawdy Day & be dry yᵉ rest of yᵉ
year, (alluding to our modern orators in Parliament) It falls
over 3 rustick arches, runs down, thro broken stone-work, to a
Bason in yᵉ midst of wᶜʰ is a Jetteau; and on each side tumuli or
little mounds of Earth artificially cast up. But this is a juvenile
Performance, & only retain'd because it *is* there & has cost
him money. After this we viewd an artificial Terrass yᵗ gives a
view of yᵉ Plain where yᵉ Battle was fought, & of yᵉ country
round. This view pleases by dint of mere *extent*, for yᵉ country
is not well variegated. From this you pass into his wood, a
slopeing Coppice like mine, but *larger*. He has here no building
worth mentioning & you pass by a winding ascent till you
have a view of a hanging Lawn enclosd on all sides with
Wood-Work. It has a wild & *Forest-like* appearance, and is

terminated at ye End by a kind of *Eye-Trap*, namely ye End of a stable finish'd in ye way of a Door & Pediment, but slightly & in Plaister-work. I lik'd this Scene ye best of any, & I had ye Comfort to hear y^t Mr. Lyttelton had done so before me. Hence you still ascend to a very large antique, octagonal Tower. The upper Room is highly finish'd in ye Gothick Taste; antique Shields blazond on ye Ceiling; Painted Glass in ye windows Gothick Niches, & Gothick Cornice. But on ye whole I am not pleas'd wth it. First, ye Stair-case breaks into ye Floor and is horrible; next ye Height is so excessive y^t I cou'd not endure to look out of ye windows; next, ye arch of ye Ceiling does not please me; & lastly, ye wretched Laboriousness & inconvenience of ye Ascent makes it not desireable to compleat a Room so expensively at that *Height*. Now as to ye Tower & Ruins he has added (for he has added a *Turret*, which is in *reality* some Poor body's chimney & a magnificent stone Arch, which is ye y^e [sic] Gate way to their House) they are to be considered from a different Point of view, namely his own House. Here I dont approve of them. First, because the Tow'r (of an extraordinary Height) attracts ye Eye too strongly, & takes from ye variety of which his Scene was capable. Next because the Ruins (tho a good deal of y^e *shatter'd* order when you are *near* 'em) at a *distance* seem too much a solid Lump, the Breaches & indeed ye Ruins themselves not being enough considerable. In ye last Place ye Top of ye Tower is detestable, & this he knows. I think I've nothing to add about his Place, but y^t he has taken advantage of a kind of separate Chappel in his Parish Church, to make himself one of ye most magnificent & handsomest Pews I ever saw. Tis elevated almost equally with ye Pulpit & he has made a neat arch thro' which he enters it from without doors. Tis neatly stucco'd, has a Cornish, & a Cove-ceiling; & is large & square; on one side of which is a plain marble monument to his Father—There is in his Churchyard ye remains of a Monument to Captain Kingsmill,[2] one of 4 Brothers y^t were slain at Edgehill Fight. Tis entirely in Ruins; little more y^n y^e *cumbent* statue of him, remaining; but this perhaps not a bad one. Is it not astonishing y^t Mr. Miller does not remove this (since the Family takes no kind of notice of it) to some solemn Area in his wood before-mention'd. Wou'd it not produce a striking effect there? as the story is both recent & real? Or, as ye Field of ye battle lies full in view & but just beneath his House, is it not strange y^t he has not one Motto, Urn, or Obelisk, that might impress y^t interesting Idea, & give a deep solemnity to his Recesses? I don't mean y^t he shou'd bring *Party* into ye Case (tho this also w^d suit *him*, or be at least consistent) but y^t he might give an Urn or so to some worthy man, y^t was kill'd there, & add some motto y^t was *moral* yet *general*—Again instead of concentrating ye View, & *forceing* ye Eye to his Castle, were it not better to have had *several* Objects in his Wood, properly subordinate to one principal Building—But his *Schemes* are yet imperfect; & excepting his Castle, he has done infinitely less y^u I expected. His Place may be greatly improved & no doubt it will; but he has a Dearth of Water, worse y^n they at Hagley & which will subdue in me all envious Sensations when I view his Castle. I am tedious, & must have done. I send your Ladyship one more Draught of a Wreath interwoven wth ye French Horn. I am quite convincd y^t it shoud be wreathed somehow after this Manner. The twining wreath was *drawn* ye worst in those Draughts I gave you, & that deceiv'd you; but whether or no this be any better, pray, my Lady, give particular orders to ye Carver to twine ye Laurel round ye French Horn. I shall be glad to hear y^r present Sentiments concerning ye Inscription. I am your Ladyship's most oblig'd & most obedient faithfull Servant,

WILL SHENSTONE.

I think on a revisal I am too censorious
in regard to Mr. Millers Place—but I saw it at
ye very worst Time of ye year, & *may* give a more favourable
Acc^t hereafter.

NOTES

[1]At Radway Grange Sanderson Miller carried out his ideas with regard to Gothic architecture.
This letter was written after a visit to Richard Jago at Harbury, near Radway, where the latter held a living. It shows that W.S. was far from complete appreciation of Miller as an architect but was, however, anxious that Miller should not know the fact, and wrote to Jago after this visit (see post, p. 262), begging him not to tell Miller of his disapproval.

[2]Hutton, *Highways and Byways in Shakespeare's Country*, pp. 29, 30, mentions a monument to Captain Henry Kingsmill, inside Radway Church. His death is celebrated by Jago in *Edge-Hill*, Book IV.

CIX

B.M. Add. MSS. 28958.

[*To* Lady LUXBOROUGH.]

THE LEASOWS, *Febr y^e* 4 1749–50.

Madam,

The Number of Lines I have wrote this day, and the unfitness of my Brain to dictate a single sentence, is past my Power of Expression. Yet am I oblig'd both by Interest and Gratitude to return the Letter you so kindly communicated. And to return it without my sincere Acknowledgment were an injury to my real Sentiments; Therefore I must accompany it with a few Lines, & promise to add *more* & *better* hereafter—I would not give up ye smallest part of the Duchess's esteem to be inaugurated King of *Corsica* to-morrow; & shou'd I neglect your Commands in respect of her Letter, I might justly risque the Danger of never seeing any more of them. In that Case what wou'd it avail, tho' She shoud preserve some little Regard for me? Yet am I not so vain as to be ignorant y^t without your Ladyship's Interposition, there cou'd be no Hopes of it's Continuance.—I think when I go to London, however, I shall have Effrontery enough, to get acquainted with that same Chaplain; Some how or other, I know not how. I like him more for approveing of y^t *simple* Performance y^n if he had applauded all I have wrote beside. Mr. Outing's Letter arriv'd at the same Time with your Ladyship's. He says little more than to this purpose that he shall be glad to execute my Commands in Town; that he is a sincere *Friend*, tho' a dilatory *Correspondent*. I know him to be so, & therefore God bless him. Twill hardly ever be in *my Power* to do him any solid service. I beseech your Ladyship to continue me in ye Remembrance of Mr. Meredyth. He is *one* Man of ingenuity & Worth in a superior station. Such an Acquaintance, as I wish; but find it difficult, to make—I wou'd willingly conclude here; but my vanity prompts me to tell your Ladyship, that the Earl of Stanford[1] call'd on me with three other Gentlemen, this week, to see my walks. Twou'd make you laugh to say that he was almost mir'd in them, but it was nearly the Case, in some particular Places. You know it is yᵉ worst of *seasons*; & I may add it was yᵉ worst of *Days*—However he was much struck with Virgil's Grove, & particularly yᵉ Cascade you were us'd to admire; gave it yᵉ Preference to yᵉ Rock work &c: at Hagley, & said obliging Things. Had he indeed curs'd & calumniated every Part beside, I cou'd not have blamd him; for we had Rain & Storms almost all yᵉ Time we were walking. He gave me many friendly Invitations to Enfield,[2] where he is building a Gothick Greenhouse; his visit does me Honour in my Neighbourhoud, & so much for this Contingency.

I take it extreme kind of Mr. Hall and am much oblig'd to your Ladyship for your Civility to Mr. Pearsall,[3] as *my Relation*. What his Book will prove, I know not; and have taken it a little ill that I have not been made acquainted with it—My obligation to you is the same. I will write again soon, & beg you woud consider this scrawl as utterly inadequate to the Respect wᵗʰ wᶜʰ I have the Honour to be your Ladyships most oblig'd

& faithful Servᵗ W. SHENSTONE.

NOTES

[1]Harry Grey, 3rd Earl, of Enville, was a landscape gardening enthusiast, and W.S. helped him with suggestions. It was after a visit to Enville in 1763 that W.S. became ill 'of a putrid fever' and died. He dedicated a root-house to Lord Stamford, and Jago in *Labour and Genius* celebrated the friendship which existed between the two:

> 'Yet still let Friendship's joys be near,
> Still, on these plains, her train appear.
> By Learning's sons my haunts be trod,
> And Stamford's feet imprint my sod.
> For Stamford oft hath deign'd to stray
> Around my Leasows flow'ry way.
> And where his honour'd steps have rov'd
> Oft have his gifts those scenes improv'd,
> To him I'll dedicate my cell,
> To him suspend the votive spell,
> His name shall heighten ev'ry charm,
> His name protect my groves from harm,
> Protect my harmless sport from blame,
> And turn obscurity to fame.'

[2]Enfield, or Enville, the seat of Lord Stamford, nine miles from Hagley.

[3]Richard Pearsall (1698–1762), religious writer in the manner of Rev. James Hervey. Some of his poems appeared in *The Gentleman's Magazine*, 1736. The book to which W.S. refers is probably *Contemplations on the Ocean, Harvest, Sickness and the last Judgment, in a series of letters to a friend*, 1753. The family of Pearsall of Hawn finds mention in Nash's *History of Worcestershire*.

CX

B.M. Add. MSS. 28958.

[*To* Lady LUXBOROUGH.]

THE LEASOWS, *March y*e 6th 1749–50.

Madam,

I ought indeed to have acknowledg'd the Favour of your Ladyship's Letter, much *sooner*, but as a *true account* of my Delay will be its best Apology, I beg Leave to offer *it* you as follows. Your Ladyship in your last Paragraph seem'd desirous yt I shou'd consider of something proper for a *Latin* Inscription to Mr. Somervile; I thought this an affair yt requir'd some Deliberation, & accordingly indulg'd myself in ye Hopes yt I might be forgiven, if I allow'd myself some time to digest my Thoughts on ye occasion; having no Creature here to advise with, & having too often experienc'd ye Fluctuation of my own Opinions. The result was yt I wrote down a Page or two by way of Specimens, from which I propos'd to select a few, for your Ladyship's Choice. But as I rememberd yt you never own'd yourself acquainted with ye Pedantry of Latin Phrases, or ye antique turn of expressions in *that Language*, I did not care to send them to you, till I had consulted with some of my Friends.

Matters were in this State, when I was call'd away to assist at ye Fishing of a large Pool near Broom, which I have there jointly with Mr. Dolman. There I spent all ye last week. Mr. and Miss are both well, and at your Ladyship's Service. I return'd too late on Sunday Evening to be able to have my Letter ready for ye Postwoman ye next Day.

I was surpriz'd & concern'd at ye Duke of Somerset's Death;[1] & considering how short a space he has had to enjoy his Honours and Estates, & to exhibit his many valuable Qualities with *Advantage*, it cannot be thought strange that his Death shou'd appear *untimely*. Even many years hence it might have done ye same. Nothing now remains, but to pray for ye Duchess; that his Graces Death may not have too bad an Effect upon her Health and Spirits, as there is too much Reason to fear it will—Your Ladyship is *ingenious* in your generosity. I do not remember yt I *presumd'* to hope for ye Duchess's

Acquaintance, when I mention'd my Intention of getting acquainted with her Chaplain. For I lik'd ye man, exclusive of his *situation*, from y^t *kind* of Character ye Duchess gave of him, & perhaps not a little for his *Partiality* to *me*—At least If I had further views, my Heart was not explicit, tho' your Ladyship, who knows my veneration for her Grace at all times, had sufficient Room to draw ye Conclusion. Sure I am that I am under ye utmost obligation for ye use you made of it.

I am almost afraid to acquaint you, y^t I had well-nigh finish'd an Ode[2] which I intended to desire your Lasp to present to her Grace. As it is now neither to be *finish'd* nor *seen*, I will venture to give you this short account of it, that it was written in ye irregular way like y^t I had ye Honour to present to you; that it turn'd chiefly on ye Pleasures of Solitude & rural Amusement, & after excluding Several Classes of Men from any Pretensions to comprehend the Beauties of Nature, fix'd upon ye Person of true Taste as ye only adequate Spectator. Don't imagine I say this to excite y^r curiosity—The Account you gave me of Outing's Journey made me laugh heartily; Outing would not desire to be Mr. Addison's Angel, or to *ride in ye whirlwind*, even tho' he could *direct ye Storm*.[3]

I am extremely glad to hear of any Accession of Happiness to Mr. Meredyth's Family, as I am likewise to hear of large Fortunes being at any time in ye Possession of generous Spirits. Lord Stamford lives about six Miles from hence, ye direct Road (betwixt me and Stourbridge) is almost one continued Grotto, in other terms a *hollow*-way; practicable for an Horse, but for no wheel-carriage; I am not sure whether there be not some other y^t may be more so. Lady Stamford[4] I never saw, but she is esteem'd greatly amongst us for her Spirit Sense and Generosity—I heard this Story lately. She & Lord Stamford din'd at Lord Ward's, where ye latter was rallying my Lord Stamford for some event y^t happen'd while he was carrying ye Sword of State 'What, my Lord, you had like to have kill'd your King! 'To which my Lady Reply'd, If Lord Stamford *had* kill'd his King, it cou'd only have been imputed to accident; whereas if *you*, my Lord, had done ye same, it wou'd have been construd Rebellion Murder & High Treason. I am not intimate with my Lord having never been

in his Company but one day y^t I din'd wth him & Lord Ward at
Himley, except at Balls, & this many years ago. On ye whole
these things consider'd I rather *wish* y^n *hope* for an *opportunity*
on my *first visit* to procure my self ye accumulative Honour of
seeing them here jointly with y^r Ladyship. And yet as I think
to cultivate this Acquaintance (for they are easy of Access) I
do hope as well as wish that I may hereafter find one.

I am oblig'd to you for ye Pleasure you gave me in mentioning y^t I was remember'd by Sr Peter Soames,[5] Mr. Allen &
Mr. Hall. I hope Sr Peter has not quite left ye Country.

And now am I to proceed to ye Subject of Urns, in regard
to which if I speak a little dogmatically, you must with your
usual Candour attribute it to the fear I have y^t Ceremony wou'd
make me tedious, & it is at best too heavy a vehicle for such
futile Opinions as mine. In the first Place then I take it for
granted y^t you prefer Latin quotations—and therefore, a
Latin Inscription, *I* say, of *course*.

You will not have Room on ye Front of ye Pedestal to intimate more than y^t you Place it, out of Friendship, to ye Memry
of W. Som: Esq: Author of ye Chase; & in my Opinion tis all y^t
you *shoud* say there.

One circumstance which made me acquiesce in an English
Inscription was, that you cannot express, '*Author of the Chase*'
in *Latin*, without a *circumlocution*.

> Perhaps Jocundi carminis de re venatica
> Auctori celeberrimo—is as *short*
as it can be express'd.)

Well but supposing thus much expressd in Latin on ye Front,
then I wou'd have '*Postquam Te* &c; on ye Side next y^e
Service Walk, & some other alluding to his *moral* Character on
ye opposite side. And thus your whole Aim is compleated.

You told Mr. Allen my *only* objection to '*multis ille bonis*'
when apply'd together with *Postquam Te Fata* &c. namely y^e
different Persons of *Te* & *Ille*. Now if he Approves of y^e
alteration of one Word in Virgils Line (tho it hurts ye Line)
Quem postquam Fata tulerunt, why then your Ladyship has
two Mottos unexceptionably expressive of Mr. S's different
Characters; & then nothing to be done but to give you an
Inscription. I cou'd acquiesce in this Proposal.

But if Mr. Allen will not allow of y^t Alteration (tho 'tis often done) why then you are to desire him to think of some *other* expressive of the *same thing*; where there is y^e *second* Person us'd instead of the *third*; & I also will think ye while as well as I can—Finally I *do* think you had better defer inscribing it for 3 weeks or a month. I will readily come over for a Day, & see it done, & a good workman will do it in little more. For some very little addition in ye expence (wch you may adjust with the Builder *when he brings ye Urn*) you may have a Person from Warwick at a Days warning; & it is a thing y^t ought to be thoroughly considerd. Positively If I furnish ye Inscription, I must consult a little; but if you persist in requiring one immediately, I desire you will let me know as soon as you are at Leisure—and I will venture my Latinity in your Ladysp's Hands. I am daily employ'd in finishing ye Scene where I have plac'd my Urn, & makeing a Path to it; & have really found y^t Part of my Farm afford more Pictures y^n I cou'd possibly have imagin'd.

Now I talk of Pictures, has not Smith brought you his '*Select Beauties*'? He was here a fortnight ago & purpos'd to wait upon you wth them. Hagley is ye best, but seems to want something. Ld Tyrconnels, next.

Your Ladyship says nothing concerning your Shell Urns— & I am afraid to enquire.

Aris furnishes me with my Paper, but I *bespeak* ye particular sort. I never buy Pens, so can, at present say nothing on y^t Head.

I am highly transported with this forward season not only as it suits my Flowers, but as it *ripens* the Hopes that spring in my Imagination about this time of ye year; I mean ye agreeable expectation of waiting upon you at ye Leasows; when I Shou'd be much more indifferent as to introducing new Improvements, if I thought they stood no Chance of entertaining *you*. I am your Ladyships most

oblig'd W.S.

NOTES

[1]The Duke of Somerset only succeeded to the title December 2, 1748. He died February 7, 1750.
[2]*Rural Elegance*.

³Cf. *The Campaign*, 1, 287, and Luxborough's *Letters*, 188.

> 'So when an angel by divine command
> With rising tempests shakes a guilty land
> Such as of late o'er pale Britannia past,
> Calm and serene he drives the furious blast;
> And pleased the Almighty's orders to perform
> Rides in the whirlwind and directs the storm.'

⁴Née Mary, only daughter of George, 2nd Earl of Warrington.

⁵Sir Peter Soame of Heydon, Essex, Baronet. In Wootton Wawen Church (Warwickshire) is a monument which runs: 'To the memory of Jane Sarah Soame, daughter of Sir Peter Soame of Heydon in the county of Essex, Baronet, and niece to Henry, Viscount St. John. The lady was born the 12th February 1703, and died unmarried on the 7th November 1744. This monumental inscription was directed by the Lady's executor and relation, Robert, Earl of Catherlough, 1765.'

CXI

Works III, 186 and
Hull, II, 12.

To the [REV. R. JAGO].

THE LEASOWS,
Mar. 15, 1749–50.

Dear Sir,

Though I have not hitherto troubled you with a letter, I have not been void either of *inquiry* or *information*, concerning the state of your affairs, and of Mr. Hardy's health. Indeed it is now several weeks since I collected some particulars from your brother, and I am now impatient for further intelligence. As to the circumstances of our friendly reception at Wroxall, Mr. John Jago has probably enough acquainted you with them. He *would*, however, seduce me to give you a distinct account; being assured, as he says, that Mr. Wren's behaviour must afford a good subject for drollery. I do not know how far this would be proper; but I think, when I write again to my friend Wren, to give *him* a sketch of his own character, just as it appeared to us during the time of our visit. Perhaps it may avail a little. Amidst his violent passion for gardening, if he would but prune away some wild excrescences from one or two branches of his character, he might bring himself to bear good fruit. He should *weed* his *mind* a little; where there has sprung up a most luxuriant crop of puns, that threaten to cloak all its wholesome productions—'Spinas animo fortius quam agro evellat.'[1] He has good sense and good-nature; pity he should disguise them.—Not but that it is better to have the *substance* alone than the *forms alone*, and so I conclude. Since I came home, I have done little else than plant bushes, hazel, hawthorn, crabtree, elder, &c. together with some flowering shrubs that I have had given me, and some that I have purchased to the amount of twenty shillings. I think nothing remarkable has occurred; only, one miserable tempestuous day, I had my Lord Stamford, who called to see my walks. My Lord promised to come again in the summer, and invited me more than once to Enville. By the way, he is now building a Gothic green-house by Mr. Miller's direction, and intends to build castles, and God-knows-what. By all accounts, the place is well worth seeing when you come into the country, which I hope you will not fail to do this spring. Pray do not you embroil me with Mr. Miller, in regard to *any* observations I made in his walks. Remember, there were a great many things with which I was highly delighted; and forget that there were a few also which I seemed less to admire. Indeed, I thought it idle to regulate my expressions, amongst friends only, by the same rules which I ought to observe in mixed company, I say *ought*, for *he* has been exceedingly favourable to *me* in his representation of The Leasows.—I hope to see Mr. Fancourt with you, when you come this spring; and why not your brother? he can spend half a week now and then at Wroxal.

I have nothing to *insert* or *inclose* in this letter that can render it at all agreeable.—I cannot *write*, I cannot *think*. I can just muster up attention enough to give orders to my workmen; I saunter about my grounds, take snuff, and read Clarissa.[2] This last part of my employment threatens to grow extremely *tedious*: not but the author is a man of *genius* and *nice observation*; but he might be less *prolix*. I will send you 'The Life of Socrates' when I can get it home from Barrels. I wish both your circumstances and mine would allow of our utter *inattention* to them; and then, I believe, our natural indolence would be a kind of match for our ambition. I shall probably enlarge my acquaintance this year; but what *doth* it? the circle of my friends with whom I can be *easy*, and *amused* much, will continue small as ever. I could dwell a good deal upon this subject; but I have only room to desire you would give me your opinion how I should inscribe my urn to Mr. Somervile. 'Author of the Chace' cannot be tolerably expressed in Latin without a circumlocution. I aim at brevity, and would therefore omit it. Pray read over the specimens I have thrown together, and *oblige* me with a speedy answer, if it extend to nothing else besides yours and Mrs. Jago's health, which I ought at this time more particularly to enquire after. I am

Your most affectionate,

and faithful friend,

W. SHENSTONE.

NOTES

[1]Horace, *Epist.* I, 14, 4-5.
[2]*Clarissa or the History of a Young Lady* was begun by Samuel Richardson in 1744. The first four volumes appeared in 1747, and the last four by the end of 1748.

CXII

B.M. Add. MSS. 28958.

[*To* LADY LUXBOROUGH.]

[Upside down, head of letter].

My Tooth is easier——
My Service to Mr. Hall.

'Tis, I think, *March ye 22^d*—1749-50.

Madam,

I cannot with any satisfaction defer writing 'till Saturday, tho' I have a perverse Tooth that sollicits me continually to attend to nothing but the Pain it gives me—The weather of late has been a mere Coquette: Sunshine enough to tempt one out of Doors, Winds fraught with Tooth-Achs, Colds, & Disappointment! Yet to catch a glimpse of this *forward* Spring, do I ramble forth at least 20 times a Day;

Well-knowing Pleasure must be bought wth Pain! To-night however I can but think ye Price too *dear;* finding ye Pain more severe y^n usual, & being troubled also in *mind* to think it shou'd interrupt me just at this time.—You can't imagine how I fretted to hear y^t your Urn was damag'd. I cou'd not forbear saying, Why did they *send* it? Why did they *bring* it, till ye Cases were ready? And yet, for ought I know, ye Damage is all *imaginary*: I *do believe* they can *cement* it so y^t it will sooner break in any other Place; & when tis painted the Piecing will be hid for ever. If so what is an *accidental Fracture* worse y^n a *natural Joint?* Not a Jott. So I beg your Ladyship may be comforted, & accept of my Congratulation——You say 'tis seen from ye several Places we propos'd, Pray, Madam, does it appear as *considerable* as you would wish it? for as to it's being handsomely executed, I do not in ye least question it. And yet three Parts in four of it's Beauty must depend upon the verdure y^t Spring has in store for it——Your Ladyship was abundantly generous to Mr. Smith. You don't know how to bestow with moderation: Otherwise you had not sent me enough Jasmin-water to serve me a twelvemonth, when I litterally meant to beg no more y^n I describ'd. But no more of this, except my Thanks——I return to Mr. Smith. I like ye Man, & I like *many* of his Landskips; these he has publish'd last, perhaps, as *little* as any. His Roman English Ruins, together with his views of Derbyshire y^e *most* of any. I cou'd wish he cou'd make Vivares execute *all* his Engravings. What an immense difference!

I will give up, if you please, ye Painting y^r Shrine of Venus after ye manner propos'd, but would likewise have your Ladyship *hesitate* a little before you make use of Moss Work &c. Is it not a Petitesse?——If not, I would however have y^e *whole back* coverd as well as ye Niche, to give ye Pillars in Front ye greater Advantage——I could wish Mr. Smith (nor myself) had never *acknowledg'd* y^t my Urn appear'd too little. I wish your Ladyship had not *heard* this previous Hint. For I am in Hopes ye Area will appear so much *contracted* when ye Trees y^t encircle it are thickn'd wth Leaves y^t it will not seem deficient in Size. If it *shou'd*, I will put a larger in the Place, & make use of this somewhere else. For I cannot agree to a Pyramid there, even if I c^d build one with rough stone as cheap as an Urn——(Mr. Smith indeed propos'd it, but it really were so diminutive so pitifull an Imitation of those in Egypt (covering 11 acres of ground to build one of 20 Feet, y^t one can't think of the latter without contemning ye former; &

sure one cannot view ye Copy without recollecting ye Original—
And yet a Pyramid has it's advantages—tis certainly a very
solemn Ornament, & a very uncommon one. However, you
will see by this y^t we vary in our Ideas of proportion, as he
thinks a Pyramid not too large, where I esteem an Urn
sufficient. You planted *Abeles*, for their *speedy Growth*, & I
acquiesc'd; little dreaming then of ye superior Excellence of
Sallows, which grow as bushy as you please, & Eleven Feet
high in a year, from little Pieces of a Foot long. Their Luxuri-
ancy itself is delightfull. I planted several this day—The
Picture of a Part of my grove will not *good*, nor *like*; yet I cou'd
have been easy had it been engrav'd by Vivares. Indeed Vivares
himself c^d not have made good Pictures of my Ld Gains-
boroughs & Lord Byron's—One of them (wth his water temple)
has as much expos'd his Taste as ever did Lord Grimstone
when he printed his 'Love in a hollow tree.'[1] By ye way is not
Smith inexcusable for admitting ye Pot-boiling Cascades &
the Stables behind ye Hermitage, (pretty in itself at my L^d
Tyrconnels)—Give me Leave, my Lady to speak to other Parts
of y^r Letter (particularly ye obligation I am under to Mr.
Meredyth) in my next. I am
most invariably, Y^r Ladyship's W.

NOTE

[1]William Lucklyn, Viscount Grimston (1683–1756), published his play, *Love in a Hollow Tree*, in 1705.

CXIII

B.M. Add. MSS. 28958.

[*To* Lady LUXBOROUGH.]

The Leasows, *March* ye 23^d 1749–50.

Madam,

I now sit down to add a word or two by way of supplement
to my last; & this is but *right*, for I know not how it comes to
pass, but your Ladyship most certainly says as much in *one*
Letter as I can in *Two*.

I don't remember what it was I said in Mr. Meredyth's
Favour which he seems so studiously to decline, & of which he

makes such profuse Acknowledgment: But if it were anything y^t regarded Generosity of Sentiment, Delicacy in his observations, or an Ease & Politeness in his expressions, your Ladyship can bear me witness that I was struck with *them* on ye sight of ye first Letter you shew'd me. Pray don't you recollect y^t you confirm'd what I then said, and also intimated, that you had always thought the same? But I will not load Mr. Meredith with anything which he may *think* a Compliment; I will endeavour to meet him, ye first opportunity, & to deserve his Acquaintance by all means in my Power.

Your Ladyship is in some Haste to see your Urn inscrib'd, & tho' I have at least 30 different methods of doing it by me, I am quite clear in my Opinion, y^t nothing more *can* be done in y^e *space that is left* on ye Front, than to mention *his Name* & his being *Author of the Chace.* All I wou'd *wish* to add there, shou'd be an Intimation of the *Friendship*, to wch you pay this tribute; & *that* I suppose, when a Person erects an Urn, is generally taken for granted—Mottos are things that one *recollects* or *finds* accidentally; so that probably by a little Patience one might think of something better y^n we now propose. I don't much *love* to alter a word in a Quotation, especially when ye verse is visibly impair'd—and as to ye Line Mr. Allen proposes, to be sure the *Sense* is exactly what one would wish there, & it is a Line of Horace's, but does your Ladyship like ye Repetition of the s.s. *multis* ille *bonis* occidit.[1] You'll say I'm too nice, & perhaps I am; nevertheless I think Mottos should be beautifull in themselves as well as pertinent; you will have them seen by *criticks;* and when they are once *cut* there will be no possibility of Alteration. I have inscrib'd mine to Mr. Somervile in a kind of *general* way, but not *cut* ye Letters, y^t I may alter them if I shou'd chuse it. 'tis thus.

Literally

GULIELMO. SOMERVILE. ARMIG^o	TO WILLIAM SOMERVILE ESQ.
DE. POESI. BONISQ: LITERIS.	WHO DESERVED VERY HIGHLY
PRÆCLARE. MERITO.	OF POETRY
HANC. SALTEM. PONI. VOLUIT	AND POLITE LEARNING
AMICITIA.	THIS AT LEAST WAS PLACD HERE
MDCCL.	BY THE DIRECTION OF
	FRIENDSHIP.

I don't much like it; if I *did*, I cou'd not offer it to your Ladyship, because you must needs have the Chace Expressly alluded to.

You'll say I have a very *glaring* Taste, when I mention, that when mine is *cut* I think to have ye Letters *gilded*. But I imagine to myself extraordinary Beauty in a gold Letter upon a simple stone colour. Another thing is, y^t it is sometimes done, & that by Persons of Taste; & lastly I will maintain, that it will not be half so *shewy* as if they were done in *black*. But I will drop this subject (of wch you must be tir'd) to resume it once more when I have heard from you—As to ye Service-walk I think you shoud make no scruple of Planting such Flowers as will grow *thro' ye Grass*, of which I fancy there are several. But what I want most of anything is to have some kind of Fence on ye outside y^t walk, y^t there may be no occasion for a Gate at ye End of ye Shrubbery. Perhaps it may be difficult to form such a Fence as you will like. I own I shou'd like to have ye Shrubbery continu'd there & a Ha Ha behind, & then your Ha-ha at ye Urn will be superfluous too—but there is no haste of this—twill be extreme beautiful in its present state. The Ode I mention'd will I believe never be finish'd—The Merit of y^e *best* stanzas is not, I fear, sufficient to deserve y^t y^e *best* shou'd be *wrote afresh*, as must be ye Case if I revis'd it— Beside by shewing it you *now*, I must very evidently seem to have laid a trap for your curiosity; which I cannot bear to think of—The green Book will soon be finish'd as to ye transcribing Part, but if I am to illuminate it & so discover my Inability to *paint* as well as to *write*, I doubt I cannot promise it at present—Ld Lovat's Tryal was lent out when I mention'd it, but if it comes home tonight, it shall accompany this Letter. I suppose the Bishop of London treats this Earth-quake[2] as a Judgment, & inscribes it to Sr Piety Caudle-cup & Dame Magdalene his wife: And yet, in the last Birmingham Paper, there are I think very cogent Reasons to suppose it was an *Air*-quake rather, & beneficial in it's Consequences—I have at last begun Clarissa, of which I have read two Volumes. I think ye Author a Person of refind understanding, but that he has needlessly spun out his Book to an extravagant Prolixity— & which he would scarce have done, had he not been a *Printer* too as well as an *Author*. Nothing, but *Fact* could authorize so much particularity, and indeed not *that*; but in a Court of Justice—I met one Mr. Chambers a week ago at Mr. Clare's,[3] (a Gentleman in our neighbourhood) who is an Acquaintance, I find of your Ladyship's—The Bishop of Cambray[4] had certainly no Invention—As for the rest, I suppose his Language is ye Language of most french Novels a mixture both of verse & Prose; & 'tis an unhappiness, I fancy, for a writer to have a genius partaking *equally* of both. I am highly honourd by every Instance of your Ladyship's goodness and am Your Ladyship's most oblig'd hum: Servt

W. SHENSTONE.

NOTES

[1]Horace, *Odes* V, XXIV, 9.
The motto finally chosen (Luxborough, *Letters*, 201) was 'Debita sparges lacryma favillam vatis amici.' Horace, *Odes* II, VI, 23, 24.

[2]There were several earthquake shocks early in 1750. It was prophesied that the last would 'swallow up London.' Walpole wrote to Mann, April 2, 1750, 'You will not wonder so much at our earthquakes as at the effect they have had. All the women in town have taken them up upon foot of Judgment, & the clergy who have had no windfalls of a long season have driven horse & foot into the opinion. There has been a shower of sermons & exhortations. Secker, the jesuitical Bishop of Oxford, began the mode.'

[3]This family receives considerable notice in Nash's *History of Worcestershire*.

[4]François de Salignac de la Motte Fénelon (1651–1715), made Archbishop of Cambrai, 1695. As preceptor to the Duke of Burgundy, grandson of Louis XIV, Fénelon wrote *Les Fables*, *Les Dialogues des Morts* and *Télémaque*, 1699. *Télémaque* is the novel referred to here, for Lady Luxborough comments on this bit of criticism with the superior knowledge of French language and literature which Shenstone owned she possessed. 'I do not think the poetical prose (which is the style of Fénelon's *Telemachus*) is at all the common style of French novels; which is, for the most part, very good; especially Marivaux's, Crebillon's & others.' *Letters*, 202. W.S. wrote *The Hermit. In the manner of Cambray* (*Works* II, 26), and there he pointed the moral as did Fénelon when writing for the instruction of his pupil.

CXIV

B.M. Add. MSS. 28958.

[*To* LADY LUXBOROUGH.]

Madam,
    I did indeed imagine that your Ladyship was gone to London upon Lady Bolingbroke's Death,[1] otherwise I shou'd have

been uneasy under ye Suspicion that I had lost that Place in your Memory which it will ever be my Ambition to retain. You are exceeding kind in condescending to make an Apology for your Silence. I do very readily allow ye weight of it, & I shou'd have considered the *condescension* itself as sufficient whether y^e *Apology* had weight or no. They tell me the Trees in Warwickshire are much more forward than ours; If so, I hope you enjoy the full Effect of ye Urn you have erected, wch I hope you find satisfactory. As to ye Method you propose of inscribing it, it has my entire Approbation; That you may believe me sincere in this, I cannot forbear mentioning that I had sent this very Motto 'Debita' &c: together with twenty different kinds of Inscription, in a Letter to a young Clergyman of my Acquaintance, for his Opinion; And This Collection was just return'd me when your Letter arriv'd. I think it surperfluous to send it you; for I don't think you can find out any better there, or even so good as that you fix upon. However I will propose a Quere or two, which you will very easily solve yourself. First then Will it be possible to inscribe this Motto upon y^e *Plinth*, in Letters of any *tolerable Size*? & if it be, will it not together with the Inscription, & ye carv'd work below, give a crowded Appearance to one side of y^r Fabrick? You know who laughs at '*Forty-five Mottos on forty-five Plinths.*' If so, will it not be better to make use of ye Side next ye Service-Walk (which is also a principal one) for ye Purpose abovemention'd. What think you of having it modeld in this manner, & inscrib'd on ye Upper Part of ye Die on this Side. As thus.

GULIELMO, SOMERVILE. ARM^O.

H. L. POSUIT. MDCCL.

DEBITA. SPARG*ENS*. LACRYMA. FAVILLAM.

VATIS AMICI.

Or else, wou'd you dislike to have y^e *Inscription alone* on ye Side of ye Service walk? as follows,

GULIELMO, SOMERVILE. ARM^O.

H.L.

SACRAM. ESSE. VOLUIT.

MDCCL.

——Then on y^e *opposite* side (for I suppose there is some Area round it)

DEBITA SPARG*ES*, &c.

You will here observe some difference between sparg*ens* & sparg*es;* as the first will apply ye concern to yourself, the latter to any one y^t passes by—You will also observe a difference of another kind, if I am not mistaken; which is, that the Letters will here be an *embellishment* to ye Pedestal, but I am fearfull in ye other Place they will seem an Encumbrance. If you dont like y^e *Application to y^{t}self,* I mean of shedding a tear over ye Ashes of your Poetical Friend, (tho I don't see *why* you shou'd disapprove it) you may use ye word Sparg^{es}, even in ye Method first propos'd.

As to what you add about ye year, had you added ye foregoing Epithet *calentem* Debita &c. it wou'd have had weight, but as it is, I cannot think it of Importance. However you may use wch year you please—I don't know how I came so precipitately to give my Opinion concerning French Novels. I dont remember y^t I ever read one; & perhaps imagin'd, too generally, that *Poetical Prose* must be like Cambrays. I am oblig'd to your Ladyship for ye Perusal of ye French Comedy. I own I do not extremely admire it. I think ye Faux Savant, as he is drawn, is much to coarse to deserve the Satyr; Another of my Objections, is, that in some Places he seems to think himself a man of Ability &c. Learning, see Pag: 65. Scene ye 9th whereas his Ignorance is so gross, y^t he must needs be *conscious* of the Contrary[2]—The People must be kept out of the Service-walk at all adventures. I would render ye Attempt to pass that way so difficult, that their Feet shou'd insensibly lead them some other. But this *will* be done when you exchange ye Rails on ye side your Service Walk for a different sort of Fence.

As to the Seals, you do me great Honour in thinking any Hint of mine deserves to be executed—For ye Rest, I must not praise ye Device because it was my own, but I may decently enough commend the Cutting which I think to be good—Will you be so kind as send me another Impression of each on *red* wax, melted wth Spirits. That you sent me of ye Urn was spoilt by the Packthread on which ye Impression was taken.—My

Wood-work is at present far from Perfection in Point of Verdure: I have also a good deal of ground fresh-leveld that is not
yet green, tho' in a fair way to be so—I must acquaint your
Ladyship (tho' my Schemes are *necessarily* limited) you will
find here many little Matters that will be entirely new to you.
I finish my Environ-Employments this week, & the next shall
begin to make some Alterations in my House.

I have read Clarissa with a great deal of *Pleasure*; will make
no Remarks at present but y^t it wants to be abridg'd by almost
one Half. You will guess by this that there are *some* very
affecting scenes in it, or I must have read it with *disgust* on
account of ye superfluities—The Author, in my opinion, was
guilty of ye same Fault in Pamela. The style (for Epistles) is
almost universally good.

Poor Mr. Hardy (whom I us'd to visit beyond Warwick)
is gone! His sale is next tuesday se'nnight. I do not know of
any thing you wou'd chuse to buy there tho' I gave a Commission to bid for some one of his better Sort of Pictures—
There is ye Model of a Ship to be [sold]. [Not legible in MS.]
A Gift of ye King of Denmark, as Mr. Hardy us'd to say, to
Sr Thomas Hardy his Father; cost £500; will sell, they say,
for £50; but for which I would not give—Five Farthings.

He was no extraordinary good Character: *humourous* and
humoursome: no generosity in the World! And yet was not I
altogether unconcern'd at his Death, as his Manner was singular, droll, & sprightly; seem'd to have no kind of Relation to,
or Connection with Death, & Death-Beds. I believe there are
generally as many disgusted as pleas'd with Falstaffs Death &
his Misfortunes preceding it—His whole Behaviour ye same
to ye last—at least mixing serious and ludicrous Things things
[sic] together so as to make a most grotesque Caracature of his
final Scene—And yet it offends one to find y^t he had not one
Friend or relation, not even his own Sister, y^t was concern'd
at his Death—Nay what is more singular, (yet very accountable) not a single Servant Male or Female but *wish'd* for his
Death, & rejoic'd *apparently* to see their Wishes Accomplish'd
—Jack Reynalds was with me this last week—What an Affair
that of Miss Prett's! I hope your Ladyship will accept of this
hasty Letter from a Person who has (at present as he may say)

both Masons, Stone-cutters, & Carpenters about him, but who is with more respect yⁿ he can now express.

Your Ladyship's most oblig'd
& most obedient Servant
W. Shenstone.

Sunday.
    May ye 6th 1750.

Since I clos'd my Letter I have determin'd to send you ye Inscriptions I had been meditating & advising with my Friend upon, that you may know I have not been idle in this Respect, & for no other purpose whatsoever—For I do most earnestly desire you wou'd adhere to ye Inscription & Motto you propose—I can't say I calculated them *merely* for y^r Ladyship's Use—for I had my own also in View; resolving nevertheless to give you your Choice & take up with some one of ye Remainder—I receiv'd them back with ye Asterisks you see, which by an agreement betwixt me & ye Person I consulted are intended to mark ye different degrees of Approbation, in proportion to ye Number he prefixes. Mr. Allen or Mr. Hall (to w^m my Compliments) will give you ye English of them) if you have any *Curiosity* to know—for as I said before you cannot do better than adhere to your own.

The first, and last-but-one are added since I had them Home. I hope for ye Favour of a speedy Letter from your Ladyship; My Correspondents are exceeding few; & in truth I don't much regret it, provided I cou'd be more often favour'd with a Line or two from Barrels.

Please to return me these Inscriptions; I have not yet quite fix'd in regard to what I shall use myself.

NOTES

[1]Lady Bolingbroke's death occurred March 18, 1750. She was Mary Claire, widow of Philip le Valois de Vilette, and daughter of Armand des Champs, Seigneur de Marcilly.

[2]Lady Luxborough wrote to W.S., April 25, 1750, 'A new comedy is acted in Paris, which I send you to read, as it is not in verse, and as it ridicules justly an ignorant Pedant; which I dare say you think (as I do) deserves the highest ridicule.' It is evident from this remark and that of W.S. in reply that the play referred to is *Le Faux Savant* of Du Vaure (1694–1778), acted in Paris 1749, being the revised draft of *L'Amour Précepteur* of 1728.

CXV

B.M. Add. MSS. 28958.

[*To* Lady LUXBOROUGH.]

The Leasows, *June* ye 5th 1750.

Madam,

I shou'd hold myself inexcusable in not sending a servant over to enquire after your Ladyship's Health, had I not been in constant Hopes of waiting upon you at Barrels before this time. Those Hopes have been hitherto frustrated; & as your Ladyship gave me a good account of your *Recovery*, & my Servant, my *only* Servant, is at this time extreme busy, I must beg you wou'd please to accept of this Letter by a more lingering conveyance. The Case is, I have been-*amus'd*, (shall I say, or *fatigued* rather) for these Six weeks with a considerable Crowd of Workmen. I believe I told your Ladyship in my last, y^t having compleated my schemes for this year out of Doors, I was then beginning upon my House. I have not been a Day since y^t time without two Masons & their Attendants, two Carpenters & some times three, a Painter, Plummer, glazier & the Lord knows who beside. My House is a bottomless Pit, as Swift said formerly of the Law:[1] Or rather it is a *whirlpool*, which sucks in all my money & that so *deep* that there is not ye least glimpse of it appears thro' ye water. Accordingly, were your Ladyship to come over (which I hope will be the Case very soon) you will hardly discover what these workmen have been doing, Why, nothing *ornamental*; but many things of a *convenient* kind, & which my Servants will more sensibly reap ye Benefit of, than either my *visitants* or *myself*. However, I must acquaint you that *one* of my Alterations has been ye Enlargement of a Drawing-Room or Library (for I know not which I shall determine to make of it) And this will be but about 19 Feet by 12; yet when finish'd will be one of ye Pleasantest Rooms I shall have. It is as yet neither floor'd nor Plaister'd, & I'm greatly afraid will not be so this Summer.

I bought two Pictures at Mr. Hardy's sale, and, considering the cheapness of *these*, am sorry I had not more. One is an admirable Portrait by Wissing;[2] the other a Flowerpiece with

T

some heterogeneous objects intermix'd; good only as far as relates to ye Flowers.

You advise me to make use of those English Lines upon Mr. Somervile's Urn, *myself*; I have some doubts concerning ye Propriety of *my* Dryads being said to have heard Mr. Somervile's Harmony, as he was never here. I wrote them in pursuance of a Plan which your Ladyship once had of having *one* motto to express his *poetical* Character, & *another* to intimate his Virtue & his Friendship. This Plan you have much better executed by y^t expressive Line which you chose from Horace.

I am oblig'd to you for sending y^e *Engraver's* Impression of ye Seals; but your Ladyship woud surely chuse to keep these *yourself*; & I wanted only such as you could very readily take off, to keep in my drawer amongst a number of others.

I had here last week, Mr. Clare, a gentleman of Fortune in our Neighbourhood; & Mr. Smart a clergymen [sic] remarkable as a Man of taste, & particularly so for drawing in Miniature[3] —They offerd to take me in a Party (of wch Admiral Smith[4] was to be one) to see Mr. Anson's,[5] wth whom Mr. Clare is acquainted. I think your Ladyship express'd y^r self much in Favour of that Place.

Not one single Jaunt have I had since I was at Barrels. I I resolve *against* Indolence, but find it making continual advances. The Fault is not in my *mind*; I want better *animal Spirits*.

Poor Mrs. Pitt (whom y^r Ladyship met in Hagley Park) died yesterday morning of a Lethargy;[6] extremely lamented by her poor neighbours, & her inferiour Friends. She had great affability, of y^e *genuine Sort*; I mean, it was ye effect of her Benevolence.

I will still hope to wait upon you shortly at Barrels for a day, y^t I may see your Shrubbery in Bloom; & present my Petition y^t you woud condescend to take a view of mine.

NOTES

[1]*History of John Bull*, Ch. VI: 'Law is a bottomless pit: it is a cormorant, a harpy that devours everything.'

[2]Willem Wissing (1656–1687), portrait painter, worked for Sir Peter Lely, and became a formidable rival to Sir Godfrey Kneller for court favour.

[3]Birmingham Directories published between 1750 and 1800 mention a clergyman by the name of Smart.
[4]Thomas Smith, of Hagley. Wyndham, *Chronicles of the Eighteenth Century.*
[5]Brother of George, Lord Anson, President of the Board of Admiralty.
[6]Christian Pitt spent the last years of her unhappy married life at Hagley Hall.

CXVI

Works III, 189.

To [Rev. R. JAGO].

June 11, 1750.

Dear Sir,

I acknowledge myself obliged to you for procuring me the pictures; I received them both very safe, as I have a pretty large assurance I *shall* do most articles of which my servant Tom has the care.—He has punctuality and management, to *atone* for his *imperfections*. He brought me those paper-sculled busts from Wroxall entirely unhurt, contrary to the expectation of all that saw them; after which, he might undertake for almost any thing.—The portrait is undoubtedly a good one. I shewed it to Mr. Smart (who is a painter himself, though a clergyman), and he allowed as much; added also, that it had something of Sir Godfrey Kneller, as well as of Sir Peter Lely. —The flower-piece is very good, so far as relates to the flowers; the dog and parrot abominable, and the grapes very exceptionable. I never considered the two flower-pieces at Icheneton with attention enough to cause a preference; having never any thoughts that *either* would fall to my share. I shall add nothing with regard to your choice; but that I sincerely *hope* yours is the better piece. I never heard of Casteels,[1] I own; nor can I find his name in any of my accounts of the painters, though they take in pretty modern ones: but I can say this for your comfort, that if he excelled in any thing, it was probably in flowers; for I see his name at the bottom of those flower pieces that I have in water colours, as the designer of them; and I think the designs are good. Though I could wish neither the Cupid nor the fruit-piece had escaped us, yet is there no blame to be laid at your door; at least supposing that you are endowed with nothing more than rational conjecture, and that you are not gifted with prophesy.

And now, having spoken, I think, to *most* parts of your letter, I proceed to say a word or two in the way of appendix. First then, after five or six weeks work of masons and carpenters, I plainly discover that my house is an unfinishable thing;—and yet, I persuade myself, there will never be wanting a room in it, where you may spend an agreeable day with your undoubted friend.—Did I ever tell you how *unseasonably* the three fiddles struck up in my grove about an hour after you left me; and how a set of ten bells was heard from my wood the evening after? It might have passed for the harmony of some aërial spirit, who was a well-wisher to us poor mortals; but that I think, had it been so, it would have been addressed to the *better sort*, and of consequence have been heard whilst *you* were *here*. This by way of introduction to what I am going to tell you. Mr. Pixell has made an agreement with his club at Birmingham, to give me a day's music in some part of my walks. The time is not yet fixed; but, if you were an idle man, and could be brought over at a day or two's notice, I would give it you, and be in hopes I could entertain you very agreeably.

You cannot think how much you gratified my vanity when you were here, by saying, that if this place were yours, you thought you should be less able to keep within the bounds of *œconomy* than myself.—God knows, it is pain and grief to me to observe her rules at *all*; and *rigidly* I never can.—How is it possible to possess improveable scenes, and not wish to improve them? and how is it possible, with œconomy, to be at the expence of improving them upon my fortune? To be continually in fear of excess in perfecting every trifling design, how irksome! to be restrained from attempting *any*, how vexatious! so that I never can enjoy my situation—that is certain.—Oeconomy, that invidious old matron! on occasion of every frivolous expence, makes such a hellish squawling, that the murmur of a cascade is utterly lost to me.—Often do I cry out with Cowley,

'O rivers! brooks! when, when in *you*, shall I
'Myself, eas'd of *un-peaceful* thoughts espy!

'O woods and groves! when, when shall I be made
'The happy tenant of your shade!'[2]

Paper fails: abruptly therefore, but sincerely and affectionately
I am, dear Sir,
Yours,
W. Shenstone.

NOTES

[1]Peter Casteels (1684–1749), painter and engraver. See Walpole's *Anecdotes of Painting*, III, 652.
[2]Cowley, *On Myself*.

'O Fountains, when in you shall I
Myself, eas'd of unpeaceful thoughts espy?
Oh fields! Oh woods! when, when shall I be made,
The happy tenant of your shade?'

CXVII

An Autograph Collection.
Lady Charnwood.

[*To* Lady LUXBOROUGH.]

The Leasows
June 27th, 1750.

Madam,

It would be an odd kind of introduction to say 'The Road by which I came *from* Barrels was one of ye pleasantest I ever came in my Life'; but that your Ladyship knows my *sentiments* too well, not to suppose that I confine my expression to ye *country* merely; and that I can by no means pretend to lessen that Regret which I never fail to experience upon leaving your company. The views thro' the Trees on ye left Hand your Port-way were charming; Wetherock Hill, which I now pass'd close by, an extreme agreeable situation. I fancy also, very much *improveable*. From thence I came along an open airy Road 'till I enter'd upon *Nor'field Common*. I left that village on ye Right & soon found myself arriv'd at *Frankley*-Beeches. These are Trees of *Note* in our Neighbourhood; are large, stand high, and have a most delightful Prospect round them. On the whole, I was surprised to think I had ever been so stupid, as to go thro' *Birmingham* to Barrels. That road, I believe, is near twice as far; destitute of all agreeable Prospects besides the tediousness of riding two or three Miles on Pebbles thro' ye Town. But when I talk thus, I speak not in regard to *Vehicles*; and yet is the road I have been mentioning practicable for *Vehicles*, 'till you come within about two Miles of my own House. Have I not *some* grounds to hope y^t I *may discover* a method of having your Ladyship conducted this way to the Leasows? And now I am enter'd upon y^t agreeable subject, you must not be angry at ye Proposal I am going to make. 'Tis only this, y^t you would please to honour me with your Company twice this Summer instead of once; and then I wou'd desire y^t your Visit might be as early ye next Month as you can conveniently with respect to Harvest; and that you wou'd condescend to accept of such accommodations as I can furnish, for three or four Days. I am well assured y^t ye Performance of this Journey in a Day, must occasion you more fatigue yn. Pleasure. Besides I have a selfish view, for I cannot shew my walks to any kind of Advantage in the usual time. We will also, if you please, see my Lord Dudley's green-house; whether he come home before that Time, or not. Tis most probable he *will*, being daily expected. And I hope this first Jaunt, you will be so good as let Mrs. Ann accompany you; as I find by Tom she would like well enough to see this Country. The *next* Visit I hope will give me ye additional happiness of Mr. and Mrs. Weymond-sell's Company. *That*, I fear, must be for a Day; for I cannot presume to offer them much worse accommodations yn. they ever met with at an Inn; tho' I would be content to expose my *Poverty*, if I could desire of *them* to sacrifice *their Ease*. Your Ladyship sees how much I presume upon Encouragement; but this is ye Extent of my present Ambition; and if it ever here-after urge me too far, your Ladyship shall rein me in with ye thread of a Spider.——I owe much acknowledgment for my elegant Reception at Barrels, and for ye Present of Fowls you were so kind as to offer me, for which I have sent my Servant ——My Four Guinea-chicks are yet alive, and also one small Pea-chick. You will imagine that this last does not want for Nursing. I have great Store of Turky-Pouts, which will be ready to kill by the time you arrive——Tho' you may have some chance of seeing my lower Rooms floor'd &c: at ye *second* visit propos'd, you can see nothing of y^t nature now. I find a difficulty in procuring Boards here, and have also *some* in detaining my workmen from all ye rest of their Masters so long as I *have* done. I'm afraid my sketch of *propos'd* Improvements (like a College Almanack) may shew you my present *unimprov'd* Fabrick to a disadvantage it is by no means adapted to bear. Whilst I was at Barrels, it seems, Admiral Smith was here, and was shown ye walks by my Servant with which he appeared much pleased, and left his Complements; I believe I must dine at Hagley tomorrow. I have reflected since I came Home that your Place (tho' so very agreeable) has not the advantage of above *one Single Skreen*. You want at least half a dozen immediately. I know no Form so good as that of a plain settee; the Back boarded, as it looks well at a distance when painted, and admits of any Inscription; ye seat consisting of bars, which let ye Wet thro. For ye Rest, they should be strong, and large enough to receive four People conveniently. You have these to procure; ye Pediment to your Pavilion to add; the Gate Pillars to remove; your Cistern to demolish; your Summer house to plaister; and I must not omit ye ground about your Urn, to turve; before Mrs. Weymondsell comes—A Carpenter makes a Skreen in ye Manner above mentioned in two days; ye Stuff being sawn to his Hands. I have just finished one, so I speak by experience; yet must I be so just as to confess that mine is hardly more yn. 8F. long. I can't help thinking, y^t your Ladyship should make y^t hedge next y^r service-walk altogether impregnable; this would perhaps be attended with some difficulty, yet I am persuaded y^r usual Workmen might effect it some time next winter. The violent changes of weather from Heat to Cold affect my constitution strangely. I have scarce had tolerable Spirits all this Summer; was bleeded yesterday but find very little Advantage from it—surely we have some better Days in reserve. May those be such which light your Ladyship to the Leasows, and shine upon you there, whatever they be that succeed them afterwards.

Tis now Thursday, June ye 20th. and I am just returned from my visit at Hagley. When I alighted at ye Stable door, I ask'd if there was Company; and the Servant told me there was *none*. Upon entering their Dining room I found Miss Lyttelton, Lady Caroline Egerton, Lady Die Egerton,[1] and Admiral Smith; a moment after (from ye Drawing room) the Duchess of Bridgwater,[2] Lrd Fielding,[3] Colonel Lyttelton and Miss West—soon after Sir Thomas Lyttelton then the Dean. It was immediately proposed by Admiral Smith and the Col'nel that they should all come here tomorrow morning; some difficulty occur'd about ye Roads, but y^t was obviated by ye Mention of one horse chairs—and ye result was that they wou'd *come*—Since I came home, have fallen some heavy Rains, which together wth ye knowledge they have of ye Roads and of my Walks being ungravell'd make it an equal Chance with me whether they will come or no. Tis now near twelve o'clock, so I must wish y^r Ladyship good-night, proposing to add a Line or two more when I have seen ye Event.

'Tis now Friday Morning, Seven o'clock; the Sky dark and lowring, and ye ground wet; so I suppose, no Lady Duchess, Lady Die, Lady Caroline, or Lord Fielding; no Colonels, Admirals, or Fine Ladies today, and *tomorrow* they all go away. What a Loss is this to my Ambition. I must trust in your Ladyship only to repair this Loss to my poor *Ambition:* and I can perceive y^t. *She* reaps very apparent Benefit from every single syllable which I have ye Honour to write to you; nor have I ye least Doubt, but that *she* will become entirely easy by the Time I shall have read your Ladyship's Answer.

Friday Noon, one o'clock.

A Sudden Change! The Day has clear'd up, and here arrives in ye First Place, Madame La Duchesse and her *elder* Daughter Lady Car, in ye next Place Lord Fielding and Miss Lyttelton on Horse-back, in the last Place Monsieur le Colonel and Lady Die in a Chair. They have all been round my Walks (which prov'd dry enough) with much seeming satisfaction. Lady Duchess whom I had yesterday an *affection* for as a good natur'd, *sans-ceremonie* woman, I today esteem as a Person of Sense and Reading. Lady Caroline, whose Person I thought yesterday only not disagreeable, I today think *handsome* (she has withal *taste* and an easy manner), Lady Di whom I yesterday thought handsome only, I today think beautifull. She is

very young—I mean about 15. Lord Fielding I hardly know
what to make of; but he surely doesn't want sense, and I think
ye *world allows* him good-nature. Miss Lyttelton was quite
obliging; offer'd to beg me a small Statue from ye Park; too
small for their Use, but transportingly beautifull, for *my Grove*.
Colonel Lyttelton desir'd they wou'd give me the Shell Urn
they have there[4]—I told him I thought ye Request wd. be too
considerable. I also enquir'd of Miss Lyttelton wt. *stress* they
laid upon their ruin'd Abby[5] (wch is near me and which I *must*
shew your Ladyship) and intimated if *that* was not *great*, I
shou'd be tempted to ask for a particular window or two to
terminate ye Vista in my wood. (Twou'd indeed be delightfull
for ye Purpose). And I had encouragement to hope I might
succeed. Further particulars of this visit I reserve for ye Tete-
a-Tete discourse in wch your Ladyship very kindly indulges
me. I believe I must end—but not without a Reflection—
Visits of this kind are of *real importance* to one in my Station—
that is, they give one some Weight amongst the People with
whom one is to live—one's Parishioners—and here I can't
but acknowledge how much indebted I am to your Ladyship,
Tis easy enough it shou'd seem for Persons of Rank to distinguish any *unpresuming* Person whom they do *not disesteem*—
but how few *are* there who do this with ye Spirit of your Ladyship? I tire you now I am sure—I have only to add that I am
in no common degree

Your Ladyship's most *oblig'd*
and most obedient servant,
W. Shenstone.

They are gone to Hagley to dine wth my Lord of Worcester[6]
—all—(not excepting Sr. Thos.) amply prepar'd to fall foul
upon the Parson who destroy'd my Coppice—Sr. T. (and I
think 'twas said, the BP) declares ye Parson to be *mad*, but not
mad *enough*. This is a random Letter, and ought to be written
over again, but as I love Letters written at different Periods
myself, I am induc'd to hope it may not be disagreeable to an
Imagination wch either regulates mine or is naturally something
like it. Allow me this Honour—tis, I know a greater y^n I ought
to do *myself*.

Pray, my Lady, make my compliments to Mr. Hall—

excuse the writing Part, and believe me yours—Why won't Mr. Hall take an Afternoon's Ride and see me now and then? Were it not good-natur'd? And then, were it not in Character? I do most heartily abhor, detest and abjure as impious and heretical, y^t damnable doctrine and position of the Cere-monialists, 'That large Margins and large spaces and large Wastes of Paper are polite and elegant. I *must* write on, 'till my Sheet of Paper will contain no more. If y^r Ladyship have not seen this coarse (but good) Edition of Swift, I fancy you will find some things in it wch you never saw elsewhere. I must beg Mr. Pope's Pardon so far as to esteem Dr. Swift (tho' in a way rather contemptuous of regular Poetry and therefore manly) ye Poetical *Genius* of the Age he liv'd in. He had inconceivable Invention, wch was not remarkably ye Talent of ye other. I am asham'd you have not received my Lord Lovat's Tryal—but I cannot get it brought me home yet— I hope I shall be able to send it back by yr servants when you come. Pray, my Lady, let it not be long first. Tis my opinion, y^t no part of ye season is so good as when ye grass is just mow'd. A short time will now affect this. And I beg also you would be so kind as establish me (as far as you well can) in ye good opinion of Mr. and Mrs. Weymondsell, and Mr. Meredyth—My *Place* also; y^t I may have a sure and certain hope of ye Honour you mention'd, Give me Leave here, my good Lady! to mention what a Change there is in my Scheme since I first began to lay out my little Farm in Paths, etc. At First I meant them merely as Melancholy Amusements for a Person whose circumstances required a solitary Life. They *were* so; but I ever found ye solitude too deep to be agreeable. Of *late* encourag'd by your Ladyship and some others I begin to covet to have my Place *esteem'd* agreeable in its way; to have it *frequented*; to meet now and then an human Face unawares— to enjoy even ye Gape and Stare of ye Mob (wch Miss Lytt: tells me I mustn't value of a Rush) but above all possible Contingencies to have it honour'd wth ye Company of your Ladyship and your Acquaintance. And now I wish yr. Ladys. some Harts-horn.

NOTES

[1]The daughters of the Duchess of Bridgewater.

[2]The Duchess of Bridgewater, married secondly Colonel Richard Lyttelton, December 14, 1745, but W.S. still refers to her by the title of her first marriage.
Horace Walpole to Sir Horace Mann, May 14, 1761, 'You will be happy too in Sir Richard Lyttelton and his Duchess; they are the best humoured people in the world.'
[3]Basil (Feilding), Earl of Denbigh, styled Viscount Feilding till 1755. Lord Feilding afterwards became prominent as a Tory and held posts in the households of George I and George II.
Horace Walpole described him in 1773 as 'the most officious of the Court tools.'
[4]Lady Luxborough (*Letters*, 209) wrote, 'I love Colonel Lyttelton for wanting to give you their shell-urn, which would have a good effect on many spots of the Leasowes; and is I think very ill placed in their garden. I hope Miss Lyttelton will get you the small statue and the old Abbey-windows.'
[5]Nash, *History of Worcester*, I, 490, gives a plate showing the remains of Halesowen Abbey.
[6]Isaac Maddox (1697–1759), became Bishop of Worcester, 1743.

CXVIII

B.M. Add. MSS. 28958.

[*To* Lady LUXBOROUGH.]

Sunday, July ye 15. 1750.

Madam,

With the utmost Thankfullness for ye agreeable Hopes you give me of waiting upon your Ladyship at the Leasows about ye 17th of this Month, I am oblig'd to sit down in order to defer my own Happiness for about a week longer. My Hay-harvest is but now compleated, & My Servants have been so universally employ'd in [illegible in MS.] I shall be utterly unable to put my walks in order in less time than a week. But I shall with ye utmost pleasure wait upon your Ladyship ye beginning of ye week after, I mean on Monday or Tuesday se'nnight, as I shall make use of the mean time to render my Environs less unworthy of your Notice. There will be a Bed for y^r Ladyship, another for Mr. Hall, a third for Mrs. Ann & one & an half for your Servants of ye other sex. There are many *Improvements* I wou'd wish compleated before you came, but should I give ye least way to Views of that kind, the Lord knows when I shou'd have a Chance of seeing you. Let it suffice my Ambition, for ye Present, y^t if your Ladyship & I live, I may *hereafter* have an opportunity of accomodating you in less vulgar manner y^n I *now* can possibly do. I beg you would please to make my Compliments to Mr. Hall, & ac-

quaint him with how much I desire to see him. I hope he did
not *mistake* me when I ask'd why he would not take—de some
afternoon. I alluded only to yᵉ Shortness of yᵉ Way, & not to
the Space of time I wou'd wish to share his Company.

I had yesterday a morning's visit from Dean Lyttelton wᵗʰ
Mr. Meadowcourt of Worcester.[1] He says he lays no great
stress on yᵉ old Abby, wonders I should be afraid of *him*, &
will promote my Application all that lies in his Power—Were
your Ladyship to know yᵉ whole extent of my Petition, you
wou'd not imagine it yᵉ most unreasonable that ever was—
Yet am I in some doubt whether I shall succeed.

As you are pleas'd to observe, there is Pleasure enough in
forming a Plan & seeing it's progress, if we speak with relation
to [illegible in MS.] of mere *amusement*; but in Projects yᵗ
are altogether of yᵉ *convenient* or *necessary* kind (such as many
I have lately engag'd in) One wishes to have them dispatch'd
with as much expedition as possible. I must do but little more
by way of *ornament* 'till next Winter: but in order to get a
habitable Room below stairs, much must I *undergo* before
winter arrives. With this Prospect before me I cannot avoid
crying out with Aeneas 'O Fortunati &c:'

Thrice Happy You, whose walls *already rise*!

And yet I love, as does your Ladyship to see Workmen
about me, but my Finances will not let me see them, without
connecting an Idea of yᵉ expences they occasion.

What does your Ladyship think of a small Excursion to
my Lord Stamford's? The Family is now at Lord Walling-
fords[2] & will continue there till the End of August. I am apt to
think we may *get thither* if the Roads continue good; For they
tell me Hagley-Lanes have nothing disagreeable in them,
except *Dust*—a thing extremely uncommon. And I dont know
yᵗ we shall find it above 7 Miles thither, half yᵉ way over level
Downs & Commons. His Chinese house, Rotonde, Gothick
Greenhouse &c will be new to your Laship as well as to myself.
But of this more hereafter Many thanks to your Ladyship for
yʳ rural Presents: rural indeed, but having an Air of Elegance
as every thing must yᵗ comes from Barrels. As to yᵉ Sp: Geese
Don Pedro has all yᵉ stateliness of a Swan: Donna Elvira, his

faithfull Consort, filled all my Vallies with Complaint for three long Summer's Days. Nor was there any Dervise here to interpret her Language, save ye learned Mrs. Arnold; who told us she was expostulating about ye loss of Some young y^t she had left behind her, & endeavouring to let them know ye Present Place of her Abode—If this was *not* ye Case, she was lamenting her Removal from Plenty & Splendour to Poverty and Obscurity. But she now seems contented under both.

I hear no more of ye small Figure y^t was talkd of. Sure I am that in their *Park* it is a mere *Concetti*, whereas it wou'd be proportionate & adapted to many Places in my Grove.

They do now entirely discard their Shell Urn, whatever is the Reason.

Why don't your Ladyship throw all y^r Haystacks into ye Form of Pyramids, & chuse out places where they may look agreeably? T'is no inconvenient Form for an Hay-stack, & they are made with as much ease, as any. I have executed one so— but alas! *mine*—is little bigger y^n an Hen-pen.

Tho the Beginning of this Letter bespeaks some Delay, I am truly *impatient* to wait upon your Ladyship, & hope you will not add to y^t Delay by defering my Pleasure any longer y^n ye Beginning of next Week.

> I am, Madam,
> Your oblig'd & most obedient Servt
> W. Shenstone.

Lord Dudley not yet come down; but the Bells here rang about two days ago for the Termination of his Law-suit wth my Ld Ward.

> To
> The Right Honourable
> Lady Luxborough
> at Barrels.

NOTES

[1]Unidentified.
[2]Charles Knollys, Earl of Banbury, son of William Knollys, styled Viscount Wallingford. His seat was at Burford.

CXIX

B.M. Add. MSS. 28958.

[*To* Lady LUXBOROUGH.]

Tis now August ye 8th 1750.

Madam,

The Return of Mr. Moore[1] affords me an opportunity of acknowledging ye Receipt of your last Letter, by which I am allow'd to expect ye Pleasure of waiting upon you soon. Indeed I grow a little *impatient* upon that Head; as the *weeds*, which I had been carefull to subdue in my Walks, begin again to rebell, at ye Instigation of these late Rains. But you promise to make Amends for your Delay by ye Addition of Mrs. Wymondsold & Mrs. Davis's Company. I should be a little sollicitous concerning ye Amusement wch so mean a Cottage as mine can afford them, but that I am assur'd their *goodnature* must receive some satisfaction from the Pleasure they will occasion *me*—I depend upon your Ladyship's giveing me a Day or two's Notice—There is no Joke in *surprizing* such a mortal as me; whom you might find, very probably sitting down to a single Pigeon; & throw me into *Confusion* by ye same means thro' which you *famish'd* yourselves. I should be heartily glad to see Mr. Outing, to whom I beg my Compliments.

I am quite sorry I cannot employ Mr. Moore, both on account of your Ladyship's recommendation, & of his own Appearance; which to *Me* promises better things than that of Crosbie, who has been here twice on ye same Occasion; & to whom I gave a Promise that, when my Room was done, *he* should be ye Person employ'd. I do not know much of Crosbie's Merits: I know he workd for Ld Ward: but I then thought to have only plain walls & a plain Cornice: whereas I am now thinking to indulge myself in two or three slight Festoons—but all this must be *defer'd*.

Your Ladyship determines very justly; It will much improve my Lord Bolingbroke's Bust to have it painted in ye same manner wth mine of Mr. Pope. Beside it will appear doubly better in a *Stucco-Room*.

You will no doubt make ye wash for your Summer House of a Stone-colour. You may try ye Colour first on an hot Brick on which it will dry immediately. You have a good Sand near you. It should be done twice at *least*.

Your Ladyship has had much agreeable Company; I will not say more than your *Share*, because I think you deserve every thing y^t can contribute to your Happiness; & I am persuaded the Company of your Friends bids fairest so to do— Is it improbable Sr Peter Soames shou'd ever travel thro' my Neighbourhood?

My Lord of Dudley came Home last Saturday, as I am well assur'd by Intelligence from ye Steeple & other concurrent Intimations; for I have not yet seen him.

That very religious Tyrant our Parson (who destroy'd my neighbouring coppice) attack'd last Sunday a most Noble & renowned Captain, in ye midst of his Sermon; taxing him wth snorting & sneezing to ye great scandal of him & his Congregation; comparing him to a Beast y^t perisheth; even to a Hog. And this was nothing more it seems y^n either a natural Imperfection, or a Habit wch the Man had got. Does it not put your Ladyship in mind of the Montague's And the Capulet's Servants in Shakespeare? 'Do you bite your Thumb at *me*, Sir' 'No, Sir! but I *bite* my *Thumb*, Sir.'[2]

At other time's he has condescended to attack his neighbour Parson's Children of about Four years old & under, telling them they are damn'd, For being seen out of Doors on a Sunday & not reading the Bible.

Nay, at other times he hath stoop'd so low as to *pun* from his, Pulpit; making Hales-owen and Hell's-own to be in his Opinion Synonimous terms.

But I tire your Ladyship wth what regards you no otherwise y^n as it fell from a Person who has impaird ye Pleasure you us'd to take in my Scenery. I am your Ladyship's most oblig'd & faithfull Servant

WILL: SHENSTONE.

NOTES

[1]Mr. Moore of Warwick. 'plaisterer.'
[2]*Romeo and Juliet*, Act I, Sc. 1.

CXX

Works III, 193.

To C[HRISTOPHER] W[REN], Esq.

THE LEASOWS,
Sept. 9, 1750.

Dear Sir,

Pray, is laziness an excuse for not writing? Tell me.—
However, if it be so, I am afraid I shall want an excuse for
laziness: like the philosopher, who, supposing the world
might rest upon a tortoise's back, found himself no less embarrassed for a pedestal to support his tortoise. I have, indeed,
been pretty busy at home raising a pool-dam, and have interchanged a few visits with such of my acquaintance as live
within three miles.—What then?—I abominate all excuses
that are grounded upon the business or amusements of an idle
man.—As if such a person's time was so wholly filled up, that
he could not find half an hour to write a line to his friend. It is
best to acknowledge laziness at first, and that there are particular intervals, when one is much less disposed to write even
a few lines than at others. And then, as to laziness, one has
nothing to do but to plead human frailty; which, if a person
has not too many frailties besides, may perhaps be indulged
him. However, 'Veniam petimusque, damusque,'[1a] will not
fail to weigh with every good-natured man. The chief dealing
I have with Harris the Jew is, for the intelligence which he
brings me concerning you and Mrs. W[ren]; but it seldom
amounts to much more than that you are well, and in your
garden.

He is an Ebrew Jew, or he would tell me you had
purchased a couple of genteel horses, or a chaise and pair,
and were coming over to The Leasows to spend a week
with me.

Nevertheless, I hope to see you soon; but *en passant* I
assure you, I shall go in about a month to Mr. Jago's, and
from thence to Mr. Miller's; who, I believe I told you, was
here, with Mr. Lyttelton, Lady Aylesbury, Colonel Conway,
&c.[1] I think I never answered your quere concerning Colonel
Lyttelton.—He is the same person that you remember, and

your prophesy concerning him has been literally accomplished. He is a man of courage, genius, generosity, and politeness; has been fortunate in the world; was made a Colonel at about six and twenty; distinguished himself in several campaigns; married the Duchess of Bridgewater; and had the other day about sixteen thousand pounds left him by Colonel Jefferies, a very distant relation. He has a seat, and speaks in the House of Commons; has bought a town and country-house; the latter of which he is ornamenting in the modern way. His Dutchess the most unceremonious even-tempered woman that lives.—So enjoy the spirit of prophesy, and exert it again.—It needs little more than good sense. Which of the historians is it, that foretold in his history a very remarkable series of events, by dint of this alone, and which were all accomplished? Let me know what you are doing now. Have you repaired the farm-house you talked of?—and have you remembered to make the man a couple of good large niches in his chimney-corner, where he, and his family, may spend a more comfortable evening than was ever spent by any first minister in Christen-dom;—perhaps also converse more to the purpose You tell me nothing of your Mr. Jago, Seignior Benedict, the new-married man. Tell him to leave his wife and family for a day or two, saddle his mule, and come over to The Leasows.—Tell him, all pleasures are heightened by a little discontinuance.—Tell him, did I say?—how can you for shame advise him so contrarily to your own practice?

> Believe me, dear Sir,
> Very faithfully yours,
> W. SHENSTONE.

NOTES

[1]a Horace, *Ars Poet.* II.

[1]Lady Aylesbury married secondly Henry Seymour Conway of Park Place, Henley-on-Thames. Their daughter became Mrs. Damer, friend of Horace Walpole.

Lady Luxborough, (*Letters*, 221), wrote, 'You, Sir, have also had an agreeable Lady at your house, who has the further advantage of youth and beauty; I mean the Countess of Aylesbury, whose charms and whose conduct have always been equally admired by those I have heard speak of her. I have been told she was a lover of retirement in her old Lord's time: I do not know what she may be in her young Colonel's. She is, you know, daughter to General Campbell, and to Miss Bellandine, who was so celebrated when Maid of Honour to Queen Caroline. It is no wonder that she is pleasing.'

U

CXXI

Hull, I, 50.

To the RIGHT HON. LADY LUXBOROUGH, *at Barrels.*

[1750?][1]

Madam,

I was much concerned to hear by Mr. WILLIAMS's Account, last *Thursday*, that your Ladyship has been greatly indisposed. The Particulars of your Disorder he does not mention, but tells me, he was desired to give it as a Reason that I did not hear from you before. It is as natural for me to make Enquiry concerning the Recovery of your Health, as it is for me to wish it, which I very earnestly do; I have, therefore, sent an honest Neighbour of mine upon this Errand, who will be glad of an Opportunity of seeing *Barrels*. Poor TOM, my trusty Servant, has, ever since I came from *Barrels*, been in a very dangerous way; and whether he ever may regain the small Share of Health he has been used to, is a great Question, else I had sent something sooner. But I must request your Ladyship not to write, if you find it the least troublesome. A verbal Message will be very sufficient, till such Time as you can write me a full Account of your Recovery.

I have no Particulars that can tempt me to enlarge this Letter, and, indeed, I hardly wish for any, lest I should accidentally let fall any Thing that might tempt you, at this Time, to write an Answer; which, tho' so highly agreeable to me at a more favourable Season, can afford me little Satisfaction, when I conjecture that you write in Pain.

I hope Mr. HALL is recovered by this Time. As my rural Scenery could not attract him hither in Summer, I have little Hopes that my Conversation can have that Effect in Winter. Few Persons care to ride twelve dirty Miles in Winter, be their Charity ever so great, 'To see the dullest of the Sons of Men,' for such am I, without any Affectation, during the Winter-Season; although absorbed in what I think they call *Swiss-Meditation*, that is, *thinking upon Nothing*. A very unjoyous Circumstance this, for such of my Friends as vouchsafe to read my Letters.—But I digress—I pray for your Ladyship's Health and Happiness, hoping my Messenger may bring me an Account of both, agreeable to the Wishes of

Your Ladyship's

most obliged and obedient Servant,

W. SHENSTONE.

'Tis now *Oct.* 18th—but this Letter was wrote, in order to have been sent last Week. I sate up late with Lord DUDLEY one Night this Week. He often proposes your Ladyship's Health, and drinks it very respectfully.

The Inhabitants of our Parish have presented our Parson at the Visitation; on which Occasion, I have given myself the generous Air of observing a strict Neutrality—in other Words, I am a Person unconcerned.

NOTE

[1]The date of this letter is probably October 1750, as Luxborough letters show that at this time Mr. Hall had broken his arm and her Ladyship was suffering from a complication of disorders.

A MS. version of the letter is in the R. B. Adam Collection at the University of Rochester Library but I discovered the fact too late to use it. The version, however, differs but slightly from Hull's.

CXXII

Works III, 196.

To C[HRISTOPHER] W[REN].

THE LEASOWS,

Nov. 2, 1750.

Dear Sir,

It never can be that I owe you for three letters; as to two, I will agree with you; one that I received together with my books, and the other soon after, but that I am indebted for more than these—

'Credat Judæus Apella,

'Non ego.'[1]

Even that same 'Judæus Apella,' who affords me this very opportunity of sending my compliments to you and Mrs. W[ren], and of assuring you, that if I had not purposed to have seen you, I had wrote to you long ago.

Master Harris talks very respectfully of your garden; and we have no dispute, save only on one point. He says, that you labour very hard in your vocation; whereas, I am not willing to allow that all the work you ever did, or will do in it, is worth a single bunch of radishes. However, I dare not contradict him too much, because he waits for my letter.

How happy are you, that can hold up your spade, and cry, 'Avaunt, Satan!' when a toyman offers you his deceitful vanities! Do not you rejoice inwardly, and pride yourself greatly in your own philosophy?

"Twas thus—
'The wise Athenian cross'd a glitt'ring fair:
'Unmov'd by tongues and sights he walk'd the place,
'Thro' tape, tags, tinsel, gimp, perfume, and lace.
'Then bends from Mars's Hill his awful eyes,
'And, "What a world I never want!" he cries.'

PARNEL.[2]

Mean time, do not despise others that can find any needful amusement in what, I think, Bunyan very aptly calls *Vanity Fair*. I have been at it many times this season, and have bought many kinds of merchandize there. It is a part of philosophy, to adapt one's passions to one's way of life; and the solitary, unsocial sphere in which I move makes me think it happy that I can retain a relish for such trifles as I can draw into it. Mean time, I dare not reason too much upon this head. Reason, like the famous concave mirrour at Paris, would, in two minutes, vitrify all the Jew's pack: I mean, that it would immediately destroy all the form, colour, and beauty, of every thing that is not merely useful.—But I ramble too far, and you do not want such speculations. My intent, when I sat down, was to tell you, that I shall probably see you very soon, and certainly remain in the mean time, and at all times, Sir,

Yours obliged,
and very faithful servant,
W. SHENSTONE.

NOTES

[1] Horace, *Satiræ*, I, 5, 100.
[2] Chalmers, *Poets*, IX, 362. *An Elegy to an old Beauty.*

CXXIII

Works III, 205.

To MR. GRAVES.

THE LEASOWS,
Feb. 16, 1750–1.

Dear Mr. Graves,

Since I received your letter, I have been a week at W[hit-church][1] I believe I may have told you, that I never was fond of that place. There is too much trivial elegance, too much punctilio for me; and perhaps, as you express it, too much *speculation*. But I was fearful I might entirely lose Mr. Whistler's acquaintance, if I did not make an effort once in five years to return his visit. Besides, I should have had no hopes of seeing him at The Leasows hereafter; and I am extremely desirous of seeing both *him* and *you* here, having made many alterations which I do not undertake but with an eye to the approbation of my more ingenious friends; but he seems, to my great surprize, to renounce the thing called *taste* in buildings, gardens, &c. is grown weary of his own little embellishments at W[hitchurch], and longs to settle in London for the greater part of his time. This, I believe, he would put in execution immediately; but that he thinks it might give some uneasiness to his mother, if he should quit the house that she with so much difficulty obtained for him. I too am sick of the word *taste*; but I think the *thing* itself the only proper *ambition*, and the *specific pleasure* of all who have any share in the faculty of imagination. I need not mention my reasons; you will soon conceive them. And, however the case be, there in one branch of it which so totally engrosses the persons with whom I principally converse, that I was astonished to hear him speak even with indifference concerning the reigning taste for rural decorations. I could ill forbear telling Mr. Whistler, that he was now *literally* a beau in a band-box;[2] but the freedom might have given more offence than the joke was worth. He has improved the place extremely; but I do not like his colonnades. You know, nothing of that kind is tolerable, unless regularly executed in stone: that is one thing. Another is, that colonnades are ornaments which will not *bear* to be very *diminutive*. Mr.——

(whose house only I saw) has been at the expence of a large cornice round it, in most elaborate brick-work; but with regard to his stucco-work *within* doors, he is quite *extravagant.* —I mention these things upon a supposition that you may like to hear *any* thing that regards the place; but indeed they are so mighty trifling, that I ought to doubt my supposition. I supped with Mr. P——'s family once at Mr. W——'s, and once at Mr. W——'s, and all was mighty well; only I happen to have a violent aversion to card-playing, and at W[hitchurch] I think they do nothing *else.* So that, on account of my ignorance at quadrille, or any creditable game, I was forced to lose my money, and two evenings out of my seven, at Pope Joan with Mr. P——'s children. Mr. W——, to make me amends, invited me to breakfast, and shewed me your verses. I assure you, you have no occasion for a better advocate than Mr. W——; whether with regard to his *judgement,* or his zeal in behalf of the subject, the verses, or the poet. I would fain have obtained a copy; but he did not care to give one without your commission. I hope *you* will oblige me so far. I like them very much; the subject is genteel, and the verses easy and elegant. We agreed upon one or two different readings; and one stanza that concerns cards should, I think, be corrected. Not that I would have you less severe upon cards neither; I was even glad to find, that you gave them so little quarter. I sometimes thought that Mr. W——'s seeming fondness for them was a kind of *contre-coeur.*—Be that as it will, his objection to the stanza, as well as mine, was solely founded on the versification, not the sentiment. I liked his Latin verses; but they do not interfere with yours. Send me a copy, and confine my use of it by what limitations you please. My reigning toy at present is a pocket-book; and I glory as much in furnishing it with the verses of my acquaintance, as others would with bank-bills. I did not know when I went to W[hitchurch], but I might have heard Mrs. G[raves] *accused of certain questions touching their law* (I mean of forms and ceremonies); but I did *not.* On the contrary, I had the satisfaction of hearing her person, her temper, and her understanding, much commended; but this I did not want. The delicacy of your taste is equal with me to a thousand commendations. Mrs. W[alker] is really so much

altered by her indisposition, that I did not know her. She talks
of going to Bath this season.—I talked of it too, and wish it
of all earthly things. You must know, I could not have come
to Claverton[3] *instead* of going to W[hitchurch], as I did not determine on the expedition at home; but at a friend's house, where
I was betwixt twenty and thirty miles on my way thither.
Besides, I would allow myself more time when I turn my face
towards Bath, than I could this winter. Your invitation, as it is
very obliging, so it has many concurring circumstances to
recommend it at this time. I want to recover my health, which
must be recovered by Bath, or *nothing*. I want to have you read
some trifles of mine, which must be ratified by you, or *no one*;
but principally, and above all, do I long to see you, my old
friend, and Mrs. G[raves], whom I expect you should render
my new one.—I am obliged for your charitable endeavours to
support my spirits. Your company would do it effectually, but
scarce any thing less, in *winter*. Solitary life, limited circumstances, a phlegmatic habit, and disagreeable events, have
given me a melancholy turn, that is hardly dissipated by the
most serene sky; but in a north-east wind is quite intolerable.
After a long state of this kind, upon every access of amusement,
one is apt to think it is not *right* to be happy; that it is one of
Wollaston's implicit lyes; a treating things contrary to what
they *deserve*.—Your situation at Claverton is admired by most
people; and, if you could connect some little matter in the
neighbourhood, would be as surely envied.

It is now high time to release you.—This is not a letter,
but an olio. I desire my compliments to Mrs. G[raves], and
am affectionately and invariably

Yours,

W. SHENSTONE.

As I must now use a frank, I will send you a few inscriptions:
your imagination will supply the scenery, on which, what merit
they may have, depends. There *were* different readings in the
first copy, of which I beg your opinion.

Stanza the first.

'At least this calm sequester'd shade
'Ambition never dares invade
'No, &c.

'But shuns, &c.'

Stanza the second.
'Hither the plaintive *halcyon hies*,
'Avoiding all the race that flies.'[4]

My design was only to convey some pleasing ideas of things, which, though proper to the place, a person might not chance to see there once in twenty times. Mr. Lyttelton and Lady Aylesbury *necessitated* me to give them copies, though they probably did it out of complaisance only: I gave them in the manner I send them you. I hope *you* have not entirely dropt your love for rural scenes, of which you were once so fond. I will allow your taste for medals to preponderate.—I beg, dear Sir, you would neglect no *opportunity* of calling on me.—I will come to Claverton when I can.

NOTES

[1]This was the occasion, when, according to Graves (*Recollection*, 141) W.S. took a 'cool leave' of Whistler, and on the return journey at Edgehill wrote:
'Whoe'er has travell'd life's dull round,
Where'er his stages may have been,
May sigh to think he still has found
The warmest welcome at an inn.'
The place of writing of these well-known lines was undoubtedly The Sunrising, at Edgehill, and the ascribing them to the inn at Henley-in-Arden, Dodsley's mistake, for they do not appear thus until the edition of W.S.'s *Works*, 1764.

[2]Whistler wrote to Shenstone, Hull, I, 104: 'As for my Retreat, it is not worth describing; or, to describe it at once, I may call it a Band-Box, viz., "The Citizen's Delight".' In *The Connoisseur*, No. 33, September 12, 1754, a citizen's week-end is described. 'Their boxes (as they are modestly called) are generally built in a row, to resemble as much as possible the streets in London.'

[3]Graves was rector of Claverton near Bath for fifty-six years, during which time he was not absent from his church for a single Sunday. After mingling with the circle which gathered at Prior Park, he became a member of Lady Miller's circle at Batheaston. See Hutton, *Burford Papers*.

[4]*Works* II, 366. The inscription, with some alterations, was used on 'a seat at the bottom of a large root on the side of a slope' in W.S.'s garden.

CXXIV (*a*)

B.M. Add. MSS. 28958.[1]

[*To* LADY LUXBOROUGH.]

THE LEASOWS, *March ye 10th* 1750–1.

Madam,

I can very faithfully assure your Ladyship y^t the Pleasure I receiv'd from your French Letter was altogether equal to what

I expected: & as I can hardly form an expression y^t implies my Approbation more fully, I ought perhaps to add nothing more upon this Head. However I can ill avoid being more explicit; for besides that your Choice of words gives me an agreeable Idea of the French Language, there is I don't know what kind of Pleasure arises upon seeing common or domestick Affairs treated of in a Language foreign to one's own. Perhaps it may however be all resolv'd into one's *vanity*, as it seems to give them an Air of greater Importance. I wish it may not be one Day my Lot to hazard a few French Lines to your Ladyship; tho' I fear I have in a great measure forgot ye terminations of my moods & Tenses; & should of course make a thousand blunders in regard to ye peculiar Idiom. But if I *should*, I trust your Ladyship would be prevail'd upon to burn what I wrote *immediately*. You, Madam, have not only the Idiom, but seem even to *think* in French; if I may guess by the excessive Complaisance you are pleas'd to discover: And surely it is oweing to the Delicacy of your *Choice*, or ye French have great Numbers of words more expressive than our own. For Instance 'Trop bonne pour avoir besoin de cet *Assaisonnement*.' I know not of any English word y^t would be proper here beside '*Recommendation*' which is greatly inferiour. I have observ'd ye same of many others: But I confine my Partiality to their Prose; & I dare say your Ladyship who know so well all y^e *Beauties* of their Language, is also not unacquainted with ye Imperfections of it; by which means you find yourself so well enabled to disguise ye latter, at ye same time y^t you are displaying ye former to so great an advantage— Notwithstanding ye suppos'd Qualifications of the Glums & the Gawries excites one's curiosity, the Book does not I think deserve a Place in your Ladyship's Library. It makes two vols in 12 ves. Price six shillings.[2] It came into my way, so I read it, giving it just attention enough to let it amuse me. And this is all I have allotted to any Book y^t I have read for some months past. As to what I said of the *Scribleriad*,[3] you will observe I had read nothing but a few Quotations; & am now to request your Ladyship's Opinion who have receiv'd y^e *Book*— Believe me, my good Lady, I am not *happy* in my subjection to *Indolence*. I long for nothing so much as to subdue the *Old*

Wizard,[4] who keeps me close confin'd; &, tho' he allows me y[e] use of Pen Ink & Paper, stupifies me to such a Degree y[t] I can use them to no sort of Purpose. I long for y[e] nearer approach of Spring, to send him packing after his old Father Winter; y[t] I may be able to acquit myself of *my* share of y[e] correspondence, & to deserve y[e] vivacity of *yours* somewhat better y[n] I do. But when I shall be able to exchange y[e] Cypress grove, in which I am wandering at present, for y[e] more agreeable verdure of y[e] Myrtle & the Laurel, is a Question I cannot pretend to solve. Very pedantick truly this! but to proceed—I wrote many ludicrous things at College,[5] & in y[e] former part of my Life; & one or two of these I am thinking to enclose to you, now & then, during this inspid Season. Perhaps, taking, like Wood-cocks y[e] Advantage of a Fog, they may hope for something better Quarter; but in truth they are much too *silly*, & your Judgment too *penetrating* to give any kind of Room for such an expectation. As to Printing, I will not say y[t] I *never* intend it, but I must first be able to spend a few weeks with a College Acquaintance,[6] who is a Person of great Delicacy, and whose Friendship to me may perhaps induce him to examine my trifles with more attention y[n] they deserve. No very agreeable task, to him or any one else! Mean time y[e] Complaint you make of y[r] present want of Amusement affords me an occasion to pour in Floods of my written Impertinence— 'The Progress of Taste[7] I meant to have shewn you long ago— 'The Snuff-box[8] (which by interweaving another Poem is now grown I see, a mere piece of Patch-work, & appears before you for no other Reason but y[t] it happen'd to be transcrib'd in y[e] *same Book* wth y[e] former) is interested in my desiring you not to read a Line of it. I send also y[e] ode I mention'd, to the Dutchess, & would ask your Ladyship in the first Place whether it *deserve* correction. If you happen to think it may be render'd tolerable, will you be so kind as to mark (in this Copy) any Improprieties, or propose any Hints of Improvement, which may occur to your Ladyship upon reading it. And this *can* be no difficult Task, if you will care to engage in it; whether in regard to y[e] Incorrectness of y[e] present Draught, y[e] brightness of your Genius, or y[e] knowledge you have of her Grace's Situation. I calculated y[e] *subject* as well as I cou'd;

but, I fear, I have made it produce nothing but commonplace Thoughts. I think my verses in general smell too much of King-cups & Daffodils; & considering how I pass my time they can scarce do otherwise. I would desire your Ladyship not to shew any thing I send in this Packet at least to any critick, & shou'd be glad to have them return'd in about Nine days or a Fortnight—A Word or two now in regard to ye propos'd alteration in your *Room*. If your Ladyship doesn't chuse to go to the expence of a *Carv'd*-frame, what think you of a white oval Frame to your glass in y^e *Middle*, & a Festoon on each side? This year ye Stucco need amount to no more y^n about Four guineas. But the Room is mighty well, even now; & you are yourself ye Judge whether ye propos'd Alteration would afford you an answerable Amusement. I am greatly pleas'd with what your Ladyship mentions of coming to The Leasows; for tho' you will see but little *new* this year yet by allowing yourself some *time* you will see the *same* with much greater Ease y^n you could before: If I shou'd add 'Pleasure, I hope you wou'd indulge it to my Fondness for a Place y^t has engross'd my Care so long. You complain, Madam, of ye Want of *fresh Ideas* (which I never observ'd in your Conversation or Letters, at any time or tide) what then must be my Case? who see nothing Day after Day, but

Bleak Mountains & wild staring Rocks!
The wretched result of my Pains!
The swains greater Brutes y^n their Flocks!
And the Nymphs—as polite as ye Swains.⁹

Vid. Y^e answer
to Collins'
Complaint.

I once thought to have inscrib'd these on a seat, but now I think my very Spleen forsakes me—I sent Tom with this Packet because it might not otherwise have arriv'd the Lord knows when. Mr. Williams *can* seldom send but on a thursday, & sometimes you do not receive anything till long after—I am your Ladyship's most oblig'd & most faithfull H.S.

W. SHENSTONE.

My Brother, who is here at present, desires his Complimts.

NOTES

¹I have given the Bodleian version of this letter and the B.M. version as it is interesting to compare the two and to realize the fact that Shenstone did, at any rate sometimes,

make more than one copy of his letters. The letter given by Hull, I, 113, follows the Bodleian MS. more closely than the B.M. MS.

²Luxborough, *Letters*, 240.

³*The Scribleriad, an Heroic Poem in six Books*, 1751, by Richard Owen Cambridge (1717–1802), advertised in *The Gentleman's Magazine*, January, 1751, 95. See Austin Dobson, *Eighteenth Century Vignettes*, III.

⁴The reference is to the wizard Archimage, in Thomson's *Castle of Indolence*.

⁵*Poems upon Various Occasions*, Oxford, 1737. W.S. took much trouble to suppress this volume, & now copies are very rare. See I. A. Williams, *Seven Eighteenth Century Bibliographies*, 51.

⁶The Bodleian MS. mentions Richard Graves as the College acquaintance.

⁷*The Progress of Taste or the Fate of Delicacy* was first printed in the *Works*, 1764.

⁸*The Snuff-box*, 'Immortal Parnel has divinely sung,' appeared in the 1737 volume but was not reprinted.

⁹*Colin's Complaint*, by Nicholas Rowe (1674–1718), and *Reply by another hand*, were in the stanza form adopted by W.S. for the *Pastoral Ballad*.

CXXIV (*b*)

Bodl. Lib.
(MS. Montagu d. 18).
and Hull, I, 113.

[*To* LADY LUXBOROUGH.]

THE LEASOWS, *March* 1750–1.

Madam,

I can very faithfully assure your Ladyship yᵗ the Pleasure I receiv'd from your French Letter was equal to what I expected; & as I can hardly form an expression that implies my approbation more fully, I ought perhaps to add nothing more upon this Head. However, I can ill avoid being more explicit; for besides yᵗ your choice of words gives me an agreeable Idea of yᵉ French Language, there is I don't know what kind of Pleasure arises upon seeing common or domestick affairs treated of in a Language foreign to one's own. I wish it may not one Day tempt me to hazard a few French Lines to your Ladyship Altho' I have in a great measure forgot yᵉ termination of my Moods & Tenses, & should of course make a thousand blunders in regard to yᵉ proper Idiom. But if I should, I trust your Ladyship wou'd be prevail'd upon to burn what I wrote immediately. Surely it is either oweing to the Delicacy of your Choice, or the French have great numbers of words more expressive yⁿ our own. For Instance 'trop bonne pour avoir besoin de cet Assaisonnement.' I know not of any

English Word y^t wou'd be proper here besides 'Recommendation; which is greatly inferior. I have observ'd ye same of
many others. But I confine my partiality to their *Prose*, & I
dare say your Ladyship (who knows so well all y^e *Beauties* of
their Language) is also not unacquainted with the Imperfections of it, by which means you find yourself so well enabled
to disguise ye latter, at ye same time y^t you are displaying y^e
former—Notwithstanding ye suppos'd Qualifications of the
Glums & the Gawries excites excites [sic] one's curiosity,
The Book does not I think deserve a Place in your Ladyship's
Library; & I wou'd not have you purchase it. It makes 2 vols
in 12 ves Price 6 shillings. It came into my way, so I read it;
giving it just attention enough to let it amuse me with y^e
Imaginary scenes it describes. As to what I said of ye Scribleriad you will observe I had read nothing but a few Quotations,
& am now to request your Ladyships Opinion, who have
receiv'd ye Book. Believe me, my Lady, I am not Lazy in
Mind. I long for nothing so much as bodily health & Spirits
to be able to acquit myself better of *my* share of ye Correspondence, and to deserve ye vivacity of *yours* somewhat more y^n
I do. But when I shall be able to exchange ye Cypress grove in
wch I am wandering at present for ye more agreeable verdure
of the Myrtle or ye Laurel, is a question I cannot pretend to
solve. Very pedantick truly this! but to proceed—I wrote
many Ludicrous things at College in ye former part of my
Life, & one or two of these am I thinking to enclose dureing
this insipid season. Perhaps takeing, like Wood-cocks, y^e
Advantage of a Fog, they may hope at such a time for something better quarter, tho to speak ye truth they are much too
silly and your Judgment too penetrating to give them any room
for such an Expectation—As to printing I will not say y^t I
never intend it; but I must first be able to spend a few weeks
with my Friend Graves, who is a Person of great Delicacy, &
whose Friendship may perhaps induce him to examine my
trifles with some Attention. No very agreeable Task for him,
or any one else. Mean time ye complaint you make of y^e
present want of Amusement gives me an occasion to pour in
floods of my *written* Impertinence. The Progress of Taste I
meant to shew you long ago: The Snuff-box (which by inter-

weaving another Poem or Two is now I see a mere Piece of Patch-work) appears before you for no other Reason in ye World but y^t it happens to be transcribed in ye same Book with ye former; & is interested in my desiring you not to read a Line of it. I send also the ode I mention'd to the Duchess, and would ask in ye first Place whether it *deserve* correction. If you wou'd not chuse I shou'd immediately destroy it, will you be so kind as to mark any Improprieties, or propose any Improvements to me? I hope you will be in no concern about defacing ye Copy, in that Case; for I woud write it over, ever so often, if I cou'd by that means add a syllable y^t was more expressive of my veneration for her Grace, or y^t tended to give her a moments amusement. I calculated ye subject as well as I could; but I am fearfull you will discover nothing but Common-place thoughts. I think most of my verses smell of Nothing but Field-flow'rs, & considering how I spend my time they can scarce do otherwise. A word more in regard to ye propos'd Alteration in your Room. If y^r Ladyship doesn't chuse to go to the expence of ye carv'd Frame, what think you of a white oval Frame to y^r glass in ye middle & a Festoon on each side. This with ye Stucco need amount to no more y^n Four guineas—But the Room is mighty well, as it *is*; & you are yourself ye Judge whether ye expence of ye alteration wou'd afford you an answerable Amusement. I am greatly pleas'd wth what your Ladyship mentions of comeing to the Leasows; for tho' you will see but little new this year, yet by allowing yourself some little time you will see ye same with much greater Ease y^n you could before, And, if I should add, Pleasure, I hope you will allow it to my Fondness for a Place y^t has engross'd my Care so long—You complain, Madam, of ye want of fresh Ideas (wch I never yet observ'd in your Conversation or Letters, at any time or tide) guess, however, what must be *my* Case, who see nothing from Day to Day but

> Black mountains & wild stareing Rocks!
> The wretched result of my Pains!
> The swains greater brutes y^n their flocks
> And ye Nymphs as polite as ye Swains.

I once thought of inscribing these, on a seat, but now my very spleen forsakes me.

CXXV

Works III, 201.

To the [REV. R. JAGO].

THE LEASOWS,

Mar. 28, 1751.

Dear Sir,

What a stupid fool was I, to shew you those letters of my friend Graves, wherein he declares himself so freely against a regular correspondence! see the effects of it! You have taken immediate advantage of his exam le, and I must never more expect an answer to any letter that I send you, in less than half a century. I wrote to you after I came home, to thank you for all your kindness at I[cheneton], &c. but not a syllable have I been able to receive from you, or a word that I could hear concerning you. I could, however, very easily convince you, that Mr. Graves (your precedent) is not altogether so hardened an offender as you may imagine. His last letter is a very affectionate recantation. I inclose that part of it which regards Mr. F[ancourt].

What a number of schemes are irreparably broken by the sudden death of the Prince of Wales![1] Yours, my good friend, which seems to be destroyed amongst the rest, has, I think, of late given you no solicitude. Your interest in Mr. N—— will remain the same, I suppose; and if he would but serve you nearer *home*, I will have no sort of quarrel with him that he did not transplant you into Cornwall,—It is at least some gratification to a person's self-love, when one finds the more *ambitious* hopes of more *aspiring* people as liable to be suddenly extinguished as one's own. However, the death of the Prince gave me a good deal of concern, though it no way affected my *particular* interest, as he had all the humane, affable, and generous qualities, which could recommend him to one's *affection*.[2]

Mr. Graves has sent me two copies of verses. One on Medals,[3] to Mr. Walker;[4] and the other, on the late Memoirs of the London Heroines, Lady V[ane],[5] Mrs. Pilkington and Mrs. Phillips.[6] Both good in their way, which you shall see when you come over.

Have you seen the first books of the Scribleriad, by Mr. Cambridge?—The Verses written in a Country Chirch-yard?[7] —Mr. W. Whitehead's Ode to the Nymph of Bristol Spring?[8] —or, what *have* you seen?—You live infinitely more in the world than I do; who hear nothing, see nothing, do nothing, and *am* nothing. Remedy this unhappiness, by sending me somewhat that may rouse my attention.—I must except what I hear from my Lady Luxborough, who indulges me now and then with a letter in French.

If you should think this letter more than usually *dull*, you must know, that, since I saw you, I have been *generally* dispirited; till about a fortnight ago I found some nervous disorders that I greatly disliked, and upon examination was told I had a nervous fever. For this I have been taking saline draughts and bolus's, and *hope* I am something better; though I am far from well. I would not indeed have written to you at this time, but I chose not to defer sending the inclosed post-script.—You who have shared many of my *happiest* hours, will excuse the produce of a more than ordinarily dull one.

Mrs. Arnold comes up to enquire after my health, and wishes I may get better, that I may stir out and see the *pretty creatures in the barn*. It seems, she has a cow or two that have calved since I kept my room.

Why should I prolong a letter that has no kind of chance to afford you any amusement? Make my compliments to Mrs. [Jago], and believe me to be ever most affectionately

Yours,

W. SHENSTONE.

I have just taken and signed a lease for life of the terrace beyond my wood, for which I am to pay annually the sum of one shilling.—Am not I a man of worldly importance, to purchase ground and take leases thus?—What matters it whether the articles that *secure* the premises to me would also *cover* them or not?

My service to Mr. F[ancour]t;—why will he not come and spend a week with me?—I think you cannot both be absent at a time.

NOTES

[1]The death of Frederick, Prince of Wales, occurred on March 20, 1751. Probably

W.S. was thinking of the affairs of his neighbours the Lytteltons, whose fortunes were mixed up with those of the Prince. The whole question is dealt with at length by Wyndham, *op. cit.*, I, Ch. XI.

[2]The feelings of the nation on the death of the Prince were expressed in the following elegy:

> 'Here lies Fred,
> Who was alive and is dead.
> Had it been his father,
> I had much rather.
> Had it been his brother,
> Still better than another.
> Had it been his sister,
> No one would have missed her.
> Had it been the whole generation,
> Still better for the nation;
> But since 'tis only Fred,
> Who was alive and is dead;
> Then there is no more to be said.'

[3]Dodsley's *Collection*, IV, 323 and 328.
[4]The Rev. Samuel Walker stood for the character of Wilmot, in Graves's *Spiritual Quixote*.
[5]Frances Anne Vane (1713–1788) wrote *Memoirs of a Lady of Quality*, which were inscribed by Smollett in *Peregrine Pickle*, Ch. LXXXI.
[6]Teresia Constantia Phillips (1709–1765), wrote in 1748, *An Apology for the Conduct of Mrs. Teresia Constantia Phillips, more particularly that part of it which relates to her Marriage with an eminent Dutch Merchant.*
[7]*The Elegy written in a Country Churchyard* was printed hastily by Dodsley in the spring of 1751, because a copy of it had fallen into the hands of *The Magazine of Magazines*. See letters of Gray to Walpole, February 11, 1751, and Ash Wednesday, 1751.
[8]*Hymn to the Nymph of Bristol Spring*. 1s. 6d. Dodsley, advertised in *The Gentleman's Magazine*, January, 1751, 33, 48.

CXXVI

B.M. Add. MSS. 28958.

[*To* LADY LUXBOROUGH.]

Madam,

I have only Leisure to give your Ladyship a very short Account of what has *befell* me since I had last ye Pleasure of writing to Barrels.

I believe I complaind, more y^n once, to you, of an unusual Depression of Spirits, in my Letters. Soon after this, I found some disagreeable Symptoms in my Nerves, wch alarm'd me; & my Disorder was hereupon term'd a nervous Fever; for which I took a multitude of Draughts and Bolus's, tho' I am now convinc'd, a Blister had been ye properest Application.

x

I had no Physician, & indeed was not so much apprehensive of *Danger* as to substitute *that* in Place of less disagreeable Means. *Somewhat* better I have been since; However, if it really *were* a Fever upon ye nerves, I think, in some Degree I am but rarely free from it.

After this my Brother was seiz'd here with a very dangerous Inflammation upon his Lungs: This Dr. Hervey[1] calls a true Peripneumony. 'Twas attended, at Intervals, with such inexpressible difficulty of Respiration, y^t I thought it impossible he shou'd survive many Hours. Dr. Wilks[2] was sent for at 12 o clock at Night, in Hopes he might be brought to join Dr. Hervey (whom we kept with us) ye next Day: but he refus'd this, & even a *second* Application, tho' we us'd the Interest of a Neighbour for whom he pretends a Personal Friendship. Had not my Brother's Disorder remitted, I purpos'd to send for Dr. Wall from Worster.[3] I can't here be *explicit* upon any Event. My Brother, we think now, is in a fair way of being Recover'd by Dr. Hervey; & tho' he is in a very languid Condition, we hope for great Advantages from a Vomit, so soon as the Physician can assure us, y^t it may be safely administred.

These are melancholy Scenes, compard wth the Pleasures of your Ladyship's Correspondence, which has been so long intermitted! My Spirits have of late been so low, so much injur'd by watching, & so much varyd by sudden Hopes & Fears, y^t I believe any more *violent* shock superadded wou'd have gone near to have kill'd me. The Effects of the *Mind* upon weak & sensible Nerves, are as much unknown to one half of ye World, as ye violent shocks of Electrical Experiments were to our Ancestors a thousand years ago.

But I now own y^t my *Hopes* preponderate; & y^t I shall with ye utmost gratitude receive a Line from your Ladyship, when you find it Convenient—I expected your Servant *before* (or) I wou'd have made Shift to have acquainted you in a few scrawling Lines with our late Situation; pursuant to ye Freedom in which you indulge me, & ye Friendship wth which I have the Honour to be your Ladyship's

most oblig'd & faithfull Servant,

April ye 24. 1751.   WILL: SHENSTONE.
          The Leasows.

My Brother desires his Compliments to your Ladyship—
we desire to be remembered to Mr. Hall—Upon my Brother's
dangerous Illness, I applyd to a gentlewoman in my neighbourhood, a good motherly sort of woman, y^t puts me in mind
of y^r Mrs. Holyoak; she is now in my Room, & will continue
sometime.

To
The Right Honourable
Lady Luxborough.

To be forwarded by   at Barrels.
     Mr. Williams.

NOTES

[1]Neighbouring doctors. Dr. Hervey married one of the sisters of Lord Dudley.

[2]'Dr. Wilks' figures in the Hagley correspondence, (Wyndham II). Mrs. Huntback
wrote to Dean Lyttelton, March 29, 1760, 'He (i.e. Wilkes) is little lamented but for
his judgment in physick. He was without all dispute a good physician but no charity
. . .'

[3]Dr. Wall was Lady Luxborough's physician. *Letters*, 229, 232, 233.

CXXVII (*a*)

B.M. Add. MSS. 28958.

[*To* LADY LUXBOROUGH.]

THE LEASOWS, *May y^e* 24. 1751.[1]

Dear Madam,

I hasten to acquaint your Ladyship, in my first Paragraph,
y^t my Brother is now greatly better; and, as we all Hope, in a
very fair way of Recovery.

What small Hopes I have entertain'd for most part of y^e
time since I wrote last to Barrels, have been rather owing to a
kind of Self-*flattery* & an unwillingness to *despair*, y^n any proper Foundation. But, these three last Days, his Disorder is so
much abated that *they* seem to receive some Sanction from
Reason. Not that I am *entirely* free from Apprehensions. The
Asthmatical Complaint is fallen down into his Legs, where it
continues at present: But what by means of Ass's Milk, (w^{ch}
agrees with him) the Advantage of a few fair days in which
he has been carried, Sedan-fashion, about my grounds, & y^e

most scrupulous Care in regard to what we suffer him to eat or drink, his Spirits Pulse, Complexion, strength, & stomach are wonderfully restor'd.

I will not detain your Ladyship any longer on this Head, yⁿ to acquaint you that I have thought *about* writing to Barrels every day since your Servant was here; but finding, all along, such frequent Changes in yᵉ Disorder, & being utterly unable to give your Ladyship any *satisfactory* Account, I had not yᵉ Spirit to set Pen to Paper.

This has been to me the most disagreeable Season, for a continuance, I ever pass'd in my Life. Betwixt sleepless Nights, *sudden* Alarms, *constant* sollicitude, the Return of my nervous Disorder, Confinement, & an entire Alteration in my way of Living, I found my own situation not a little endanger'd. I might add to these, the uncertainty of Physicians, the difficulty of obtaining satisfactory Advice, & yᵉ no less Difficulty of prevailing on my Brother to follow even a *small Part* of it. Such Persons as He ought always to be *well;* I mean to *guard more* than others against Diseases, as they have so little Patience in Reserve to submit to the Means of Cure—But to lead yʳ Ladyship from yᵉ sick Room into the open Air, a little. I am now beginning for yᵉ first time to brush up my walks. The Trees & Shrubs are in full bloom, all of a sudden. I mean so far as concerns their green Leaves, for the *latter* have not yet *flower'd.* The Servants are now busy in cleaning my Grove &c: whither I now stray once or twice a day with great Complacency.

And yet I now begin to feel (more than I *could* before) for the misfortunes of my Friends. I doubt yᵉ Death of poor Mr. Hall's Brother, will occasion him much worldly perplexity, as well as concern at present. I would otherwise press him to spend a week with us at The Leasows, as some kind of Relief to *him*; & a great Pleasure to *us*. I think a Change of Place after such an Affliction is very often of no small Service. That Book of Mr. Pearsall's which your Ladyship subscrib'd to, is come out, I *hear*; but I have had no Copies sent me hitherto. Your Ladyship I know intended to oblige *me* by your subscription. *That* Point you can never fail to obtain; But I am sorry you shou'd *suffer* by these Marks of your generosity. More I am not at liberty to say. You will please to mention this Publication to Mr. Hall. I sent *his* Name, tho' I am not sure y^t he subscrib'd, knowing he would be ye readiest of Men to serve an old Schoolfellow. I hear no more of Mr. Smith & *his* Devices. I begin to be asham'd for him.

Would your Ladyship be so kind as lend me Pompey the little?[2] I have read, as I said before, little beside Physick-books for this two-months & I want now to be indulg'd with something more amusing. I won't pretend to your Ladyship that I am a very great *Physician*, but I consider myself as qualify'd to make ye best Nurse of any in the three Kingdoms— I said *little besides Physick-books*, but I have seen Whitehead's Ode to the Bristol-Spring; which I dont much like; & the Verses in ye country Church-yard w^{ch} (as ye Hagley-gardiner said of my Grove) I like *too well*. Pray whose are they? If your Ladyship have any thing new besides, I would return it in a week. I hope your Ladyship will now speak about a time when I may have the long-wish'd-for happiness of waiting on you at the Leasows. In ye mean time I am to return my Brothers Thanks, with my own, for every obliging Instance of your Regard, & to subscribe myself inviolably your Ladyship's most dutifull

& most obedient Servant,

WILL: SHENSTONE.

May ye 25.

I shou'd have sent ye foregoing *Account* yesterday, but I find nothing in my Brother's situation that need tend to discolour *it*. I will *yet* hope, Madam, that there is some good in Reserve for us, which may in some *measure* compensate for ye gloomy season we have past—I know not from *what Quarter*, but I still *confide*—I hope your Ladyship does.

I did not propose *many* Alterations about my House this year, & I now shall effect *nothing*. But I know your Ladyship will feel some Pleasure upon finding me tolerably chearfull & content that Matters are not *worse*—I hope with this good weather your Ladyship's wonted Spirits will return, & that I too shall be able to correspond with; or to *see* you with greater Alacrity y^n I fear'd of late It wou'd be in my Power to do. Miss

Dolman desir'd her Compliments to your Ladyship, when she went from hence—I see I cannot yet write with any *Sort* of Spirit, so I will relieve your Ladyship at once from so many Insipid nothings, as I shoud probably add, if I proceeded. ——26th.

We all continue on ye mending Hand—Tom was to have taken this *to-day*, but cannot possibly be spar'd, as my Brother is yet assisted in moving from Room to Room—He shall positively go to-morrow morning. ——27.

I have nothing to add that is material. Mr. Pixell has undertaken to copy Mr. Somervile's Picture,[3] but has not yet done it—There has been a Blight in my Grove which has injurd the Shade—but yet your Ladyship will own it is still pleasant.

NOTES

[1]The letter in Hull differs verbally at several points from the B.M. MS. It makes no mention of *The Ode to the Bristol Spring* or of *The Verses in the Country Churchyard*, omits the postscripts of May 26 and 27, and follows more closely the Pierpont Morgan Library A.L.

[2]*The History of Pompey the Little, or the Life of a Lap-Dog*, by Francis Coventry (d. 1759). The publication was a satirical romance which Lady Mary Wortley Montagu preferred to *Peregrine Pickle*.

[3]The picture to be copied was lent by Lady Luxborough (*Letters*, 260, 276), and was by Thomas Worlidge (1700–1766), a painter and etcher of some note.

CXXVII (*b*)

Pierpont Morgan Library
and Hull, I, 119.

[*To* Lady LUXBOROUGH.]

The Leasows, *May y^e* 24th 1751.

Dear Madam,

I hasten to acquaint your Ladyship y^t my Brother is now greatly better, and, as we all hope, in a fair way of Recovery.

What small *hopes* I have entertain'd for most part of ye time since I wrote last to Barrels, have been rather owing to a kind of Self-flattery, and an unwillingness to despair, than any proper Foundation. But, these three last Days, his Disorder is so much abated, y^t *they* seem to receive some Sanction from *Reason*. Not y^t I am entirely free from Apprehensions. The Asthmatical Disorder is fallen down into his Legs, where it continues at present. But what by means of Ass's Milk, wch agrees with him, the Advantage of a few fair days in wch he has been carried, Sedan-fashion, about my grounds, & ye most scrupulous Care in regard to what we *suffer* him to eat or drink, his Spirits, Pulse, and Complexion are astonishingly recoverd, & his Strength and Stomach proportionably restor'd.

I will not detain your Ladyship any longer on this Head, y^n to acquaint you y^t I have thought about writing to Barrels every Day since your Servant was here; but finding, all along, such frequent Changes in ye Disorder, & being utterly incapable to give your Ladyship any *satisfactory* Account, I had not ye spirit to set Pen to Paper.

This has been to me ye most disagreeable Season, for a continuance, I ever spent in my Life; Betwixt sleepless Nights, painfull Apprehensions, Constant sollicitude, Confinement, and an entire Alteration in regard to my Way of Life, I found my own Situation not a little endanger'd. But as the Original Cause begins to cease, I hope the effect will—I might have added to ye former vexations, the difficulty of procuring good advice & ye no less Difficulty of prevailing on my Brother to follow it. Such Persons as he ought always to be well; I mean, to guard more y^n *others* against Diseases, as they have so little Patience in reserve to submit to ye Means of Cure—But to lead your Ladyship from the Sick Room into ye open Air, a little. I am now beginning for ye first time to brush up my walks. The trees and Shrubs are in full bloom, all of a sudden. I mean so far as concerns ye green leaves, for the latter have not yet flower'd. The Servants are now very busy in cleaning my grove &c: whither I stray now, two or three times a day, with great Complacency. I doubt the Death of poor Mr. Hall's Brother will occasion him much worldly Perplexity as well as Concern, at present. I would otherwise press him to spend a week with me at the Leasows as some kind of Relief to him, & a great Pleasure to us. I think a Change of Place after such an Affliction is very often of no small Service. That Book of Mr. Pearsall's wch your Ladyship subscribed for, is come out, I hear; but I have had no Copies sent yet. Your Ladyship, I know, intended to oblige *me* by your Subscription, & *That* Point you can never fail to obtain. More I am not at Liberty to say. You will please to mention this Publication to Mr. Hall. I sent *his* Name, tho' I'm not *sure* y^t he subscrib'd; but I knew he wou'd be ye readiest of Men to serve an old School fellow— Wou'd your Ladyship be so kind as lend me Pompey ye Little? I have read, as I said before, nothing but Physick-Books for this last Six-weeks, & I want now to be endulg'd with somewhat more amusing. I wont pretend to your Ladyship y^t I am a very great *Physician*, but I consider myself as qualify'd to make ye best *Nurse* of any body in the three Kingdoms—I hope soon to be able to adjust a time when I may have ye long-wish'd for Happiness of waiting on your Ladyship at the Leasows. In ye mean time I am to return my Brother's Thanks wth my own for every obliging Instance of y^r regard, and to subscribe myself inviolably your Ladyship's most

dutifull & obedient Servt

WILL: SHENSTONE.

May 2 5th.

P.S.

I shou'd have sent the foregoing Account, yesterday when it was wrote; but I find nothing to add hither to y^t may *discolour* ye favourable Relation I have been giving of my Brothers Recovery—I *will* yet hope y^t there is some good in Reserve for us, wch may in *some measure* compensate for ye gloomy Season we have past—I dont know from what quarter—but I still confide. I hope y^r Ladyship does.

I did not propose to do *much* about my House this year, & I now shall do *nothing*. But I know your Ladyship will find some Pleasure in ye conjecture y^t the Money wch might have been expended upon Rooms or Furniture, has been spent with some Effect upon my Brothers Recovery: without which the Leasows wou'd have afforded no Pleasure of one while—I hope, with this good weather, y^r Ladyship's wonted Spirits will return; I hope also y^t I shall henceforth be able to correspond with you upon more agreeable Subjects y^n I could of late. Miss Dolman desir'd her Compliments when she was here last, wch was about a week ago—I cannot yet write wth

any sort of Spirit; so I will relieve your Ladyship at once from so many insipid Nothings, as I shou'd probably add, if I proceeded.

CXXVIII

B.M. Add. MSS. 28958.

[*To* LADY LUXBOROUGH.]

THE LEASOWS, *June* y*ͤ* 14*th* 1751.

Dear Madam,

I had just been writing two Pages of a Letter, in order to send it in yͤ Morning to Mr. Williams, when, stepping out o'Doors to take a Peep at my Masons, I saw your Ladyship's servant arrive—Now I mention *Masons*, I will just add here, that I am doing a small matter to my Windows, wᶜʰ I expected would give some thing of a better Air to my Front; but I now believe I shan't like it when 'tis done. When one has an old House to manage so irregular in all respects as mine, tis seldom yͤ Embellishments give us any Pleasure. It seems only *maturing* & *perfecting* an *Error*. And to *correct* it, I am not able.

Joe tells me he is in great Haste, wᶜʰ puts me upon hurrying on, faster yⁿ my usual Speed, so yᵗ I shall be sure to *stumble*. When I *do*, *your* Ladyship will excuse it, knowing it is not any Fault of *mine* yᵗ I am not a Race-horse.

My Lord Bolingbroke's Misfortune[1] is a very severe one, & I am truly concern'd for it. I hope, if he finds not yᵗ Redress from yͤ French Parliament, which I wish him, he will however find a good deal from his own Philosophy—of wᶜʰ no one seems to have more—I will keep secret, tho' I am exceedingly glad to hear of, the Probability there is yᵗ you may see him at Barrels. I think yͤ visit cannot fail of proving very agreeable to *Him*, as I am sure it will, to your Ladyship. You will please to observe yᵗ I cannot speak above a Word in answer to any thing you have so kindly communicated. I believe Joe thinks I am even now sealing up my Letter—whereas I fully purpose to write a Page or two more—

A great many thanks to your Ladyship for y^r Eau de Mille-fleurs. If Mrs. Weymondsold be so very good as to remember me when she sends for Perfumes &c: I wish I could with any Propriety suggest to her, y^t, as I use them chiefly in *Snuff*; I shou'd be mighty thankfull if she would procure me ever so small a Bottle of the Chymical *Oil* of Jessamin, rather y^n the *Water*; wch last when drop't into Snuff very soon evaporates. I beg my Compliments, there.

I beg my Compliments also to Mr. Hall & will *Recommend* it to him to *spend* a little time at the Leasows, after ye Fatigue of his Accounts &c: is over—I speak *interestedly* tho' for we shall be extremely glad to see him.

The King seems *unfeignedly* fond of the Princess & her Children—& it is a very aimiable Feature in his Character—He shew'd something of ye same tenderness, upon ye Death of ye late Queen.[2]

I think wth y^r Ladyship in regard to Miss Greens Behaviour; & did so upon first reading ye Paragraph in ye Newspapers—One is too apt to think one's own Afflictions greatest—What can exceed ye Anguish wch this Event must occasion to old Mr. Dalton? Or Perhaps, Miss Green.[3]

I approve of ye Paper ornaments for any Ceiling at Barrels, where Fretwork may be proper.—

I detest Lord Hallifax's making use of those Bristol-stone Pillars *within* his *House*.[4] These stones will serve to embellish some little grott or Cell in your Coppice with great Propriety; I cannot invent any Form to please myself, unless I were upon ye Spot—Your Ladyship can, very readily, in my Absence.

The Apology you are so condescending as to make for delaying your Journey to ye Leasows is fraught with very important Articles indeed! I can say no more y^n this, y^t when I have hopes given me of waiting upon y^r Ladyship, I always think ye sooner ye better—the dryer ye roads the better—the longer the Days the better & the more in order my walks, & ye greener my Trees, so much ye better—As for the rest I think your Apology of undoubted Weight; & I shall be very proud to wait upon your Ladyship when *Fortune* (for ye Crime now is her's alone) will permit.

I had yesterday afternoon Captn West & his Lady &

Children, Miss Lyttelton & Miss West, who walk'd round the walks & drank tea with me in ye Grove. NB. The Grove I mention has receiv'd some little Improvement—Mrs. West is a Woman of Taste.

Latter End of last week I met a Party in my Walks, the Men well dress'd, the Women in handsome lac'd Jackets, whom I took some Pains to escorte & entertain—& who were as I found afterwards, a couple of Actresses from Birmingham—an Actor &c:

Mr. Pixell took this Copy of Mr. Somervile, which I altered with my own Hand, 'till I thought it *something* like—'tis not so good, as your Original by a great deal, w^n compar'd—He is doing what he *intends* shall be *better*—*This* was never quite finish'd—but I send it as an Echantillon.

I propos'd it one day to Mr. Dolman to take a Ride in his Chair to Barrels, for a Night, when he was over last, (viz) about a Fortnight ago) & the Scheme was only broken thro' by something y^t he found deficient in regard to his Dress; for wch I was angry at him.

It is probable I shall *some* day (within a short time) but as yet an unfix'd & uncertain Day, do myself ye Honour & Pleasure of walking with your Ladyship thro' ye Shrubbery, and ye Coppice; the Walks of wch are now, Tom tells me, extremely elegant.

My Brother continues on ye mending Hand—desires his best Respects to your Ladyship.

I shall be as glad to see Autumn triumph over Spring, this year, as your Ladyship. She never certainly had so fair an opportunity. For my Part I can fairly say that I have neither had a Pleasure budded in my Imagination, nor (scarce) a Flower blossomd on my *Shrubs*, all this Spring. Y^r Ladyship excells in ye Products of both. May y^r Ladyship live long to enjoy ye Pleasures of y^r Imagination, & the Beauties of your Environs, & may I long enjoy ye satisfaction & Honour of subscribing myself your Ladyships most oblig'd & most obedient humble.

Servant,

I suppose I've made 50   W<small>ILL</small> S<small>HENSTONE</small>.
Blunders; for I wrote full-stretch.

NOTES

[1]Lady Luxborough (*Letters*, LXVII), deals with Lord Bolingbroke's misfortune which was a law-suit in France, following on the death of his wife.

[2]Luxborough, *Letters*, 286.

[3]Ibid., 271, 272.

[4]George Montague Dunk (1716–1771), 2nd Earl of Halifax. Lady Luxborough told W.S. (*Letters*, 223) that 'Lord Halifax is cutting off part of a gallery with four pillars of these stones, which will cost him £500 each; & fixes branches for candles in them, to reflect the light . . . invent something for me to make . . . of those beautiful Bristol stones of all colours.'

CXXIX

B.M. Add. MSS. 28958.

[*To* LADY LUXBOROUGH.]

THE LEASOWS, *August y*[e] *8*[th] *1751.*

I was extremely sorry, dear Madam, to discover by the whole Cast of your Letter y[t] Depression of Spirits of which you so seldom Complain. I too have had my Share, as your Ladyship can witness, for all the former Part of This Season. But there is nothing of *Importance* in this World, beside the *Life* or *Death* of *Friends*. The misfortune is that we seldom esteem any Thing so *trivial* as we *ought*. However, very inexcuseable should I be, if I kept silence long together, when your Ladyship so *obligingly* intimates y[t] what I write may afford you some small Amusement—The Verses & the Letter I enclose will serve to clear up y[e] Mystery of what I wrote before—you will not *admire*, but you will wonder—All I shall say is, that I think Colonel Lyttelton has a *Heart*; & as I hope, Friendship enough to deserve this from me—His Letter remov'd y[e] Anxiety I was under, by shewing me in some Sort y[t] my Compliment was not *ill receiv'd*; & as to any thing farther it is hard enough to say— Some other Persons here complimented have been civil— Your Ladyship has every Claim to my Respect. You will please, Madam, to observe that the *Subject* of these Verses,[1] the known Regard I bear you, together with my real Inclination, all requir'd y[t] your Name should not be omitted on an Occasion like This.[2] Why I did not ask your Leave in the *first*

Place, & why I made use of a compliment wch you formerly accepted from me, were both owing to the same Reason: I mean *Precipitation*. Had I detain'd ye Verses longer I did not know but the Dutchess[3] &c: might be gone from Hagley; (tho' I think by reason of ye Colonel's Indisposition, she remains there still.) Another thing, Lord Stamford dineing that day at Hagley, I chose rather y^t he should see ye Comp^t paid him,[4] as it were *accidentally* & at a third place, than have a Copy giv'n him, or at least be told of it in a more *formal* way. All this put together occasion'd me to take the Lines in an awkward hurry out of my Pocket Book, & send them without a Cover by an absolute stranger, Mr. Burgess; who was with me & at a distance in the walks when the Colonel went away. So y^t you have here my Reasons for y^t painfull suspence I mention'd; for my not adviseing with your Ladyship; & for any Confusion you may observe in ye Combination of Ranks, Characters, & Things. I have been forc'd to write out this from Scraps no bigger y^n a Cheese-paring; & as I have no other Copy, must desire your Ladyship to return this: wch must undergo some Corrections. Pray likewise, write me word as soon as possible, y^t you excuse me—And if you wou'd please to send me any Hints for it's Improvement, it would add to ye Obligation. I write from my Bed-side, upon my right Elbow, & in a very awkward Posture; so y^t you must forgive me, if I drop my Pen, after it has faithfully assur'd you that I am your Ladyship's *most* affectionate

& oblig'd hum: Servt

WILL: SHENSTONE.

Masons & Carpenters! The Lord
deliver me!

NOTES

[1]The verses to Colonel Lyttelton appeared, *Works* I, 174, under the title *A Pastoral Ode to the Honourable Sir Richard Lyttelton*.

[2]Lady Luxborough was celebrated under the name of Cynthia as 'the nymph that guides their way.'

[3]The Duchess is eulogized in the *Ode*, Stanza 6.

> 'Amazement chill'd the shepherd's frame,
> To think Bridgwater's honoured name
> Should grace his rustic cell;
> That she, on all whose motions wait
> Distinctions, titles, rank and state,
> Should rove where shepherds dwell.'

⁴Stanza 17 celebrates Lord Stamford.

> 'Scarce faded is the vernal flower,
> Since Stamford left his honour'd bower,
> To smile familiar here:
> O form'd by nature to disclose
> How fair that courtesy which flows
> From social warmth sincere.'

CXXX

Works III, 211.

To a Friend [Rev. R. GRAVES.]

The Leasows,
Sept. 17, 1751.

Dear Mr. G[raves]

I am very sensibly obliged to you for the *diligence* and *expedition* which you have shewn in answering my last request: I cannot feel the very *tenderness* of friendship to be at all abated in me by our long separation; nor will it at any time be possible I should, so long as I receive such testimonies of your usual *kindness* and *ingenuity*.——I have no sort of exceptions to make against the province in which you were engaged at Cheltenham, nor the light in which you appeared. What you lost in any one's opinion of your independency, you would gain in their idea of your merit, genius, and learning; and then you had all those other advantages *par dessu*.——As to the compliments that were paid to Mrs. G[raves], you have something the same sort of reason to be pleased with them, that I have to be pleased with those that are given to my place; which I consider as naturally possessed of many beauties, each of them brought to light, and perfected through my own discernment, care, and cultivation. And then your pleasure ought to be so much greater than mine, as you have a nobler subject to enjoy. ——Mrs. G[raves] has too much sense to object against the freedom of this similitude.

I cannot help adding a few strokes to your picture of Mrs. ———. I think her an extremely *superficial* female-pedant: for, after an interval of many years, since I first conversed with her at Mr. ———'s, I found her conversation turn solely upon the same *topics*, *definitions*, and *quotations*. I believe, I could easily enough have recommended myself to a greater degree of her favour: but her vanity and affectations were beyond what I could bear—Your account of —— is very picturesque, and agreeable to the idea I always had of him; but I believe that idea was perfected by what observations I made when I had some of his company at London.—There was something accountable enough to me in their burlesquing Mr. L[yttelton]'s monody. He is, you know, engaged in a party; and his poem (though an extraordinary fine composition) was too tender for the public ear. It should have been printed privately,[1] and a number of copies dispersed only among their friends and acquaintance; but even so it would have been republished; and it was too good to suppress. I wish the burlesquers of such *ingenuous* profusions could be punished, consistently with English liberty. 'Where were ye, Muses, &c.' is imitated from Milton,[2] and taken by Milton from Theocritus. I write Greek wretchedly, but you will remember the passage,

Πᾶ ῶοκ' ἄρ ῆθ' ὄκα Δάφνις ἐτάκετο; ῶα ῶόκα, Νύμφαι;[3]

I heard, once before, it was burlesqued under the title of 'An Elegy on the Death of a favourite Cat;'[4] but the burlesque will die, and the poem will survive.—You tell me, 'The author of Peregrine Pickle says, if you will flatter Mr. Lyttelton well, he will at last make you a Middlesex Justice;'[5] and it happened oddly that, whilst I was reading your letter, a neighbour told me I was put in the commission of the peace. I have never received a single line from Mr. Whistler, and I believe my journey to W[hitchurch] has given the final blow to our friendship. Pray was not Mr. Blandy some relation of theirs, or only their attorney? The affair is uncommonly shocking; and I fancy the *genuine* accounts that Mr. W[histler] sends you will be curious anecdotes at Bath.—I suppose you have painted your room with oil-colours, and made it *really* handsome.— I drew out a festoon and a medal some time ago, for a pannel over Mr. P——'s chimney; but they knew not what to make of the medal, and had only the festoon executed in stone colour, by a common painter; yours is better, and in character.—I am a degree more frugal than you; for I only use quicklime, and either blue or yellow sand, to take away the objection which I have to whited walls.

I paid a visit to Mr. Lyttelton, the Dean, &c. since he came down; but had little of their company, for they thought Sir Thomas was dying: however, by unparalleled strength of constitution, he lingered in violent pain till last Saturday, when he died, very much lamented.[6] He had good natural parts, well improved by reading modern writers, and by the knowledge of the world: extremely prudent, considerate, humane, polite, and charitable.—I have jumbled his more obvious qualities together, that you may not think I am usurping the province of a news-man. Sir George will lose no time in building a new house, or doing what is more than *equivalent* to the old one.

I want no *temptation* to come immediately to C[laverton]. This is a melancholy *season* with me always; whether it be owing to the scenes I see, or to the effect of hazy skies upon an ill-perspiring skin.—I can say no more at *present*, than that I most ardently desire to see you, and desire my humble service to Mrs. G[raves]. I have a chalybeat spring[7] in the middle of my grotto: what think you of this inscription:

> 'FONS FERRUGINEUS
> 'DIVARUM OPTUMAE
> 'SALUTI SACER.'

Is it antique?

I am, dear Mr. G[raves],
Your most affectionate
W. SHENSTONE.

NOTES

[1]The elegy was published anonymously, but the author was at once recognized and his poem greeted with praise by some and abuse by others.

[2]Milton, *Lycidas*, 50.

[3]Theocritus, Idyll I, 66.

[4]By Gray. The poem was included in Dodsley's *Collection*, II, 274.

[5]Fielding, Pitt and George Lyttelton were contemporaries at Eton, and through Lyttelton, Fielding was made a Bow Street magistrate. *Tom Jones* was dedicated to Lyttelton and the character of Squire Allworthy drawn partly from him and partly from Ralph Allen. Smollett was angry because Lyttelton would not help him with a comedy, so he burlesqued Lyttelton's *Monody*. In *Peregrine Pickle* he drew a scurrilous portrait of him under the name of *Sir Gosling Scrag*. This was removed from the second edition, and the author owned that he had given way to 'the suggestion of personal resentment.'

[6]Sir Thomas Lyttelton died September 14, 1751. Wyndham, *op. cit.*, gives an intimate account of his last days. W.S.'s opinion of Sir Thomas Lyttelton was borne out by all who knew him.

[7]W.S. too was interested in the health-giving properties of certain waters, for he lived at the time when the spas were very popular.

CXXXI (*a*)

University of Texas MS.[1]

[*To* Lady LUXBOROUGH.]

Dear Madam,

Tho' I think it is a sort of Maxim y^t a Person in London seldom complains y^t he is forgotten by his Friends in the Country, yet I cannot by any means prevail upon my Conscience to acquit me of a kind of disrespectful Silence since your Ladyship went to Town. It was neither y^e *Politicks* nor y^e *Amusements* of our great Metropolis, y^t could make the letters of your Friends appear either impertinent, or even indifferent to you. And tho' the sublime Entertainment you must receive from the Conversation of so great a Man as my Lord Bollingbroke might bid the fairest to do so, yet was I not without Conviction y^t your Ladyship would feel some sort of Complacency upon ye sight of a scrip of Paper which should acquaint you y^t I was alive.

Alive indeed I am; if at least it may be call'd so to exist amongst a set of People, whose Employments Passions & Sentiments are entirely foreign to my own, & where I see & hear & do nothing but what I think may as well be left unseen, unheard & un-done. What can your Ladyship expect from a Correspondent so situated, beside pure Respect and Friendship, & many artless Assurances of their Reality & their Continuance?

Mr. Outing stay'd pretty near a week with me. He has, I think, strict Honour, good-nature, & good-sense. W^t he seems to want, in *my Eye*, is a little genuine *Taste*. For tho' good-sense may by Degrees enable a Person to *discover* ye Beauties of Nature or Art, yet it never can furnish him with any extraordinary Relish or Enjoyment of them, which is the Effect of Taste alone; and differs as widely from ye former as the Palate differs from the *Brain*. Your Ladyship has, I dare say, frequently made the same observation.

Sr Thomas Lyttelton (notwithstanding ye Head-ach was his general Complaint) was found to have dy'd of a Polypus in the great Artery; It is not material y^t the Physicians never

Y

suspected, what they cou'd not have cur'd had it been ever so apparent. You must imagine y^t his Death has thrown a kind of Gloom round the villages in this Neighbourhood. The residence of a numerous & fashionable Family animates a Country-Place to an inconceivable Degree. The Family at Hagley will be immediately dispers'd. Miss Lyttelton goes to Lady Litchfield's,[2] to the Colonel's, to London &c: & does not think to settle. Miss West goes first to Stowe and then designs to board wth her Brother the Commodore. Sir George & his Lady set out for London this day, & as they Purpose to build next spring upon y^e *old Foundation*, it may be many years before they come to reside amongst us[3] even for a *small Part* of the Summer.

Lord Dudley & I din'd together at Hagley last Wednesday, where we found Mr. Anson, & some other Company. Mr. Miller unluckily ask'd me at Table how I lik'd the new situation of their Column, wch threw me under a Necessity of offending either against the *Rules* of Politeness, or (what are more sacred with me) the *Laws* of Sincerity. The Truth is, I do *not* like it, upon *many* Accounts; & am persuaded, before many years are past, they will be of the same Mind.

Mr. Smith has so mangled & disfigur'd my Grove in his Draught, y^t I dare not send it to your Ladyship 'till he has alter'd the Plate so as to render it less intolerable. Fluellen, as I remember, in Shakespear, speaking of ye near Resemblance betwixt Macedon & Monmouth observes 'There is a River in Macedon, there is a River also in Monmouth—peradventure there be Fish in both—wou'd you desire better similitude?'[4] Smith being a modest Man, seems to content himself with some such Degree of Resemblance as Fluellen's; but I wish him well, & will cause him one Day to do the Place Justice for *his* sake as well as my *own*. For *his*, as this Piece will be seen by many who know the Place, and for mine as the Place is known to afford the best scene I have.

If your Ladyship ask how I have of late employ'd myself, I can give you but a sorry Account; but the *truth* is, y^t I have been bestowing Alterations upon an old House which it does not deserve; exhibiting my Walks to Persons y^t have no Taste; & making Concerts in my Neighbourhood for People that have no Ear. I write without Thought, and read without Attention; and for all these gallant Exploits they are going to make me a right worshipfull Justice of the Peace. You will guess that I shall prove a very *inactive* one: But I shall make ye fewer Blunders.

My Lord Dudley keeps me in Countenance. He is far more indolent y^n myself. He makes a very honest, humane & hospitable Neighbour; often enquires after your Ladyship and as often drinks your Health.

There was a neighbouring Clergyman went with us to Hagley, who has 10 Children to maintain upon a trifling Income, and whose wife has a Cancer. I was advancing there, that Lord Bolingbroke's Cancer was cur'd; but it was immediately deny'd that my Lord's Disorder *was* a Cancer.[5] Pray, my Lady, speak to this Point, y^t I may if possible give some Comfort to the poor Clergyman.

Amidst all my Indolence, I have still some Ambition, & one of ye warmest wishes it produces, is y^t I may one day have the Honour of seeing my Lord Bolingbroke at Barrels. I beg you wou'd recommend me to his Lordship as a modest inoffensive Man, who has always manifested a Desire to be esteemd, Mad^m your Ladyship's most dutifull

and most obedient Servant,

WILL SHENSTONE.

Octob^r 21, 1751.

NOTES

[1]Hull's version of this letter has been given as well as the MS. version as they differ considerably.

[2]Dinah, daughter of Sir Thomas Frankland of Thirleby, Yorks, wife of George Henry Lee, Earl of Lichfield.

[3]Wyndham, *op. cit.*, II, 269 etc., describes at length the building operations at Hagley, and the part which Sanderson Miller had in the alterations. So many negotiations were entered upon, that it was not till the summer of 1754 that the foundations were finally dug.

[4]*Henry V*, IV, 7.

[5]Luxborough, *Letters*, 287–9.

CXXXI (*b*)

Hull, I, 62.

To Lady LUXBOROUGH.

The Leasowes.

Dear Madam,

Tho' I think it is a Sort of Maxim, that a Person in *London* seldom *complains* he is forgotten by his Friends in the Country, yet I cannot, by any Means, prevail upon my Conscience to acquit me of a Sort of disrespectful Silence, since your Ladyship went to Town. It was not either the Politics or the Amusements of our great Metropolis, that could make the Letters of your Friends appear impertinent, or even indifferent to you; and tho' the sublime Entertainment you must receive from the Conversation of so great a Man as Lord Bolingbroke, might bid the fairest to do so, yet was I not without Conviction, that your Ladyship would feel some sort of Complacency upon the Sight of a Scrip of Paper, which should acquaint you that I was alive.

Alive, indeed, I am; at least, if it may be called so, to exist among a Set of People, whose Employments, Passions, and Sentiments, are entirely foreign to my own; and where I see, and hear, and do nothing but what I think may as well be left unseen, unheard, and undone. What can your Ladyship expect from a Correspondent so situated, beside pure Respect and Friendship, and many artless Assurances of their Reality and Continuance?

Mr. O[uting] stayed pretty near a Week with me. He has, I think, strict Honour, Good-nature, and good Sense. What he wants, in my Eye, is a little genuine *Taste*; for tho' good Sense may, by Degrees, enable a Person to discover the Beauties of Nature or Art, yet it can never furnish him with any extraordinary Relish or Enjoyment of them, which is the Effect of innate Taste alone, and which differs as widely from the former, as the Palate differs from the Brain. Your Ladyship has, I dare say, frequently made the same observation.

You will hear Sir Thomas Lyttelton, notwithstanding he complained always of his *Head*, died of a *Polypus* in the *great Artery*; which, I do not find, was ever, in the least, suspected by his Physicians; but which, if it had been ever so apparent, they could not possibly have cured. You will imagine that his Death must have thrown a Sort of Gloom round the Villages in his Neighbourhood. A numerous and fashionable Family animates a Country-Place to an inconceivable Degree. The Family at *Hagley* will be immediately dispersed. Miss LYTTELTON goes to Lady LITCHFIELD's, to the *Colonel's*, to *London*, and does not think to settle. Miss WEST goes first to *Stow*, and then intends to reside with her Brother the *Commodore*. Sir GEORGE and his Lady set out for *London* to-morrow, and as they propose to build, next Spring, upon the *old Foundation*, it may be many Years ere they come to reside amongst us, even for a small Part of the Summer.

Lord DUDLEY and I dined together at *Hagley* last *Wednesday*, where we found Lord ANSON's Brother, and some other Company. Mr. MILLER unluckily asked me at Table, how I liked the new Situation of their Column; which threw me under a Necessity of offending either against the Rules of Politeness, or (what is more sacred with me) the Laws of Sincerity. The Truth is, I do not like it upon many Accounts; and am persuaded, before many Years are past, they will be of the same Mind. But least of all, do I approve their Intentions of building three new Fronts, and altering every Room by a gothic Model, and that with an Eye to Frugality, at the same Time that they have not an Inch of Gothicism about the House, to warp their Imagination that Way. But this Subject never fails to lead me too far; nor can I explain myself to the full, unless I could shew your Ladyship their Plan. The fine Situation they have, within an hundred Yards, they neglect;— in short, as it appears to me, they are going to sacrifice an Opportunity of rendering their Place compleat, for the Sake of an imperfect, but expensive Specimen of gothic Architecture; which, not having its Foundation either in Truth or Proportion, will fall into Disgrace again in the Course of a few Years—Can one then forbear crying out, 'The Graces droop' —'Am I in *Greece* or in *Gothland*?' But as their Resolution seems fixed, I mention this in Confidence, and must, for the future, lay my Finger on my Mouth.

Mr. S[mith] has so mangled and disfigured my *Grove*, that

I dare not send it to your Ladyship, till he has altered the Plate, so as to render it less intolerable. FLUELLIN, as I remember, in SHAKESPEARE, speaking of the near Resemblance betwixt *Macedon*, and *Monmouth*, observes, 'There is a River in *Macedon*, there is a River also in *Monmouth*—peradventure, there be Fish in both.—Would you desire better Similitude?'. S[mith] being a modest Man, has seemed to content himself with some such Degree of Resemblance: but I wish him well, and will cause him, one Day, to do the Place Justice, for his own Sake as well as mine—for his own, as his Piece will be seen by many who know the Place, and for mine, as the Place is known to afford the best Scene I have.

I am, &c.

W. SHENSTONE.

CXXXII

James Kenward, Harborne and its Surroundings, 39.

[*To* MR. SMITH[1] *of Tennal.*]
Sir,

I have sent to demand the Hare which was cours'd in my Brother's Grounds, kill'd by my Dogs, and taken from my Servants. I little expected this usage from the Persons that were concern'd in it.

I am, your Servt

WILL. SHENSTONE.

NOTE

[1]James Kenward, *Harborne and its Surroundings*, 39, writes :—'In the period 1734–1747 certainly, and probably earlier and later than those years, Tennel Hall was inhabited by Thomas Smith, Attorney at Law; and the poet Shenstone seems to have visited him there frequently. Mr. Thomas Sargeant kindly showed me in 1877, several original letters from Shenstone to Smith, addressed to "Tennal" and to "Lapall" or "Lapwell," Halesowen, (1757–9) ; and to Birchy Close (1761–2). I give three of these letters which are of interest. It is not pleasant to think that such a sport as coursing was favoured by the author of the "Pastoral Ballad," who could write—

> ' " For he ne'er could be true, she averred,
> Who could rob a poor bird of its young ;
> And I loved her the more when I heard
> Such tenderness fall from her tongue." '

The two undated letters to Mr. Smith must be placed prior to that which announces the death of Shenstone's brother.

CXXXIII

James Kenward, *Harborne and its Surroundings.*

[*To* Mr SMITH *of Tennal.*]

Sir,

  I was inform'd and I believe with truth, that your Dogs had cours'd the Hare previously, but *lost* her, that the Hare coming accidentally into a Field where *my* Dogs were, the noise generally made upon those occasions introduc'd *yours* a second time, whilst *mine* were in the Pursuit, that She was kill'd in my Br.^s grounds by my Dogs, and torn from them not without some Violence. I leave you to consider the Nature of this Behaviour which I can only be induc'd to over-look by your Promise to send me one of y.^r next Hares you kill.

I am, y.^r hum: Servt

WILL. SHENSTONE.

  As ye Hare was design'd for Cous. Shenstone if you give *him* y^r next Hare 'twill be consider'd in ye same light.

CXXXIV

B.M. Add. MSS. 28958.
Hull, I, 127.

[*To* LADY LUXBOROUGH.]

THE LEASOWS, *Jan: ye first* 1752.

Dear Madam,

  I had wrote to your Ladyship long before this time, to acknowledge the Kindness of your Letter & Present; but I have a most deplorable Account to give of my Delay, & what so good a Friend as yourself will not read without a sigh. Alas! dear Madam! I have lost my only Brother! A more sincere or *truly* affectionate *one* never bore the Name. I cannot now add more, tho' I should not want matter to expatiate upon his *Merit*, were I not at y^e *same time* to revive & lament the Loss of *it*. The Impetuosity of youth & Temper, wch alone could in y^e

least obscure *it*, were beginning to subside apace—But it has been his Lot to go *before* me, in yᵉ very *Prime* of his Days, & ere yᵉ Force of his Understanding, or yᵉ Benevolence of his Heart has been half *exerted* or *known*.

Future Letters, & other Conversations may afford me an opportunity to pour out all my soul. At present I am not enough master of myself. I find all my Views intercepted; All my schemes & measures, (& I may add my Heart itself) to be well nigh broke on this occasion! Every Object round me, every Source of my former Amusement, revives a train of Ideas which I am not able to support. I have procur'd a set of low Friends to accompany me, & to draw of my Attention; but (to confess my weakness to a Friend) my *principal* Relief, since yᵉ fatal *Close of November*, has been drawn from mere Stupefaction.

Pardon me, my good Lady; I did not mean to make a display of my affliction: It insensibly steals into my Letter.

> 'I cannot but remember such men *were*,
> And were most *dear* to me.'[1]

Since this unhappy Catastrophe, it has been my Fortune to hear of another which must nearly affect your Ladyship.[2] Believe me, Madam, I am far from an *unconcernd* Observer of Events yᵗ must naturally afford you either Pleasure or Pain: But I am not in a Condition to *receive* Relief; & how can I pretend to *give* it. One thing however I will venture to suggest —I think Cæsar acknowledg'd (at an earlier Period of Life yⁿ what my Lord Bolingbroke arriv'd at), that He had liv'd enough either in Regard to *Nature* or to *Glory*.

During yᵉ Height of our Afflictions, we can scarce believe it possible they should *ever* wear off. In *my* Case there are some Particulars wᶜʰ render it most improbable they *should*. Yet *Time*, we find, alleviates the sorrows of *others*; & it is fitting we should hope *implicitly* yᵗ it may some-how diminish *our own*.

I am altogether ignorant where this Letter will find you; but I hope you will be so kind as to *write* or to *dictate* a Letter to me, & I will not cease praying that it may be the *former*. Let your subject be what you please; assure me only of yᵉ continuance of your *Esteem*, & it will be of greater Service to me y^n whole volumes of Philosophy. But this is doing you Injustice, for I have found my *Philosophy* of *none:* And there is nothing so satisfactory, upon ye Death of Friends, as to receive fresh testimonies of Kindness from the *Best* of those that survive.

> I am, Dear Madam,
> (With all ye tenderness of my present situation)
> Your most oblig'd, faithfull, & ever-affectionate
> Servant
> WILL SHENSTONE.

This is ye third time I have begun to write to you, but I hope I shall find less difficulty when I am to answer you next. Above all things do I long to see you; & please myself with ye Thoughts of it, when I hear you are return'd to Barrels —At present I am taking Med'cines within-doors, for a kind of nervous Fever. *Some* Assistance I may hope from them, & that, I think but *little*: Tis taking *Drugs* from y^e *Shops*, to cure *Anxiety* of *Mind*.

NOTES

[1]W.S. misquotes *Macbeth*, IV. 3.

> 'I cannot but remember such things were
> That were most precious to me.'

Joseph Shenstone finds more frequent mention in Lady Luxborough's *Letters* than in his brother's. She wrote of him on one occasion as a man 'whose obliging temper is to be liked by all, and is much regarded by me.'

[2]The death of Lord Bolingbroke occurred December 12, 1751, the cause of death being cancer of the face. Luxborough, *Letters*, 287–9.

CXXXV

B.M. Add. MSS. 28958.

[*To* LADY LUXBOROUGH.]

THE LEASOWS, *Jan.* ye 25 1752.

Dear Madam,

Very truly did I rejoice at the sight of your trusty servant, who has deliver'd your Packet with great Care & Expedition. Your Ladyship honours me with your Friendship, revives me by your Letters, and amuses me by a succession of elegant

Presents, for All which Favours I can do no more than *thank* you; & that in y^e *vulgar* & *customary* way, like a Person not half so sensible of the Obligation, as I feel myself to be.

I am very glad to hear, & I *think* also, that the Bath-waters bid fair for your *Recovery*. I hope you will partake likewise of the *Pleasures* of the place;[1] which, as your Complaints are nervous, must have an undoubted tendency to further *it*. What you say with regard to *my* coming to Bath is very just; & the manner in which you invite me, extremely kind & obliging. There is nothing could attract me thither *so powerfully* as the satisfaction I shou'd find in conversing with you: And yet I have other Inducements at this time, & those no way inconsiderable; The Melancholy y^t I feel at *Home*, the *suitableness* of the Bath-waters, & an Invitation from Mr. Graves to Clarton within two Miles of ye Place; one of ye most familiar Friends I have, and of the most ingenious Men, I know—But before I must *think* of this Expedition I have a scene of Business to pass thro', which is a task as necessary, as it will be painfull.

It is not more irksome for your Ladyship's *hand* to write, than it is for my *Head* to express a single Sentiment; for which reason I avoid writing at present to any Person in ye world but You. Since I wrote last, I have been *forc'd* to drop ye method of raising my Spirits by Liquor &c: and have had Recourse to Amusements; which are another kind of *Inebriation*. I have bought an old Romish Missal on Vellum[2] highly illuminated &c: which contains some Indulgences y^t are very remarkable. I have had Toys from Birmingham for this Purpose, Patterns of Paper for my Drawing Room, (where I live *continually*) and my Servants were gone out on such Sort of Errands, when your Joe pass'd by my window—Thus when the Evil Day arrives a Child may often support himself as well as a Philosopher. But perhaps it may *be* Philosophy to avocate one's Thoughts by any trifles whatever. This may be true; but yet we cannot always do so, without a *Consciousness* y^t we are defrauding sorrow of its *lawfull claim*.

My Lord Dudley desir'd his Compliments to your Ladyship. He & two of his Sisters spent five Days wth me this Week. He will be in London to-morrow from whence I am given to hope that he will send me his Picture. I shall value it, as he is a truly benevolent Man, & one who has shewn me many Instances of Civility.

Mr. Mallet seems handsomely rewarded for his Attachment to Lord Bolingbroke. I suppose He will publish Manuscripts wch must prove exceedingly advantageous.

I have found much Entertainment in ye Perusal of Lord Orrerys Narrative; & was glad to find that he gives your Brothers Character with so much Justice, Elegance & Propriety.[3]

I have since glanc'd upon Mr. Warburton's Edition of Pope's Works;[4] which abounds in scurrilities thrown upon his *own* Enemies & in perversions of his Author's Meaning.

I trespass upon Joe's Patience, if not upon your Ladyship's; but I must ask your Leave to mention one more particular. 'Tis probable you may want Servants upon your Return to Barrels; & I shou'd take it as a great Favour if you wou'd please to make Tryal of my Servant's Sister. She has good Sense, good Temper & a good Person, & it is my Opinion she would please your Ladyship. I am sure she would be zealous to do so—But if after Experience she shou'd be so unfortunate as to be disapprov'd, I *promise* it shall give no offence.

I am, dear Madam, with ye truest sense of all y^r Favours,
        Your most oblig'd & faithfull Servt
                                    WILL. SHENSTONE.

NOTES

[1]Cf. Luxborough *Letters*, LXXIX, for a lively account of Bath under Beau Nash. Lady Luxborough went there so that 'bathing and pumping' might restore the use of her hands, but 'the pleasures of the place' played a large part in her cure. 'We can offer you friendly conversation, friendly springs, friendly rides and walks, friendly pastimes to dissipate gloomy thoughts; friendly book-sellers, who for five shillings for the season will furnish you with all the new books; friendly chairmen, who will carry you through storms and tempests for sixpence, & seldom else, for Duchesses trudge the streets here unattended. . . .'

[2]This passage is interesting as casting light on the wide taste shown by W.S. as a collector, and reminds one of the 'rare monkish manuscripts,' of Pope's *Moral Essays*. Ep. Iv.

[3]John Boyle, Earl of Orrery, published his *Remarks on the Life and Writings of Dr. Swift* in 1751. See p. 220 and following pages. 'The triumvirate, to whom we owe an elegance and propriety unknown to our forefathers, are Swift, Addison, and Bolingbroke. At the sight of such names, no dispute can arise in preferring the English moderns to the English antients . . . he (i.e. Bolingbroke) shone out in his retirement with a lustre peculiar to himself; though not seen by vulgar eyes. The gay statesman was changed into a philosopher equal to any of the sages of antiquity. The wisdom of Socrates, the dignity and ease of Pliny, and the wit of Horace, appeared in all his writings and conversation.'

[4]William Warburton (1698–1779). Pope left all properties to Warburton after his death, and in 1751 Warburton published an edition of Pope's *Works*.

CXXXVI

Works III, 216.

To Mr. GRAVES, *on the Death of Mr. Shenstone's Brother.*

The Leasows,

Feb. 14, 1752.

Dear Mr. Graves,

You will be amazed at my long silence; and it might reasonably excite some disgust if my days had passed of late in the manner they used to do: but I am not the man I was; perhaps I never *shall* be. Alas! my dearest friend! I have lost my only brother! and, since the fatal close of November, I have had neither peace nor respite from agonising thoughts![1]

You, I think, have *seen* my brother; but perhaps had no opportunity of distinguishing him from the groupe of others whom we call *good-natured* men. This part of his character was so visible in his countenance, that he was generally beloved at sight; I, who must be allowed to know him, do assure you, that his understanding was no way inferior to his benevolence. He had not only a sound judgement, but a lively wit and genuine humour. As these were many times eclipsed by his native bashfulness, so his benevolence only suffered by being shewn to an excess. I here mean his giving too indiscriminately into those jovial meetings of company, where the warmth of a social temper is discovered with least reserve; but the virtues of his head and heart would soon have shone without alloy. The foibles of his youth were wearing off; and his affection for me and regard to my advice, with his own good sense, would soon have rendered him all that I could have wished in a successor. I never in my life knew a person more sincere in the expression of his love or dislike. But it was the *former* that suited the propensity of his heart; the *latter* was as transient as the starts of passion that occasioned it. In short, with much true genius and real fortitude, he was, according to the *English* acceptation, 'a truly honest man;' and I think I may also add, a truly English character; but 'habeo, dixi? immo *habui* fratrem & amicum, Chreme!'[2] All this have I *lost* in him. He is now in regard to *this* world no more than a mere idea. And this idea, therefore, though deeply tinged with melancholy, I must, and surely *ought* to, cherish and preserve.

I believe I wrote you some account of his illness last spring; from which to all appearance he was tolerably well recovered. He took the air, and visited about with me, during the warmer months of summer; but my pleasure was of short duration. 'Hæsit lateri lethalis arundo!'³ The peripneumony under which he laboured in the spring had terminated in an adhesion of the lungs to the pleura, so that he could never lie but upon his right side; and this, as the weather grew colder, occasioned an obstruction that could never be surmounted.

Though my reason forewarned me of the event, I was not the more prepared for it.—Let me not dwell upon it.—It is altogether insupportable in *every respect*; and my imagination seems more assiduous in educing pain from this occasion, than I ever yet found it in administering to my pleasure.—This hurts me to no purpose—I know it; and yet, when I have avocated my thoughts, and fixed them for a while upon common amusements, I suffer the same sort of consciousness as if I were guilty of a crime. Believe me, this has been the most sensible affliction I ever felt in my life; and you, who know my anxiety when I had far less reason to complain, will more easily *conceive* it now, than I am able to describe it.

I cannot pretend to fill up my paper with my usual subjects—I should thank you for your remarks upon my poetry; but I despise poetry: and I might tell you of all my little rural improvements; but I hate them.—What can I now expect from my solitary rambles through them, but a series of melancholy reflections and irksome anticipations?—Even the pleasure I should take in shewing them to *you*, the greatest they can afford me, must be now greatly inferior to what it might formerly have been.

How have I prostituted my sorrow on occasions that little concerned me! I am ashamed to think of that idle 'Elegy upon Autumn,'⁴ when I have so much more important cause to hate and to condemn it *now*; but the glare and gaiety of the Spring is what I *principally* dread; when I shall find all things restored but my poor brother, and something like those lines of Milton will run for ever in my thoughts:

'Thus, with a year,
'*Seasons* return, but not to *me* returns
'A brother's cordial smile, at eve or morn.'[5]

I shall then seem to wake from amusements, company; every *sort* of inebriation with which I have been endeavouring to lull my grief asleep, as from a dream; and I shall feel as if I were, *that instant*, despoiled of all I have chiefly valued for thirty years together; of all my present happiness, and all my future prospects. The melody of birds, which he no more must hear; the chearful beams of the sun, of which he no more must partake; *every* wonted pleasure will produce that *sort* of pain to which my temper is most obnoxious. Do not consider this as poetry.— Poetry on such occasions is no more than literal truth.   In the present case it is *less;* for half the tenderness I feel is altogether shapeless and inexpressible.

After all, the wisdom of the world may perhaps esteem me a gainer. Ill do they judge of this event, who think that any shadow of amends can be made for the death of a brother, and the disappointment of all my schemes, by the accession of some fortune, which I never can enjoy!

This is a mournful narrative: I will not, therefore, enlarge it. —Amongst all changes and chances, I often think of you; and pray there may be no suspicion of jealousy betwixt us during the rest of our lives.

I am, dear Sir,
most affectionately yours,
W. SHENSTONE.

NOTES

[1]'Mr. Shenstone's own letters on the death of his brother, are the genuine effusions of a feeling heart, pierced with the most poignant grief and affliction.' *Recollection,* 175. Joseph Shenstone's tomb is beside William's in Halesowen Churchyard.
[2]Terence, *Phormio,* IV, I, 1.
[3]Virgil, *Aen.* IV, 73.
[4]*Verses written towards the close of the Year* 1748, *to William Lyttelton, Esq. Works,* I, 181.
[5]*Paradise Lost,* III, 40.

CXXXVII

Works III, 221.

To C[HRISTOPHER] W[REN], Esǫ.

Alas! dear Mr. W[ren]! the terrible event has happened! I have lost the best of brothers; and you are to pity, not to condemn, your unfortunate correspondent.

About the middle of November I had prepared a letter for you, which lies now amongst my papers. At that time, amidst all my apprehensions, I had some hopes to support me; but before I could send it, my situation was greatly altered, and the month did not wholly expire, till it had effectually rendered me the most wretched of mankind.

Thus much it was necessary I should tell you; you will pardon me, if I do not descend any farther into an account of merit that is lost, and of sorrow which is too apt to revive of itself. Be assured, it is to me a loss which the whole world cannot compensate; and an affliction which the longest time I can live will not be able to erase.

You said, you would let Master W[ren] come and spend a few days with me.—I beseech you do.—It will be some relief to me; and, God knows, I have occasion enough for every assistance than [sic] can be drawn from correspondence, company, or amusement.

You, Sir, I presume, proceed in the innocent recreations of your garden, and those may at least prove a balance for any small disquiets that attend you. If greater ills befal you, you have persons near you to alleviate them.—A wife, family, visitants, male and female friends in abundance, and a table sufficiently hospitable to attract even your enemies. With me the case is otherwise. What I have undergone this winter, may you never feel so much as in apprehension!

Believe me, my friend,
    affectionately and invariably yours,
            W. SHENSTONE.

CXXXVIII

B.M. Add. MSS. 28958.

[*To* LADY LUXBOROUGH.]

Dear Madam,

I am glad to observe that your Ladyship's Handwriting is greatly mended, from which I please myself with drawing many agreeable Conclusions—Such as, that the Bath-waters agree with you, that your Spirits also are better, that you will soon return to Barrels, and that I shall have more frequent Letters from you. The terrible Events that have pass'd, since I *wrote* to Barrels with so much tranquillity, & *receiv'd* Letters from thence with so much satisfaction, seem to have been attended likewise with many other Irregularities. And tho' my unparallel'd Misfortune can never be repair'd to me, yet I shall feel much easier to myself, when my remaining Friendships and Amusements return to their wonted Course. In other words, whatever has pleas'd me during my poor Brother's Life-time, seems now even more pleasing than it did at the Time; & I shall seem to regain some of those former Satisfactions, when you begin to date from Barrels, and to describe again your Employments there. Bath is, *must* be, to me, for the present, quite out of the Question. For besides all other Impediments, I know not but such sprightly Assemblies, when one's Health or Spirits are disorder'd, rather give Pain than Pleasure! Tis like the Glare of Sunshine to Eyes that have been lately couch'd—But I have done; & I hope that your *Ladyship's* Spirits are good, or that you find by *Experience* that my Observation is not *true*.

I have amus'd myself of late with the Choice of Paper for two Rooms; & having seen more than fifty Sorts, have at last fix'd upon two y^t are flock'd: The One, a green and Buff-colour; the other a Red and Buff-colour. I have seen a small specimen of the chew'd Paper for Ceilings; 'Tis pretty, but I think them *unreasonably* dear in ye Price of it.

Mr. Allen's House I saw, when ye Shell of it was almost finish'd; by wch you will collect y^t it is long since I was at Bath. I remember I thought ye situation pleasing, & the View from his middle Room delightfull: He is, I think one, amongst many other Instances, that Persons of the truest *native* Genius, are also Persons of the sublimest Generosity.[1]

I shall be glad to hear from your Ladyship, whenever you find it least painfull to write, and just so much as you can write with Ease. I hear from few besides, nor are there many besides from whom I would wish to hear. Family Losses are of too tender a nature to be touch'd upon by a dull Instrument or an unskillfull Hand: And I receiv'd yesterday morning a Compliment of Condoleance; the Shock of which I did not recover during the rest of the Day. Yet this was from a Man of Sense, and one that seem'd to wish me well.

I return your Ladyship many thanks for accepting the Servant I propos'd to you. I have not often interferd on such occasions, & I began to think myself as unlucky in recommending *others*, as *myself For* the Day after I had written, the Girl was taken ill, & it was as much as they could do to recover her in due time. She sets out from hence with Mr. Joseph to-day; & my own maid with her, to return tomorrow. This I hope you will excuse. If her Health continues, I do not question but after some little time she will merit your Approbation. Her Family are honest, orderly People; & she will, at worst, prove *faithfull*; tho' your Ladyship shall not hire a Servant that will be *more* so, than, Dear Madam,

Your most oblig'd

& most obedient Servant, Will Shenstone.

The Leasows, *March y^e* 14th 1752.

NOTE

[1]Ralph Allen (1694–1764), was famous for his generosity, especially to men of letters, and most of the well-known writers of the day were among his friends. He was of obscure parentage but became wealthy through his own efforts and shrewdness in connection with the postal system. Out of his own quarries he built a magnificent mansion, Prior Park, Bath, which was begun in 1736 and finished in 1743. Everyone spoke well of him. W.S. had probably heard of his generosity to Graves at Claverton. Later, we know from Graves's *Anecdotes of Ralph Allen of Prior Park*, Allen was a constant benefactor.

CXXXIX

Hull, I, 134.

[*To* LADY LUXBOROUGH.]

THE LEASOWS,
June 6, 1752.

My Conversation, dear Lady LUXBOROUGH, is by no Means equal to the Reception I find at *Barrels*, and if you return me Thanks upon *that* Score, you make me doubly sensible how unable I am to make a due Acknowledgement.

The Day after I left *Barrels*, I had a Morning Visit from Admiral SMITH, Captain WHOOD,[1] Mrs. STANLEY, and her two Daughters, who engaged me to dine with Sir G. LYTTELTON. These are Ladies of Taste, I think; but Admiral SMITH is the Delight of Mankind; I forgot to mention Mr. MILLER, who seems to recommend my Walks with great Cordiality. I see they condescend to look upon *modern* Plans at *Hagley*, and if they build anew, I suppose it will be in that Style.

Since this I have seen a good deal of Company, more of whom arrive to see my *Walks* than *me;* yet I am not jealous or invidious: my Walks are truly more deserving of this Favour.

Yesterday, I had the Company of Miss LEA, and Mr. HILTON,[2] a very modest and ingenious Man, who came with Lord DUDLEY from *London;* besides two other Parties of Visitants, who engrossed my whole Day.

And now I sit down by *Five* in the Morning to answer your Queries concerning *Papier-Machée*. It is bought of Mr. BROMWICH, at the *Golden-Lion*, upon *Ludgate-Hill*. What you will want, will be an Ornament for the Middle, and four Spandrells for the Corners. I have taken down the Pine-Apple from the middle of my Cieling, and send it you to see, together with some other Ornaments which were never yet fixed up. They will cost (I mean a middle and four corner Ornaments) somewhere about eight Shillings. You may ornament it *more* or *less* tho' as you please. As to the Cracks of your Cieling, (which I don't remember) if they are not violently bad, they may be mended by a common Mason, and the *Colour* will disguise them. As for putting them up, I will send you over a very agreeable Neighbour of mine, who was once an eminent Upholsterer, but now lives upon his Fortune, who seems glad of the Opportunity it will give him to see *Barrels*, and the Honour it will afford him of being serviceable to your Lady-ship. They should be painted with Flake White and thin Starch; but all this he will manage to your entire Satisfaction. He is a Person of Taste, has seen a good deal of Life; and tho' he has had his Share of Difficulties, always chearful. You must not offer him any Thing. Thus have I been as short as I can, in pointing out your quickest Method of embellishing your Cieling. The whole Cove (except the Moulding) should be washed with Oker; but this you may defer, if you please, till Mr. PIXELL arrives.

I beg my Thanks to Mrs. WEYMONDESOLD, for her kind Remembrance of me: am a little fearful her Visit will be too late in the Year; but 'tis in Mrs. WEYMONDESOLD's Power to make *all* Seasons pleasing.

My Lord DUDLEY will be extremely glad to wait on Mr. OUTING: but he must come hither first, and we will adjust the Remainder.

I have taken the Liberty to send this by my Servant Girl, who is desirous to see her Sister and *Barrels*; and really my Man is so much Assistant in the Way of fitting up my Room (which engages me) that I could very ill spare him.

I hope Mr. PRICE[3] is recovered, by the Mention you make of his going again to *London*. I did not merely ask, but wish to see him here. And now I must leave your Ladyship for the Company of my Carpenters; yet am ever *uniformly* your Lady-ship's most obliged

W. SHENSTONE.

NOTES

[1]Can this be one of the famous brothers Hood, probably Samuel, protegé of Admiral Smith? Actually Samuel Hood did not receive command of a ship till 1754. Wyndham, *op. cit.*

[2]John Scott Hylton, of Lepall House, Halesowen, virtuoso friend and correspondent of Shenstone. Hull gives Hylton's replies to Shenstone's letters. The epistles appear, he fears, 'a mere FARRAGO LITTERARIUM, or more properly like a Welsh Dish, called a SALMAGUNDY, which hungry People may eat, but not well digest.' The letters endear to us this boyish correspondent.

He was a small poet and the song marked J. S. H. supplied by W.S. for Dodsley's *Collection* IV, 305 was the work of Hylton. Courtney, 104, gives an account of him.

[3]Lady Luxborough's servant.

CXL

Works III, 223.

To [CHRISTOPHER WREN].

July 22, 1752.

Dear Mr. W[ren],

I do not know why I made you a promise of a pretty long letter. What I now write will be but a moderate one, both in regard to length and stile; yet write I must, *par maniere d'acquit*, and you have brought four-pence expence upon yourself for a parcel of nonsense, and to no manner of purpose. This is not tautology, you must observe; for nonsense sometimes answers very considerable purposes.—In love, it is eloquence itself.—In friendship, therefore, by all the rules of sound logic, you must allow it to be something; what I cannot say, 'nequeo monstrare, & sentio tantum.'[1] The principal part of a correspondence betwixt two idle men consists in two important enquiries—what we do, and how we do; but as all persons ought to give satisfaction before they expect to receive it, I am to tell you in the first place, that my own health is tolerably good, or rather what I must call good, being, I think, much better than it has been this last half-year.—Then as touching my occupation, alas! 'Othello's occupation's gone!' I neither read nor write aught besides a few letters; and I give myself up entirely to scenes of dissipation; lounge at my Lord Dudley's for near a week together; make dinners; accept of invitations; sit up till three o'clock in the morning with young sprightly married women, over white port and *vin de paysans*; ramble over my fields; issue out orders to my hay-makers; foretel rain and fair weather; enjoy the fragrance of hay, the cocks, and the wind-rows; admire that universal lawn which is produced by the scythe; sometimes inspect, and draw mouldings for my carpenters; sometimes paper my walls, and at other times my cielings; do every social office that falls in my way, but never seek out for any.

'Sed vos quid tandem? quæ circumvolitas agilis thyma? non tu corpus eras sine pectore. Non tibi parvum ingenium, non incultum est!'[2] In short, what do you? and how do you do?— that is all.

Tell my young pupil, your son, he must by all manner of means send me a Latin letter: and if he have any billet in French, for Miss Lea at The Grange, or even in Hebrew, Coptic, or Syriac, I will engage it shall be received very graciously. Thither am I going to dinner this day, and there 'implebor veteris Bacchi, pinguisque ferinæ.'[3]

All this looks like extreme jollity; but is this the true state of the case, or may I not more properly apply the

'Spem vultu simulat, premit atrum corde dolorem?'[4]

Accept this scrawl in place of a letter and believe me
Ever most affectionately yours,
W. SHENSTONE.

NOTES

[1] Juvenal, *Sat.* 7, 56.
[2] Horace, *Epistolae*, I, 4, 6.
[3] Virgil, *Aeneid*, I, 219.
[4] Virgil, *Aeneid*, I, 209.

CXLI

B.M. Add. MSS. 28958.

[*To* LADY LUXBOROUGH.]

THE LEASOWS, *Sept.* ye 30th 1752.

Dear Madam,

Your Ladyship is extremely complaisant with regard to y^e *number* & the *Choice* of Epithets you bestow upon ye Entertainment I was capable of affording you at The Leasows. Sure I am, that whether your Ladyship *makes* Visits or *receives* them, the Persons with whom you *converse* must ever think themselves Very greatly honour'd, oblig'd, & entertain'd.

I sup'd with Ld Dudley at the Grange on Wednesday last, where I deliverd y^r Compliments; & found my Lord very much at your Service, & very stedfast in his Resolution of waiting upon you soon. We did not fix a Day, but I guess it will be towards ye End of a Fortnight; before wch Time you shall hear from me again.

I have order'd the Farrier to bring his Bill to me, & to take Care he *charg'd* no otherwise than if it had been my own Affair, as whatever concerns *your* Interest may be truly said to be.

Your Breakfast Room I am sure must be extremely handsome; your Design for ye upper Part of ye Frame to Ld Rochester's Picture, ye best y^t can be imagin'd; if you chuse to have the Break Continued: And in regard to *this*, I can hardly pronounce, unless I were to *see* the whole Effect.

The Honour of serving y^r Ladyship, and meeting with y^r Approbation, has render'd my Friend Pixell so vain, y^t it will take about five or Six Weeks Mortification to bring him down to the Standard of other vain-glorious Men; during wch time, I must not allow him his way in any single Article. He told me, before he enter'd my Hall, that he had been forc'd to *undo* what I had been doing in y^r Room; & before he had talk'd much more, discover'd that he had added many Things, which *I* must insist upon seeing undone. Y^r Ladyship must by all means bestow a little Carv'd Work over y^r Windows & Doors, wch was all I meant to suggest by my *Charcoal-Operations;* of wch I find Master Pixell has made a quite serious Affair. But real Festoons will not do upon Paper, much less, my ridiculous extravaganzas—Consequently the Wainscoat s^d remain. He has more over made something, he says, round ye Marble Chimney piece with a bit of Flock Paper, wch must needs be sometime supply'd by a small wood-moulding. The Room is really an handsome one, & need not owe anything at all to Whim or Concetti—After all Mr. Pixell is extremely sensible of your Ladyship's Civility, & comes this moment to my little Room-door to desire his Duty to you——

The Day I came Home from Barrels, I had two Persons, it seems, of *Taste* & *Fashion* to see my Walks—from Hereford; who told my Servant there was a Gentleman to come hither from thence in a Coach to see the same, to-Day. Who it is *I* do not know, but He has a Park of his *own*, with Urns, Statues, Vistas & so forth—& how he'll get hither from Stourbridge, (where he lay last Night)—the Lord knows.

I expect Sr George Lyttelton's Family next Week; who, I *feard*, had taken offence that I had not visited them yet at Hagley: But I find all is well there.

The Middle of my Drawing Room Cieling was renderd like to y^r Ladyships ye Monday after I came Home.

I thank your Laship, for my Love-Apples, & will beg ye Favour of some Seed at a proper time of year: I hope you will suffer your Gardener to come to the Leasows, see ye Greenhouse in my Neighbourhood, & take in my Walks; & as it runs strongly in my Head y^t Mrs. Lane[1] has an *admirable Taste* & would find some Pleasure here, I hope y^r Lasp will, when opportunity offers, give her Leave to come over—Poor Mr. Joseph will be impatient; I must therefore hastily beg with my kind Services to Mrs. Davies & Mr. Outing, & to be ever esteem'd y^r most oblig'd and most

Obedient Servt.

W. SHENSTONE.

Mrs. Pearsall, whom I saw on Thursday, is very much your Ladyship's Servant; was full of y^r Encomiums, & thought herself quite unfortunate y^t she had so little of y^r Company.

To

The Right Honourable
Lady Luxborough.

NOTE

[1]Lady Luxborough's servant.

CXLII

Works III, 226.

To MR. G[RAVES], *on the Receipt of his Picture.*

THE LEASOWS,

Oct. 3, 1752.

Dear Mr. G[raves],

I am unfeignedly ashamed to reflect how long it is since I received your present, and how much longer it is since I received your letter. I have been resolving to write to you almost daily ever since you left me; yet have foolishly enough permitted avocations (of infinitely less importance than your correspondence) to interfere with my gratitude, my interest, and my inclination. What apology I have to make, though no way adequate to my negligence, is in short as follows. After the receipt of your letter, I deferred writing till I could speak of the arrival of your picture.—This did not happen till about a month or five weeks ago, when I was embarrassed with masons, carvers, carpenters, and company, all at a time. And though it were idle enough to say, that I could not find *one* vacant hour for my purpose, yet in truth my head was so confused by these multifarious distractions, that I could have written nothing satisfactory either to *myself* or *you:* nothing worth a single *penny*, supposing the postage were to cost you no more. The workmen had not *finished my rooms* a minute, when Lady Luxborough, Mrs. Davies, and Mr. Outing arrived, with *five* servants and a *set* of horses, to stay with me for some time. After a nine days visit, I returned with them to Barrels, where I continued for a week; and whither (by the way) I go again with Lord Dudley in about a fortnight's time. Other company filled up the interstices of my summer; and I hope my dear friend will accept this apology for so long a chasm of silence, during which I have been uniformly at his service, and true to that inviolable friendship I shall ever bear him.

I proceed now to thank you for the *distinction* you shew me, in sending me your picture: I do it very sincerely. It is assuredly a strong likeness, as my Lady Luxborough with all her servants that have *seen you* pronounce, as well as I; consequently more valuable to a *friend* than a face he does not know, though it were one of Raphael's. The smile about the mouth is bad; as it agrees but ill with the gravity of the eyes, and as a smile, ever so little *outré*, has a bad effect in a picture where it is *constant*, though it may be ever so graceful in a person where it is *transitory*. However, this may be altered, when I can meet with a good painter. I have no *other* objection, but to the prominence of the belly. The hair, I think, is good; and the coat and band no way exceptionable. I have given it all the advantage I can: it has a good light, and makes part of an elegant chimneypiece in a genteel, though little breakfast-room, at the end of my house.

Mr. Whistler and I are now upon good terms, and two or three friendly letters have been interchanged betwixt us. He presses me to come to Whitchurch, and I *him* to come over to The Leasows; but the winter cometh, when no man can visit.— The dispute is adjusted by *time*, whilst we are arguing it by *expostulation*.—No uncommon event in most sublunary projects.

Lady Luxborough said very extraordinary things in praise of Mrs. G[raves], after you left us at Barrels; yet I sincerely believe no more than she deserves. I took the liberty of shewing her your letter here, as it included a compliment to her which I thought particularly genteel.—She will always consider you as a person of genius, and her friend.

During most of this summer (wherein I have seen much company either here or at Lord Dudley's), I have been almost constantly engaged in one continued scene of *jollity*. I endeavoured to find *relief* from such sort of dissipation; and, when I had once given in to it, I was obliged to proceed; as, they say, is the case when persons disguise their faces with paint. *Mine* was a sort of *painting* applied to my temper— 'Spem vultu simulare, premere atrum corde dolorem.'[1] And the moment I left it off, my soul appeared again all haggard and forlorn. My company has now deserted me; the spleen-fogs begin to rise; and the *terrible* incidents of last winter revive apace in my memory. This is my state of mind, while I write you these few lines; yet, I thank God, my health is not much amiss.

I did not forget my promise of a box, &c. to Mrs. G[raves]. I had a dozen sent me, one or two of which I could have liked, had they been better *finished*. They were of a good oval, white enamel, with flowers, &c. but horribly gilt, and not accurately painted. I beg my best service to her, and will make a fresh essay. My dearest friend, accept this awkward letter for the present.—In a few posts, I will write again.—Believe me yours from the bottom of my soul.

W. Shenstone.

I will send you a label for made-wine, after my own plan. It is enamel, with grapes, shepherd's pipe, &c. The motto VIN DE PAISAN.

NOTE

[1]Virgil, *Aeneid* I, 209.

CXLIII

Works III, 230.

To Mr. JAGO.

The Leasows,
Nov. 15, 1752.

Dear Mr. Jago,

Could I with convenience mount my horse, and ride to Harbury this instant, I should much more willingly do so than begin this letter. Such terrible events have happened to us, since we saw each other last, that, however irksome it may be to dwell upon them, it is in the same degree unnatural to substitute any subject in their place.

I do sincerely forgive your long silence, my good friend, indeed I do; though it gave me uneasiness. I hope you do the same by mine. I own, I could not readily account for the *former* period of yours, any otherwise than by supposing that I had said or done something, in the levity of my heart, which had given you disgust; but being conscious to myself of the most sincere regard for you, and believing it could never be discredited for any *trivial* inadvertencies, I remember, I continued still in expectation of a letter, and did not dream of writing till such time as I had received one. I trusted you would write at *last;* and that, by all my past endeavours to demonstrate my *friendship*, you would believe the *tree* was rooted in my heart, whatever irregularity you might observe in the *branches.*

This was my situation before that dreadful æra which gave me such a shock as to banish my best friends for a time out of my memory. And when they recurred, as they did the first of any thing, I was made acquainted with that deplorable misfortune of yours![1] Believe me, I sympathized in *your* affliction, notwithstanding my own; but alas! what comfort could I administer, who had need of every possible assistance to support myself? I wrote indeed a few letters with *difficulty;* amongst the rest, one to my friend Graves; but it was to vent my complaint.——I will send you the letter, if you please, as it is by far my least painful method of conveying you some account of my situation. Let it convince you, that I could have written nothing at that time, which could have been of any service to

you: let it afford you, at least, a faint sketch of my dearest
brother's character; but let it not appear an ostentatious display of sorrow, of which I am by no means guilty. I know but
too well that I discovered upon the occasion, what some would
call, an unmanly tenderness; but I know also, that sorrow upon
such subjects as these is very consistent with virtue, and with
the most absolute resignation to the just decrees of Providence
—'Hominis est enim affici dolore, *sentire;* resistere tamen &
solatia admittere, non solatiis non egere.' Pliny.²—I drank,
purchased amusements, never suffered myself to be a minute
without company, no matter what, so it was but continual. At
length, by an attention to such conversation and such amusements as I could at other times despise, I forgot so far as to be
chearful.—And after this, the summer, through an almost
constant succession of lively and agreeable visitants, proved
even a scene of jollity.—It was inebriation all, though of a
mingled nature; yet has it maintained a sort of truce with
grief, till time can assist me more effectually by throwing back
the event to a distance.—Now, indeed, that my company has
all forsaken me, and I am delivered up to winter, silence, and
reflection, the incidents of the last year revive apace in my
memory; and I am even astonished to think of the gaiety of my
summer. The fatal anniversary, the 'dies quem semper acer-
bum, &c.'³ is beginning to approach, and every face of the sky
suggests the ideas of last winter.—Yet I find myself chearful
in *company;* nor would I recommend it to you to be much
alone.—You would lay the highest obligation upon me by
coming over at this time.—I pressed your brother, whom I
saw at Birmingham, to use his influence with you; but if you
can by no means undertake the journey, I will take my speedi-
est opportunity of seeing you at Harbury.—Mr. Miller
invited me strenuously to meet Dr. Lyttelton at his house; but
I believe my most convenient season will be, when my Lord
Dudley goes to Barrels; for I can but ill bear the pensiveness of
a long and lonely expedition. After all, if you *could* come hither
first, it would afford me the most entire satisfaction.—I have
been making alterations in my house that would amuse you,
and have many matters to discourse with you, which it would
be endless to mention upon paper.—Adieu! my dear friend!

may your merit be known to some one who has greater *power* to serve you than myself; but be assured, at the same time, that no one loves you better, or esteems you more.

W. SHENSTONE.

NOTES

[1]Death of his wife in 1751.
[2]Pliny, *Epist. VIII,* 16.
[3]Virg. *Aen. V,* 49–50.

CXLIV

Works III, 234.

To the [REV. RICHARD JAGO].

THE LEASOWS,
Jan. 29, 1753.

Dear Mr. Jago,

Although I have many reasons to urge why I did not write to you before, or visit you from Barrels as I fully intended, I will venture to wave all particulars till I see you; and only assure you in the general, that I was never able to write any thing satisfactory, or to visit you, at that time, with any sort of convenience.

Believe me, my good friend, if *inclination* might have ruled, I had been with you at Harbury many weeks ago. Sure I am, they must be the *cares* of a home, and not the *pleasures* of it, that *ever were* sufficient to detain me during the *winter season.* Nor do I think I have any enemy that wishes me more miserable than I have almost constantly found myself ever since the beginning of *it.*

I cannot even now fix a time when I can see you; and perhaps it may be deferred till Mr. Miller's place will have received some advantage from the Spring; and, in that case, I would infallibly see my Lord Guilford's;[1] but I leave this undetermined: and I hope, if you *can* wander from home with any kind of satisfaction, you will do me the justice to believe, that you have no friend alive who will more gladly receive you than myself.

I have papered some rooms this last year, and would willingly have you see them before their colours are vanished;

which I think, will unavoidably be the case of *one*, before a second summer be half concluded.

Thus is beauty as uncertain as either fortune or fame.

I suppose you have heard there is a citation from Doctors Commons, and a writ of 'Ne exeat' out against Mr. W——— for an intrigue with ———. If you have not, be not *precipitate* in spreading the story.—They say, he has fled into France on the occasion.—What a shocking affair is this! so early in life! so extensive, so lasting, so irremediable in its consequences! but,

'Sic visum Veneri! cui placet *impares*
'*Formas* atque *animos*, sub juga ahenea,
'*Saevo* mittere cum joco!'[2]

Your misfortune and mine incline *us*, almost, to love *all* people that are miserable; but how will the daughters of the Philistines rejoice on the occasion; nay, almost countenance another's loss of virtue by manifesting their own apparent want of humanity!

There is a most admirable piece of allegory on this head in the Female Fables, by Brooks,[3] if I mistake not; to whom the author in his preface acknowledges himself greatly indebted.

I am truly sorry to understand how much you are alone; I really imagined you were much happier in point of company than myself, as you live in a much politer neighbourhood; amongst persons of genius, learning, and humanity. And happier you *are*; for however I make a shift to scrape some company around me, they are such as can affect me with little else besides the spleen.

Do not dwell too much on subjects that make you thoughtful; superficial amusements are our point, till some time hence; I am an ill adviser; but I prescribe you the methods which I have found most effectual with myself.

I have not been forgetful of the task that you enjoined me, to give my observations on the verses which you inclosed.—I will write my sentiments on a separate paper. Do not punish me with silence and suspence concerning you, but write. I can ardently desire what I but little deserve, being

Your most affectionate friend,
W.S.

NOTES

[1]Francis, seventh Lord North and first Earl of Guilford, whose seat, Wroxton Abbey, was only a few miles from Radway Grange.

[2]Horace, *Carm.* I, 33, 10–12.

[3]Henry Brooke (1703?–1783), contributed some of the best pieces in *Fables for the Female Sex*, 1744, published by Edward Moore, author of *The Gamester*.

CXLV

Hull, I, 145.

To Mr. ——

THE LEASOWS, *Jan.* 1753.

Dear Sir,

The Letter with which you favoured me deserves my earliest Acknowledgments, and will prove not a little serviceable, in regard to the Subscription we have in Hand. The whole Account of that Affair is as follows: I have been assured by Persons of Veracity, (amongst which I may safely name Lord DUDLEY, Mr. PIXELL, and THO. COTTEREL)[1] that you had generously made an Offer of twenty Guineas towards the Addition of two new Bells to our present Set; and that in Case the Parish would supply what was wanting, it would be a Pleasure to you, Sir, to have your Offer accepted. Upon this Encouragement, I determined to make Trial what a Subscription would produce, and accordingly drew up a Form for that Purpose; intending to write you an Account of the Undertaking, so soon as I could form a Conjecture of its Success. This I was upon the Point of doing, when I had the Pleasure of a Letter from you, which, nevertheless, was extremely seasonable, as it immediately removed a Doubt that began to spread, in Regard to your Concurrence.

There is now subscribed, (exclusive of your Benefaction) the Sum of fifty Guineas; and I make no Scruple of raising twenty more, by an Application to such Persons as have not yet been solicited. Be our Progress what it will, I purpose in a few Weeks to give you a further Account of it; in the mean Time, can assure you, that the Subscription will be pushed forward with all possible Diligence, that it may give us the earlier Chance for the Pleasure of your Company. I have only to add, that the Bells will never sound more agreeably, than when they ring for your Arrival; will be heard no where more advantageously than from some Parts of my Farm, and that you will find no one more desirous of making the Country agreeable to you than

Your most obedient humble Servant,
W. SHENSTONE.

NOTE

¹A Birmingham tradesman.

CXLVI

Works III, 238.

To the [REV. R. JAGO].

THE LEASOWS,
Feb. 27, 1753.

Dear Mr. Jago,

I wrote you some account of myself, and inclosed some trivial criticisms, in a letter I sent you about a fortnight ago, which I hope you have received.—Tom comes now to enquire after your health, and to bring back my ode to Colonel Lyttelton; in regard to which, I desire, that you will not be sparing of your animadversions. I whispered my difficulties to Mr. Miller at Hagley, how delicate I found the subject, and how hard it was to satisfy either myself or others; in all which points he agreed with me. Nevertheless, having twice broken my *promise* of sending a corrected copy to Sir George, I was obliged to make my peace by a *fresh* one, which I suppose, I must of necessity, perform.—Give me your whole sentiments hereupon, I beseech you; in particular and in general, as a critic and as a friend.—The bad state of spirits which I complained of in my last, for a long time together made me utterly irresolute: every thing occasioned me suspence; and I did nothing with appetite.—This was owing in a great measure to a slow nervous fever, as I have since discovered by many concurrent symptoms. It is now, I think, wearing off by degrees. I seem to anticipate a little of that 'vernal delight' which Milton mentions, and thinks

'Able to chase
'All sadness, but despair.'[1]

At least, I begin to resume my silly clue of hopes and expectations; which I know, however, *will* not guide me to any thing more satisfactory than before.

I have read scarce any new books this season. Voltaire's new Tragedy[2] was sent me from London; but what has given me the most amusement, *has* been the 'Lettres de Madame de Maintenon.'[3] You have probably read them already in English, and then I need not recommend them. The Life of Lord Bolingbroke[4] is entirely his *public* life, and the book three parts filled with political remarks.

As to *writing*, I have not attempted it this year and more; nor do I know when I shall again.—However, I would be glad to correct that Ode 'To the Dutchess of Somerset,'[5] when once I can find in whose hands it is deposited. I was *shewn* a very elegant letter of hers, the other day; wherein she asks for it with great politeness. And as it includes nothing but a love of rural life, and such sort of amusements as she herself approves, I shall stand a good chance of having it received with partiality. She lives the life of a *religieuse*. She has *written* my Lady Luxborough a very serious letter of condolence upon the misfortune in her family;[6] and need enough has Lady Luxborough of so unchangeable a friend! for sure nothing could have happened to a person in her situation more *specifically* unfortunate.
—Mr. Reynolds has been at Barrels, I hear, and has brought her a machine that goes into a coat-pocket, yet answers the end of 'a jack for boots, a reading-desk, a cribbage-board, a pair of snuffers, a ruler, an eighteen-inch rule, three pair of nut-cracks, a lemon-squeezer, two candlesticks, a picquetboard, and the Lord knows what beside.'—Can you form an idea of it? if you can, do you not think it must give me pain to reflect, that I myself am useful for *no* sort of purpose, when a paltry bit of wood can answer so *many?* but, indeed, whilst it *pretends* to these exploits, it performs nothing *well*; and therein I agree with it. So true it is, with regard to me, what I told you long ago.

'Multa & præclara minantem
'Vivere nec recte, nec suaviter!'[7]

We have a turnpike-bill upon the point of being brought into the House of Commons: it will convey you about half the way betwixt Birmingham and Hales, and from thence to Hagley; but, I trust, there will be a *left-hand* attraction, which will always make you deviate from the strait line.

I should be ashamed to reflect how much I have dwelt upon *myself* in this letter; but that I seriously approve of egotism in letters: and were I *not* to do so, I should not have any other subject. I have not a single neighbour, that is either fraught with politeness, literature, or intelligence; much less have I a tide of spirits to set my invention afloat; but the less I am able to amuse *you*, the more desirous am I of your letters; which afford me the truest entertainment, even when my spirits are ever so much depressed.

That universal chearfulness which is the lot of some people, persons that you and I may *envy* at the same time that we *despise*, is worth all that either fortune or nature can bestow.

I am, with entire affection,

Yours,

W. SHENSTONE.

NOTES

[1] *Paradise Lost*, IV, 154.
[2] *Rome Sauvée*, probably referred to here, belongs to the year 1752.
[3] The letters of Madame de Maintenon were many times translated into English during the eighteenth century. A copy was lent to Shenstone by Lady Luxborough, *Letters*, XCII.
[4] *Memoirs of the Life and Ministerial Conduct etc. of the late Lord Bolingbroke.* 4s. Sew'd. Baldwin with a great margin, advertised, *The Gentleman's Magazine*, 1752, p. 481.
[5] *Rural Elegance.*
[6] Elopement of her daughter.
[7] Horace, *Epistles* I, 8, 3.

CXLVII

Works III, 242.

To Mr. GRAVES.

THE LEASOWS,

Mar. 28, 1753.

Dear Mr. Graves,

I am vexed to find you have no copy of those verses.—I must make a fresh enquiry; and should they happen to accompany

2 A

this letter, as I fear they will *not*, be so good as to assist me all you can in the way of *hints* and *corrections*. Corrections of what *is*, and hints of what *may be*. I do not reckon much upon these verses, or the patronage which you mention; though the Dutchess is a woman of high reputation, and has as much benevolence as any woman upon earth.

I do *not* include the design of visiting Bath as a public place: I have long since given up such schemes of gaiety and expence. I visit *you* and *Mrs. Graves;* at the least, I mean to do so.

Inoculation is a point on which I never speak a syllable in the way of *pro* or *con:* I mean, not so as to influence particulars; for, in the general, I esteem it both right and salutary; and even *right* because we *find* it *salutary*.

I do not know whether I could not bear the *dishonour* of friends or relations better than their *death*.—It must afford one no small satisfaction to give them one's affection and assistance under every frailty to which human nature is exposed; at least, so long as they are true to friendship. It is Mr. Whistler's opinion, as well as mine. But Mr. ——'s case is altogether different; and I make no question that he thinks as you do upon the occasion.

Poor Danver's death affects me more than you would perhaps imagine. If you remember, I was at M[ickleton?] when the scheme of his going abroad was in agitation. I think how this event must affect Mrs. T——, whose concern will not be *lessened* by her long separation from him. I dare say he reckoned upon his relations here as his *best estate*, whatever he might gain elsewhere; and, no doubt, the hope of retiring amongst them has been a constant spur to his diligence.—The event was always uncertain, and has proved at last unfortunate; yet, as Melmoth says very justly, 'The course of human affairs requires that we should act with vigour upon very precarious contingencies.'—I desire you would give me a sight of the Latin inscription.

I think it was the Gentleman's Magazine in which I was shewn your verses.[1]

I have a particular and lively idea of your place; though I do not remember to have seen even such *parts* of a scene as I have united together in my imagination. I cannot think otherwise than that the front door opens here, the garden-door there, the stream runs in this place, &c. &c.

'Hac ibat Simois, haec est Sigeia tellus.'[2]

The sight of the place could not impress my imagination more deeply; though the impression I *am to* acquire will hardly leave one line of my present one remaining. *Cabbage-garden ornée*[3] is very high burlesque, and affects the improvements of your friend too nearly.

Let me know in what manner Mrs. Graves and you are drawn. Be as particular as you please.

I could not be clear from your letter whether you had received the box or not. That, together with the tallies, lay on the table before me while I wrote to you last; and went with my letter to Birmingham.—Pray satisfy me directly whether you received them.—They are trifles indeed; but, as they acquit me of my promise, they are virtually of consequence.

Mr. Whistler has not answered a letter which I sent him about two months ago: nay, I think, a quarter of a year.

You are rich.—I have only to wish the continuance of your riches, with some diminution of your fatigue. And yet the most laborious man in the world is, I am fully assured, more happy than the *laziest*.

'The Rival Brothers'[4] has some of Dr. Young's affectations; and I question if the moral be absolutely true—at least, Mr. Addison is in some measure against it; but, on the whole, I think it a noble Tragedy; abounding as much with refined sentiments and elevated expressions, as 'The Gamester'[5] and 'The Earl of Essex'[6] are deficient in *both*.

My verses are not yet sent to Sir George Lyttelton;[7] I start new difficulties, and cannot make them to my mind: yet have promised him a copy, and disappointed him thrice; and can hardly defer it much longer without great offence.

I have scarce been twenty yards from home this winter. Last night I visited one of my neighbours; and what with wine, sitting up late, a perfect flux of discourse, and a return home through the dark, found myself *vertiginous* before I was aware. Never did Prior's manly description, 'I drank, I liked it not, &c.'[8] seem so natural to me as it does to-day. I am absolutely vile in my own sight, and I abhor myself in dust and ashes. I was *never* so intoxicated as not to know what I said, or to talk mere nonsense; and yet how many things could I wish unsaid that I let fall last night!

We are going to add two new bells to our present set of six; to have a turnpike road from Hagley to Birmingham, through Hales; and to emerge a little from our obscurity. I am, dear Sir, with compliments to Mrs. Graves,

Ever most affectionately yours,
W. SHENSTONE.

NOTES

[1] No verses of Graves appear about this time in *The Gentleman's Magazine*.
[2] Ovid, *Heroides* I, 33.
[3] W.S. habitually referred to The Leasowes as a 'ferme ornée.'
[4] *The Brothers* 1753, a tragedy by Dr. Edward Young (1693–1765). Shenstone's opinion of Young as a poet was not as high as his opinion of him as a dramatist. See *ante*, p. 144.
[5] *The Gamester* by Ed. Moore (1712–1757), was produced at Drury Lane on February 7, 1753. It was written in prose and was a great success.
[6] *The Earl of Essex*, 1752, a tragedy, by Henry Jones (1721–1770), poet and dramatist. The success of *The Earl of Essex* ruined Jones, who died in poverty. Luxborough, *Letters*, 332–3.
[7] *A Pastoral Ode, to the honourable Sir Richard Lyttelton.*
[8] *Solomon*, Bk. II, 106.

CXLVIII

B.M. Add. MSS. 28958.
Hull, I, 155.[1]

[*To* LADY LUXBOROUGH.]

THE LEASOWS, *April y.* 2.ᵈ 1753.

Dear Madam,

Your Ladyship's Spirits appear no less perennial than your Genius; Mine alas! to say all in a few words, have been very little better than they were the last fatal winter! And tho' I was conscious wᵗ *apparent* cause I gave you to be angry with my silence, yet I could not bear the Thoughts of answering so polite a Letter as your last, with a Heart utterly depress'd & a Head equally confus'd—Les Morts n'ecrivent point, says Madame de Maintenon, & je me comptois de leur Nombre—

I am here to thank you, Madam, for ye very strikeing Amusement I receiv'd from those Letters. I read them twice; and as I have sully'd the Copy you were so good as to lend me, I will send another wch I bespoke for myself, as soon as it arrives— The Memoirs of Ld Bolingbroke's Life abound too much with Politicks for *me*; I believe The *World* also would be as well pleas'd with ye more domestick Incidents relating to so great a Man. For this your *Ladyship* is in *all* Respects best qualify'd; & I could wish you to engage in something of this Sort; if not for ye Publick, at least as an amusement to yourself & your Friends—or as a suitable Present to the *now* Ld Bolingbroke.

Since I have begun to mention Books, Let me finish ye subject. The Gamester I have read no more of than what I glean'd from the Quotations in ye Magazine. I never had any opinion of ye Genius of Mr. Moore; and hardly think I shall change my sentiments on acc^t of this Performance. The Dedication I see is fantastical & affected—The Moral, must on all Hands be allow'd to be truly *reasonable*—

The Earl of Essex I have read. The unfortunate Earl of Essex! whose Story, whatever it may deserve, has never *yet* produc'd a good Line, & now scarce ever *will*. I am willing, with y^r Ladyship to make all Allowances for the Writer.

The Brothers wch I have also read is I think a noble Tragedy; full of refind & elevated Sentiments, and generally speaking, of suitable expressions. I am not blind to many of it's Faults; Dr. Young must be Dr. Young; but I have read no Tragedy of late years that has affected me so much.

I don't remember to have heard you mention anything of Voltaire's last Play. I therefore send it. These I think are all the new Pamphlets that I have seen this Winter.

I am truly glad to hear y^t you had Mrs. Davies so long at Barrels, to *counter-plot* the effects of this unjoyous season. For my own Part, I should have been glad to have joind in that Contrivance, & to have been introduc'd to your Ladyship as regularly as y^r *Laurustinus*. But I have been little better in bodily health, than I have been in Mind. And *Home*, when one is not truly well, has more Attractions than Elysium. Pardon this unpolite Intimation, which seems to partake of selfishness.

And yet it were *as* unpolite at least, to offer one's Company to another when one is not pleas'd with it one's self.

The Jack[2] was sent to Cotterell soon after it came hither: 'Tis possible your servant may find it ready to be taken home. I mean the Copy together with ye original.

I was two or three times in Company wth Captn Somerville[3] when he went to Westminster school. I would be glad to send my Compliments if there was a probability of his remembering me, sufficient to render it *proper*.

I hear now and then of Mr. Outing by means of Mr. Hylton. Last week they were going upon a small expedition, & he said, Outing blam'd him for not traveling, as *he* did, like an apostle viz. with *one* Coat, *one* Shirt, *one* Pair of Stockings &c: They were going to Charles Walker's *Villa*.[4] Not his *Cabbage-garden orné*, as Mr. Graves denominates his Place at Claverton & For wch I rebuk'd him. The Burlesque might spread too far.

I have promoted and accomplish'd ye addition of two new Bells to our present Six: towards wch however I give only two guineas.

I drew up a rough draught of a Petition to Sr G. Lyttelton in regard to our Turn-pike, meaning if it was approv'd to correct & transcribe it—And Lo! the People of our Parish have sign'd & sent the Echantillon.

Pardon me if I stop here—I have many things to add if I had *Leisure* & *Spirits;* but y^r Servant waits, I am not *now* to assert y^t I am dull. I desire your Ladyship would make my Compliments to Mrs. Davies. I am far from what I was when she saw me, but I am entirely at her Service. I desire also to be remembered to the rest of your Friends, & am madam

Your Ladyship's most oblig'd

& most obedient Servant

WILL SHENSTONE.

Mr. Whistler has had ye Gout, ye most inconsistent of all disorders with ye Idea his complexion [illegible in MS.]—Mr. Graves and Mrs. Graves have been just drawn by a second-hand at Bath. He approves his own Picture, and says only y^t *Mrs.* Graves's is as good as he *expected*.

To the Right honourable

Lady Luxborough.

NOTES

[1]There are considerable verbal differences in the two versions of this letter. Hull ends simply 'yours' and adds no postscript.
[2]See Luxborough, *Letters*, XCII.
[3]Son of Lord Somervile, of Somervile's Aston, relation of Somervile, the poet, and of Lady Luxborough. See her *Letters*, 333.
[4]Charles Walker of Purford's Green. Hull, I, 150.

CXLIX

B.M. Add. MSS. 28958.

[*To* LADY LUXBOROUGH.]

THE LEASOWS, *May y.* 13*th*. 1753.

Dear Madam,

I am *well aware* y^t my Pegasus is one of those dull Horses which will not bear to be *hurry'd*. Allow him but his *Time*, and he may jogg on *safely;* but urge him to move faster, and he is sure to break one's neck. Your Ladyship's, on the other Hand, is of a different strain; and is never known to stumble, 'tho He have all the Celerity of a Race-Horse. This Account being *literally* Fact, you must in justice excuse ye Defects of this Letter. Your Gardener is urgent to return this Evening, and I have defer'd rather too long to *begin* my notable epistle.

The first thing y^t occurs to be consider'd is my Friend Pixell's affair. I will not fail to *communicate* and to *press* Mr. Reynolds's advice to him: As for y^e *Event* he must trust to Fortune, and has reason to acquit his Friends.[1]

I am glad to hear y^t your Lasp's Health is mended; and y^t your Complaints, tho' grievous while they *last*, are such as do not after threaten to continue: I too have had better Health & Spirits for these three last Days, a greater *Quantity* of both, could they be weigh'd, y^n I have been forc'd to *subsist* upon ever since I saw you at Barrels. I had reason to suspect some Inward Inflammation in ye winter; I liv'd maigre, & pursu'd a Regimen of warm diluters within-Doors, till I found my nerves were totally relax'd, & my Skin not proof against an airing in my kitchen-garden. Hence Wind ye sure consequence of obstructed Perspiration, viscid Juices, & eternal Lassitude, hence also the numberless effects of wind upon the Nerves; Watching, when one should sleep; or sleep more anxious & less refreshing than watchfullness. I now begin to try the Bark in little Portions & by degrees; and my Spirits, to speak ye truth, are now not much amiss: Only my Head is *confus'd* as My letter will testify.

I shall be extremely glad to meet Mrs. Davies at Barrels, & I shall be extremely glad to meet Sr William Meredyth at Barrels; & one or the other it shall go hard with me, but I *will* meet. In the meantime, let me *seriously* assert that your Ladyship's Menace is altogether too severe. Give my *Vanity* at least an opportunity of experimenting, whether I cannot make the Leasows new to you, as long as we live.

I beg my Compliments & *Thanks* to Mrs. Davies, when you see her. I am glad you like the few Lines to Sr William Meredyth: I know his *general* Accomplishments; I only wanted to consult your Ladyship about a *Propriety* of Compliment.

Mr. Hylton *has* y^t disposition your Ladyship observ'd in him; & has also, (what you had not here any *time* to observe,) no despicable share of Politeness Genius & Literature.

You might well laugh at ye Correspondence betwixt Lord Dudley & me. He is too diffident of his Abilities; and it would be no Discredit to his Character if he would write more frequent letters.[2]

Your Ladyship may be justly allow'd to laugh at my Apothecary's Apprehensions: But you cannot with so much Justice laugh at my contribution to ye Bells. I live but at ye Distance of *Half* a mile, upon an opposite Hill to that on wch the Church is built; a fine Valley betwixt, with a pretty large Piece of Water. Finally, there is no Place in the Parish where the Bells will sound more harmoniously y^n The Leasowes. And, by y^e *bye*, I knew from ye beginning.

I never hear from Mr. Outing, & I never write to him. All I know is that

'*He* is contented, so am *I*!'

but I think him a truly honest Man, and wish him Prosperity.

I agree with y^r Ladyship y^t Madame de Maintenon had

much more worldly *Art* & Design y^n is suitable to a Person who so often uses the expression 'pour faire mon salut' & 'songez a votre salut.' which are ever in her Mouth.

I have spoke to many Parts of your Ladyship's Letter—If your Gardener *must* go to-night, I ought to fill ye rest of my Paper with my Thanks for ye offer of his Assistance, ye Love-Apple, & ye Brocoli-seeds. He has been shewn Ld Dudley's Green-house this Morning; and is now walk'd out to take a View of my Farm: But as the Day is rainy, & the Verdure of my groves, immature, I cannot give your Ladyship an Acquittance in Full for ye Promise you made y^t he should have a *sight of ye Leasows* . . . I am ever

Your Ladyship's most oblig'd
& most obedient Servt
WILL: SHENSTONE.

Mr. Hume[3] is return'd, & seems highly delighted indeed! He has not seen ye Beau-monde of Hales here, on account of ye weather, but I hope he will however say enough to draw Mrs. Lane hither whenever she is at Leisure.

NOTES

[1]Luxborough, *Letters*, 335–6.
[2]Graves, *op. cit.*, 96, remarks on Lord Dudley's lack of education.
[3]Lady Luxborough's Scottish gardener, often mentioned in her letters. Boswell on one occasion told Dr. Johnson 'that England was obliged to us for gardeners, almost all their good gardeners being Scotsmen.'

CL

B.M. Add. MSS. 28958.

[*To* LADY LUXBOROUGH.]

THE LEASOWES, *June y^e* 22. 1753.

Dear Madam,

It is now a great Length of time since I last had the Honour of a few Lines from your Ladyship; at least according to the *Chronology* of a Person who wishes to hear of your Health & Happiness so sincerely as myself. Mrs. Davies did indeed inform me some weeks ago, that she had prevail'd upon you

to take a View of ye Perfections of your Shrubbery &c: I hope
to hear by ye Return of my servant that such walks as these
have been frequently repeated; and y^t by enjoying them a little
at first, you furnish yourself with strength & Spirits to enjoy
them more & more. For my own Part, tho' I am greatly better
y^n I was dureing the Winter, & have had a continuance of
weather not at all unfavourable to the Views of the Country, yet
I cannot yet fancy to myself y^t I have *begun* my *Season;* & am
mighty willing to hope that I have much greater Happiness
in *Reserve.*

Sir George Lyttelton has been at Hagley for a week or nine
Days, & return'd yesterday to London. I did not see him all y^e
Time: Tho' I have thrice broke my Promise to him of sending
him y^t Ode to his Brother; & tho' the rest of our Turn-pike-
Commissioners all din'd with him on Wednesday last.   Such
is my *Impropriety* of Behaviour to all my Friends; & ye odd
vicissitudes of my Health, (which I cannot easily *explain* to
them) are ye real cause: I hope y^t your Ladyship will not be my
severest Accuser; tho' I have not paid my Respects to your
Ladyship in ye manner my *Inclination* tells me I should have
done.

I have after an unavoidable Delay, & some Difficulty,
transcrib'd a copy of this Ode To The Dutchess of Somerset,
I have indeed accompany'd it with a few stiff Lines to her
Grace; but I must absolutely depend upon your Ladyship to
be presented *properly:* I mean with all that *Respect* & *Deference*
of which you know me to be truly conscious for her Grace's
exalted *Character*, & with all that profound *Humility* with w^{ch}
I ought to inscribe so *superficial* a Poem.

The Bookseller made my Paper-Books too little; yet I could
not endure to wait longer for others; However if your Ladyship
thinks this Decorum may *not* be *dispens'd* with, I will once
more transcribe this Ode &c:

Ld Dudley is expected at The Grange next Tuesday. I
long to see him for his *Honesty;* In such a scoundrell Parish as
ours, it really *Shines.*

I have seen but little *first*-Rate Company this Season. *Some*,
I have, but strangers. One mighty agreeable young Lady whose
Name was Offley; Yorkshire Two gentlemen, yesterday (wth

serv^{ts}) one whose Name was Coom. They took a *minute* description of ye Place & every single Motto &c: I met them comeing up to the House; and had only a few Minutes' Conversation. As for Tradesmen & w^t I am to call middlin sort of People, I have had more this year yⁿ any of the Preceding.

Outing seems to me to be very frequently wth Lord Dudley in Town, & I should not be surpriz'd to see y^t He *returns* with Him.

My aimiable Friend, & your Ladyship's most faithfull Servant, Mr. Hylton, will be down in a Fortnight. Either with Him, or young Pixell, do I then purpose to wait upon your Ladyship at Barrels—I hope Mrs. Davies contributes often to your Amusement: I am sure she much wishes it. I beg my Compliments to all your Ladyship's Friends and am your Ladyship's most oblig'd

              & most obedient hum: Servt

                    WILL: SHENSTONE.

I hope your Ladysp will renew to me the Promise of a visit this Summer—I answer'd Mrs. Davies's Letter.

CLI

                       Hull, I, 179.

To the DUCHESS OF SOMERSET.

                    June 23, 1753.

Madam,

I find myself at length enabled to obey your Grace's Commands, after a Delay, but ill expressive of the Pleasure with which I received them. But by some Means or other, the Original of this Ode was mislaid, and it was not immediately in my Power, from scattered Materials, to give it once more the Form, in which it now appears.

I fear it is no less requisite to make an Apology for the Freedom of inscribing it to your Grace from the Beginning. In this Respect, I have but little to offer, beside the flattering Imagination, that the *Subject* might recommend it. It would be no small Vanity in me to presume, that in Regard to the more elegant Amusements of a Country Life, I had the Honour to entertain the same Sentiments with your Grace; however, something of this Kind I must of Necessity confess, if I would give a genuine Account of the Liberty I have taken.

The additional Fragment was originally intended as an Episode to a much larger Poem on the Subject. It was thrown into its present Form soon after the Rebellion, and it is now transcribed, because I would not send a vacant Space in my Paper, wherein I had the most distant Chance of contributing to your Grace's Amusement.

Lady LUXBOROUGH, who does me the Honour of communicating these trifling Productions to your Grace, will not fail to do me the *Justice* of declaring the singular Veneration I have for your Grace's Character. She will testify, with how much Diffidence I offer you such imperfect Compositions, written at a Distance from every judicious Friend with too much Inaccuracy, by the Side of Meadows and Streams, from which little can be expected, but a Group of rural Allusions. Above all she will be so obliging as to suggest, how little I am influenced by any other Ambition, compared with that of being esteemed,

Madam,
Your Grace's most devoted
and most obedient Servant,
W. SHENSTONE.

CLII

Works III, 247.

To the [REV. R. GRAVES], *with Observations on Arms, Inscriptions, &c.*

THE LEASOWS,
July 15, 1753.

Dear Mr. Graves,

I send you my Ode, as I sent it to the Dutchess some weeks ago. Why I pitched upon one reading sooner than another, I will not now explain: nor will I trouble you to make any fresh remarks upon it at present; only, when you happen to read it over at your leisure, if any thing occurs to you that would tend to perfect it, I would beg you occasionally to make some memorandums. I have not yet received an answer; but, as I accompanied the verses with a letter, I suppose I shall receive one in return. I also added, to fill a blank space in my paper book, a poem which I call 'The Vista;'[1] and which you may perhaps recollect; how properly I know not, for I had the benefit of no person's *judgement* or advice.

Lord Dudley made Mr. Dolman a present of a piece of plate, a large cup, in consideration of his sister's being at Broom about half a year. There was on it, one supporter awkwardly enough holding up the coronet in his paw; and from the coronet proceeded a label, with 'amoris ergo Dudley.' I do not know who was the manager, or whence he had the inscription; but I think, from Dr. H——. This is *elegant* and *enough*. Nevertheless, as there may be some convenience in dazzling the eyes of the people where I dwell, and as *such* eyes as theirs are not to be dazzled, and hardly *struck*, by *elegance* alone, I chose the method that was most *magnificent*.—I wish they are not invidious enough to say, that *his* arms are engraved there for want of some of my *own*: so I would not be long before I remove their notable suggestion.—I have truly so low an opinion of arms since they became purchaseable by money and since the present unlimited use of them, that, were I to find a coat to my name in the office which I did not like, I would not use it; but substitute what was more agreeable: yet some *sort* of *right* or *claim* is requisite to satisfy one's delicacy with an opinion of *property*; and indeed, to fix one's *choice*, where one has the whole furniture of the universe for *its* object.—After all, the vulgar are more struck with arms than any thing; 'stupet in titulis & imaginibus;'[2] and, I believe, there were near two hundred people gathered round Lady Luxborough's landeau at Birmingham, and declaring her arms to be very *noble*, or otherwise.—I do not, therefore, chuse to employ a vulgar *mind* about this matter.—Were you to go to London, I should gladly solicit *you;* or if you have any friend you could write to in town, to search the office; for really I have none that I like *for the purpose*. It will not cost above a couple of shillings.—I will send you a draught of the lid of my standish when it arrives—for I really do not know what Mr. Hylton will put upon it: I find, he consults with Dr. B——, my Lord's physician.—'*De* Dudley' would run most abominably, and 'Baro Dudley' may be authorized by the frequent practice of Maittaire.[3]—If it is inscribed 'Dudley' *alone*, I can add the rest if I should hereafter think proper; and I wish it may be so.

My verses to the Colonel are not yet transcribed.

I think the Latin inscription to your brother very elegant; and I should not care to have any part of it omitted—I would, by all means, have this little history of his life perpetuated.— 'His saltem, &c.' And were you to put it into English, it would be too long for an inscription; unless you were, by means of a printed elegy with notes, or any other such method, to produce the same effect; and then you might make the epitaph as short as you pleased.—After all, the *first* method is perhaps as eligible. When the affair is nearer a conclusion, I should be glad to be of any service.—I will think, and write again about it.

And now, having spoke to such matters as have been the subject of our late correspondence, I am at liberty to diversify my letter as I may.—I should be glad to know in your next, whether you have heard of late from Mr. Whistler; and whether he is confined at home as usual by his mother's state of health. I almost despair of ever seeing him again at The Leasows, though there is hardly any pleasure I so much covet as that of surprizing him with the *alterations* I have *made*, and the *articles* I have *purchased*, during the five years since he was in Shropshire: add to this, the several *acquaintances* I have formed which he would like, and the amusing visits I could pay hereabouts with freedom.—I do not know whether you saw Mr. Davenport[4] and his family at Bath this spring. He is laying out his environs, and I am by appointment to go over the week after next. He has also a painter at this time taking views round his house; which is one of the most magnificent in our county; yet I never leave home but with reluctance. I really *love* no place so well; and it is a great favour in me to allot any one a

week of my *summer*.—Add to this, that my constitution requires nursing; and I am most *happy*, where I am most *free*.
It is in vain to say, they *allow* you all freedom, where you can
not allow it *yourself*. For this reason, I never more enjoy myself,
than I do at The Grange; and yet this to some may appear
paradoxical.

I yesterday embellished my chalybeate spring.—The
inscription that is *cut* on the stone is as follows, viz.

'FONS FERRUGINEUS.
'DIVAE QUAE SECESSU ISTO
'FRUI CONCEDIT
'SALUTI. S.'

Yet I question whether some of the following be not preferable; if they are, I beg you will tell me. One shilling and six-
pence produces the alteration:

'FONS FERRUGINEUS.
'DIVAE PER QUAM LICET
'HOC SECESSU FRUI, &C.
'SAL. &C.
or,
'DIVAE PER QUAM LATEBRAE
'QUAEVIS OBLECTANT '&C.'
or,
'DIVAE LOCORUM OMNIUM
'COMMENDATRICI, &C.'
or,
'DIVAE NIMIRUM RUSTICAE
'SALUTI SACER.'
or,
'DIVAE CUI DEBETUR
'LOCORUM OMNIUM AMOENITAS '&C.'
or,
'DIVAE PER QUAM LICET
'INORNATO RURE LAETARI.'

Believe me ever, with my best compliments to Mrs. Graves,
Your most obliged
and most affectionate servant,
W. SHENSTONE.

NOTES

[1]No poem with this title appears among W.S.'s published poems. I am, however, indebted to a correspondent for information contained in an unpublished letter of Graves, who, writing to Dodsley certain recommendations for the arrangement of the 1764 edition of W.S.'s poems, says, 'He having met with fresh difficulties—by the Bishop's being gone out of town, has had but little time to attend to the MSS. However, has read over the *Vista* (very unproperly so call'd) which with short notes referring to ye several King's reigns and a few corrections would pass very well—The story of the *Spanish Lady* or "*Love* and *Honour* is an excellent thing, to my taste—and the *progress of Delicacy* very pretty."' These few words identify the poem as *The Ruin'd Abby; or, The Effects of Superstition*. 'Ye several King's reigns' are there and, it is the poem preceding *Love and Honour* which is next mentioned by Graves.

[2]Horace, *Satires*, I, 6, 17.

[3]Michael Maittaire (1688–1747), classical scholar and typographer.

[4]Sherrington Davenport of Worfield, neighbour and correspondent of W.S., to whom he introduced Percy. *Recollection*, 162.

CLIII

B.M. Add. MSS. 28958.

[*To* LADY LUXBOROUGH.]

THE LEASOWES, *July y*[e] 19th 1753.

Dear Lady Luxborough,

Tho' I have not yet had the Opportunity, which I *soon expect*, of bringing one of my Friends to wait upon your Ladyship at Barrels, I am by no means void of Anxiety in regard to your Health: And the Last Account of it being so far short of what I could wish, I send Tom purely in Hopes of receiving a *better*. Should *that* be the Case, I would begin to flatter myself with the agreeable *Consequences* of your Recovery; amongst y[e] rest, the annual Visit you have hitherto been so good to make me. Tis owing to your Ladyship's Indulgence, y[t] the Prospect of this visit revives, with each returning year, as regularly in my Imagination, as the Leaves upon y[e] Trees, or the Flowers upon the Meadowes. May no unkindly Star contribute to *robb* me of y[e] Pleasure of your Company, or y[e] Beauty of a Season, so long as I live! At least may the Goddess *Health* be never averse to it, to whom I have of late been dedicating my *Chalybeate* Spring! The Inscription is as follows 'FONS FERRUGINEUS &c: 'The Chalybeate Fountain; sacred to the Goddess *Health*, by whose Favour alone we enjoy this Retirement—' There is a little *Art* appears in the stone-work round this Spring; & I think it not amiss; but I will not *anticipate* your Ladyship's opinion.

Ld Dudley has been arriv'd this Fortnight. He has made me a 4 Days visit since he came; proposes your Ladyship's Health to his Company & will be extremely glad to wait upon you—I suppose when you come into this Country you will think it requisite to dine *there* the first Day; & I will afterwards beg ye Honour of conducting you to The Leasowes. My Lord *himself* does not regard the Ceremonial; but He has some *about* him, I know, that *do*—Your Intimation concerning Miss L[ea] and Sally Rock[1] was coincident with ye mention of it by some Company in my Drawing Room—& the first I *heard* of it. It seems Miss Lea has made a Conquest of Mr. Warren a Buckinghamshire Gentleman, who is about Seventy; & poor man, violently afflicted wth the Gout; but will come to the Grange this Summer, if he be *able*. He offers a Landau & Four, unlimited Indulgence; & to put her Fortune in ye Stocks for ye Benefit of y^e *younger* Children—The Event I do not know: but it will, I *think*, be a Match.

But Miss L., all this while, has a Regard for Mr. Hilton; Mr. Hylton on ye other hand is enamour'd of Sally Rock (a secret) & how Fortune is to manage ye Catastrophe of this tragicomedy, is past my comprehension to determine.

> The Maid for lovely Fore-head fam'd
> With Cyrus' beauties is enflam'd:
> While Pholoe, of haughty Charms,
> The panting Breast of Cyrus warms: ⎫
> So Venus wills! whose Power controuls ⎬ ill-translated
> The fond affections of our Souls! ⎭
> With sportive Cruelty, who binds
> Unequal Forms, unequal Minds!
>
> Francis's Horace Vol. I.[2]
> Page 121.

Mr. Hylton arriv'd at ye Grange & visited me yesterday; I hope very shortly to come with him to Barrels. He is zealously your Servant, &, if you will excuse ye familiarity of ye Sound, your *Friend*—I am going to dine with my Lord to-day upon Venison, where we shall wish it were as easy to *promote* your Ladyship's Health, as to *drink* it.

I am for my own part arriv'd at what I am to *call* Health; namely as good a state of it as I shall probably enjoy this Summer; perhaps, ever. More of *Happiness* I shall partake when your Ladyship arrives.

Our Turnpikes take place—but will I fear produce but little Alteration this Year.

I have nothing to add y^t can amuse you, so may as well conclude—Only let me beg, if writing be troublesome to your Ladyship, y^t Mrs. Lane may be permitted, now & then, to give me some Account of your Health—I am with ye most ardent wishes for it, Madam, your Ladyship's most oblig'd

& most invariable Servant,

WILL: SHENSTONE.

I never hear from Mrs. Davies.

NOTES

[1]'Sally Rock,' several times mentioned in Shenstone's Letters, was apparently a member of Lord Dudley's household.

[2]Philip Francis (1708?–1773), miscellaneous writer, Dr. Johnson said of his translation: 'The Lyrical part of Horace can never be perfectly translated. Francis has done it the best.'

CLIV

B.M. Add. MSS. 28958.

[*To* LADY LUXBOROUGH.]

THE LEASOWS, *August the* 26, 1753.

Dear Lady Luxborough,

I wrote a few lines to Mrs. Davies this afternoon, purposing to defer my Letter to your Ladysp, 'till I could spare my Servant for a Day; by which means I might receive an *immediate* Answer in regard to your Ladyship's Health. But considering y^t I have but one only Servant about ye House, in Case any Company should arrive, I find it expedient to apply once more to my good Friend Mr. Williams, who has always hitherto been punctual in furthering any Packet you were pleas'd to send me, I beg therefore, if your Ladyship does not care to write, that you would permit Mrs. Lane to give me some account of your Recovery, by ye very first opportunity that occurrs. There is no Friend you have yt wishes your Health more sollicitously than myself; but as the sincerest Wishes of ye most faithfull Friends are mighty ineffectual Things, unless seconded by your own Endeavours, I really want to offer you something more *significant* yn the mere Expression of my Wishes. *Advise* your Ladyship I cannot, without Presumption; but *Remind* you I *may;* for I am well assured you will not call *that* Presumption, which flows alone from Gratitude for many unmerited obligations. Without further Preamble I mean No more than this, that you would omit Nothing (for this and the two next Months) yt has been found so serviceable to your Health while Sr Peter Soame was at Barrels. I believe the principal of this Advice was Exercise & Regular Hours, & I add the two next Months, because one Part of this Prescription may not afterwards be so conveniently follow'd. Let me Add that I mention this for ye sake of yourself, who wish ye Happiness of your Acquaintance; for ye sake of your Friends who derive great Pleasure from your Conversation; & for ye sake of my own Sincerity, which ought ever to be held inviolable.

I mention'd to Mrs. Davies in a Letter wch She will shew you, if at Barrels, what an Inundation of Company I have had since I came Home. I will not repeat the List, for this Reason. But I should act ungratefully if I should forget, on this Occasion, *who* it was that did me this Sort of Honour *primarily;* who it was yt has never miss'd an opportunity of recommending either my Place or Me, And that with Spirit, & Ingenuity; And So long as I do not forget these Things, it is impossible yt *Any* Visitants can erase the Memory of ye Obligations I have to Lady Luxborough. I need not say erase, for they tend naturally to revive it.

Lady Plymouth[1] is a most aimiable Person, & I really think a very desireable Match for my Lord. I am to dine there sometime in a Fortnight.

Lady Gough[2] seems a very friendly Sort of Woman; her

Person but indifferent; She made much Enquiry after your Ladyships Villa, & I believe has a Longing to see your Shrubbery. I am to visit there also.

Miss Banks[3] is a Person to fall in Love with; but, I am told, is too celebrated, & withall a Court-Lady.

L[d] Temple[4] was chiefly struck with y[e] View from my House, my Terras, & my Grove: Ask'd me to call on him & take a View of Stowe—To make your Ladyship laugh a little, if you please. L[d] Dudley had stay'd a Night here, & Mrs. Rock had been teizing him to dress, telling him she was sure some Company would drop in, and surprize him. He, in a kind of Pett, swore he would not stir a step let who the *Devil would* come; And that selfsame Instant enterd L[d] Temple and Miss. Banks & caught him in his Night-Cap &c.

The Paragraph to Dean Lyttelton (in y[e] Ode you know of)[5] made L[d] Temple laugh abundantly. That with the Ode To the Dutchess of Somerset[6], & The Verses upon Autumn,[7] were read at Hagley-Table, & were all more extoll'd than they had any Pretence to deserve. Some Particulars, in regard to the Colonels Ode, I would mention, but have neither Room nor Time Nor indeed are they much material.

Mr. Hylton is gone to dine with L[d] Dudley to day: Otherwise I should have many Compliments & Acknowledgm[ts] to make on his Behalf. But He talks of conveying them in a Letter of his own.

If your Ladyship *should* have an opportunity of writing, I should be very highly delighted with a Line of your own. If not, I'm well assured you will suffer Mrs. Lane to write to Me. I am,

> Dear Lady Luxborough!
> Your most oblig'd and ever obedient
> hum: Servt WILL: SHENSTONE.

NOTES

[1]Uther Lewis, Earl of Plymouth, of Hewel Grange, married Catherine, first daughter of Thomas Archer, Baron of Umberslade. W.S. was consulted concerning landscape gardening operations at Hewel. *Recollection*, 144–5.

[2]Wife of Sir Henry Gough, *née* Barbara, only daughter of Reynolds Calthorpe, of Elvetham, Hants.

[3]She married Henry Grenville, brother of Lord Temple. Dickins & Stanton, *An Eighteenth Century Correspondence*.

[4]Richard, first Earl Temple of Stowe. Richard Grenville succeeded his uncle, Viscount Cobham, in 1749, and later became Earl Temple on the death of his mother.

[5]*A Pastoral Ode to the Honourable Sir Richard Lyttelton. Works*, I, 174. Dean Lyttelton is there celebrated under the name of Philo.

> 'While Philo, to whose favour'd sight,
> Antiquity with full delight,
> Her inmost wealth displays;
> Beneath your ruins moulder'd wall
> Shall muse, & with his friend recall
> The pomp of ancient days.'

[6]*Rural Elegance.*

[7]*Verses written towards the close of the year*, 1748 *to William Lyttelton, Esq.: Works*, I, 181.

CLV

B.M. Add. MSS. 28958.

[*To* LADY LUXBOROUGH.]

Septr ye 18.th 1753.

Dear Madam,

I hope your Ladyship will readily enough believe that an Account of your Recovery, from your own Hand, was the most agreeable Intelligence I could possibly receive. Somewhat heighten'd I may now confess, it was, by the *surprize* it gave me; For tho' I really thought it in your *Power* to recover, when I saw you last; I was not a little fearfull that you would not use ye Means which to Me seem'd absolutely indispensable. Your Ladyship will see so many Instances of ye Joy it gives your Friends to find you on ye mending Hand, that I hope your natural Philanthropy will induce you to persist in such a Regimen as you have found to be of Service. And what if after a little time your strength should be so much advanc'd, that I should pronounce it not only possible, but expedient for you to make a Journey to the Leasowes, by way of Exercise? I doubt your Physician has too much Integrity to accept a Bribe, or I would infallibly take a Ride to Worster, & endeavour to make him of my Party.

I have had a perpetual succession of Company ever since I wrote to you. L^d & Lady Ward sent to have the Roads examin'd—& I was told by Captn Whood that I was likely to see L^d & Lady Anson,[1] with Mr. Anson, this Week; when they were to be at Hagley. Sr George Lyttelton; Admiral

Smith & Mr. Berkeley,[2] Member for Glostershire, have been here, But I will not fill this Letter with Names; I may perhaps, when the Season is over, make tryal how brilliant a List I can furnish, for y^r Amusement. Sir George made very friendly Enquiries after your Ladyship's Health, & seem'd truly concern'd at the Account I gave Him. Glad I am that it is now in my Power to give one more *agreeable*.

I have engag'd my Vote to Mr. Coventry; & as it is entirely my Lord Foley's[3] Resentment y^t prevents a Compromise, I could wish your Ladyship would support me in my Endeavours to serve Ld Coventry.[4] There are a Number of Votes, I think, in Oldbarrow, for wch I, last Election, apply'd to Mr. Somervile. If you want a List I will procure one: But in the mean time it will give me great Pleasure to find y^t I have ye Honour *to think wth your Ladyship*, when I am *forc'd* to turn my Thoughts towards a Subject on which I think so *little*, as Party. The Probability, & Danger of a Minority seems as far as I can judge to demand a Whig-Parliament.

I desire my Compliments to Mr. & Mrs. Holyoake & if I am not impertinent, would request their Assistance in the same Cause. My Lord Dudley will be excessively glad to return them his Thanks at The Grange. He din'd here yesterday, & is *zealously* at your Service.

I forget *what* I said of Miss. Peggy Banks; but I could hardly say *too much*. She lives mostly wth Lord Temple, goes in Parties with the Pelhams, is as remarkable for her Taste & Reading as her Beauty & Behaviour. I most solemnly assure your Ladyship that I did not know when I wrote my last Letter, that she would be an 100,000ll Fortune.

I beg the Favour of your Ladyship to convince Mr. Reynalds y^t I wish impatiently to see him, & will infallibly see him ye first opportunity that offers. He does not well, to be angry with a Person who so truly esteems him—I must defer my Letter to Mrs. Davies for a day or two, & shall be in *Woefull Plight*, if *she* takes it amiss, I'm sure. But pray, my Lady, ask her one Question; Why Part of a select Company may not make an autumnal visit, & unite with ye rest to make another in the Spring? Winter is too dark a Medium for me to look thro, at least clearly.

I have Mr. Hylton's Prints & Pictures here, wch I shew to my Company, & it adds to their Entertainment—It has been unlucky for me this year that any of their Visitants at Hagley cannot *walk*—I believe I should else have had the *Duke of Beaufort* wth his Dutchess (Mr. Berkeley's Sister)[5] Sr *Richard Lyttelton* with his new Ribband,[6] & her Grace his Wife; & I am just now forc'd to hear y^t *Ld Anson* is a miserable Walker— But I shall have no Cause to complain having far out-shone all my Neighbours in y^e *Splendour* & y^e *Number* of my Visitants. I was us'd to consider your Ladyship as a Star y^t was particularly friendly to me, as well as distinguishedly bright.— Y^r Absence will be a terrible Draw-back upon the Lustre of this Year; & I wou'd give fifty of my *Lesser* Stars for Your Appearance. But I fear it will not be—I must take Leave upon another Paper—I have now determin'd to send Tom with my Letter hopeing your Ladyship will please to dispatch him in the Morning, because I have Company that dines with Me to-morrow—It would be of great Importance to me, if your Ladyship would be so good as to send me a favourable Answer in regard to the Votes at Oldbarrow; at least such as I might repeat with Propriety to Sr George Lyttelton, whom I shall see again this Week. He either has more Insincerity than I *suspect* in Him, or He is very respectfully y^r Ladyship's Friend—

If y^r Ladyship have Plenty of Melons, I am tempted to be so impertinent as to beg one by Tom's Return.

My Pen is in a rambling Humour—& if I cou'd detain Tom any longer, It would tell you a Multitude of Things— Nothing however more true or so important to me, as that I have the honour to be, Madam, y^r Ladyship's most obliged
    To   W Shenstone.
The Right honourable
    Lady Luxborough
        at Barrels

    To be left with
    Mr. Williams in Birmingham.

NOTES

[1]George Anson, son of William Anson of Shugborough, Co. Stafford, Admiral, created Lord Anson, Baron Soberton, 1747.

[2]Norborne Berkeley, only son & heir of John Syme Berkeley of Stoke Gifford, Co. Gloucester, M.P. (Tory) for Gloucester in four parliaments, 1741–1763.

[3]Thomas Foley, Baron Foley of Kidderminster, of Witley Court, Co. Worcester, was much interested in W.S.'s landscape gardening. *Recollection*, 144.

[4]George William Coventry, 6th Earl, of Croome Court.

[5]Charles Noel (Somerset) Duke of Beaufort, married Elizabeth, sister of Norborne Berkeley, Lord Botetourt.

[6]Colonel Lyttelton was made a Knight of the Bath in 1753.

CLVI

B.M. Add. MSS. 28958.

[*To* LADY LUXBOROUGH.]

Friday, Septr 1753.

Dear Madam,

I write a *few* Lines to give your Ladyship my Reasons why I cannot write a *Many*. Your Servant found me at the Grange with Lord Dudley; who, by the way, desires his best Compliments & Thanks for your Endeavours to serve Mr. Coventry —But before I could well open your Letter, Mr. Joseph told me that Captn Somerville & Mr. John Reynolds were that Moment arriv'd at the Leasowes. *This* brought me home in an Instant; & *This* also is ye Reason yt I cannot allot more y{n} a few Moments of the few Hours they stay with me to express how much I think myself oblig'd by yr Applications at Oldbarrow. They are now gone wth a Servant to see one *half* of the Walks *before Dinner*. The Paths I fear mighty slippery, & the Hedges wet—But the Sun I see shines out, & we may hope a fine Afternoon—I have scarce pass'd a single Day without a *Deal* of Company, ever since I wrote to you last. Lady Lyttelton with Miss Lyttelton, Miss West, & two officers, here I think last Tuesday—Allowd the Roads to be quite good, & had a favourable Day; was in Appearance greatly struck with my little Scenery, (having never seen our Parish before) and talks of coming again this Season.

I heard since I wrote to yr Ladyship that Miss Banks's Fortune is only 10,000ll. So that I cannot make out ye 100,000ll. any otherwise than by presuming She has 90,000 Pounds worth of extrinsick & intrinsick Merit.

My best Compliments to Mrs. Bartlett[1] & Mrs. Davies.

I *do* owe Mrs. Davies a Letter wch I will shortly fill with my Acknowledgements for ye laborious & unpleasing Task She undertakes at my Request. I din'd on Wednesday at Sr Harry Gough's, & yesterday wth my Ld Dudley at Admiral Smiths; *He* was indeed from Home, but we found *an* Admiral Cotterel there, and three very agreeable young Sea-officers, Capt^{ns} Hamilton,[2] Beecher, Whood. I shortly go wth Ld Dudley to visit Lord & Lady Plymouth—By the Way, L^{dy} Plymouth had a *Triumph* at Sr John Packington's[3] wch I want room & Time to display—Rejoice my good Lady at every Acquisition of Acquaintance I make & be well assurd that every Friend of Mine Shall be a Friend of yours if it be in my Power to make Him so. I am wth much unmannerly haste—but the utmost Respect

Y^r most oblig'd
W.S.

NOTES

[1] Mother-in-law of Mrs. Davies. Luxborough, *Letters*, 327.

[2] Sailor friend of Admiral Smith, mentioned in Hagley correspondence.

[3] Sir John Pakington of Westwood Park, Co. Worcester. William Pitt in a letter to William Lyttelton from Bath, Autumn 1753, described Westwood as 'a noble proud place, but as pride is generally made, the house has something little within.'

CLVII

Messrs. Maggs, and Hull, I, 170.

[*To* REV. R. GRAVES.]

THE LEASOWES,
October ye 24*th* 1753.

Dear Mr. Graves,

After a long season of vanity and universal Dissipation, I return with *unfeigned* Pleasure to a Correspondence with my dearest & most familiar Friends. So just is your Notion of the Permanency of my Affection; & so true it is, that *much greater* Civilities, than any *yet* shewn me by the *Great*, can never alter my opinion of the valuableness of your Friendship. Will you believe my simple assertion, or shall I take Pains to prove it by the very nature of Things? I cannot esteem it necessary.

Your Account of Mrs. Walker's Death was new to me. I will write to Mr Whistler shortly, & am in Hopes I shall *now* prevail with him to give me some weeks of his Company. Amongst the Strangers who visited my Walks this summer, there were three or more, as their servants inform'd us, who had Recourse to these Amusements on the Death of their Relations. Perhaps ye Sight of an old Friend is no less serviceable on such occasions.

Your Stream, I find, is very considerable—I dare say Horace's was not larger tho' mention'd as 'rivo dare nomen idoneus; ut nec *Frigidior* Thracum, nec *purior* ambiat Hebrum.'[1]

And you are mistaken in imagining that there is no *notice* taken of it, for I assure I have heard it commended here, this Summer: I forget by *whom*. You shew excessive Delicacy in your Dislike of it's running over water-cresses, as Pot-herbs. Pray what can at once have more *beauty* & more Propriety; supposing your stream to pass through ye Kitchen-garden! But I will not quarrel with you about y^e *Kind* of aquatick, if you will allow me to think nothing more pleasing than *greens beneath transparent water*.

When I can fix upon a Painter to draw me an head of Ld Dudley, (for wch he promises to sit at the Leasowes) I will endeavour to get your Picture alter'd; tho' Bond,[2] whose Paintings I have heard much celebrated, made no scruple to pronounce it an admirable Portrait.

I am glad enough to hear of y^r Encrease of Salary; & begin to think a sort of affluence a little more *essential* to *Happiness* than I have formerly done. Only remember you are *thin;* and— Do not injure your Constitution.

I enclose you a Copy of that Ode to The Dutchess. It would *admit* of many emendations, if it do not *want* many *Corrections;* but I know not when it will receive either, & I chuse moreover to send it in the Dress it wore at Hagley-table. I would send you moreover the Ode to Sr Richard Lyttelton, but that it would be grievously irksome to transcribe it at this time— The *Antiquary* Character given the Dean is not approv'd—I vindicated it as far as was decent for me; but I believe I must exchange it for a Compliment upon his *Humanity!*

Sr George, The Dean, Mr Lyttelton &c. made me a Morning's Visit yesterday, & took me with them to dinner at the Grange. Sr George goes next week to London, & the Family will disperse.

Dodsley adds this winter a 4th Vol. to his Miscellanies;[3] He wrote to me last week to beg a few Copies of Verses; I shall send him 'the Autumn-verses,' & two copies y^t are upon my Seats 'O let me haunt this &c:' and 'O you that bathe in courtlye Blysse' in old characters—Give me y^r Opinion, what else of mine And whether I shall send any Copy of yours. They will be read by the polite world. What do you think of getting y^r Verses upon Medals inserted? But He talks in his Letter as if they must be sent *immediately*.

I desire my Compliments to Mrs Graves, and am satisfy'd I can never be otherwise than what I am at present, your most affectionate Friend & most obedient Servant.

WILL SHENSTONE.

Excuse this villainous Scrawl; I am not half in Spirits.

NOTES

[1]Horace, *Epistles*, I, XVI, 12, 13.

[2]Daniel Bond (1725–1803). Hull, I, 172, adds this note: 'Mr. Bond, a Painter in Birmingham, an Artist of great Taste and Ability. The Editor of these Letters is in Possession of an admirable Likeness of Mr. Shenstone, painted by this Gentleman, for which he is proud to make this public Acknowledgement.'

[3]Vol. IV, Dodsley's *Collection*, appeared March, 1755. It contained thirteen poems of W.S.

CLVIII

Hull, I, 174.

To MR. H[YLTO]N.

THE LEASOWES,
Oct. 25, 1753.

Dear Mr. H[ylto]n,

This can prove no other than an heavy, stupid Letter, agreeable to the present Disposition of my Mind. The most it can pretend, is to acquaint you, in vulgar Terms, that you retain your usual Place in my Affection and Esteem; yet this may be no trivial Information, now you have accepted a Place at Court, and have left your Friends at Liberty to form Conjectures about your future Conduct; to continue, or to dismiss you, as our Electors do their Representatives. Be this as it will, I confess that I rechuse you, and wish that every Court in *Europe* consisted of as honest Men.

You are in the right to decline taking M——s, if you find the Scheme too expensive; and as he could not have come into your Service, without purchasing his Time out from his Master, I believe it will now be his Point to continue with him till the Expiration of his Indentures.

I am now in some Sort of Doubt, concerning the Management of my Snuff-Box; whether to have it repaired in the cheapest Way, with a figured Tortoise Shell on the Top, and a plain Tortoise Shell in the Bottom; or to exchange the Gold of it, and have a figured Tortoise Shell Box with a gold Rim, *like yours with a gilt one*, only in the Shape of an oblong Square, a little rounded at the Corners. I should have no Thoughts of this, but that my own seems too little and unmanly. Give me your Opinion soon; though, if this latter Scheme includes much Expence, proceed with the former, if you please, immediately.

I desire my gold Clasp and Rim may be directly exchanged; I shall have a new gold Clasp and Rim: perhaps, may enclose a Pattern for the former, before I seal this Letter. *Quaere*, therefore, whether the Man, who makes it, will now allow most in the Exchange.

I believe I shall defer the Purchase of my favourite Waistcoat till the Spring. My Visitants begin to fail me, (though Sir GEORGE LYTTELTON, the Dean, and Mr. LYTTELTON, were here yesterday) my Verdure abandons me, and I have little else to do, than go to sleep for the Winter.

Pray send me the Verses on Miss B——R, by the honourable Personage. As to mine, you may give Copies, if you please; but as they are not fully corrected, I hope whoever has those Copies, will take care they be not printed. I can say nothing polite at present, so must defer my Acknowledgments to the Ladies at *Woolston*, till I write to you again.

Your Letter to Lady LUXBOROUGH was promised, so I think you should by all Means write, though I confess it appears to have been rather too long deferred.

And now having spoke to the principal Parts of your Letter, let me consider what I have to add.

First then, your Tenant, old Mr. P——s, of the Hill Top, was carried in a Hearse, through my Grounds, to be buried yesterday. Mr. I[ng?] has been two or three days in this Country adjusting Matters with your Tenants. . . . .

.   .   .   .   .

C[RAWLE]Y[1] tells me, you may have your Place supplied at the Expence of five Pounds *per* Year. If so, is it not your Point to come down and live at *Lappal?* I do not herein speak merely for my own Sake. Sir GEORGE told me yesterday, that he had secured me BLOOMER's Cottage. I said, I was obliged to him, but did not ask, after what Manner. He promised to come and dine, and stay a Night with me next Year. In the mean Time, I am beguiled of his dining with me, by *your* venerable D[ean]; for having had an Offer from him, from Mr. LYTTELTON and the Dean, to take a Dinner here this Week, the D[ean], through his great Address, conveyed all these Honours to the *Grange;* and to-morrow, it seems, Sir GEORGE dines with Master PEARSALL. I remonstrated upon this to Mr. LYTTELTON, at the *Grange*, in a Manner pretty forcible, and yet tolerably decent. He excused for himself and them in a Manner that made me quite satisfied with *him*. He is an excellent young Man.

Let these Things serve as Lessons to you, who are a Courtier, not to hope from Ambition to receive the '*Plaisir sans Peine.*'

Adieu!

I am truly yours,

W. SHENSTONE.

NOTE

[1]Is this Mr. Crawley, an attorney, mentioned post, p. 412?

CLIX

B.M. Add. MSS. 28958.

[*To* LADY LUXBOROUGH.]

THE LEASOWES,
Novr 11th 1753.

Dear Madam,

It is now so long since I had the Honour of hearing from you, that I begin to be not a little anxious about the Progress of your Recovery. I do beseech your Ladyship to believe me so much your Friend as to deserve at least some Intelligence concerning the State of your Health. Tho' I will not entertain a Doubt of my preserving some Place in your Esteem, I cannot avoid Some awkward Sensations on the Account of your unusual Silence. It appears, some how or other, as if you were in Some Degree estrang'd to me.

Since I wrote last to your Ladyship, I have had no great Share of Company; & it grows expedient for me to make Some *Winter*-friends amongst my own *Parishioners*. I had the *offer* of a visit from the Captains Somerville, Mr. Outing & Mr. Reynalds, but could on no account receive them, thro' a Pre engagement at Lord Plymouths. Thither I went with Lord Dudley & stay'd from Thursday 'till Saturday. I was receiv'd with so much Politeness by both L^d & L^{dy} Plimouth y^t I am morally certain Some good Friend of mine had been prejudiceing them in my Favour: & I am much inclin'd to suspect your Ladyship of this Sinisterity—

Since this I have *made* three visits; to Admiral Smith; to Mr. Pitt at Hagley, & to Mr. Clare at Clent. The week following I had Sir George Lyttelton; who enquir'd after your Ladyship in a very friendly manner, & seem'd truly glad to hear the account I gave him of your Recovery. I did not fail to acquaint him of the Progress you had made amongst your voters. I *hope* the Opposition is over, but I am sure our separate obligations must continue—The same week produc'd me a Visit from the very venerable The Dean of Exeter, with Durant their Parson.[1] From Mr. Lyttelton *twice*, who came the second time to dine with me; From Mr. Miller twice, who came the *first* time to dine with me; From the Captains Hamil-

ton & Whood, two of the Admiral's Domesticks. Mr. Lyttelton at present stands higher in my Esteem than ever; The
Dean something lower, Mr. Miller, the same.

Other Visitants of any Importance have I not seen; saving
that this Morning, Ld Plimouth wth some Company surpriz'd
me about Breakfast time. I enquir'd whether his Lordship had
heard of late from Barrels, & he told me, No; but intended to
Send over soon. They stay'd till after two, & then went to
dine at Stourbridge. I look upon my Season as now entirely
over; wch has been both *open'd* & *clos'd* very magnificently by
Ld Plimouth.

Mr. Hylton is now in Town; whither he has *hawl'd* a
thousand guineas in order to buy his Place at Court; has dis-
agreed with the Proprietor & lodg'd his money in the Funds;
is twenty Pounds out of Pocket, he says, by the *trifling* of a
bonny Scot, & vows to have no dealings with any of his nation
more—For my Part I am no way concern'd for his Disappointment as I never *greatly* approv'd his Bargain. He purposes to
write to your Ladyship Soon, & to make his Acknowledg-
ments for ye Civilities he receiv'd at Barrels; but he is not a
little embarass'd about an Apology for his neglect of doing this
before.

That Ode of mine to the Dutchess is got into several Hands,
& I am not a little suspicious y^t it may arrive at the Press in
some way or other which I shall not approve. Dodsley, for the
conveyance of whose loitering Epistle, I am truly oblig'd to
your Ladyship, would be glad to print that Ode. He is now,
at this very time, publishing an additional vol: of his Miscellanies.[2] I have nothing in my Hands correct, nor have I time
to get anything corrected by reason of the Distance of my
Friends; but I think this Ode as correct as anything I *have*; &
if it would not be disagreeable to her Grace, I should be glad
of her Permission to print it, at this time. I look upon Dodsley's
as a reputable Collection, that will be seen by ye best of Judges,
yet so as that their Censure cannot fall wholly upon any *one*
Piece—But the late arrival of his Letter allows me no time for
Application—What would your Ladyship advise me, in this
Case? I think to send him something of Mr. Whistler's, &
something of Mr. Graves,[3] to-morrow.

Mrs. Davies, to whom I desire my *Thanks*, a better word than my *compliments*, is at this very Instant accusing me of Ingratitude—I will write to her speedily, but to-day it is impossible.

I want to *tell* you forty things relating to our visit at Hewell-grange; but I cannot think of *writing* them. L^d & L^dy Plimouth are very highly in *my* good graces; I think I have some little share in *theirs*. I guess'd once that L^ds Plimouth & Dudley would become extravagantly intimate; you know that the virtues of benevolence, & uprightness of heart, are common to them both—Yet I never in my Life beheld so striking a Contraste! I shall, I believe, have some little Share in ye disposition of L^d P's environnes; & I sincerely think I could do him some service. I only wish I had known his Lordship before he began that Piece of water. I told both him & L^dy P. my mind very emphatically & *ingenuously* ye very Day I came, & they had both the good-sense to hear me, and to thank me for it. That side ought apparently either to have been coverd with water, at any given expence, for near an 100 yards lower; or it ought to have been thrown into a broad serpentine River, the fens drein'd; & the ground slop'd down to it, from about the Present hahah. The stream is sufficient for any sort of purpose. The *Cascades* might have been *display'd*, or the *stoppages* where they *were*, conceal'd wth aquatick Plants, as had been thought most agreeable; & I think, by proper *management*, the expence of either of these Schemes might have been less than the Present. The Reasons I go upon will appear yet more striking when the opposite ground becomes a Part of their Park, wth garden Seats; from wch the House will make a very magnificent Figure—Enough of this. The Management of their Rooms has my thorough approbation.

Hagley-House is to be fix'd at last in the very grounds where I always wish'd it;[4] It affords me a triumph; in *my own breast;* For I never dar'd speak freely on ye Subject; nor is it *my* Opinion that has given the least turn to it—at least not that I know of.

I have been makeing a little Alteration in ye Room over my Hall; wch is now my Library upon a Somewhat a better Foot y^n it has hitherto been; yet I retain my Press bed in it for unexceptionable Reasons. My little breakfast Room has a glass, & is become my Dressing-Room.

Mr. Hylton makes enquiry how far our Freedom *over ye Bottle* & *upon* the Bottle at yʳ Ladyship's House, has disgruntled Mr. Outing. I told him I could not say, for that I neither see nor hear from him.

Other Matter know I not, saving that Lᵈ Dudley, who often drinks your Health, has much irritated his great toe by hitting it against the Beds-foot whilst he was stroling thro' the Dark in full Quest of the Chamber-pot. It is now on the mending Hand.

We met Mr. Winnington[5] & his Lady at Hewell, & I went with Lᵈ P. & him, on the Friday, to Mr. Vernon's of Hanbury.[6] There I saw Mr. Coventry; Mr. Payne;[7] Mr. Greatheed's brother,[8] & a Room full of Company—My expedition on the whole was greatly entertaining.

Your Ladyship must permit me to talk in this Manner upon Paper, as I should do in Company. I have neither a Head to contrive, a Correspondent to supply, or a Neighbourhood to produce any *amusing* materials—Yet I *wish* you Amusement, Health, & Happiness; every *sort* of Happiness wᶜʰ I wish for myself. I beg you would write me as much as you can without Fatigue, & believe me ever more respectfully

Your Ladyship's most oblig'd
& most Obedient Servant
WILL: SHENSTONE.

My Service to Mr. & Mrs.
& Miss Holyoake.

NOTES

[1] Rector of Hagley.

[2] Vol. V. Dodsley's *Collection*, published March 1758.

[3] In Vol. IV, Dodsley's *Collection*, *Flowers*, 320, and *Song*, 322, were by Whistler, *The Cabinet*, 323, *Panacea*, 326, *The Heroines*, 328, and *The Parting*, 329, by Graves.

[4] After many delays caused by much consultation of friends the building of the new Hagley Hall was finally begun in the summer of 1754, and the fine building replaced 'an immeasurably old & bad house.' Dickins & Stanton, *An Eighteenth Century Correspondence*, Chap. XVIII.

[5] Edward Winnington, of Stanford Court, Co. Worcester.

[6] The manor of Hanbury, 3½ miles E. of Droitwich, was owned by the Vernon Family. Thomas Vernon, d. 1771, is apparently the one mentioned here. Nash, *History of Worcestershire*.

[7] Nash says that Dennis Payne, M.A. was incumbent of the Church at Hanbury, September 11, 1732, and that Thomas Vernon, Esq. was patron.

[8] The Greatheed family—that of Bertie Greatheed, the artist—lived at Guy's Cliff, Warwick.

CLX

B.M. Add. MSS. 28958.

[*To* Lady LUXBOROUGH.]

THE LEASOWES *Dec*! *y*! 12, 1753.

Dear Madam,

I am truly impatient to receive a few Lines from your Ladyship, & accordingly have sent Tom, th'rough roads not a little formidable, (with your permission) to stay all night. I hope you will not regulate your answer by the Lines I now am scribbling, but will also remember the size of the Packet I sent before.

There are no Incidents occurr to me, which will afford your Ladyship the least amusement. Ld Dudley with his sisters & domesticks spent some days with me here last week; but he was *ill*, & indispos'd for conversation, to a degree that he may *reasonably expect*. His Coal-mines will prove advantageous; but what are they to *me*? unless he will take such care of his health, as will give Hopes that he may long enjoy them: otherwise they may only tend to animate *benumb'd serpents*. you remember the Fable;

If Mr. Hylton have not acquitted himself of his Letter to your Ladyship, pray notifye, that I will wrap a large Flea in a piece of white paper, & will cause the Postboy to put it in his ear. It shall be one of ye more active sort, nor shall He, without some difficulty, get shut of his troublesome *inmate*—The extract I gave you from his Letter was genuine; & if your Ladyship will permit him to send you the news of the town, there is no doubt y^t he has Leisure & opportunity.

The Scene is chang'd with me, from what I found it in the Summer. Instead of the daily arrival of truly fashionable company, I see nothing but Robin Redbreasts driv'n to visit me by stress of weather; or Tom-Tits seeking out where they may secure themselves for ye winter; yet the Red-breasts give me their song, & it is infinitely better than *my own*.

Lonesom as I am, I see no objects of envy near me: for were all ye amusements of my neighbours group'd together & given me in a Dish or Punch-bowl they would not tend to render me one whit happier than I am. I could venture to assert the same concerning the principal Amusements of our metropolis. And, I think, your Ladyship will be ready to join me.

Dodsley sent me his Agriculture;[1] & least *peradventure* you may not have seen it, I give it Tom for your perusal. How far the Town will relish it, I know not; but it is written with much *art*, & infinitely beyond what they cou'd reasonably *expect* from him. While your Ladyship reads Page y[e] 59, Canto the third, should you not be apt to imagine he had seen Virgil's grove? or, from some of y[e] preceding Lines, should you not be apt to think he had seen Barrels? Had he appropriated these Lines to either of our Places, we should hardly envy the compliments he pays Chiswick, Esher, Woburne or Hagley[2]—But of this enough, for I do not pretend to criticise —He is, at this instant of time, expecting a large cargo of my verses—but my cargo will not *yet* set forwards, & when it does, will not be large—Truth is, my mind is somewhat alter'd—I cannot bear to send him *stuff;* and as to my *better* compositions, my friends induce Me to think I might print them in a more advantageous manner, both with regard to *Reputation* & *Profit*. For Instance, The Elegy on Autumn, Ballad on Princess Elizabeth, Ode to Memory, Inscriptions[3] and a few things more might have made me a 1s pamphlett y[t] would have had some chance to have been acceptable—but I proceeded *unadvisedly*, & must extricate myself as I can. My Friend Graves, & I have had a might [sic] *busy* correspondence. He has a talent for criticism, wherein *over-delicacy* is scarce a Fault—at least when 'tis ballanc'd by my own excessive Indolence. I receiv'd the Fable I enclose from him, which he offers to address to me.[4] But, whatever Answer I return him, The Fable itself is humorous—You will laugh at his 'doughty disputants—& return me y[e] composition.

S[r] Charles Grandison[5] is much admired—& if I cannot borrow, I will purchase it—but I should be glad to have y[e] concluding volume promisd us, at a time less *indefinite*—If y[r] Ladyship have any new Pamphletts you will I know be so good to lend me some.

I could be glad, were it agreeable to y[r] Ladyship, y[t] our Servants might be a little harrass'd with alternate Journeys to

Barrels & to the Leasowes. It would exhilarate this dull
Season. At least it would have that effect wth me—My Letters
would pretend to little more than a repetition of good wishes &
My Compliments to all Friends—To keep one's pen in motion
when one has nothing to say, is like rapping at a Door when one
has no sort of business. It alarms, not gratifies the attention.
Tis better pass by in Silence, especially as y^r Ladyship knows
me for what I truly am, namely,

Y^r most oblig'd & most obed^t

W. Shenstone.

Friday, Decr. the 14^{th 6}

One Day has past & it has been *impossible* for Tom to proceed so far as Barrels. I trust he will be able to set forward
tomorrow.

I had the Honour of answering the Dutchess's Letter last
Thursday se'nnight; but was too late for the Post; & she
would not receive my Letter till *tuesday* last. I promis'd to obey
her commands most punctually, but I *said nothing* about my
Intention of with-holding y^t Ode[7] from Dodsley—If your
Ladyship writes to her, I desire you would do *the same;* & only
assure her grace of my entire respect, & implicit obedience to
her commands at all times—I think it would be *suitable* enough
to *Dodsley,* agreeable to Mr. Somerviles *Friends,* & no *injustice*
to his *memory,* if some few of his stragling Pieces[8] were inserted
in this collection. If your Ladyship thinks with me, I will
transcribe for the Press any little Pieces you are pleasd to send
me & will make no alteration but where the verse is *manifestly*
deficient. But as, I hinted before, this must be done *soon,* or
quite omitted—I told your Ladyship that I had, one night,
added a stanza to ye enclos'd Verses. I therefore enclose a copy
& should be glad if you could be prevail'd on to give me your
opinion of their merit, with ye same Frankness as tho' they
were written upon any other person.

I have nothing to add—why cease I therefore to wrap these
Papers in a Cover, after I have bid your Ladyship once more
Adieu?

I talk'd of sending Dodsley's Agriculture—but lo! it is lent
out; & I am oblig'd to defer it 'till another opportunity.

NOTES

[1]*Agriculture, A Poem*, 1753. *On the new art of Landscape Gardening*, by R. Dodsley.

[2]Lord Burlington's garden at Chiswick, planned by Edward Kent, was the first example in England of the new taste for informal landscape gardens which copied pictures. Walpole in his *Essay on Modern Gardening* proved carefully that Kent was the initiator of the new national taste. Esher also was laid out by Kent and Woburn Farm was the original ferme ornée, planned by Philip Southcote. Mason in *The English Garden* extolled Southcote and Shenstone as inventors of the ferme ornée.

The lines wherein Dodsley praised these examples of landscape gardening come from Canto II.

> 'And lo! the progress of thy steps appears
> In fair improvements scatter'd round the land.
> Earliest in Chiswick's beauteous model seen:
> There thy first favourite, in the happy shade
> To Nature introduc'd, the goddess woo'd,
> And in sweet rapture there enjoy'd her charms
>
> .   .   .   .   .
>
> in the lovely vale
> Of Esher, where the Mole glides lingering, loath
> To leave such scenes of sweet simplicity,
> In Woburn's ornamented fields, where gay
> Variety, where mingled lights and shades,
> Where lawns and groves, and opening prospects break
> With sweet surprise, upon the wandering eye.
> On Hagley's hills, irregular and wild,
> Where thro' romantic scenes of hanging woods,
> And vallies green, and rocks, and hollow dales,
> While echo talks, and nymphs and dryads play,
> Thou rov'st enamour'd; leading by the hand
> Its master; who, inspir'd with all thy art,
> Adds beauties to what Nature plann'd so fair.'

[3]All these appeared in Dodsley's *Collection*, IV.

[4]*The Pepper-box & Salt-seller. A Fable To . . . Esq:*, Dodsley's *Collection* V, 63. The moral runs thus,

> 'Thus *real* genius is respected!
> Conceit and folly thus neglected!
> And, O my Shenstone! let the vain
> With misbecoming pride, explain
> Their splendor, influence, wealth or birth;
> —Tis men of *sense* are men of worth.'

[5]*The History of Sir Charles Grandison*, 1753, by Samuel Richardson.

[6]The postscript to this letter is misplaced in the B.M. MS. where it appears after letter of August 8, 1750, but internal evidence, mention of the dedication of *Rural Elegance* to the Duchess of Somerset, and of the publication of Dodsley's *Agriculture*, fixes the date as 1753.

[7]*Rural Elegance.* I have not traced the letter to which Shenstone refers here, but the Duchess of Somerset's reply is included in Hull, I, 195, and is dated December 18, 1753.

[8]Dodsley's *Collection*, IV, contained *An Address to his Elbow Chair new cloath'd* by the late W. Somervile Esq: Author of *The Chace*, and *Song*, 'As o'er Asteria's fields I rove.' In Vol. V appeared *Paraphrase upon a French Song*.

CLXI

Hull, II, 20.

To [THOMAS PERCY?]

[1753?][1]

Dear Sir,

WHEN I promised you some Poetry for Mr. S——, I am afraid that, through my Desire of recommending myself to his Family, my Tongue out-run my Wit. If I laid any Sort of *Stress* upon what I was to send, I am very sure it did so; and when you have read the Trifles enclosed, you will be of the same Opinion.

It is probable, however, that I had an Eye to a larger Ode of mine, upon the Subject of rural Elegance, which I have not now Time either to correct or to transcribe; but which I will not fail to communicate to them upon some future Occasion.

Or if my Promise regarded a Translation of the Mottos *here*, I shall have the best Opportunity of performing it, when I take the Freedoms you have allowed me, with your polite Description of my Farm.

Am I wrong in detaining that Paper?—For positively, these last few Days I have found myself a good deal feverish, and my Head has been so much confused, that I was almost tempted to omit this Message. In this Case, I think your Good-nature would have acquitted me of *Disrespect*: but I could not suffer you to leave the Country with so bad an Opinion of my punctuality.

It remains, that I present my best Respects to Dr. TURTON[2] and his Lady, and that I wish you an agreeable Journey to *Oxford*. I purpose, in a few Weeks, that you shall be enabled to say something more particular, in Regard to M——'s Poetry; in the mean Time, I desire that he would accept my Compliments, and my Thanks for the Pleasure his Verses have afforded me. Above all Things, assure Mr. ARNOLD of my most unfeigned Esteem; and if he discovers any Partiality for my Place or me, encourage it, that it may induce him, on a proper Occasion, to favour me once more with his Company. You see, I am availing myself of *your* Interest, to make all your Friends my own; and to attone for this Piece of Selfish-

ness, it shall not be my Fault, if every Friend I have be not yours, at least, with some Share of that Regard with which I am,
dear Sir,
your most faithful, humble Servant,
W. SHENSTONE.

NOTES

[1]This letter probably belongs to 1753, for W.S. was then occupied with *Rural Elegance*. Moreover a note of Percy's in the B.M. MS. tells us that he 'had drawn up hastily in 1753' a 'Description of the Leasowes.'

Thomas Percy (1729–1811), afterwards Bishop of Dromore, was compiler of *Reliques of Ancient English Poetry*, 1765. In the Preface to his work, Percy writes, 'The plan of the work was settled in concert with the late elegant Mr. Shenstone, who was to have borne a joint share in it had not death unhappily prevented him. Most of the modern pieces were of his selection and arrangement, and the Editor hopes to be pardoned if he has retained some things out of partiality to the judgment of his friend. . . .' A certain amount of discussion took place after W.S.'s death concerning the small amount of credit he received for the part he had in *The Reliques*. This part the letters in this volume show to be considerable.

[2]Possibly Dr. John Turton of Wolverhampton.

CLXII

MS. Messrs. Francis Edwards.
Works III, 253.
Hull I, 189.

[*To* REV. R. JAGO.]

THE LEASOWS, *Jan.* 29, 1754.[1]

Dear Mr. Jago,

I am at a Loss how to begin this Letter. I will not however, in the usual way, give you a tedious List of Apologies in the Front of it. Some account of my Silence you will find dispers'd throughout the Letter, & as for what is deficient, I will depend upon your Friendship.

There has not been a Person here since you left me, of whom I could obtain the least Intelligence concerning you. And as an Enquiry by the Post was my only obvious method, & as I both ow'd & promis'd you a Letter at Parting, I do acknowledge myself to blame, notwithstanding all the Excuses I can make.

Amidst all that conflux of visitants w^m I receiv'd this last Season, I was hardly once *so* happy as I was in *your* Company. I was the happier on seeing *you* so; and if you remember I took notice, at the time, how little your vivacity was impair'd in comparison of mine. If I was then but a sorry companion, it was not Solitude & winter that would make me a better *correspondent*. That Gaiety & Humour which you were once so partial as to discover in my Letters, will hardly appear again there any more even to the Eyes of my most partial Friend. At least, they will not enliven any Letter that I write in winter. Yet Friendship still remains; Friendship, like the root of some perennial Flower, perhaps even then gathers strength in secret y^t it may produce a better display of it's colours in the Spring.

This, I do not pretend to be an adequate Apology. I know my dearest Friend, that you both like to see and hear from me at all times, but it proves that you have no *great* Loss eith [sic] of my Letters or my Company.

I am, as the Phrase is, deeply penetrated by the Civility of your Neighbour Mr Miller. He took a short Dinner with me once, dropping Sir George at Mr Pearsalls. He c^d not have pleased me better. He afterwards breakfasted here, & seem'd in general fond of every opportunity of bringing good company to my Hole the Leasowes.² Do you think that Radway or that Harbury have no attractions for me. You know me too well to imagine it. But I truly am not well enough to dare to be from home. Friends will say 'you may be as free at my House as at your own. And they will mean what they say But what is this to the Purpose if you cannot make yourself so.

I cannot pretend to give you a detail of what pass'd since I saw you. Ld D. with myself made one visit to Hewell. I will not say that his L^sp only, for I also was receiv'd in the politest manner Imaginable. We met M^r & Mrs Winnington. We took a trip to Mr Vernons where we met also Mr Coventry, & a deal of other Company. All this w^d afford subject for conversation betwixt you & me, but I must not assign too much of my Paper to this Purpose.

Lord Plymouths Piece of water should have been only a large serpentine stream. I can give you many reasons. I think him such a sort of character as may *shine* in Company, upon growing older—he is & must be belovd already. He has been here once since, & talks of causing me to come & design for him in his Park—The Plan for the House is right, supposing it right to continue it. His Park may have many Beauties. I hope sometime to meet *you* there.

My Ode after Long Delay has been sent to the D. of Somerset. It has produc'd me two genteel Letters from her Grace—& I am pleas'd wth the Event, for some Reasons wch I could mention.

Soon after this Dodsley ask'd me to contribute to 4 vol of his miscellanies. I meant at first to do so pretty largely—but I afterwards chang'd my mind, and determin'd to send only little Pieces—I did send him several of my own, some of my Frd Whist [sic] Graves, and some accidental Pieces of others wch lay in my Drawer. I meant to send something of yours, of my own accord if I was hurry'd, otherwise not without applying for Consent. He wrote me word last week that his Public [sic] must be defer'd upon account of the Elections. So y^t we shall now have time enough to meet or write upon ye Subject— What I purpos'd was your Linnets—'I owe etc.' Dick Graves send me the Inclos'd little comical Fable. I made some few alterations & put it into Dodsleys Hands. Be so good as to return it, as I have now no other Copy.

Some correspondence I have had this winter with Mr Hylton about Toys & Trinkets which he gets done for me in London. He is by far a better Friend & Correspondent than a Poet. Should you take a Trip to Town he would be quite *proud* to see you. He lives at Mr Evans in Brook-street. Make my Com. to Mrs. Catts.

I am like ye rest of the world perusing Sir C. Grandison. I do'nt know whether that world joins me in preferring the Authors Clarissa. He wants ye Art of abridgement in everything he has yet wrote.

My dear Friend Pardon this Flegmatick Letter & cherish & preserve your own vivacity. If occasion *offers*, do not neglect to call upon me for my own sake & believe you have not alive a more lasting or more Affectionate Friend.

W.S.

NOTES

[1]The version of this letter given by Hull differs in many details from the MS. letter and from that given *Works* III, 222.

[2]*Works* III, adds here, 'To him I owe Miss Banks and Lord Temple.'

CLXIII

R. B. Adam, Esq.
& Hull, I, 208.[1]

[*To* J. S. HYLTON.]

March ye 29.th 1754.

Dear Mr Hylton,

I wonder Mr Crawley did not give me some Intimation of Miss Dolman's Illness, before. However, all her Relations will think themselves lastingly indebted both to him, & to every one else who have contributed their kind Endeavours to further her Recovery. We are under a terrible anxiety concerning her. Satisfy'd as I am of the Abilities & vigilance of Dr Batt, & convinc'd of the friendly care of her Acquaintance that attend her, I shall dread to look into the Letter that I expect by tomorrow's Post. God grant it may be favourable. I have Hopes given me, tonight. Mr Dolman sends me word that the Letter he receivd on Thursday, (probably written after yours) acquainted him that the Pustules began to turn; that she was then better, & that they hop'd the worst was past.

Believe me *uniformly* your Friend, but do not expect me to dwell upon many particulars tonight. . . . I sent, yesterday evening, for John Taylor, & Aaron & Aaron's wife. *John* & Aaron's *wife* came. The Husband was at the Ale-house; & they were fearfull, I find, that if they had *brought* him he would behave with *Insolence*. I doubt you will not endure to live much at Lappal while he is there. However, I propos'd y.^r boarding &c: to the Woman, who said she should be glad to serve you. I then propos'd to John some few Questions about y.^r Parlour; when lo! Those Tenants are yet in it; & say, Mr Ing bid them continue 'till they had further legal warning. Of consequence, I find of late they have not *thought* of removal; yet perhaps I could *bring* them to remove. Tell me therefore once more if you think you can live with Aaron; if not, why do you remove these under-tenants, till you can bribe Him to relinquish. Shall I offer him any further sum? Blame not *me* for any Delay in regard to your matters here; blame rather the *inconsistent & contradictory* measures pursu'd at different times, separately, by you and M.ʳ Ing. But believe *me* ready to do anything you would *have* me; in consequence of y.ʳ true affection with which I am ever

Yours
WILL: SHENSTONE.

Don't let anything I've said discourage you, in y.ʳ scheme of retiring into this Country. Will not the *Grange* or *Leasowes* be *endureable* for one half year; And that the Summer half year, when they dress themselves afresh to please you? But y.ʳ *under*-tenant may remove.

Yʳ Cabinet, nor oysters are not *yet* brought me whatever the Reason.

Leave my Compliments to Dear Miss Dolman & all that attend on her—Send me five Lines at least every Post next week. Adieu.

Y.ʳ Tenants meet M.ʳ Ing at Birm. the Thursday after old L. Day.

NOTE

[1]The MS. letter differs much from that given by Hull.

CLXIV

Works III, 258.

To MR. GRAVES, *on the Alternations of Pleasure and Pain.*

THE LEASOWS,
April 19, 1754.

Dear Mr. Graves,

It is a long, long time, according to the computation of friendship, since I had the pleasure of a line from you; and I write chiefly to remind you of it; not with any hopes of affording you the amusement of a single minute. In truth, I have not spirits for it. The severity, the duration, the solitude, of this winter have well-nigh exhausted them.—The succession, the regular succession, of pain and pleasure becomes every day more clear to me. It begins to seem as ordinary as the course of day and night. Thus my last summer was the most amusing I ever saw; my winter the most disagreeable—allow me to except one only: I mean, that ever-mournful winter which robbed me of my dearest relation. Sometimes this pain and pleasure are contrasted within the compass of a day. Sometimes, in different weeks, &c. &c. However, do not think me superstitious: There is hardly a person that is *less* so. Yet I am firmly persuaded of the alternation, either in the mind, or in the events themselves. My summer, I said before, was highly entertaining; my winter rendered equally disagreeable, by a long-continued squabble amongst our principal parishioners, and by the death of my best-beloved and the most accomplished of my relations, M[aria] D[olman].[1] She risqued going to London for the sake of finding something *new;* was seized with the small-pox, and died in all her bloom.—The natural consequence which we should draw from observations of this sort is, equanimity; 'æquam memento rebus, &c.'[2] and again, 'sperat infestis, metuit secundis, &c.'[3] Enough of this, which I should not mention, but that the fact itself strikes me continually more and more; and were I to mark the pleasing and unpleasing parts of my existence in an almanac, as the Romans did their *Fasti* and *Nefasti*, I know not if, at the year's end, the black and white marks would not nearly balance each other.

I have bought Hogarth's Analysis:[4] it is really entertaining: and has, in some measure, adjusted my notions with regard to beauty in general. For instance, were I to draw a shield, I could give you reasons from hence why the shape was pleasing or disagreeable. I would have you *borrow* and read it.

Grandison I cannot think equal to Clarissa, though, were merit in this age to be preferred, the author of it deserves a bishoprick.

Jago has been fortunate for once; but the value of his livings must be exaggerated in the newspapers.[5]

If Mr. Whistler would give me a visit in the height of my season this year, I should look upon it as one of the most pleasing events that could happen to the remainder of my life; and I would not presume to hope that fate would ever allow me a repetition of it.

My love of toys is not quite exhausted.—I have purchased, or rather renovated, some that are both rich and beautiful, though short of what I meant them. I have amused myself with designing little ornaments this winter, some of which may turn to account under the management of some Birmingham mechanic.—To atchieve *ease*, in that season, is the most that I can *hope*; and it is more than I often *obtain*.

Excuse this worthless letter; which *must* cost you money, as they tell me franks are useless. I could not avoid some uneasiness upon reflecting how long you have been silent. Present my best compliments to Mrs. Graves; and pay a tribute of one single half-sheet to that affection with which I am ever

Yours,

W. SHENSTONE.

NOTES

[1]Hull, I, 205, gives Hylton's letter from London telling Shenstone of his cousin's death.

[2]Horace, *Carmina*, II, 3, 1.

[3]Horace, *Carmina*, II, 10, 13.

[4]*The Analysis of Beauty*, 1753, by William Hogarth set up 'the sensibilities' rather than the reason as an aid to beauty.

[5]In 1754, Lord Clare, by his interest with Dr. Maddox, Bishop of Worcester, secured the vicarage of Smitterfield for Jago. The value of the living was £140.

CLXV

Works III, 262.

To the [REV. RICHARD GRAVES] *on the Death of Mr. Whistler.*

THE LEASOWS,
June 7, 1754.

Dear Mr. Graves,

The melancholy account of our dear friend Whistler's death was conveyed to me, at the same instant, by yours and by his brother's letter. I have written to his brother this post; though

I am very ill able to write upon the subject, and would willingly have waved it longer, but for decency. The triumvirate which was the greatest happiness, and the greatest pride, of my life is broken! The fabric of an ingenuous and disinterested friendship has lost a noble column! yet it may, and *will*, I trust, endure till one of us be laid as low. In truth, one can so little satisfy one's self with what we say upon such sad occasions, that I made three or four essays before I could *endure* what I had written to his brother.—Be so good as excuse me to him as well as you can, and establish me in the good opinion of him and Mr. Walker.

Poor Mr. Whistler! how do all our little strifes and bickerments appear to us at this time! yet we may with comfort reflect, that they were not of a *sort* that touched the *vitals* of our friendship; and I may say, that we fondly loved and esteemed each other, of necessity—'Tales animas *oportuit* esse concordes.' Poor Mr. Whistler! not a single acquaintance have I made, not a single picture or curiosity have I purchased, not a single embellishment have I given to my place, since he was last here, but I have had his approbation and his amusement in my eye. I will assuredly inscribe my larger urn to his memory; nor shall I pass it without a pleasing melancholy during the remainder of my days. We have each of us received a pleasure from *his* conversation, which no other conversation can afford us at our present time of life.

Adieu! my dear friend! may our remembrance of the person we have lost be the strong and everlasting cement of our affection! Assure Mr. John Whistler of the regard I have for him, upon his *own* account, as well as his brother's. Write to me; directly if you have opportunity. Whether you have or no, believe me to be ever most affectionately yours,

W. Shenstone.

I beg my compliments to Mrs. Graves.

CLXVI

Works III, 272.

To Mr. JAGO.

THE LEASOWS,
June 16, 1754.

Dear Mr. Jago,

Were I to pronounce my sentence upon the long suspension of our correspondence, I should impute the blame of it, in almost *equal* measure, to *yourself* and to *me*. To *you*, for an omission of the letter you *promised* me when last in town; to me, for waiting in expectation of it, and for neglecting to do *justice* to the sentiments of my heart on the occasion of your late preferment. Great were the hopes I had indeed conceived, that your increase of revenue had been accompanied with a place of residence which was more *to your mind* than that where you at present abide; but I do not find by any accounts that you propose to leave Harbury: for which, no doubt, you have reasons which I do not yet penetrate; but which may demand my assent the moment you discover them. I have but little to say of the life I have led since you received some account of me from Mr. Hylton in London. The Winter, or at least its *ministers*, continued to tyrannize during the *minority* of Spring; and the Spring has alike been slow in giving up the reins to Summer. Of consequence, I seem in a sort of middle state, betwixt a dull half-animated grub and an insignificant loco-motive fly. Neither in the *one* state or *other* am I of the least importance; but, from the advances which I have *already* made, you are *somewhat* the more likely to find me in your garden. About a fortnight ago I received a line or two from our intimate acquaintance and school-fellow Mr. Hall. It was brought me by Sir Edward Boughton's[1] gardener; a fellow of good taste, to whom Mr. Hall desired I would cause The Leasowes to be shewn. I find you have delighted Mrs. Hall by some alterations which you propose for their environs, and which they thoroughly resolve to put in execution. When I come over into Warwickshire, as I hope to do soon, I shall be very glad to make them a visit in your company. My spirits, though far from good, are better, in the main, than they were in winter; and, on some peculiar days, are raised as high as to *alacrity*; *very* seldom higher; seldom so high.

You must (from hence at least) take matters in the order or rather *disorder* in which they occur: Mr. Miller I saw on Wednesday last in Lady Lyttelton's coach, who stopped two minutes at my gate on her return from London. I enquired concerning you; but could gather no intelligence.—Mr. Hylton, who is now in Warwickshire (if he have not strolled to London), has been with me several months this summer. He is adding a room or two to his place, which lies very near me; and purposes to reside there so soon as it is finished. The situation is not void of beauties; but, if you will pardon the vanity, must veil its bonnet to mine. I have heard of planting hollies, pyracanthas, and other berry-bearing greens, to attract those Blackbirds which you have so effectually celebrated: it shall be *my* ambition to plant good neighbours; and, what with Lord Dudley and his exotics, Mr. Hylton with his fossils, and myself with my *ferme ornée*, is there not some room to expect that we may attract the tasters this way? but first we must take some care to *advertise* them where their treasures lie.—Another day is passed, and Mr. Miller, &c. has again been with me, and waked me out of a sound sleep to breakfast.—He mentions with what reluctance he *left* a surveyor at Radway, employed in taking plans of the field of battle near Edge-hill. This he purposes to enrich with a number of anecdotes, gleaned from his neighbourhood; which must probably render it extremely entertaining: and surely Edge-hill fight was never more unfortunate to the nation, than it was lucky for Mr. Miller! He prints, together with this plan, another sheet of Radway Castle. I approve his design. He will, by this means, turn every bank and hillock of his estate there, if not into *classical*, at least into *historical* ground.

I have done mighty little about my grounds since last winter. As indolence has on *many* occasions contributed to *impair* my finances, it is but just that it should sometimes contribute to *restore* them. Yet I am not quite destitute of something new for your amusement.

Of late I have neither *read* nor *written* a syllable. What pleased me last was Hogarth's Analysis. I expect Dodsley down every week; and as he will spend a few days with me, I could wish you were to meet him. His genius is truly poetical, and his sentiments altogether liberal and ingenuous.

I am, at present, a surveyor of roads; employed in repairing my lane to the turnpike. How glad should I be to meet you, and to shew you its *beauties!* to shew you Mr. Hylton's new series of coins;—his *designs* as well as his *performances* at Lappal —how glad should I be to see you! yea, I would hardly fail to return with you to Harbury; were you to add this one obligation. I left Mr. Miller in doubt whether he would not see me at Radway some time next week. Evil and capricious health (the particulars of which would make a detail of no importance) destroys all my punctuality, and bids me promise with *fear*. You, I trust, are mostly at home; and were you to be at Snitterfield, I would follow you without reluctance. So, with hopes to see you shortly, either in Warwickshire or Shropshire, I relinquish the subject.

I have reserved a very melancholy subject for the last. May you, and Mr. Graves, and myself, stand firm to support the fabric of friendship, which has lost a very beautiful column in poor Mr. Whistler! he died of a sore-throat, which in a few days time turned to an inward mortification.—I will say no more on the occasion: very affecting has it been to me.—God preserve your life, your happiness, and your friendships! and may you ever be *assured* of *that* with which I am, dear Sir,
Your most affectionate humble servant,
W. SHENSTONE.

Shall I beg a line from you, as soon as may be?—I do, most earnestly.

I am given to understand that I may expect a visit this summer from the Bishop of Worcester; from Lord Ward, Lord Coventry, and Lord Guernsey.—It may be so; but honours of *this sort*, which would formerly have affected me, perhaps *too* deeply, have now lost much of their wonted poignancy. Can *such* persons bear to see the scenes *riant*, and to find the *owner* gloomy? Let *them*, as they are *able*, make my circumstances more affluent; and they shall find the *reflection* in *my* face and in *their* reception; but, as this will never be, it is no compliment to declare, that an hour or two's interview with you or Mr. Graves outweighs the arrival of the whole British Peerage.

Something else I have to say. Young Pixell last winter told me, that the organist of Worcester had set your Ode (The Blackbirds) to musick;[2] that he *liked* the musick; and that he would sing it next evening at the Birmingham concert. I have not heard him mention it *since*, and I *forgot* to enquire; but, if you happen to have the notes, I should be glad if you would inclose them for me.

I have been of late much bent upon the encrease of *horns* in this neighbourhood.—Do not interpret me *perversely;* I mean French-horns only. My Lord Dudley has had a person to teach two of his servants—nothing—at my instigation; but your old acquaintance Maurice, *who lives* at *the corner of my coppice*, will exceed them in a week by means of a good ear. I have borrowed a horn for him. Adieu!

NOTES

[1] Sir Edward Boughton, 8th Baronet, Co. Warwick, Parson Hall's patron.
[2] I have been unable to trace an organist of Worcester who set Jago's *Blackbirds* to music.

CLXVII

Works III, 278.

To C[HRISTOPHER] W[REN] Esq;

July 6, 1754.

Dear Mr. W[ren],

You do me justice in believing that I am truly sorry you have not been well. A degree or two of regularity more than what you have already will, I fancy, restore your health, and my satisfaction; and I beg you will afford me the earliest account of your recovery.

I considered Master W[ren]'s visit as an absolute engagement, and remained at home in constant expectation of him for a fortnight together.—I am, however, not sorry, for his own sake, that he is gone to Oxford, especially as you seem to have an assurance of its proving advantageous. Pray assure him of my earnest wishes for his happiness, and that The Leasowes will be always at his service, whenever, through the fickleness of human nature, he thinks proper to give up a Muse for a Water-nymph.

I expect Mr. Hylton daily.—He was last week in London, and is now, I believe, at Coventry.—He will probably visit you before he comes into this country.—He talked of it when he left me.—I am obliged to be brief.

Post-woman waits for me, 'multa gemens.'[1] Dodsley is the man for your purpose—He has, with good genius, a liberal turn of mind.—I expect him to spend a few days here every week.—I will, if he returns through Warwickshire, occasion him to call upon you; but you know he is often lame with the gout, and will hardly be able to make any long digression.

Your case is exactly mine.—You say, you cannot bear wrongs with patience, but you can sleep and *forget* them.—So can I—so do I.—Did I never tell you (if not, I do so now) that indolence will, in a thousand instances, give one all the advantages of philosophy? and pray, if you call me lazy any more, take care that you do not use an expression by way of disparagement, which I consider as the highest honour. I am a fool, however, for discovering my secret. What a number of compliments might you have made me unwittingly!

> 'Tacitus pasci si posset corvus, haberet
> 'Plus dapis, & rixæ minus, invidiæque.'[2]

Had I time, I could comfort you under your ill-usage, by discovering to you the similitude of my own situation.

Excuse this scrawl; accept my compliments; carry them to Mrs. and Miss W[ren]; and believe me ever your obliged and most obedient humble servant,

W. Shenstone.

NOTES

[1]Virg. *Aen.* I, 464–5.
[2]Horace, *Epistolae*, I, 17, 50.

CLXVIII

Works III, 264.

To the [REV. R. GRAVES].

THE LEASOWES,
July 15, 1754.

Dear Mr. Graves,

The *particulars* relating to our poor friend's departure occasioned me much concern, and indeed some tears: yet as *those* particulars are what one covets to hear, and the melancholy which they produce is never unmixed with pleasure, I think myself much obliged to you for the care you took to convey them. It is possible, the letters I wrote to you and Mr. J. Whistler might appear too tender from a *mere* friend of the deceased; but there is a sympathy betwixt friends, which is not always found amongst relations; nor does *kindred* imply *friendship* a whit more than *friendship* does *kindred*. It is not many weeks ago, that I had a bill filed against me in Chancery by young D[olman], the only near relation I have by the mother's side; and the next in lineal succession to my share of the Penn's estate.—Do not let this surprize you.—I believe the affair will be accommodated.—He only wanted to procure a division of the Harborough estate at a large expence, which might be better adjusted without *any*; in other words, to run his head against a stone-wall, that he might have a chance of causing it to tumble upon *me*. Would you consent that I should suffer him to have the mansion-house at Harborough thrown into his lot? Were I so to do, I could make it advantageous to myself, and the dispute were at an end; but I have a kind of romantic veneration for that *place* and *family;* which, if you remember, I have expressed in one of my best elegies.[1]*

Pray what will become of our letters to Mr. Whistler? as I am not conscious of any thing dishonourable in mine (and I am *sure* I may say the same of yours), methinks I could wish that they might not be destroyed. It is from a few letters of my own or others alone, accidentally preserved, that I am able to recollect what I have been doing since I was born.

I met, when I was last at Barrels, a surgeon of Bath, whose name, I think, was Cleland.[2] He knew your name and place;

but, I find, was not personally acquainted with you.—I am glad enough to hear that your place gets into vogue. It is, I think, what you should *chuse*, upon all accounts. Let the beauty of the place guide them to the merits of its *owner*. I have often thought, myself, that were a person to live at The Leasowes, of more merit than myself, and a few degrees more worldly prudence, he could scarce want opportunities to procure his own advancement. My rural embellishments are perhaps more considerable than yours; but then the vicinity of Bath might occasion you a greater conflux.—Your unexpensive illuminations please me highly.—I have purposed these many years to purchase a set of tin-lamps, of about four-pence a-piece, to stick against trees, and to use upon occasion in my coppice; or rather in my grove, where some of the water-falls would not fail to shew delightfully.

You asked me about Jago's preferment. The living *last given* him by the Bishop of Worcester is, I believe, near an hundred pounds a year. With this, he has Harbury, of about fifty; and Chesterton, a sort of chapel of ease, about forty; in the *whole*, therefore, about an hundred and ninety; but then he is obliged to keep a curate; and what I think yet worse is, that he cannot make it *convenient* to *live* at his new situation, which is a pretty one.

I have had some visitants this season; indeed as many, and as considerable, as such a sort of season could afford me. A Scotch peer called upon me in his way through Birmingham: his title was D[almeny].[3] He seemed to have a very clear head, a very polite and easy manner, and all the refinement of true taste, *without* the warmth or appetite.—I could not help thinking him, on many accounts, characteristic of the Scottish nation.

Would to God I could see you and Mrs. Graves here this summer! I have the same wish it may be *my* lot to visit *you*, next autumn. Be assured, I *purpose* it.

I expect Dodsley every week. He will, I am convinced, be for publishing his Miscellany next winter. Would Mr. W[histler], think you, agree, that you and I should be allowed to publish such of poor Mr. Whistler's papers there, as we judged were most likely to do credit to his memory?

Adieu! dear Mr. Graves. Let us reconcile our affections to the ordinary events of life; and let us adopt my friend Jago into our second triumvirate. I am, however, always, with *peculiar* attachment, yours,

W. SHENSTONE.

My best compliments to Mrs. Graves.

P.S. Since I wrote the foregoing, I have had Mr. Davenport of Davenport-house, with all his family.—His brother, the clergyman, remembered you by your picture.—His wife is the finest *person*, &c. I have seen here, except Lady Aylesbury— ingenious, easy-behaved, and of an excellent temper.—They come to Bath in a fortnight.

Since that time, Sir George Lyttelton, Mr. Lyttelton, and Miss Lyttelton.—Sir George thinks some alterations requisite in my verses, to which I cannot bring myself easily to conform —but must.

I look upon my scheme of embellishing my farm as the only lucky one I ever pursued in my life.—My place now brings the world home to me, when I have too much indolence to go forth in quest of it.

NOTES

[1]*Footnote:—'*Elegy* XV.'
[2]Unidentified.
[3]John Primrose, styled Lord Dalmeny.

CLXIX

B.M. Add. MSS. 28958.

[*To* Lady LUXBOROUGH.]

THE LEASOWES, *July the* 17*th* 1754.

Dear Madam,

They say the dullest ecclesiastick may *remind* the ablest scholar of matters wherein he is not capable to *instruct* him. Such is *my* Plea; who though I am not to inform your Lady-ship what Pleasure your visits afford me, & how much it is your duty to communicate happiness, yet may, allowably I hope, *remind* you that ye year rolls on apace. Sorry am I to observe that it has carry'd off your noble Friend, the pious, the benevolent, and all-accomplish'd Dutchess of Somerset. It would be presumption in me to lament *my* share in the Loss of her. Notwithstanding ye veneration I had for her character, notwithstanding ye gratefull sense I entertain of her many civilities, it will perhaps much better become *me* to condole with your Ladyship for *yours*. . . . What an uncomfortable Summer is This! Scarce one single Day that ye sun is not obscur'd Either by rains or clouds, or it's efficacy destroy'd by raw unwholesome winds. I have seen but little company this year as yet; & my walks have been so much neglected in expectation of better weather, that I have hardly *wish'd* for any visitant y^t should be drawn by mere *curiosity*. Twas in such a wretched condition y^t they were seen, some weeks ago, by a Lord Delmany: A Scotch Peer, who made an excursion hither from his Road thro' Birmingham to Scotland. Pray, does your Ladyship remember any such title? for, hearing it only *whisper'd* to me, I am not sure that I spell or pronounce it right. He has an Estate pretty near Lord Somervile, & is, I think, related to Ld Primrose. Admiral Smith I see *often* here, who comes in a friendly way, & takes such a dinner as I can provide for him, extempore. I will not make my Letter a muster-roll of Names; only Lord Dudley I must add, who spent a few days with me last week; drank *deeply* to your Health, & wishes *cordially* to see you. Did you say nothing when I was at Barrels that connects July & Sir Peter Soames? Certain it is, that He & Barrels & July occurr together in my Imagination; & I cannot, any other way, be able to account for it. Should it be preternatural Inspiration & Truth, I beg you would offer him my most respectful compliments & wishes for the Honour of shewing him the Leasowes.

I have done but little since your Ladyship was here; & yet, supposing I had done a great *deal*, can you think me so *unpolitical* as to lessen your surprize by *previous* Delineations. I know too well; & am too much interested in ye Impression I wish you to receive from ye Place it self. Thus much however Let me tell you, my little Pavilion in ye water is no more! I yesterday enjoy'd it in Ruins, but my Pleasure was mix'd with

melancholy; as the case would be, were I to survey yᵉ noblest
Ruins upon earth.

Your Ladyship afforded me a Precedent when you pull'd
down your Temple in yᵉ Avenue. I appeal to you therefore
whether it be not *fortunate* to raise such[1] Sort of buildings
　　　　　　　　　　Rise　　　　　　　Destruction
whereof the raising and the destroying affords almost equal
Pleasure. Every constituent part of the universe is changeable;
& *beauty* itself is not more necessarily pleasing to yᵉ Imagination, than *variety*. Let us keep the secret to our selves, my
Lady; & not let yᵉ silly *world* understand how idly they
calculate, when they endeavour to produce objects of *perpetual*
amusement.

Were it not for Fear of treason, I should almost presume to
advise your Ladyship to demolish yᵉ Pavilion at yᵉ End of
your Bowling-green, upon yᵉ foremention'd principles. Sure
I am yᵗ, for a trifle of *expence*, Your Ladysp̄ might give that
Place a new & I *think* more elegant appearance.

The Bricks to be us'd in building a Strong wall at yᵉ back of yʳ
Pheasantry. A Slope & a gothick skreen (wood) to be plac'd
agst it. Shrubbery, continu'd to yᵉ end of it, to hide any part of
yᵉ House wᶜʰ you do not wish to appear, what ground is
gain'd to be added to the green: & this, I should think, *all* yᵗ
the *Place itself requires*. But I remember, this moment, yᵗ you
once propos'd a green-house there. I therefore drop my suggestion, with this only remark, that *refinement* is an *endless
Thing*; & as the *value* of such amusements is in proportion to

yᵉ *appetite*, no person living should pretend to fix how far another should pursue it.

This needs explanation. All I mean is that as your Ladsps Fortune has enabled you to gratify your taste for elegance more than mine has done your *relish* may become *weaker*, tho more *distinguishing* than mine.

I remember I took a scanty Leave of every-body when I left Barrels. Mrs. Reynalds did not visit me. Mrs. Davies I must write to. Lady Luxborough will, I hope, let me hear from her soon, & believe me ever her most oblig'd
& most obedient servant
WILL: SHENSTONE.

My Comp. to yᵉ Family at Oldbarrow.

NOTE

¹W.S.'s note at the bottom of the page—'neither very good nor very bad.'

CLXX

B.M. Add. MSS. 28958.

[*To* LADY LUXBOROUGH.]

THE LEASOWES, *Sept:* 29. 1754.

Dear Madam,

After assuring your Ladyship of the great Pleasure I receiv'd during the Time I had the Honour of your company at the Leasowes, I am to hope for the additional satisfaction of hearing that you feel no Inconvenience from your Journey. . . . When I left your Chaise at yᵉ End of Birmingham, I purpos'd only to beg a Draught of Perry at Mr. Baskerville's¹ Door; but was soon prevail'd on to alight, & spent an hour or two very agreeably. They both seem'd extremely sorry that your Lady-ship had not *time* to call; which I assur'd them was the Case. I found them sitting in their Parlour with a Busto-maker hard at work in finishing the Bustos of Mr. & Mrs. Baskerville; 'serving God with his Talent,' as I think, was Sir Godfrey Kneller's Phrase, when he painted on a Sunday. The Bustos are greatly like, & if well manag'd in Point of Hair and Drapery, will, I think, be very genteel ones. His Price is two Guineas. But as he came thither from Stratford you may possibly have heard the maker's Character. I should make ye frightfullest of *Bustos*,[2] or I do not know but I should employ him. . . . On Monday I was surpriz'd By Lord Sandys[3] & his Son whom I accompany'd round the *greater Part* of my walks; but who shewd less *Appetite*, (if not less *Discernment*) for matters of this kind, than almost any Persons I have seen here. The Son however seems to have more Taste than the Father. On tuesday I receivd the Northfield-Family, agreeable to ye message you saw: Ld Dudley met them here; & the greater Part of the Company, Mr. Lloyd especially, had Taste and Politeness enough to make my Day very satisfactory. I will not however trouble your Ladyship with a Detail of my Visitants, more or fewer of which have arrivd every Day this week. Pray does your Ladyship know a Mr. Bingley or Dingley? He seem'd a Person of Fashion, & came hither with his wife & a large Party to see my new Cascade by moon-light on Friday. Your Ladyship will please to observe from what has been said, that I could not with the least convenience send a servant to Barrels upon this Errand *before*. I hope, sincerely hope, that Mrs. Davies has not yet left Barrels. I mean chiefly, that I wish her to be *long* or very *often* with your Ladyship; but at present I mean also that you should assure her of my *unfeigned* Thanks for her company, & her assistance in makeing the Leasowes once more agreeable to Lady Luxborough. I desire also my compliments & Thanks to good Mr. Holyoak; hopeing, e'er long, that Mrs. Holyoak will deserve my thanks on ye same occasion; and, in the mean while, will accept my Compliments. I have an odd kind of Favour to beg of your Ladyship; but wch, if attended with the least Inconvenience, I *as* sincerely beg you would refuse me. I had a small Fruit-piece (a Painting) sent me of a Present last week, for which I want a Frame; & having heard, accidentally, that your Ladyship has many Frames you do not use, am tempted to enquire whether you could conveniently supply me with any that might be made to fit a Picture of two feet two, by Seventeen Inches or rather better. I beg, if inconvenient, you would make no sort of scruple to refuse it. . . . I suppose, so long as this weather continues, (and the Glass I see is high) my occupations will be much the same as you found them, at the Leasowes. But after the first Day's rain, the Face of things will be revers'd. I may then take the Cynick's Lanthorn, & creep about with my Friend Hylton in search of one conversible creature, by Day-light: But I rather *believe* we shall take a different method, & move directly to Barrels, where we shall be well assur'd of finding all that we can wish from Genius, Taste, Politeness, & hospitality. I am with veneration ever yours

WILL: SHENSTONE.

NOTES

[1] John Baskerville (1706–1775), the famous Birmingham printer, inventor of the Baskerville type. Straus and Dent, *John Baskerville—A Memoir*.

[2] W.S. apparently did have a 'busto' of himself made, for the frontispiece of the *Works* shows one, which, if not 'the frightfullest of *Bustos*,' is at any rate unattractive.

[3] Samuel Sandys, Lord Sandys, Baron of Ombersley, Co. Worcester.

CLXXI

B.M. Add. MSS. 28958.

[*To* LADY LUXBOROUGH.]

THE LEASOWES,
October y 13. 1754.

Dear Madam,

After the perusal of your Letter, I wrote immediately to Lord Dudley upon the subject of it; and thought proper that your Coach-man should accompany my servant to The Grange. Accordingly they both are gone, with orders to wait 'till they receive an Answer from Mrs. Rock. What the Event will be, I do not know; but am willing to hope the best; & am well assur'd it must give no small Pain to his Lordship either to leave his Priviledge unsupported, or to refuse any Request that your Ladyship is pleas'd to make.

I am afraid my Letters henceforth will begin to savour much of Winter, of whose un-joyous approach we have had no trivial Specimens. Yet I *guess* that Autumn will oblige us with some smiles at *Parting;* enough at least to render agreeable the small Excursion your Ladyship proposes. I also have a Journey, or two to perform, & that to Places which are ambitious of being seen in their proper Season. However, as to this next Week, I must devote it wholly to my *own;* and considering how much *Time* & *Labour* has been bestow'd upon it, this year, my Friends will not take it amiss if I seem attentive to the Produce of *Them.*

I expect Mr. Hylton here to-day, or to-morrow: How long he means to stay, is unknown to *me;* perhaps also to *Himself,* but I hope it will be long enough to accompany me to Barrels.

I return your Ladyship my best Thanks for ye beautifull Frame you were so kind to send, but, on the other Hand, it gives me some Confusion to think that even the least capital of your Pictures should so suffer by my Impertinence.

The Servants are return'd, & my Lord desires *I* would write to Mr. Crawley, an attorney in London, & his intimate Acquaintance. I suppose he means to *Sign* what I write; and as for the rest I purpose y^t ye Letter shall go by to-morrow's Post.

I beg my Compliments to all the good Friends, y^t were so kind as to send me *theirs.* I can add nothing to amuse your Ladyship: I can only add a certain truth, that I am ever most respectfully your Ladyship's most oblig'd & most obedient Servant

WILL: SHENSTONE.

I will detain Mr. Belchier's [1] Letter as it may assist me in the Letter I have to write.

NOTE

[1] 'Our troublesome little Parson' of the Luxborough *Letters*, 408, for whom she asked assistance from W.S. and Lord Dudley (376). He proved unworthy (398, 402 397).

CLXXII

Works III, 268.

To the [REV. R. GRAVES], *on hearing that his Letters to Mr. Whistler were destroyed.*

THE LEASOWES,
Oct. 23, 1754.

Dear Mr. Graves,

It is certainly some argument of a *peculiarity* in the esteem I bear you, that I feel a readiness to acquaint you with *more* of my foibles than I care to trust with any other person. I believe nothing shews us more plainly either the different *degrees* or *kinds* of regard that we entertain for our several friends (I may also add the *difference* of their *characters*), than the ordinary style and tenour of the letters we address to them.

I confess to *you*, that I am considerably mortified by Mr. John W[histler]'s conduct in regard to my letters to his brother; and, rather than they should have been so unnecessarily destroyed, would have given more money than it is allowable for me to mention with *decency*. I look upon my letters as some of *my* chef-d'œuvres; and, could I be supposed to have the least pretensions to propriety of style or sentiment, I should imagine it must appear, principally, in my letters to his brother, and one or two more friends. I considered them as the records of a *friendship* that will be always *dear* to me; and as the *history* of my *mind* for these twenty years last past. The amusement I should have found in the perusal of them would have been altogether innocent; and I would gladly have preserved them, if it were only to explain those which I shall preserve of his brother's. Why he should allow either *me* or *them* so very little weight as not to *consult* me with regard to them, I can by no means conceive. I suppose it is not *uncustomary* to return them to the surviving friend. I had no answer to the letter which I wrote Mr. J. W[histler]. I received a ring from him; but as I thought it an inadequate memorial of the friendship which his brother had for me, I gave it to my servant the moment I received it; at the same time I have a neat standish, on which I caused the lines Mr. W[histler] left with it to be inscribed; and which appears to me a much more agreeable remembrancer.

I have read your new production with pleasure; and as this letter begins with a confession of foibles, I will own, that through mere laziness I have sent you back your copy, in which I have made some erasements, instead of giving you my reasons on which those erasements were founded. Truth is, it seems to me to want mighty few variations from what is now the present text; and that, upon one more perusal, you will be able to give it as much perfection as you mean it to have. And yet, did I suppose you would insert it in Dodsley's Collection, as I see no reason you have to the contrary, I would take any pains about it that you should desire me. I must beg another copy, at your leisure.

I should like the inscription you mention upon a real stone-urn, which you purchase very reasonable at Bath: but you must not risque it upon the vase you mention, on any account whatever.

Now I mention Bath, I must acquaint you, that I have received intelligence from the younger Dodsley,[1] that his brother is now there, and that none of the papers I sent him are yet *sent to press;* that he expects his brother home about the fourth or fifth of November, when he proceeds with his publication. Possibly you may go to Bath whilst he is there, and, if so, may chuse to have an interview.

I shall send two or three little pieces of my own, in hopes that you will adjust the reading, and return them as soon as you conveniently can. All I can send to-night is this 'Ode to Memory.' I shall in the last place desire your opinion as to the manner of *placing* what is sent. The first pages of his Miscellany must be already fixed. I think to propose ours for the last; but as to the *order*, it will depend entirely upon you.

Adieu! in other words, God bless you!—I have company at the table all the time I am writing. Your ever most affectionate

W. SHENSTONE.

NOTE

[1] James Dodsley (1724–1797), was taken into partnership by Robert, at The Tully's Head, the firm being that of 'R. & J. Dodsley, in Pall Mall.'

CLXXIII

To Mr. D[AVENPORT].

THE LEASOWES, *Nov.* 13, 1754.

Sir,

The Arrival of your Servant gave me a retrospective View of my own intolerable Omissions, and oppressed me with somewhat like the Load of an evil Conscience. I must allow that Appearances make against me; and yet I must and will assert, that there is no one has a truer Respect for Mr. D[avenport], a deeper Sense of his Civilities, a greater Relish for his Company, or a more lively Desire to partake of those Beauties which he is daily distributing round his Situation. Of these last, Miss F[anny] F[letcher?] has sometimes favoured me with the greatest Encomiums: I am sure she knew how much I should enjoy them, and might also mean them as Inducements (which I never yet wanted) to hasten the Visit I intended to you at W[orfield]. Alas! neither her Pleasure in giving me these Descriptions, nor mine in receiving them, were unmixed with Pain; as she was too often forced to adjoin but an indifferent Account of poor Miss D[avenport]'s Health. For this, and for the Affliction it occasions you and Mrs. D[avenport], I really feel a Concern that I am not satisfied to express in the ordinary Forms of Condolence.

I have passed this Summer in a Series of Dissipation; betwixt some Events disagreeable enough, and others that wear at least the Appearance of Pleasure. I have done (what I must call) a good deal round my Place. Company produced new Operations, and new Operations produced almost daily Company. The Line of my Path is now almost universally extended to the Sides of Hedges, and, together with some slighter Improvements, have been added two new Cascades: of the first of these, I believe you have heard some Account; it is really, if you'll pardon such an Expression from the Proprietor, a very *great* Thing for the *Size* of it.

My Servant has been *weekly* upon the Point of setting out for D(avenport) House, ever since the Time I first heard of your Return to it: but as he is here much less of the Footman or Groom, than the River-God, he has been almost continually called upon to unlock and conduct his Rivulets; for this Fortnight, indeed, or three Weeks last, he has been less importuned on that Score; but then, during that Space, arrived a Visitant, who is now with me in the House, and, till the Time of whose Departure was ascertained, I was unable to fix a Day when I could wait upon you and Mrs. D[avenport]: I hope to do so about the Middle of next Week; and will not fail to send Tom over upon *Monday* or *Tuesday*. If he can be of any possible Service, in regard to the Cascades you proposed (and I think his Head a clear one) you are welcome to command him over as often as you please. I have detained your Servant much beyond the Time he purposed to return. I can therefore only desire my best Compliments to Mrs. D[avenport], and assure her, that my Muse is not less at her Service, and beg your Acceptance of this Ode to, &c. and would, I am sure, esteem it greater Honour to embellish your Place than mine. I wish you do not find it obscure; however, if it discover but an ordinary Talent for Poetry, it will discover at least a warm Attachment to rural Improvement. With this I shall be quite contented, so long as I think it has the least Tendency to recommend me to Mr. D[avenport]'s good Opinion.

I am,

dear Sir,

yours and Mrs. D[avenport]'s, &c.

CLXXIV

B.M. Add. MSS. 28958.

[*To* Lady LUXBOROUGH.]

The Leasowes, *Dec.* 8.*th* 1754.

Dear Madam,

I know not what to say. I wish it were in my Power to draw up an apology in as clear and forcible a manner as you have brought my accusation. But to dispose and give weight to an hundred little excuses, (each of which, when taken separately, can pretend to small Importance) would be a task very difficult for *me*; & to your *Ladyship*, I think, extremely unamusive. Pardon me therefore, my good Lady, *implicitly*; & believe that in so doing you have escap'd a most tedious narrative. I have met with numerous avocations of a very different nature: Some regarding *business*, and utterly displeasing; others of a mixt kind, & neither pleasurable nor painfull;—very few, since I saw your Ladyship, which I have thoroughly enjoy'd.

When Mr. Belchier's Messenger arriv'd here, my Lord Dudley had been gone to London about a week. I therefore wrote that gentleman a short message, intimating my wishes for his Freedom Health and Happiness; acquainting him, that I had, at your Request, done all that lay in my power to serve him; and that All I could do, from that time, was to transmit his Letter to my Lord D. in London; which I would not fail to do by the following Thursday's Post. Indeed the Servant's own account of his master *here* gave me some cause to conclude that your Ladyship was deceiv'd in Him. I trust what you will further collect from yᵉ Letters I have enclos'd may indeed occasion you to compassionate his distress, but will at the same time discover how improper it must have been for my Lord to appear in support of his written Protection.

Sir William Meredyth does me a great deal of Honour in his remembrance of me; & whatever I receive from him will of course be very acceptable. I heartily wish him all the Pleasure which his situation, his time of Life, & his numerous accomplishments so fairly promise him; & 'tis none of my least ardent wishes that I may one Day meet him at Barrels. Mean time, The little quotation he gives you from Horace Walpole's speech[1] is truly humorous; & I am glad that Sir Williams Correspondence restores to your Ladyship some of that Amusement, of which London robbs the country at this time of the year. I beg yᵗ when you write you would offer him my best Respects.

I am sorry to hear of poor Mr. Bradley's Death;[2] who appear'd to me to be a Person of great good-nature, & of a true natural *Taste* under the disadvantages of worldly Business. I beg my humble Service to Mrs. Bradley.

My Lord Dudley & Miss Lea are now in London; where

my Lord has purchas'd a new Coach & a Pair of Horses; which are expected to convey them to the Grange before Christmas.

Mr. Hylton has been with me for these six or seven weeks past; & purposes to reside in this neighbourhood all the winter. Could I have remov'd the Panic apprehensions under which he labours as an *Horse*-man, he would long ago have waited upon your Ladyship at Barrels. I trust however I shall be able to bring him with me, before the Close of this present December.

I am at this time embarrass'd with a Promise which I made last year to Dodsley. I then offer'd to contribute some few Pieces towards his Miscellany; either of my own; or of my Friends, whose Permission I could procure. Accordingly I have taken some Pains in His behalf; and am willing enough to send him half a score of my smaller Madrigals. But then it is a Point with me not to publish aught that may be altogether unreputable; or y^t may prejudice the Publick against any thing I may print hereafter. And, in this respect, I am irresolute what to send him. Will your Ladyship be so kind as to honour me with your Opinion, in regard to a Song or two which I enclose for your Perusal.

There is a Song or two written by your Ladyship, y^t I think extremely elegant. 'Hark to the Blackbird's &c:' and 'The Sun his gladsome beams' &c: The latter of these equal to any song in the Language. I think it pity they should be suppress'd and should be heartily glad if you would permit him to print them with any Limitations you think proper for me to mention.[3] I am clear & positive in my opinion of their *Merit*.

I beg y^t your Ladyship would wave all sort of Compliment in respect of the Pieces wch I send for your Perusal; *Severity* is ye most *friendly* when one is upon the Brink of the Press. I beg my Complim^{ts} to Mr. Outing, who will not refuse me his assistance also. I trust that, before the Close of Christmas I shall see him in Warwickshire, if not in Shropshire. I desire always to be esteem'd

Your Ladyship's most oblig'd
& most obedient hum: Servt
WILL SHENSTONE.

I shall probably write
again before the Close of this week; as I

have some other little Pieces wch I have
thoughts of sending to Dodsley: at least
if I find by your Ladyship's answer [illegible in MS.]
the Trouble I give you is not imp[illegible in MS.].

To
The R^t Hon.
Lady Luxborough.

NOTES

[1]Luxborough, *Letters*, 399.
[2]Mr. Bradley, of Edstone, a neighbour of Lady Luxborough. *Ibid.*, 402.
[3]*The Bulfinch in Town* (*Collection*, IV, 306) and *Song Written in Winter* 1745 (*Ibid.*, 307), are referred to here.

CLXXV

B.M. Add. MSS. 28958.

[*To* Lady LUXBOROUGH.]

THE LEASOWS, *Dec^r* 12 1754.

Dear Madam,

It is my *misfortune*, not my *Fault*, to write to your Ladyship in the greatest *Hurry*. I am sure your goodness will therefore excuse me, if everything I say in this Letter be expressive of it. I hope also that Mr. Outing will accept my Thanks at present, & allow me to answer his Letter when I have a better opportunity.

Shall I tell your Ladyship a Secret? I was so thoroughly convinc'd of the Merit of your little Pieces, that I sent them to Dodsley very near a Month ago. It is true, had I not obtain'd your Leave to print them (which I always meant to sollicit) I would, most assuredly, have stop'd the Publication: but far happier am *I* in the Liberty that you have given me.

I believe the Press waits for my Contributions at this very time: I purpose therefore to compleat what I mean to add of my own, by next Saturday's Post; & should think myself oblig'd, if you would please to return the Copies I now send, (together with what I sent before) by the Servant. As to those I now Send, I need not give your Ladyship or Mr. Outing much trouble. There seem not to be above two that have y^e *least* pretensions to appear in Print. The one 'those Stanzas ad-dress'd to your Ladyship upon furnishing y^r Library;[1] The other, 'that Ode to Lucio.[2] However I shall be very glad to receive an Opinion so just as yours, or His.

I wrote to Mr. Crawley on Monday last; &, in the Letter, took the Liberty of assuring Lord Dudley that your Ladyship would altogether acquiesce in his Conduct towards Mr. Belchier. I also left him no Room to blame either your Lady-ship or myself.

I dare detain Tom no longer. He will as it *is*, arrive much later at Barrels than I wish Him. I beg however that your Ladyship, with Mr. Outing, will afford me what assistance you can at this Juncture; & I will write again to Barrels by ye way of Birmingham, when I hope to signify a week when Mr. Hylton & myself may have ye Pleasure of waiting on you. I am, Madam,

> Your Ladyship's most oblig'd
> & most obedient hum: Servt
> WILL SHENSTONE.

To
the Right Hon.
Lady Luxborough.

NOTES

[1]Dodsley's *Collection*, V, 24.
[2]*The Ode to Lucio*, 'So dear my Lucio is to me,' appeared first in the *Works*, 1764, I, 172.

CLXXVI

B.M. Add. MSS. 28958.

[*To* LADY LUXBOROUGH.]

THE LEASOWS,
Jan. 10, 1755.

Dear Madam,

I do not wonder that your Ladyship esteems my silence *unaccountable*, as I have the strongest *Inducements* to write that either *Pleasure* or *Gratitude* can afford me. And yet the total

Reason why I did not write before, was oweing to the necessity I was under of attending to Dodsley's publication; & the state of my health and Spirits at this time of the year. It has been my wayward Fate to study the Refinements of Poetry, when my Head was hardly sufficient to indite a Piece of common Prose. Much indeed am I oblig'd to your Ladyship & Mr. Outing for the Propriety of the Remarks you sent me; & yet in *one* Respect they gave me Pain, as they discover'd how much more *wisely* I had acted, had I come over to Barrels about a Month ago, brought my Madrigals in my Pocket, & *there* finish'd this affair with Dodsley agreeable to our joint Opinions.

Your Ladyship has so admirable a talent at Impromptus (I speak very *seriously*) that I cannot forbear asking the assistance you can lend me in an *hour or two's* time, this Evening. The Objections you made to the Canto on *Sollicitude*[1] I believe are entirely just. I have therefore omitted a considerable part of it, and endeavour'd to improve the rest; but with what *success*, I want greatly to be satisfy'd. Never was I puzzled more than in tricking out that pastoral Fop Sir Paridel;[2] yet I think, that when my head is *clearest*, there is no kind of Humour on which I could more *easily* succeed. The Stanzas in particular, wherein he compliments his Mistress by the trite resemblance of Flowers, cost me no small Pains. Your Ladyship, if you cannot any way *approve* them, will I'm sure *assist* a poor bewilder'd Poet who applies to you as a *Genius*, a *Florist*, and a *Friend*.

That you may be more easily induc'd to make free with *my* said performance, I discover to your Ladyship y[e] Liberties which I have taken with *yours*. Amongst the Rest, that of sending it to Dodsley is what I beg you would forgive. I really thought it would appear well at the Close of your other pieces;
contempt for
as it shews a becoming disdain of an art in which you cou'd so easily excell.[3]

I shall be glad if your Ladyship and Mr. Outing approve this Copy of the Princess Elizabeth; as I shall not have time to make any important alteration. The Autumn-Verses have been in Dodsley's hands this twelve-month; & I *hope* they do not *want* an amendment, which I'm *sure* they will not *have*, as matters are circumstanc'd.

I have not time to express my sense of Sir William Meredyths complaisance, but will take some other opportunity.
Pray, what was Mr. Pit's Embarasment?

Mr. Belchier's is an handsome Letter; & I am glad for his
own sake that he has not miss'd his voyage. I will the first
convenient opportunity return his Protection to Lord Dudley.

You have *read* that Mr. W. Lyttelton is appointed Governor
of S. Carolina;[4] but you may not have *heard* that Admiral
Smith stands Candidate for Bewdley[5] in his Room, & is oppos'd
by Mr. Winnington.

Mr. Hylton desires his most respectfull compliments to
your Ladyship; & returns you many thanks for ye honour of
your Intelligence concerning a Horse that would suit him.
This really *would* suit him; & he would be extremely safe in
dealing with Mr. Holyoak; but it seems he *now* does not purpose to buy *any*, amusing himself with the *Mere Possession* of a
Keffel he dares not bestride.

Your Ladyship is extremely kind in *asking* my Company,
at a time of year when neither my head, my spirits, nor my
temper renders me worth any one's company, correspondence,
or Notice. For this week or nine days past, I have indeed been
more particularly heavy & dispirited. I will however wait upon
your Ladyship soon; as soon as it becomes possible you should
receive any Amusement from my Company. Mr. Hylton
intends to come with me; & in the meantime, I will *write*.
Your Ladyship says nothing of *your* Health; I will therefore,
for *my own* sake, believe that you are well. You would *always*
be both well and happy, if health and happiness depended *less*
upon externals, and more upon the inmost wishes of, Madam,

Your Ladyship's most oblig'd

& most obedient hum: Ser^t

WILL SHENSTONE.

NOTES

[1] *Solicitude* is the title given to Part III, *A Pastoral Ballad in four Parts*, which first
appeared in Dodsley's *Collection*, IV, 348.

[2] *Collection*, IV, 353.

[3] Presumably the reference is to the end of the lines *Written to a near Neighbour in a
tempestuous Night*, 1748, placed third in the *Collection*, where Lady Luxborough dis-
claims the power of writing poetry and calls upon Morpheus.

'Wisely at least he'll stop my pen,
And with his poppies crown my brow:
Better by far in lonesome den
To sleep unheard of—than to glow
With treach'rous wildfire of the brain,
Th' intoxicated poet's bane.'

[4]Appointed January 1855, an advancement due mainly to the efforts of William Pitt. Wyndham, II, 106, 200.

[5]Bewdley was a neighbouring borough in the interest of the Lyttelton family, and here William Lyttelton made his first entry into politics. Wyndham, II, 200.

CLXXVII

Works III, 280.

To MR. JAGO, *on their Contribution to Dodsley's Miscellanies.*

THE LEASOWES,
Jan. 22, 1755.

Dear Mr. Jago,

I am sure you must be puzzled how to account for my silence, after the honour you have done me by your verses, and the request you made that I would *write*.—I am also as much at a loss how to give a proper weight to my apology. To say I have been ill, would perhaps imply too much; when I would only allude to that state of heaviness and dejection which is so frequently my lot at this time of the year; and which renders me both *averse* to writing, and utterly dissatisfied with every thing that I *do* write.

If at any time my head grew a little less confused than ordinary, I was obliged to devote my attention to the affair in which I had so *foolishly* involved myself with Dodsley. You are unable to conceive what vexation it has given me: I could not endure to *disappoint* him: of consequence, it has been my lot to study the delicacies of *poetry* when my brain was not sufficient to indite a piece of common prose; but as the *Mouse* (by which I mean my *own* performances) will so soon make its ridiculous appearance, it were totally impolitic in me to expatiate on the labours of the *Mountain*.—The first letter I received from you left me greatly dissatisfied. I was then to send D[odsley] my *final* instructions in a post or two.—You took little notice of any query I made; and intimated a disapprobation, which agreed *too well* with my own internal sentiments.—I knew not but you were *angry* at the *liberties* I had taken; though I could have suppressed any single paper which I had then conveyed to London.—Little did I *then* imagine that it was in my power to have protracted the affair till *now*. Had that been the case, I should have troubled you with repeated embassies; for I abhor the tediousness of the post, and my servants do little at this time of the year, that is of more importance than their master's poetry.

Your next letter convinced me, that you had taken no offence: and so far I was happy; but then I wanted to have your Gold-finches as correct as your Black-birds; there were *some* things I wished you to alter; and others in regard to which I was desirous to speak my *sentiments*. Add to this, my own *verses*, with which I was infinitely *more* dissatisfied. Why then did I not write?—The true reason was, that I was pressed by D[odsley] to send conclusions every post; and though I have had all this leisure (as it *happens*) since you wrote, I never could *depend* upon more than the space of a day or two. Besides, criticisms in the way of letter are extremely tedious and dissatisfactory; insomuch, that I am thoroughly determined never to print any thing for the future, unless I have the company of my friends when I send to the press. Hurried as I then was, I sent up your two copies, and what I proposed for him of my own, with a kind of *discretionary* power to select the best readings. How you would approve of this measure I knew not; but I had this to plead in my behalf, that D[odsley] was a person of taste *himself*; that he had, as I imagined, many learned friends to assist him; that his *interest* was concerned in the perfection of his Miscellany; and that I submitted my own pieces to the same judgement.

After all, I am but indifferently satisfied with the present state of these contributions. D[odsley] writes just so much as he deems *necessary* in the way of business, and passes by a thousand points in my letters which deserve an answer. His last acquaints me, that he has spent a whole day in the arrangement of what I have sent him; and that he purposes to send me *proof-sheets* before the close of this week, desiring I would send them back by the return of the post. Whether they arrive on Saturday or on Monday, I can keep them till the Thursday following.

And this brings me, in the last place, to the main purpose of this letter.—It is a request on which I lay great stress; and which you must not refuse me upon almost any consideration. —I beg, in short, that you would promise me the favour of your company on Monday (or even Tuesday) next, if possible; and let us jointly fix the readings of *your* pieces, of my *own*, and those of our common *friends*.—You will immediately comprehend the *expediency* of this; now, in particular, that our names are to appear. *Some* alterations I think *necessary* in your Gold-finches, and there are two or three stanzas which I think you might improve.—Nevertheless, I will not pretend that this journey is so *requisite* upon your *own* account as *mine;* and will recommend it upon no other footing than the pleasure you will receive by the obligation which you will confer.

I thought to have concluded here; but, as an envelope is now become altogether necessary, have a temptation to proceed which I did not see before.

It is now become Friday the twenty-fourth of January. The packets I send, and the request that I make upon so *little* warning, will, at first, astonish you.—Unforeseen interruptions would not suffer me to dispatch my courier sooner.— What then remains, but that I endeavour to adjust this affair agreeably to its *present* circumstances?

You will readily conceive from what you observe in my packets, how desirable your company is to me at this juncture. Supposing it then in your *power* to come over on Monday, Tuesday, or even Wednesday, I am inclined to believe you *will.* Supposing it *not* so, I can foresee you will not have leisure to satisfy my queries by the return of the bearer; and what I would *next* propose is, that you would either suffer me to send again to you betwixt this time and Thursday next; or that you would yourself dispatch a purpose-messenger, and allow me to pay for his journey.—In either of these *latter* cases, I am sure you so well know the nature of my present irresolution, that you will endeavour to afford me all the assistance you are able.

Adieu! my dear friend! and depend upon my best services on every possible occasion.

I am ever your most affectionate
and most obedient servant,
W. SHENSTONE.

CLXXVIII

Works III, 286.

To the [REV. RICHARD JAGO], *on the same Subject.*

THE LEASOWES,
Feb. 22, 1755.

Dear Mr. Jago,

I received a letter from Dodsley, dated the fifteenth of February; informing me that you were then in town, had been with him, and left your directions whither he might send you a set of Miscellanies.

February the twentieth, and not *before*, arrived young H[ylton?] with your letter; very obligingly intended to give me previous notice of your journey; but which, by the iniquity of chance, tended only to acquaint me with an opportunity which I had *lost*.

There is nothing could have been so fortunate as your journey to London, had Mr. H[ylton?] thought proper to bring your letter in due time.——What excuse he made for his neglect, or whether he made any, I have really forgot. This I know, that the whole affair has been unlucky. There has been abundant time for consultation, and a perfect series of opportunities of which we have not been suffered to avail ourselves.——It is now three weeks or a month since I corrected the proof-sheets; was so hurried in the doing of it that I scarce knew what I wrote; and yet, in spite of all this hurry, the book is hitherto unpublished. *Now*, indeed, it must be much too late for alterations, as D[odsley] has given me some room to expect a book this very day.——I know but little what he has done in consequence of that discretionary power with which I, through haste, was obliged to intrust him: but in what I have done, *myself*, you may expect to find all the effects of *dulness precipitated*.

It is now the twenty-third of February, and I have received no fresh account of our friend Dodsley's proceedings; nor am I able to *trace* them, as I expected, in the newspapers.

As to your share of this Miscellany,[1] you can have no cause to be dissatisfied.—After what manner he has thought proper to print Lady L[uxborough]'s verses, I am a good deal uncertain; but I apprehend he has not followed her own readings very precisely, and that the blame thereof is to be thrown upon me.—I am concerned for the memory of my poor friend Whistler; and regret that his *better* pieces did not fall into my hands. I think that Dodsley, however, would have done him greater justice, had he inserted his translation of 'Horace and Lydia.' It is true, the translations of that Ode are out of number; but *his*, if I mistake not, had many beauties of its own.—I do not know whether I ever hinted to you, that *his* genius and that of Ovid were apparently congenial—Had he cultivated his with equal care, perhaps the similitude had been as obvious as that of your twin-daughters.—Mr. Graves has one small well polished gem in his collection; his verses upon Medals.—His little conjugal Love-song is also natural and easy.—I *told* you what I least disliked of my *own* puerilities. If the printing of my Rural Inscriptions be *invidious*, it was altogether owing to the instigation of Sir G[eorge] L[yttelton]. There are four or five little matters, which, if he have printed with my name, incorrect as they are, I shall be utterly disconsolate; at least, till I get sight of a succeeding impression.—For though I am not much solicitous about a poetical reputation (and indeed it is of little importance to so *domestic* an animal as myself), yet I could ill endure to pass for an affected, powerless *pretender*.

And now no more upon the subject.—I have nothing to add that can the least amuse you.—You, who have been conversant with all the busy and the splendid scenes of life, can want no materials to make a letter entertaining.—Indeed you never *did*.—I shall be glad, however, to receive a *long* one, upon what subjects you please.

I have passed a very dull and unamusive winter; my health indeed rather better than I experienced it last year; but my head *as* confused, and my spirits *as* low. I live in hopes of an opportunity of seeing you at Harbury; but I begin now to receive visits as an honest beggar does an alms, with my humblest thanks for the favour, and with a despair of making a return.

Perhaps my next letter may discover somewhat more *resolution:* inclination I never want; being at all times with singular affection yours,

W. SHENSTONE.

NOTE

[1]W.S. supplied the poems, 293–357, Vol. IV. These included some of his own poems, and poems by Jago, Somervile, Graves, Lady Luxborough, Whistler and J. Scott Hyl on.

CLXXIX

Messrs. Maggs, & Hull, I, 223.

[*To* LADY LUXBOROUGH.]

THE LEASOWES,
Feb. 27, 1755.

Dear Madam,

I find it necessary to write to your Ladyship this week; not being able to endure that you should think hardly of me, during the time that may elapse before I can *possibly* see you. When I have the Honour of doing so, I trust that I can eraze any unfavourable Impressions, & very fairly acquit myself of all *voluntary* neglect. Mean While, let me only beg that you would suspend your accusation. I wish I could *fix* a time for the Performance of this visit; but it is not in my power. Such weather as the present, does not only numb one's Limbs, but extend it's severity to our very *purposes* and *resolutions.* Your Ladyship well knows how Winter affects *me*; & has more than once remark'd it in the very style of my Letters. I am dull enough to be unworthy of a conversation much inferior to yours; & if I add that I am a little peevish withall, I should do myself no Injustice. Were it possible to retain the same *venomous* or *torpid* Qualities, when arriv'd upon the Coast of Barrels, I ought in common Policy to confine myself at Home. But I *have* been, and *am* confin'd upon a different score; a kind of partition—treaty betwixt myself and master Dolman : and when this is concluded or broken off, (as I trust will soon be the case) I shall not then draw excuses from the stupidity with which it is my Lot to be *visited* in winter. I have indeed sometimes imagin'd that I brighten'd up in your company, when I had before esteem'd it as impossible as that you should polish a piece of *Cynder*, or of *Spunge*. No very promising materials!— I have expected to see Dodsley's miscellany advertis'd these six weeks ago. Had he llow'd me but one *Half* of this time to deliberate, I could have adjusted the share we have in it much more to my satisfaction. I know but little what he has finally done, in pursuance of that discretionary Power with which I, thro' absolute Haste, found it requisite to intrust Him; and that possibly at a time when his *own* Hurry was as great as *mine*. But *this* I know, that, in what I did *myself* towards the last, you must expect to trace the Finger of 'stupidity precipitated.

Stupidity however is many an honest man's Lot; Presumption is less excuseable: and I am therefore most humbly to crave your Ladyship's pardon for proposing what I *thought* might be some Improvement of your verses. I have this to plead in my behalf, that you write these lively pieces almost extempore; that you lay no stress upon them & hardly ever revise them that, on these accounts only, I thought it possible an expression not altogether exact might here & there escape you; that finding my proposals disapprov'd at Barrels, I did all my *time* would then *allow* to cause Dodsley to have recourse to your original Readings; And if he have *not* done so, *universally* (as I apprehend may be the Case) the Fault may be repair'd in some future Impression, & is, even now, not altogether *mine*—I will resume this subject upon some other occasion; at present, Let me only add, that Dodsley, when last I heard from Him, desir'd my opinion whether or no he should be thought *impertinent* if he presented your Ladyship with a compleat Sett of his Miscellanies. It seems the *three first* volumes are out of Print, at this time; but will be reprinted in about a month. The New volume, he gives me reason to expect every Day.

I am particularly pleas'd to find that your Health continues tolerable during this *severe weather*. Tis a Circumstance that leaves room to conceive yᵉ advantage you may derive from *better*. How truly do I long for the approach of Spring! Methinks I could travel many leagues to meet it; were it possible, by so doing, to bring it faster on it's way. And yet unless it should supply me with *Health* as well as with *Com-*
Daffadils [sic]
pany; with *Spirits* as well as Spring-flowers; &, in one word, re-enliven *both* the Farmer & the Farm, what would it avail? The two Canary-birds, that were given me about three weeks ago, sing whilst I am writing; sing from morn to Night; & that with all the vigour which the Spring itself can inspire. Yet I do but half enjoy them: my mind is not in tune. The Commencement of *my* Spring must receive its date at Barrels. I am with invariable attachment your Ladyship's most oblig'd humble Servᵗ

W. SHENSTONE.

CLXXX

The F.L. Pleadwell Collection, Library of Congress.

[*To* JOHN SCOTT HYLTON.]

Feb. 28—1755.

My compliments to Mr. Hylton, whose list of Grievances I have been shewing to Mr. Pixell—If Aaron persists in taken Floyd's House, I could wish he might be acquainted that he will never obtain a license for selling Ale; nor ever be permitted to encroach an Inch upon the Waste—My cages are come, & a sort of Instrument-Case from Giles's[1]—Let not Mr. Hylton forget to obviate any *claim* yᵗ Aaron may lay to yʳ 20th.

W. S.

NOTE

[1]Five men of the name of Giles are mentioned in a Birmingham directory for 1770. Two were engravers, one a 'painter in general,' one a joiner, one an apothecary and

surgeon. W.S.'s letter to Lady Luxborough, April 17, 1755, establishes the fact that the Giles of their letters was an engraver. Presumably the engraver to whom 'copies' of 'an idle ballad' were sent, was Joseph Giles, who published in 1771, *Miscellaneous Poems on Various Subjects and Occasions. Revised and corrected by the late Mr. William Shenstone. Some Reflections on hearing the Bell toll for the Death of a Friend, The Robin— An Elegy, and An Epitaph,* W.S. sent to Dodsley on behalf of Giles, and these found a place in Dodsley's *Collection,* V, 87–93.

CLXXXI

B.M. Add. MSS. 28959,
& Straus, *Robert Dodsley.*

[*To* R. DODSLEY.][1]

THE LEASOWES,
March 4th 1755.

Dear Sir,

I return you many thanks for the Compliment you make my Friends & Me in the offer of a sett of miscellanies. I dare say L[dy] Luxborough will take it well to be included in it. My Expectation of seeing the last volume advertis'd, was the reason I have not made you this acknowledgment before.

The Delay has given me some Pain; not thro' the least Impatience of seeing my Trifles made publick; for I am really fearfull of the appearance, & could wish a longer time to adjust the state of my contributions. But this very Wish makes me reflect upon the time that has elaps'd since I wrote to you; & of which, I trust, I could have avail'd myself to your satisfaction & my own. I suppose that the Impression must now be taken off; if otherwise, & that for any particular Reason you have chosen it should be deferd I should be glad that you would afford me y[e] earliest Intelligence.

I am ever faithfully
& affectionately yours
WILL: SHENSTONE.

My Lord Dudley will accept my respectfull Compliments & pardon my Freedom in requesting y[t] he would frank me these few Covers. We are told here y[t] my L[d] has lately taken a House in Town.

which seems to f

NOTE

[1]In the B.M. MS. the following note is placed before the letters from Dodsley to W.S., and W.S. to Dodsley:—

Letters from my worthy Friend
Mr. Robert Dodsley;

A very eminent Bookseller in London; Author of the Miller of *Mansfield*, (his native place) the Toyshop, the Œconomy of Life; above all, Cleone & Melpomene; with many other Pieces. A Person whose writings I esteem in common with the Publick; But of whose Simplicity, Benevolence, Humanity, & true Politeness, I have had repeated & particular experience.
May 22, 1759.   WILL. SHENSTONE.

CLXXXII

Hull, I, 227.

To MR. GRAVES.

THE LEASOWES, *March* 21, 1755.

Dear Mr. GRAVES,

Pardon the Arrival of this one more Letter without a Frank; I have sent some Covers to my Lord of D[udley], who is down, and shall probably enough receive them before I write again.

There is nothing that I can less forgive the World than your Want of Leisure. Do not misinterpret me, or take amiss what I say. I know you to be infinitely more happy than myself, who am cloyed with it; but it would add something to my Happiness, if not to your own, that you had more vacant Spaces or Intervals of Time to employ in those refined Amusements, for which you are so exquisitely qualified.

I am in doubt, whether I should add Mottos to my Seal, or not rather cause the Circumference, which at present is rather of the largest, to be contracted. Should you have struck out any Thing since you wrote to me, you will be so good as to let me know.

As to Sun-Dials, I never much affected the Things themselves, nor indeed any Mottos with which I have seen them inscribed; perhaps this Indifference may arise from no very commendable Sources, a Reflection upon my own Want of Proficiency in Mathematics, and an habitual Consciousness of my own Waste of Time. However, I have often had Thoughts

of placing a slight one somewhere upon my Premises, for the
Sake of inscribing it with a Couple of Lines from VIRGIL:

> *Sed fugit interea fugit, irreparabile tempus,*[1]
> *Singula dum capti circumvectamur amore.*

All the Lines in VIRGIL afford me that Sort of Pleasure which
one receives from melancholy Music, and I believe I am often
struck with the Turn and Harmony of his Expression, where a
Person less attached to these can discover no great Beauty.

I told you, how much I was vexed that DODSLEY did not
suffer me to avail myself of the Time that passed from the
Correction of the Proof-Sheets to the Publication of his Book.
He has at last sent me a Copy, which I received last *Thursday*
Se'en-night. I wish the last Stanza of WHISTLER's Verses upon
Flowers had remained as he himself wrote it: but being somewhat dissatisfied with the original Reading, and having no
Time left to improve it myself, I left it to D——, who I think
has made it worse; however, in this Respect, and some others,
it may be proper to fix one's Eye upon a subsequent Impression; and DODSLEY has acted as discreetly as it was possible for
him to do, considering what instructions were given him, and
how *much* was left to his Discretion. Our Contributions may be
said to begin with Mr. SOMERVILLE's *Address*, &c. Page 302;
amongst which he has inserted two Odes (Pages 305 and 307)
to which I am a Stranger.[2] The Song marked J.S.H. is my
Neighbour Mr. H[ylton]'s, who has a pretty Collection of
Drawings, Petrefactions, and Coins. The *Lady of Quality* you
know; and as to the Pieces that follow, you know the Authors
of them as well as I do. I will not anticipate your own Observations; but I cannot help remarking that MILTON's *Il Pen-
seroso* has drove half our Poets crazy: it has, however, produced
some admirable Odes to *Fancy*, amongst which, that of WHAR-
TON (not in this Volume)[3] I think deserves the Preference; and
after his MERRICK's,[4] PENSHURST,[5] and the Ode on *Solitude*[6]
are of the same Tribe, and are good. The *Pleasures of Melancholy*,[7] and MARIOTT's Ode to *Fancy*,[8] of the same Tribe, are
indifferent. There is nothing I am more pleased with, than
Father FRANCIS's Prayer,[9] Mrs. BERKLEY repeated it to me in
my Root-House this last Summer, and, I think, said it was Mr.

WEST'S. I could wish I had made you some Compliments in this Volume, for particular Reasons, and had resolutely done so, had your own Diffidence permitted me.

I have now and then some Thoughts of printing that *Ode to the Duchess*, together with something sufficient to make a twelve or an eighteen-penny Pamphlet, about the Time the Parliament rises; but not unless it sits till *June* as was reported, and not unless you will promise me the Favour of your Assistance.

'Tis the Property of great Delicacy, to be often-times too diffident; possibly then you may not long persevere in that Manner of spelling your Name, which you seem at present to prefer; yet is nothing so clear to me, as that yourself and your Relations should spell their Name GREAVES to the End of the World—*Nati Natorum & qui nascentur ab illis*.[9a]

COWPER'S Performance is all that you think it: but would you see both his Style and his Sentiments effectually demolished, look into the Account of Books in that *Gentleman's Magazine* where it was first advertised.[10]

You will guess that I shall want impatiently to hear from you, when you have received your Set of Books, or perused them elsewhere.

I am,
ever-more affectionately yours,
W. SHENSTONE.

NOTES

[1]Virgil, *Georgics*, III, 284–5.
[2]*Ode to a Friend wounded in a Duel*. (By Charles Parrott, Fellow of New College). *Ode to Night*. By the same. This ode first appeared in *The World*, 74, May 30, 1754. Courtney, 42.
[3]Dodsley's *Collection*, III, 109. The author was Joseph Warton.
[4]Ibid., IV, 181. *An Ode to Fancy* by the Rev. Mr. Merrick.
[5]Francis Coventry, d. 1759, published in 1750. *Penshurst, a poem, inscribed to William Perry, Esq. and the Hon. Mrs. Elizabeth Perry*. This was reprinted in Dodsley's *Collection*, IV.
[6]Ibid., IV, 229. *Solitude. An Ode* by Dr. Grainger.
[7]Ibid., IV, 210. *The Pleasures of Melancholy. Written in the Year* 1745: By Mr. Thomas Warton.
[8]Ibid., 287.
[9]Ibid., 258. *Father Francis's Prayer*, by Gilbert West (1703–1756).
[9a]Virgil, *Aen*. III, 98.
[10]John Gilbert Cooper published in 1754 *Letters on Taste*. These were advertised in *The Gentleman's Magazine* for December 1754, and the author's sentiments on the ruins of a castle which enliven a prospect and on the beauty of streams, etc. were ridiculed. Probably W.S. is referring to this publication,

CLXXXIII

B.M. Add. MSS. 28959,
and Straus, *Robert Dodsley*.

[*To* R. DODSLEY.]

THE LEASOWES,
March the 23^d 1755.

Dear Sir,

I had the Pleasure of receiving the fourth volume of your miscellanies, which arriv'd as I remember last thursday was se'nnight. I am oblig'd to you for the care you took to forward it, when printed, as well as for all that Trouble I occasion'd you, *before*. Some Improvements may be made in a subsequent Impression; & whenever this is propos'd I dare say you will give me notice. In general, you have done all that I could expect from a Person of Genius and a Friend.

It remains for me to wish that the Book may fully recompense you, I will not only say, for the Pains you have taken, but for the Discernment you have shewn. It contains many excellent pieces, that are entirely new to me: & if others that are no less excellent have been printed before, it cannot reasonably be objected by such as consider your first Design.

Is it impertinent to ask the Names of those Persons who have not inserted them?[1] If so, I drop my enquiry. The Pages, where their Lines occurr, are, 73. 114. 119. 170. 200. 202. 227. 228. 233. 250. 253. 265. 267. 305. 307.

Should the Parliament sit till June, I have some thoughts of printing my ode upon Rural elegance; together with some such other Pieces as may make a 12 penny pamphlett—But if my Purpose continues you will hear from me again soon, & I shall send you up a copy, about half-correct, for your Opinion.

I hope Mr. Baskerville meets in London with the encouragement he deserves. I long to hear from you upon all accounts, am, your most affectionate

& most obedient Servant
WILL SHENSTONE.

NOTE

[1]Courtney gives the names of most of the contributors.

CLXXXIV

B.M. Add. MSS. 28958.
[*To* Lady LUXBOROUGH.]

The Leasowes,
March the 29, 1755.

Dear Madam,

It was not before yesterday that I receiv'd this Parcell from
Dodsley; & it is with Pleasure I hasten to execute his commission. The several Setts he mentions were bound so much
alike, that it was impossible for me to make your Ladyship any
particular Compliment. The Sett which I have sent, is at least
as handsome as any; & I cannot pretend to think it *handsomer*,
till it has receiv'd your Arms at the Beginning. As to the Share
we have in this volume, There is nothing I can well *add* to
what I said in my last Letter: This however I would *repeat*,
that whatever your Ladyship disapproves may be rectify'd in
some future Impression; & that I beg you would in no sort
condemn me, 'till you have heard the whole I have to say.
The Volume has many good Pieces in it which are new to me;
and if some others, perhaps as good, have been printed formerly in Pamphletts, it is allowable enough as it is consistent
with Mr. Dodsley's first Proposal. There is one little Piece
which strikes my Fancy greatly. Tis Father Francis's Prayer, in
Lord Westmorland's Hermitage. Mr. Berkley repeated it to
me in my Root-house last Summer, and, as I remember, told
me it was written by Mr. West—But I mean to see your Ladyship soon; I should hope in a Fort-night's time; & shall then
find much more Pleasure in discovering my Sentiments on this
occasion. On Monday next, I think to write to Mr. Dodsley; &
am glad of the Liberty you allow me to oblige him with a sight
of your Letter.

Thus having at last brought this affair to a conclusion, &
being *willing* at least to hope that I have done my Friend some
service, I no further concern myself about such Laurels as the
World can *bestow* upon me, but fix my Thoughts on such as I
can *purchase* at Coventry of Mr. Whittingham. I mean that I
am daily expecting a score or two from that quarter, to shade

the wretchedness of my Barns & out-houses. The mighty
Cæsar, whose Head was bald, you know, priz'd Laurels upon
such another score; and was not more delighted with any
Decree of Senate y^n that which allow'd him to wear a wreath
perpetually.

I receiv'd Mr Outing's Epistle with Pleasure; but as I have
nothing to communicate beside what this Letter contains, &
as he left it somewhat uncertain whether he should remain
at Barrels 'till now, I have not indeed wrote, but am entirely
at his Service. It is a prodigious long time since I heard anything of Mrs. Davis: I should be oblig'd if your Ladyship w^d
give me some Intelligence concerning her. Governor Hylton,
as Mr. Outing styles him, has gott Possession of his Castle.
But as a Sportsman *buys* Game and then pretends that he *shott*
it, or as Pyrrhus *bought* Towns & then boasted that he *took*
them, Even so —— Plain enough does it appear to me that he
has given his tenant a year's rent to which he had no sort of
Pretensions; and that in the making of this *separate* Treaty he
has had no regard to the satisfaction of me his Friend and *Ally*
—He has of late given away his Keffel; but this upon such
terms as to leave me quite uncertain, whether Mrs. Stanton,
when she *sold* Him the Horse, us'd him worse, than He has
done his Landlady when he *made her* a *Present* of Him. Notwithstanding all this, He shall accompany me to Barrels; & is
perhaps more likely to do so, now this *Shadow* of a Horse is
remov'd.

Your Ladyship bids me scatter Flowers upon the road I
have to pass. Do you not here, in other words, bid me be happy,
& be well? I am sure at least you *wish* me so; but as there Few,
in comparison, that equal you in Point of Genius, there are I
think *almost* as Few y^t equal you in Point of Spirits. Let me
add, that, Universal *Chearfullness* is the Gift of Nature only,
and is worth every other advantage that she or Fortune can
bestow. I am ever, Madam,

Your Ladyship's most oblig'd,
& most obedient Servant,
WILL: SHENSTONE.

I do not think it
quite *fair* for me to take advantage

of Dodsley's offer; but If I should cause
Him to give any other sett away, He should, I
think, present one to Lord Grey.

Y^r Ladyship will please to return me Dodsley's Letter.

University of Texas MS.

'Tis now Sunday March the thirtieth. After having wrote y^e
foregoing Part of my Letter yesterday, I was induc'd to take a
Ride to Edgbaston, & pay a visit to my Friend Pixell. This is
truly the first excursion I have made, of many months, & is
assuredly a good Omen with regard to *greater* Undertakings.

Upon revising my Letter, methinks the Close of it has an
Air of *Peevishness*. Do me the Justice to believe, that this is
foreign to my Temper upon all occasions when I write to
you.

I was shewn a Letter yesterday from Sr Harry Gough to
Mr. Pixell, which said Sir H. laments that the Town at Present
is much fonder of Arne than Handel—I wou'd willingly have
engag'd Arne to sett the three remain^g: parts of my Ballad,
each to different Musick. I enclose his Answer, which is very
rational. However I am going to write to him once more, and
[indiscipherable in MS.] if he will sett it for his *own* Collection.
What he *has* done is reckon'd good, and I cannot be content
with any other Composer.[1]

Your Ladyship may well wonder how I manage my *sealing-
wax* to look so. What you deem sealing-wax, was really no
other yⁿ ye Inner Bark of a Birch-tree & bear y^r Impression
of a seal wch is now cutting for me by Mr. Giles; from w^m
I rec^d that specimen.

I beg to be remember'd to Mr. & Mrs. Holyoak, & the
rest of your neighbours. I hope you will favour me with a *long*
Letter; if you do not find writing disagreeable. My *appetite* for
Amusement begins now to encrease a little; but Appetite,
without Food to satisfy it, is not surely preferable to Food
without an Appetite. Hylton & I are poorly off in the Winter-
Season, when it has remov'd all that is beautifull from ye Face
of our Parish, and left us nothing in place to contemplate,
but the Inhabitants! I write this, as I lie abed; but ye Painfull

posture in wch I do so cannot diminish ye satisfaction I always find in subscribing myself (once more) Madam

Your Ladyship's ever

obedient Servt

W. SHENSTONE.

NOTE

¹The B.M. preserves a letter of Dr. Arne on the subject of the musical setting of *The Pastoral Ballad*. (Add. MSS. 28959.)

Nov. ye 30th 1754.

By the hands of Mr. Dodsley, I receiv'd your very obliging Letter, & wou'd for my own Pleasure comply with your Request, but Mr. Dodsley's Interest in this Particular interferes with mine, for, if he prints my music in his publication, I shall loose the Sale of it to Mr. Walsh, (the King's Music Printer) who gives me 20 guineas for every Collection I compose consisting of eight or nine Songs, & who would not give a Shilling for any thing that another had publish'd.

Of this I acquainted Mr. Dodsley, who did not seem inclin'd to make any Gratuity for the Loss.

Any Song, Cantata or Dramatic Piece, from so delicate a Pen whereby I shou'd not considerably lose to promote another's Gain, wou'd be the most welcome present I cou'd receive, stamp an additional Reputation on my Music, & highly oblige Sir,

Your most Obed^t Servt

THOS. AUG^{NE} ARNE.

Charles Street,
     Covent Garden.

Arne finally wrote some music, for Vol. IV, of Dodsley's *Collection* contains it. But negotiations still went on for setting the 'three remaining parts' of the Ballad to music.

CLXXXV

Works III, 289.

To [REV. R. JAGO].

THE LEASOWES,
April 3, 1755.

Dear Mr. Jago,

I have so long expected the favour of a few lines from you, that I begin at last to question whether you received the letter I sent you. It was inclosed in one to Mr. M[iller?], whom I requested to further it with all convenient expedition. I am neither able to recollect the whole contents of it; nor indeed, if I *were*, could I endure the thoughts of transcribing them. The chief intention of it, however, was to acquaint you of Mr. H[ylton?]'s unhappy delay in the delivery of that letter with which you favoured me from Radway.

What confirms me in a suspicion that my last letter miscarried, is, that Mr. Wren lately acquainted me of your being at Wroxall upon business, and of your making some slight mention of Mr. Dodsley's publication, without intimating that you discovered any design you had of writing to me. This is mere preamble and stuff: implying nothing more than the desire I have to *hear* from you, when it ought also to express how impatiently I long to *see* you. Worldly concerns and my winterly state of health have detained me at home for these many months past: worldly concerns may have confined you likewise; but as your health and spirits are universally better than mine, and as you have much less dislike to travelling than myself, I would hope that my absence from Harbury will never cause you to *neglect* any *opportunity* of coming hither. For my own part, I have been meditating upon a visit to you all this winter; and do, at this time, resolve most strenuously to perform it before June. But the many such schemes of pleasure in which I have been disappointed are a sort of check upon my expressions, and make me promise with *fear*. As to Dodsley's performance, which you must have received before this time, I will make no observations till I have the pleasure of seeing you: and yet there are many points I would discuss, and many accounts I want to give you. So many indeed, that they would furnish out perhaps a superficial drawling letter; but would serve infinitely better for conversation, with the book before us. The volume, I am told, is well received in town; though political intelligence must engross much of its present attention.

Mr. Hylton is in my neighbourhood, and upon the point of settling at his farm. Could you possibly spend a week with us, we would try to make it agreeable. At all events, I beg to hear from you; and that, not merely as it will afford me great pleasure, but as, at the same time, it will ease me of some solicitude. I will not make this a long letter, though I wish to receive a long one in return; having a head very little qualified to add any thing that may amuse you, though a heart very sincerely and affectionately at your service.

W. SHENSTONE.

CLXXXVI

Works III, 295.

To MR. GRAVES, *with some Account of Politics and Poetry.*

THE LEASOWES,
April 4, 1755.

Dear Mr. Graves,

You will be harrassed with my letters till you condemn my excessive leisure as loudly as I have lamented that you should ever feel the *want* of it. Nor is it a point so easily decided *which* of us may be the greater *sufferer;* you through my *officiousness*, or I by your long *silence*. Yet the partiality which you have ever shewn me will, I think, dispose you to receive my letters more patiently than it is in my power to sustain the loss of *yours*. After all, I should not write at present, but that the Miscellanies with which Dodsley compliments us arrived last week at The Leasowes. I desire therefore you would acquaint me, whether the sett that he means for you should remain here till your arrival; or if you chuse that I should send it by the Birmingham-stage to Bath. Having made this enquiry, I was thinking to conclude; but cannot reconcile myself to the *novelty* of sending *you* three empty pages. The Parliament will rise too soon for the publication of my 'Rural Elegance;' and having performed my promise to Dodsley, I think no more about such *laurels* as the *public* can bestow upon me, but am giving all my attention to such as I can purchase of my nursery-man. I wish, however, that the volume may recompence Dodsley for his trouble: I may also add, for his ingenuity, and for his politeness in giving each of us a compleat sett. They are elegantly bound, and all as much alike as possible.

The present crisis of state-affairs does not seem to favour his publication, as the attention of the public must lean greatly to that quarter. I saw a letter from Sir William M[eredith] (who corresponds with Lady Luxborough), which placed the struggles of the ministry in a clearer light than they had yet appeared to me. It seems that persons of all denominations are for carrying on the war with vigour; and the King's application for a Vote of Credit was received with general approbation. The zeal of the Parliament was indeed so remarkable on this occasion, that, instead of the £600,000 at first intended, it was thought proper to propose a million. But the services were ascertained, and the Chancellor of the Exchequer made accountable for the application of it. The augmentation of the fleet with 20,000 seamen; the raising 5000 marines on a plan of dividing them into small companies, which will render them more useful both by sea and land; the completion and reinforcement of the Irish regiments; are the uses to which this million is to be appropriated. Mr. Fox[1] and his land-war-party sat mute, whilst Mr. Legge[2] with great openness and perspicuity explained the present schemes; as they were calculated, to exert our whole strength at sea, and, if possible, nowhere else. Mr. Dodington,[3] who, it seems, has not spoke of many years, charmed every body. His wit did not only entertain, but animate and affect his hearers. '*It were better*, he said, *than lose the dominion of the Ocean, that the Ocean should overwhelm us: for what Briton could wish to leave a posterity crawling upon this island, only to feel the tyranny, and swell the victories, of France?*' It seems, F[ox], in his opposition to the Duke of Newcastle,[4] is supported by the Duke of Cumberland,[5] his army, and the Scotch: that the ministry (or the D. of N[ewcastle]'s party) seem not displeased with a prospect of uniting with the Tories, who now hold the balance; and it seems the Tories, by Sir William's letter, are as little displeased to unite with the Ministry.

You will guess that good part of this political account is *transcribed;* and you will guess aright. I had some thoughts that it might amuse you, and had no occasion to use other expressions.—Let me now, once more, return to the futile objects of my *own* amusement. The impression upon this letter will be taken from my new seal. The motto that I have pitched upon is, SUPEREST MEMORIA: though I yet retain some hankering after the single word PRAETERITIS. Probably this, however, is not the last seal that I shall cause this man to cut in steel. The altar is not yet finished: ANTE OMNIA MUSAE; but it does not quite satisfy me.—I will inclose the two last letters I received from Mr. Dodsley; but you must not think I build too much upon any compliment which he there makes me.—It is true,

I think him a very sincere man; but he cannot have been conversant so long with modern-writers, but he must conjecture, when their piece is published, that they a little hunger for applause. I am now uncertain whether you will receive a letter from him; as he has, unaccountably I think, sent your books *hither*, and not to Bath. I am, however, fully satisfied, that your first and last pieces, more *especially*, do credit to his collection, and must please all persons of taste.

I desire my best respects to Mrs. Graves, who will be pleased to see the affection that subsists betwixt you perpetuated. She will also feel some satisfaction in the professions of friendship that are made you by your most affectionate and faithful humble servant,

W. SHENSTONE.

NOTES

[1]Henry Fox, 1st Baron Holland (1705–1774), was Secretary of War in Newcastle's administration, but he and Pitt joined to make Newcastle's position intolerable. Newcastle, however, managed to win him over and Fox became leader of the House of Commons.

[2]Henry Bilson Legge (1708–1764), Chancellor of the Exchequer, fourth son of William, 1st Earl of Dartmouth.

[3]Dodington had a great reputation as a wit in his day. He received, as a result of his tactics in 1755, the post of Treasurer of the Navy, under Fox and Newcastle.

[4]The Duke of Newcastle became first Lord of the Treasury in March 1754, and found himself in opposition to Fox because he insisted on dissociating himself from all participation in the disposal of the Secret Service Money.

[5]William Augustus, Duke of Cumberland (1721–1765), military Commander, third son of George II.

CLXXXVII

B.M. Add. MSS. 28958.

[*To* LADY LUXBOROUGH.]

THE LEASOWES,

April 17th 1755.

Dear Madam,

Tho' I have nothing to communicate which can prove the least entertaining, yet it is expedient that I should return Sir William Meredyth's Letter, lest I should any way appear

ingratefull for the Pleasure it afforded me. The Disputes of
Senators, the Division & subdivision of Parties are for the
most part as little *known* to me, as what passes in the Star
Aldebaran. I will not confess that I am as indifferent *concerning*
them: my Ignorance not so properly arising from the want of
publick spirit, as from a voluntary Inattention to matters I
can no way influence. However a little first-rate Intelligence, at
Intervals, affords me Pleasure; & Sir William's Letter, being
entirely of that sort, has given me a *competent* knowledge of
what is doing at the Helm. I do entirely think with your Ladyship that the Ministry should take advantage of the national Ardor
to make now a very vigorous effort at Sea. I have no Reasons
to give but what are obvious to all the world; yet reasons of this
kind are sometimes not the weakest—Since the arrival of your
Letter I have had *other* fresh Intelligence, that the Ministry,
if they can possibly avoid it, will make no war at *All*.

I have not heard from Mr. Dodsley since I wrote to you
last. Indeed I did not write to *Him* before last Monday, when I
convey'd to him your Thanks & compliments in your Ladyship's own Hand-writing. I then wrote also to Mr. Arne; whom
I requested to *compleat* the musick to my Pastoral. But as I
offer'd him no *Money*, & have no hopes of prevailing but by
Dint of *Complaisance*, it is possible, nay probable, that He may
not comply.

Mr. Giles, who cuts my Seal, is a most exquisite Hand in
Steel. I shall soon, I hope, be able to give you a better Impression; but am not myself yet master of the method by which
he gives them upon Bark. Tis some-how done with the Stroke
of a Hammer, & of Consequence hardly practicable after the
Seal has been Sett. 'Tis to be observ'd also that common Clay
is a yet better material, as I can sufficiently demonstrate when
occasion serves.

Did your Ladyship ever see the four Roman Ruins publish'd
by Arthur Pond?[1] They cost me twelve Shillings. I caus'd
Aris to procure them for me, & have ask'd Mr. Hylton to
colour them. You cannot conceive the magnificence of their
effect in a Camera.

The weather is beginning to amend, & promises a pretty
forward Spring. I hope your Ladyship will reap the Benefit

both in Point of Health & Pleasure. I exhibited my Place to some Company yesterday, which is the first time I have done so ever since last November.

Lord Dudley remains in Town—I feel myself grow dull, & will therefore bring my Letter to a conclusion whilst I am *aware* of it. Your Ladyship will present my Compliments to Mr. Holyoak & his Family, & believe me to be ever

Your most oblig'd & most obedient

H. servant

WILL SHENSTONE.

NOTE

[1]Arthur Pond (1705–1758), painter and engraver. There is in the B.M. a 1760 *Catalogue of the genuine, entire & well known Collection of Etchings and Prints; by Masters of the Greatest Eminence, purchased by Sir Edward Astley Bart. of Mr. Arthur Pond, lately deceas'd, (among which are those very scarce and valuable Prints by Rembrandt, which Mr. Pond had, with the Greatest Care, been many Years Collecting).*

CLXXXVIII

The F.L. Pleadwell Collection,
Library of Congress,
and B.M. Add. MSS. 27548.

[*To* JOHN SCOTT HYLTON.]

April 1755.

I desire my Compliments to Mr. Hylton; and am tolerably well: Have however taken a Second Purge today, and intend to take another on Friday, by which means I hope to acquire at least a little more agility for ye ensuing Spring yn has been my Lot this Winter—Many thanks for ye Picture which (wth ye exception of one or two Faults) is in ye main a very laudable Performance.—You do right to keep Robin in constant employ—Priest brought 4 Loads of Lime & I sent him positive orders to take you two of them to Lapell; which he as positively refus'd to do—I went to him in a sort of Pett; but upon his assuring me yt he would take you some in a day or two, and upon hearing a very good Character of his Honesty, was induc'd to let him have his way—wch *possibly* too, I could not have prevented. You do right in planting Poplars, if you can find them suitable Places. I must myself put a Period to my Plantation &c for this Season; and endeavour to get my Walks in some sort of order to be exhibited—As far as I can find, their new Chancel at Hagley is a mere Mausoleum; and contains such a *Display* of Pedigree &c: as one would think must prove invidious to ye last Degree—I will tell you more of it wn I see you. As I understand, ye Dean & all ye living Part of the Family have their arms there, distinct; with their Names &c: beneath. Mr. Kendal[1] brought some Company here yesterday, from whom I gain'd my Intelligence—Adieu

WxSx

Young Lea[2] call'd on me yesterday on his Way to London; where he is to be ordain'd on Sunday next, & after that go on board ye Ship that is appointed for him. He apologiz'd for not calling on you, and desir'd me to make his Compliments.

1755. *April.*

To John Scott Hylton Esq.

NOTES

[1]Lady Luxborough mentions visits to and from a Mrs. Kendal of Stratford.
[2]Sailor son of Parson Lea.

CLXXXIX

Messrs. Maggs.

[*To* J. S. HYLTON.]

Saturday, May 3d 1755.

My Compliments &c. I have just parted with Mr Perry who din'd with me, & with whom I have had a long Conference in regard to Dolman's affair. Perhaps I may tell you something more of it, when I see you; but if I should not do so of my own accord, you may take it for granted it is painfull to me. I think he brought me no News, but that my painted glass is near finish'd; & that ye Admiral took Durant to Portsmouth in order to shew him ye Fleet. I very greatly approve of ye Pill prescrib'd for Tom; & hope it will recover Him to his ordinary Pitch of Health. He has brought a Box of them from Hales, and, as his stomach was empty, I bid him take a few directly, & not go out of Doors. I believe you used not hurry yourself about painting Moll's new Book tho I cannot say how far she piques herself upon having her new treasure in Possession—*Red* [sic] it, she has already. It is probable I may surprize you in ye midst of your Masons, tho' I have matters upon my Hands which I must no way neglect—Thus far have I written before the Post-woman's arrival.

The Bells are ringing furiously, & perhaps my L^d of Dudley is at the Grange: Perhaps also it may be oweing to ye sight of y^r Morning's Letter, which, upon poor Tom's Account, I thought it proper to shew Mr Gaunt.[1]

Parker finds everything insipid but Ambition; Let him experience how far he can find *That* satisfactory.

Mary is come & brings neither of us any Letter.

I have not a syllable to add—beside

A—Dieu

W.S.

Dolman

Supposing you were to give Molly D. that aimiable Character she deserv'd, then introduce her as appearing to her Brother & expostulating about his Treatment of Miss Milward[2] & me, from ye time of her Death. As for metre, such as follows,

> 'The Sun was sunk beneath ye Hill'
> 'The Western Sky was edg'd with gold' &c

or suppose you made her write Him a Letter only, in this Metre? Wou'd it give you any Amusement? If so, indulge y^r Fancy.

Once more Adieu—'till I see Robin again; who is now waiting for a Fancy, when I have not one Idea.

To John Scott Hylton Esq:

NOTES

[1] A Joseph Gaunt appears as a witness to W.S.'s will.

[2] Miss Milward was with Maria Dolman in London, at the time of the latter's death. Hull, I, 202. She was probably a member of the family which lived at Tennall Hall—Nash, *History of Worcestershire*, gives record of many monuments to the family in Knighton Chapel.

CXC

B.M. Add. MSS. 28958.

[*To* Lady LUXBOROUGH.]

The Leasowes, *May the* 14*th* 1755.

Dear Madam,

Appearances are much against me; and if your Ladyship be inclin'd to *trust* them, I do not doubt but at this time I lye under your Displeasure—yet were I to relate but one Half of my story, I could sure turn every part of your *Disgust* into *Compassion*. For were I to relate *Half*, your *Penetration* would guess the rest, & I am sure you are too much my Friend not to sympathize in my Distress. What I allude to here is my vexatious Dispute with little Dolman. For, what betwixt his own Perversness & the Insidiousness of his Attorney, I ought to be —somewhat else than what I am, to cope with them. When I wrote to your Ladysyp last, a Negotiation was upon the Carpet, & proposals passing on each side. In the midst of this, & without ye least Notice, They abruptly caus'd my *answer* to be demanded in Chancery. The Consequences of *delaying* this may be disagreeable to the last degree; And I do not question but this little Fellow may have malignity enough—to cut my throat. At least his Behaviour of late makes me think so, who in return for such Services as he could not easily requite, has offer'd me such Injuries as he cannot possibly compensate— This is Truth; & my Embarrassment must be my Excuse for the Present, & God knows how much longer. Mr. Hylton when he writes, shall give your Ladyship concurrent evidence. He indeed is now become the perfect 'Squire of Dames & has been in constant Employment ever since my Lord's Family arriv'd.

The Letter I enclose is one of the politest I have yet receiv'd from Mr. Dodsley; & I take it for granted y^t I do no wrong in shewing it. All His last Letters to me remain at present unanswer'd; So do many Overtures of Friendship from Persons I respect: Lord Stamford sent his Compliments as he *went up* to London, & I promis'd to wait on Him the Moment He came down. He return'd back to Enfield with his Family last

Sunday, sent three Servants with a Request that a Sir Harry (Some-body) might see ye new Cascade—I am much in the same situation with regard to Mr. Davenport & Mr. Dean—Do not imagine, I beg your Ladyship, that I speak this out of *Vanity*—I wish I was as guiltless of every sin as I am of Vanity *at this time*—But rather observe, y^t I am quite a stranger to every Pleasurable Hope or Purpose, &, for this reason only, defer the mention of ye visit I would make at Barrels—My Walks are indeed pleasant, for any one besides myself: I hope your Ladyship's afford *you* the same Pleasure they do to others.

Mr. Clare, whom you have heard mention'd by Mr. Chambers of Kidderminster,[1] is made Deputy-Cofferer in ye Place of Mr. W. Lyttleton[2]—This affords me some surprice, not only ye offer, but ye Acceptance—Admiral Smith is yet in Town, & in case of war proclaim'd, which may not be the Case, will be sent, it is reported, with an honourable Command to the West-Indies. Sir George Lyttelton comes down in June, & his Chancel-window is compleated. Perhaps in some future Letter I may give a Description of this chancel—But what talk I of future Letters, when if my Dispute should happen to be ended, I should immediately fly to wait on y^u in Person? Mr. & Mrs. Graves are to arrive here next saturday Se'nnight—I could not bear to *decline* a visit which is offer'd me so very seldom; else am I greatly apprehensive that I shall be ill at Leisure to receive them.

I am moreover under a Promise to accompany them to Barrels—God grant y^t Events may prove happier y^n I foresee! 'Tis all I can say at present—I must needs see Guy-cliff.[3]

I am with unvaried respect & gratitude

Your Ladyship's most oblig'd

W. SHENSTONE.

NOTES

[1]Did Mr. Chambers of Kidderminster inspire the poem, *Works* I, 210, *On Mr. C.—— of Kidderminster's Poetry?*

[2]William Lyttelton became sub-cofferer to the Household in 1754, under his brother George. He did not hold the office long as he was made Governor of South Carolina.

[3]Lady Luxborough, *Letters*, 411, was charmed with Guy's Cliff, Warwick, which was a well known show place in the eighteenth century. 'The prettiest thing I ever saw of the kind, is the shell-room at Guy's Cliff: Mr. Greethead and Lady Mary have executed it all with their own hands: bed-hangings, chimney-boards, pictures over the doors, etc.'

Jago celebrates it thus, in *Edge-Hill*, Book II.

> '. . . . . . thy example, Guy!
> Calls me from scenes of pomp, and earthly pride,
> To muse with thee in thy sequestered cell,
> Here the calm scene lulls the tumultuous breast
> To sweet composure. Here the gliding stream,
> That winds its wat'ry path in many a maze,
> As loth to leave the enchanted spot, invites
> To moralize on fleeting time and life,
> With all its treacherous sweets and fading joys,
> In emblem shown, by many a short- liv'd flow'r,
> That on its margin smiles, and smiling falls
> To join its parent earth!'

CXCI

Messrs. Maggs.

[*To* J. S. HYLTON.]

June the first, 1755.

My Compliments to Mr Hylton; am glad enough if He have escap'd from such a Bevy of Charmers with so small a Wound as what he complains of in his Wrist return Him thanks for ye Sight of Dr Betts Letter; wch I think an extreme polite one, & wch I would have him shew my Lord have had Parties of Company all this week: this afternoon, M^r and Mrs Amphlett of Hadsor, M^rs and Mr Amphlett of Clent[1] wth Miss Briscoe[2] in Mr Amphlett's Coach: have not yet receiv'd Mr Davenport, nor any Message *not* to expect Him. Mr Hylton will Guess my Embarrassament [sic] thro tantalizing scenes of amusement wch I am not suffer'd to enjoy—

Adieu.

WILL SHENSTONE.

To John Scott Hylton Esq;

NOTES

[1] This family receives lengthy notice in Nash's *Worcestershire*.

[2] Elizabeth Lea, youngest sister of Lord Dudley, married July 14, 1759, the Rev. Benjamin Briscoe, afterwards incumbent of Stanton. Probably this lady belonged to the same family.

CXCII

Hull, I, 232.

To Mr. B[INNEL?].

THE LEASOWES,

Oct. 1755.

Dear Mr. B[innel?],

The affectionate Letter I received from you ought to have been answered by the next Post; it had been so, if I had pursued the Dictates of a Heart, I will not say, altogether happy in our Reconciliation, but more properly in the Manifestation of our ever-undivided Friendship.   I have had a large Conflux of Visitants this Summer, and the Dissipation they have occasioned me, was for the most Part very agreeable. But it must not be by any Accession of *Pleasure*, that I attempt to excuse my unseasonable Neglect of writing; for Pleasure I have in writing to my Friends, when my Mind is free from Anxiety, and that Pleasure connected with a Duty I owe to Friendship, superior to what is claimable by any mere Visitant or Acquaintance; yet I cannot but confess the Change which a very few Years have wrought in me; for surely it is not long since I wearied you, and the rest of my Correspondents, with my *Assiduity;* where I now write *one* Letter, I then wrote *twenty:* mean while, the Warmth of my Heart is not diminished, with regard to Friendship; I know it from the Pleasure which the Receipt of your Letter gave me. Of this Kind are the only Pleasures which accompany us through Life; they encrease upon Repetition, and grow more lively from Indulgence. '*Vient l' Appetit en mangeant*,' was, I think, an Answer made by a *French* Courtier to his Sovereign, when it was objected to him by the latter, that there was no End of his Importunities. But whatever odd Instances may be found of a perverted Appetite, the Maxim is only universal, in regard to social Pleasure. The Case is not the same, with regard to Pleasures of Sense; it is not so even with regard to Pleasures of Imagination. Accordingly, though I first embellished my Farm, with an Eye to the Satisfaction I should receive from its Beauty, I am now grown dependent upon the Friends it brings me, for the principal Enjoyment it affords; I am pleased to find them pleased, and enjoy its Beauties by Reflection. And thus the durable Part of my Pleasure appears to be, at the last, of the social Kind.

With much Willingness would I have waited upon your Friend Colonel C—— this Year, but for the perplexing Law-Suit in which I am involved with young D[olman]. It has made me rude to my Superiors, deaf to all inviting Offers, and neglectful, at once, to my old Friends and my new. Pray make my Compliments to him, and assure him how sensible I am of the Honour he has done me. Another Year, if I live, will, I hope, make me some Amends for this, by affording me an Opportunity of waiting upon him and you.

Pray also make my Compliments to Mr. and Mrs. P——, and Dr. C——, and my Peace with the A[ccleto?]n Family, or any other where you visit, that may mistake Necessity for Disrespect. Above all, recommend me to Mrs. B[innel?] in the best Manner you are able, which, I take it, is by assuring her, that I ever have been, and am, and will be while I live,

Dear Mr. B[innel?]
your affectionate Friend,
W. SHENSTONE.

CXCIII

Colvile, Worthies of Warwickshire, 488.

[*To the* REV. W. HOLYOAK.]

THE LEASOWES, April 21, 1756.

Dear Sir,

It is not easy for me to express how much I think myself obliged to you for the particulars with which you favour'd me on this mournfull occasion. I receiv'd only a few lines from M^r [sic] Davies and Mr Outing, excusing themselves on account of their melancholy situation, that on the loss of so intimate a Friend as Lady Luxborough, one is anxious to become acquainted with every little circumstance that attended it. For this I am indebted to you, Sir, and Mrs Holyoake: so indeed is every one indebted who wish'd well to Lady Luxborough. For I know of nothing that was so much a ballance for the variety of her affections, as the advantage of two such compassionate & ever hospitable Neighbours. To you she had recourse upon many a severe and pressing occasion, and had great reason to be convinc'd how much preferable your Friendship was to that of the more gay & more capricious world. Even on the last & most important occasion, your best offices were not wanting: and if we consider her advantage merely, I know not whether her best Friends ought to wish her Life prolong'd. Her enjoyments of Life must have diminish'd yet farther, and it is not very improbable that her mortifications would have encreas'd. In regard indeed to ourselves the case is much otherwise; and whatever may be now expended upon embellishments at Barrels, it can hardly ever be, the agreeable object from your House that it has been. I do therefore sincerely condole with you upon the loss of your accomplish'd neighbour, and the loss of all those chearfull ev'nings which we might have expected to pass in her company. But as pleasures of this kind are to be no more our lot at Barrels, let me beg leave to put Mrs Holyoake in mind of a promise she once made me; the acquittance for which will not be valid, unless deliver'd to her at the Leasowes. On the death of one's Friends, one ever finds a propensity to think on those that remain; let me therefore have ye comfort of considering your Family in that Light, and the pleasure of subscribing myself.

> Dear Sir,
> Your ever affectionate,
> and obliged, humble servant,
> WILL SHENSTONE.

CXCIV

Messrs. Maggs.

[*To* J. S. HYLTON.]

26 *May* 1756 [*in another hand*].

My Compliments to the Mr Hyltons. Positively I will not see Lapall on Friday, unless the Poles are painted; being

morally sure that Jo: Connop could paint them before breakfast, any Day; & being not a little *disgusted* with or perhaps
envying Mr Hylton's want of Taste. For surely where *Taste* is,
it is ever attended with *Impatience*—I am not mighty well
to-day, & entirely splenetick; but if Mr H. & his B^r will
favour me so far as to call here, will go with them to M^r
Lea's Pixell cannot come.

W. Shenstone.

What other knives I have are so remarkable y^t every Body
would know them.

To John Scott Hylton Esq;

CXCV

B.M. Add. MSS. 28959.

[*To* Mr. MILWARD.]

[*Back of Dodsley's letter, June* 1756.]

M^r M[ilward][1]
The Bearer M. Rice has a number of Children, & One
whom I would recommend to Ld Foleys Hospital[2]—I believe
him to be a proper object of this Charity no way disqualify'd,
& should be glad if he could be sent as one for the Choice of
the [illegible word]. If you or Mr Cox can be of any service in
y^s affair, I should be at all times ready to acknowledge my
share of ye Obligation

I am your faith.
hum. Ser.
W. S.

NOTES

[1]Of Welsh House and Tennall Hall, Harborne.
[2]At Old Swinford.

CXCVI

Works III, 299.

To the [Rev. R. GRAVES], *with a Recommendation of Mr. Dodsley to his Acquaintance.*

From Mr. Baskerville's,
Birmingham, *July* 27,
1756.

Dear Mr. Graves,

It were needless for me to recommend to you a person whom you so truly esteem as Mr. Dodsley; and from whom you will gladly receive a visit, not more upon *my* account, than upon *his* and your *own*.—All I beg is, that, considering the shortness of his time at Bath, you will be acquainted with him at first sight; which, I think, should ever be a maxim with persons of genius and humanity.—He has made a few days extremely agreeable to me at The Leasowes; has been shewing me his new Tragedy,[1] which I wished you also might peruse. If I be not unaccountably imposed upon by my friendship for the writer, the extraordinary merit of this performance is altogether unquestionable.—I will not inform you through what hands it has passed in town; because I would have you communicate your sentiments to him with entire freedom, being assured the delicacy of them may *yet* be of service, and that the openness with which you communicate them will be infinitely pleasing to Mr. Dodsley. He has done me the honour to ask me for an epilogue;:—I *wish*, but *fear* to undertake it.—Should any lucky hint occur to *you*, I well know how much you are able to manage it to advantage. In that case, I would beg a line from you the first opportunity.—What talk I of a line from you, who am, at this very time, many letters and apologies in your debt? but I cannot add many syllables to the letter I am writing.—I will write again in a few days. Mean time, my compliments to Mrs. Graves; and remember, that Mr. Dodsley and you become well acquainted at first sight.

I am ever, dear Mr. Graves,

Your most affectionate humble servant,

W. SHENSTONE.

NOTE

[1] *Cleone.*

CXCVII

Hull, I, 236.

To Mr. S[AUNDERS].[1]

THE LEASOWES, *Aug.* 24, 1756.

Dear S[aunders]

I am truly glad to hear of your Reception with our worthy Admiral,[2] to whom I will take the first Occasion of conveying my Acknowledgments. It is not quite clear from your Letter, whether you are Mate or Midshipman; but whatever your Post may be, I hope, and make no Doubt, that you will endeavour to fill it as becomes you. Should you happen to be continued in the Admiral's own Ship, you will have the Honour to serve more immediately under the most generous Man alive; whose Penetration will not suffer any Degree of Merit to escape his Notice, and who will allow yours the more Consideration, on Account of his Regard for me. As the best Means, therefore, of promoting your Interest, you will need to concern yourself little further, than to deserve well; and this by an uniform Course of Diligence and Sobriety, by the strictest Attention to Honour and your Duty, and by a Conduct entirely free from all Artifice and Disguise. You have an honest, open Countenance; I do not in the least question that you will verify it in your Behaviour; neither do I drop *any* of these Hints, as though I mistrusted your Conduct; I do unfeignedly believe them to be every one superfluous: however, it may prove a Satisfaction for you to reflect, that the Temper, which I trust is natural to you, is what I think most likely to recommend you to the Admiral. And be assured, that you shall acquire no Reputation in the Service, which shall not be seconded by all the Interest and good Offices of your affectionate Kinsman,

W. SHENSTONE.

NOTES

[1]Tom Saunders, Shenstone's cousin.
[2]Admiral Thomas Smith, who was interested in Tom Saunders.

CXCVIII

Messrs. Maggs.

[*To* J. S. HYLTON.]

26 *Aug*st 1756 [*in another hand*].

My Compliments with abundance of Thanks to Mr. H. for the Beauties he has added to my Picture. I like it well in general; but cannot absolutely forego my Opinion that he *contrastes* ye colours of the stone more y^n is necessary; that he uses *some* that are much too glaring; that there is too much of a greenish cast? in ye Pantheon, of purple elsewhere. These are all ye Faults y^t occurr to me at present. But I am destitute of leisure to enumerate ye Beauties of his work, or the Thanks of his oblig'd & affect^{te} h.s.

W. SHENSTONE.

Some-time when I come to Lapall we will pitch upon a stone-colour. Mr Perry dines here—my head aches most intolerably.

To John Scott Hylton, Esq;

CXCIX

Messrs. Maggs.

[*To* J. S. HYLTON.]

My Compliments to Mr Hylton; and if the Dullness of the Day can reconcile Him to a dull Companion, should be glad that he would pass it with *me*, of all men living: For true it is, that I have no better Pretensions to *Illumination*, this Day, than the sucking-Pig which I mean to roast for his Dinner. If Mr Hylton come, I would get him to bring with him enough Elixir of Vitriol to medicate three or four Gallons from my Spa.

WILL SHENSTONE.

Sept. 26 [*& in another hand*]
    Sunday Morn: 1756.

CC

[*To* J. S. HYLTON.]

*Saturday 6th Novem*ʳ 1756.
[*in another hand.*]

My Compliments to Mʳ Hylton. Indeed I do *not* purpose to
see the Grange this afternoon; being not extremely well, &
(if I were to go from Home at *all*) being more *inclin'd* to go to
Lapall. Yet on this must Mʳ Hylton not depend, so as to drop
any excursion which he purposes to make after Dinner. All
imaginable thanks are return'd for yᵉ Pictures Mʳ H. has taken
yᵉ Pains to colour; & he will be entitled to a repetition of the
same, whenever his Conveniency shall enable him to compleat
yᵉ rest. I am sorry to keep Mʳ Hylton so long out of yᵉ Wine
I borrow'd of him; but if he be at Fault & will procure some
from Beete's I will immediately reimburse him. Tom is gone
to Woolescott upon Tenant's Business.

WILL SHENSTONE.

To John Scott Hylton, Esq.

CCI

[*To* J. S. HYLTON.]

My Compliments to Mʳ Hylton—whom I could wish to
call *here*, as he goes to Hales in the Morning—this I look upon
as yᵉ *shortest* method of concluding treaties for yᵉ Afternoon—
Mʳ P(erry) [written in another hand] is no bad Companion;
but does perhaps in some *degree* deserve yᵉ Character Mʳ H.
gives Him. All I am apprehensive of at *Present*, is, yᵗ he should
borrow a few Pieces of Mʳ Dodsley. The two noble Lords, it is
very evident, will never come to any Rupture—Both Lords &
Commons in Halesowen, The Natives of High-street & of Rum-
bo, must yield Obedience to *One* only—All we have to wish, is,
yᵗ the *one* to wᶜʰ I allude may be directed by a worthy Ministry.

And who more worthy than the Durants—? According to the *express Words* of Jo: Powell '*There is not a damn'der worthier Fellow living in all the World than Jack Durant.*'

The *Grange-Ministry* (to wit Baker, Mrs Rock & Coley) are, I hear, in high Spirits upon excluding me from Mrs Garlands Charity—What would they say, if I should get a Letter from Lord Lyttelton in my Behalf?

I know not what *sort* of Firs I am to expect from his Ldships Gardiner; but I *do* remember something yt he spoke to me of *Pinasters*—*This* I know, that I *can* have nothing equal to Six Icthyodontes Scutillati.

Jenny's Purge is well-tim'd and will I guess remove her Disorder. Those Verses wch Mr Hylton mentions, *can* be no other yn what he says—Shaw's Practice of Physick was here[1]— as I remember, a year or two ago—but it was borrow'd by Jo: Gaunt; & it is at least a year, since I saw ye Face of it. I am to-night tolerably well; but my Spirits too much owing to a few glasses extraordinary—Mr. Hylton's Health, & Bon repos—

WILL SHENSTONE.

Decr 11, 1756.

To John Scott Hylton, Esq;

NOTE

[1]Peter Shaw (1694–1763) wrote *A New Practice of Physic*, 1726, which reached a seventh edition in 1753.

CCII

Works III, 292.

To the [REV. R. JAGO].

THE LEASOWES,
Dec. 14, 1756.

Dear Mr. Jago,

Though the silence that has prevailed for so long a time betwixt us be, I fear, to be placed to *my* account, yet do I by no means imagine, that you will desire me to fill half this letter with apologies. Suffice it, that I owe all the world, at this time, either letters, visits, or money: yet that my *heart* is as well disposed in each of these respects, as that of any one person who is insolvent. The regard indeed that I owe to you has been a troublesome inmate within my bosom for some time past; making daily remonstrances against the injustice which I have done it; and urging me strenuously to take horse, and make my *personal* apologies at Harbury.—I return you many thanks for Mr. S——'s company, and for the sight of the manuscript which he shewed me. Alas! that I cannot spare money to drain and to improve my lands, or to put almost any part of his excellent rules in execution! and yet that Mr. Childe of Kinlett[1] (hearing my place always termed a *farm*) should come expecting to find all things managed here according to the perfection of *husbandry*! As little *can* I pretend to improve Mr. S——'s treatise, as his treatise *will* my farm: no farther at *most*, than in what regards the *stile*, or *plan* of his performance. Yet could I wish to see both *it* and *him* again before he prints it; wishing him all the success which his very *endeavour* deserves. Assuredly the present is not the *time* for his publication: more *immediate* remedies than can be derived from agriculture are become absolutely requisite to relieve the sufferings of this nation.—I should be extremely well-pleased to visit you at Harbury, but cannot even propose to myself that happiness at *present*; and were I even to *promise*, have but too much reason to know the *uncertainty* of my *performance*. Yet am I sensible enough we *ought to meet*, if we purpose that what we print should have the advantage of our mutual criticisms. Let me then *conjure* you to come over, at your convenience, for a few days, that we may agree at least upon some *general* points, and make no worse a figure in the future Miscellany, than we have done in the foregoing.[2]—But I have really more things to *say* than I will pretend to *scrawl* upon *paper;* nor can I endure to retail a few particulars, while I am impatient to communicate the whole.

Let me acquaint you while I remember, that there is at this time a Mr. Duncombe and his son, clergymen, that are publishing a new translation of Horace.[3] Whatever you may think of their *success*, after *Francis*, I believe I may pronounce them men of real merit, and in no wise destitute of learning or genius. They have requested me to communicate any *version* or *imitation* that I can furnish, either of my own or of any friends; wherefore, if you *have* any thing of this sort, I should be glad if you would put it in my power to oblige them. The son has an 'Ode to Health' in the fourth volume of Dodsley's Miscellany.[4]

Under the head of intelligence, I have mighty little to convey.—The house at Hagley is, in a manner, finished, so far as concerns the shell; and wants nothing besides a portico to be as compleat as most in England.—Pray remember me to Mr. Talbot,[5] Mr. Miller, and Mr. Holbeach;[6] should they call upon me next year, they will find my place better worth their notice.

I am, and *have* been ever, cordially and most affectionately,

Your most obedient servant,

W. SHENSTONE.

NOTES

[1]In Shropshire.

[2]*Works* III, 293, has the note: '*See the Edinburgh Review, No. 1.' The Bodleian Library contains, in W.S.'s hand, a long extract from the above-mentioned copy of *The Edinburgh Review*—'Pagina nostri memor vide The Edinburgh Review, No. 1, 1755. ('Dodsley, IVth Volume, p. 58)'—and a passage from *The Monthly Review*, May 17th. Both criticisms are laudatory.

[3]William Duncombe (1690–1769), was partially responsible for *The Works of Horace in English Verse*, 1757.

[4]Dodsley's *Collection*, IV, 268, *Ode to Health*, by Mr. Duncombe, Fellow of Corpus Christi College, Cambridge. John Duncombe (1729–1786).

[5]John Ivory Talbot of Lacock Abbey, Wilts. Sanderson Miller assisted in the work of fitting up Lacock Abbey in the Gothic taste. Dickins and Stanton, *An Eighteenth Century Correspondence*, XIX.

[6]Jago, *Edge-Hill*, Book I, celebrates Farnborough, the seat of William Holbech.

> 'Where the tall pillar lifts its taper head,
> Her spacious terrace, and surrounding lawns,
> Deck'd with no sparing cost of planted tufts,
> Or ornamented building, Farnborough boasts.'

CCIII

Messrs. Maggs.

[*To* J. S. HYLTON.]

My Compliments to Mr. Hylton—whom I had Thoughts of seeing to-day at Lapall—but not being very well, and having

received Mrs. Southwell, I must defer it sometime longer.
To-morrow, as I said before, Mr. Hollier dines here; & very
glad should I be were our Meeting upon the score of *Pleasure*.
I shou'd then have no more to do than to sollicit Mr. Hylton's
Company—but Necessity requires that it should be turn'd to
other account—Perhaps it may *import* Mr. Hylton to know y^t
Dr. Watt was expected to dine at the Grange to-day, & to
stay there all night; being sent for on account of ye Inflamma-
tion in my Lord's Leg—I was going to ask Mr. Hylton's
Company at tea this afternoon, but thought it too late—
However if Mr. Hylton go to the Grange, & will call here, I
shall be glad—I have receiv'd my Franks—

Adieu.

WILL: SHENSTONE.

Mrs. Southwell's Compliments.

Jan: 18, 1757.

CCIV

Works III, 301.

To the [Rev. R. GRAVES] *on Mr. Dodsley and his Works.*

THE LEASOWES,

Mar. 7, 1757.

Dear Mr. Graves,

I have passed a very dull and unamusive winter here—the
worse, for being neither *disposed* nor *qualified* to keep up a
correspondence with my friends: with *you*, among the *chief;* and
yet, it is upon you that I must depend to make up my defici-
ences with Mr. Dodsley.—The poor man has been afflicted with
the most *lasting* fit of the gout he ever underwent before.—
His patience, on these occasions, is inimitable.—His excursion
to the *Regions of Terror and Pity*[1] is not the only instance of his
ability to compose verses in the midst of pain. When he sent
me a copy of it, he let me know, that he had transmitted another
to you by the same post. I should be glad to receive your remarks upon it, ere I communicate my own. I have, for some
weeks past, found my head so terribly confused, that it has been

with difficulty I could *think* or *express* myself on the most superficial topic. I hope, in a little time, to be able to examine it more attentively than I can at present: yet, in the mean while, must acknowledge, that I think his subject capable of furnishing extraordinary beauties for an Ode: and *such*, I think, he should *call* it; dropping the narrative parts, and the connexions as much as possible. I cannot wish him to print it without very *material* alterations; and what would occasion almost the same trouble as it would require to *new-write* it. I do not mean this as a condemnation of what he has already done; so much, as a proof of my opinion how much he will be able to improve it. *After all*, it will scarce affect me half so much as his Tragedy. He is so *honest* a man, that the work he has to give the world is much better than the specimen: or, to borrow an idea from my *situation*, the grain that he has to deliver will prove much better than the sample. It is with shame I acknowledge I have not yet sent him his epilogue; and I feel the greater compunction of mind upon this score, as it is possible he may impute my neglect to Garrick's refusal of his play.[2] This weighs nothing with you or me; a thousand motives may affect a manager that have little or nothing to do with the merit of the performance; yet he may so far thank Mr. Garrick, that whatever his refusal takes from the *reputation* of his Tragedy, it will, through Dodsley's industry, add apparently to its value. I have not yet been able to satisfy myself with every part of your epilogue, and must either omit sending it at present, or must send him an imperfect copy. If you write to him, let me beg you to give the most favourable account you *can* of me.

Somebody acquainted me (I think it was Mr. Talbot), that your old friend Ballard[3] had bequeathed you his coins for a legacy. I was truly glad to hear it; but have wondered since, that you never once informed me of so considerable an acquisition.

I remember a poem of yours, called [*To Morgan Graves, Esq?*], upon the present taste in gardening; which you will not wonder if my late employments make me wish once more to see. Be so kind as to send me a copy of this, as well as of any other little pieces that you have in your bureau. Some of yours deserve a better place than what is assigned them in the Magazine. In particular, I remember that upon Enigmas, and Mopsy. Be assured, I will make no *use* of *any* without your previous consent. You know, I suppose, that Dodsley's other Miscellanies do not appear before next winter.[4] I received from him, together with his Ode, a few Elegies published by Mr. Whitehead.[5] They are, I think, worth your perusal; and designed by my worthy friend to excite my emulation.—Alas! that I am so ill able to deserve the encouragements which I receive from him!

My neighbour Baskerville, at the close of this month, publishes his fine edition of Virgil.[6] It will, for *type* and *paper*, be a perfect curiosity. He follows the Cambridge edition.

What think you of their management in regard to Mr. Byng?[7] I cannot help thinking the King should *pardon* him. The Court-martial, by acquitting him of cowardice or disaffection, have left no *motive* for his *negligence*, beside an *error of his judgement*: for we *cannot* impute it to *supineness, indifference*, or *inattention*. And then to sentence a man for error, is to expect infallibility. That twelfth article of war is most undoubtedly ill-expressed.—Pray do not forget my best respects to Mrs. Graves.—Let me hear from you soon, and believe me ever   Yours,

W. SHENSTONE.

NOTES

[1]*Melpomene, or The Regions of Terror and Pity*, was issued anonymously by Dodsley, in November 1757, and it met with immediate success from the critics.

[2]See R. Straus, *Robert Dodsley*.

This refusal of Cleone was one of Garrick's notable mistakes. He also refused Home's *Douglas*.

[3]George Ballard (1706–1755), a Gloucestershire antiquary of repute. Thomas Hearne, a great friend of Graves's father, describes in his *Diary* a visit paid to Ballard, March 2, 1727, and calls him 'an ingenious, curious young man, who hath picked up an abundance of old coins, some of which he showed me.' Later Ballard frequently visited Hearne at Oxford and told him many of the details about the Graves family which find mention in the *Diary*.

[4]Vols. V, and VI appeared March, 1758.

[5]William Whitehead's *Elegies—with an Ode to the Tiber*, I.s, were published by Dodsley on February 4. Straus, *op. cit*, 361.

[6]See Straus and Dent, *John Baskerville* (Bibliography), p. 67.

[7]Admiral John Byng was court-martialled and sentenced to death for his failure off Port Mahon. Wyndham: *op. cit*., ch. XII.

CCV

[*To* J. S. HYLTON.]

My Compliments to Mr Hylton, & to M^r & Mrs Smith—
I arriv'd at home very safe, & my Cold to-night is somewhat
better y^n it was last night—I have sent ye News, wch for y^e
use of my Servants, I should be glad to have return'd, to-
morrow. The Conduct of Bing's C.M. is now to me incomprehensible, & ye Burlesque upon their address is not without
it's humour or Poignancy. Mr Amos Green[1] call'd here this
Morning together with a very well-bred & ingenious Man,
one Mr Gwyn from London. He mention'd him as a famous
Architect, & as Person who has given us an admirable Draught
of ye Section of St. Pauls.[2] He told me a good deal concerning
ye Contest about Mr Bing. That Mr Pitt has been so much his
advocate, as to have prejudic'd his own Popularity with y^e
Citizens of London. That he was severely reprimanded by y^e
Speaker, for bringing a Message from ye King relating to
Bing's Reprieve; *before* the House had given ye King any
formal acc^t of ye motion made in it. Commodore Keppel,[3]
it seems, was ye Person y^t mov'd to be absolv'd from his Oath
of Secrecy. He says moreover y^t Admiral West wrote a Letter
to Ld Temple wch was deliver'd to him at ye Admirals.[4] The
purport was, y^t if Adm^l Bing suffer'd upon ye 12th Article of
War, He & his Brother Officers w^d seem to go to Sea with a
Halter about their Necks—that ye Article therefore ought to
be repealed &c &c. Ld Temple was he says so far from laying
Stress upon his Cousin's Letter, y^t he oblig'd him to write a
Recantation, or threaten'd to try him for Contempt—The Duke
of Devonshire[5] is Mr Bing's Advocate, also the Townshends
& many others. So Mr Hylton may see my Sentiments are not
unsupported by some of ye Prime Geniuses in ye Kingdom. It
was said likewise y^t if Bing suffers (as he *doubtless* will) *his*
Friends will all *unite* in ye prosecution of Ld Anson. Mr Green
&c left me about dinner-time, to whom I gave an Invitation
to take a bit of dinner here another Day. Gwyn is really an
agreeable Man—& I wish'd for more of his Company—M^r
Green goes next week to London—And so much for this Party.

I am glad enough to hear y^t Mr Soley has oblig'd Mr Hylton—& shewn this act of mercy to ye wretched Victims of ye Spiritual Court.

Tom is gone to Harborough upon ye affair of Letting a Farm—If ye Comet would *only* vitrify or purverize *Law-Suits*, it's approach towards us would be as well-come as ye arrival of May-day. Had I know ye weather w^d prove so bad, Tom s^d have defer'd his Journey at all adventures. Tis now intolerable. When Robin came, I lay upon ye bed—&, since I came down stairs, I have doubled my Diligence y^t I might not detain him too long, & yet furnish out some Intelligence. I have now no more to say—but in Order to piece-out my Packet, have sent a new Edition of Perry's Verses—in which (if Mr H. please to Compare it wth ye first) he will find I have been taking very unaccountable Freedoms—I hope to atcheive a Letter for Mr Dodsley to morrow, wch together wth Mr Graves's may produce a Message to Birmingham—I think I have no more to add. Adieu.

W. SHENSTONE.

March ye 8th 1757.

Admiral Norris[6]
Commodore Keppel
Captn Moore[7] ye 3 Dissentients.

NOTES

[1] Amos Green (1735–1807), was a native of Halesowen, and was employed by Matthew Boulton to paint boxes, etc. He came under the notice of W.S. who, according to the *Memoir of Amos Green, Esq., written by his late Widow*, 'cultivated his acquaintance and often had him at The Leasowes. . . . His intercourse with Shenstone afforded him great pleasure: he said he was singularly agreeable, when in spirits: but he was full of foibles and faults, and their friendship was not lasting.'

[2] John Gwyn, d. 1786, friend of Dr. Johnson, exhibited 'A section of S. Paul's,' an architectural drawing, at the Society of Artists in 1764.

[3] Hon. Augustus Keppel, one of the members of the court–martial.

[4] Admiral Smith was President.

[5] William, 4th Duke of Devonshire.

[6] Henry Norris, Rear–Admiral of the White.

[7] John Moore.

CCVI

Works III, 305.

[*To* Rev. R. GRAVES.]

The Leasowes,

April 8, 1757.

Dear Mr. Graves,

What remarks I had to make upon our friend Dodsley's Ode, I sent him the last post. I would gladly have occasioned them to pass by Claverton; but, having delayed them so long, I was impatient to convince him that I had not *wholly* disregarded his request. They are indeed pretty copious: and yet I have reserved to myself the privilege of re-criticising when I see his altered copy. I recommended to him the addition which you proposed, and some others; and if he will but take the pains that I have chalked out for him, I doubt not that he will render it an excellent Ode, though he may not find it a very *popular* one. I have also sent him a copy of our epilogue, not much different from what you saw;[1] to these I added my little Ode on Lady Luxborough's furnishing her library, and Perry's Verses upon the Malvern-waters.[2] At the close of these last, there appears (with Perry's approbation), a short address to Dr. Wall of Worcester; a very eminent physician, and the great patron of this mineral, who has promoted a subscription in the county towards *building*, near this well, for the accommodation of strangers.[3]

I purpose also to give Dodsley the little Ode I inclose; and would beg the favour of you to advise me concerning the additional stanzas, to fix the readings in the rest, and to return me the copy.

I come now to analyze your remark on Ballard's legacy; which is indeed very ingenious, but will scarce bear examination: nor do I think that you rather wish to have *found* that set of medals, than to have them *given* you by a deceased friend. Assuredly, if we do not allow pleasure to be *predominant* in this kind of melancholy, we destroy the foundation of all tragic or elegiac writings. Melpomene has no place amongst the Muses; and the pains that we have taken with our friend Dodsley's pensive Ode have been employed to no purpose. But you want not these pedantic flourishes, and are wholly of my mind.

Martin's Magazine is, I believe, pretty obscure; and I wonder where you got a sight of it. It was, however, fortunate enough for *me* that you gave no copy of 'James Dawson.' I never yet saw your verses, *on that Grotto*,[4] or from *Phædrus*,[5] and I want to see your W———once more, concerning which you are silent. Your 'Pepper-box' and 'Mopsy' might, I think, appear in Dodsley's Miscellany,[6] either *with* or *without* your name. I also want a copy of your verses upon Riddles;[7] and whenever you have a leisure hour, should be glad if you would look them out and send them.

Go, and think yourself an happy man; at least, if your children be recovered, as I am inclined to think they are; and give my service to Mrs. Graves, for the happiness that she occasions you; of which I cannot but partake, being, with constant and sincere affection, your most obliged humble servant,

W. SHENSTONE.

NOTES

[1]The epilogue to Dodsley's *Cleone* was finally published under W.S.'s name. *Works* I, 239.
    The story of the writing of the epilogue is told by Straus, *Robert Dodsley*, X. Dodsley wrote to W.S., 1756, 'I could have wish'd for your Name, as it is better known, and would have done me more Honour.'
[2]Dodsley's *Collection*, V, 84.
[3]   'Ev'n I at these fair fountains eas'd of pain,
            To you, my friend, address one votive strain:
            To you the Naiad of this balmy well
            Reveals the wonders of her secret cell:
            To you transfers the lay, whose active mind,
            Like her own stream from earthly dregs refin'd,
            Explores a panacea for mankind.'

[4]Dodsley's *Collection*, V, 62. *To Lady Fane on her Grotto at Basildon*.
[5]These were not included in the *Collection*. *Euphrosyne*, pp. 149–152 contains various fables from Phædrus.
[6]*Collection*, V, 63.
    Mopsy did not appear in the *Collection*.
[7]*Collection*, V, 57 and 58 contains verses on riddles supplied by W.S.

CCVII

Carnegie Book Shop, New York.

[*To* J. S. HYLTON.]

I desire my Compliments to Mr. Hylton, & that he wou'd send me a Purge—I think, of Manna & Crem: of tartar.

Yesterday I had Mr. James Pixell, and after him, Capt. Wight, who kept me up 'till about eleven—However in ye afternoon I sent to enquire after Ld Dudley's health, & whether they expected Dr. Wall to make a *second* visit at the Grange. The latter I did, at Mrs. Fieldhouse's request, but it seems they do not expect him, unless they send a purpose message.

My L^d's Disorder was an apoplexy, which makes me think his Indisposition was *once before* of ye same sort—Could Mr. Hylton contrive, or could I help him to contrive a second visit from ye Doctor—for ye general Advantage, for unless Mr. Hylton find himself better to-morrow, I woud wish *him* to take advice, as well as Mrs. Fieldhouse.

Com omnia sint in incerto, fare Tibis.

WILL: SHENSTONE.

21 *May* 1757.

I have been greatly feverish and out of order, all to-day; Mr. Barker found me very unfit to receive him, but I gave him an Invitation to see the Leasowes at a better time. Since they went, I had James and Evers; on ye Subject of ye Captain's building; and then betwixt one thing and another my spirits have been wholly dissipated—Adieu.

CCVIII

B.M. Add. MSS. 27548.

[*To* JOHN SCOTT HYLTON.]

Augs^t 18^t 1757.

Our Compliments to Mr. Hylton—We are inclin'd to think y^e *Time* He should pitch upon for his Eclogue[1]—should be y^t of Montezuma's Death or then-abouts. That the speakers should deplore the revolution in their affairs & alternately, recollect ye prodigies &c: preceding ye appearance of ye Spaniards; should describe the Light in wch their artillery Shipping &c appeared to them &c &c: and that in ye course of the Dialogue should be interspers'd *continual* allusions to ye particularities of their Country; whether in regard to Dress-Fruits, Diet, Customs &c &c: In short Mr. H. is to remember y^t the Beauty of his Eclogue must turn upon American Peculiarities.

W.S.

Mr. Hylton.

NOTE

[1]Dodsley was staying with W.S. for his usual summer visit, and was engaged in revising *Cleone*. He was also collecting material for a further volume of his Miscellany. In a letter written October 29, 1757, Dodsley says, 'Where is Mr. Hylton's Indian Eclogue? Is he gone thither to learn their manners? If not, pray give my Compliments to him, and bid him make haste or he will come too late.' Apparently Hylton's poem did come too late for no Indian Eclogue is found in Vols. V. or VI of the *Collection*, which appeared March 1758. Vol. VI, 280, *True Resignation*, is the work of Hylton. See also IV, 305–6.

CCIX

Messrs. Maggs.

[*To* J. S. HYLTON.]

18th *October*, 1757.

My Compliments to Mr Hylton, to whom I have sent a Taste of ye true *Faternian* grape: So *very* genuine, y^t I am in doubt whether he should preserve ye whole of it amongst his Fossils, or drink a glass of it after his supper. But I know y^t if he drink it, he will neither forget my Health, or Mr Davenport's; & y^t he *deserves* y^e *Liberty* if he likes y^e *wine*, of drinking ye whole Pint this Evening—If Mr H. have heard aught of Mr A. Green's success, he will inform me by ye Bearer. I think ye wine a very rich One.

WILL: SHENSTONE.

To John Scott Hylton, Esq;

CCX

Messrs. Maggs.

[*To* J. S. HYLTON.]

All-saints' Day, 1757.

My Compliments to Mr Hylton—to whom I return his Brother's Letter—and truly sorry I am for aught that affords him vexation; at ye same time y^t I must acknowledge, *I* could neither communicate my Griefs to Friends, nor hear them mention'd to me, in ye manner he does, & *has* done. 'Tis perhaps a Foible in my Character, & an excellence in His; but every one has his *own*, & ye Parts of each are connected.

I have little or no Objection to Mr Smith's Proposal, but that Mr Karver is my Acquaintance, & I should rather, I think, have a stranger for my Creditor—However I have written to Mr Smith on ye Occasion, & requested his assistance so far as to go to old Parks & assure him of ye Payment. Should it so happen, y^t some other Person's money should be prefer'd at last, I trust Mr Smith would not take it ill, & I woud endeavour to make Him Amends upon some future Occasion—but I will determine in a Day's time.

WILL. SHENSTONE.

I have been not a little out of Order ever since I came Home; but hope, by proper regimen, to recover my Health & Spirits.

To John Scott Hylton, Esq;

CCXI

Messrs. Maggs.

[*To* J. S. HYLTON.]

My Compliments to Mr Hylton—with my Thanks for his transcript of poor Whistler's verses.[1] They want a few alterations (wch however will cost some pains) & *then* would be not unproper to insert in Dodsley's miscellany. I thought to have sent a sheet to Birm^m this Evening; but have not, cannot do so 'till to-morrow. Mr H. may transcribe ye verses, & read ye Letters at any time—I found upon reading ye rest as I lay in

Bed, a Copy of those on riddles wch were printed in ye Magazine—They may amuse Mr H. for a minute. I strol'd down to Hales-bridge this Morning—no great Part of wch is fallen in; & ye accident seems chiefly oweing either to y^e *Fright*, or *Spirit* of ye Horses.

The King of Prussia's victory[2] consists of 4000 killed, 4000 wounded, 3000 Prisoners, 60 Pieces of Cannon taken, with all ye Baggage &c: eleven general officers; & many other advantages. Sr John Mordaunt's case seems desperate[3]— Somebody will, unquestionably, go from the Leasowes to Birm^m tomorrow. I am really *far* from well, & instead of seeing Mr Perry, have only received a Letter wch gives me no sort of satisfaction. I am afraid that Mr Dovey[4] will discover more of ye attorney yⁿ y^e *Gentleman*—(But this betwixt you and me). I would send you Perry's Letter, but must write some answer to it by his Messenger. How few are there in ye world who will not take some advantage of their own *occasional* Importance!—Adieu.

WILL. SHENSTONE.

Novr 21, 1757.
To John Scott Hylton, Esq;

NOTES

[1]Whistler's verses in Dodsley's *Collection*.

[2]The November number of *The Gentleman's Magazine* contains *The London Gazette* account of 'the glorious victory which the King of Prussia gained over his enemies on the 5th of this month in Thuringia.'

[3]General Mordaunt, an old man, was, by the insistance of the King, put in command of ten battalions, and with Hawke made a raid on the coast of France. Little was achieved and the nation was nearly as angry with Mordaunt as with Byng, and a court-martial was demanded. This and other raids awed Europe, as Pitt hoped they would.

[4]Possibly Rupert Dovey of the Hagley letters. (Wyndham, *op. cit.*)

CCXII

Messrs. Maggs.

[*To* J. S. HYLTON.]

Novr 29, 1757 (*or* 9).[1]

Arbusta humilesque myricae, are Mr Hylton's proper Object— . . . Laurustinus is ye most desireable, on account of the Figure it makes in Winter. The Laurel mention'd by young Mr Wren, If I comprehend it right, is extremely pretty —I am in No Haste about ye return of the Poem—It is possible I may send a Packet to Birming: this afternoon. I am daily making ineffectual efforts to further M^r D's Publication —but alas! at ye times I do not *love* Poetry, I *hate* it—almost as bad as business. I shall be likewise distress'd for Franks. I am often wishing for my Friends to come help me in ye correc- tion of my Poetry; but I know by experience, y^t *when* they arrive I rather chuse to converse with them y^n employ them. The Floods (inter nos) have brought me 4 Fine trouts, & lodg'd them on my *walk*. It is not at all improbable, that They have given more of mine to other People. Adieu.

W.S.

To John Scott Hylton Esq:

NOTE

[1]The date is probably 1757, when W.S. was employed in 'furthering' Dodsley's *Miscellany*.

CCXIII

Works III, 307.

[*To* Rev. R. GRAVES] *on* [*Mr. Dodsley and his Works*].

About 1757.

Dear Mr. Graves,

Do you know my hand-writing?—It is really such a length of time since you had demands upon me for letters, that I am hardly able to enumerate the several causes of my neglect. *This* I know, that scarce a day has passed, during this interval of silence, in which I have not *remembered* you with the most affectionate esteem.—I *hope* you correspond with our friend Dodsley; and that it is not altogether disagreeable to you, to find he is printing some of your verses. He has many, alas! *too* many, of mine; which I suffered him to take away in sum- mer, and which the state of my winter health and spirits renders me but ill able to revise. I believe, I am, even now, the principal cause that his two volumes remain yet unpublished; nor can I express the pain it gives me, to be thus detrimental to his interests; and to delay the publication of so much better pieces than my own. I am also dissatisfied upon *another score:* I mean, that I have been wanting to myself, in not asking the benefit of your advice; which I have heretofore experienced to be at once so *comfortable* and *so advantageous;* but although the scheme was projected in summer, the business of correction was (by *me* at least) deferred till winter, and then I had neither spirits to *correct* or to *correspond.*

I am really as much obliged to you for the pains which you took on my behalf in London, as though the *subject* of your enquiry were a thing of more *importance* to me; but, indeed, you can hardly conceive how indifferent I am now grown, not only as to articles of *that sort*, but to aught that regards external splendour.

I really have not time to enter upon the merits of inoculation; but am very sure that Mrs. G[raves]'s danger was enough to influence your determination. I am heartily glad to hear of her recovery; and can but look upon the weeks which I purpose to pass some time hereafter with you at Claverton, as the most agreeable of any that belong to the remainder of my life. I am sensible, that if I *coveted* to *shine* in poetry, I should lose no time in visiting public places: but my wishes of that sort are most extremely limited, and I shall visit *you* on the account of *friendship;* that is (past all doubt), on a much *better principle.*

I have *long* meant to write to you, and have accordingly given *some* answer to most parts of your last letter. Nevertheless, the occasion of this present letter is quite of another kind. —A young painter of my acquaintance is advised to go to Bath;[1] has a recommendation to the Bishop of B[ath], who will introduce him to the Duke of N[ewcastle]. And though I cannot so easily bring him acquainted with nobles or prime-ministers, I can give him directions to my friend, who, in point of taste, is their superior. The person then, who, I suppose, will be the bearer of this letter, has, by dint of mere ingenuity, risen to a considerable eminence in fruit-pieces, &c. He has been employed by Lord Lyttelton, and is much admired at Oxford: for my own part, I believe you will think he is in few respects inferior to, and has (if I am not mistaken) some advantages of, Stranover;[2] but you will see his pieces. All I have to say further on the occasion is, that he is a native of our parish, and a particular friend of *mine;* and if it were in your power to promote his interest at Bath, you would not only highly gratify *me,* but at the same time do a service to one of the least assuming, most ingenious, and most amiable men I know.—I beg my best respects to your family, and am, dear Mr. Graves, most affectionately

Yours,

W. SHENSTONE.

NOTES

[1] Amos Green.

[2] Tobias Stranover (1684–1724?), bird and fruit painter, not mentioned in Walpole's *Anecdotes of Painting*.

CCXIV

B.M. Add. MSS. 28959.

[*To* R. DODSLEY.]

Tuesday, De^{cr} 21. 1757.

Dear Sir,

I receiv'd your Letter this morning to my no small Confusion—Yet blame I *no* one beside *myself;* or rather that Incapacity I feel for *Criticism* which alone can makes me wish, in any sort desire, to delay your publication. When I sent my last Packet, I purpos'd by ye next post to explain the uses for which it was intended—I have *not* done so—I have not been *able* to do so—& *now* am *surpriz'd* to find y^t another Sheet is gone to the Press—for According to ye construction I put upon y^r last Letter, I thought it might be not altogether too *late,* if I *regulated* ye whole by X^{tmas} I hope y^e *Elegy* is not yet begun in Sheet B; and even thus, if it were not inconvenient to stop ye press a little, I would rather it were done, y^n otherwise—Too many of my Pieces are entirely so   .   .
I think to write again, & have reserv'd my *only* Frank, for tomorrow, Mean time I give you my Thoughts in regard to

yᵉ Compositions *your Letter mentions*.[1] In yᵉ Ode to Health, I could propose no better word yⁿ *falling* instead of *mouldering*,[2] and if you happen to prefer yᵉ Latter, I will by no means disagree with you.

In regard to the Song 'I told my nymph' I desire yᵗ you would follow *all* yᵉ readings you propose. (The same, as to yᵉ Compliment 1743.) As to yᵉ Ode 1739. I am neither wholly satisfy'd with yʳ reading or my *own*. However; does not *Aid* in yᵉ first Line *run* better yⁿ Charms? Love's *imperial pow'r was known* is flat, & Love *here* is a *Person*, tho' a *Passion* in yᵉ 5th Line—But I leave you to *penetrate* my reasons, why I propose yᵉ following alterations, for yʳ *Choice*.

I.	II.
'Twas not by Beauty's aid alone	'Twas not thro' Beauty's aid alone,
That Love usurp'd his Fancy'd airy throne,	That Love's insidious pow'r was known
His fancy'd magic powr display'd	Or ever breast, betray'd
His tyrant sceptre sway'd	A mutual kindness, &c.[3]
Which &c.	

I think yᵉ *second* preferable; as '*insidious*' suits better with '*betrayd*' in yᵉ *next* Line, & not ill with 'was known' *in this*. The '*betrayd*' us'd in yᵉ next stanza may be exchangd for *reveal'd*, or some word of equal Import. I don't know *why* I prefer 'Lips at once and Eyes' &c. so very probably you are in yᵉ right—*Quick* Lightnings doesn't *run* so well as 'the Lightnings &c: but is is [sic] perhaps preferable on *another* score—As to the rest, please to follow your own readings in regard to this Ode—The Plate will require but very trifling alterations, if any and may be sent at a Minutes warning.

I have but a mean Opinion of two or three amongst yᵉ songs, and was thinking, (with this last ode, Lysander[4] & some few other Pieces in my Manuscript) yᵗ I could have supply'd their Place to advantage.

Do you remember yᵉ Verses on yᵉ Kid?[5]—but I will write again to-morrow, & speak more Explicitly on the Occasion.—

Do you think Mʳ H. Walpole wou'd oblige me wᵗʰ a Copy

of yᵉ Travels he has lately printed? (Hetznerus,[6] I think is yᵉ Name—) I do not mean any otherwise than thro' *your* Mediation.

You judge rightly of me in thinking how much it pains me to print precipitately—My *gratitude* suffers equally in subjecting you to Inconvenience. I am therefore truly under much anxiety—but wᵗʰ abundance of good-will, Dear Mʳ Dodsley,

Yʳˢ very affectionately
W. SHENSTONE.

Pray write.

To Mr. Dodsley,
at Tully's Head, in
Pell-Mall
London.

NOTES

[1] A long letter of December 18 with many suggestions, B.M. MSS. Add. 28959.
[2] Dodsley preserved 'mouldering.' *Collection*, V, p. 23, l. 17.
[3] The verse appeared finally (V. 34) thus:

> "Twas not by beauty's aid alone,
> That love usurp'd his airy throne,
> His boasted power display'd:
> 'Tis kindness that secures his aim,
> 'Tis hope that feeds the kindling flame,
> Which beauty first conveyed.'

[4] *Lysander to Cloe, Cloe to Lysander*, appeared Vol. VI, 213–15, but were not included in *Works*, 1764.
[5] Vol. V, 36.
[6] Horace Walpole set up his printing press at Strawberry Hill, in July 1757. The book mentioned, Hentzer—*Journey into England*—was printed at Strawberry, 1757.

CCXV

B.M. MSS. Add. 28221,
and Hecht, 6.

[*To* THOMAS PERCY.]

THE LEASOWES, *Jan.* 4*th* 1758.

Dear Sir,

The beginning of your Letter puzzled me; being conscious that, a few weeks before, I had sent your Elegy and Song to Mr. Dodsley,[1] *without* that regular examination which you desired me to bestow upon it; & which Nothing but a total want of Leisure could have caus'd me to decline. However, upon second Thoughts, I recollected that Mr Dodsley & myself had formerly taken some Pains, (and, I believe, some *Liberties* too), with the Pieces to which you alluded. Be this as it will, you are most evidently in ye right for not adopting *implicitly* what was done in your absence; nor can Mr. Dodsley or myself wish to debarr you of a Privilege, which, on a similar occasion, we should be so ready to demand *Ourselves*.

Upon ballancing the account of our Pamphletts and so forth, there appears due to you certain Portions of *Apology* & *Acknowledgement*, which if you are so good as to accept, I need say no more upon the subject. I like the *Sentiments* in general which run thro' Mr. Cambridge's Epistles,² but, as to the *species of writing*, think it not very material whether we import *that*, or the French Gawses.

I have enclos'd the Ballad of Gill Morrice for your Perusal: at the same time that I very much question whether *Child* Morrice be not the juster title. You pique my Curiosity extremely by the mention of that antient Manuscript;³ as there is nothing gives me greater Pleasure than the *simplicity* of *style* & *sentiment* that is observable in old English ballads. If aught could add to that Pleasure, it would be an opportunity of perusing them in your company at the Leasowes, & pray do not think of *publishing* them, until you have *given* me that opportunity—And what, if at the same time, I should recommend the example to you, of my Neighbour XXX [Hylton] who would esteem no one *Coin* or *Fossil* he possesses, of a Rush, if he knew the world, for the merest trifle, could obtain possession of a *duplicate*? But this you'll say is a kind of selfishness allowable only in a *Virtuoso*.—Suppose then you consider your M.S. as an hoard of gold, somewhat defac'd by Time; from which however you may be able to draw supplies upon occasion, and with which you may enrich ye world hereafter under more *current* Impressions.

Do you hear that Mr. Johnson's Shakespear will be published this Winter?⁴ I have a Prejudice (if *Prejudice* it may be call'd) in favour of all he undertakes; and wish ye world may recompence him for a Degree of Industry very seldom connected with so much real Genius. I am likewise impatient to see the new Tibullus—⁵ or *should* be so, had I finish'd the Proof-sheets which I detain from Mr. Dodsley.

I should be heartily glad if I could give you a better account of my *Punctuality* as a Correspondent; but your Candor, I trust, will make up yᵉ deficiency, as you will never find me wanting in the sincerity of my Esteem. I am

Sir,

Your most affectionate

humble Servt

WILL: SHENSTONE.

Let me beg yᵉ Favor of a Line
from you, when you are at Leisure.

To

The Revʳᵈ Mʳ Percy.

Gill Morice.

In place of yᵉ 14ᵗʰ stanza read yᵉ three following—

14

Gill Morice sate in gude grene wood,
He whistled & he sang:
O what mean A' the folk coming?
My Mother tarries lang.
His hair was like the threeds of gold
Shot frae yᵉ burning Sun;
His lips like roses drapping dew
When as his race (yᵉ Sun's) was run.*
His breath was a perfume.

¹I wish you wᵈ mend this Rhime. 'tis Pity &c.

15

His brow was like yᵉ mountain snae
Gilt by yᵉ morning beam;
His Cheeks like living Rose's glow;
His een like azure stream.
The boy was clad in robes of green,
Sweet as yᵉ infant spring;
And like the Mavis in yᵉ bush,
He gart yᵉ vallies ring.

16

The baron came to ye grene wood,
Wi' mickle dule & care,
And there he first spy'd Gill Morice
Kameing his yellow hair,
That sweetly wav'd around his Face;
That Face beyond compare!
He sang sae sweet it might dispell
A'rage but fell despair.

Nae wonder &c:

[Note written lengthwise in MS.]

*This, considering Addisons Note upon Milton's 'able to chase "All sadness but despair" looks a little more modern y^n ye rest—but may not *be* so—

NOTES

[1]Dodsley's *Collection*, VI, 233, *A Song* by T. P . . . cy. 'O Nancy, wilt thou go with me.' (This song was addressed to Anne Gutteridge, whom Percy married in 1759.) Dodsley's *Collection*, VI, 234, *Cynthia, an Elegiac Poem*, by the same. 'Beneath an aged oak's embow'ring shade.'

[2]*Epistles to the Great, from Aristippus in Retirement*, 1757, Dodsley. 1758, *The Call of Aristippus. Epistle IV. To Mark Akenside, M.D. By the Author of the three former Epistles of Aristippus*. These were not by Richard Owen Cambridge, but by John Gilbert Cooper.

[3]The letters of Shenstone and Percy throw considerable light upon the sources of the *Reliques*, which consisted, according to Percy's title, of *Old Heroic Ballads, Songs, and other Pieces of our Earlier Poets (chiefly of the Lyric kind). Together with some few of later Date.*

[4]Johnson's edition of Shakespeare did not appear until October 1765.

[5]*A Poetical Translation of the Elegies of Tibullus and of the Poems of Sulpicia with the Original Text and Notes Critical and Explanatory*. 2 vols. by James Grainger (1721–1766), friend of Percy and Shenstone.

CCXVI

Works III, 311.

[*To* Rev. R. GRAVES] *on* [*Mr. Dodsley and his Works*].

THE LEASOWES,
May 30, 1758.

Dear Mr. Graves,

I thank God, I have recovered a tolerable degree of health this spring; though by no means free from so much heaviness and lassitude, as renders me averse to all activity of body and mind. In the course of my disorder, so long as I could bear to think of *any* sublunary enjoyment, I remembered my friends, and of course thought much of *you*; but its advances were so precipitate, when I sent for the physicians, that I soon received a *wrench* from every object of this world: and it was by slow degrees, even after my recovery, that my mind took so much root again, as appears necessary for its immediate support. I suppose you have been informed that my fever was in great measure hypochrondriacal; and left my nerves so extremely sensible, that, even on no very interesting subject, I could readily think myself into a vertigo: I had almost said an epilepsy; for surely I was oftentimes near it. It became, therefore, expedient for my recovery, to amuse myself with a succession of the most trivial objects I could find; and this kind of carelessness I have indulged till it is grown into an habit. Even letters to my friends are hardly consistent with my rule of health; yet I could be no longer silent with regard to *you*, without feeling a sensation that would hurt me *more*. This may fairly enough be termed the first *letter* I have wrote since my recovery; wherein if I should tell you one half that I am inclined to do, relating to this dreadful illness, what room should I then leave to speak on any other subject? I must, therefore, tell these things by word of mouth, or write them some other time. The journies which my friends, and indeed physicians, propose for me, are what certainly bid fairest for the completion of my cure: yet there are many, many things, which, however unfit for the task, I must endeavour to adjust before I can leave home, with any possibility of enjoyment. Need I mention any other than my cursed embarrassment with D[olman]? Who, during my *danger*, was induced to stop proceedings; but is now beginning law afresh, and, by the removal of tenants from *his* share of the Harborough estate, has now wriggled himself into possession of almost one half of *mine*? However, I am not without hopes of seeing all terminated in a little time; nor entirely without a prospect of seeing you at Claverton this summer. That you may think this the more probable, I am pressed by two young gentlemen, whom I very much esteem, to accompany them on a visit to Mr. Bamfylde in

2 1

Somersetshire.[1] These two gentlemen are Mr. Dean and Mr. Knight.[2] Perhaps you may have heard of Mr. Bamfylde, who is very much at Bath; is there now with his lady, or has left the place but lately; and whose fortune, person, figure, and accomplishments, can hardly leave him long unnoticed in any place where he resides. Yet my visit to Estercomb, must be of secondary consequence to me, whilst you live by the road-side. I am much obliged to you for your compliment on my Poematia in Dodsley's Miscellanies; which came very seasonably, considering how I had been mortified by the first sight of what was done. To speak the truth, there are many things appear there very contrary to my intentions; but which I am more desirous may be attributed to the unseasonableness of my fever, than to my friend D[odsley]'s precipitation. My purpose was to acknowledge as *mine*, none of the pieces which now follow the longer Ode to Lady Luxborough. Her name was actually erased; as also my own at the close of your Fable. The verses by Mrs. Bennet to Mr. Richardson were absolutely new to me; where my name occurs again.[3] All this is against me; as a thing in itself invidious to have one's name recur so often, and as my *own lines contradict* th merit which my friends so liberally allow me.—The verses of mine in the sixth volume (which was printed before the fifth)[4] were printed without my knowledge; and when I sent up an improved copy, it arrived a good deal too late. As things happen, I am made to own several things of inferior merit to those which I *do not* own.—All this is against me; but my thoughts are avocated from this edition, and wholly fixed upon a future; wherein, I hope, Dodsley will be prevailed upon to omit some things also from *other* hands which discredit his collection: and, to balance *all my discomforts* on this head, the world will know that I am esteemed by a person, whom I esteem so much as you.—I know not how it happens, but the taste for humorous poetry does not prevail at this time: yet I cannot agree with Mr. J. Warton, that it is no poetry *at all*, any more than that a good representation of Dutch boors is not a picture.—His brother, the Professor, is to be here with his pupil Lord Donnegal,[5] &c. this summer.—Mr. Spence and Mr. Dodsley will stay a day or two here this month on their way to Scotland; and Mr. Home, the author of Douglas,[6] &c.

called on me, and we spent an evening together at Admiral Smith's. Thus my *ferme ornée* procures me interviews with persons whom it might otherwise be my wish, rather than my good-fortune to see. Would to God, it could attract *you*, whom I more long to see than any one; and let me tell you, there were considerable additions made to it last year: Dodsley's present of Faunus;[7] a new, Gothic-building, or rather a skreen, which cost ten pounds; and the ruins of a Priory,[8] which, however, make a tenant's house, that pays me tolerable pound-age. —I am growing a little into *your* taste: why should not you advance farther into *mine?* I mean, I have a love for medals, by means of some that have been given me: yet do not think that I shall ever rival *you*.—My object is only *beauty*, and I love only those of exquisite workmanship; so that this is no more a rivalship than that of two persons who admire the sex, but love different individuals; a rivalship, which, I trust, is more likely to cement our friendship than disunite us; which it is my *conviction* and my *comfort* no *sort* of rivalship will ever do. I have hardly room to express my good wishes for long health and happiness to Mrs. Graves and your little family, and to sub-scribe myself, my dear friend,

Your ever affectionate humble servant,
W. SHENSTONE.

NOTES

[1]Copplestone Warre Bamfylde, d. 1791, landscape painter, of Hestercombe in Somersetshire.

The New Bath Guide of 1796 urges the 'curious traveller' to visit the delightful seat of Mr. Bampfylde of Hestercomb. 'The gardens and rural beauties at Hestercomb are the striking object. An hermitage in it, with the figure of an old witch painted in the center pannel, occasioned the following genteel compliment from the late Dr. Langhorne:

> "O'er Bampfylde's woods by various nature grac'd,
> A witch presides! but then that witch is taste." '

[2]Mr. Edward Knight of Wolverley, often mentioned by W.S. He made a fortune in the iron-trade. 'Mr. E. Knight, of Portland-Place, a gentlemen well known for his extensive learning, and his taste for fine art, has happily applied the character of Hesiod, from Vellenus Paterculus, to Mr. Shenstone, at his seat at Wooverley, in Worcester-shire.' *Recollection*, 187.

[3]*Verses by Mrs. Bennet to Mr. Richardson, upon an Alcove now at Parson's Green*, Dodsley's *Collection*, V, 296. Mrs. Bennet's brother married Samuel Richardson's daughter. Courtney, *op. cit*., 57, gives an account of Mrs. Bennet. The compliment to W.S. ran thus:

> 'O Favorite Muse of Shenstone hear!
> And leave awhile his blissful groves;
> Aid me this sweet alcove to sing,
> The Author's seat whom Shenstone loves.'

[4]Vol. VI, 211–216.
The remark on the order of printing is interesting.
[5]Thomas Warton (1728–1790), author of the *History of English Poetry*, was elected professor of poetry at Oxford in 1757. His pupil, Arthur (Chichester) Earl of Donegall, matriculated at Trinity College, Oxford, November 25, 1757, aged 19.
[6]John Home (1722–1808). His tragedy, *Douglas*, was written in 1758.
[7]Dodsley's *Description of The Leasowes*, Shenstone, *Works* II, 342. 'And now passing through a kind of thicket, we arrive at a natural bower of almost circular oaks, inscribed in the manner following:

> 'To Mr. Dodsley.
> 'Come then, my friend, thy sylvan taste display,
> 'Come here thy Faunus tune his rustic lay;
> 'Ah, rather come, and in these dells disown
> 'The care of other strains, and tune thine own.'

On the bank above it, amid the fore-mentioned shrubs, is a statue of the piping fawn which not only embellishes this scene, but is also seen from the court before the house and from other places.'
[8]The Priory is still to be seen, now 'ruinated' indeed.

CCXVII

Library of The Assay Office, Birmingham.

[*To* MATTHEW BOULTON.][1]

Dear Sir,

I am employ'd by my Friend, Mr. Hylton to request you would procure for him an electrical apparatus; and this, with all the expedition that shall be consistent with your own convenience. He wishes it to be such as may effectually exhibit all the common experiments in electricity; & This he leaves entirely to your Judgment who are so much better vers'd in it: At ye same time he wishes it *plain*, and not to partake of *Any* elegance that tends to heighten the expence—Thus much for my Friend Hylton; and now, as touching myself, I confess I could find much Pleasure in Researches of this sort; but as I have other avocations, and Lapul is so near, I have agreed with my Neighbour for certain Portions of electrical Fire, for which I am to furnish him with Cascade-water as often as he finds occasion.[2] To be more serious, there is *one* Advantage I chiefly hope from his Lucubrations, I mean, that they will draw you oftener into this county, of whose Conversation I am at all times very desirous to partake. I return you many thanks for the Honour done me by Mr. Franklyn,[3] and hope, whenever you have opportunity, you will oblige me with Favors of the same kind. I am, dear Sir,

> your most obligd and very
> > affectionate Friend,
> > > WILL SHENSTONE.

July ye 19th 1758.

N.B. Mr. Hylton thinks y^t *Oak* may supply all ye purposes of Mahogany in ye Frame.

> To Mr. Boulton,
> > on Snow-hill,
> > > Birmingham.

NOTES

[1] The famous manufacturer and partner of James Watt, of Snowhill, Birmingham. Jago celebrated him in *Labour and Genius* when the stream boasts its power to

> 'furnish stuff for many a trinket,
> Which, though so fine, you scarce would think it,
> When Boulton's skill has fixed their beauty,
> To my rough toil first ow'd their duty.'

[2] W.S. seems to have been much interested in the powers of the waters of his cascade and so connects himself with the growing prosperity of his district. May 20, 1762 he recommends his 'principal cascade' to Graves as a subject for poetry and goes on to show that though its appearance suggested 'the playfulness of infancy' yet later in its course as the Stour it supplied 'more iron-works than almost any single river in the Kingdom.' The contrast here suggested supplies the basis for Jago's *Labour and Genius*. Is it too much to suppose that W.S. suggested the idea to his friend?

[3] Benjamin Franklin (1706–1790), who came to England in 1757, was a friend of Dr. Small, by whom he was probably introduced to Birmingham celebrities. It is interesting to see that Shenstone numbered him among his acquaintance. Franklin had been carrying out experiments with lightning conductors.

CCXVIII

Works III, 316.

[*To the* REV. R. GRAVES] *on* [*Mr. Dodsley and his Works*].

July 22, 1758.

Dear Mr. Graves,

It gives me great anxiety when I reflect how long I have waited for the satisfaction of a line from you. I beg, if you are alive and well, you will let me know so by the next post.

Mr. Dodsley and Mr. Spence have been here and stayed a week with me. The former was in certain hopes of seeing you in town; but I do not find that he either saw or heard from you, which *adds* to my anxiety.

I have seen few whom I like so much, upon so little acquaintance, as Mr. Spence; extremely polite, friendly, chearful, and master of an infinite fund of subjects for agreeable conversation. Had my affairs permitted me, they had certainly drawn me with them into Scotland; whither they are gone, for about a month, upon a journey of curiosity.

I believe it will give you pleasure to hear that my law-suit with D[olman] is accommodated, by the generous interposition of my Lord Stamford; concerning whose benevolence and magnanimity it is impossible for me to speak in the terms which they deserve. It is ended, I hope, not very *disadvantageously* for me; apparently with *one* advantage, of beng intirely exculpated in the opinion of all mankind. The common method (as M. Bruyere[1] observes) is to condemn *both* on these occasions. This suits people's indolence, and favours their impartiality. And though the equitableness of my whole conduct in this affair was self-evident to all that were near me, yet I found many that were inclined to blame us *both*, and *some* that I could never convince till *now* that the fault was not *wholly* mine.

Your 'Pepper-box and Salt-seller' are in one of the Chronicles.—They pillage Dodsley's two last volumes of all that is worth perusal.[2]—I surely have some friend amongst the writers of the Monthly Review;[3] for I have not only escaped a flogging, but am treated with great civility.

I *never* know how to leave off when I begin writing to you, having always a great deal to say: I only purposed you a few lines, to desire you would write directly. Pray make my best compliments to Mrs. Graves, and believe me ever yours most invariably.

W. Shenstone.

NOTES

[1]Capt. F. L. Pleadwell of Washington writes to say that 'The Works of Monsieur de la Bruyere. In Two Volumes. xx Sixth Edition xx with an original chapter by N. Rowe, Esq' has come into his hands. Shenstone's name is on the flyleaf, and the book is heavily annotated. A note on the fly-leaf reads thus: 'Whoever reads Bruyere finds a

great many truths he has himself observ'd, but never lay'd sufficient *stress* on. Dr, Young seems to have study'd his Peculiarities and Affectations: I shou'd Imagine there must have been a greater similitude betwixt his *soul*, & y^t of Bruyere, yⁿ betwixt ye Features & Lineaments of any Persons whatever.' A note in pencil, partially obliterated through rubbing reads thus:—

> 'Read Bruyere Novr 20 1755 (?)
> who with his affectations, d(iscovers)
> much wit & a thorough I(nsight into y^e)
> Nature of Mankind.'

Captain Pleadwell says Volume II contains many single words of criticism and many marginal dashes. There are, too, many small sketches—evidently similar to those in W.S.'s letters.

²Some items from Dodsley's *Collection* are in the July and August numbers of *The London Chronicle* and in the May number of *The Gentleman's Magazine*. I have not found *The Pepper-box and Salt-seller*.

³*The Monthly Review*, June 1758, 533. 'Perhaps a more excellent Miscellany is not to be met with in any language. . . . As a more expanded advertisement of this publication might be thought to convey but little entertainment to our Readers; and would, indeed, fail of answering every purpose of a Review, we shall close the article with a transcript of two of Mr. Shenstone's elegant and truly poetical pieces; the first, entitled, *An Ode to Health;* the second, *An Irregular Ode after Sickness*.'

CCIX

Messrs. Maggs.

[*To* J. S. HYLTON.]

Augt 1758.

My Compliments. I expected Jack this morning, but *suppose* & *hope* y^t he may be gone from Lapall to Birm— Mr Amos Green is here, and we want some of ye same (or same sort of) gold size wch Mr Green says he gave Mr Hylton —I went yesterday to dine wth Mr Dolman, calling by ye way & staying about 3 Hours at ye Admiral's, where were Miss West & her Guittar[?]; Captⁿ Hood with ye most elegant snuff-box I ever yet saw; Mr Midwinter¹ with a Canister of ye Queen o' Spain's snuff; & Admiral Smith in a new Peruke— On my return, I found I had had some Company, whom I should have been glad to have attended—the Mr Dean's of Whittington & a Mr Turton of Staffordshire (who dind here) M^r and Mrs Kendall wth M^r and Mrs Jones &c &c. If Mr H. care to walk over, & will *promise* not to see aught y^t is in agitation 'till to-morrow when all will be compleated, we shall be glad to see Him (*after* Dinner time for I know of no dinner we are like to have) But if he should be seduc'd by Mr Green to peep—he will be struck blind for ever after—As I remember, there is an Image at Coventry y^t may afford him proper warning—

The Gold-size by ye Bearer—

W. SHENSTONE.

Sunday 6th Augt 1758 [*in another hand*]

To John Scott Hylton, Esq;

NOTE

[1]Mrs. Midwinter, widow of Capt. John Midwinter, intimate friend of Admiral Smith, later kept house for the admiral.   (Wyndham, *op. cit.*)

CCXX

Messrs. Maggs.

[*To* J. S. HYLTON.]

Tuesday, 8th Aug^st 1758.

My Compliments to Mr. Hylton—Since he was here arriv'd Mr. and Mrs. Clare with a Party; who enquir'd after Mr. Hylton, had heard he was going to lay out *much money* upon y^t *damn'd old place*, before he had mended his Roads y^t lead to it—Mr. H. knows Mrs. *Clare*, &, as he also knows *me*, he will suppose I made an answer not wholly improper upon ye occasion—My Ld Warrington, it seems, dy'd about a week ago, an event of ye utmost Importance to Ld Stamford[1]— the disposal of his affairs not yet known, even at Enville. I beg y^t Mr. H. w^d examine ye sense of ye word *Integet*.

WILL: SHENSTONE.

To

John Scott Hylton Esq.;

NOTE

[1]At the death of his father-in-law Lord Stamford inherited estates in Cheshire and Lancashire.

CCXXI

Library of the Assay Office, Birmingham.

[*To* MATTHEW BOULTON.]

The Leasowes, *Aug^{st} y^e* 14th 1758.

My best respects to Mr. Bolton; and if the corner Ornaments for the Chaire are finish'd, I should be glad enough to receive them—as also to know, whether any step be taken in regard to my four Bells.

Mr. Hylton, I presume, purposes to wait upon Mr. Boulton, this Week—I have burnt my Fingers with electricity already; having told ye story of Mr. Franklyn's bottling up ye Lightning, till I am thought as great a Lyar as a Popish Legendary.

I desire Mr. Bolton would let me see Him here, as *soon* and as *often* as is Consistent with his better Employments—

WILL SHENSTONE.

To Mr. Bolton.

CCXXII

Assay Office Library, Birmingham.

[*To* MATTHEW BOULTON.]

My best Respects to Mr. Boulton, with abundance of thanks for ye Letter with which he favours me—Mr. Green did not shew me ye Pattern before monday last, when I found it expedient to alter ye *delicacy* of my first draught, for something y^t was more likely to make a Figure at a *Distance*. Mr. Boulton will see my Intention, & will be so good as get ye Ornaments cast by saturday, & gilt in ye manner he proposes —Mr. Hylton is yet at Home, but I will take care to shew him Mr. Boulton's Letter, & I'm very sure he will be much obligd by Mr. Boulton's Invitation—The best & shortest method

has been taken with regard to the Bells; I can only say I am
sensibly obligd by Mr. Bolton's readiness to serve me, & can
only wish for occasions of testifying ye Esteem with which I am
his very affectionate Friend etc:

WILL: SHENSTONE.

Wednesday,
August ye 16th 1758.

To Mr. Bolton,
    on Snow-hill,
        Birmingham.

CCXXIII

Assay Office Library, Birmingham.

[*To* MATTHEW BOULTON.]

August ye 17. 1758.

My best respects to Mr. Bolton, with abundance of thanks
for ye favour of his Letter—Mr. Green did not bring me ye
Pattern before monday last; when I found it expedient to
change ye *delicacy* of ye Model, for somewhat y^t was better
calculated to make a Figure at a distance—Mr. Bolton will see
my Intentions when Mr. Green returns ye pattern; which I
beg he would get executed as soon as possible, & gilt in ye
manner he proposes. The best and ye shortest method has been
taken in regard to the Bells. I am ashamed to give Mr. Bolton
all this trouble, but shall be glad on every occasion to testify
ye Esteem with which I am his very affectionate Friend etc.

WILL SHENSTONE.

To Mr. Boulton,
    on Snow-hill,
        Birmingham.

CCXXIV

Assay Office Library, Birmingham.

[*To* MATTHEW BOULTON.]

Aug. 23. 1758.

I desire my best Respects to Mr. Boulton; and if the P. chaise ornaments happen to be *cast*, should be oblig'd to Him for a sight of them, before he gives orders for ye gilding.

I am told, Mr. Boulton has a Dove that is a *widower;* and in case he do not purpose to provide him a companion, should be almost tempted to request y^t he might cohabit with some of mine. Mr. Boulton will please to observe y^t the request is quite *conditional.*

The enclosed Impromptu may amuse Mr. Boulton for a moment; but he must give me his word & honour y^t he will make no other use of it, before I see Him.

WILL: SHENSTONE.

To Mr. Boulton, on
Snow-hill.

CCXXV

Assay Office Library, Birmingham.

[*To* MATTHEW BOULTON.]

My Comp. to Mr. Boulton, who will discover by ye enclosed what I know of the affair—I could indeed wish, ye Copy I sent Mr. Boulton were either *return'd* me or *burnt;* and any others destroy'd, if Mr. B^n knows of any. I could also wish y^t Mr. B^n would take no Notice of Giles's Letter; which I only send as the *laziest* method of explaining my present situation. Finally I could wish, y^t Mr. Baskerville would not be so extremely idle as to give a Construction to this Trifle, which cannot possibly be countenanc'd by any *one* Consideration.

Mr; Boulton will be so good as acquaint me when I may

expect the Chaise-Ornaments; Mr. Knight, who is going to bespeak a Chaise at Birm. prefers this very Form to all others.

WILL SHENSTONE.

Septr 18*th* 1758.

To Mr. Boulton,
   on Snow-hill,
     Birmingham.

CCXXVI

Assay Office Library, Birmingham.

[*To* MATTHEW BOULTON.]

Septr 25*th* 1758.

I desire my Compliments to Mr. Boulton; & if the Chaise Ornaments happen to be ready, should be glad enough to have them sent by ye bearer.

I hope y^t Mr. Baskerville has by this time been induc'd to construe y^t idle ballad according to ye sense that was obviously intended; & y^t I shall have no further occasion to say any thing on that subject. I have receiv'd ye 2 copies I gave to Mr. B^n and Mr. Giles. Had I given Copies to Mr. Baskerville's enemies, ye case had been very different.

Pray when is Mr. Hylton furnish'd wth his electrical Apparatus? and when is Amos Green expected.

WILL: SHENSTONE.

To Mr. Boulton
   On Snow Hill.

CCXXVII

Assay Office Library, Birmingham.

[*To* MATTHEW BOULTON.]

Sept. 27, 1758.

My Compliments to Mr. Boulton with many Thanks for his Care in ye execution of ye Pine-apples. They will do mighty well; nevertheless the *Leaves* or *lower part* of the Fruit would shew much better if it were a little *fuller* & more plain. I am to bespeak a sett for Mr. Knight; &, if it be not much *trouble, would* propose this alteration; not otherwise. I am now dispos'd to give Mr. Boulton some additional plague about ye *Bells.* See ye trouble he brings upon himself by his *known Inclination* to oblige; especially when it is once discover'd by a person of a scheming turn. What does Mr. B. think of a scheme for enamel'd stars for Horses fore-heads?—Would to God, I could discover a Scheme by wch I could oblige Mr. Boulton in return.

WILL: SHENSTONE.

To Mr. Boulton
    on Snow-hill
      Birmingham.

CCXXVIII

Assay Office Library, Birmingham.

[*To* MATTHEW BOULTON.]

My Compliments to Mr. Boulton, & I would beg ye Favor of Him to send me two or three pair of shoes and knee-buckles, for Choice—

I am sorry to clogg my offer of a Pair of Guinea-fowl,[1] with any stipulation : I cannot, will not stipulate; for I'm very sure if my Breed should fail, & Mr. Boulton's prove prolific, he will very readily supply me with a pair of young ones, some-time hereafter—If they ate not rightly pair'd Mr. B. will send me Word. It is a Species in wch ye distinction of sexes is not easily discernible.—

    Septr 30. 1758.   WILL: SHENSTONE.

[Letter torn, name missing.]
    Snow-hill,
      Birmingham.

NOTE

[1]The guinea-fowl were probably raised from stock from Barrels. Luxborough, *Letters,* 116.

CCXXIX

Works III, 318.

To the [REV. R. GRAVES], *containing an Account of his Excursions
and Amusements.*

THE LEASOWES,
Nov. 25, 1758.

Dear Mr. Graves,

I have had daily expectations of a line from you these two
months: conscious, however, that I did not deserve any; and
affording a manifest instance of the infatuations of self-love.
The last letter that I received of yours is dated the close of July,
since which time I have been chiefly engaged in my customary
amusements; embellishing my farm, and receiving the company that came to see it. My principal *excursions* have been to
Enville, on Lord Grey's birth-day; to Lord Ward's, upon
another invitation; and to the Worcester Music-meeting. I
need not mention what an appearance there was of company at
Worcester; dazzling enough, you may suppose, to a person
who, like me, has not seen a public place these ten years. Yet
I made a shift to enjoy the splendour, as well as the music that
was prepared for us. I presume, nothing in the way of harmony
can possibly go further than the Oratorio of The Messiah.[1] It
seems the best composer's best composition. Yet I fancied I
could observe *some parts* in it, wherein Handel's judgement
failed him; where the music was not equal, or was even *opposite*,
to what the words required. Very many of the noblesse, whom
I had seen at The Leasowes, were as complaisant to me as
possible; whereas it was my *former* fate, in public places, to be
as little regarded as a journeyman shoe-maker.—There I first
saw our present Bishop, also our late Bishop's monument,
which is fine.[2]—Lastly, there I first saw my Lady Coventry; to
whom, I believe, one must allow all that the world allows in
point of beauty.[3] She is certainly the most *unexceptionable*
figure of a woman I ever saw; and made most of the ladies there
seem of almost another *species*. On the whole, I was not a little
pleased that I had made this excursion; and returned with
double relish to the *enjoyment* of my *farm*. It is now high time

to take some notice of your obliging letter.—I think I was not told the purport of the journey you made to London; so can only say, I am very sorry for the aggravating circumstances of your disappointment; and hope, long before this time, that Mrs. Graves is quite recovered.—Did I forget to make your excuses to Dodsley or no?—he was here (as I remember) soon after, with Mr. Spence, in their way to Scotland.—Mr. Spence, the man *you* would like, and who would like *you*, of all mankind. He took my Elegies into Scotland, and sent them back on his return, with a sheet or two of criticisms, and an handsome letter.—How much am I interested in the preservation of his friendship!—and yet, such is my *destiny* (for I can give it no other name), I have never wrote to him *since*. This *impartiality* of my neglect, you must accept *yourself* as *some* apology: but to proceed; Mr. Spence chose himself an oak here for a seat, which I have inscribed to him,

('SPENCE'S OAK.)
'EXIMIO. NOSTRO. CRITONI.
'CVI. DICARI.[4] VELLET.
'MUSARUM. OMNIUM. ET. GRATIARUM. CHORUS.
'DICAT. AMICITIA.'

I absolutely *forgot* to talk to Dodsley about your [*Spiritual Quixote?*], and I am vexed; because I could, with a safe conscience, have raised his idea of your abilities. However, it is not too late, even if you care to publish it this winter.—His play comes on (I fancy, *this very night*) at Covent-garden. What he says in behalf of this step is, that there was no glimpse of probability, that Garrick would ever admit it at the other house.[5] Mrs. Bellamy[6] is his Cleone, and speaks the epilogue, of which more anon. I suppose he acts by Lord Chesterfield's [7]opinion: for I know, when he was going to print it (since he came home) with a *proper* dedication to Mr. Garrick, my Lord then prevented him, telling him, it *would* be acted one day or other.— Did I ever send you a copy of the epilogue, with all the additions and alterations? Dodsley first liked, then disliked it, and lastly liked it again; only desiring me to soften the satire, shorten the whole (for it was upwards of sixty lines), and add a complimentary close to the *boxes*.—All this I have endeavoured, and sent it him last Monday. *You* would not care to own it: and he would fain have *me;* but I think neither of us should run the risque, where so little honour is to be acquired; yet Mr. Melmoth's name to the prologue is an inducement.[8]—I was very near surprizing you at Claverton this autumn, with my friend young Knight, in his way to Mr. Bamfyld's; but he goes *again* in spring, and I shall certainly accompany him; I have *bespoke,* but not yet *procured* any, horses for my chaise. It is a neat one, you will find; and I have made two or three excursions in it.—I saw Mr. Patchen's Topographical Letters[9] soon after they were published.—If you continue to me the honour of a shield in your Gothic alcove, the field should be either 'Or, three king-fishers proper,' or, with the addition of a chief gules, three trefoils argent—no bar, cheveron bend, &c.— More of this when I write again. Motto, FLUMINA AMEM, SYLVASQUE INGLORIUS—RURA MIHI.[9a]

I cannot recollect my company of the season, to tell it you.— Sir Francis Dashwood,[10] Lord Litchfield,[11] and Mr. Sheldon,[12] were here together in the beginning of the autumn; and I have strong invitations to visit them.—I have a very genteel letter from Sir Francis, offering me gold-fishes; and I have a double inducement to visit Mr. Sheldon, as he lives near Mickleton, and is the most agreeable man alive.—Your acquaintance Lord W——dined and spent good part of a day with me. Under a sort of gloomy appearance, a man of admirable sense and some humour. I put him in mind of you, and the remarkable monument at Cambden.—Mr. Thomas Warton was also here with Lord Donegal, and has since sent me his 'Inscriptions,'[13] which are rather too simple, even for my taste.—Bishop of Worcester with his family and company—Lord Willoughby— Lord Foley—I mention Lord Foley the rather, because I shall call on your friend Dr. Charleton [14] (who was also here) to pass a day or two with me at Whitley.—I shall pass also a day or two at our Bishop's, whom I met since at Enville. These two (*propose* what I *will* besides) will probably be the principal, or only excursions that I shall make this winter.—God send it may no more affect my health than it has hitherto done.—I am at present tolerably well, and live more temperately than before. —Would to God you could come over; go with me to Dr.

Charleton's, and Lord Foley's, and Lord Stamford's, and pass a week here! I would meet you with my chaise at Worcester, or even farther. I have finished a building opposite to the new stable, which I think you saw.—They together give my house a degree of splendour. Did you see my Priory?—a tenant's house, one room whereof is to have Gothic shields round the cornice.—I am in some doubt whether to make it an House of Lords or House of Commons; if the former, my private friends will have shields round my Gothic bed-chamber.—The wretch is cursed that *begins* a letter with no better a pen than I *finish* one with. My dear friend, write directly a long letter.—Keep me alive in the memory of Mrs. Graves, and believe me ever yours most affectionately,

W. Shenstone.[15]

NOTES

[1]Handel's *Messiah*, first heard in Dublin in 1741, having been completed in twenty three days, rapidly became popular.

[2]Dr. John Hough (1651–1743) preceded Dr. Isaac Maddox as Bishop of Worcester. His monument was the work of Roubilliac and is considered the most beautiful monument in the Cathedral. 'It represents the bishop in a reclining posture over a sarcophagus, with his head turned upwards, and his hands clasped, as if in an act of devotion. On the top of the pedestal stands Religion, holding in her right hand the Bible open, and with her left holding back part of the drapery, which would seem to be falling over the basso-relievo on the front of the sarcophagus, etc.' *A Concise History and Description of the City and Cathedral of Worcester*, 1829.

[3]Maria, Countess of Coventry (1733–1760), was one of the famous Misses Gunning. She and her sister Elizabeth were considered to be the most beautiful women of their day.

[4]Note, *Works III*, 320. 'Sub intellige sedem istam (hanc).'

[5]Note, *Works III*, 'He says, the players liked it, and seemed to take pains with it,'

[6]George Anne Bellamy (1731–?1788,) a well-known eighteenth century actress. See *An Apology for the Life of George Anne Bellamy, written by herself*.

[7]Lord Chesterfield, Lord Lyttelton and Dr. Johnson were all interested in *Cleone*. Dr. Johnson to Bennet Langton, January 9, 1759, 'Cleone was well acted by all the characters, but Miss Bellamy left nothing to be desired. I went to the first night and supported it as well as I might; for Doddy, you know, is my patron, and I would not desert him. The play was very well received. Doddy, after the danger was over, went every night to the stage side, and cried at the distress of poor Cleone.'

[8]William Melmoth was a friend of Dodsley. The prologue which he contributed to *Cleone* is most amusing.

[9]Dodsley published April 18, 1757, *Four Topographical Letters, written in 1755 on a Journey thro' the Counties of Bedford, Northants*, etc. Possibly the reference is to these.

[9a]Virgil, *Geor*. II, 486.

[10]Sir Francis Dashwood, Bart. of West Wycombe.

[11]George Henry Lee, Earl of Lichfield.

[12]Weston, the seat of William Sheldon, is celebrated by Jago, in *Edge-Hill*, Book I.

[13]Messrs. James Tregaskis & Son, in a catalogue of May 1931, advertised Shenstone's copy of Thomas Warton's *Inscriptions*, which contained the following:—'Mr. Tho. Warton, the editor, to Mr. Shenton(e). October ye 22, 1758.'

Thomas Warton's *Inscriptionum Romanorum Metricarum Delectus* was published by R. & J. Dodsley in 1758.

2 K

¹⁴Rice Charleton, M.D. (1710–1789) author of *A Chemical Analysis of Bath Waters,* 1750.

¹⁵Later editions of W.S.'s *Letters* contained the following postscript: 'I have received a present of the Edinburgh Homer (2 vols. folio) from the Solicitor General Mr. Pringle: and many other books from other gentlemen of Scotland.'

Andrew Pringle, d. 1776, was made Solicitor General of Scotland, July 5, 1755, and was raised to the bench as Lord Alemoor in 1759.

CCXXX

Henry E. Huntington Library.

[*To* J. S. HYLTON.]

*Nov.*ʳ 26, 1758.

Dick is going to Birm., and shall take yᵉ Letters yᵗ [   ] been sent—I can't *account* for yᵉ expensiveness of yʳ M[   ] Journey to Coventry—surely he wᵈ need to lodge but one Ni[ght] there, & wᵈ have his Victuals at Mʳ Inge's—I know V[ery?] few Instances of *Attorneys*, where both yᵉ *Gent*ⁿ & even yᵉ M[an?] are not swallow'd up in yᵉ *Lawyer*—'He will make you a schedule *thereof*; & at yᵉ bottom *thereof;* will remain a blank space for you to sign yʳ Name *thereon*'—But let us comfort ourselves that it is much less eligible to *be* Lawyers, yⁿ to *suffer by* em—

Mʳ Hylton may write to Mʳ Percy when he pleases; but ought not to send any accᵗ from yᵉ Leasowes 'till I can enable Him; wᶜʰ? at present cannot be—

WILL: SHENSTONE—

CCXXXI

B.M. Add. MSS. 28221. and Hecht, 11,

[*To* THOMAS PERCY.]

Rec.ᵈ *Dec.*ʳ 1ˢᵗ 1758 [*in Percy's handwriting*]

Dear Sir,

It is really a shame to acknowledge *now,* the Favour I receiv'd from you so very long *ago;* but it would be a much *greater,* not to acknowledge it at *all:* And indeed it were a very *preposterous* kind of Hypocrisy, to conceal the Pleasure I have receiv'd, on which I am to ground the Hopes I entertain of your Correspondence. I have perform'd about one *half* of ye request you were so *complaisant* to make, with regard to your Poetry. The rest, with your Leave, I must defer a little longer. I think y^r Elegy on Ld Sussex[1] extremely easy and genteel. Pardon ye Hints I have interlin'd, and only use what you approve of them. When you have so done, I should esteem it a Favour, if you would please to send me a fresh Copy. I have enclos'd a few Pieces for your *Amusement*; which I send with no other Limitation, y^n that you will keep them from the *Press*. Possibly I may be one day tempted to furnish out a small Miscellany; having a press in my own *Neighbourhood*,[2] so very favorable to my *Indolence*. Y^r. Friend, Dr. Grainger, with a Mr. Luard pass'd a Day with me: And a very agreeable Day it *was*; not inferior to any one I have spent, since I had ye Pleasure of seeing you. The Doctor, on reading y^t urnal Inscription (Postquam Te Fata tulerunt Ipsa Pales agros, atque ipse reliquit Apollo)[3] made me a Compliment on ye Subject, as polite as it was extemporaneous.:

> 'S—with you I'd weep ye Dead;
> 'With you of Fate complain—
> But tho' Apollo's self be fled
> And Pales—*you* remain.'

They were going into Scotland: *both*, Persons of Taste— The Dr. a Person of much real Genius, & Learning; & I cou'd wish to see them oft'ner.

I met Mr. Wright at Enville, upon Ld Grey's Birth-day— Mr. Baldwyn[4] also and Colonel Cotes were here; & as I remember (or am *inclin'd* to remember) made honorable Mention of *you*.

Mr. Spence and Mr. Dodsley render'd a week here very agreeable to me. Mr. Spence chose himself an oak; on wch I put ye following Inscription:

SPENCE'S OAK.
Peramabili . nostro . Critoni
Cui . dicari . vellet .
Musarum . omnium . & Gratiarum
Chorus .
Dicat . Amicitia.

Other additional Inscriptions—with Some y[t] are intended, I reserve for a future Letter—amongst which, you must not be angry, if you happen to trace y[r] own Name.

Dodsley's Play[5] has either *been* acted, or comes on, at y[e] new House,[6] this Week. It is a point I have much at Heart to see this Play triumph over it's Antagonists. You will not want a *Foundation* to do it some Honour as you see Occasion; but Let y[e] Author's merit & my request incline you to be rather luxuriant in it's Commendation.[7]

Baskerville's Milton,[8] they tell me comes out in y[e] X[tmas] holidays—I have company while I write, & must, *unwillingly*, take my Leave at present.—Be so good as to return me y[e] printed Verses upon the Leasows,[9] and believe me ever and most affectionately yours,

WILL: SHENSTONE.

Mr. Pitt of Shifnel (here wth Mr. Slaney) says he gave you those old Ballads.—The Pilgrim you sent me is mighty pretty, as y[e] Plan is different from what one has ever seen. I have had y[e] Edinburgh Homer,[10] A miscellany of Allan Ramsays, Scotch Proverbs, Scotch Ballads,[11] presented me from Caledonia, & am grown almost a Scotch-man.—Excuse this.—

NOTES

[1]Percy's note: *Verses on the Improvements designed at Easton Maud$_t$*, 1758. Lord Sussex was Percy's patron and first Lord of the Bedchamber to the Prince of Wales. He died prematurely and so a life 'of the greatest worth and brightest hopes' was cut short.

[2]Baskerville's press.

[3]Virgil, *Eclogues* V, 35.

[4]Percy's note: 'Afterwards Member of Parliament for the County of Salop.'

[5]Percy's note: 'Cleone, a Tragedy.'

[6]Covent Garden.

[7]Shenstone's note at the bottom of the MS.: 'I could indeed wish, y[t] you wou'd give him a copy of commendatory verses.'

[8]Straus and Dent, *John Baskerville. A Memoir*, 68, 69. Different editions of Milton's poems occupied Baskerville for the whole of 1758.

[9]Possibly that printed work, *Works II*, 380–82. *On his first arrival at the Leasowes*, 1754, by R. Dodsley.

[10]In 1758 an edition of Homer was issued by E. Ruddiman of Edinburgh, but the more famous editions of the *Iliad*, 1756, and the *Odyssey*, 1758, 4 folio vols., came from the well known Foulis press at Glasgow, and were perhaps the finest editions it produced.

[11]Allan Ramsay (1686–1758), was a correspondent of William Somervile. 1724–27 Ramsay published 3 vols. of miscellaneous poems, which contained traditional ballads, lyrics and some songs of his own. The 1728 quarto volume included *The Gentle Shepherd*. In 1737 he published a collection of Scots Proverbs.

In the B.M. there is a volume of *The Gentle Shepherd* with MS. notes by W.S.

CCXXXII

Works III, 324.

To the [REV. R. GRAVES], *in Expectation of a Visit.*

Christmas, 1758.

Dear Mr. Graves,

There *can* be nothing more welcome to me than the intelligence which you give of your intended visit at The Leasowes. —God knows how few of these interviews may for the future be allotted to us; and I should be glad at least to testify the joy which they afford me, by meeting you at Birmingham, or elsewhere within one day's journey for my chaise.—Pray be so good as to give me one more letter before you set out.— Very glad should I be to pay my respects to your brother at Mickleton, for whom I have the truest respect; but dare not give encouragement, for fear that ought should interfere.—I have ten thousand things to say to you; but will defer them, I think, *all.* I am positive your [*Spiritual Quixote?*] may be made *advantageous* to you by means of Dodsley; and even *reputable,* if you so please.—Will not Mrs. G[raves] accompany you? pray convince her of my sincere regard.

I want to congratulate you on your escape from the small-pox, in a manner *different* from your ordinary acquaintance; yet am not able to express my sentiments—guess the rest; knowing, and sufficiently knowing, that I am, with constancy and ardour, your most affectionate friend,

W. SHENSTONE.

CCXXXIII

Works III, 325.

To MR. JAGO.

THE LEASOWES,
Jan. 6, 1759.

Dear Mr. Jago,

If you know the maxims on which I conduct myself, you might call me perhaps *unpolite;* but, I think, by no means *unfriendly;* I mean with respect to the *ordinary congratulations* on your *marriage.*[1] Were you and I less intimate, less experienced, and less assured friends, it had been no venial omission to have neglected such a ceremony. Perhaps I should not have neglected it; but as I have the satisfaction of believing that you would rejoice in any success of mine, so I hope you would not distrust my sentiments upon any change of your condition which you yourself esteemed for the *better.* I do indeed, my worthy friend, wish you much joy, both *now,* and at *all* times; and you will ever discern it in my face, as often as fortune grants us an interview. Mr. S—— is a benevolent man, and I am sure would withhold no information that tended to *illustrate* our friendship on either side.

I have thoughts of proceeding on to Harbury, whenever I come to Mr. Wren's; as I have long enough made my friend a promise, and intend ere long to do. Many reasons occur why I cannot set forward to-morrow morning: are these reasons substantial, or no other than the sly and sophistical insinuations of indolence?—surely the former.

Dodsley, and indeed Mr. Spence, both expect me in town this February.—I fear it will not *be;* but if it *should,* how readily would I give notice, and become obliged to you for your company.

Though I should have *expected* you would select a partner whose society you could enjoy, yet I was not a little satisfied with the hint given me in your letter, as well as in one I had before received from Mr. S——. It is not for such ladies as you and I esteem, that Mrs. Bellamy's extraordinary lecture was intended;[2] and a *lecture* it would have been with a vengeance, had not D[odsley] omitted some thirty lines, and substituted about twelve or fourteen of his own. However, he is now going to print his fourth edition of it; in which the original epilogue will be restored, as well as considerable improvements introduced into his play. He sold two thousand of his first edition, the very first day he published it.

I have so *much* to tell you, and of so *various* kinds, that I am afraid to expatiate upon *any* one article. Cannot you make a shift to call upon me, before *my public life* arrives?—I would send my chaise to meet you at any place you should appoint.

I have passed my winter hitherto pretty chearfully amongst my books, in what I *call* my library. It now better deserves that name, by the form I have given it, and the volumes I have added. Mr. S— would tell you something of my *other* occupations.

I could wish that you would favour me with a copy of your Essay on Electricity, and with any new copy of verses of your own, or of your friends.—Be not apprehensive: there shall nothing appear in print of your composition any more, without your explicit consent.—And yet I have thoughts of amusing myself with the publication of a small Miscellany from neighbour Baskerville's press, if I can save myself harmless as to expence—I purpose it no larger than a 'Lansdown's,'[3] a 'Philips's,' or a 'Pomfret's Poems.'[4]

Have you read my friend Dr. Grainger's Tibullus? It affords you an elegant edition of a good translation and of the text. He is engaged in a war with S[mollett][5], and has just sent me his pamphlet; which I could wish you to read, in order to form a judgement of S[mollett]'s character.—Spence, I see, has advertised his 'Parallel betwixt Malliabecqui and his Taylor.'[6] It is merely a charitable design: and such are now all Spence's views.

What remains of my paper must be employed not in *mere* ceremony, although in something that bears the form of it: in my best compliments to Mrs. Jago, and my offer, not indeed of a part of the friendship which I owe you, but rather of an equal quantity; in an assurance of the cordiality with which I shall rejoice to see both her and you; and in confirmation of that affection with which I have ever been, and am, my good friend, your most obedient servant,

W. SHENSTONE.

NOTES

[1] Jago married secondly, in October 1758, Margaret, daughter of James Underwood, of Rugeley.

[2] A note *Works* III, 326, reads: See Epilogue to *Cleone*. The Epilogue to *Cleone* takes the form of a lament for the time

> 'When women hid their necks and veil'd their faces,
> Nor romp'd, nor rak'd, nor star'd at public places,
> Nor took the airs of amazons for gaces.'

> The 'modish fair' are urged 'to bring those days agen,
> And form anew the hearts of thoughtless men.'

[3]George Granville, Lord Lansdowne (1667-1735), verse writer and dramatist.

[4]John Pomfret (1667-1702).

[5]*Critical Review*, December 1758, 475, gives a lengthy review by Smollett of *Tibullus*, with selections 'to show that the doctor has not found it an easy task to preserve the elegance and harmony of his original.' Smollett's criticism was really biting, whereas that which appeared in *The Monthly Review*, 1759, Vol. 20, was thoroughly laudatory. Comment was made upon Smollet's Review in *The Gentleman's Magazine*, 1759, 83.

[6]Spence's *A Parallel in the Manner of Plutarch between Robert Hill, the learned tailor and Magliabecchi*, 1757, was included in Dodsley's *Fugitive Pieces*, 1761.

CCXXXIV

B.M. Add. MSS. 27548.

[*To* JOHN SCOTT HYLTON.]

*March. 2d—*1759.

The Green is right—I wish I *could* get some Liquid Verdigrease; but have many times endeavoured to make it, without effect—you must not speak one word against taking this Sett of Lettering types; as I myself take an octavo Sett, and ye opportunity of borrowing each other's, will be so wonderfully convenient—you will Learn to Letter in a days time; and may make *immediate* experim^{ts} on some of y^r blue Paper; first rubbing it over wth glare of egg; then, slightly, wth sweet oil: then lay on L. gold—then apply ye Letter just so hot as not to burn—I will tell Mr. Dodsley how ye small sett is dispos'd— they will be about 7^s or thereab^{ts}. Mr. Mc Leod says—It is impossible to find a *slip* tonight—were I as low a Punster as Pixell, I wou'd say y^r Boy may find *Many*.

Mr. Hylton.

CCXXXV

B.M. Add. MSS. 27548.

[*To* JOHN SCOTT HYLTON.]

Sunday, 11th *March* 1759.

My Compliments—I return *Some* of Mr. H's Books, & will e'er long dismiss ye remainder—Fiddian may go with Dick, if he will be here by six o'clock to-morrow morning—

Otherwise, Miss Wight[1] comes this afternoon to see what can be done by means of Mr. H's threepence. At present, it lies *wholly* upon *me* to fetch both news and Letters—I mean for a *certainty*—nor can I, even thus, answer by return of Post; without sending twice the same Day—'Twould be prodigiously *convenient* to have Letters &c arrive regularly, by 12 o'Clock, on Post-days—Mrs. Acton *has* some turn for *Elegance*, (unless Miss Wight be *too much* attach'd to her)—and would have given them a better Turn both in point of *happiness* and *Figure*, might she have had her own way—Mr. Hylton's review never came—but I will give Aris a trimming, tomorrow. Mine I send; which will occasion me to buy a Book or two—Poor Grainger has *not quite Justice* done him.

I had yesterday 2 Letters from Tom Saunders at Guadalope; which I directly sent to Admiral Smith; and now, to his sister Wilkinson—He is Lieutenant (now,) in ye Berwick—Mr. H. heard of our success there—I have got ye Admiral's Douglas &c: with a second double entendre—Mr. Dodsley (wth a short Letter) has sent me a pair of Swans from London, in a Cage as big as Mr. Hylton's Shop—they come home tomorrow—The Cutts to Pamela are elegant, but not so *accurate* as I wish 'em; and must be returned by Fiddian in ye morn: being M'acleod's. I will get Mr. H. some Russia L. at Birm: if he will; but there are *two* sufficient reasons why he must not trust to this at John Taylors[2]—Let ye Emrald go.

NOTES

[1]Miss Wight and Captain Wight appear to have been near neighbours.

[2]Possibly John Taylor, a Birmingham tradesman, who did japanning and lacquering in Crooked Lane. Hill, *The Bookmakers of Old Birmingham*, 91.

CCXXXVI

Historical Society of Pennsylvania.

[*To* Mr. MILWARD.]

Dear Sir,

I sent you a Letter, sometime ago, under Cover to my Friend Dodsley, and as I trust he would not fail to forward it, was in Hopes, before this time, to have receiv'd some Answer to the Case in Question. I beg you would press for the Council's opinion, by as much application as you think decent. Dolman gives me now no sort of Answer to anything I ask or propose; refuses to fish the Pool, tho' he wants Fish as well as myself, and tho', whether *by* ye Article or without it, I have a Claim to half the Fish there. I am in no sort of apprehension for aught they can recollect of my expressions at the Stour-bridge-meeting. It is possible, I might say, during the Course of our Conversation, that 'I should hardly trouble myself any more about it' or 'I believe I never shall go to Law for it' or some such kind of Phrase, in regard to ye Berkswell estate; without however it's being *propos'd* to me as a *Condition* of our agreement; or my ever purposing to *make* it *so*. Saunders, as I am told, recollects some words of this sort—Ld Stamford, I *hear*, does *not*; and Hollier remembers nothing said about it.

All this while he witholds my Money; with an eye to which I have done many things, which I needed *not* have done this year; & how far he will be dispos'd to pay Interest for ye same, I know not. Unless he *do*, I have not my Equivalent. Besides all my affairs are so unsettled, thro' Default of this Paym^t & Accommodation, that I fear it will be greatly in his Power to distress me by his Delay—It seems to be his intended Point—Nevertheless, I am still fully purposed to renounce no *real* claim to Berkswell.

Wednesday last, I had ye Favor of a visit from the Miss Milwards, Miss Batchelor, Mr. Meredyth & Mrs. Cookes; who din'd here, & were intirely well: seem'd to expect you in a Fortnight. However, Let me beg that you wou'd favor me, with a few Lines on the receipt of these.

I am, Sir,

Y^r most obed^t hum: Ser:

WILL: SHENSTONE.

Sunday, March ye 12th
1759.

To
Mr. Milward, at
Mr. Henrick's, in Bell-yard
near Temple-barr;
London.

CCXXXVII

Hull, I, 253.

To Mr. DODSLEY.

March 31, 1759.

Dear Mr. DODSLEY,

I am afraid you think me negligent: know then that I sat down last Thursday, to write you a long Letter, about seven o'Clock at Night, when I discovered that the Post went out at that very Hour I sat down to write. I had immediate Recourse to such Consolation as the Case admitted; and supposed a Letter received on *Monday* Morning, might do near as well as one on *Saturday* Night, considering that *Sunday* intervened, which must be a leisure Day, *even* for *Printers*. But in good Earnest now, do you *think* me lazy? Or have you, under your present *Dissipation*, an *heavier* Complaint against my *Diligence*? You and I shall hardly agree about the *Means* of *estimating* Letters; you, conscious of your own Genius, are desirous to value them by their *Weight*; while I, conscious of my late *Industry*, would fix their Value by the Number of *Words*. What Pretensions, pray, can you suggest, for so very *perverse* a Manner of Reckoning? Is not *Industry* a *Moral Virtue*? And are not many written Words a *Proof* of Industry? But though your *Ingenuity* be even a Miracle, you will hardly prove it to be *a moral Virtue*, unless indeed, in the *Way you manage it;* and *so, all* your Faculties are moral Virtues: however, we less *artful*, or less *heroick* Personages, must magnify the Virtues that we *have;* of these, Industry is one, though perhaps *this* had scarce been *allowed* me, till within these three or four Months past. I say, that we, who are the *Animæ nil magnæ Laudis egentes;* we, the *Animæ viles, inhumata infletaque turba:*[1] In other Words, the *Numerus*, and the '*nati Fruges consumere* if *we* would appear considerable, pray what Method can we take? I know, indeed, but two; the one of disparaging *your* Abilities which is not quite so feasible; the other, of taking all occasion to magnify our own good Qualities. If then, Industry be a Virtue, I am possessed of it very remarkably: Not a Moment of my Time passes, but I am employed, either in overseeing Labourers; reading ROBINSON'S *History of Scotland;*[2] writing in my Paper Books, ('tis not material *what*, but writing;) perplexing the *Birmingham* Artists with Sketches for Improvements in their Manufactures, which they *will* not understand; and lastly, and finally, feeding my Poultry, my Ducks, my Pigeons, and my Swans; which last give me as much Pleasure, as what I had before gave me Vexation. No inconsiderable Panegyrick, I'll assure you! And surely this is not only *Industry*, but an *Industry* of a *better Kind* than what employs the *Animæ viles* of a Drawing-room. And now this *last Instance* of my great Industry puts me in Mind of asking you a Question:

Pray now, you that are a Mythologist, what an absurd Man you are, not to jump at an Invitation to come directly to the *Leasowes?* Here am I, (like your Friend ÆSOP, before OGILBY'S *Fables*;[3] or like ADAM, in our old *Bibles*) sitting once or twice a Day with every created Animal before me. Is not this the only Residence for a Person that is writing Fables? 'Tis true, this very Person may contemplate better in a *Crowd*, than *another* in the Depth of Solitude: *you* may far surpass *me*, who thus *converse* with *Birds*, while he describes a Sparrow from *Pall-Mall*, or a King-fisher from *Charing-Cross*: but *Imagination* is a prodigious *Heightener*, and unless he paints them from Life, may he not *attribute* to a *King-fisher* much finer Feathers than he in Truth possesses? Pray take the Opinion of Mr. SPENCE—How I blush, while I recollect that Name! And yet, were it not for my *own* Omissions, it must revive *only* my most *favourite* Ideas. Surely 'tis written in the Book of Fate, that I shall discharge my Debt within a Post or two, for Fate evidently enough interferes, or I could never have been so long silent. I am almost ashamed to desire my humble Respects to him, and yet it is impossible for me to suppress my Feelings.

I must now proceed to Business. Past six o'Clock once more; but the Post now goes out at ten. If you *can* procure me the quarto Cuts for MILTON, it will be a very desirable Favour.

Mr. BOND has made some Alterations in your *Grove*, which I thought very pretty on its *Arrival;* yet, perhaps, he may be right enough, if Mr. GRIGNION[4] can comprehend his Meaning. The Trees he means *on the wrong Side the Water*, are some of those opposite to the Letter S, which I have put upon the Back: but I am fearful of *spoiling;* and must beg Mr. GRIGNION would re-compare the Print with Mr. BOND's original Drawing, then retouch his Plate, and let me have a few more Proof-Sheets of both the Prints. Give me one or two Lines by *Return* of Post, if possible.

No Books ready? I want MALLET's Works, bound in *Russia* Leather, and lettered on Green. Pray excuse this last vile Page. I have wasted my Time, and now am utterly at a Fault for it.

W. SHENSTONE.

NOTES

[1]Virgil, *Aeneid*, XI, 372.

[2]William Robertson's (1721–1793) *History of Scotland* appeared February 1, 1759. Robinson is probably a misprint for Robertson. Robertson was in London in the spring of 1758, making arrangements for the publication of his history, and he returned on horseback by way of Birmingham and the Leasowes. W.S. makes no mention of this. John Home, friend of Robertson, is mentioned as calling on W.S., Letter to Dodsley, May 30, 1758.

[3]A rhyming paraphrase of Æsop's *Fables*, published by Ogilby in 4to in 1651.

[4]Charles Grignion (1717–1810), line engraver, obtained much work from the booksellers and illustrated books chiefly from the designs of Gravelot, F. Hayman, S. Wale and J. H. Mortimer.

CCXXXVIII

Works III, 329.

To MR. GRAVES, *on their several Situations and Compositions.*

THE LEASOWES,

April 18, 1759.

Dear Mr. Graves,

You will think my silence long; and I should be sorry to *have* you quite regardless of it; although, I fear, it must be my fate to trespass frequently upon your kind solicitude.—I have no excuse to make, beside some frivolous avocations, and *much* of that heaviness and lassitude which disinclines one to write letters.—I passed the former part of my winter with more vivacity than I did the latter, or even the incipient spring; owing, possibly, to these cold winds, which will not permit me to use my wonted exercise. You will laugh at the word *vivacity*, when applied to so dull an animal; but I speak comparatively of that unmeaning drowsiness which is my lot at other times, and *was*, in some sort, while you were here.

Mr. Dodsley tells me, he received a letter from you, acquainting him that Cleone would be played at Bath: I should be glad to receive from you any particulars of its success. He is publishing an elegant edition of it, which I expect by this very post. The new plate of my grove, which will appear at the end of his Melpomene, is perhaps liable to some exceptions; but, by much, the best that has yet appeared. Do not forget to send me your objections to it. As to the epilogue, I have totally banished, I think, every one of the lines which he *substituted;* have left to him the choice of two or three readings for the four last lines; and though none of them quite please me, yet the epilogue, on the whole, discovers more of genius, is more spirited, and less inaccurate. I shall be glad to find that you think the same with me.

In regard to your place, so far as I can form an idea of it, I would have you consult *self*-amusement; I mean, without too much regard to what *others* say or think. As to distinguishing your ingenuity (which I unfeignedly desire you may), the press affords you more *adequate* materials than either your fortune or, perhaps, your place. Do not imagine, however, that I shall not be much delighted with every stroke I trace of yours at Claverton. My faculties are very strongly intuitive in respect of every thing belonging to you; and I should be ashamed if any nook or angle that you had rounded; any wall that you had ruinated; any stream that you had diverted; or any single shrub that you had planted; should elude my discovery: yet you will shine *more* by means of the press; and if I said any thing concerning your [*Spiritual Quixote?*], that did not *encourage* you to perfect it, I am sure, I must use terms very inexpressive of my meaning. Without any more words, let me *intreat* you to proceed with it; give a *full scope* to your imagination; and if there should be aught one would wish *retrenched*, it is mighty *easily done*.

I have indeed *thoughts* (for I *never* use the word *resolutions*) of publishing my Elegies next winter—you will gainsay, when I tell you my intention of publishing also my very farm; at least, about eight or ten scenes taken from it, by way of top and tail-pieces for those Elegies.—The world will perhaps tax my vanity; but I do not in the least care.—The pleasure which that world gives me, I am very conscious, will not be too *high;* and I am determined that the pain it may seek to give shall bear proportion: yet should I be sorry to obtrude stuff upon it, either from the pencil or the pen; and my good friend Mr. Dodsley has sometimes pained me, not a little.

I tell you, you *cannot* allow for winter.—That very scene near Priory-gate shews not a bit of road in *summer;* though the consciousness of a firm rail there would add to my tranquillity. —Mr. Knight has given me Strange's[1] prints, which, I hear, are fine. Dodsley gives me swans: but for these two months past I have been a librarian, or rather a bookbinder; yet nothing more *unfeignedly,* than yours and Mrs. Graves's most affectionate humble servant.

W. SHENSTONE.

NOTE

[1]Sir Robert Strange (1721–1792), engraver.

CCXXXIX

B.M. Add. MSS. 27548.

[*To* JOHN SCOTT HYLTON.]

24. *Apr.* 1759.

This Picture will go near to please Miss Lea—As for *precision,* it is in vain to think of it, till I can procure some Impressions in blue; on a Paper y^t is Less exceptionable. I c^d wish ye Light had fallen on ye Birds back, which Amos Green w^d not allow—'Tis *there* ye blue is so very *lively,* as to make y^e *whole bird* appear of y^t colour.

Mr. Hylton had better attempt no other, till we have fresh impressions, and ye body of a K. fisher. I go to-morrow to Mr. Deans, and from thence, perhaps, to Mr. Knight's, where I am ask'd to meet Mr. Palmey Family—I hear no news saving w^t Mr. Wight and Dr. Altree tell me, y^t Parson Wilmot, and Parson Lea had a sort of Brush in Hagley Lane—last week —Parson Lea sent me his Son's Letter to ye Admiral, with a

circumstantial and ever pompous acc^t of their Capture. The
£
Adm^l says 700 to 'em at *Least*.

The little girl said 'four of them Little ones were to visit
Parson Boyce at Whitsuntide—but did not know how they
s^d get thither: told me Mrs. Boyce said I was a mighty good-
natur'd man and y^t she didn't doubt I shoud very readily
lend 'em my P. Chaise. Such are ye words of *pertness* mix^t wth
Cunning—wch I am never inclin'd to gratify—Dodsley's Play
is worse in one or two places, but better in an hundred and
fifty—inexpressibly amended.

CCXL (a)

B.M. Add. MSS. 28221.
Hull, I, 258.
Hecht, 16.

[*To* THOMAS PERCY.]

THE LEASOWES,
June the 6th 1759.

Dear Sir,

It is perhaps no uncommon Case for ye Magnitude of a
Debt to *preclude*, or at least to *retard* every step towards a Discharge. In truth, the many Favors you have confer'd upon
me by the Packets I have received from Easton-mauduit, have
made me quite asham'd of such a *partial* Payment, as my *Health*
and *Leisure* would have permitted me to make. When I complain of indifferent Health, I mean no other y^n a kind of
Drowsihed or *Lentor*, which has somewhat infested me all this
Season: Perhaps it were better *express'd* by the disreputable
name *stupidity*. Be that however as it may; It is by *this* alone I
have been disqualify'd for those refin'd sorts of Amusement, in
which your obliging Letters, & the Packets enclos'd in them,
requir'd me to engage.—I have been expected to pass a week
at Shifnall[1] ever since the beginning of May; where I was by
particular appointment to meet our Friend Mr. Binnel. The
visit *is not* laid aside; but will probably not take Place till after
a Fortnight or three weeks. One Pleasure I expect from it

(besides what I shall receive from Mr. Pitt and Mr. Slaney's Company) turns upon the opportunity it will afford me of reading over with Binnel y^r Translation of Ovid's Epistles:[2] And it has been with *this* view, in some measure, that I have defer'd ye examination you desir'd me to bestow upon it. In *general*, I wou'd wish you to make it as just to the Author, and to y^r own Sentiments, as you can; and *afterwards* employ *me* as a *mere* Musick-master, whom you would wish to tune y^r Harpsichord: At *most*, to retrench any little Incroachments upon Simplicity, ease of Style, and Harmony.

I want to communicate *many* things, but must defer *most* of them 'till I *see* you. And pray, Let Mrs. Percy know that I am one of your *peculiar* Friends; and then I hope she will not scruple to recompence me with an *irregular* Visit by way of *Distinction*. I brought my Friend Jago's new Bride to pay me that Compliment ye other Day.

Mr. Dodsley, in his last Letter, desir'd I would present you with his new Edition of Cleone; which is y^e *only* one you should preserve. It is, according to my exactest calculation, *improv'd* in about an 100 Places; merely alter'd in about 6; and perhaps injur'd in about 4. I will either keep it till you come; or send it *directly* if you will acquaint me *How*.

I had retouch'd and transcrib'd both Edom of Gordon & the Gentle Heardsman, long before ye arrival of y^r Letter. The *former* I read to a *Scotchman*, who seem'd a good deal pleas'd with it. Your *supplemental* stanzas to ye g. Herdsman, must undoubtedly approach much nearer to what was y^e *orig: reading*, than those which I have substituted; having not ye final words to direct me—I will not send them you *now;* because I would multiply your Inducements to pass a Day or two at the Leasows, at this best season of ye year.

You must by all means read Dr. Young's 'Conjectures on original Composition; even tho' it shou'd dissuade you, when you have compleated Ovid, from undertaking any more *translations*. I should not *murmur* at y^e *effect*; provided it stimulate you to write *Originals*.[3] I have Likewise read y^e 'Essay on the present State of Learning &c written by a Dr. Goldsmith, whom you know; & whom such as read it, will *desire* to know. I dissent from him however in his Partiality to Rhime (I mean

2L

in works of Length) but as to ye present pomp & Haughtiness of style *instead* of *sentiment*, am entirely of his Opinion.[4] Caractacus[5] I've not yet seen. La Motte[6] has lately afforded me not a Little entertainment: I read it on acct. of *Dodsley*, who, you know is writing *Fables*, & ask'd my Thoughts upon the *subject*.[7]

Pray keep me well with Dr. Grainger. I'm quite asham'd of my neglect. Had I known his Intention of *answering* Smollet, I would have us'd my endeavours to dissuade him. The *properest* answer had been convey'd in a few short notes in ye next Edition of his Tibullus. Pray have you seen Smollet's reply? I suppose, sufficiently scurrilous.—Y^r Friend Mr. Johnson was so good as to send me a Little Poem call'd ye Parish Clerk (by Vernon)[8] including a Comp. on my Schoolmistress. I am surprisd at the *Language* and *Harmony* of Period—shall send for his whole Book; & wish to do the Man some real Good.

Y^e 'Bacco-stopper[9] you gave to [Hylton] has been ye occasion of a Plot, at the *Denouement* of which, It will be worth y^r while to be at the Leasowes.

Suffice it, that I accompany'd y^r Favor[10] with a forgd Letter from Mr. Moody; mentioning y^e *Deposition* of of [sic] one Mr. Fitzdottrel, Cabinet-Maker (of whom ye said Moody is feign'd to buy ye Stopper) before ye Mayor of Stratford, in regard to its *authenticity* offering to join Mr. [Hylton] in ye purchase of y^e *whole Tree*. Mr. [Hylton]'s reply (*intercepted*) desires only a *part* of the Tree to make a *Cup;* whereon he purposes something carv'd in Basso Relievo. Moody is made to answer, y^t he has purchased the Tree, & sends H. one large *Arm* thereof wrapt up in brown-Paper. Moreover, (according to ye natural Propensity of Tradesmen) gets him the Cup *made* and *Carv'd.*—In *one* Compartment, Fitzdotterel making Oath before ye Mayor of Stratford—In another, Shakespear, with a gardiners apron, planting ye very tree; & Moody, in the *Middle*, shewing it to Mr. [Hylton] on the *right*—The Cup is now in my Bureau with ye Figures well-enough executed. Moody also is made to tell of a Man at Nottingham y^t has a Large Collection *in His way*, which he thinks he would be glad to part with, having a Family of 10 Children to whom y^e

Money would do more good. Moody is then desir'd to procure *the List:* and *here* you must assist me. I have gott for Him, the Spoon wth which old Parr[11] eat Buttermilk; and am promis'd a real King William's-Bib., for Mr. [Hylton] to wear on y[e] Day of his Patron-saint—But with regard to these things at *present,* Lay y[r] Finger upon y[r] upper Lip.

I had y[e] enclos'd *King-fisher* engrav'd for me—purposing to assume it for Arms—but this the *profane* and *vulgar* must not know; on whom *Arms* strike no small Impression. (Qui stupet in titulis & imaginibus. Hor.)[12]

This *grove* you will have more agreeably at y[e] End of Dodsley's Cleone.—My best respects to Mrs. Percy.—

I am with great Regard
Y[r] most obedt.
W. SHENSTONE.

Pray write directly.

To the Rev[d]. Mr. Percy.

NOTES

[1]Percy's note: 'With Mr. Humphrey Pitt, Uncle to Mr. Binnel.'

[2]Grainger's translation of Hero and Leander was for Percy's projected edition of Ovid's *Epistles* (Nichols, *Illustrations of Literature*, VII). Grainger wrote to Percy, January 10, 1759: 'Last night I compared it (version of Ovid's Epistle [Leander to Hero]) accurately with the original and was amazed to find it so exact, and at the same time so flowing and easy.' On February 17, 1759, he wrote: 'I have spoken both to Millar and Dodsley about Ovid, but neither of them seems inclined to make a purchase of the work. I doubt not, however, but that either of them would readily print the Epistles, and become joint partners with you in profit and loss. Perhaps, too, this would be your most profitable scheme, as I am confident your book, whenever it appears, will cut out both Dryden, and Barrett, who is neither a poet nor a lover.'

[3]Edward Young's *A letter to Richardson, Conjectures on Original Composition*, 1759, was written when the author was nearly eighty years old.

Young says that no imitation, however good, can be of as much worth as an original. 'We read imitation with somewhat of his languor, who listens to a twice-told tale. Our spirits rouze at an Original that is a perfect stranger, and all throng to learn what news from a foreign land. . . . But why are Originals so few? not because the writer's harvest is over, the great reapers of antiquity having left nothing to be gleaned after them; nor because the human mind's teeming time is past, or because it is incapable of putting forth unprecedented births; but because illustrious examples engross, prejudice, and intimidate.' See Modern Language Texts, Reprint, pp. 7 & 9. This very lively bit of criticism received comment from many of the notable people of the day.

[4]Oliver Goldsmith's *Enquiry into the Present State of Polite Learning*, was published by Dodsley, 1759. 'Those who are acquainted with writing know that our language runs almost naturally into blank verse. The writers of our novels, romances, and all of this class who have no notion of style, naturally hobble into this unharmonious measure. If rhymes, therefore, be more difficult, for that very reason I would have our poets write in rhyme. Such a restriction upon the thought of a good poet, often lifts and increases the vehemence of every sentiment; for fancy, like a fountain, plays highest by diminishing the aperture.' Ch. IX.

Ibid XI. 'The solemnity worn by many of our modern writers is, I fear, often the mask of dulness; . . . It were to be wished, therefore, that we no longer found pleasure with the inflated style that has for some years been looked upon as fine writing, and which every young writer is now obliged to adopt, if he chooses to be read. We should now dispense with loaded epithet and dressing up trifles with dignity. For, to use an obvious instance, it is not those who make the greatest noise with their wares in the streets that have most to sell. Let us instead of writing finely, try to write naturally: not hunt after lofty expressions to deliver mean ideas, nor be for ever gaping, when we only mean to deliver a whisper.'

[5]William Mason (1724–1797), friend and biographer of Gray published *Caractacus*, a Dramatic Poem, in 1759.

[6]Antoine Houdart de la Motte (1672–1731), poet, critic. His *Fables* are his only poetic work remembered now.

[7]Percy's note: 'Thus far this Letter is printed in Mr. Hull's Select Letters 1778. Vol. I. Letter 65, p. 258.'

[8]Percy's note: 'A common soldier, originally bred a Buckle-maker at Wolverhampton.' William Vernon wrote *The Parish Clerk*, 1759, and *Poems on Several Occasions*, 1758, the title page of which describes him as 'a Private Soldier in the Buffs.' The compliment on *The Schoolmistress* ran thus:

> 'Let courtly bards in polish'd phrase endite
> Soft madrigals, to celebrate the fair;
> Or paint the splendor of a birth-day night,
> Where Peers and Dames in shining robes appear;
> The task be mine neglected worth to praise,
> Alas! too often found, in these degen'rate days.
>
> O gentle Shenstone! could the self-taught Muse,
> Who joys, like thine, in rural shades to stay,
> Could she, like thine, while she her theme pursues,
> With native beauties deck the pleasing lay;
> Then should the humble Clerk of Barton-Dean
> An equal meed of praise with thy *School-Mistress* gain.'

[9]Percy's note: 'Mr. Moody, who kept the great Toy-shop at Birmingham, had to sell a Parcel of Tobacco-Stoppers; the Top of wch consisted of a Head of Shakespeare indifferently cut, made of Mulberry Wood from a Tree pretended to have been planted by Shakespeare. I bought One for a Shilling and sent it to Mr. (Hylton) who collected curiosities.'

[10]Percy's note: 'The Tobacco-Stopper had been left at Mr. Shenstone's in order to be conveyed to Mr. (Hylton).'

[11]Thomas Parr (1483?–1635), of Shropshire, was reputed to have lived to the age of 169, when he was exhibited at Court. This change in his life brought about his death. He was buried in Westminster Abbey.

[12]Horace, *Satires*, I, VI, 17.

CCXL (*b*)

Messrs. Rosenbach MS.

[*To* THOMAS PERCY.]

THE LEASOWES, *June ye 6th*, 1759.

Dear Sir:

It is perhaps no uncommon case for the Magnitude of a Debt, to prevent or at least retard every *step* towards a Discharge. It truth, the many Favors you have confer'd upon me, by the Packets I have receiv'd from East-on Mauduit, have made me asham'd of such a partial Payment as my Health & Leisure would permit. When I complain of Health, I mean no other than a kind of *Drowsihed* & Lentor which has somewhat infested me at this season: Perhaps it were better express'd by the disreputable name, Stupidity: Be that however as it may, It is by this chiefly I have been disqualify'd from those refin'd sorts of Amusements in which your Letters & Packets requir'd me to engage. I have been expected to pass a week at Shifnall ever since ye beginning of May: where I was by particular appointment to meet our Friend Mr. Binnel. The Visit is not laid aside, but will probably take place in about a fortnight's time or Less. One Pleasure I expect from it, beside what I shall reap from Mr. Pitt & Mr. Slaney's Company & that turns upon the opportunity it will afford me of perusing your Ovid in conjunction with Mr. Binnel: And it has been *this* view, in some measure that I have deferd the examination you desir'd me to bestow upon it. In general, I would wish you to make it as just to the Author's sense, & to your own sentiments as you can, and afterwards consider me as a mere musick-master whom you would employ as a proper person to tune yr. Harpsichord: In other words, to retrench any little encroach-ments upon Simplicity, ease of style, or Harmony.

I want to communicate many things, but must defer most of them 'till I can see you. And pray let Mrs. Percy know me for one of your *peculiar* Friends; & then I hope she will not scruple to reward me wth an irregular visit by way of Distinc-tion. I brought my friend Jago's new Bride to pay me that Compliment the other Day.

Mr. Dodsley in his last letter desir'd I would present you with his new Edition of Cleone, which is the only one you should preserve. It is, according to my best calculation, improv'd in about an 100 places, merely alter'd in about six, & perhaps injur'd in about Four. I will either keep it till you come, or send it to you, if you will shew me *How*.

I had retouched & transcrib'd both the gentle Herdsman & Edom of Gordon, long before your Letter arriv'd; Your supplemental stanzas must undoubtly approach nearer to

what was ye original reading than those which I have substituted, and which I will not send you now, because I will
multiply your Inducements to visit my Place in the proper
season.

You must, by all means, read Dr. Younge's new 'Conjectures on original Composition, & Let it deterr you, when you
have compleated Ovid, from engaging in any more translations. I have also read ye essay on ye present state of Learning
written by a Dr. Goldsmith whom you know, & whom such as
read it will desire to know. La Motte also has afforded me no
little entertainment. I read it on account of Dodsley who you
may remember is writing Fables, & who has requested me to
send him my thoughts upon ye Subject.

> Dr. Granger
> King fisher—
> Vernons P
> Hyltons Cup. Ye Denouement.

[Not signed].

CCXLI

Pierpont Morgan Library.

[*To* J. S. HYLTON.]

My Complim^{ts}—We are all risen, & in great Forwardness
—Hark away! Hark away! Fly to y^e [indiscipherable in MS.]
Hark away!

I beg Mr. Hylton w^d bring with Him six more Papers of
ye Bark—& a Paper of Hearts-ease pounded for Miss Fanny.

W. SHENSTONE.

{ *Monday, Aug^{st} 6th* 1759 [*in another hand*]
  Received the Above before Six o'Clock
  in the Morning.

CCXLII

B.M. Add. MSS. 27548.

[*To* JOHN SCOTT HYLTON.]

11 *Aug.* 1759.[1]

Our Compliments to Mr. Hylton—who will be so good as Let me know how far John Taylor has proceeded with Mr. Dean's Cage—(He seems extremely angry, y^t it is defer'd—) We want also to hear how the Bodies of the Darbies are to be dispos'd of—I *mean* principally, *where*.

Will Mr Hylton be so good as Look *himself*, or *Lend me Books* to Examine, how far ye word dicat—or dat, dicat &c: may be us'd (wth Authority) without an accusative Case after it; to intimate ye thing inscrib'd—I am forc'd, thro hurry of servants to send will back with this; & to desire he may return again when he shall be immediately dispatch'd to Birm—Mr Dodsley is writing for ye Post——

We met Mr Knight & a flashy West Indian (one Mr Marchant) at the Inn at Enville—went to Worfield in ye Evening, where we found Mr Davenp^t gone to Breden; lay here; din'd yesterday wth the same Gen^{men} at Hagley; saw ye House ag^n & Park; & returnd home pretty late—I expect ye same Gent. wth others about 5 this afternoon; when we shall be glad of M^r H's Company. What a Metamorp: at ye Grange!

W.S.

Did Mr Hylton steal any of Mr Dodsley's Fables—He misses his Earthquake & Thunderstorm, & (as he thinks) some one besides.

NOTE

[1] The letter apparently belongs to the year 1759, though the date of the MS. looks more like 1757. In the summer of 1759 Dodsley was at The Leasowes preparing his edition of Fables which Baskerville was to print. The postscript to this letter suggests that he was busy with Fables.

CCXLIII

B.M. Add MSS. 28221.
Hecht, 24.

[*To* THOMAS PERCY.]

THE LEASOWES, *Octr 3^d* 1759.

Dear Sir,

May I wish you Joy of your Deliverance from the Crew of Workmen of which you complain'd, & of the Pleasure you receive from the Birth of an Infant,[1] come to divert you in their Room? Tis upon *your* account only, I can forgive him for the Interruption he gave to the visit you intended me; and yet forgive Him, I believe I must; provided he will not disturb you while you are engag'd in writing to me. I hope some time to wait upon you in Northamptonshire; but this year it was impracticable. I certainly owe all the world either visits Letters or Money. I began to *fancy* I had perform'd Feats this season; but now I sit down to reflect I can trace nothing but neglected civilities & broken engagements in all the Counties round me. Neglected, I mean, & & [sic] broken by myself. What a Temptation, to Me, is your old Folio of MS. ballads! At present Let me thank you for the Spanish Ballad you were so kind to send me; which is indeed a good one, & admirably well translated. Edom of Gordon, of which you desire a Copy, must receive great alteration towards the Close, before I can *endure* that you should see it; and as to the Heardsman, I will indeed send you *my* additional readings if you still desire them; tho' they can only afford you ample Reason to be perfectly satisfy'd with your *own*.—If you do not receive your Cleone by this Post, I will take particular care that you shall receive it, in a Post or two.—I was going to color you a Kingfisher &c., when Mr Hylton requested *He* might have the *merit* of coloring & conveying them to your hands. I can spare you a few more of each, if you have any Fr^d that would be oblig'd by them.— Mr Binnel I have not yet seen, and must needs be under disgrace in the neighbourhood of Shifnal; yet have I offer'd to return home with *him* from the Leasowes, come when he will. —There is one or two fine Odes in Caractacus. As for the Epigoniad, if you will excuse me, I will wholly decline the reading of it. My head will bear but a limited application; & it must be Books from which I have greater expectations, to which for the future I allott a part of mine. Rhime seems *actually* to have lost much ground in all Poems of this Nature; & were Pope's Homer to make it's first appearance now, he would be *greatly* blam'd for making use of it.[2]—I told M^r—— about the Etymologicon,[3] & presume he has acquainted you with it's arrival. By the way, I made a visit to Mr Stratford, at Merevale in Warwickshire, who was complaining, y^t (tho' a subscriber) he had never yet receiv'd Mr Lye's book. I told him I would cause Mr Lye to be inform'd of it, and did not doubt but I could procure the Book.[4]—I will occasion Pixell, when I see him next, to send ye Music-b: to my Lord Sussex. —The Plott is not unravell'd y^t concerns [Hylton]. The L^{dy}, who acted as my Amanuensis, is but just return'd from Bath. Pixell gave me ye enclos'd List, which however is too ludicrous for any one to swallow—your Coin & your Nemean Lion will be wonderfully to my purpose; as likewise your shell, ye definition of which made Dodsley and me laugh abundantly.— As to any account of Inscriptions or Improvements at the Leasowes, I will defer it till I can send you a Little Plan of my Farm, which I have lately had survey'd, & reduc'd to a small scale. I shall there with a very few words, give you a full Idea of all that's done.—And now, I think, I have taken notice of all ye topics in your Letter; except y^r request for a Motto to y^r Bee-hive; which does not *yet* occurr to me. Is there, however, no stanza you could adapt to your purpose in ye First of Dr Akenside's Odes:[5] Ego apis matinae &c.?

I have been reading, with some Pleasure, the Letters of Mme de Sevigné.[6] The Translation, which fell in my way, is very inaccurate yet somewhat spirited; seems the *hasty* production of some *French*-man, by no means void of *Genius*.

Mr Cambridge, Author of the Scribleriad and many other pieces, calld & din'd with me about a fortnight ago. He seems to have genius; &, the excrescence of genius, somewhat of Caprice & Concetto. Dodsley, who stay'd wth me about 5 weeks, went from Birm^m to Bath; where he is now, I believe, with Spence & Whitehead, & in full expectation of seeing me. This is one of ye many broken engagements, which I alluded to, before—I took Dodsley to Mr Davenport's, but, as it was a week later y^n we had appointed, had ye mortification to find the Family from Home. To *divert* vexation, on my Return back, I compos'd the Lines I send, for ye Venus in His Grotto. Tis, you know, ye Venus of Medici;[7] which has a more bashfull attitude y^n any other, & is almost hid there in a Recess. Give me y^r opinion of y^m, or propose any Improvement. There is none knows of them but Dodsley. Excuse w^t I have scrawld in a paroxysm of dullness, as it is the dullness

of your very faithfull & very affectionate

W.S.

NOTES

[1]W.S.'s note in MS. at the top of the page upside down: 'I am congratulating you on ye Birth of an imaginary Child, yet am ignorant whether you wish y^t your Child shou'd be born so soon.'

[2]William Wilkie, known as 'the Scottish Homer,' (1721–1772), published The *Epigoniad*, 1757, based on *The Iliad*, IV. It was written in heroic couplets after the manner of Pope.

[3]*Etymologicum Anglicanum*, of Francis Junius, was edited in 1743 by Edward Lye (1694–1767), Anglo-Saxon and Gothic scholar.

[4]W.S.'s note in MS.: 'He said he subscrib'd to some Doctor.'

[5]*Odes on Several Subjects*, 1745.

[6]Mme de Sevigné's letters were translated into English and published in 1758, 7 vols. 12 mo.

[7]*Works* II, 370–71.

CCXLIV

Works III, 332.

[*To the* REV. R. GRAVES], *on Fables, Mottoes, Urns, Inscriptions, &c.*

THE LEASOWES,

Oct. 3, 1759.

Dear Mr. Graves,

Depend upon it, I shall see Claverton before winter.—The mischief is, that, with as violent a propensity as ever person felt, I shall not be able to reach your hemisphere while Mr. Spence, Mr. Dodsley, and Mr. Whitehead give it such peculiar lustre, in my eyes. This I did not despair of doing at the time Mr. Dodsley left me at Birmingham. It turned upon an event,

which I did not indeed explain to him, the accommodation
of the affair with D[olman]; which concerns near one half of
my little fortune, and which, if I have any luck on my side,
must now be perfected within a fortnight. I was shewn the
rough sketch of our *conveyances* last Saturday.—Once for all,
my *indolence* is not in fault; my health and my worldly em-
barrassments *have* often been so, and at present *are*. 'Pol me
miserum, patrone, vocares, si verum, &c.'[1]

Dodsley to give his book eclat,[2] should allow himself time
to *abridge* and *polish*. It is not enough, in my opinion, merely to
surpass L'Estrange[3] and Croxall.[4] The grand *exception* to
Fables consists in giving *speech* to animals, &c. a greater
violation of *truth* than appears in any other kind of writing!
This objection is insurmountable. Their peculiar *advantage* is
to remove the offensiveness of advice; in order to which, one
should perhaps pursue a medium betwixt the superfluous
garniture of La Fontaine, &c. and the naked simplicity and
laconism of Phædrus. In respect of his own new-invented
Fables, I wish him to devise uncommon subjects, and to incul-
cate refined morals. But pray send me *your* two directly, which
will answer all that I expect in Fables.

Did Mr. Dodsley tell you of that seat in my shrubbery
which I had taken the freedom to inscribe to you? I could not
satisfy myself in an inscription; and, from a kind of spleen and
aversion to delay, made use of the shortest that I could devise.
The seat and scroll are elegant. The inscription, only,

'AMICITIAE ET MERITIS
'RICHARDI GRAVES.
'—IPSAE TE, TITYRE, PINUS, IPSI TE FONTES, &C.
'VOCABUNT.'

I will not be so affected as to pretend that the much greater
compliment you design *me* is more offensive to my modesty
than it is pleasing to my friendship. I wish however it could
be a little shortened. The 'inter hortensis elegantiæ studiosos'
seems a little too verbose for inscription. Beside, I had *rather*
the compliment were not thrown with so much *emphasis* upon
any skill I have in gardening; but in some sort *divided* betwixt
that and *poetry*, if you perceive no great objection; suppose,

'AMICITIAE G. S.
'QUI,
'NAIADAS PARITER AC MUSAS
'EXCOLENDO,
'SIMUL ET VILLAM EIUS ELEGANTISSIMAM
'NOMENQUE SUUM
'ILLUSTRAVIT.'

or,

'AMICITIAE G. S.
'QUI,
'NAIDAS PARITER AC MUSAS
'FELICITER EXCOLENDO,
'SIMUL ET PATERNA RURA
'NOMENQUE EIUS
'ILLUSTRAVIT,
'ET NOMINI SUO
'NON EXIGUUM DECUS
'ADDIDIT.'

'AMICITIAE G. S.
'QUI
'BENIGNAS PARITER EXPERTUS EST
'NAIADAS ET MUSAS.'

or,

'CUIUS VOTIS
'FAVERUNT PARITER NAIADESQUE, &c.'

A motto,
'(FORTUNATUS ET ILLE DEOS QUI NOVIT
'AGRESTES)
'PANAQUE, SILVANUMQUE, SENEM, NYMPHAS-
'QUE SORORES.' Virg. [5]

'Illustravit' seems an happy word here, if it do not savour too much of *nobility*: villa, I presume, implies no more than a country mansion-house.—But I leave the whole to your discretion.

Now you speak of *our* Arcadias, pray, did you ever see a print or drawing of Poussin's Arcadia?[6] The *idea* of it is so very pleasing to me, that I had no peace till I had used the inscription on one side of Miss Dolman's urn, 'Et in Arcadia Ego.' Mr. Anson has the two shepherds with the monument and inscription in alto relievo at Shugborough. Mr. Dodsley will borrow me a drawing of it from Mr. Spence. See it described, vol. 1, page 53, of the Abbe du Bos, 'sur la poesie et la peinture.'[7]

Tell Mr. Dodsley, if he be yet at Bath, that Mr. Cambridge called and dined with me; answering precisely to the idea which I had conceived of him from Mr. D[odsley]'s account. I wish to God he may have brought you acquainted with Mr. Spence; to whom you are, in my estimation, the most *like* of any one I know. Is Mr. Spence yet at Bath? Mr. D[odsley] is gone, or going. Either he or the former told me that anecdote[8] of Pope and the Prince of Wales long ago. Pray read Madame De Sevigné's Letters—they have amused me much of late. I hope, within a post, to send you a neat plan of my farm, &c: the same to Mr. Spence by your means, if he be at Bath. Do you hear who is to be Bishop of Worcester?[9] Give me the earliest intelligence you can gather. The late Bishop visited me last year; and intended, I hear, to have done so this. I wish we may have another as obliging and polite as I always found his late Lordship.

I want to inclose some little engravings, &c. to you, but must wait till I can get a frank. Write *directly*, for this once, I beg you, though you prove dilatory another time. Of all books whatever, read Burke (second edit.) 'Of the Sublime and Beautiful;'[10] and of all points whatever, believe that I am, with my best good wishes to Mrs. Graves, dear Sir, ever your most affectionate and invariable friend,

W. Shenstone.

'DI MEMORIA NUDRISSI PIU QUE DI SPEME.'

How do you like this motto for an urn?

My best compliments to Mr. Spence and Mr. Dodsley, if at Bath. I will write soon to each of them—your garden is as pretty as you can make it.

NOTES

[1]Horace, *Epistles* I, 7, 92–3.

[2]Dodsley's edition of Fables, *Select Fables of Esop and other Fabulists*, printed by Baskerville for Dodsley, February 9, 1761.

[3]Sir Roger L'Estrange (1616–1704), published 1692, *The Fables of Æsop and other eminent Mythologists with Moral Reflections.*

[4]Samuel Croxall, D.D. (d. 1752), published 1722 *Fables of Æsop and others, newly done into English, with an application to each Fable, illustrated with cuts.*

[5]Virgil, *Georgics*, II, 493.

[6]Gaspar Poussin (1613–1670), and Nicholas Poussin (1594–1665), had a great influence on eighteenth century garden art, and one finds frequent mention of their names during the period. See Manwaring, *Italian Landscape in the 18th Century.*

[7]Jean-Baptiste Dubos (1679–1742), wrote *Reflexions Critiques sur la Poésie et la Peinture,* 1719.

[8]Footnote *Works* III, 336: 'On the Prince's asking Pope, how he could be glad to see him, when he expressed so much contempt of Kings; Pope answered, "Though he did not like old Lyons, he loved the young ones before their claws grew".'

[9]Isaac Maddox died September 27, 1759, and was succeeded by Dr. James Johnson (1705–1774), who earned for himself a reputation as a very kindly, amiable man.

[10]Edmund Burke's (1729–1797), *A Philosophical Inquiry into the Origin of our Ideas of the Sublime and the Beautiful,* 1757. The second edition was published by Dodsley, January 10, 1759.

Dr. Jacob Schwartz showed me W.S.'s copy of the first edition of *The Sublime & Beautiful,* which afterwards became the property of Richard Graves, and contains on the end-paper the inscription: 'Ric. Graves 1763. e Musaeo defuncti amici G. Shenstone.' The volume contains criticisms in the margin, some in the hand of W.S. and some in that of Graves, and a general critical note on the end-paper, in the hand of W.S.

CCXLV

MS. Messrs. Francis Edwards.

To Mr. HYLTON.

My Service—I should be glad if Mr. Hylton would send me a Dose of Rhubarb and Crem. Tartar, as before—If his Brother's Letter be yet arriv'd, I should likewise be glad to peruse it.

W.S.

Oct[r] 18, 1759.

CCXLVI

Works III, 338.

To the [REV. R. GRAVES].

THE LEASOWES,
Oct. 26, 1759.

Dear Mr. Graves,

I want no conviction of the pleasure which you will receive from the termination of my infernal lawsuit. It must, if I have *any* luck, be finally adjusted in about nine days time; after having robbed me of my peace for six of the best years of my life. During the *former* part of life, I languished for an acquaintance somewhat more extensive; and when the company that flocked to see my place removed all grounds of *that* complaint, this accursed dispute arose, and mixed with every enjoyment that was offered me.—I have sometimes found entertainment in balancing the good and evil that has been allotted me in general; and have in the end imagined the good prevalent, and that I have great reason to be thankful for more happiness than I deserve. Yet are there many awkward circumstances that forbid the *scale* to fall *precipitately;* among the chief, I place the distance to which I see you and one or two others removed. This is indeed an heavy article, and, were it not for letters, would be insupportable.

As to Mr. Dodsley's collection of Fables, you are mistaken if you think that I perused the quarto book. I dipped into it here and there, and thought there wanted *much* alteration. There was a little book with a paper-cover, on which I bestowed no small pains; and when I had so done, crossed the Fables which I thought might well enough pass muster. Addison would have been the best writer of Fables of any author I know—the purity of style—the conciseness—the dry humour—and the familiar manner. As to Dodsley's publishing this winter, he may possibly do so, without loss of credit; but when one considers that they are, or ought to be, the standard for years to come, one can hardly avoid wishing him to give them the polish of another summer. 'Twas fortunate that you pitched upon 'The Raven and Magpie'[1] to transcribe for me; as Mr. Dodsley had sent me 'The Sun-flower and the Tuberose'[2] *before.* I think the last somewhat inferior, but will reconsider it before I write again. The Fable which I literally translated from Phædrus was 'The Wolf and the Crane,'[3] in order to give Dodsley an idea on *what* Rollin[4] laid the stress in Fables.

As to the inscription, I will endeavour to adjust it to your mind—'Meritisque reconditoribus' may do, but is not explicit enough. I want fully to express a character that shines remarkably among select acquaintance, and yet (through extreme refinement) makes less figure in the public eye.

I had made the same objection to Burke's chapter upon *words*—and yet there seems to be something right in it. Du Bos (which I have only seen in *French*, but which I believe is also translated) consists of three volumes, 12mo. His subjects are pleasing, and his knowledge may be entertaining; but his genius seems not very profound, from the little that I have consulted in him.

Dodsley is *precisely* what you say of him; an object of esteem and love, and in some *degree* of admiration. His *ear* does not wholly please me in writing, and yet he is intimately affected with musick—Lord L[yttelton]'s ear is perhaps the reverse. I mean, he does not much regard music, yet writes harmoniously in verse and prose.

Robertson I think to buy—Butler[5] also, though I shall not admire him—Lord Clarendon,[6] when I am *rich*—Rasselas[7] has a few refined sentiments thinly scattered, but is upon the whole below Mr. J[ohnson]. Did I tell you I had a letter from Johnson, inclosing Vernon's Parish-clerk? Pray take Dodsley's advice in regard to your [*Spiritual Quixote?*]; and heighten the ridiculousness of your *heroe*, which *his* kind of *lunacy* will countenance, yet admit him to say good things. But do not make *any* alteration in the narrative of your own story—at least, till I have again perused it.—Do not spurn this fifty pounds. It will procure you numerous conveniences, which you would perhaps otherwise deny yourself.

I have passed four or five days, betwixt this week and last, at my Lord Ward's at Hinley. This has furnished me with franks, beside the consolation I derive from *having paid* a visit of *this kind*. It is 'spinis è pluribus una saltem exempta.'[8] The *restraint* renders them *spinæ*. I hope I may say so without umbrage, or giving an appearance of disrespect. For Mr. W——is an agreeable man, and my reception was very polite.

I have three or four more of these superb visits to make, and which I may not omit without giving real offence. To Lord Plymouth, next week; Lord Stamford's, the week after; then to Lord Lyttelton, at our Admiral's; and then to Lord Foley, if your friend Dr. Charleton will accompany me; then, *&c.* alas! alas! 'Quid me exempta juvat spina?'[9]—I must conclude upon a separate paper. That your *expectation* may not *deceive* you in regard to the plan I promised, I inclose a survey of my farm, reduced to miniature by a neighbouring artist. Let me know if it bring the place to your memory. I think to have a plate (which may be done at Birmingham for six or eight shillings), that shall leave me no trouble but to tinge the impressions with colors; in order to give my friends. But do you advise me to engrave *this*, or another that is twice as large?

I have purchased 'Gerard upon Taste,' the author of which is a Professor at Edinburgh, and the book commended in the Review—you will say that the Reviewers are partial to Scotchpeople[10]—I know nothing of that, but the book is learned, and on a pleasing subject—I may perhaps add a very *important* one —for surely it is altogether unquestionable that taste *naturally* leads to virtue. I am however in some doubt whether it will give you that amusement which Burke's has done.—I *must* now take my leave, having engagements of a different kind; but not till I have desired my hearty respects to Mrs. Graves, and her acceptance of this 'Grove and King-fisher.' I am, dear Mr. Graves, ever and most entirely, your very affectionate.

W. Shenstone.

NOTES

[1]Dodsley's *Select Fables*, III, 154.

[2]Ibid III, 153.

[3]Ibid I, 22.

[4]Charles Rollin (1661–1741), French historian and professor of belles-lettres.

[5]The papers of Samuel Butler remained untouched for many years. In 1759 two very interesting volumes, *The Genuine Remains in Verse and Prose of Mr. Samuel Butler* were printed. Presumably W.S. refers to these.

[6]Edward Hyde, 1st Earl of Clarendon (1609–74), author of the *History of the Rebellion*. In 1759 appeared *The Life of Edward, Earl of Clarendon, ... Being a Continuation of the History of the Grand Rebellion from the Restoration to his Banishment in 1667. Written by Himself*. Oxford, 1759.

[7]*Rasselas. Prince of Abissinia, A Tale*, was advertised to appear in two weeks in *The London Chronicle*, April 10–12, 1759. It was published by Dodsley, April 19.

[8]Horace, *Epistles* II, 2, 212.

[9]Horace, *Epistles* II, 2, 212.

[10]*The Monthly Review*, 1759, Vol. 20, p. 533, notices at length *An Essay on Taste By Alexander Gerard, M.A. Professor of moral philosophy and logic, in the Marischal College of Aberdeen. With three dissertations on the same subject, by M. de Voltaire, M. D'Alembert, F.R.S., M. de Montesquieu*. 8vo. 4s. Millar. 'Mr. Gerard has treated his subject, not in a loose and superficial manner, but has entered into it with the spirit and abilities of a philosopher.'

CCXLVII

B.M. Add. MSS. 23239.

[*To* JOHN SCOTT HYLTON.]

13. *Novem:* 1759.

My Comp^ts—It is indeed impossible for me to help Mr Hylton (or Any one else) to Money before Dolman pays me: which however I expect, *weekly*. It was in full *assurance* of this Payment, that I incurr'd expences *Last* year, which have, during ye Course of *This*, both distress'd me & injur'd my creditors.

What I send, wth ye 2^d part of Jorlin,[1] is all I receiv'd from Heron—I did not subscribe so much by way of Amusement, as thro' mere compassion——

Thoughts of ye Author of y^e 'Essay on Spirit' (B^p of Clogher,[2] I presume; *who* is He?) are written in a Masterly way.

Any good News from Coventry? It appears from ye Lines Mr H. wrote with Litmus, y^t it keeps its color *best* in y : *fullest strokes*—an argument perhaps y^t it should be *thicker*.

I want my Polygraphici,[3] as we have now some small-Beer Wort.

The Lines at ye End of ye impartial Review are good,—& as, I conjecture, our Friend Percy's.[4]

Admiral Smith goes to Hawn daily, & *certainly* intends to carry off ye Widow.

Alcock[5] shou'd, by *promise*, have come *yesterday*—but he regards neither promise, nor Politeness—What he does for *me*, I mean to be done *last*.

W. Shenstone.

Novr 13. 1759.

I shall, when Alcock comes, borrow all kinds of Heads Mr Hylton has, to chuse an Attitude.

NOTES

[1] Engelbert Jorlin wrote, in 1759, *Plantae tinctoriae . . . specimen botanico œconomicum . . .* (Upsala). Shenstone, later in the letter, talks of litmus, which is a planta tinctoria.

[2] Robert Clayton (1695–1758), was Bishop of Clogher from 1745–1758. *The Essay on Spirit wherein the doctrine of the Trinity is considered in the light of Nature & Reason*, by R. C. belonged to 1751, ran through several editions and caused a good deal of discussion in pamphlets.

³The polygraphici or 'manifold writer' is presumably the 'sett of lettering types' of which W.S. wrote to Hylton, March 2, 1759.

⁴Thomas Percy, by his contribution to *The Impartial Review* took part in the controversy which was aroused by Smollett's criticism of Grainger's *Tibullus* in *The Critical Review* of December 1758.

⁵Edward Alcock painted W.S.'s portrait now in the National Portrait Gallery. It was exchanged by W.S. for one of Dodsley by Reynolds.

CCXLVIII

B.M. Add. MSS. 28221.

Hecht, 26.

[*To* THOMAS PERCY.]

THE LEASOWES, *Nov*ʳ 23 1759.

Dear Sir,

What an aversion have I to writing, unless to such a Friend as you, who will allow me to write with perfect Freedom! The rest is mere 'taedet, it irketh; oportet, it behooveth,' and perhaps' taedet, it irketh,' *because* 'oportet, it behooveth.' This I learnt from Lily's Grammar.¹—Pray, No more of your *ideal* Brat, that you say is to be dropt at the Door of the Publick. I am a simple-minded Man; & have nothing to do with Metaphor or any such Vanities. In truth, I meant no other yⁿ a mere corporeal Child; with down-right Legs & Arms; of an *original* Composition, & true *English* Constitution; the perfect Picture of his Father and Mother; &, in one word, yᵉ Joint Production of yourself and good Mʳˢ Percy. Indeed, before I seald up my Letter, I began to entertain a Doubt whether I was not *premature* in my Congratulations.

I know nothing of yᵉ Work you *now* discover yourself to have undertaken;² but am very sure I shall be right glad to be favor'd with any Piece of your Publication.

I never see Smollett's Reviews—But pray tell me, Did you write that Libel on Him, which appears at the End of a Review, lately publish'd, and styld the *Impartial*? The Verses are correct and spirited; & I had good Reason to think them yours.

You have injoin'd me a very difficult Task in regard to the Willow-tree, especially if you lay me under that restraint, which you have observ'd *yourself*, in regard to the Rhimes. I own, I am not quite satisfy'd with either of yᵉ Versions. I return them; & if aught occurr to me y^t tends to their Improvement, will communicate it. In ye mean time, by the Paper accompanying them, you will partly see what I *wish* effected.

The Verses on ye Venus Marina,^{3} I have shewn to my Friend Graves; & they will be so much *alter'd* in Consequence of a Hint he gives me, that I beg you w^d burn the present Copy. I could wish, moreover, that you may have said nothing concerning them; For as M^r D[avenpor]t is gone to *live* at Bath, I may perhaps like to make some other use of Them.

G. Herdsman, Boy & Mantle, & Edom of Gordon; when I have *time;* but why not rather, when I have the Pleasure of seeing you at the Leasowes? A Grove & Kingfisher or two, I enclose.

I do not like y^r Bee-motto—as being neither *moral,* nor *affecting;* which, when Mottoes are *not,* they had certainly better be quite omitted—For what need of Intimation, y^t a Bee makes Honey out of Flowers? I will transcribe Akenside's Ode for you, but it cannot come by the Present Post.

M^r [Hylton] is impatient for his *Curiosities;* tho He is at this time sitting for his Picture, which you will say, perdie, is *None.* He s*hall* not be offended 'at the Receipt of aught you send Him. I swear by the Ventle-trap itself—by the Icthyodontes cuspidatus—Nay even by King William's Bibb; & by the Porringer of old Parr.

Ovid is safe in my Bureau—and when you tell me y^t you wait on *my account,* I will be as expeditious, as Crispinus. But I really propos'd myself a double Pleasure, in ye examination of it with our Friend Binnel.

Positively, I never will *attempt* to translate that Epigram.^{4} Do you know that I *hate* Epigrams? & more particularly such very quaint Ones, where it wou'd give No Pleasure to succeed. Pardon me, for not complying with your Request; which w^d be indeed a *different* & a *real* Pleasure.

Have you seen Gerard on Taste? Dr Smith on Moral Sentiments?^{5} Hurd's Dialogues Moral & Political?^{6} All of which I've bought, but not quite read—S^r Ed. Lyttelton^7 says, Hurd's *first Dialogue* will be *omitted* in (the) next Edition—It sneers Dodsley, very causelessly; & is also infinitely *below* the Author.^{8}

Mr Duncomb sent me his first Vol. of Horace, together with One of ye Satyrs *inscribed to me* in M.S. But Lo! on purchasing ye 2^d vol., he has chang'd *my* Name to *Dr. Hawkesworth*—[9] This I have *occasion'd* & indeed *deserv'd*, by not answering his obliging Letter. However, you see what I lose by writing to *you* instead other persons; and ought surely to make it up to me, whenever occasion Serves.—Pardon the *Freedom* of this Letter—I indulg'd ye Humour that was predominant, as every true-born Poet *should*—I hope I've said nothing inconsistent with ye respect I bear to you & Mrs Percy. Adieu!

W. S—e.

NOTES

[1]William Lily's (1468–1522) short Grammar enjoyed extraordinary popularity for many years.

[2]Percy's note in MS: 'Hau Kiou Choaan, a Chinese Novel. 4 Vols. 12 mo.' *Hau Kiou Choaan or The Pleasing History. A Translation from the Chinese Language,* published by R. & J. Dodsley. 1761.

[3]*Works* II, 370–71.

[4]Percy's note in MS: 'An Epigram sent to Mr. Shenstone at the request of Dr. Stonehouse of Northampton.' Sir James Stonehouse (1716–1795), baronet, physician, and clergyman, was a close friend of Philip Doddridge and the Rev. James Hervey.

[5]Adam Smith (1723–1790). *Theory of Moral Sentiments,* 1759. Smith was elected to the Chair of Logic in Glasgow, 1751, and to the Chair of Moral Philosophy, 1752.

[6]Richard Hurd (1720–1808), friend of Mason and Gray, Chaplain to Bishop Warburton, Bishop of Lichfield and Worcester, published *Moral and Political Dialogues,* 1759. His more famous *Letters on Chivalry and Romance* were published 1762.

[7]Edward Littleton was a pupil of Hurd's and his old schoolfellow. There was a close friendship between them.

[8]The reference is apparently to the introductory dialogue, by way of Preface, between the bookseller and the editor. . . . 'What, I pray you, are the most admired and correct works of the time?' asks the editor. 'The *Connoisseur,* you will tell me, or the *World.* Your brother Dodsley declares positively for the *World.* . . . And for matter of authority, ten to one the names of Cowley, Waller, Addison, Arbuthnot, etc. may go as far with some readers as those of C.M.B.J. or even Mr. Dodsley himself.'

[9]John Hawkesworth (1715?–1773), miscellaneous writer.

CCXLIX

Works III, 343.

To the [REV. R. GRAVES], *on his Want of Leisure.*

THE LEASOWES,
Nov. 24. 1759.

Dear Mr. Graves,

Though I write to you again so soon, yet it really grieves me to hear the complaint which you so often make for want of time. I, who have time to *waste*, by lustres, cannot have patience with the world, that suffers *you* to want the leisure which you would employ to so much better purposes. Perhaps, however, you are as *happy* as more leisure could *make* you; the case is not so *clear*, as to leave me satisfied of the contrary. And yet, as the pleasures of imagination have an undoubted claim to a real existence, they must surely afford very *lively* sensations to persons of your sensibility and refinement.—Be this as it may, I *will* always *murmur*, that you can so ill spare time for literary amusement. Nevertheless, make *one* effort, and finish the task you have now before you. I must confess, you may naturally reply, that I am now become an interested person; but *this*, I am sure, will be no check to your activity.

Mr. William Duncombe sent (with the first volume of Horace) one of the satires in Ms. *inscribed to me*. Upon purchasing, however, the second volume, I find *my* name is changed to Hawkesworth.—Who knows but I lost this compliment by writing to you, my friend, while I should have been writing to him?—if so, indeed, you ought to make it up to me; and I am sure I shall prize *your* compliment beyond that of which I have been deprived.

The view of [Belton], which you mention, I have indeed seen a long time ago; but surely the *water-fall* is quite detestable. There is something on each side, as I remember, that puts one in mind of a porridge-pot boiling over beneath the pot-lid. The appearance of the house and the back-ground is better; this was adjusted by the painter, the other (as I think Smith told me) by an old house-steward of Lord T[yrconnel]'s.

I have inclosed another copy of the lines to Venus, for your emendation.—Thank you for the stanza you introduced.—I meant, indeed, *before*, to allude to *natural* beauty more than *moral*; but did not fully enough express myself. There remains no transition now but from *animal* beauty to *inanimate*; which is easier.

You will observe, that I take great liberties with the Fables you ask me to revise.—Dodsley must think me *very* fantastical or *worse*, while I was correcting those he wrote at The Leasowes. —I find my *ear* much more apt to take offence than most other people's; and, as *his* is far less delicate than mine, he must of course believe, in many places, that I altered merely for alteration's sake. I cannot be easy without some certain proportion betwixt one sentence and another; betwixt one member of a sentence and another; without a melody at the close of a paragraph almost as agreeable as your 'magnificent salon.'

I have not written to Dodsley any decent letter since he arrived at his house in London.—I must now apply myself to write half a score Fables, and, if he chuses it, a translation of La Motte's Discourse upon the subject.—Your reply in regard to the delay of *my* publication cannot be answered; that is certain.

Whitfield's Journal,[1] I *fear*, is purged of its *most* ridiculous passages.—Dodsley brought one down hither for Mr. Deane to shew my Lord D[artmou]th;[2] but he tells me, there remains nothing of that *gross* absurdity which I saw in your brother's at Mickleton.

The painter whom I just mentioned to have taken some portraits through my recommendation, and to have painted a ruin for my green-room, offers to give me my picture if I chuse to sit.—Were you here to lend me your assistance, I should certainly comply.—Mean while, tell me what you think of some of the attitudes that I inclose. What I myself prefer at present is, to *lessen* my *dimensions* (which of itself gives a kind of beauty), and to appear in a kind of night-gown agreeable to the attitude marked AA. The man evidently hits off likenesses, and is esteemed to *shine* among the painters of Birmingham. I shall be forced to have your picture copied by him, which, by means of dampness, flies off the canvas; so that, on the whole, I shall re-pay his compliment.—This last article puts me in mind that I owe you my picture, whenever you demand it; but I would chuse to defer it till the spring, for some certain reasons regarding œconomy. Remember me *always* to good Mrs. [Graves]; and believe me yours, with all possible affection.

W. Shenstone.

NOTES

[1] In 1756 Whitefield published *The Two First Parts of his Life, with his Journals revised, corrected, and abridged.* The seven 'Journals' were issued between 1738 and 1741.

²William (Legge), Earl of Dartmouth, married in 1755 Frances Catherine Gunter, only daughter of Sir Charles Gunter Nicoll, K.B. Both Lord Dartmouth and his wife are frequently mentioned by W.S. and his correspondents. Mrs. Delany remarked on the virtue and goodness of heart of the couple.

CCL

B.M. Add. MSS. 23239.

[*To* JOHN SCOTT HYLTON.]

My Service to Mr Hylton; who I presume by this time begins to think himself not much oblig'd to Mr Alcock—But what better can he expect from a Painter, that has been employ'd to exhibit ye royal Face, to 5000 Spectators?—For no Less appear'd in Birmingham-streets, at ye Display of ye Fireworks yester-night. However, I would have Mr Hylton write to demand the Finishment of his Picture—(as Capt. Wight will go near to do same)—and Let his Boy sett out, pretty early.

I have not been quite so well, since my Expedition at Ridge-acre[1]—and am to-night, rather Low in spirit—How goes on ye Damm, and what News.?

This is ye best blue I can obtain from Litmus by any operation, whatsoever. I observe y^t on Different Papers, (as differently charg'd wth Alum, perhaps) it has a different effect. It will appear bluer by Day y^n Candle-Light.[2]

W. SHENSTONE.

Tis now, I think, November the XXX. MDCCLIX.

NOTES

[1]Anne, eldest sister of Lord Dudley, married William Smith of Stoke Prior and Ridgacre.
[2]In MS. is a design in bright pink.

CCLI

B.M. Add. MSS. 27548.

[*To* JOHN SCOTT HYLTON.]

Friday 7th *December* 1759 [*in another hand*].

My Comp^{ts} I receivd this Parcell from Mr. Percy yesterday, with a *Few Lines* only, importing that he w^d write again soon, and give Mr. H. some acc^t of Particulars—I don't yet see matter of much Importance in them; It is possible Mr Hylton *may*.

If Mr H. have done any more to his old Ballad, I shall be glad to revise it—It really appears to *me*, more y^n an adequate Return.[1] And yet I fancy Mr Percy esteems his Present very respectable. Mr Alcock is now here, and has begun to dead-color my *Drapery* in y^e *first* place—I have slept ill, and am not perfectly well to-day; wch gives me Little Spirit For him to transfuse into my Portrait——

Mr Hollier here yesterday; and on Friday next Mr. H. is, with me, to meet him at Mr Clare's.

Perry also dind here at my Request, and went home ab^t 8.

The Journey thro Italy[2] is entertaining—not however thro any remarkable degree of Connoisance in ye Writer—His Jests are often as rouzing Puns as ever were escap'd Pixell, Hobbs,[3] or even Dr. Parker[4] himself—yet were the Book mine, I w^d neatly bind it in 2 vols—I have gott Smolletts Don Quixote here, wth new Quarto cutts by Hayman[5]—I do not like them better y^n those of Coypell[6]—Write me a Long Billet & return ye Letters.

(Will arriv'd.)

W.S.

The other R. Ruin is at Birm. but Mr. Alcock shall send it back—unless Mr H. means his Book of Arches. Let Will go in ye Morn^g if he does n't hear from me. I rather think the *men* bestow'd some *superfluous* Pains *before* (for their own reasons) y^n that they proceed too fast now. M^r. Hylton *must* be safe in *this* Respect, because ye standing of ye Damm is warranted, for a time y^t must imply it's Durability.

I saw no Letter for Mr. H.

The Telescope is, doubtless, a very good one—What if Mr. H. attempts a K. Fisher taken off the *blue* on to good Paper.

NOTES

[1]Apparently Hylton among others was collecting and revising Ballads.

[2]I have been unable to trace any *Journey through Italy* appearing about 1759.

[3]The reference is probably to Thomas Hobbes (1588–1679), the philosopher of *The Leviathan*, famous for his gift of repartee at the court of Charles II.

[4]William Parker, D.D. (1714–1802), well-known pulpit orator, whose native place was Coventry.

[5]Francis Hayman (1708–1776), one of the founders of the Royal Academy, whose original drawings for these Don Quixote illustrations are in the print room at the B.M.

[6]Charles Antoine Coypell, (1694–1752). *Les Aventures de Don Quichotte de Cervantes, peintes par C. Coypell et N. Cohin* belongs to 1723.

CCLII

MS. Montague d. 1.

Bodl. Summ. Catalogue No. 25427.

[*To* JOHN SCOTT HYLTON.]

Dec. 9. 1759.

My Service ——

Will was here about half a Hour, not more, before I wak'd, when I immediately dispatched him.

The Knives will be return'd—Mr. Hylton had better not disparage Mr Percy's Present (to *Him*)—before he hears what he has to say for it; wch I expect to do, in a Day or two—Mr Alcock is engag'd to Capt. Wight, to-morrow-morning—but if my own Picture dries, I believe I shall cause him to break thro y^t engage^t, in order to get it finishd,—He says, he shall finish Mr Hylton's at ye next time he comes to Lapall. I desire Mr. H. w^d send me ab^t half a Dozen Papers of Bark.

Mr. Hodgetts[1] is just arriv'd; & I cannot possibly stir out to-day.

There is a rumour of extreme good news by Sea—& *as* bad or worse, in Germany—but No assurance of Either——

I don't know justly *when* I shall send any one to Birm^m but Mr Hodgetts will go near to return to-morrow, & will carry any small Parcel——

I do not find y^t Mr Hylton's pool goes on so very fast——
Does Mr H. chuse to Look at a Pair of those Pistols I
mention'd? Capt. Wight bought a Pair of ye same yesterday,
by my recommendation—but I think reel Ebony w^d make
them elegant *indeed*—Wight has also bespoke Furniture; but
I heard not, of what kind.

I shall endeavour to keep Alcock to-morrow; for he has
scarce done any stroke at my Face—Tuesday Cap. Wight
goes to Kedderminster, Bewdley &c: dines at ye Adm^{ls}
on Wednesday so y^t *one* of those Days Mr Alcock may come
to Lapall—He finishes highly in miniature—& I am apt to
think y^t the *Appendages* at least of my Picture will be very
pleasing—Has Mr H. heard from Ridgacre—If I ask them
this week, I shall hope y^t some of them will sit for their Picture
—I should rather *wish* Miss Fanny—tho It be more *requisite* y^t
no time should be Lost by her Mama.

Desire Mr H. w^d write me a Long Answer—Good Night.

WxSx

NOTE

[1]John Hodgetts of Hagley, cousin of W.S. He was executor to the poet's will, and
jointly with Richard Graves erected an urn to Shenstone's memory in Halesowen
Church. He caused Lady Luxborough's *Letters* to Shenstone to be published in 1775
(see Advertisement to the *Letters*), and also published Jago's poems.

CCLIII

Messrs. Maggs.

[*To* J. S. HYLTON.]

(*About* 7th [*in another hand*]) *Jan;* 1760.

My Compliments. As to Ambrose Foley's old Ballads, I am
greatly fearfull y^t I burnt them one night, when I was sorting
my poetical Papers. At Least I can find nothing of it at the
present. If they *should* be consum'd, Mr Ambrose must comfort himself, y^t he has lost Nothing but what is infinitely
inferior to what he is able to write himself. As to game, I know
no other Method of procuring any, y^n what Mr Hylton does
Himself. Two Partridges w^d be much too inconsiderable a a

[sic] present to send to town—& I shou'd imagine many *Hares* are at this time brought into Birm^m which (by means of a Friend there) may come on reasonable terms.

Poor Heron sends this parcell which Mr Hylton may keep longer, or return to me directly. The *Sketches* are worth M^r H's buying. I think I *have* 'em (Dr Armstrongs) The Dictionary I've not examin'd.

The Man will call here on his return. Cou'd Mr Hylton send me a Little Shell-gold. I begin to use, & Like, the Shell Silver.

Why doesn't Mr H. get some People, & head a party of Tracers?

Governor Littleton gone against some Indians at ye Head of 2000 Men.

Mr Alcock is now here, & proceeding on my Picture, with a promise to finish before he leaves it. Mr Ireland ye Painter, here also.

Will Mr Hylton lend me some pretty female Faces for Him to copy. Particularly y^t Little Print from Raphael of ye Madonna & ye Bambino. Not a Large print. the Roundness of ye Figures remarkable. Mr Hylton may make up a Parcell & send safely by this Man.

W.S.

CCLIV

B.M. Add. MSS. 28221.
Hecht, 29.

[*To* THOMAS PERCY.]

Jan. 7th 1760.

My best Compliments to M^r and Mrs Percy, with many thanks for ye last packet—I will not fail to write soon.—Is it y^e *Tune* which makes me Like this little French trifle, or has it any merit y^t can induce Mr Percy to give it us in English? I suppose him as *quick*, as he is happy in productions of this Nature.

Mr P.'s acc^t of ye Farm[1] here must be a Little adjusted—

mean time I can not but smile to see, what an important
Figure my Little Hut makes in His representation.

I've, this minute, receiv'd two Folio pages of blank verse
from my Friend Dodsley upon yᵉ same magnificent subject.²
However, yᵉ Lines are musical, & spirited.

Chanson.

Assis sur l'Herbete,
Tyrsis, l'autre Jour,
Dessus sa musette,
Chantoit son amour:
'Cruelle Bergere,
'Qui scais tous charmer!
'Pourquoi scais tu plaire,
'Sans scavoir aimer?' etc.

2

'Dessus cette Herbete,
'Y a t'il un Berger
'Qui soit moins volage?
'Qui soit moins leger?
'Cruelle etc.'

3

'Depuis que tes charmes
'Ont ravis mon Cœur,
'Je vis en allarmes;
'Je tombe en Langueur.
'Cruelle etc.'

4

'Cesse, cesse, cher Sylvandre,
'Le douče[?] entretient:
'Ton Cœur est trop tendre;
'Je crains pour le mien.
'A Force d'entendre,
'Que Je puis charmer,
'Je pourrois apprendre,
'Que Je puis aimer.'

5

'Au bord du Rivage
'Nous jouons, tous deux;
'Je t'offre pour gage
'Mes plus tendres Feux [sic]
'Aimable Bergere,
'Qui puis tous charmer!
'Tu scais *plus* que plaire;
'Car tu scais aimer.'

NOTES

[1]Percy's note in M.S: 'a Description of the Leasowes, wch I had drawn up hastily in 1753.'
[2]*Verses by Mr. Dodsley on his first arrival at The Leasowes*, 1754. Shenstone, *Works* II, 380–82.

CCLV

Works III, 347.

To the [REV. R. GRAVES], *with an Account of a Design for his own Picture.*

THE LEASOWES,

Jan. 8, 1760.

Dear Mr. Graves,

Were I to regulate my compliments by the arrival of *times* and seasons, I should congratulate you upon a *correspondence* which now enters upon its three and twentieth year. Our *friendship* is of something older date; and is not this an *atchievement* that deserves the honour of a *triumph* both for you and me too?—More, I am sure, than the regular destruction of fifteen or twenty thousand wretches in the field; considering how *uncommon* we find friendships of so long a duration, and how *cheap* we find such victories, not only on the Prussian, but on the Austrian side.

Mr. Cambridge (Scriblerus), who called here this autumn, was considering this massacre rather in a philosophical than political view; and, indeed, it does not appear to me that plague, earthquake, or famine, are more pernicious to the human race, than what the world calls Heroes; but enough of this.

Your want of leisure gives me pain; surely, if I may guess by one or two of your last letters, you have enlarged the number of your scholars, and extended your domestic cares, beyond what your circumstances *require*.[1]

You must not judge of my painter's abilities by the small sketch I inclose.—I desired him to give me a *slight* one; and have, perhaps, ruined even *that* by endeavouring to bring it nearer to what the picture now is *myself*. It will give you a tolerable idea in most points, except the Pan, which has his face turned towards the front; and is not near so considerable.—I chose to have this *term* introduced, not only as he carried my favourite reeds, but as he is the principal *sylvan* deity.—The Water-nymph below has the word 'Stour' on the mouth of her urn; which, in some sort, rises at The Leasowes. On the scroll is, 'Flumina amem sylvasque inglorius.' alluding to them *both*. —The Pan, you will perhaps observe, hurts the *simplicity* of the picture—not much, as we have managed him; and the intention here is, I think, a balance.

The dog on the other side is my faithful Lucy,[2] which you perhaps remember; and who *must* be *nearer* the *body* than she perhaps would, if we had more room. However I believe, I shall cause her head to cut off that little cluster of angles, where the balustrade joins the base of the arch. The balustrade is an improvement we made the other day; it is, I think, a great one; not only as it gives a symmetry or balance to the curtain of which you complained; but as it extends the *area* on which I stand, and shortens the *length* of this *half-arch*. The painter objected to a tree; I know not why; unless that we could introduce no *stem* without encroaching too much upon the landscape: but the reason he gave was, it would be an injury to the face. The console is an Apollo's head. The impost does not go further than the pilaster, which ends the corner; and here the drawing is erroneous. We are, I think, to have a carpet, though we know not well how to manage it.

And now, I must tell you the dimensions.—The figure itself is three feet, three inches and a half; the whole picture four feet, eleven inches, by two feet, three inches and three-quarters.—The colour of the gown, a sea-green; waistcoat and breeches, buff-colour; stockings white, or rather pearl-colour; curtain a terra-sienna, or very rich reddish brown.—I think the whole will have a good effect; but beseech you to send me your opinion *directly*. There are some things we can alter; but there are others we must not.

You shall have one of the size you desire in the spring; but will you not calculate for some one place in your room? The painter takes very strong likenesses; is young; rather daring than delicate in his manner, though he paints well in enamel; good-natured; slovenly; would improve much by application. Adieu!

W.S.

NOTES

[1]Claverton Rectory was enlarged by Ralph Allen, of Prior Park, Bath, who owned the Manor house at Claverton and whose body rests in Claverton Churchyard. After the enlargement of the rectory, Graves was able to take pupils.

'In the year 1859, Mr. Allen purchased the manor of Claverton, where, after having repaired, improved and built a gallery in the church; finding that the rector had several young gentlemen of family and fortune under his care; and a very indifferent house for their accommodation, Mr. Allen offered to build him a room, which he immediately executed; building a room twenty-five feet by sixteen, with two bed chambers over it, which he observed would serve for a school, as long as he continued that employment; and might afterwards be converted into a good parlour, as it is at present.'—Graves, *The Triflers*, 66.

[2]Seen in the National Portrait Gallery portrait of W.S.

CCLVI

Messrs. Maggs.

[*To* J. S. HYLTON.]

My Compliments—and if Mr H. should not be return'd from Ridgeacre at ye arrival of This, I wou'd beg ye Favor of him, on his return, to send me what I mention'd yesterday. Mr Alcock will want ye yellow.

We are at a Fault for some Greenhouse Plant, to put in a Flower-pot in my Picture. Can Mr Hylton contrive to give me any Idea of ye scarlet-Geranium or has he any Draught of any Flower y^t might be of use to us?

The Parish-paper was transcrib'd handsomely, which I was

glad enough to see. I should think they will hardly fail of Lord
Lyttelton's assent. The chief difficulty will remain afterwards,
to obviate which, Mr Hylton must assist me in endeavouring
to bring over Mr Barnsley. He is already for the removal of
Shern; but People in general & myself for One, are clearly
convinc'd it were better put an End to a sort of Establishm^t
which, in *our* Parish at least is like for ever to prove a Jobb.

Our levies are really higher y^n ever; and were y^e *old way*
to cost us *more*, People wou'd be better contented without a
Workhouse.

My Picture now draws towards a Conclusion, & will be
finish'd when I can get a good day to sit three or four Hours
together.

W. Shenstone.

Wednesday
Jan. 16^*th* 1760.

CCLVII

B.M. MSS. Add. 28221.
Hecht, 29.

[*To* THOMAS PERCY.]

My best Compliments to M^r and Mrs Percy—I observed
in his Letter to Mr Hylton, y^t he desir'd a Copy of these Verses
—what else, I do not remember; for I fancy Mr Hylton has
taken ye Letter Home.

Dodsley's Lines want some Correction—and indeed are
not equal to a Little sketch of a Complim^t in short verses &
Rhyme, y^t he shew'd me at the Leasowes.

Could not Mr. P. procure M^r [Hylton] one of those Locks
of Amazonian Hair, by which the Amazons are reported to
have suckled children behind their Shoulders?

I think entirely with Mr P. with regard to Baskerville's
bible[1]—& mention'd ye same to Him long ago.

Mr Percy, I conceive, held ye Little *Chanson* rather too
cheap—The translation will not do, either in point of metre,

2 N

or expression. But, perhaps, to give it as good an English Dress as it has a French one, might cost more Pains that [sic] it deserves at best.

I will not fail to answer Mr Percy's Letter ye first moment I can find Leisure and a Frame of mind; which, verily are not my Lot at present—He will therefore give me Credit for a Letter, yet continue himself to *write* or to *enclose;* as well knowing y^t I am his very faithfull

& affectionate

h: Servt W.S.

Feb. 5. 1760.
To the Rev^rd Mr. Percy.

NOTE

[1]Straus and Dent, *John Baskerville. A Memoir,* 48–50, 69–70. The Bible did not appear till 1763, and like so many of Baskerville's books was not a financial success.

CCLVIII

MS. Messrs. Francis Edwards.

[*To* J. S. HYLTON.]

[*Early* 1760?][1]

Dear Sir— —

> This great world's but a trouble,
> Where all must their fortunes bear;
> Make the best of a bubble—
> 'Tis but a *Neighbour's Fare.*

Such is ye Sense or Nonsense of a song wh. was once extremely popular—Be this as it will; be assur'd, you have no vexation belongs to you, but your Neighbour has its counterpart; and if you expect comfort from Him, he has ye self same reason to demand comfort from you. Perhaps it were best therefore, to give mutual Acquittances; and have recourse to such assistance as we can draw from Philosophy.

The Persons I sent to Harborough, I am very well assur'd gave me their sincere Opinions—I am almost tir'd with advising you about Aaron—but you had better, by some Intimation or other, *prevent* the sale of yr. Cyder-mill—It is extremely

manifest to all with whom I have consulted, that you have
offer'd Aaron more than he can *prudently* refuse—

Mrs. Hollier spent a qr. of an hour here this afternoon.
Our Discourse chiefly turn'd upon the Harborough Estate—
NB. People are going instantly to plant Harborough Hill with
Trees; and the House D[olman] means to build, will answer
all their Purposes as an Object to the Park—I have nothing to
add which is fit to add upon *Paper;* but mean to call upon you
at yr. Lodge in a Day's time—Adieu.

W. Shenstone.

There is something in *one* or *two* Parts of this Magazine
which will amuse you—suppose you call upon me on yr.
way to Cradely—I have about as much Intelligence as can be
spoke in five sentences—

My spirits are neither very high nor low; but my head is
muddy.

Nothing till I see you.

NOTE

[1]The letter has been placed here as it may belong to the early months of 1760.
Bitterness concerning the Harborough estate seems to have died away and W.S. to be
taking an interest in Dolman.

CCLIX

Works III, 350.

To the [Rev. R. Graves], *on Fable, and other Articles of Taste
and Literature.*

The Leasowes,
Feb. 9, 1760.

Dear Mr. Graves,

I could not understand, by Mr. Dodsley's last letter to me
that he had any *sort* of intention to publish his Fables this
winter. Presuming upon this delay, and having neither had the
leisure nor the *frame* of mind fit to take his preface into consideration, I have hitherto deferred to do so; and can only say
in *general*, that I could wish you had happened to be more
copious in your observations. La Motte's Discourse on Fables

is a most excellent performance; containing, as appears to *me*, all that need be said upon the subject, and this expressed with all imaginable elegance and perspicuity. I believe I shall advise our friend D[odsley] to make more ample use of this dissertation. There is a translation of La Motte into *prose*, which is altogether *below contempt*; and yet, for aught I know, the *only* one. The word *naïve* is very probably *that* for which he has substituted the word *lively*; though by no means of similar import. *Natural* approaches nearer it; but according to La Motte is not precise: and, as the words *Naïf* and *Naïveté* seem of late to become more in vogue, I will here give you an extract of what he says upon the subject: 'Je ne souhaiterois plus rien à l'auteur de Fables, si ce n'est d'être fidele au sentiment, & de le peindre toujours avec la Naïveté qui le caractérise; car j'ose encore distinguer le *Naturel* & le *Naïf*. Le *Naturel* renferme une idée plus vague, & il est opposé en général au *Recherché*, au *Forcé*; au lieu, que le *Naïf* l'est particulierement au *Refléchi*, & n'appartient qu'au *sentiment*.'

'Le *sublime*, selon cette idée, peut être *Naïf*. La reponse du vieil Horace à la question qu'on lui fait sur la conduite de son fils; que vouliez-vous qu'il fit contre trois? *Qu'il mourut*. Cette response est *naïve*; parce que c'est l'expression toute nuë du *sentiment* de ce Romain; qui préfére la mort de son fils à sa honte. Il ne *répond* pas précisément à ce qu'on lui demande; il dit seulement ce qu'il *sent*. Ce n'est que dans la vers suivant que la *Réflexion* succéde à la *Naïveté*:

'Ou qu'un beau désespoir alors le secourut.

Il *raisonne* dans ce vers; il n'a fait que *sentir* dans le premier.

'Les occasions du *Naïf* sont, peut-étre, plus fréquentes dans la Fable; & l'éloge de La Fountaine est de n'en avoir gueres manquées; dans la Fable du Pot au Lait, le discours qu'il prête à sa Latiere est un chef-d'œuvre de *Naïveté*, d'autant plus singulier, que sous *l'apparence du raisonnement* le plus suivi, le *sentiment* se montre dans toute sa force; ou pour mieux dire, dans toute son *yvresse*.'

And now, let me know what English word you would employ to interpret *Naïf*. *Sentimental* has some pretensions; but is not wholly to one's mind.

I bought the quarto edition of La Motte's Fables, to which

this essay is prefixed; though the vaunted cuts which tempted me to this extravagance did not answer my expectation. The author, with much address, begs the Duke of Orleans to be at the expence of them; which, to the best of my remembrance, was 'deux mille ecus.'

Mr. Hurd, you see, is one of Dr. Warburton's Chaplains. I bought his Dialogues Moral and Political, almost as soon as they were published. Sir Edward Lyttelton told me, the introductory one would be omitted in the next edition. The three following are very ingenious; but the two former are a little ambiguous in regard to his intended moral: the two last are wholly political, and I have not yet perused them, though esteemed the *best*.

Have you seen Dr. Smith's 'Theory of Moral Sentiments,' which is prodigiously commended, and which I have bought, but not read?—You will see an account of this in the Monthly Review.[1]

I have lately been reading one or two volumes of The Rambler;[2] who, excepting against some few hardnesses in his manner,[3] and the want of more examples to enliven, is one of the most *nervous*, most *perspicuous*, most concise, and most harmonious prose-writers I know.—A learned diction improves by time.

I am sorry to find no mention of your [*Spiritual Quixote?*] in all the letters which I have received of late. Do not think of *dropping* or even *delaying* the publication of it; only, if you please, before it goes to the press, let me peruse it once deliberately.—What think you, if Dodsley approve it, of admitting cuts into your scheme?

And now, from *cuts* I proceed to *pictures*. Alcock's portrait of me is in a manner finished; and has been hung up for these nine days past, in its carved frame opposite to the fire-place in my library. *They say* it is a likeness, allowing for the diminution of size. Indeed, if I can conclude any thing from the strong resemblance which he has produced of *others* here, I may form some *conjecture* that he has not failed in mine.—Be this as it will, the picture is, upon the whole, a tolerably pleasing one; and this is the *most* I must dare to say, considering my own person makes so large a part of it.

What think you of a tawney or reddish brown for the robe or night gown, with black for the waistcoat and breeches, reserving green for the curtain? though green is, with me at least, no very gay colour, nor has it that effect which you apprehended in the drapery. Terra-sienna is a delightful colour; so, I think, is Roman ocre burnt. Let me know then, what objections you have to the drapery just now proposed. Let me know also any design that you think most pleasing for a background; or any story of two or three figures, that would be suitable for a relievo.

From *pictures* I proceed to *painters*. I believe, Alcock would go and settle at Bath, if Amos Green could be induced to join him. Amos Green is the name of the painter whom I recommended to you *before my fever*. He is esteemed inferior to no one in England for fruit. He also paints flowers, insects, and dead-game, *very* well. To this he would adjoin the business of water-painting. Alcock would paint portraits in oil; and to this he would add enamel-painting: both of them the best-natured young fellows in the world. Now suppose them also *ingenious*, and tell me whether they would have a chance to *thrive*.

You ought to have very considerable *amends*, if you are to be plagued with writing and with music-masters.—I believe I rate your time and trouble at a much higher price than you do yourself.

Dr. Blackstone[4] has raised himself to a very eminent figure, indeed, in the world of letters. I rejoice at it, without one particle of envy, both as he is your friend, and a person of merit. I believe no one, besides yourself, would have dreamt of your odd analogy betwixt him and me.—I know not *how* they came to insert that insipid Song of mine in the Chronicle.[5]—What sensation it caused in me, was that of disapprobation; as it looked like laying stress on what one knows to be of no importance.

The chief points wherein my picture varies from your drawing is in the corner below the base of the pedestal; where an antique vase is introduced with a flower and two or three leaves of the scarlet Geranium. The gilt vase agrees well enough with the gold fringe on the edge of the curtain; but the whole is so *subdued*, as not to catch the eye too strongly. It was chiefly meant to obviate the disagreeableness of the *parallel* lines and angles occasioned by the step in that corner; but it crowds that side a little, if one look from top to bottom; and, though a pleasing object, it is hard to say whether it do more good or harm.

It is time now to take my leave, with my hearty respects to Mrs. Graves, and with the usual assurance, that I remain your most affectionate and faithful friend,

W. Shenstone.

Do write soon.

NOTES

[1]*The Monthly Review*, July 1759, '... in a word, without any partiality to the author, he is one of the most elegant and agreeable writers, upon morals, that we are acquainted with.'

[2]Johnson started *The Rambler* in 1750, in imitation of *The Spectator*. It was published twice a week and continued until March, 1752.

[3]Footnote, *Works* III, 354. 'He too often makes use of the *abstract* for the *concrete*.'

[4]William Blackstone (1723-1780), legal writer and judge, was knighted February 1770. He was a contemporary of W.S. and Graves at Pembroke College, Oxford, and is mentioned by Dr. Johnson, in Boswell's *Life*, as in the 'nest of singing birds.' He was a lifelong friend of Graves. 'I was chosen from Pembroke College to a fellowship in All Soul's, and Sir William Blackstone followed me thither, from the same college a few years afterwards, we became particularly intimate and he communicated to me without reserve, his youthful projects and productions.' Graves, *The Triflers*, 53.

[5]*The London Chronicle*, or *Universal Evening Post*, Wednesday, January 2, 1760, published W.S.'s *The Skylark*, 'Go tuneful bird.'

CCLX

B.M. Add. MSS. 28221.
Hecht, 30.

[*To* THOMAS PERCY.]

The Leasowes, *Feb.* 15th 1760.

Dear Sir,

I forget what fine Lady recommends it to her Husband, always to quarrel *en Abregé*. Sure I am, that want of Leisure, & the manifold Articles to which I've not reply'd, make it expedient for Me at present to *correspond* in the *same Manner*.

The Old Ballads I pretended to adjust cannot possibly *appear* with my consent, had I ever so much Leisure to transcribe them. They are corrected indeed, but that in a manner so very contrary to my present Sentiments, y^t I cannot endure to transcribe them as they *are;* nor have I opportunity, or a State of mind, proper for making Alterations.

I never see y^e *Critical* Review—so y^t I know not upon what Paragraph there, you ground ye Apprehensions from Dr Smollet. He advertises, I see, a *Licence* for his original Papers in the Brit. Magaz:[1] Is not this stooping pretty *Low,* for one that writes ye History of England?[2] But you'll perhaps deny it to be a *Condescension.* I have no knowledge yet of ye Nature of your Chinese Publication. Pardon me, however, if I propose One Question to you. Are you never prejudiced by y^e *Air of Learning,* y^e *obscurity,* y^e *rarity,* and, perhaps, the *Difficulty,* of your work, to imagine something in it more extraordinary, y^n the Publick will perhaps discover? One is many times led by ye foresaid circumstances, to incurr ye blunder of a Mole, & to fancy one's self *deep,* when one is extremely *near ye surface.* This is, Tibi Soli, as ye Jesuits say: and I can guess but Little of your undertaking. But I have known a Person of ye truest genius take great Pains to translate a Poem, when with one tenth Part of ye Labour he could have compos'd a Poem ten times better. For instance Merrick & his Tryphiodorus.[3] See Dr Young on orig^l Composition, & y^r Friend Dr Goldsmith's book.[4]

For my Part, I am much pleasd with many parts of that Volume; particularly the station he assigns to *Taste,* of reconciling Literature & the Sciences to Common-Sense. It has ever been my own notion; and I was glad to find it so well authoriz'd. My Maxim, almost invariably, is, to take no Notice of undeserv'd Censure. If a Person's object be reputation, Let him press forward toward the Goal. Not even stop, unless *quite* necessary, to lash a Dog that attacks his Horse.

The Orientals afforded a new, & very fertile subject for eclogues. Poor Collins[5] did not wholly satisfy me; having by no means sufficiently availd himself of their many local peculiarities.

I cannot positively say, whether I sent those Notes to John de Reeve *without a Cover,* or not. I suppose you would have me always use a Cover.

Maupertuis's Letter on possible Discoveries[6] I had before

observ'd. It put me in mind of an Improvement that I've long thought might be made in our Magazines; were ye proprietors to give encouragement for persons to point Defects in all arts & sciences; for others to propose improvements in em; and to allot a Page or two, for these Purposes, only.

I have now, I think, taken *some* notice, of all y^t was pass'd over in y^r former Letters. I have now to add about a Page de novo & so conclude.

M^r [Hylton] is making a Pool, which will add much *Lustre* to his situation. 'Tis really a well-judg'd Piece of work; if he find no occasion to regret y^e *expence* of it. It answers many important Purposes—It repairs his Road for an 100 yards, where it would least admit of reparation: It supplies him with as many Fish, as he can possibly want, from year to year: It gives his House some Figure as you approach it, & is a beautifull object from his Windows. These are important works & —— w^t you please.

As for me who was, last year, a *Book-binder*, I am become, this year, a *Painter*, I mean my *Amusement* has been to sit beside a Painter, who has taken mine and about half a dozen other Portraits of persons in the neighbourhood, at my House: [Hylton]'s for One, with a noble *Conch* in his left hand; & his Pool *&c.* in ye back-ground. Motto (for *Conchyology* I regard not) is proposd to be:

> J[ohn] S[cott] of [H——] heare stand I,
> Who built a new shit-house, & made ye Pool bye.

As to reading, I have, for the first time, perus'd a vol: or two of ye rambler, & think for *Judgment* & *perspicuity* he equals any writer I ever read—& for ye musick of well-turn'd Periods, I do not *know* his equal. For I am hardly *satisfy'd* with any one in ye eng: Language, *beside* Him.

Have you read y^e 'Theory of moral Sentiments' by Dr. Smith, a Scotchman? or ye 'Dial: moral and political,' by Mr Hurd? Both which I purchas'd.

My Ode to Venus is not yet, to my Mind—so that I shall *probably* make Alterations—I think, if a proper Reference c^d be made from y^e *beauty* we *admire* in this Venus, to *what* we require in a modern Garden, it might furnish out a madrigal, not wholly inelegant—But I have, however, sent you my *present* Edition of it.

What think you of ye Valentine, receiv'd yesterday by my Under-servant Hannah? With some Difficulty, I obtain'd a sight of it; and have given you ye best Idea of it, I was able.

Such employm^ts, you will naturally say, do not suppose a want of Leisure: and indeed they do not—but they suppose a mind willing to amuse you, & which for ye sake of y^t event, will trespass a Little upon ye time wch is really requir'd for other purposes. Believe me with Compt^s to Mrs Percy, y^r most affec^ate

W. SHENSTONE.

NOTES

[1]*The British Magazine* was a new sixpenny monthly magazine started in January 1760. The imitation of Don Quixote—*The Adventures of Sir Launcelot Greaves*—a poor work of Smollett, ran through the early numbers. Serial publication in a monthly magazine was a new venture.

[2]Begun in the 'fifties definitely to take away from the success of Hume's History. Vol. 1 appeared 1761, 2, 3 and 4 in 1762, and volume 5 brought the work down to 1765.

[3]James Merrick (1720–1769), published 1739 *The Destruction of Troy. Being the Sequel of the Iliad, Translated from the Greek of Tryphiodorus.*

[4]Percy's note in MS.: 'Review of Polite Literature in Europe, 12°.'

[5]William Collins (1721–1759), published his *Persian Eclogues*, 1742.

[6]Pierre Louis Moreau de Maupertius (1698–1759) French mathematician and astronomer.

CCLXI

Inside Draft Copy of *RELIQUES*: Harvard.

[*To* J. S. HYLTON.]

My service, & I have sent ye Chief Musician to bring ye Pencils—Poor Heron's Letters. particularly his account of the *thriving* trade he carries on, are as humorous as may be. He seems to have wit, and a ready application of ye promiscuous matters he has perused—I would advise him not to waste his talent upon epistles, but to write a Novel; or detach'd Characters; or Little essays, or somew^t, by wch he may get money and recommend himself to Friends.

My Pencils came fro' the maker whom Mr H. recommended. I heard last Night y^t Mrs Briscoe was deliver'd of as
mere a *Child*, as *Herself*—A Boy—Is this time?—Dick is
gone to Birm^m. Mr Hylton, methinks, shou'd not delay to
exert his Authority as a Surveyor—I am really more & more
delighted wth the Pool, & w^d not by any means have it cramp'd
in ye extent—Another Servt offer'd yesterday, y^t seem'd more
promising that that [sic] from Rewley—

W. SHENSTONE.

Saturday:
March, ye 8. 1760
Will Mr H. call here this afternoon?

CCLXII

Works III, 357.

To the [REV. R. GRAVES], *on his neglecting his Correspondence.*

THE LEASOWES,
July 7, 1760.

Dear Mr. Graves,
   I must confess that I do not altogether find your argument
conclusive.—An hurry of business *may* be necessary, and somewhat inconsistent with frequent correspondence; but a state of
leisure, which I wished you, does not imply a course of *dissipation;* which makes your present apology for not writing to
me before. And so, betwixt business at one time, and dissipation at another, I am to be defrauded of a correspondence that
is quite essential to my well-being. Pardon me, if, on such
occasion, you find me extremely clear-sighted in the foibles
of my friends; and do not say with the man in Horace, 'Cur
in amicorum vitiis, &c.'[1a] The *matter* is too *important* for me to
connive at any sort of sophism.—However, to make you easy
on this head, I am convinced the letter was owing to *you;* for
which I will draw my apology neither from *business* nor dissipation: and yet how justly might I palliate my long silence

upon *either* footing! Since I wrote to you, I have been *busied*
in bringing about a conclusion with D[olman]. The letters,
journies, &c. *previous* and *posterior* to the execution of articles,
would afford me noble matter for excuse.—The constant
attendance upon workmen (of which I have fourteen or fifteen
this very day), making a piece of water below my Priory, would
produce more on the score of *dissipation*—you remember the
place. This, at present, is my chief employment, although
Alcock is drawing on the side of my table.—I wonder you do
not get some little urns turned, in any sort of wood, about
fourteen or fifteen inches high, and painted on the side with
figures, in the manner of some antique basso-relievo. He has
done something of this sort for me. You may, if you so please,
have the ground a dark *bronze*, and the figures a *light* one. I
am of late grown fond of bronze (which you yourself may
easily execute), and I think it always was your taste.—Dodsley
comes hither in about a fortnight, and prints *one* edition of his
Fables by means of Baskerville's press and paper. *Mean time*,
he is to *give* me his picture done by Reynolds;[1] and to *send* me
two bronzed plaster urns, of about twelve inches, with basso-
relievo; and two figures (ditto) of Homer and Virgil (of about
twenty-one inches) for two niches in my library. The parcel is
to be pieced out with Ogilby's Virgil, which I want for the
sake of the landscape.[2]—And now to the particulars of your
letter.

I can readily conceive how much greater pleasure you must
receive from the *retinue* of your journey, than an Archbishop
can from all his equipage; and I can truly assure you, I find
a pleasure in every pleasure you enjoy.

Your room, indeed, will be a noble one; but be sure remember the 'Imploravit opes hominis, fraenumque recepit.'[3] and
guard against it.—To speak my sentiments, I think you will.
I think with you in regard to Tristram Shandy; so does the
author of The Monthly Review,[4] you will see. I bought Webb
instantly;[5] but have not read it. Lord Lyttelton is *allowedly*
the author of those Dialogues;[6] whose, the very last, I do not
know.[7] There is a noble specimen of Scotch poetry translated
from the Erse language.[8]—I have had two copies sent me from
Scotland; and, had I two franks, would send you one. 'Chrysal,

or The Adventures of a Guinea' (real characters intended),[9] will amuse you. Something *ever* occurs that obstructs my travelling at all—and though I long *ardently* to visit you, the Lord knows when it will be; yet *be* it certainly will, when I accompany Mr. Knight to Mr. Bamfield's: where I am pressingly invited by that gentleman and his neighbours, Lady Egmont,[10] Sir Charles Tynte,[11] &c.—I have about an hundred things more to say; which I must defer till I have heard from you.—God bless you and yours.

W. SHENSTONE.

NOTES

[1a] Horace, *Serm.*, I, 3, 26.

[1] Dodsley's portrait by Sir Joshua Reynolds is in the possession of H. Yates Thompson, Esq., and is reproduced in Straus's, *Robert Dodsley*.

[2] Published 1649, beautifully reprinted 1654, 1665.

[3] Horace, *Ep.* I, 10, 106.

[4] In *The Monthly Review*, July 1760, p. 83, appeared the following: '*The Life and opinions of Miss Sukey Shandy*. A writer of one of the magazines observes, that "if Tristram Shandy has done any mischief it is raising such a swarm of filthy Pamphleteers." This is certainly one of the bad consequences following the licentious manner in which the Writer has indulged himself; and Mr. S— is so far reprehensible for it, as every man, and more especially a Teacher of men, ought to be rendered accountable for the bad example he sets others.'

[5] Daniel Webb (1719?–1798). *An Enquiry into the Beauties of Painting and into the Merits of the most Celebrated Painters, Ancient and Modern* was issued by Dodsley, February 18, 1760.

[6] Lord Lyttelton's *Dialogues of The Dead* were advertised at 4s. in *The Gentleman's Magazine* for May 1760.

[7] Mrs. Elizabeth Montague (1720–1800), 'Queen of the Blues,' friend of George Lyttelton and Dr. Johnson, contributed anonymously Nos. XXVI, XXVII and XXVIII to the *Dialogues of the Dead*. This contribution showed considerable literary talent.

[8] James Macpherson's *Fragments of Ancient Poetry, Gallic and Erse*, published by Dodsley at 1s., August 20, 1760.

[9] Charles Johnston (1719?–1800?), wrote *Chrysal, or the Adventures of a Guinea*, and it was advertised as published by Becket, 2 vols. 12 mo. 6s., in *The Gentleman's Magazine*, May 1760. Much of the satire was political.

[10] John (Perceval) Earl of Egmont, married secondly, January 26, 1756, Catherine, third daughter of the Hon. Charles Compton.

[11] Sir Charles Kemeys Tynte, Bart. of Haleswell.

CCLXIII

B.M. Add. MSS. 28221.
Hecht, 39.

[*To* THOMAS PERCY.]

THE LEASOWES,
August 11, 1760.

Dear Sir,

I should be extremely glad, if the *slow arrival* of any Letters you expect from Me, might in no sort interfere with any *good Intention* of your *own*. I can at best claim to be no other yⁿ a very *desultory* correspondent, who may at *one* time make Amends, for what he is deficient at *Another*. However, I ought *now* more *particularly* to apologize for my Delay, being yᵉ result of a little too much Inattention to your Desire of an Answer by *return* of the *Post*.—Indeed I do indulge myself in yᵉ Hope of seeing you some time in Northamptonshire; as I do, likewise in *that* of seeing many *other* pleasing sights, perhaps infinitely less affecting yⁿ the sight of an Ingenious Friend. The Hope affords me present Pleasure—But when! or where—I'm weary of Conjectures!—having too often been mistaken in my visionary schemes of Happiness.—Were I to say all yᵗ occurrs in regard to Master [Hylton]; it would engross my whole sheet of Paper, which I do not intend, it *shall*. He has indeed, for some *time*, held but a Low place in my Esteem: altho' what Quarrel we have at *present*, is altogether of his *own* Contrivance: For I by no means wish'd to *break* with Him; on account of yᵗ *amusement* which our Connexion afforded *each* of us, and of which he will hardly say that he had *Less* yⁿ an equal share. The Discovery regarding Moody & the Mulberry-tree was posterior to our Fray: and employ'd by Him as an *after-thought* to account for much *preceding* Impertinence. The Advice you gave Him was obviously right; but thrown away on One, who cannot distinguish between solid Censure & harmless Raillery. On the whole, he has of late display'd so much of the *froward child* & the *officious Gossip*, yᵗ we shall scarce be again upon civil terms, till he have made Concessions which he may not approve—I ought to have told you of our Fray before; yᵗ ye Letter he wrote might not surprize you. I have never *yet* sent Him your *Catalogue* of Rarities; nor a parcell of Curiosities from y^r Friend Miss Hickman. But a Friend of Mine has, thro' my Hands, presented Him with upwards of 300 Medals; which, as I'm just beginning to make a Collection, I almost wish I had secur'd for *Myself.*

I thank you heartily for your Letter to Johnson.[1] I do very unfeignedly respect both the *Writer* & the *Man*; and should be sorry to forfeit, by a neglect on my side, any degree of Esteem he discovers for Me. I am also truly glad to hear of your Friend Grainger's success.[2] I hope however he will not sacrifice too *much* of his Life, *abroad.* When he can once qualify himself to make a little *external* Figure Here, his *intrinsick* merit will ensure success at *Home;* And *then,* I should expect that Home would be more *agreeable* to Him—if I am not blinded by ye Pleasure I propose to myself from his farther acquaintance. I am oblig'd to you for y^e *Incidents* you offer, relating to my ludicrous essay on false Taste.[3] Pray fail not not [sic] to communicate, aught you observe of ye same stamp. I fear y^e *white-wash'd* tree will appear some^wt incredible— however, I'll see what may be done, whenever I have *Leisure* and *good spirits.* My good Friend Mr Spence intends a whole *Pamphlett* of *this kind;* which he calls y^e *History* of false Taste: but I do not expect any great matter, from a subject of *Humour* in my Friend's Hands. *Dodsley* gave me this Intimation; who resides here for near two months, to correct ye edition of Fables begun by Baskerville. He has given me a Portrait of his head by Reynolds, ye Price of which I am asham'd to mention. He seems to entertain no doubt, y^t your Chinese novel will excite Curiosity—You will perhaps be desirous to know what I have of late been doing about my Farm. One Piece of water below my Priory has *confin'd* me, *employ'd* my servants, and *enslav'd* my Horses all this year—I hope to finish it, the next week; but have often been *deluded* by such expectations. I have had a large conflux of visitants; and expect *more,* when L^d. Lyttelton brings all ye world to his new Palace. Pray how do you like his Dialogues? or who is ye Author of ye Remarks, that is so partial as to mention *me* with honour? As to *other* Books, you *must instantly* procure y^e 'antient Fragments' of Scotch 'Erse' Poetry.—I would wish you to read 'Webb's treatise on Painting,' 'Elegies descriptive & moral'[4] and, if you love *mischief*, the two Odes y^t ridicule Grays & Mason's manner.[5] Have you ever yet seen the '*Prolusions*' containing Overbury's wife, the Notbrowne Mayde, Sackville's Induction, ye tragedy of Edwd III (as suppos'd, by Shakespear) & a Poem of Sir John Davies?[6] Tis indeed a specimen of *type* & *paper* y^t is meant to *alarm* my neighbour Baskerville; & had not ye Editor admitted so many *affectations*, I should hardly know where to assign ye Palm. However, Tonson,[7] having sent it to Baskerville, is to find it surpass'd in Dodsley's Fables. I presume ye inclos'd to be ye Papers you *mean*. I wish I had happened to take a copy of them. I will attend to Ovid ye first Leisure moment, if you will believe me to be, on all occasions, yours & Mrs Percy's most true & faithfull Servant,

W. SHENSTONE.

NOTES

[1]Percy wrote, July 29, 1760, 'I not long since wrote to Johnson and took occasion to repeat the Apology you made for not having answered his Letter. . . . I concluded with repeating some of the civil and respectful things I have heard you say of him, and doubt not but he will remain very well satisfied.'

[2]Ibid. 'I had a letter last post from Dr. Grainger at St. Kitts, wherein he desired his Compliments to you. He is happily married there, hath got into a course of practise in which he hopes to clear 100£ per añn: Intends to lay up for a few years and then come and spend his days in England.'

[3]Ibid. 'When I saw you, you talked of giving a short History of false taste: I can furnish you with one or two real facts that are not unpleasant. Last year died a Mr. W., who had a seat at M. and who was possessed by the very demon of Caprice. He came into possession of an Old Mansion that commanded a fine view down a most pleasing Vale; he contrived to intercept it by two straight rows of Elms that ran in an oblique direction across it, and which led the Eye to a pyramidical Obelisk composed of one single board set up endways and painted by the joiner of the Village; this obelisk however was soon removed by the first puff of wind.

'In view of one of his windows grew a noble large spreading Ash, which, tho' spontaneous gift of Nature, was really a fine object, and by its stately figure and chearful Verdure afforded a most pleasing relief to the Eye; you will stare when I tell you, that Mr. W. had this Tree painted white—leaves and all; it is true the leaves soon fell off and the tree died, but the Skeleton still remains, as a Monument of its owner's Wisdom and Ingenuity.'

[4]John Scott (1730-1783), published in April 1760, *Four Elegies, Descriptive and Moral*. (Dodsley.)

[5]The *Odes to Obscurity and Oblivion*, published anonymously in 1760, were by Robert Lloyd (1733-1764), and George Colman (1732-1794). Grainger writes to Percy: 'I have read the Odes (to Obscurity and Oblivion, by Bob. Lloyd, etc.) with uncommon satisfaction, and hope they will produce a proper change in the future compositions of Mason and Gray. I ever thought these gentlemen, especially in their lyric performances, too obscure; indeed, I have read some of their stanzas which were so poetical as to be scarcely sense.'

[6]*Prolusions or Select Pieces of Antient Poetry—compil'd with great Care from their several Originals, and offer'd to the Publick as Specimens of the Integrity that should be*

found in the Editions of worthy Authors—in three Parts, published by Tonson, in 1760, for Edward Capell (1713–1781).

⁷The firm of Tonson 'in the Strand' belonged to the brothers J. & R. Tonson, but Jacob Tonson, d. 1767, was head of the business.

CCLXIV

B.M. Add. MSS. 28221.
Hecht, 43.

[*To* THOMAS PERCY.]

THE LEASOWES, *Oct*ʳ 1, 1760.

Dear Sir,

I am truly glad that you deriv'd any Pleasure from your visit, which afforded Me a very considerable One: And I shall esteem myself yet *more* fortunate, if any Pleasure it gave you, may induce you to repeat it, when you find a proper Conveniency. There will indeed by no *end* of *writing* all we have to say on the present occasion: A week's Conference on the Subject, when things are in somewhat greater Forwardness, will be more effectual than fifty Packets, as much distended as your last—Besides, I'm a little suspicious that my *winter-Spirits* may render me Less punctual yⁿ you will expect me to be. I will, however, *try* to return your Parcells within a Post or two; together with my Judgment of *acceptance* or *reprobation.* After this, I would have you transcribe what you think proper, in a Large Paper-book, & let me reconsider them *all together,* before they are sent away to Press. Many of those in *Print* need not be transcribd *at all;* only their *Titles* regularly inserted in those *Places* that you shall allott them.¹

As to *Placing* them, I would not have yᵉ *Long* ones *ever* follow one Another; unless there happen to be some very *particular* reason for their so doing. My Motive is, that Any that think them dull, should esteem *doubly* so, on account of their *Length;* and then—you know yᵉ Consequence.

I believe I shall *never* make any objection to such *Improvements* as *you* bestow upon them; unless you were plainly to *contradict* Antiquity, which I am pretty sure will never be the Case.

2 O

As to alterations of a *word or two*, I do not esteem it a point of *Conscience* to *particularize* them on *this* occasion. Perhaps, where a whole *Line* or *More* is alter'd, it may be proper enough to give some Intimation of it. The Italick type may answer this purpose, if you do not employ it on other occasions. It will have the appearance of a modern *Toe* or *Finger*, which is *allowably* added to the best old Statues: And I think I should always let the Publick imagine, that these were owing to Gaps, rather yⁿ to *faulty Passages*.

I have *us'd* myself to these three marks of approbation, + for the least, ⧺ for the next, and ⧻ for the highest. I shall therefore employ them in the present Case, but I would not have you *insert* any Pieces that sink *below* the *second* Mark.

I could indeed wish you not to place your Thoughts on extending the *size* of your Publication. However, I shall not object to 3 such vols as Mallet's,[2] if you can by any means fill them *properly*, even with yᵉ addition of *Scotch* Ballads.

You did well in ordering me that Collection of old Ballads:[3] I doubt, however, I shall not be able here to borrow 'Dryden's Miscellanies.'[4]

I am more fearfull of your *admitting* what may not suit the Class that will be your principal Readers; than I am of your *omitting* a few good pieces, which may, at worst, be added in some future Volume.

With Regard to the Celtic Poem, I think there is something *good* in it. The absolute *Necessity* of Notes, will be the Rock that you may chance to split upon. I hope they will be as short as possible, & either at the end of every *Piece;* or thrown into yᵉ Form of Glossary at the end of the *Collection*. Perhaps some small Preface at the Beginning also, may supersede the Use of *Many*. I would rather chuse to have yᵉ translation be a kind of *flowing* yet *pompous Prose;* & printed in *Paragraphs* accordingly—The Original, I should think, had much better be omitted; partly for yᵉ Reasons you give yourself, and partly, lest this, *together with* the Notes, may *load* the text more yⁿ is agreeable. I should be glad enough to revise, *with you*, this whole Collection when tis put together; In the mean time, would not trouble you to send me each particular Piece, as it is very probable I shall not have means to afford you much assistance.

A Question of yours remains with regard to y^e *smaller* Fragments of ye Celtick Poetry.—There should be *certainly* nothing of this kind inserted, y^t is *Less* considerable y^n what you send me; And as to these, and a *Few* of the Kind, they, perhaps, may not be much exceptionable. However, if it be ye least necessary to add *notes* by way of *explanation*, One may readily enough conclude y^t they had better all be totally *omitted*.

Thus I think I have shewn my Obedience to your Injunctions for the Present; & if I ever happen to do otherwise, I hope it will not be imputed to want of *Inclination*. Dodsley is gone to spurr *Baskerville;* returns on Friday to spurr *me*, when I will deliver him your Compliments, & make *this very Letter* my *Excuse*. Mr Melmoth is not yet come, but is expected every Day. I am also made to expect a very clever woman, one Mrs Gataker,[5] with a party of ingenious Persons from London, in a fortnights time. I shall be truly glad to see Mr. Thornton,[6] but I hope he will by no means scruple to make himself known to me on his arrival. I believe Dodsley's original Fables will be printed off in about a Fortnight; when I shall find myself more at *Leisure*.

The printed Ballads you sent, are, I think, by no means worth preserving.

I will here conclude myself very affectionately both yours & Mrs Percy's; if I think of any thing more I will not fail to add it by way of Postscript.

W. SHENSTONE.

Eight o'Clock; Tis now time y^t my Packet should be *made up*, ready for to-morrow morning. I have nothing more to add, except that I have been attending on a Sir J. Mostyn with a Party of Ladies & Militia-Gentlemen,[7] y^t have been long quartered at Bridgnorth. They seemd very good sort of People, without any great Depth of *Taste*.

NOTES

[1]Percy's note in MS: 'viz. The proposed Collection of Reliques of ancient Poetry, etc.'

[2]Publ. 1759. *Edwin and Emma* and numerous other ballads were by Mallet and *William and Margaret* was long thought to be his work. See *The Beginnings of the English Romantic Movement*, Phelps, pp. 177–182.

³Percy's note in MS: 'That in 3 Vols. 12 mo. 1727.'
⁴Dryden's *Miscellany Poems* in 6 volumes appeared in 1684–1708.
⁵Mrs. Gataker is possibly the wife of Thomas Gataker, a surgeon at Charing X
Hospital and author of several medical pamphlets published by Dodsley.
⁶Bonnel Thornton, journalist (1724–1768), friend and fellow student of Percy at
Christ Church, Oxford. With George Colman (1733–1794), he ran the *Connoisseur*,
and also had a hand in the *S. James's Chronicle*.
⁷Percy's note in MS: 'Among these was my Relation Mr. Price of Bringpeice,
Flintshire.'

CCLXV

B.M. Add. MSS. 28221.
Hecht, 46.

[*To* THOMAS PERCY.]

THE LEASOWES, *Nov*ʳ. 10ᵗʰ 1760.

Dear Sir,

I send these few Lines, merely to acquaint you, that I have
not yet received the Collection of Ballads from London; &,
of consequence, am not enabled to write such an answer as
you may expect from me. I am going with Mʳ Dodsley this
afternoon, as far as Birmingham; who goes from thence to
town on Wednesday-Morning, & will order those volumes
down with all convenient expedition—I will have regard to yᵉ
improvements you mention, while the Pieces you allude to,
are under my examination.—There is no room that I can see,
to question yᵉ reception yᵗ your Work is like to meet with—If
I have any talent at Conjecture, All People of Taste, thro'out
the Kingdom, will rejoice to see a judicious, a correct & elegant
Collection of such Pieces. For after all, 'tis such Pieces, that
contain yᵉ true *Chemical* Spirit or Essence of *Poetry;* a Little
of which properly mingled is sufficient to strengthen & *keep
alive* very considerable Quantities of the kind—Tis yᵉ *voice*
of *Sentiment*, rather yⁿ the *Language* of *Reflexion;* adapted
peculiarly to *strike yᵉ Passions*, which is the only Merit of
Poetry that has obtained my regard of late.

I have been mentioning yʳ Quere to Mʳ Dodsley, about yᵉ
argument or *Introduction* to each ballad—I will say *more* in my
next Letter—At present, I shall only intimate, that I would
wish you to consult for *Simplicity* as much as possible—*Some*

old words, I presume, (which it will be perhaps necessary to preserve) must be explained by modern ones—For these alone, I would reserve the *bottom* of each Page. The remaining Quere will be, whether ye little Anecdotes y^t you insert by way of illustration, should be placed at y^e *beginning*, or at the *end* of ye ballad—If they are short, perhaps, they may not be amiss in Italicks, at ye beginning. However should you begin each Ballad at ye head of a Page, you will often have *room* for notes of a *larger extent* at the Close of ye Foregoing—and perhaps you may want here to introduce a *particular* note, as well as a *general* Argument. In this case (ye bottom, as I said, being reserv'd for mere *verbal* explanations) I would throw both ye general argument & particular notes together at the *Close;* for otherwise your text will be almost smotherd, by these incumbrances in every part—However I do not yet decide; & should be glad to hear farther what you have to say—According to this Plan, I fear ye notes would often incroach upon ye top of a Page, if you do not guard against it, while you are printing—I *doubt*, whether you ought to *sort* y^r pieces, or to *vary* them as much as possible—I will return ye old Ballad next Letter, having at present not a moments Leisure. Mr Dodsley's Fables are not quite printed off here, thro' some Mistakes y^t have occasioned ye Loss of three or four reams of Paper—However w^n fresh Paper arrives, they will be finished in 3 Day's time—Mr Dodsley desires his Compliments, as I do mine, to Mrs Percy —Pray write soon, & believe me ever yours

WILL: SHENSTONE.

To Rev^rd M. Percy.

CCLXVI

Hull, I, 279.

To Mr. HULL.

THE LEASOWES,
Jan. 7, 1761.

Dear Sir,

   I am with you aware, that the Story of the *Spanish Lady*[1] is rather too simple, too destitute of Matter for the Generality of

People who frequent the Galleries of a *London* Theatre; but might not some Incidents of Humour be extracted from the Group of Sailors, which must necessarily be introduced in the Piece? There are in real Life various, and very striking Characters among our *English* Tars. Indeed, much Use has been made of them already, and to very pleasing Purposes.

Observe, I propose (or rather merely *allow*) this Violation of the Simplicity of the Story, as a Means to make it answer the Purposes of Emolument to you, if you choose to undertake it; for, as far as relates to my own Taste, I think, even in Representation, it could not be preserved too simple.

The Consideration that an Author is compelled to forego, in many Instances, his favourite Intention, renounce a Compliance with his own Judgment, and even sometimes abolish the very Excellencies of his Genius, to gratify the vitiated Taste of a few noisy Auditors, who otherwise would condemn the Work, is rather melancholy; and could not by any Species of Reason be supported, except that which you advanced, namely, that your Theatres in *London* are maintained in these Days at a very great Expence, and that Expence must be repaid; consequently, if SHAKESPEARE cannot elicit a full House, HARLEQUIN must extort it; but woe the while for the State of Letters and Genius!—Such was not the genuine End and Intention of a Theatre. I, for my own Part, look upon it as a Temple raised to *Moral Virtue;* the Design of it is to instruct through the Medium of Delight; to shew Virtue and Vice in their respective Colours: and the Business of the Audience is, to judge, compare, define, to distinguish between what is given for Example, and what for Precaution: so conducted and preserved, a Theatre truly merits the Denomination I have given it, but if *Moral* is to submit to *Matter*, if *fine Sentiment* is to give Way to *fine Scenery*, it falls from the Purposes for which is [sic] was originally instituted, and becomes a Place of *Shew* indeed, but not of *Science*, [sic.]

All these Absurdities and Misfortunes are owing to the Audience; and it is much to be lamented, that the Conductor of an useful Place of Amusement cannot oppose and rectify them; but I clearly see he cannot. Your Anecdote of Mr. GARRICK's laudable Attempt,[2] some Years ago, to remove from public View an annual Object of Indecorum and Immorality, and substitute a Piece, which (however antique) furnished Matter for the moral HOGARTH to display his Genius on, diverts me much, and would (were I of any Country beside *England*) most probably astonish me. As an *Englishman* it does not. The Attempt was as much to the Credit of Mr. GARRICK, as the Defeat of it was disreputable to the Audience.

This Subject might, I think, by itself furnish Matter for a tolerably-sized Essay; and I marvel that some Writer, who has rather more Affection for the Use of a Pen than myself, does not adopt it. A Reflection on the very severe Trial a dramatic Writer undergoes, when he offers his Work to the Public, has frequently called forth my Compassion; the Means to procure general Approbation are so vague and precarious, that I almost wonder when I hear of any one hardy enough to stand a Candidate for it.

My Zeal in these Particulars has made me deviate from the principal Object of this Letter, which was to request you to make a little Sketch of my favourite Story upon dramatic Principles, during the Course of this Winter; and let us (*Deo favente*) when next we meet at the *Leasowes*, see how the Design appears. It may be an agreeable Amusement, if it answers no other Purpose.

Whether I may ever execute the Elegy which Mr. DODSLEY has recommended,[3] is very uncertain, though I much approve his Plan. Suppose you were to attempt it—I have some Reasons for thinking that Elegy would suit your Disposition and Abilities. The Mention of DODSLEY's Application to me has procured me *twelve* Lines,[4] for which I hold myself indebted. You do not tell me who they were written by, so I suppose I am to ask no Questions.

When you get any more such original Morsels, your communicating them will be a Kindness. While I am thus a Winter Solitudinarian, while
'Scarce one Friend my Grass-grown Threshold finds,'
You can hardly conceive how much Value such Trifles bear.

I am, dear Mr. HULL,
your very faithful and affectionate,
W. SHENSTONE.

NOTES

[1]Thomas Hull (1728–1808), actor and dramatist, produced his musical play *The Spanish Lady*, at Birmingham, on May 2, 1765. It was acted again, with alterations December 11, 1769.

[2]Hull, I, 282, adds this note: 'It had been the Custom at both the royal Theatres, for many Years, to perform the *London Cuckolds* on the Lord Mayor's day. Mr. Garrick, from Motives of Propriety, endeavoured to substitute the old Play of *Eastward-Hoe*; but the Audience exploded it.'

[3]Dodsley suggested an elegy on the death of General Wolfe. Hull, I, 272.

[4]Hull, I, 284, adds the twelve lines received by W.S.

CCLXVII

B.M. Add. MSS. 28221.

Hecht, 51.

[*To* THOMAS PERCY.]

[*Early*, 1761.]

I procured a copy of the Fables from Mr Baskerville, *before* the Cuts *were inserted*,[1] & have by help of Mr Alcock (a Painter) supplied the places of the *emblematick* prints with some devices of my own. I send you some account of them; y^t you may be induced to favour me with Hints for two or three more—which will be wanting to compleat my scheme, & which you can very readily *supply*—but which I can *not*.

A Drawing of Mr. Dodsley from Richardson.[2]

Frontispiece—One of the Graces taking away the Shield & Helmet from Minerva; while another crowns her with a wreath of Roses and the third brings her a silken robe.

Truth leading a Child along ye Margin of a precipice to ye temple of virtue, an agreeable and striking sketch, & ye Landskip very—pleasing.

A Statue of Esop—not a handsome Esop.

Two Boys busyd in reading a Book of Fables, that half covers them—makes a pretty ornament.

Boys hanging Flowers round a large Shield of Minerva.

A Sphinx &c.

A Mask, with ye Syrinx, Tibia & Laurel.

Three Boys admiring a double-headed Busto—Two staring at ye beautifull Face of a *young Lady* (ye Fable) the third, on ye other side, pointing to a Philosopher's head (the moral) a pleasing ornam^t enough—

The young Hercules strangling serpents, from the Antique —alluding to Children being taught early to triumph over Vice.

Mercury teaching Cupid to read, his Mother standing by— from a Picture of Hannibal Carracci.[3]

Aurora, with winged steeds, & ye morning star by way of Pompon, driving away ye Night—alluding to ye effects of Instruction upon Youth—(taken from Tooke's Pantheon).[4]

Children dancing round a Statue of Truth, and as it were gladdened by the rays reflected on them by her Glass—the prettiest picture amongst 'em, and used as a tail-piece at the *Conclusion*.

I can procure you ye names of the *writers* in Dodsley's Fables, if you chuse to have them—Some of them certainly are such, as ought to credit the Performance.

NOTES

[1] The date of this letter must be before February 9, on which day Baskerville published Dodsley's *Fables*.

[2] Jonathan Richardson (1665–1745) author of various works on painting and portraits. His son (1694–1771), followed in his line less successfully.

[3] Annibale Carracci (1560–1609), painter and designer. 'Hercule enfant étouffant les serpents,' at the Louvre, is his work.

[4] Andrew Tooke (1673–1732), master of the Charterhouse. *The Pantheon, representing the Fabulous Histories of the Heathen Gods and most Illustrious Heroes, illustrated with copper plates*. London, 1698.

CCLXVIII

Hull, I, 303.

To Mr. DODSLEY.

Feb. 11, 1761.

Dear Mr. DODSLEY,

I have spoken to Mr. L[ivie][1] upon the Subject of his Dedication; and he agrees with me, that there can be no properer Person to procure the Leave we want than Mr. D[alton].[2] Suppress, therefore, if you please, my Letter to Mr. L[ivie], and engage Mr. D[alton] as soon as ever you can, to do his best Offices in this Affair. They wait only for the Plates,[3] and my Lord's[4] answer, before they can order his Arms to be engraved. I blundered, in regard to L[ivie]'s University; a Blunder so much the more unlucky, as they have no Masters of Arts at *Edinburgh*: he was of *Aberdeen*. As to the rest, you will give Mr. D[alton] any proper Information my Letter affords you. L[ivie] does not expect a Present; he will be perfectly satisfied if the Work entitle him to any Degree of Lord B[ute]'s esteem: and this Mr. D[alton] may *say*, should his Lordship give him an Opportunity. Perhaps it need not be mentioned, that L[ivie] is a *Scotchman*, unless my Lord should make particular Enquiry. Betwixt Friends, I believe, that having no Establishment, he means hereafter to ask some little Matter, by Means of a *Scotch* Lady, who is my Lord's Relation.

The smaller Drawing you enclosed is really a perfect Beauty, and must be executed at all Events when I return it, which I mean to do on *Saturday;* I shall give the Engraver one or two Directions.

I wish I could think as highly of the Frontispiece. In Truth, it does not please me; and what to do, I cannot tell. The Designer does not seem to enter into the Spirit of the Story; and the Circumstance of the Shield hung upon the Pillar, (a single Pillar of the Temple had been sufficient) with the Motto being wholly omitted, throws the whole Stress upon the Merit of the two Figures in the fore Ground. I am sorry to say, these do not answer, MÆCENAS appears with no Dignity, and HORACE's Attitude I can't explain. If the Floor had been raised one Step where the Patron sits, and his Person tall, or his Chair embellished a little, &c. and if HORACE were shorter, (as his Nature was) his Attitude no Way violent, and his Head downcast, it would, perhaps, have removed some of my Objections. But if there were no Possibility of hanging a Shield, &c. on a Piece of a Temple, and so making a Back-Ground important, (as the Designer surely might have done) yet there evidently were Means of rendering it more beautiful than it appears here. HAYMAN certainly should have been the Man! But more of this when I write on *Saturday.*

When shall I see *Baptista Porta?* As also the Frontispiece only to the Ornaments, &c. of Temples and Churches?[5] The

Verses in the *London Magazine* are tolerably well printed, though my Punctuation is not observed.[6] Your Brother was to send me also the *Annual Register*,[7] all, except that for the Year 1759. I believe W—— has or will desire your Brother to supply him with the few Magazines he distributes here. This Letter is written amid much Hurry and Confusion of Brain, when I can really express nothing to my Mind, much less the Esteem and Affection with which I am,

Dear Sir,
your most obedient,
W. SHENSTONE.

NOTES

[1]John Livie was Baskerville's assistant, proof reader and corrector of the press. This letter refers to the presentation to Lord Bute of Baskerville's *Horace*, which was ready in May, 1763.

[2]Richard Dalton (1700–1791), brother of John Dalton, Lord Beauchamp's tutor, was keeper of the royal prints and medals and later of the royal pictures.

[3]The frontispiece and vignette were by Wale and Grignion, and the book bore the arms of Lord Bute at the head of the dedication page.

[4]Lord Bute's.

[5]Probably the reference is to *The Ornaments of Churches considered*, advertised in *The Gentleman's Magazine* for April, 1761, at 4s.

[6]*London Magazine*, January 1761, p. 47. *Under a Venus de Medicis, at the Leasowes*, 1759.

'To Venus, Venus here retir'd
My sober vows I pay.'

[7]*The Annual Register, or a view of the history, politicks and literature of the year* was started by R. Dodsley in 1758, and published by his house till 1790.

CCLXIX

Works III, 360.

To the [REV. R. GRAVES], *on* DODSLEY'S *Fables, and other Literary Articles.*

THE LEASOWES,
Mar. 1, 1761.

Dear Mr. Graves,

Although this interval in our correspondence must be placed, I fear, to *my* account, you will hardly think it mends the matter, to *fill* my present letter even with the best-grounded apologies—I will only mention a bad state of health, which has been my lot this winter, as a general excuse for two or three

months silence; and then declare, as with truth I may, that the
esteem and affection which you have so well deserved of me
have never undergone the least diminution or abatement. It is
with me a melancholy task, to *write* letters when I am not well;
although it be the time, of all others, when it is most necsseary
for me to *receive* them.—Our friend Dodsley, I presume, has
sent you a book of his Fables before this time. What merit
I have there, is in the *Essay;* in the *original Fables*, although I
can hardly claim a single Fable as my own; and in the *Index*,
which I caused to be thrown into the form of *Morals*, and which
are almost wholly mine. I wish to God it may sell; for he has
been at great expence about it. The two rivals which he has
to dread, are, the editions of Richardson[1] and of Croxall.—
The *Fables* in Croxall are tolerably written: his *reflections*, little
to the purpose, either for boys or grown people.—Richardson's
Improvement of L'Estrange would be a better collection, both
for the *Fables* and the *moral Reflections*, had he not admitted,
through an extravagant and mistaken love of drollery, that
vulgarity of phrase which in many places is not *common
English*.—This, I think, a true state of the case: say the best
you can in behalf of Dodsley.—As to his cuts, though to *him*
expensive, they will hardly, I fear, meet with much of your
approbation—the scale is much too small—and the emblematick prints which are larger will scarce, I fear, be understood.—
I procured a copy from Baskerville *before* the plates were
inserted, and have caused my painter (Alcock) to supply the
vacancies with some devices of my own—some account of
which I send you, as it may amuse you for a minute. I want
one or two to compleat my scheme, and should be glad if you
would propose some in your next letter.—I return you my
hearty thanks for the hints you gave for the Cambridge verses;
but when I received them it was too late, and I myself too much
indisposed, either to throw them into proper form, or even to
answer that gentleman's letter; which I thought a very genteel
one.—I know not what he did on that occasion, having seen
neither Cambridge nor Oxford verses.—Mr. Dodsley gave me
'The Environs of London.'[2]—Between friends, I wish he may
find five thousand readers, whom the management of that work
pleases more than *me*.—I will try to get you some of the *cuts*,

if you desire me to do so, though it will reflect a kind of tacit dislike of the *whole* performance.—His brother publishes this winter 'The Works of Soame Jenyns,' in three pocket-volumes;[3] and a Chinese novel from a Ms. translation revised, &c. by a friend of mine. You have perhaps heard me speak of Mr. Percy[4]—he *was* in treaty with Mr. James Dodsley, for the publication of our best old ballads in three volumes.—He has a large folio Ms. of ballads, which he shewed me, and which, with his own natural and acquired talents, would qualify him for the purpose, as well as any man in England. I proposed the scheme for him *myself*, wishing to see an elegant *edition* and good collection of this kind.—I was also to have assisted him in selecting and rejecting; and in fixing upon the best readings—But my illness broke off our correspondence, the beginning of winter—and I know not what he has done since. —There is a New Peerage going to be published—with, I believe, the draughts of the Peers houses—Lightholer called here, and said he had taken Lord Lyttelton's, and Lord Stamford's, for that purpose—the latter of which he shewed me.— Thus I have told you what I hear of new *publications*—as to what passes in the busy world, know no more than the Chronicle informs me—unless when *your* letters happen to be *rounded* with little anecdotes from Bath.—Have you seen Baskerville's new Prayer-books? My Lord Dartmouth has undertaken to present two to the King and Princess.—Do, for *charity's* sake, make me some amends for this long chasm in our correspondence, by a very early and long letter—I am sick to hear from you; being, with ardent and sincere affection, your ever faithful friend and servant,

W. Shenstone.

'Our little life is *rounded* with a sleep.'

Shakespeare.

NOTES

[1]*The London Chronicle*, November 12 to 14, 1761, 47: 'This day was published Æsop's Fables, with instructive Morals and Reflections, abstracted from all Party Considerations, adapted to all Capacities and designed to promote Religion, Morality and Universal Benevolence. By the late Mr. Samuel Richardson.'

[2]*London and its Environs* published in 6 vols. on December 6, 1760, by Dodsley, and possibly edited by him. Straus, *Robert Dodsley*, p. 372.

[3]Soame Jenyns (1704–1787), religious writer. May 16, 1761, was published *Miscellaneous Pieces in Two Volumes*. See Straus, *Robert Dodsley*, p. 374.

[4]The translation came from Dodsley's press on November 14, 1761.

CCLXX

The Historical Society of Pennsylvania.

[*To* THOMAS PERCY.]

Dear Mr. Percy,

It is now the second Day of March, 1761, a Point of time when it is become very expedient that you should see a few Lines dated from *The Leasowes*. By ye Way, I think, I have managed my *Date* with some Address. An attack of my old Fever, tho less dangerous than the former, prevented my answering your Letter at *First;* and *since,* a continuation of indifferent Health & spirits have kept me silent even 'till now. It is an unfortunate circumstance, that I find it so melancholy a task to *write* Letters, when I am not well; the very time, of all others, when it is the most comfortable to *receive* them. I desire that this may be accepted in full Discharge of all Apology; who have been the more *impatient* to recover my Health, that I might hear again from *you,* and two or three more *Friends.*

I have such a multitude of things to say, & to enquire after, that I know not where to begin much can I pretend to comprehend them in this Paper. Therefore, without observing rule or order, Let me ask in the first place when we may expect your *Chinese* Novel—The Ballads have, I fear, been postponed on *my account;* I forget if ever I acknowledg'd that I received the three volumes from Mr. J. Dodsley, just before I was taken ill; or that I read them over & marked several, according to different degrees of Approbation. I hope the scheme is not laid aside. I just intimated to Mr. Dodsley that I was sorry the Agreement was broken off, to wch he replied without the least acrimony; but seemed to think that his Brother had not acted wrong. I presume that, before this time, he has sent you a copy of his Fables, of which I shall be glad to hear your opinion. I heartily wish they may succeed; they have actually cost Him a deal of Money. You will trace *me* solely in the Essay and the *original Fables,* (where my *principal* merit lies in *additions* and *alterations*) and in the Index, which is almost wholly mine, &, but for me, would have been little more than a mere table of

Contents—Croxalls *Fables* are not much amiss, the wooden cuts are quite fine, but the *reflections* very exceptionable, whether meant for Boys or Men—Richardson's Improvement of l'Estrange has Spirit; but is full of those dirty & vulgar Phrases, which, in many places, are not common English. Surely the Field is tolerably open, & Dodsley may hope to make some Figure in it—Have you seen the *Environs* of London in 6 Vol. 8vo &c? The works of Soame Jenyns in 3 pocket-vols, were to have been published this winter—A new Peerage is coming out;[1] I believe, with Cuts of the noblemen's Houses; at least Lightholder shewed me Ld Stamford's, & said he had taken Lord Lyttelton's, which he said were intended for that work. I have made, since you were here, some addition to my Books, such as *I* must call *considerable*, & should be glad enough to shew you. I wish you were here, if only for a day, y^t we might discuss a thousand such Points, as I find, by what I have written, will make no Figure upon Paper. But if you have no Call this way, do not fail to *write* to me, Lest I should take it into my Head to fancy that I had given you some offence. I sent a Letter, of your hand-writing as it appeared, to Mr. [Hylton]. . . . & shall grow jealous of his obtaining a Correspondence y^t I have lost, if you do not write soon. You well know how great an emphasis Jealousy adds to disappointment—I have not your last Letter near me, but I remember it proposed my reconciliation with that Gent^n. I sent him a Letter about a month ago, wch I concluded with an Invitation to him, to dine here the next Day; allowing me to consider *his visit* as a *recantation* of some froward expressions he had made use of in his anger; at the same time mentioning, that if I could recollect any such I had used *myself*, I would freely allow Him to consider my *Invitation* in the *same Light*—These were the words as far as I can remember—But these words & the rest of my Letter, were constru'd otherwise y^n was intended; and an answer returned, that must throw the Quarrel upon himself.—I have behaved civilly to him since you saw us; and declare, I never once intended that our Bickerment should be perpetual—But, I think, if you saw *both* our Letters you would lay the Fault at his Door—I see I cannot write to entertain you at present and therefore will conclude; desiring you will present my best respects to Mrs. Percy & believe me ever y^r most faithfull

& very affectionate Friend,

WILL: SHENSTONE.

NOTE

¹Note at the bottom of the MS.: 'In Quarto Numbers, by Guthrie: it did not succeed.' William Guthrie (1708–1770) published 1763 a *Complete List of the English Peerage*.

CCLXXI

B.M. Add. MSS. 28221.
Hecht, 51.

[*To* THOMAS PERCY.]

I desire my best Respects to M^r and Mrs Percy, & will not be long before I return a fuller Answer to his obliging Letter—I cast my eye upon it this morning, & observed, to my utter Confusion, that the advertisement¹ should have been returned immediately—I wish it may not come too Late—chiefly that Mr Percy may be less disposed to censure my Inattention to his Request—For, in reality, I have discovered nothing that it is very material to alter.—Dodsley has sold 2000 of his Fables, & begins to talk of second & third editions.² I would have him permit Baskerville to print one more edition for the Curious, with no other decoration than a Frontispiece with new emblematical Top & Tail-pieces.—I want much to see the Chinese Novel; & will lend what assistance I can in regard to the old Ballads. I hope however that the prodigious pains Mr Percy proposes to take in this affair, will be employed rather to fill a moderate Collection with the *best readings* of good Ballads, than to swell such Collection to any very great extent.

Adieu for a Few days.

Saturday, April, 1761.

WILL: SHENSTONE.

To
The Rev^d
Mr Percy.

NOTES

[1] Percy's note in MS: 'The Advertisement prefixed to ye Fragments of Chinese Poetry, 4th vol. of Chin. Hist.'

[2] The second edition of Dodsley's *Fables* appeared April 21, 1761, and the third edition February 17, 1762.

CCLXXII

B.M. Add. MSS. 28221.
Hecht, 52.

[*To* THOMAS PERCY.]

THE LEASOWES, *April* 24, 1761.

Dear Sir,

You must accept a sort of *Piece-meal* performance of my Promise—I could indeed easily send you an account what Ballads & Songs I have marked in *those* Collections; but before I can properly recommend Any for your Insertion, it is altogether expedient that I should be well acquainted with your *Plan*. The Adjustment of This, will be a matter of Importance, & pretty intricate determination. For Instance, do you make any distinction betwixt a Ballad, & a Song, and so confine yourself to the *Former*? With the common people, I believe, a Song becomes a ballad as it grows in years; as they think an old serpent becomes a Dragon, or an old Justice, a Justice of Quorum. For my own part, I who love by means of different words to bundle up distinct Ideas, am apt to consider a Ballad as containing some little story, either real or invented. Perhaps my notion may be too *contracted*, yet, be this as it will, it may not be of much Importance to consult Etymology on this occasion, as it will be necessary herein to follow, the ordinary opinion of the world, at Last.

Again, if you admit what *I* call *Songs*, you must previously acquaint me, within what *Date* you think it best to circumscribe yourself: And this will lay you under difficulties, when I come to teize you with Horace's argument: demo unum, demo etiam unum, Dum cadat elusus &c:[1] For what will become of the new 'William & Margarett,'[2] 'Leinster fam'd for Maidens

2 P

fair'[3] & many more of a good stamp, which it will touch you
nearly, to omit? Again, what will you determine as to old
renowned songs, that perhaps have little or no Merit; & would
not have existed to this day, but for the tunes with which they
are connected? And again; how will you manage the Scotch?
Will you allow them a separate volume, & a Glossary? which
will [sic] many of them will too much require? These Points
& Many others cannot be so well adjusted as by a Conference
betwixt us at The Leasowes; where I hope you will have
Leisure to pass a day or two, when you have dispatched your
other publications.

NOTES

[1]Horace, *Epistles*, II, I, 46–47.
[2]*Reliques* II, 393 (Everyman Ed.). *Margaret's Ghost*, thought to be by David Mallet.
See ante p. 563, note 2·
[3]*Reliques*, II, 395. *Lucy and Colin*, by Thomas Tickell.

CCLXXIII

Works III, 364.

To the [REV. R. GRAVES], *with some Political Anecdotes.*

THE LEASOWES,
May 2, 1761.

Dear Mr. Graves,
I will, upon your last assurance, take it *ever* for granted, that
you do not omit writing upon any score of ceremony. This will
render your silence, at least in some *degree*, less irksome to me;
when I do not think it the effect of my own procrastination.——
Mr. Dodsley had sold two thousand of his Fables long ago;
but complained that he should *lose* thirty pounds by my
neighbour Baskerville's impression; and that he should not be
more than ten pounds gainer, upon the *whole*. I told him it was
enough, in books of *this sort*, if the first edition paved the way
for their future establishment in schools. And surely so it is:
for a book of this kind, once established, becomes an absolute
estate for many years; and brings in at least as certain and as
regular returns. I would *wish* him to give the polite world one
more edition from Baskerville's press; admitting only a *new*

sett of emblematical top and tail-pieces; and confining those empty cuts relating to each Fable to the cheap edition which he prints at London. A second edition of this latter sort will appear in a little time; and if you have any improvements to propose, he will very thankfully receive them. Mr. Spence offers him to write *the life* afresh; and Spence, Burke, Lowth, and Melmoth, advise him to discard *Italicks*. I confess he has used them to a very great *excess*, but yet I do not think they should be utterly discarded.

I did not intend that Mr. Davenport should ever hear of those verses; and how he came to do so, is past my comprehension. He seemed to me to have deserted Worfield, without any intention to return again. I therefore meant to inscribe them under my own Venus, in order to afford some novelty, at an *easy rate*, to those who are curious enough to *repeat* their visits here. Pray, if you see Mr. and Mrs. Davenport, present my best respects to them;—and as to the verses, I will send you a copy for them, if you *desire* or *advise* so me to do.—Mr. S—— is agreeable, not void of learning, has some smartness, but little taste. Mrs. S—— has *much* of the latter; and perhaps imagination, which makes a part of taste, may have had no small share in converting her to Popery.—Mr. Powys I have almost forgot.—You are ingenious and very inventive in regard to the means of giving yourself mortification. I dare to say, your new building suggests no such idea as you conceive.— And I think it sufficient in a parsonage-house, if one sees detached specimens of taste or elegance, without uniformity, or even without consistency.

I do not find but that you *figure* among the gentry near Bath. Dr. Charleton, who was here yesterday with Sir Francis[1] and Mr. Knight, gave me an account that the B[ishop] of G[loucester][2] had been to pay his respects to you. I will not enter into particulars, but would wish you to cultivate his acquaintance.—I shewed Sir Francis the dead colouring of the picture which I intend to send to you;—but you must know that Alcock is the most volatile of all creatures that have not wings. By way of improving the picture I meant for Dodsley, he has made it infinitely less like, and yet it must go to London as *it is*, for God knows when he can be brought to alter it.

I asked the Doctor, how Mr. Blackstone came to obtain a seat in Parliament; and his answer was, 'The King insisted on it, as he was a man of learning and ingenuity.'—The enmity betwixt Lord L[yttelto]n and Mr. P[itt], I find, continues in its full force; insomuch that my Lord is to have no place while Mr. P[itt] continues in the ministry.—My Lord B[ute]'s promotion was, it seems, demanded by the D. of N[ewcastle] and Mr. P[itt], as they would not be exposed to bear the blame, while he was the chief mover behind the curtain. These little particles of intelligence have, I believe, Sir—for their author. —I was told by another politician, the same day, that we were not to expect a peace—that the French, who might give up the Colonies, would not resign the Fishery.

Mr. Knight, his mother and sister, go through Bath to Mr. Bamfylde's in about three weeks, if nothing intervene. I am teazed greatly to accompany them,—by my own *inclination*, I can assure you, as well as their *importunity*. I do not say I will *not*, nor must I ever promise you *beforehand* that I *will*. I have good reasons to the contrary. They have some thoughts of bringing Dr. Charleton into the party.

Believe me ever yours and Mrs. Graves's.

W. SHENSTONE.

NOTES

[1]Sir Francis Charleton.
[2]William Warburton.

CCLXXIV

B.M. Add. MSS. 28221.
Straus & Dent, *John Baskerville*.

[*To* THOMAS PERCY.]

Wednesday, June 11th 1761.

My best Compliments to Mr Percy, who already owes me a Letter; yet would I give him credit for another, if I had *Leisure* at this time to write again—Mr Baskerville has sent me a Specimen of Horace, about twice as large as ye small Elzevirs;[1] He proposes to copy Elzevir, but ye *Punctuation* has been objected to—It seems Elzevir omits ye semi-colon universally, & is not accurate in ye application of ye 3 remaining stops—Quere, what is to be done; & whether he had not better substitute some other edition in regard to *text* as well as punctuation? As to ye Former, I was thinking of Francis— Pray tell me your Opinion—I did *not* send y^r Letter to Mr Hylton, for reasons I will give, when I have more Leisure to explain myself—I will however send the Biography, & mention y^r request, in a Day or two's time—I took ye Liberty of asking Mr Dodsley for your Chinese Novel, as I knew you were so good to intend me a copy.—

W.S.

To
　The Revd Mr Percy.

NOTE

¹Elzevir, celebrated family of printers of Amsterdam and Leyden, published their beautiful editions of the Greek and Roman classics 1594–1680.

CCLXXV

B.M. Add MSS. 28221.
Hecht, 57.

[*To* THOMAS PERCY.]

THE LEASOWES, *July ye 5th* 1761.

Dear Sir,
　I am truly glad to find that all things conspire so happily to favor your undertaking, & to further an event I have wished so long, as that of a good edition of old Ballads.—I know not how that Ballad of 'Rosamond' came to be totally omitted in my List: I found it distinguished in the Book wth a mark of second-rate approbation. *More* than this I cannot allow it; notwithstanding any merit I could discover, on a reperusal. It seems to me a melancholy Fact, smoothely & decently related, without any great indication of *poetical Spirit* in the Composer. Compare it with 'the Spanish Lady,' either in point of *Sentiment*, or poetical embellishment, &, I should imagine, you wou'd find a difference, much in Favour

of the Latter. I will only add that you should by all means *insert* it, as it will proper [sic] to have a Ballad on the Subject.

I have read 'the Hive' in 4 vols,[1] & 'the vocal miscellany in 2,[2] since I rec^d your last Letter; marking ye songs with a different number of crosses, according to ye different quantity or proportion of *poetical Spirit* I observed in them. You shall have a List, when I can find Leisure to transcribe one; or rather, I will find Leisure for that purpose, when you let me know that you require it. I must confess, the Task has been a little irksome to me; as the number of frothy & affected Pieces I found there written on ye subject of Love, has almost habituated me to read, without any sort of Attention. I rather chose, however, to admit many, for you to reject; y^n to reject one, for you to admit. I will depend upon seeing you & your collection (at least a *List* of your collection) before you send it to the Press. I told Dodsley in my last Letter y^t I was sure the work w^d be a noble one; if I might guess from y^r activity, y^r Learning, y^r Diligence, & your connexions. I wished it might be an elegant edition; & very greatly shall I be deceived, if there be not large numbers in the Kingdom y^t will be as much pleased with such a work, as *our* Friend Mr Johnson, Mr Garrick, or myself. I have a very good Friend in Scotland,[3] who has a taste for Vertû, & for Antiquity. He has made me a Present of many books from Scotland; and, I am sure, so soon as I can write to him, will gladly be of service to your undertaking.— I am glad you wrote, y^rself, to Mr Warton; for (tho' I *would* have done it in y^e *end*) yet, to my shame be it spoken, I never wrote to thank him for the Present he made me of his Critique upon Spenser.[4] The Preface to y^r Letter was very pertinent; & must engage him to serve you, to the utmost of his Power— I have only seen *extracts* from his Life of Bathurst.[5] I suppose he rather *means* it as a pious tribute to the memory of a benefactor, than a work which will much interest or entertain the Publick. I will assist you what I can in *Designs* for this Collection, but should chuse to enter on ye task, when you are here.

I have rec^d your Chinese-Novel, but have not yet had time to read it. Tis a neat edition, I see; & I wish you all success. Do you not suppose 'y^e *House* of Sussex,' a little too pompous in y^r Dedication;[6] or do you *mean* it *should* be pompous, in

Lieu of much *other* Panegyrick? The six last words in y^r Dedication had surely better been omitted—I have hitherto read no farther, & I shew a Confidence in y^r good-nature, by making thus free.—Mrs Lyttelton (ye Governor's very agreeable Lady)[7] presented me with Almoran & Hamet,[8] as a ballance for wch I gave her Dodsley's Fables, in Morocco. In truth, I cannot think Dr. H[awkesworth] by any means a first rate writer. His *taste* in writing seems defective. See his poor Task in regard to Fables in ye 18th adventurer vol. the First.[9] Mr Johnson's Rasselas deserves applause, on account of ye many *refined Sentiments* he has expressed with all possible *elegance* & *Perspicuity*——As to Almoran, I suscribe to y^r Sentiments; & have some others of my own, wch are by no means in its Favor—I cannot, however, esteem his Love-story a very pleasing one. The King's Notice may establish ye Author; but will hardly be able to establish the Book.—I think Baskerville should hardly *venture* to follow *Bentley* in his Edition of a small Horace;[10] but I am sure there are 4 or 5, at least he ought to follow, in preference to Elzevir—He is now in London.

I shall probably write to you again, in a Post or two; but do not suffer any expectation of this Sort to deprive me of a Letter, when you have Leisure to write one. I am very affectionately both

yours & Mrs Percy's
Will: Shenstone.

NOTES

[1]*The Hive, A Collection of the Most Celebrated Songs*, 4 vols. London, 1724, published anonymously, with a preface—*A Criticism on Song-Writing. By Mr. Philips; in a letter to a lady. The Hive* was popular and ran into a fourth edition in 1732.

[2]*The Vocal Miscellany*, London, 1734. These two publications belonged to a very large group of song miscellanies of the first half of the century.

[3]John MacGowan, Writer to the Signet. See Hull, II, 167–171, and *Times Literary Supplement*, July 4, 11, 18, 1929.

[4]*Observations on the Faerie Queene*, 1754.

[5]Thomas Warton published in 1761 *The Life and Literary Remains of Ralph Bathurst, President of Trinity College in Oxford*. Trinity College was Warton's own college.

[6]Percy addressed his novel to the Countess of Sussex, wife of his patron.

[7]Percy's note in MS: 'William Lyttelton, Governor of South Carolina, &c.' He married in June 1761, Mary Macartney, of Longford.

[8]*Almoran and Hamet—An Oriental Tale*, by John Hawkesworth.

[9]*The Adventurer*, Saturday, January 6, 1753, contained an essay entitled, 'Critical remarks upon fables. Fable of the dog and shadow upon a new plan.' This magazine was under the joint direction of Hawkesworth and Goldsmith.

[10]Richard Bentley (1662–1742), published his *Horace* at the end of 1711.

CCLXXVI

Historical Society of Pennsylvania.
and Hull, II, 115.

[*To* THOMAS HULL.]

I desire my Compliments to Mr. Hull & Miss Moreson,[1] with many Thanks for the Pleasure I received from last Night's Play.[2] It was indeed acted with great spirit, and as far as I could judge, afforded the Audience no small satisfaction— Not perhaps equal to what they derived from the Appearance of the *dun Cow &c.*[3] For *that* is hardly to be expected.

I think the Play has now so much *good* in it, y^t it may be worth Mr. Hull's while to give it a few more finishing Touches —Suppose a Confessor or Friar, either out of hatred to the Queen, view to his own advancement, or any *selfish* motive (which he might explain in a short soliloquy) *persuaded* Rosamond to aspire to the Throne, & to urge the King to a Divorce: that Rosamond should avow her abhorrence of such injustice to the Queen, intimating that her love had no other object than the King's person & heroick virtues: that this refusal should affront the Friar, who, in revenge, should inform the Queen that Rosemond actually *had* those very intentions with which he had been endeavouring to inspire her &c: This w^d throw more Plot into the Play, (wch it wants;) and would more sufficiently account for the Queen's sudden Change from a mild Character to a revengefull one and, as Mr. Hull thinks ye Play too short, w^d add two new scenes.—Some further Improvements I would recommend in the Close, & a few more places; but Mr. Hull's further *attention* to the play, will render it needless to point these out to Him.

down

I should esteem it as a Favor if Mr. Hull would send me a Copy of the Prologue & Epilogue as they were spoken; which I will not communicate with^t his permission. Either *His* or Miss *Morison's* Muse seem to favour them at a Minute's warning.

and thanks

Mr. Hull will please to present my Comp^ts to Miss

Ibbot's and Mrs. Younger—If their Leisure permits, I should be very glad to drink a Dish of tea wth them at the Leasowes, before they leave the town.[4]

Mr. Hodgett's, with whom I am at present, would be glad that Mr. Hull would dine here, about two, and so should I, if it be no way inconvenient to Him.

WILL: SHENSTONE.

Snow-hill Birm^m.
    Aug: 29, 1761.

I had almost forgot to thank you for the Stanza's you left at the Leasows last week when I was on a Visit to Hagley. They are well constructed for the Occasion & the Idea seems to arise from humane Sensibility warmed with honest Indignation.

William Shenstone Esqre
    To
  Mr. Hull,
    in New-street,
  Birmingham.

NOTES

[1] Thomas Hull married Miss Morrison, one of his principal actresses, in 1760.

[2] Hull's note, II, 115, 'A hasty and imperfect Compilation of some Scenes, on the subject of Rosamond, which, however, laid the Ground-Work of the present Tragedy, acted at Covent-Garden Theatre. The Public may easily discern how fully the Author has availd himself of the kind and judicious Hints contained in the Letter before us.'

[3] Hull's note, ibid., 'Introduced in a Pantomime performed the same Evening.'

[4] The passage 'Either . . . the town' is crossed out in the M.S.

CCLXXVII

Works III, 368.

To the [REV. R. GRAVES], *on the intended Publication of his* [*i.e. Shenstone's*] *Works.*

THE LEASOWES,
Sept. 14, 1761.

Dear Mr. Graves,

I ought to have thanked you many weeks ago, for a very *long* and *entertaining* letter; the *length* of which, as well as the

entertainment, was increased by a Postscript a few days after.—
But as the Winter is with me a dull and uniform season, so
the Summer is a time of universal dissipation; and very happy
do I think myself, when, after a continual succession of company, visits paid, and excursions taken, I can sit down in peace
and quietness, to attend to the business of correspondence and
friendship. Either reason, habit, or complexion tells me, that
I am never *otherwise* so properly employed.

The last digression I made was to the concert at Worcester,
to hear The Messiah well performed; to meet a number of
faces one knows; but first, and principally, to visit your brother,
without which motive I had not gone. In the two *former* respects, the journey answered my expectation:—but, alas! your
brother was gone into Herefordshire. I, however, alighted out
of the chaise; and the house-keeper very civilly shewed me his
delightful parlour, that looks into the meadows, the Prebends'
gardens, and down the Severn to Malvern-hills. A more agreeable town-house cannot possibly be found any where. But I
regretted, when I reached the inn, that I had not asked to see
his children; for I either heard them upstairs, had a glimpse of
them at the window, or fancied, to a degree of conviction, that
they were most of them within the house. I now return to
remark upon some particulars in your letter—I believe it is
that indifference you complain of, which is the *grand* detri-
ment to genius in an advanced part of life. In all *poetical*
affairs, we are too apt to cry out with Pallas, 'Non est mihi
tibia tanti.' And this renders all our efforts tame, prosaic, and
judicious. But this propensity, as well as many others, we
should guard against, upon the approach of age: change the
object of our amusements; cherish hopes, well or ill-grounded,
of finding that pleasure in the novelty of objects, which we
have not found in any individual. These are the means of
preserving our vivacity a somewhat longer time than it naturally
lasts; but how far it is *prudent* to attach ourselves to the world
that we must leave, is a point which *you* better can determine.
Refined taste, as it implies a *love* of physical beauty, has this
tendency.

There is nothing can be more rational than what you say
about the expediency of *losing no time*, if I mean to collect and

publish what I have written. You are indeed very partial to my abilities; but, allowing for *that*, what you mention *coincides* with what I have thought myself, and this for some years past. A more agreeable kind of *distraction* in summer, and an indifferent state of health and spirits in winter, have hitherto prevented any progress in the correction of my pieces. To these I might add a *suspence* about the compositions, and the manner, proper for publication. I am now most inclined to make a collection of the whole; I mean, the best of what are already printed or in Ms.; to publish them by subscription in a large *quarto* size for the sake of profit; and to apologize for this method, by mentioning the expence of top and tail-pieces, with which I mean they shall be embellished. Some of *these* (by the bye) may be taken from my farm, the rest emblematical, in an easy and careless, but, at the same time, elegant manner. I should think the instance of Mr. Pope might render this method not disreputable; and it might be advertised (as was done by Mr. Spence), that, unless a certain number were subscribed for, the whole affair should be no farther prosecuted. This would put it in the way of many friends to serve me, who (I flatter myself), *with inclination*, esteem themselves void of *opportunity*. Let me beg you to think seriously of this, as well as of a general title-page, before you write again.

Thank you kindly for all the little diverting anecdotes that are contained in your letter. I am glad to hear your *place* brings you company; partly, as it tends to amuse you; and yet more, as it tends to make your merit more conspicuous. You and I have led a life of total disinteressment. Let me advise you to seek some *advantage* from your commerce with *great men*.— The boy, who was here with you and Mrs. Graves, was here last Friday evening with a Mr. Jolliffe and his son; the latter of whom observed your name upon the bench, and seemed proud to declare that he was once your school-fellow. Mr. Stratford (to whom I had written about some gold-fishes) says in his answer, 'I had the pleasure from Bath of waiting upon Mr. G[raves], and was as much satisfied with the miniature beauties of his place, as with the polite reception I met with from the owner.' If you have an opportunity, you will oblige me by presenting my compliments to that gentlemen.—I met Dr.

Charlton at Worcester, who stands high in my esteem.—The account of Gothic architecture, &c. is curious; but I have found it in Dr. Warburton's edition of Pope—I inclose the verses on the Venus de Medicis—I told you before my intentions, &c. concerning them; and since, I hear that they have appeared in some one of the Magazines—through Dodsley's or Percy's means, for I surely gave a copy to nobody besides—and those copies must be much imperfect.—My picture shall be sent you as soon as I can possibly get Alcock over, who had promised to come every week for these three months past. I believe he *will* come soon.—I did not know of Mr. Warton's compliment; but he is very obliging to me on all ocasions, and sends me all that he publishes.—I have not yet read Dr. Robinson's History, to my shame be it spoken, though I have the honour to know the author.—I hope the King *will* oblige the Irish Peers with a place in the procession, as that people seems greatly out of temper; and, I fear, not without some reason.

I see my friend Dodsley has *let off* his little *squib* upon the marriage, in the Chronicle. '*The King sought a partner*,'[1] &c. And last night was brought me, from Baskerville's press, on the same occasion, very *pompously* printed, the most despicable Grub-street I ever saw.[2]

I have made some little improvements about my place; have taken away the wall in front, and made a handsome ring; have extended my path, in one piece of ground, greatly for the better —but the grand water in the valley will make no figure till next spring.

I have also assisted my friend Hull the comedian in altering the Tragedy of Rosamond; had it brought upon the stage to a full house at Birmingham, where it was very well received; put Hull into a way of making an indirect compliment to the present King in the ten last lines of his Epilogue, which was followed by 'God save great George,' &c. in a full chorus of the audience and actors drawn out abreast upon the stage.

Since this, there has been deposited in my hands a large collection of Poetry, by a Miss Wheatly of Walsall;[3] many of the pieces written in an excellent and truly classical style; simple, sentimental, harmonious, and more correct than I almost ever saw written by a lady. They will be published, I believe, by subscription, under the patronage of Lord Dartmouth.

But nothing in the poetical way has pleased me better than a compliment which I received about nine days ago by the post, under the feigned name *Cotswouldia*.[4]—She must be some Gloucestershire lady that has seen the place; as she raises up a Fairy in my grove, into whose mouth she puts the compliment. It seems written by somebody of fashion by the style.—Can you form any conjecture?

There was a Mr. Freeman of Betstow (or some such name) with two or three ladies in a coach and six that were here not long before; a very genteel and polite young man.

I really know not how to stop, when I begin a letter to *you*; and it is one reason why I look upon the task as too considerable to be undertaken at all times. Pray write soon, and believe me wholly yours and Mrs. Graves's.

W. SHENSTONE.

NOTES

[1]*The London Chronicle*, September 8–10, 1761, p. 248. *On The King's Marriage*.
'The King sought a Partner to soften his care,
A Partner to share in his bed and his throne;
He found one in Charlotte, the good and the fair,
To double his *pleasures* as he does our own.
Behold of high Virtues the signal reward!
What greater could Fortune for either have done?
He gains the first prize (Ladies, don't think it hard.)
And She the first Potentate under the sun.'

[2]In September 1761, came from Baskerville's press: *An Ode upon the Fleet, and the Royal Yatch (sic) going to conduct the Princess of Mecklenburg to be Queen of Great Britain*. See Straus and Dent, *John Baskerville*, 73 and 43, note. The expression used here reminds one of Johnson's definition in the Dictionary: 'Grub-street, the name of a street in London, much inhabited by writers of small histories, dictionaries, and temporary poems; whence any mean production is called Grub-street.'

[3]Mary Wheatley's *Original Poems on Several Occasions* were published by Dodsley in 1764. Miss Wheatley, who afterwards became Mrs. Darwell, belonged to a well-known Birmingham family. She published in 1794, a second collection of poems entitled *Walsall*.

[4]Shenstone, *Works* II, 376–78. *Verses received by the post, from a Lady Unknown*, 1761. The 'Lady' was Elizabeth, sister of Lord Amherst, wife of Rev. John Thomas, rector of Notgrove in Gloucestershire.

CCLXXVIII

B.M. Add. MSS. 28221.
Hecht, 62.

[*To* THOMAS PERCY.]

THE LEASOWES, *Sept^r* 1761.
Saturday.

Dear Mr Percy,

Accept a few hasty Lines, after a long series of dissipation, which must account for my late silence & my present Incoherency. The Mind takes some time to settle, after having been distracted by Concerts & Horse-races; and were I to see the Coronation,[1] which I do not mean to do, it would be stuffed with nothing but Lace, ermin, Feathers, Coronets & velvet, for this half-year.

I hardly know how to re-unite the thread of our Correspondence; But this I know, that having read Hau Kiou Choaan,[2] I ought to have returned you earlier thanks for the Pleasure it afforded me. Let me tell *you* my *truest* sentiments, at the time I tell others my most *favorable* ones; for this I think is the business of Friendship in all circumstances of this kind. The Novel, tho' in some parts not void of Merit, must certainly draw its chief support from its value as a *Curiosity;* or perhaps as an agreeable means of conveying to the generality all they *wish* or *want* to know, of the Chinese manners and constitution. I think the Publick must esteem itself as much obliged to the *Editor*, as the editor has grounds to be offended at the *Printer*. Very numerous indeed are the errors that remain, over & above what appear in the tables of errata: & very sollicitous *indeed* does ye Editor appear, least, by ye omission of any *possible* Improvement, he should disoblige the Publick. This, perhaps, to an excess of y^e *better kind*. Your Annotations have great merit; yet, on ye whole, I can form no Conjecture, what vogue it will obtain. I can only say I wish it all that you do, or even Mr J. Dodsley.

I long much to hear how you proceed in regard to your Ballads. Tis undoubtedly a popular scheme; and, with all deference to my Friend Mr Dodsley, deserves to be rendered to the Editor more advantageous yⁿ he has yet made it. You must not intimate yᵗ I *say* this; but I certainly *think* it. The names of the Ballads I selected, shall be sent you whenever you want them; & when this is, you must let me know. There was a Little good-natured, welch-man called upon me t'other Day; I think he said his Name was 'Rice,[3] &, as far as I could make out, he is Chaplain to the Earl of Bradford. He told me, yᵗ, by his means you had settled a Correspondence in Wales, & left with me a Little Welch Ode, wᵗʰ a literal translation of it in Latin.—You must send me a word how far you've gone, and whether there be any Hopes that we may see the Collection next winter.

There is a Miss Wheatly, about six Miles from hence, who has written a pretty Large Collection of Poetry—I have been attending to it for this week; & really think yᵗ many Pieces are written with a truly classic elegance. If she can obtain my Lord or Lady Dartmouth's Leave they may possibly appear this next winter, under one or other of their Names.

Company intervenes, & I must take my Leave; having many things to *say*, but Little or nothing to *write*. Is not yᵉ natural *Inference*, that you must call upon me as soon as may be?

You will find Dodsley's verses on the Leasowes, in the Gent's Magazine for *last* month,[4] ill-printed; & probably, printed better, in yᵉ London Magazine, for *This*.[5] But I have last week received a Copy of verses from some fair Lady of Glostershire, which I like much better. They are sign'd Cotswouldia & came by the Post. You shall see them soon, one way or other. My best respects to Mʳˢ Percy & my best affections wait on you.

W. Shenstone.

P.S.
Dodsley's Verses were sent both to the London-Magazine, & the Gentleman's, that I might preserve my Impartiality betwixt those two original Magazines. The Proprietors of yᵉ *Latter* printed them very incorrectly; and of the *Former* not at All. Dodsley himself, being now in Town, means to reprint them in one or other of yᵉ periodical papers: probably in the L. Chronicle,[6] or London Magazine; in each of which he has some Property.

Pray was it You or He, that caused a Copy of my Verses

on the Venus de Medicis, to be printed in some one of the Papers? For so, Mr Jago tells me, he saw them. I rather impute it to Mr Dodsley, who served me so, once or twice before. They are called, it seems, 'Directions for Taste, taken from &c.' This is quite contrary to my Maxim of never saying any thing at ye Head of an Ode which may give Intimation what you are to expect. I am vexed at Baskerville for acting otherwise, in ye Little Pocket Horace y^t he has almost printed. Any *short* argument must be imperfect & any *Long* one, utterly absurd. The scotch editor judged better, & his Edition *looks* ye better for this Omission; tho I know B. lays no small stress upon ye beauty of his *Italick* Type. But to return from this digression—These said Verses of mine are printed without a Name, or any other Circumstance relating to 'em; by which means they answer no other purpose y^n that of expletives to a Magazine. Besides this, they were printed prematurely, & are since improved by an additional stanza. Clear yourself of this affair[7]

Let ye Liberties taken by the Translator of the Erse-Fragments be a Precedent for You. Many old Pieces, *without* some alteration, will do nothing; & with your amendments, will be striking.   W.S.

   17 *Sept^r* 1761.

Pray what do you hear of the Queen?

Do not fail to write soon—I have had here a Little Mr Derrick who publish'd a translation of a Satyr in Juvenal.[8]
   To
         The Rev^rd Mr Percy.

NOTES

[1] The Coronation of George III took place on September 22, 1761.

[2] W.S.'s note in MS.: 'Lady Gough borrowed it, kept it a Fortnight, and read nothing but ye dedication.'

[3] Percy's note in MS: 'Rice Williams, Rector of Weston near Shiftnal and Newport, Shropshire.'

[4] *The Gentleman's Magazine*, August 1761, 374. *Verses occasioned by an Incident at the Seat of Wm. Shenstone, Esq. By Mr. Dodsley.* 'How shall I fix my wand'ring eye.'

[5] The verses did not appear in *The London Magazine*.

[6] *The London Chronicle*, September 22, 1761.

[7] Percy's note in MS: 'They were printed by Dodsley.'

[8] Samuel Derrick (1724–1769), author of *The Third Satire of Juvenal, translated into English Verse*, 1755. Boswell records that Dr. Johnson liked Derrick but on being asked

whether he or Smart was the better poet, he said there was 'no settling the point of precedency between a louse and a flea.' Soon after the death of Beau Nash, Derrick became Master of Ceremonies at Bath.

CCLXXIX

MS. Prof. Tinker, of Harvard.

To Mr. J. C.[1]
To be left with Mr. Dilly,[2]
Bookseller in the Poultry,
London.

THE LEASOWES, *Septr.* 17, 1761.

I should be glad enough to be better acquainted with the Gentleman who asked my Opinion of three small Copies of Verses, in June last, under the Name J: C: The Message not being answered at *First*, was laid by, & forgot; tho' I read the Lines with Pleasure, & thought them written in *good Taste*.

He will permit me to propose some Queries; which, whether rational or not, are at least well intended.

In the Paraphrase on Habakkuck, Line ye I. & 2d *Fades* & *Heads* are rhimes not quite so accurate, as one wishes in these *small* Compositions; where, as in gems, one expects the highest degree of Polishing—suppose

> Tho' the green blade desert the —— —— mead
> And withering blossoms hang the languid head.   q.

more particularly as the 'Fields yielding no meat' is intended by the Prophet for the *immediate* cause of the Cattle's death.

Some *tense* also should be pitched upon, & preserved; & I am afraid the *Future* would be most consonant to the Prophet's Design; which would require an alteration of some difficulty, in some of the rhimes.

Line ye. 12th 'I lisp the feeble strain &c' tho' beautifull in itself, yet differs from the Prophets Idea of *joying* & *rejoicing*.

Line ye 13. '*Rapture* here does not well suit with '*Rest*' in ye next Line, as it makes a sort of Anti-climax. It should be some word that expresses Constancy, Firmness &c.

2Q

Line the Last, thro *Life's sad* &c. I could wish the s s did not clash here.

Inscription for an Hermitage.

Line the 5th To find within this lone recess.   q.
Line the 12 Yon rill, in silence, seeks the main   q.
Line 17 & 18. Here, hail at Eve that power divine,
              Who made these tranquil moments, Thine.
Perhaps *tranquil* in ye 4th Line, or this, had better be changed for peacefull or &c.

Ode to Health.

Line 2d And the Satrap's &c   q.
Line 16 Sighs for Health, *or* Liberty. The Line *otherwise* gives *Liberty* too large a share, in what is called an Ode to Health.
Line 21 Bermuda's radiant Isle &c q: (*pleasing* is used before.)

Ode to Content.

Line ye 4th Near sheltering wood or shaded rill &c   q.
Line 5 & 9—Why not write ye name of the river & village at length?
Line 10th Thy *Presence* chear'd q.
Line 20th Yet Thou, Content, be still &c   q.
N.B. some of these alterations are proposed merely for ye sake of Euphony.

WILL: SHENSTONE.

NOTES

[1] I have been unable to trace anyone with initials J.C. writing a paraphrase of Habakkuk at this time, though the subject appears to have been most popular.
[2] Charles Dilly (1739–1807), with his brother Edward were well known for their hospitality. Dr. Johnson was frequently a guest at their table, and there the famous meeting with John Wilkes took place.

CCLXXX

Edinburgh Annual Register, 1809, 549.

To Mr. MacGOWAN, *late of Edinburgh.*

THE LEASOWES,
Sept. 24, 1761.

Dear Sir,

I have indeed been guilty of the most absurd hypocrisy that ever was, having suffered an appearance of neglect to rob me of the pleasure of your correspondence, when no one living could have been more sensible of the obligation it laid me under. Sure I am that I must be greatly indebted to Mr. Roebuck's[1] representation for the place I still retain in your esteem, and which I should utterly have given up for lost, had not your goodness, by many ouvert acts, lately convinced me of the contrary.

'Twas indeed the view of accompanying my letter with something worthy of your acceptance, that has kept me silent so long, in spite of all your friendly provocations. I wanted to transcribe one or two pieces of greater length than the trifles I inclose. Alas, that I have not, even now an opportunity of so doing! Dr. Roebuck goes tomorrow, and you must accept of an irregular, disjointed letter, in which I find it my duty to acknowledge so many different favours.

The Scotch press, of which you sent me so many agreeable specimens, has, I think, not a rival in the world, unless it be that of my neighbour Baskerville. Here I find myself unable or unwilling to decide the preference. Amongst friends, however, I would whisper, that Baskerville's impressions are more striking to the eye, either on account of his ink, his paper, or his type; yet, at the same time, it may be much doubted whether the Scotch editions will not be deemed the best for use. Martial has expressed what *may* prove the case at the close of one of his epigrams:

'Laudant illa, sed ista legunt.'[2]

As to corrections, the Scotch seems to have hitherto the advantage;[3] but if Baskerville find encouragement to print many Latin books, he purposes, I believe, to employ a Latin editor. There will shortly appear an Elzevir Horace from the press, revised by Mr. Levy, which you will probably like to see.

As to the Erse fragments, you judged very rightly, that, amidst the applause they were sure of receiving from the world, they would not fail to afford me a very peculiar satisfaction. I am unfeignedly thankful for the early copy you sent me, and for the ingenious letter which accompanied them. It seems, indeed, from a former version by the same translator, (which Mr. Gray, the poet, received from him, and shewed my friend Percy,) that he has taken pretty considerable freedoms in adapting them to the present reader. I do not in the least disapprove of this; knowing by experience, that trivial amendments in these old compositions often render them highly striking, which would be otherwise quite neglected. And surely, under all the infirmities of age, they may be said to have an absolute claim to some indulgencies of this kind. I presume the editor follows the same model of translation in what he is now going to publish. I would wish him particularly attentive to the melody of his cadences, when it may be done without impeachment of his fidelity. The melody of our verse has been perhaps carried to its utmost perfection; that of prose seems to have been more neglected, and to be capable of greater than it has yet attained. It seems to be a very favourable era for the appearance of such irregular poetry. The taste of the age, so far as it regards plan and style, seems to have been carried to its utmost height, as may appear in the works of Akenside, Gray's Odes and Church-yard Verses, and Mason's Monody and Elfrida.[4] The public has seen all that art can do, and they want the more striking efforts of wild, original, enthusiastic genius. It seems to exclaim aloud with the chorus in Julius Caesar,

> 'Oh rather than be slaves to these deep learned men,
> Give us our wildness and our woods, our huts and caves
> again!'

I know not how far you will allow the distinction or the principle on which I build my remark, namely, that the taste of the present age is somewhat higher than its genius. This turn, you see, favours the work the translator has to publish, or has published already. Here is indeed pure original genius! The very quintessence of poetry; a few drops of which, properly managed, are enough to give a flavour to quart-bottles. And yet one or two of these pieces (the first, for instance, together with the second) are undoubtedly as well planned as any ode we find in Horace.

I have perused the Gentle Shepherd with all imaginable pleasure; and here again am indebted to you, sir, for the assistance of your glossary. 'Tis rare to find a poem of this length, where simplicity of sentiment and of language are so very well sustained. The metre is generally musical; and the old Scottish words form an admirable kind of Doric. Good sense, expressed naturally, in a phrase easy, perspicuous, and not wholly void of ornament, seems the talent of Ramsay, whose taste in composition was perhaps more remarkable than his genius; and in whom greater fire and invention would certainly have deprived his readers of the Gentle Shepherd.

And now having thanked you for the Scotch snuff, (better than any I ever tasted before,) I come to ask, whether you have any old Scotch ballads, which you would wish preserved in a neat edition. I have occasioned a friend of mine to publish a fair collection of the best old English and Scotch ballads; a work I have long had much at heart. Mr. Percy, the collector and publisher, is a man of learning, taste, and indefatigable industry; is chaplain to the Earl of Sussex. It so happens, that he has himself a folio collection of this kind of MSS; which has many things truly curious, and from which he selects the best. I am only afraid that his fondness for antiquity should tempt him to admit pieces that have no other sort of merit. However, he has offered me a rejecting power, of which I mean to make considerable use. He is encouraged in his undertaking by Sam. Johnson, Garrick and many persons of note, who lend him such assistance as is within their power. He has brought Mr. Jo. Warton (the poetry professor) to ransack the Oxford libraries;[5] and has resided and employed six amanuenses to transcribe from Pepys's Collection at Cambridge,[6] consisting of five volumes of old ballads in folio. He says justly that it is in the remote parts of the kingdom that he has most reason to expect the curiosities he wants—that in the southern parts fashion and novelty cause such things to be neglected. Accordingly he has settled a correspondence in Wales, in the wilds of Staffordshire and Derbyshire, in the West Indies, in Ireland, and, if he can obtain your assistance, in Scotland, hopes to draw materials from the whole British empire. He tells me there is, in the collection of Mag. Coll. Libr. a very curious collection of antient Scottish songs and poems, he thinks not published or known: many of Dumbar,[7] [sic] Maitland of Lethington, and one allegorical poem of Gawain Douglas,[8] too obsolete for his collection; and one yet more obsolete, called 'Peebles in the Play,' mentioned in Christ's Kirk on the Green.[9] He met Mr. Gray in the university library, who is going to write the Hist. of English Poetry.[10] But, to put an end to this long article! his collection will be printed in two or three small octavos, with suitable decorations; and if you find an opportunity of sending aught that may be proper for his insertion, I think I can safely answer for his thankfulness as well as my own.

He shewed me an old ballad in his folio MS., under the name of Adam Carr: three parts in four coincide so much with your Edom of Gordon, that the former name seems to me an odd corruption of the latter. His MS. will, however, tend to enrich Edom of Gordon with two of the prettiest stanzas I ever saw, beside many other improvements. He has also a MS. of Gill Morrice, called in his copy Childe Morice. Of this more another time. I must at present take my leave. Should you see Mr. (Douglas) Hume, Mr. Alexander,[11] or Dr. Robertson, I desire my best respects to them. And should you see my good Lord Alemoor and Mr. Professor Smith, I beg you would please to assert how unfeignedly I am their servant. I hope to muster up sufficient assurance, even now, to acknowledge by letter their acceptable presents of books; however the fire of gratitude was not less intense for having lain concealed and produced no blaze. I have many more Scotch friends whom I wish to particularize; but these, if I am not mistaken, live in the neighbourhood of Edinburgh. I am, dear sir, your most obliged humble servant,

WILL SHENSTONE.

I will endeavour to procure and send you a copy of Percy's translation of a genuine Chinese novel, in four small vols., printed months ago, but not to be published before winter.
To. Mr. MacGowan.

NOTES

[1]John Roebuck, M.D. (1718–1794), when resident in Birmingham was connected with John Baskerville and other Birmingham worthies, and spent his time in applying chemistry to the many industries of Birmingham.

[2]Martial, *Epigrams* IV, XLIXI.

[3]When Robert Foulis was appointed printer to the University of Glasgow, the 'immaculate' Horace was printed 1744. The story goes that the proof sheets were hung up in college and a reward offered for every inaccuracy discovered.

[4]In 1744 Mason wrote*Musæus*, a monody on Pope's death, in imitation of *Lycidas*. *Elfrida*, a dramatic poem on the model of the classics, appeared in 1752.

[5]Joseph Warton was headmaster of Winchester School. It was Thomas, Professor of Poetry at Oxford, who assisted Percy in collecting ballads.

[6]Sir Richard Maitland, Lord Lethington (1496–1586), made a famous collection of early Scottish poems, which were given to Samuel Pepys by the Duke of Lauderdale, and these are preserved in the Pepysian Library at Magdalene College, Cambridge.

[7]William Dunbar (1465?–1530?), Scottish poet. His work was forgotten for about two hundred years, until Ramsay introduced specimens of it into *The Evergeen*, 1724. Poems of his were preserved in the Magdalene College collection.

[8]Gawin Douglas (1474?–1522), Scottish poet and bishop. *King Hart* and *Conscience* were included in Maitland's collection.

[9]*Christ's Kirk on the Green—a merrie Ballad,* ascribed to King James V of Scotland.

[10]About 1761 Gray sketched out a plan for a History of English Poetry, but he never got beyond the preliminary sketch. Some months after, Thomas Warton published the first volume of his history, Gray sent his skeleton plan to Warton. The latter's history, however, owes nothing to Gray.

[11]John Alexander (1736–1765), Presbyterian minister at Longdon, twelve miles from Birmingham, was a well-known Greek scholar of the time. Does W.S. refer to him?

CCLXXXI

B.M. Add. MSS. 28221.
Hecht, 65.

[*To* THOMAS PERCY.]

Oct.: 1761.

Dear Sir,

To *reward*, or rather, to *distinguish*, your Fidelity, I enclose what I think a better Copy of those verses upon the Venus, than any that has *yet* appeared. Some Places remain yet; y^t require correction, or would admit of Improvement: and it convinces me, what *Pains* are requisite to give a degree of accuracy to the merest Trifle. Well enough may one conceive how Horace bestowed years upon the correction of an Ode, that was to endure the test of Ages. Nothing, I believe, can have duration *without* this; and, *with* it, Nothing that is not written in a dead Language.

I will teize you no more with my Hints about the Necessity of an *exclusion*-bill. It is very true, y^t, in a larger Collection, you may have a greater chance to find pieces of Merit; but it is also true, that, from a Larger Heap, one is apt to help one's self more liberally, than from a small one: and my only Fear has been, that mere Antiquity should sometimes impose upon you, in the Garb of merit. But I have *said enough* on this Head, & I believe you are upon *your guard*. As to your First Quere, it would have a very odd appearance, were you to leave such *large* Intervals, as you necessarily must *sometimes*, were you to assign a fresh Page to the beginning of every Ballad. The Notes, (which, I think, you place at the Close of each), would *sometimes happen* to fill this vacancy; but, at *others*, to make a fresh one. Well-judged & elegant wooden tail-pieces (an ornam much wanting to every Press in Europe) would leave you at Liberty to pursue this Scheme; but unless *your* Press affords you some that are *tolerable*, I would have you think no more about it. II. I should greatly approve your method of beginning with the *oldest* (and this, for the reasons you yourself lay down), *but* on account of the Danger you would incurr of throwing too many ballads *together*, that were irregular in point of Metre, or subobscure in point of Language; And this, at the *beginning of your work*, might perhaps be liable to give disgust. If you can surmount this Objection, Suppose you were to class them according to aeras of 20, 40, or 50 years. III. your third quere puzzles me. However, I should think it *safer* to defer the publication of such old Pieces as have rather more merit in the Light of *Curiosity* than *Poetry* (such as the tragick one of 'the Fight at Otterburne' and the comick one of 'John the Reeve') 'till you have experienced the Publick's reception of the two First Vols: which reception will be rule sufficient in regard to all that are to follow.

The *Lists* I will send you so soon as you can inform me

what you have received already; for I declare I have forgott.

It were impossible for *my* Arrangement of *those ballads here* to be of Service to you; because I take it for granted y^t many of them will require to be intermix'd with your other Pieces. However, were *you here*, much of this work might be done in a day or two.

I am truly glad to hear what you tell me of the King and Queen. I hope she will rather *promote* than *discourage* any Favor he may shew to the Arts and Sciences. The prettiest verses I have seen yet on occasion of their Nuptials are an Ode of one Pullein's in the London Magazine.[1]

I believe I have marked most of the typographical errata in Hau Kiou Choaan; but would by no means advise you to affix any thing *more* of *this nature* to the volume. I have some thoughts of sending a Sett in boards to John MGouan Esq., writer to the Signet in Edingburgh. This you must know is the Gentleman wth whom I mean to bring you acquainted. I wrote him a long acc^t of your present scheme, about a Fortnight ago; but Dr. Roebuck who was to convey the Letter, postponed his Journey till this week. I will send you the first Letter I receive from him; which will be in No long time. He is a generous spirited Man; a person of Taste, & a Scholar, with a considerable tincture of the antiquarian.

Perhaps I can make you smile by giving you a specimen of the comical Humours of Lady G[ough]. She was here wth L^{dy} Sanderson,[2] &, *before* I could come to receive them in the Parlour, L^{dy} G[ough] had peep'd into a Letter of Dodsley's, that lay upon ye marble Slabb. This passed—but upon her return, she desired Pixell would counsell me to break off all correspondence wth that *Dodwell*;[3] for that she had heard he was an Infidel—You will easily unriddle the mystery: Peeping into a folded Letter (wch by the way she *ought not* to have done) as the De'il would have it, she mistook the name of our Friend *Dodsley* for *Dodwell* — She has since accused our Friend Dodsley of no Less than Blasphemy; by reason y^t he in his verses makes so free wth *silvan Gods* & *rural deities*, & even compliments me with being such a genius, as to have no occasion for their Assistance. Would you have thought she could have been so ignorant? but she is also subject to *Envy*, and her chaplain P. (under the Rose) now & then diverts himself in finding it employment.

The printed Copy of Dodsley's verses, in wch I caused ye Birm^m Press to make some alterations, I have sent; but beg you to return it with the other M.S. Copy, of Lady Cotswouldia's Encomiasticon. Who she is, the Lord knows; but there is something ingenious in her Design, & Execution.

Ld Lyttelton was here last Thursday, wth Lord & L^{dy} For'scue, & his Children;[4] but I happened to be at Birmingham.

Baskerville's Horace will be *printed* about ye End of this month, but not *published* before X^{tmas}. It is really a beauty— —and upon ye whole as good a *Text* as any we have *yet*—but excuse my vanity; who think I could have rendered it *better*, if they had suffered me to have the *final* determination of *it*. You know B. imagines y^t his *Letter* is *every thing*, on wch ye merit of a book depends; he was nevertheless *induc'd* to employ a Mr Levy, residing as a private Tutor at Dr. Roebucks, no bad Grammarian or Classick, and, *now & then*, they have suffered me to have a Finger in the Pye. Samby's is but an indifferent Text, it seems,[5] the Scotch Edit^n but so so; A little Edition of mine printed at Hamburgh,[6] much superior to either, that I did not cause them to print it *precisely* according to Bentley.—Pray my Comp^{ts} to Mrs Percy—Write soon, & believe me yours most affectionately

W. SHENSTONE.

Is there any small edition of Bentley?

2nd Postscript.[7]

I hope that you yourself allow some consideration for the space of *time taken up by the Post;* which you recommend so much to mine. Pray how prospers Hau Kiou Choaan?

How happens it, I beseech you, that you have suppressed the *Runick Fragments* &c., 'till M^r M'Pherson has published *His* Poem? Why will you suffer the Publick to be quite *cloyed* with this kind of writing, ere you avail y^{r}self of their *Appetite*? I cannot say whether you should *now* defer the publication, or publish directly.

I asked Dr Roebuck to subscribe my Name, for Fingal,[8]

in Scotland; if I did not commission him too late: at the same time, I abominate *Quartos;* and think most writers in a Conspiracy to plague me. What reason is there that a Quarto-shape shou'd please more in a *Book* yⁿ in an *human Figure?*— I found indeed M'Pherson's account of the Fragments, & some extracts from his Poem, in yᵉ Chronicle of yesterday.⁹ I think a translator of a finer *Ear*, might cause these things to strike infinitely *more*, & yet be faithfull to the Sense.

I fancy Dodsley thinks of causing Baskerville very soon to print a new Edition of his Fables; & to have the Designs I shewed you, engraved for it. 'Twould be attended with Labour expence, & Hazard—*otherwise*, it would, in my Opinion, make his Scheme more perfect, to assign one entire volume to old Fables; & another to *modern* & *new-invented* ones. There are many *Old*, & many *modern* Fables, of singular merit, left out of his Collection. After all, if he means it principally for yᵉ use of Schools, perhaps it *ought*, or *need*, not to be more voluminous; and yet Rousseau, with a sly sarcasm, intimates yᵗ Children are not his proper Readers.

The Little Echantillon¹⁰ I have enclosed will make you wonder—However send me yʳ Opinion, if you please, without saying a tittle of yᵉ affair to any one, 'till you hear from me yᵗ I am *quite determined.* I have just mentioned it in a Letter to Mʳ Graves & to Mʳ Dodsley, *only*—I should like to collect my trifles in some such manner, yᵗ a Friend may buy them together, at a Bookseller's. To print them *elegantly, without assistance*, implies a risque I do not chuse to run; nor would it be consistent with *Prudence* for me so to do. On the other Hand: if yᵉ Publication in this manner could be made *advantageous* without being *disreputable*, I see no reason why I should decline it—Let me see what can be said *for* it, in my particular Case—and with such regulations &c. as I would lay it under—First, I will not suppose yᵉ book so *very* worthless as to make *no kind* of recompence for yᵉ subscriber's money— Next, I fancy the Degree of Acquaintance wᶜʰ my Ferme ornee has occasioned me wᵗʰ numbers of Gentry, will preclude any Necessity for *overurgent* applications—At least I do not mean to use them—Come wᵗʰ a good will, or come not at all' as the Children say at Play; &, further, to avoid yᵉ air of a mendicant, I can plead the expence of Printing & offer, in failure of a decent number, to return yᵉ money yᵗ shall be received. Next, Does not the Subscription-method save One from the *gross* mortification of seeing one's books remain unsold? Lastly, Is there not something agreeable in collecting together yᵉ Names of Numbers, which one must imagine to have a good Opinion either of one's Genius or one's disposition?—After all, *the Method* has been so vilely prostituted, yᵗ the Name of it, at first, will sound disreputably. And yet this method was in no much better Name, when Pope, & Spence condescended to make use of it—you will say, 'wᵗ a difference of Cases!—but however—*Some* temptation I must have, to go thro' yᵉ trouble of revising my pieces: & what temptation were yᵉ View of Fame (even supposing there were yᵉ least *chance*) to so *domestick* a wretch as I? To see a neat edition of one's Poems, wᵗʰ elegant decorations, & to acquire *some* Money, which I value only for yᵉ sake of employing it—These might be some temptations—Consider then of these matters, and wᵗ are yᵉ best methods of evading yᵉ *discredit* of a Subscription. Some will say it renders a man dependent—but has not the Subscriber an elegant & amusive toy for his money? I should, no doubt, think yᵉ better of my Friends for subscribing, but none the better of myself for accepting yᵉ subscription.

NOTES

[1]*The London Magazine*, 1761, 499–500. *On the King's Marriage*, by Samuel Pullein.

[2]Sister of Sir Henry Gough.

[3]Henry Dodwell (d. 1784), wrote *Christianity not founded in Argument*, 1741.

[4]Lord Lyttelton's second wife was not allowed to have charge of her step-daughter, Lucy, who stayed with her uncle, Lord Fortescue. Mrs. Montagu, Queen of the Blues, often mentions her in letters to the Hagley family. The other child of Lord Lyttelton's first marriage was a boy, Thomas.

[5]Horace's *Opera* were published by William Sanby, in 2 volumes, in 1759.

[6]W.S. tells Percy, Letter CCXC: 'The best Livie cᵈ find was a small one I lent him of Merveillius printed at Hamburgh, comprehendˢ wᵗ is good in Bentley, Cuningham and Sanadon.'

[7]Percy's note in MS.: 'N.B. The first Postscript was returned to Mr. Shenstone. N.B. The first P.S. related to Mˢ Shˢ own Poems by Subscription.'

[8]*Fingal, an Ancient Epic Poem. Translated from the Gaelic Language by James Macpherson*, 1761.

[9]*The London Chronicle*, December 1–3, 1761, 531–3.

[10]Percy's note in MS.: 'Proposals for an Editⁿ of his Poems by Subscription.'

CCLXXXII

Hull, II, 120.

To MR. HULL, *at Covent-Garden Theatre, London.*

THE LEASOWES,
Oct. 18, 1761.

Dear Mr. HULL,

IF I recollect aright, both you and NED ALCOCK were here this last Autumn, on the Evening when my Fish-Ponds had been robbed, and the Fish destroyed. You were an Eye-Witness of the Circumstances, therefore cannot but retain them in your Memory. I find I have been arraigned of *Lenity*, by several conscientiously-upright Neighbours. '*I have screened a Robber from Justice;*'—'*I have given Encouragement to future Thefts*,' &c.¹ Such are the Aspersions wherewith I have been loaded. I make a material Distinction between a *Robber* and a *Pilferer;* nor can I assign the former Appellation to a poor Wretch, who, in his Hunger, has taken two or three *Fishes*, or as many *Loaves*. It is true, I would rather have given more than the Value of them, to have prevented my *finny Friends* being disturbed in, or taken away, from their elemental Habitation; it is also as true, that, in my first Warmth, on the Report that the Fellow had bruised the poor Creatures to Death against the Stumps and Roots of Trees, I could not only have delivered him over to Justice, but have been almost induced to become myself his Punisher; but when that Warmth submitted to cool Reflection, I *felt it impossible* to resist his Argument, of having a Wife with five Children at Home, and not a Doit to procure them a Meal. I verily believe too he spoke the Truth. Poverty and Affliction seemed to work and plead within him, and his Words were the Words of Nature.

I cannot be so severe against these petty Misdemeanours as many are; nor can I, though I revere the Call of Justice, be a rigorous Supporter of its Claims, except in atrocious Cases. Beside, what had it availed me, to have consigned the Offender to the Power of a Magistrate? Rather say, what Pain and Inconvenience should I not have entailed on myself? I should have had the Trouble of attending the Examination; have had the Fellow imprisoned many Days; and the additional Mortification of travelling, perhaps to *Warwick*, or *Worcester*, in order to convict him. And after all, no Restitution is made for my Loss, though it were ten Times more valuable than a whole *Draught of Fishes*. There is surely something deficient in our Laws, concerning the *Meum* & *Tuum;* the Person robbed not only abides the Loss without Amends, but is even put to Expence, as well as Inconvenience, to get the Robber punished.

Then again, the Wife and five Children!—The poor Fellow subsists, chief Part of the Year, only by carrying News-Papers round the Country. Had He been shut up, what was to have supported the ragged Family meanwhile? I am beside inclined to think, that half a Crown, and a little wholesome Admonition, that is, if he be not a practised and stubborn Offender, might go as far towards amending his Morals, as an Acquaintance with the Inside of a Prison, and the Conversation of such Associates as he might find there.

I have suffered myself sometimes to doubt the Excellence of our Laws, relative to Life and Death, notwithstanding I know it has been asserted by many People, that they are wiser than those of any other Nation. What then? Is the Man who takes a few Guineas from you on the Highway, on a Level with him who commits a deliberate Murder? And is there no Punishment to be found more adequate to the first Transgression, than taking away the Life? Surely, one Example made by a visible Brand, a Mark of Disgrace, which could never be washed away, would more avail towards the Prevention of future Crimes, than half the Executions in the Kingdom, which have now, from too great Frequency, lost the chief Part of their Purpose and Terror. The Punishment which was inflicted by a Regent in some Part of the East, (I think the Circumstance is related in the *Arabian Nights Entertainments*) on a Judge who had been induced, by Gold, to give an unjust Decision, is admirable. The Brand, placed on his Habitation, in legible Characters, 'Here lives a corrupt Judge,' was, in the highest Degree, consonant to Justice, inasmuch as *it* made the Crime its own Punishment.

I have been led into these Reflections by finding how severely I have been arraigned, only for having been *an innocent De-*

frauder of the Law: so have troubled you with them; but here I come to a Conclusion. You are at Liberty to draw what Inferences you please from, or make what Objections you like to, my Opinion.

I am now to thank you for the Anecdotes you have given me, as well as for the Perusal of the enclosed Ballad.[2] I am particularly pleased with the Image,

'Appear they not as drizling Dews
Fresh'ning some faded Flower?'
I am, dear Sir, very faithfully,
Your Friend and Servant,
W. SHENSTONE.

NOTES

[1]An interesting story, bearing testimony to the kindliness of Shenstone's character was told in *The Birmingham Weekly Post*, July 27, 1912, where it was retold from *The Mirror* of 1823. 'Shenstone was one day walking through his romantic retreat, in company with his Delia (whose real name was Wilmot), when a person rushed out of a thicket, and presenting a pistol to his breast, demanded his money. Shenstone was surprised, and Delia fainted. "Money" says he, "is not worth struggling for. You cannot be poorer than I am; therefore, unhappy man, take it (throwing him his purse), and fly as quickly as possible." The man did so: he threw his pistol into the water, and in a moment disappeared. Shenstone ordered the foot-boy, who followed behind them, to pursue the robber at a distance, and observe whither he went. In a short time the boy returned, and informed his master that he followed the man to Halesowen, where he lived; that he went to the very door of his house, peeped through the keyhole; that as soon as the man entered, he threw the purse on the ground, and addressing himself to his wife, "take (says he) the dear-bought price of my honesty," then taking two of his children, one on each knee, he said to them, "I have ruined my soul to keep you from starving," and immediately burst into a flood of tears. Shenstone enquired after the man's character, and found that he was a labourer who was reputed honest and industrious, but oppressed by want and a numerous family. He went to his house, when the man kneeled down at his feet, and implored mercy. Shenstone not only forgave him, but gave him employment as long as he lived.'

[2]Hull, II, 125.

CCLXXXIII

Hull, II, 132.

To MR. HULL.

THE LEASOWES,
Nov. 26, 1761.

Dear Mr. HULL,

I ESTEEM myself beholden to you, for having made me acquainted with the Reality of the two Writers, Dr. LANCAS-

TER[1] and HENRY.[2] I have admired them both in their Pages, but knew only their Names. In fact, when I first read the *Essay on Delicacy*, I imagined the Name of LANCASTER to be fictitious, and that the Work might be the Production of the Author of *Sir Thomas Fitz-Osborne's Letters*. There is great Spirit, fine Sentiment, and true Elegance of Style throughout; and my Friend DODSLEY's preserving it in his *Fugitive Pieces*[3] is truly meritorious. It well deserves to be rescued from Oblivion. But what a Pity that your Uncle does not make a more frequent Use of his Pen! the World does not abound too much in such Writers. How much likewise is it to be lamented, that a Man of such Abilities should lie concealed in an obscure Part of *Essex*! He should have remained in the World—that is, I mean, for the Sake of the World; to his own Happiness, probably, Retirement was most conducive. It is most certain, that no Men are fit for Solitude, but those who find the Source of Amusement and Employment in themselves. Fancy, Reflection, and a Love of Reading, are indispensably necessary for such a Situation. It is downright Lunacy for a Man who has passed his Life in a Compting-House, or a Shop; who possesses, possibly, but a moderate Share of natural Understanding, that Understanding too not cultivated by Education, and who has never known what it is was [sic] to look into a Book— It is, I repeat, downright Lunacy, for such a Man to think of *retiring*. He knows not, the Fatigue he is going to encounter: he will want Employment for his Hours; most probably, may shorten his Existence, and while he retains it, it will be one continued State of Apathy, if not Disorder.

HENRY, you say, is a Mr. GRIFFITH, of the County of *Kilkenny* in *Ireland*. A Friend brought me over the Letters of HENRY and FRANCES, when they were first published in *Dublin;* they are most admirably clever and comprehensive; I have enjoyed and re-enjoyed them; and while I have admired the Writings, have loved the Writers. In the private Character you have given me of this amiable *Pair*, I feel as if I were acquainted with them. Before the Information received from you, I have sometimes suffered myself to think, and even communicated to an intimate Friend or two, that there was a Similitude of Disposition between HENRY and myself; but

when I look on your Description of him, I entertain much
Doubt. In the active Parts of his Philosophy, his Perseverance,
and Resolution, I fear I am far behind him. He is a Man
qualified for any State or Situation; Business or Amusement,
Solitude or a Crowd.—And you have spent Months with him
at *Kilkenny*!—I give you Joy of such an Happiness.

Again I thank you for the Enclosures you are ever and anon
sending, and am,

Dear Mr. HULL,
yours very affectionately,
W. SHENSTONE.

NOTES

¹Hull's note, II, 137: 'The Editor's Uncle.'

²In 1757, at the instance of Margaret, Countess of Cork, Mrs. Elizabeth Griffith
(1720–1793), published with her husband, Richard Griffith, anonymously, a series of
Genuine Letters between Henry and Frances, 2 vols., a selection from her correspondence
with her husband before marriage. This sentimental production met with great success.

³*Fugitive Pieces*, 1761, contained work by Burke, Spence, Lord Whitworth and Sir
Harry Beaumont.

CCLXXXIV

Hull, II, 143.

To MISS M——

THE LEASOWES,
Dec. 8, 1761.

Dear Miss M——,

I OUGHT to have returned Thanks for your agreeable Account of the Excursion to *Chepstow*,¹ some Time ago; but these
are Duties which I do not always perform so soon as I ought—
you know I don't—Neither will I waste my Time and Paper
in apologising for a Failing which you are so ready to forgive,
convinced that I am not less grateful on that Account.

I have great Joy in reading these little pleasurable Travels,
in a private Letter, related, as yours are, without Formality,
describing, with Ease and Simplicity, every little Occurrence
as it falls out. I can journey with you in Imagination, and partake every trivial Difficulty and every Delight. *You* are fond of
these little *Parties of Pleasure*, as they are called, and in you it is,
by no Means, reprovable; but in general, they are very dan-

2 R

gerous to young Folks. *You* have Means and Time, at your own Disposal; your Party is small and select, both in Point of Reputation and Understanding; you likewise turn your Excursion to some Advantage, you make Observations on all you see, form nice Distinctions between different Places, Points, and Characters, and draw just Conclusions from them —But, as I said before, these Parties too often are hazardous; the Mind once indulged in them, is apt to covet them too often; they are sometimes the Means of drawing a Female into improper Company; they encroach on Means and Time, neither of which, probably, can with Propriety be bestowed; they have their Source in Dissipation, are continually attended with Hazard, and too often end in the Worst of Mischiefs. In short, I would wish all young Folks, who have neither Leisure nor Money at Command, to shut their Ears against the very Name of a *Party of Pleasure*.

More than once in my Life, I have been solicited by Friends to visit foreign Climes. I had an Invitation of this Kind lately; but it is now too late; at least, I think so— Besides, why should a Man go so far for Objects of Curiosity, who has seen too little of his own Country? Many Parts of *England*, *Wales*, and *Scotland* equally (I should think) deserve our Admiration, and we need not risque Winds and Waves, to which I feel *some* Objection. Numbers of our travelling Gentry peregrinate too early in Life, before the Mind is sufficiently formed to make proper Observations on what they see and hear.

A Friend once related an Anecdote, which is apposite to my Subject. A very young Man, of good natural Understanding, and Heir to an affluent Fortune, would needs be one of these inconsiderate Travellers. In the Course of his Adventures, he fell into Company, in *Naples*, with some well-travelled, and well-informed Foreigners. They were conversing on what they had seen in *England;* and some little Difference of Opinion arising about the Architecture of *Windsor*-Castle, they naturally referred themselves to the young *Englishman* for a Decision. With much Confusion and Hesitation he was compelled to confess, he had never seen the Building in Question. The Company, with true foreign Politeness, only testified their Admiration in a silent Smile—but the Reflection instantly struck, and pained the young Gentleman. The Result was, that he returned for *England* within two Days, rationally determined to instruct himself in the Knowledge of his own Country, before he pryed into those afar off. His Reflection and Determination did equal Credit to his Understanding.

Our Friend HULL has, as usual, been amusing us with as good a Drama, as our neighbouring Town can give Encouragement to; but says, he returns no more. I know many who will be sorry on this Account. He has not departed however, without having excited Curiosity in a very peculiar Way; on a small Plan, indeed, but to a very commendable Purpose. He enticed with him his two principal Actresses, Miss MORRISON and Miss IBBOT, (both possessed of great Merit in their Profession) some few of his Band, two Voices, and gave an Evening's Entertainment of *Singing* and *Reading*, at the little Town of *Stourbridge*, some few Miles off; the Profits devoted to the Assistance of a Tradesman, who had suffered under repeated Misfortunes. The Success, I hear, more than answered his Expectations; the little Assembly-Room was crouded, and with much Company. A slight Cold made me fearful of being out late, but the Particulars were given me by a neighbouring Clergyman who was present. The Pieces selected for Reading were well-chosen. I do not remember the whole Number, but I recollect that *Miss* CARTER's *Ode to Wisdom*,[2] PRIOR's *Henry and Emma*,[3] and GRAY's *Elegy in a Country Church-Yard* were amongst them. The latter gave particular Satisfaction, my Friend told me, to the Gentlemen of the Pulpit, of whom he counted seven. The whole was received with great Approbation. You are to observe that HULL and his Party, so far from proposing any Emolument to themselves, declined even to be re-imbursed the Expences they were at in going, and the Master of the Assembly-Room *gave* the Use of it. From this confined Instance of such a Scheme, I am apt to think an Union of Poetry and Music, executed on a larger Plan, would be an admirable Two-Hours-Entertainment, either in a public Room or private Family.

I enclose a Piece of Writing, which a Friend of mine sent me

in a Frank last Week.[4] I think the Subject calculated for your
Liking. It was planned, and partly written, in Mr. HOARE's
lovely Grounds, at *Stourton* in *Wiltshire*;[5] and the Thought
suggested by surveying, from an Eminence there, a woody
Vale, wherein ALFRED is reported to have once concealed
himself from the *Danes*. Send it back, when you have done
with it.

Adieu, dear Miss M——,

Yours very faithfully,

W. SHENSTONE.

NOTES

[1]The letter from Miss M— of Bath to Shenstone, dated July 21, 1760, is printed by
Hull, I, 285. It contains a glowing account of a visit to Percefield, the seat of Mr.
Morris. 'Such a Place for the variety and Beauty of its Prospects, I never saw.'
The New Bath Guide of 1796 says, 'it possesses the most beautiful and magnificent
scenery, take it in all its parts and varieties, of any place in the kingdom. From a small
shrubbery you are led to a spot railed in, called from its frightful eminence the Lover's
Leap, the perpendicular height of which is computed at 300 feet. It commands the
conflux of the Wye and the Severn, and looks down the latter to the Bristol channel,
while stupendous rocks, immense woods, distant prospects, and all the softer beauties of
elegant improvements render Percefield a scene that fills the beholder with the most
ravishing admiration.'

[2]Elizabeth Carter (1717–1806), translator of Epictetus, was greatly admired by Dr.
Johnson for her scholarship, and was friend or correspondent of most of the well-
known literary people of her day. Her famous *Ode to Wisdom* was introduced by
Richardson into *Clarissa*.

[3]Matthew Prior (1664–1721). *Henry and Emma*, to be found in *Poems on Several
Occasions* was particularly admired by W.S. whose copy of Prior's *Poems* (see ante,
p. 178, note 1) contains a mark of approbation beside *Henry and Emma*, thus ▦▦▦▦
This signifies very keen approval.

[4]Hull, II, 149. *Cadwal: A Legendary Tale*.

[5]Stourhead, or Stourton, Wiltshire, was a famous show place in the eighteenth
century. *The New Bath Guide* of 1796 urges the visitor to see it. 'This seat (which is
25 miles from Bath) is not large, yet has an air of grandeur, and is well dignified for
pleasure and convenience.' The Guide praises the interior of the house and its exterior
and grounds. 'From Alfred's Tower to the house, the eye is charmed with a number of
delightful views; and in many other parts of the garden are interspersed temples, statues,
and other buildings which altogether display the most exquisite taste.'

CCLXXXV

Hull, II, 135.

To MR. HULL, *at Covent-Garden* Theatre.

Sir,

I AM greatly obliged both to you and Miss MORRISON,
for the Ballads you were so good as to inclose to me.[1] The

Speed you have used in sending them, testifies the Reality of that Delight you seemed to express at the *Leasowes*, when I first communicated my Friend Dr. PERCY's Design. I sent them directly to him; he has begun to print off his venerable Collection,[2] with an Eye to the Publication of it sometime next Winter. One of your Ballads is truly beautily [sic] and extremely proper to his Purpose. It has that *Naiveté*, which is so very essential in Ballads of all Kind; and which requires no more than, that *sublime*, or *elegant*; or *tender* Sentiments be expressed in a simple and unaffected Manner—*Sentimental* Language would be no ill Term for it; or, perhaps, the Essay before DODSLEY's *Fables* does not improperly stile it, the *Voice* of Sentiment, in Opposition to the *Language* of Reflection.

As to the *other*, Miss M[orrison] well distinguishes, that the Merit of it is almost wholly confined to the Sentiment at last. This is both *natural* and *tender*; and would *she* take the Pains to new-write the *whole* on this Account, (for even this Sentiment is not *expressed* so very simply as one could wish it) I dare say it is in his Power to render it very pleasing. I know not how far I am *singular*; but as I love to avail myself of different Words, to bundle up Ideas in different Parcels, it is become habitual to me, to call *that* a *Ballad* which describes or implies some *Action*; on the other Hand, I term that a *Song*, which contains only an Expression of *Sentiment*. According to this Account, I believe one of your Pieces would appear a *Ballad*, and the other a *Song*.

The *Play-House* Coronations answer the Purpose of all those who chuse to compound the Matter betwixt *Indolence* and *Curiosity*. Mr. GARRICK has given a very genteel Turn to this Taste among the Citizens, in his Epilogue to the new Play.[3] I have not *yet* seen this Performance; and should be glad if you would give me some Account of its Appearance on the Stage. Why does not Dr. LANCASTER compleat his *Essay upon Delicacy?* I read it, since I wrote last, in DODSLEY's *Fugitive Pieces*, and think it mighty well deserves the Labour necessary to its Continuation.

'Tis true, that Specimens of Wit or Humour have been dispensed this Winter but sparingly from the Press; and even there in *political* Pamphlets, where I am least inclined to seek them. But we must swim with the Tide, if we would collect the Shells and Corals that it leaves behind; accordingly I have read two or three of these Pamphlets which have answered my Expectations. Should any other appear that strikes you, be so good as to enclose it to me in a Frank. As to *Lavinia*, or other dramatic Schemes, I must defer them till I see you at the *Leasowes*, which whenever it happens, will afford me Pleasure, being very faithfully and affectionately,

your most obedient Servant,

W. SHENSTONE.

Christmas-Eve, 1761.

NOTES

[1]Hull, II, 139–143. The two ballads were not given by Percy in his *Reliques*.

[2]Hull's note, II, 136: '*Antient Poetry*, now published in three Volumes; the universal Estimation and Encouragement of which Work sufficiently testifies its Excellence.'

[3]Hull's note, II, 137: 'Epilogue to the Tragedy of *Hecuba*, produced that year at Drury-Lane Theatre.'

Dr. John Delap (1725–1812), poet and dramatist, author of *Hecuba*, wrote several plays but met with little success. Robert Lloyd wrote the prologue to Delap's *Hecuba* and Garrick the Epilogue. The lines to which W.S. refers ran thus:

> 'With us, there's no compulsive law that can
> Make a live girl to wed a quite dead man;
> Had I been wedded to some ancient King
> I mean a *Grecian*—Ancient's not the thing;
> Then had our bard made ample reparation,
> Then had you seen a *Grecian coronation!*
> Sneer not, ye criticks, at this rage for shew,
> That honest heart at coronations glow!
> Nor snarl that our faint copies glad their eyes,
> When from the thing itself such blessings rise.'

CCLXXXVI

Assay Office Library, Birmingham.

[*To* MATTHEW BOULTON.]

Decr 25. 1761.

My Christmas Compliments to Mr. and Mrs. Bolton. I hope Mr. Bolton's engagements at the Sohoe[1] will turn out much more advantageous to *Him*, than they have done to *me;* if it be to *them* that I am to attribute his Long absence from the

Leasowes. Mr. Perrott, his neighbour[2] dines here on Sunday:
and as *this*, at least, must be a Day when he will be disengaged
from his attendance upon workmen; if he have no *other*
Avocation, I shall be truly glad of his Company.

WILL: SHENSTONE.

To Mr. Bolton,
        on Snowhill,
            Birmingham.

NOTES

[1]Boulton was engaged at the time of the writing of this letter in building his new house
and factory at Soho. Here he made the coins admired by J. S. Hylton in a letter in
the collection at the Assay Office Library, Birmingham.
[2]Owner of Bell Hall, Belbroughton—'F. Perrott of Belbroughton' appears among a
list of Birmingham medical practitioners of the middle of the eighteenth century.

CCLXXXVII

B.M. Add. MSS. 28221.

Hecht, 73.

[*To* THOMAS PERCY.]

Jany 1761-2.

Dear Sir,
    I sincerely thank you for the *delicacy* with which you express
your Sentiments on my Publication: very judicious in all
respects; except the too great Partiality therein shewn to y[r]
Friends abilities.
    Should the affair *proceed*, and would the Publick excuse the
mere *Act* of asking a Subscription, they shall be *sure* to find
nothing illiberal or disingenuous in y[e] conduct of it. I think I
may promise *this*, Let the *Loss* or *Gain* be what it will.
    The Mistake I observe in my Date (1762 instead of 1763)
may *possibly* have led you to suppose that my Collection was to
appear *this* Spring—Alas, it will be as much as I can possibly
do (even *presuming upon* y[e] enjoyment of tolerable health &
Freedom of Spirits) to prepare Matters, against Spring following—I find y[r] Advice extremely rational, 'to be very carefull
how I restrain myself by naming too early a Day.' I also

approve what you say wth regard to stipulating for a *number* of Subscribers—I did it chiefly in order to give myself some Air of *Indifference*, as to the Publication—*Consider* this *motive* if you please—I did *not* use ye term *Essays* for ye sake of introducing a red Letter &c. I thought *essays* (or 'Attempts') a more *modest* Intimation of what the Publick was to *expect*—namely a Sort of *tryals of ones hand* in different *kinds* of Poetry—made chiefly in ye younger part of Life—& in order to convince *myself*, w^t *Kind* suited with my Cast of Genius.

I hoped also for somewhat more indulgence, on acc^t of the variety, or different *Kinds*, of Poetry. There will be time enough to consider this before Febry; w^ch, Mr Dodsley says, is allowedly the properest time for these advertisements—you should have considered what I sent rather as a Model for *Proposals*, y^n a Title-page to the *Book itself;* in which Light, at least, it might not be improper to Let ye Publick into some Particulars—For Instance, that my *Elegies* are to be in the Collection &c:

I am not partial to a Full title-page—being a Passionate Lover of *Simplicity*—You need not fear therefore, but I shall take care that Mine shall not offend you by its number of Parts—To say a Piece looks *busy* (crowded) is, w^th *Baskerville*, one of the highest terms of Approbation—as it is with *Me*, a term of Reproach.

I am, *myself*, dissatisfy'd with my new Orthographies of ye word 'Leasowes.' The Chief Point was to banish ye Preposition wch however I find impracticable.

You will hardly convince me y^t any Pains of mine, in point of revisal or correction, have a tendency to *hurt* the *little* Pieces I produce. This I believe is very *seldom* the Case, when a Person's taste is not notoriously *perverted*—My chief endeavour, on these occasions, has been to produce *ease* & Simplicity, if not melody of expression, so far as this c^d be effected without *impoverishing* the Sentiment. And were I *not* to employ this Labour, Many of my Trifles w^d appear ye most affected, & the most *laboured* things that ever were. Pastoral Poetry, in my opinion, should exhibit almost *naked sentiment*. Tis possible y^t some parts in y^r Copy of my ballad, may appear preferable to those y^t were finally inserted—But this was not owing to *over-correction*: but to the decision of Friends, who on my shewing them a number of stanzas (*upon* whose merit I could not determine) occasioned me to reject some, & admit others, as their Tastes were more or less fond of *Art*. In short I believe many of y^e *rejected*, and the inserted stanzas, were written almost simultaneously—There *is* however a time when this Labour does mischief—Tis when writers (of w^m you may recollect some) think they can not too much *stiffen*, or *raise*, or alienate their Language from ye common Idiom. By this they procure a Kind of Homage, parallel to w^t is acquired by a *reserved behaviour*—the Dignity of Distance—the awe pertaining to Eastern monarchs—but never once ye more valuable effects of genuine affection or sincere *applause*. But too much of this—

Adieu.

CCLXXXVIII

B.M. Add. MSS. 28221.
Hecht, 75.

[*To* THOMAS PERCY.]

My Compliments.—I am afraid that my Awards[1] hitherto have resembled the Umpirage of Chaos 'who by Decision more embroils the Fray'[2]—However, I would have you allow yourself *time* for the *thorough* examination of this dilemma that occurs at *First*. For my own part, I ever considered y^r old M.SS. as the noblest treasure in a *Poet's hands;* even as pure gold in dust or Ingots, which the Owner might either mint himself, or dispose of in the shape he found it, for the Benefit of other *Artists*. Remember I use ye word *Artists*—for if you publish these old pieces *unimproved only*, I consider them as not every one's money, but as a prize merely for either *virtuosoes*, or else the *manufacturers* in this kind of ware. The Poets namely. The purchasers however, of this sort, will lie under a disadvantage not incident to ye present owner; who possesses his treasure in Secret, & not in common wth all mankind. Quere then, whether you yourself chuse to wave both the trouble & the Credit that would accrue from such improvements as you are well able to bestow.—I am really not sufficiently sanguine to *dictate*, on this Head, yet hope the Hints I throw out at times, & the different Lights in which I place things, may be of some little use to you in y^r determination at Last.

Quere: What if you proceed from old to newer ballads *in every distinct vol^{me}*, supposing y^r improved Copies to appear towards the Close, & there be just refer'd to the *original* Copies? This would at least prevent ye first volume from being too much loaded with obsolete pieces, which were not agreeable to the *general* Taste—And So, make First, second, & third series, in *every distinct* volume. Consider well wth y^{r}self, the *advantages* this would give you. I think I begin to like it.

If you consider *improved* Copies as the *standard or principal* ones, & give *them* a first place, I do not see y^t you need hereby violate y^r purpose of arranging according to the date—They may still rank as old Barons, let the robes they wear be ever so modern.

From all this you will conclude that I really know not what to say.—

Chaos.

From Mr Shenstone's Brain
Feb. 3^d 1762.

P.S. Dr. Roebuck comes home to-day, by whom I depend upon hearing from M^r M'Gouan in Scotland. Lend your Assistance in ye following Whim—I am making a sett of *boxes* y^t are to appear on ye outside like books, & each to be Lettered —the titles used in Lettering might have some wit or humour, in lieu of w^t *these books* may want *within;* and such may be drawn either from titles that are, Puritanical,—such as 'a new round to Jacob's Ladder'—'A spiritual shove'—'Valley of holy shot' &c. &c. &c. Quaint & antiquated—such as 'a tragedie of plesaunte thinges' &c. such as Skelton &c. of old time may easily furnish[3]—Witty & Satyrical—on such subjects as make a good Figure in Ld Rochester[4] *Nothing*—'Dutch wit'—'French Probity, or Ridicule upon false Science—or grave and frivolous Disquisitions upon unimportant subjects—the virtuoso — taste —Coins— mosses— Butterflies— Roman

Fibulas &c. &c. &c. But you will find yᵉ field *too* large, *without* these hints of mine—only remember the titles must be expressible in in [sic] a *few short words*—I *have* some Few. What say you to Fingal—? I've only seen extracts, waiting for an 8ᵛᵒ Edit. They are, however, fine indeed! What a treasure *there* for a modern Poet, before they were published!

NOTES

¹Percy's note in MS.: 'On the subject of the Ancient Reliques of Poetry.'

²*Paradise Lost*, II, 907–9.

³John Skelton (1460?–1529), is chiefly remembered for his satire. The first collected edition of his work appeared under the title *Pithy, pleasaunt and profitable workes of Maister Skelton, Poete Laureate.*

⁴John Wilmot, second Earl of Rochester (1647–1680)poet at the court of Charles II.

CCCXXXIX

B.M. Add. MSS. 28221.

Hecht, 78.

[*To* THOMAS PERCY.]

3ᵈ *March*, 1762.

[*In Percy's handwriting.*]

I think *with you*, in regard to what I've yet read of Fingal, or rather of the Pieces annexed to that Poem; for my head has been so bad of Late, yᵗ I durst not undertake to read, wᵗ is *called* an *Epick-poem*—I admire many detached Sentiments &c. in Ossian; but have *many* Objections to his Translator's management, wherein I think wᵗʰ you. Thank you for yʳ humorous titles¹—you did not observe, yᵗ they consist in general of more *words* than can be inserted—Beside this, my Scheme is *changed*—As these books are *really* boxes to contain yᵉ Letters of some chosen Correspondents, I shall Letter yᵉ Backs wᵗʰ my Friends' names.

I've been plagu'd much of Late wᵗʰ Designs for yᵉ Ornamᵗˢ to Baskerville's Horace Lᵈ Bute accepts the Dedication & the Ornamᵗˢ I hope will be somewhat agreeable

I've also been busyd in contributing my joint Endeavours to procure a new turn-pike road to Stourbridge.

[My Lord B——]² has caused our toll-gate petition to be

postponed, 'till ye merits of ye cause can be further examined. We cannot *now obtain an act*, before ye latter end of next year —Nor perhaps get our road mended sooner y^n ye end of 2 years, after that. I hate the affectedly-wise Face of unnecessary *deliberation*; 'tis ye mien of *wisdom*, but ye marque of *Folly*.

Have you seen Miss Carter's Poems?[3]

I am y^r most affectionate & faithfull Friend

W.S.

To The Revd Mr Percy.

NOTES

[1]At the end of this letter in the MS. is a sheet containing Percy's handwriting— 'N.B. Some of the titles I sent Mr. Shenstone in compliance with his Request were:—

A cordial dram for a drooping Saint.

A mouse-trap for a nibbling sinner.

Warburton on humility.

Pitt on resignation.

Spiritual Spicery, or choice comfits of Devotion.'

[2]Crossed out in MS.

[3]*Poems on Several Occasions*, dedicated to William Pulteney, Earl of Bath, were published 1762.

CCXC

B.M. Add. MSS. 28221.
Hecht, 78.

[*To* THOMAS PERCY.]

[*March ?*, 1762.]

I really have not heard *yet* from Scotland, wch amazes me— but I do believe M'Gouan is endeavouring to procure some-thing y^t he may enclose for you—He sent me word (a month ago) y^t he w^d then write in a weeks time.

I desired Mr Livie (who is gone up to town about ye publication of Bask^s Horace, of wch he is ye Editor) as he had Letters for Mr Warton, to make him also my Comp^ts & tell him 'what pleasure it gave me to find y^t he countenanced y^r Undertaking. The said Horace will be extremely beautifull;

& tho it have not every *reading* I could wish, is on the whole more to my mind, y^n any other that is extant—Sandby's is bad, it seems—& the best Livie c^d find was a small one I lent him of Merveillius printed at Hamburgh, comprehend^g w^t is good in Bentley, Cuningham & Sanadon—I will send you a Copy; if you'll tell me, after what manner it is practicable.

Have you seen Horace Walpole's book on Painters[1]—I was quite divided, *after* I had read it, whether I should purchase it or no—The Cuts turned ye scale; & I bespoke it. His *own* remarks are sprightly & judicious—but these are thinly inter-spersed—& a very great part of the 3 vols. consists of ye most trifling anecdotes of inconsiderable Artists—I never knew so much Genius as Walpole's in such a Bigot to Antiquity—For, tho' I call you an Antiquarian, yet you are not near so great a Bigot—He is extremely inaccurate in his Language, tho he says it was corrected by Gray.—I've also purchased Lord Kaims on Critism[2] [sic]: from wch I hope some Entertainment on acc^t of his *Subjects*—tho I scarce expect to find him, any ways, equal to my Fr^d Burke. I have for these 3 weeks been much out of order, but am sorry to hear ye same of you. I am now rather better; and when *you* are so, pray let me reap ye benefit.

W.S.

NOTES

[1] His *Anecdotes of Painting in England*, from Vertue's MSS. came from Strawberry Hill Press in 1762. The four volumes were completed in 1771.
[2] Henry Home, Lord Kames (1696–1782), Scottish judge, published *Elements of Criticism* (1762), in 3 volumes.

CCXCI

MS. R. N. Carew Hunt, Esq.

[*To* J. LIVIE.]

My compliments to Mr Livie; who will present them also to the Doctor's[1] Family—If Dr *Lowth's* Introduction to English Grammar[2] be yet arrived, and M. Livie have read it and can spare it, I should gladly be favoured with a a [sic] sight of it.

It is to be presumed that the *translator* of Fingal has *given* a classical turn to many of the Phrases; or at least encreased it, when 'twas found. To show how surprisingly they agree w.th ye Classicks, & also for ye sake of foreign nations, I could wish that some such Nat. Poet as Holdisworth,[3] or Dobson, would turn ye whole into Latin Heroicks. The *Descriptions* and *Sentiments* are inimitably fine —— Pray is not this a fault in ye Horace Mercatorne vagus, *cnltorne* viventis agelli Should it not be *cultorve?* or the Line differently stop'd?—I saw this by chance, for M'Leod has not yet afforded me an opportunity of examining the Whole—

W. SHENSTONE—

Thursday, March, 1762.

NOTES

[1] John Livie was tutor to the family of Dr. Roebuck.
[2] 1762, *A Short Introduction to English Grammar.*
[3] Edward Holdsworth (1684–1746), classical scholar. Spence in *Polymetis* praised Holdsworth for understanding Virgil the best of any man he knew. After Holdsworth's death he edited some of his work.

CCXCII

B.M. Add. MSS. 22548.

[*To* J. LIVIE.]

March ye Last, 1752.

Mr Shenstone's Compliments to Mr Livie, and to the Doctor and Mrs. Roebuck.

Mr Livie will please to let me know (either by the Bearer, or from London) *where* a Letter will find him in our great Metropolis.

At all Events he will give me a Line, within a few Days after he arrives in town.

Should he see Mr Warton, (on his Road thro Oxford) I desire my Compliments to that Gentleman; and that He may be acquainted with the Pleasure it gives me, to find that He assists my Friend, Mr. Percy—He will readily know that I allude to the *antient Ballads* Mr. Percy is collecting; a scheme

I've long wished, and am now likely, to see executed with success.

Mr. Livie mentioned, I think, that either Dr Ash[1] or Mr Peeke had purchased 'Mr Walpole's Lives of the Painters'— Would it not be possible to procure a Sight of it for a Few Days, from one or other of those Gentlemen?

If I should like it, I shall certainly purchase it—Mr Livie will I hope lend me his good offices on this occasion. I have not ye Pleasure of being so well acquainted with Mr *Peake*, as I could *wish*. The Bearer may wait for Mr Livies Answer, if he should order him to do so.

To Mr Livie.

NOTE

[1]John Ash, M.D. (1723–1798) of Temple Row, friend of Dr. Small, who lived with him, and of Dr. Roebuck, and founder of Birmingham General Hospital.

CCXCIII

MS. Eng. letters d. 59.
Bodleian Library.

[*To* THOMAS PERCY.]

Sunday, May 9th 1762.

— Shenstone's best respects to M^r and M^{rs} [   ]cy— I have, this moment, received the inclosed from M^r M'Gouan; which I *send*, less for the sake of these *partial* compliments with which he oppresses me, than to communicate his kind Intentions with regard to Mr Percy's Publication. Dr Roebuck, who with two Scotch Gentlemen (a Mr Stuart and a Mr Murray) dined with me this day, has kept the Letter, according to his usual Flightiness, this month past in his Bureau.

I am not yet recovered of my Cold; which renders me unfit for every critical, or indeed, social office—but it is at all times a pleasure to me to receive a Line from Mr Percy; and I beg he would not fail me, when his Health or Leisure enables him to write

W. SHENSTONE.

return M^r M'Gouan's
    if you please.

CCXCIV

B.M. Add. MSS. 28221.
Hecht, 79.

[*To* THOMAS PERCY.]

THE LEASOWES,
May 16*th* 1762.

Dear Mr. Percy,

I am really sorry that my last Remarks did not arrive in due time; as I am not conscious that I *delayed* to send them, & as I thought myself perfectly *clear* in most things that I proposed —In regard to the present Packet, I have less to say. You will think it proper to insert something that comprizes the actions of this great Champion Guy, as well as those of King Arthur; and yet there is evidently not a single particle of poetical Merit in *either* of the Ballads. Once for all, it is extremely certain that an *Over*-proportion of *this Kind* of *Ballast*, will sink your vessel to the Bottom of the Sea. Therefore be upon your guard, in time: Neither have you Any reason to be apprehensive that your vols. should be deficient in point of *Bulk*. You are not to accost the Publick, as Terry Hopkinson did his Customer 'Sir, you must consider that these volumes have all together a *deal of Stuff* in them.' But I've perhaps harped upon this string too Long, & will leave these matters to your own decision. It is not *necessary* that your 3 vols. should be any thicker than 'the Hive.'—I am sorry to find that the mention of *Coventry* in my Superscription does not make my Letters arrive a Jott the sooner.—I will take Care to leave an Horace for you, so soon as I can receive the Few y^t are allotted me, & can get one bound. I believe y^t you will not find it disappoint your expectations. Why it was not published near a Month ago, or what the Gravers &c. are doing, is much beyond my comprehension. —I have read Webb, who has something clever in his Essay upon Poetry;[1] but he is too Laconic, & does not say enough for what his title implies. Besides, there are some of his Illustrations from Shakespear, y^t seem not greatly *to his purpose*. On the whole you must needs read it; but I think you will not esteem it equal, to His treatise upon Painting. His account of the Distinction betwixt Wit, Taste, & Genius, is very clear &

satisfactory; and of these three accomplishments that of Taste seems to be the *Author's* Portion—I begun to read Ld Kaims; but found the introductory part too abstracted for the *then* state of my Brain. I hope, erewhile, to make a fresh Essay— The *Indies* themselves should hardly bribe me to read over Cambridge's *Indian-War*.[2] I saw ye book at a Friend's House, where I read his preface, & *dipt* into other parts. The Author once did me the Honour to dine here; & is a Person of multifarious Knowledge; wit, humour, & Imagination. His Hobby-horse (or Foible) is the Construction of *Boats*, calculated to swim in different waters, & according to the models of different Countries. But how he came to write a Book of *this* *Stamp*, can be explained only by the God of *Whim*. Let me, however, do a piece of Justice to his Character. He is a truly worthy & good-natured Man, & much esteemed by all his Acquaintance—The best thing in Mallet's Poems (2^s) is, his verses upon Mr Charles Stanhope,[3] which are truly characteristick. His Emma[4] has not y^t simplicity or Beauty, which one would expect from so tender a subject.

> '*She, shivering, sigh'd, & died* '

A notable Line this, for a Conclusion! Have you seen ye pompous Edition of Thomson's works?[5] And does not his Monument put you in Mind of what the Publick owes to Mr *Richardson?*[6] For my own part, I never Look into his works, but with greater Admiration of his Genius—and then, if we regard ye extensive good they were *so well* calculated to promote, there are Few Characters to whom the Nation may be said to *owe* greater Honours.—Baskerville has of late been seized with a violent Inclination to publish Hudibras, his favorite Poem, in a pompous Quarto,[7] with an entire new sett of Cutts.—Dr Warburton has, I hear, also engaged Him to publish a Quarto-Edition of Mr Pope[8]—Pity but Guthrie had employed him to print his account of the British Peerage; wch is to be so highly decorated with the Arms, seats, Robes, &c. &c. &c. to come out in 5^s Quarto-Numbers, & to amount perhaps to 12 or 14 Pounds—Hume (Douglas) is writing a tragedy upon some Subject in Fingal;[9] wch abounds with Hints enough of that Kind, for any person of *true* Genius.—

A Friend of Mine wants an Edition of Plutarch's Lives in English: Can you inform me what Editions there are? I saw a neat sett in 8 vols, bought the other day at a Sale, with medals of the chief persons, but not above half as a big [sic] as a common 12mo; than wch no Edition should be *Smaller*.—I shall probably buy Dr. Goldsmith's Book *directly*.[10]—This Letter is already a perfect Hotch-potch; and so I proceed to tell you that there is a place near me that is called 'the Ganno-green' and also an inclosure, that is called 'the Bewspers'—Tell me ye Etymology of y^e *former*; & whether I am right in deriving the *Latter* from 'Beau Esperance.'[11]

I have of Late been meditating a Place for inserting a Seat to you in my Shrubbery; by which I class you with two Prime Friends, of whose Fidelity I have had experience ever since I was at School, with One, & University, with t'other. Mr Graves & Mr Jago; Both Men of Literature, Taste & Genius; with some distinction however of Character.

The *Renovation* of Spring has given me a pleasure in my Walks, which I always despair in *Winter* of their ever more affording me. But the *truest* Pleasure such things give, is of the social & *only-lasting* Sort; I mean the Pleasure *reflected* upon the Proprietor from ye Pleasure they *give a Friend*. Should *you* come over & be delighted here, the Pleasure w^d be encreased an hundred-fold. For *New* Objects are always found necessary to Self-*amusem^t*; but the *same* Objects, if they give pleasure to a Friend, will never be indifferent to ye well-disposed Owner.

W.S.

NOTES

[1]Daniel Webb (1719?–1798). *Remarks on the Beauties of Poetry* was published by Dodsley, March 6, 1762.

[2]*An Account of the War in India, between the English and French, on the Coast of Coromandel. From 1750 to 1760*, published 1761.

[3]*Poems on Several Occasions*, 1762. *The Reward, or Apollo's Acknowledgments to Charles Stanhope. Written in* 1757, 19–24.

[4]Ibid., *Edwin and Emma*, 57–69.

[5]Thomson's friend, Patrick Murdoch, issued an edition of Thomson's works in 1762, with a memoir.

[6]Many people felt that the public owed much to Richardson because of the highly moral tone of his work. See *Dialogues of the Dead* for Mrs. Montague's ideas on the subject.

Shenstone's note in the MS.: 'I want an elegant 8vo edition of Richardson, with fine Cuts.'

[7]This is an interesting indication of Baskerville's literary tastes, but apparently the publication was not carried through. Straus and Dent, *John Baskerville* (Bibliography).

[8]Warburton's wish was not carried out. Straus and Dent, *op. cit.*

[9]The *Fatal Discovery* was produced at Drury Lane, February 23, 1769.

[10]*Letters from a Citizen of the World to his Friends in the East*, 1762. During 1760 Goldsmith contributed *Chinese Letters* to *The Public Ledger*, and these were printed in 2 vols. 1762.

[11]W.S.'s note in MS.: 'Beau and Belle have been used indiscriminately. Beau desert and Bel-desert etc.' This place is commonly known among the inhabitants as 'Belser.'

CCXCV

Works III, 375.

To the [REV. R. GRAVES], *suggesting to him a Subject for Poetry.*

THE LEASOWES,
May 20, 1762.

Dear Mr. Graves,

I find you will *not* write, unless I give a regular answer to your letters; and yet, God knows, I have a better excuse for my delay, than I wish my friend to have for his punctilio—I mean, indisposition.—Whence it has happened, I cannot say, unless I may blame these continual east winds; but I have suffered more from the smiles of spring, than I have really done from the frowns of winter.

Having premised thus much, I lay your letter before me. The expence of printing a sheet of those commendatory verses at a common press is eighteen shillings; and at Baskerville's about three pounds, ten shillings: nor do I mean any decorations, unless perhaps 'The King-fisher,' or 'View of my Grove,' which, you know, I *have* engraven ready to *my* hands. So you see that *this* offering to vanity is not likely to be the most expensive.

I wish you had bestowed somewhat more attention upon *the title;* in which case, I really believe the job had been executed long ago. Pray be so kind as to re-consider it.—Is not 'The Garland of Friendship' a little too quaint? for that, as I remember, was what I proposed.—The *motto* which you proposed was a very good one; and I think also, that the addition of the next line would be an improvement to it; 'Et isti errori, nomen virtus posuisset honestum.'[1a] But I do not love *double* mottoes; so, if I admit this, I must exclude what I proposed; which, to speak the truth, was of my own invention.

The custom of prefixing commendatory verses to collections of poetry is now seemingly grown obsolete. Besides, in my case, they would only shew, that I had *taken* up more fame than my funds would answer. I return you many thanks for *your* poetical benevolence; but why do you mention it under the name of *Epigram*? I do not even chuse that it should have the air of *simile* from the *beginning:*

> 'Lo the tall youth, by partial fate's decree,
> 'To affluence born, and from restraint set free;
> 'How pleas'd he, &c.'[1]

I have taken *this* and some *other* liberties with it, and shall insert it among the rest; unless you chuse to *redeem* it, with something more to your satisfaction; for, to speak with frankness, I think it better calculated to do *me* honour than *yourself;* though I could esteem it *good*, if it came from a person whose abilities I respected less than yours. There is a subject here, which I would recommend to you, if by so doing I should lay you under no *restraint*. It is my principal cascade.[2] Its appearance well resembles the playfulness of infancy; skipping from side to side, with a thousand antic motions, that answer no other purpose than the mere amusement of the proprietor.— Other similitudes, &c. would here occur:

> 'Cui enim nascenti faciles arriserunt Musæ, &c.'

It then proceeds a few hundred yards, where it *rolls* and *slits iron* for manufactures of all kinds; resembling the graver toils of manhood, either in acquiring money, or furnishing the conveniencies, comforts, or ornaments of life: and, in this manner, it proceeds, under the name of The Stour, supplying works for casting, forging, and shaping iron, for every civil or military purpose. Perhaps you may not know that my rills are the principal sources of this river; or that this river supplies *more* ironworks than almost any single river in the kingdom: for so my friend Mr. Knight told me.

The Mr. D——you enquire after, and who wrote the *best* address Sir Robert Walpole ever *received*, is Mr. Dodington.[3] —Did I never send you a list of all the concealed names in that Miscellany?—I began to transcribe one from my own set; but find one part of my list is lost; I however send it, and will piece it out when I find an opportunity; as I purpose also to give you some account of our several merits in Dodsley's Fables. By the way, do not the verses to Dr. Cornwallis (now Bishop) affect you sensibly, vol. VI, p. 138?[4]—they do *me*, whenever I read them; and I cannot help applying them to myself. I feel somewhat of the same sensation when I read 'The Letters of Henry and Frances;' in which (from self-partiality, no doubt) I find myself extremely like Henry.

Pray let me hear, if you please, of Mr. Davenport.—I wish I had learnt to *draw* well in early life. It would have given me some very great advantages.—Let me hear also much of Mr. Melmoth, who, I presume, has left you long before this time. I did once design to have sent you down my proposals for a subscription, and requested the favour of *you two* to settle them finally, without any further reference to myself; but my head and spirits have been too bad to undertake even a common letter.—What think you of Dr. Lowth's Grammar?— Livie met him at Mr. Dodsley's; and says, he is well pleased with *our* frontispiece, &c. to Horace. Livie could not present his book to Lord Bute, *himself*, on account of my Lord's indisposition. Mr. Dalton (Dr. Dalton's brother), who teaches the King to draw, presented it. It seems, this Mr. Dalton (who gave the drawing of Lord Bute's arms) has lodgings in the palace, and sees the King every day. *While* Livie was *with* him, word came that the King was coming into his room; upon which, Livie was sent out another way.—The King asked Dalton, whom he had with him?—and was answered, an editor of Horace, who had inscribed it to Lord Bute.—Dalton is to present a copy to the King.

I inclose to you a specimen of the decorated parts of Horace, with the frontispiece.—The book will be published in a month's time, when I mean you a copy from those that are allotted to me.

My Lord Bute's arms are unexceptionably well-finished.—

The other plates, either through negligence, or the wilfulness of the designer and engraver, have given me infinite trouble and vexation. However, with about *two-thirds* of my directions observed, they will, I hope, afford you some pleasure; and discover somewhat more *beauty* and *spirit* than one commonly finds in such designs.—Send me your remarks very particularly, I beseech you.

W.S.

NOTES

[1a] Horace, *Serm.*, I, 3, 42.
[1] *The Festoon* (Graves), 173.
[2] *Euphrosyne* (Graves), 263. *The Cascade*

> 'Curio, ambitious of a taste,
> Having his little garden grac'd
> With every object for the eye . . . '

[3] Dodsley's *Collection*, VI, 129. To *the Right Hon. Sir Robert Walpole. By the Honourable Mr. D——.*

[4] *To the Worthy, Humane, Generous, Rev. and noble Mr. F. C. now Lord Bishop of Litchfield, by Dr. D. Written in the Year* 1743. Sneyd Davies (1709–1769), was the author, and the verses were favourites of Hazlitt and known to Lamb.

CCXCVI

B.M. Add. MSS. 22548.

[*To* J. LIVIE.]

Mr Shenstone desires his Comp^ts to Mr Livie—I have, for this Fortnight past, lost my Faculty of Speech; as well as been otherwise indisposed—I hope however that I shall be able, in a couple of days, to bid Mr. Livie welcome here, somewhat more plainly than in *Whispers;* as I conceive Hopes that my Voice is beginning to return.

I have procured a Book from London, bound I *presume*, precisely Like the Horace given to Ld Bute. If it be reasonable, I should be glad to get my remaining Copies of Horace delivered to Mr. Hodgetts,[1] to whom I've given Instructions about the Binding.

The Leasowes, *June* 15. 1762.

Dodsley comes hither the 29th.

To Mr Livie.

NOTE

[1]William Hodgetts was a notable Birmingham bookseller of the beginning of the nineteenth century. Apparently others of the same name carried on a similar business in the eighteenth century. Whether John Hodgetts, cousin of Shenstone, was of the firm I have not been able to discover.

CCXCVII

B.M. Add MSS. 12113.

[*To* J. LIVIE.]

Mr Shenstone's, with Mr. Dodsley's, best respects to Mr. Livie; who will, present ye same to Mr Baskerville and his Family—I believe we shall both dine at a Friend's in Birmm on Friday—and ye hay-harvest will not be quite compleated this week, so yt I cannot help wishing ye Favour intended me by Mr. Stuart's Family[1] may be defer'd till ye week after—If Mr Livie chuses to ride over, *before*, he will find us at home, and glad to receive him, upon any other day yn Friday.

July 7. 1762.

Any purple Leather yet arrived?

To Mr. Livie,
at Mr. Baskerville's.

NOTE

[1]W.S. wrote to Graves—November 20, 1762 (see post, p. 638) that among his summer visitors he had 'Mr. Stuart the painter and publisher of "Athenian Ruins".' So that Mr. Stuart of this letter is probably James Stuart (1713–1788), painter and architect, who in 1748 published a *Description of the Antiquities of Athens.*

CCXCVIII

B.M. Add. MSS. 28221.
Hecht, 84.

[*To* THOMAS PERCY.]

THE LEASOWES, *Augst* 10, 1762.

Dear Sir,

I was upon the Point of sending the inclosed, & giving you an account of my late silence, when I received yr Letter which

informs me that you would spend a day or two here next week[1]
—I will apologize therefore when I see you; & only mention
at present that I shall be at Home, & very *glad* to see you, at
the time proposed—I build much on D[r] Grainger's Poem,[2]
both on account of his *Subject* & His *Abilities;* which I think
extremely happy—He has taken Possession of a Field for
Poetry, which is both *large,* & *fertile,* & yet *un-occupied;* And
the Cultivation of which must be a *popular* measure to Many
Amongst us—But I say no more, till I see you & the Poem;
only, if you write to Him directly, please to present my best
respects.

I have been under a strange mistake with regard to what you
call *Revises,* which I understood to mean *Sheets that were finally
printed off.* I therefore kept them y[t] I might see y[e] appearance
of y[r] ballads as they succeeded one another—whereas I now
find that I have been expected to send these Revises directly
to you—Pardon the Mistake—It was indeed a Foolish one.

I have been tolerably well this last month or six weeks, since
the time I got rid of my Cold.

I have an Horace at y[r] Service, either in scarlet or in Purple
—Baskerville has begun to print a Virgil of y[e] *size* of the
Spectator;[3] which I think a better y[n] that of his Horace. *I* have
also *some* things to say; but may as well reserve them 'till I
see you—So wishing you a good Journey, I remain y[r] ever
affectionate

WILL: SHENSTONE.

To

the Rev[rd]
M[r]. Percy.

NOTES

[1]Percy's note in MS.: 'The Visit was afterw[ds] deferred till the end of September and
I took Mrs. Percy.'
[2]*The Sugar Cane—a Poem in Four Books,* by James Grainger, 1764.
[3]Baskerville's Virgil did not appear till 1776.

CCXCIX

James Kenward's *Harborne and its Surroundings*, 40.

[*To* MR. SMITH.]

Mr. Shenstone's service to Mr. & M^rs· Smith. I expect the Harborne tenant to come about my Farm[1] to day, but cannot well tell at what time. If Mr. Smith shall be at Home I will let him know so soon as the man comes; and shall be glad to have him step over and assist me in the Letting it.

Saturday, Aug. 27, 1762.

To Mr. Smith at
    Birchy-Close.

NOTE

[1]Probably Ivy Farm. In his Will, dated February 5, 1763, W.S. stated, 'I give to my Cousin John Shenstone and his Heirs all that my Estate at the Quinton in the parish of Halesowen called Ivey Farm.'

CCC

B.M. Add. MSS. 28221.
Hecht, 87.

[*To* THOMAS PERCY.]

Nov. 14, 1762. [*In Percy's handwriting.*]

My friend Whistler, of whom you have heard me speak, was never above half pleased with my Pastoral ballad; which used to give me some mortification. Let us however be of good courage—We have, I think, a more distinguished party on the other side ye Question. Pardon my quoting my own performance; it was ye same, with regard to *other* Ballads— and he was passionately fond of Smith's Phædra & Hippolitus,[1] where ye Language is lifted to much more y^n ye Sentiment. Mr Dryden a Man of *Fire*, was not less favorable to our Cause, y^n Mr Addison a man of *Delicacy*;[2] and amongst *my* Acquaintance, y^u will have a Mr Graves to ballance a Mr Jago.—The Novelty, & romantic Air of ye Plan, in ye gentle heardsman, gives an additional value to it's other beauties. Quocirca vivite fortes! &c.[2a] As to y^r being known to ye world in ye Light *merely* of a Ballad-monger, you may be told, once for all, y^t I never mention you as such, without throwing in other matters, to prevent *this* passing for y^r *chef* d'oeuvre. Depend upon't, y^r Character shall not suffer by any discovery I make on this head; & that I am well aware a *general* & *indiscriminate* explanation of this sort would not only hurt you wth some Folks, but would lay you under improper restraint in ye execution of y^r Plan.

You must dun me once more for 'The Boy & the Mantle,' & then it shall be ready—As to Head-pieces, it doesn't appear to me y^t you can *want* them, before the whole be printed off. I would always have them relate to the *whole* book y^t follows, whether they be allegorical or not—Some of y^rs seem to *promise* well—but I have not yet had Leisure to consider them so attentively as I could wish; & should be better able to do so, were I to see ye whole Volume together.

Alas no more has yet been done in regard to the Description you mention.[3] My Head has not of Late been fit for it—*Indeed* it has not—and yet I have had ye boldness to offer myself as a companion to great Folks, having made a weeks excursion, & passed a few days at Ld Foley's—He is a very lively agreeable Man (almost ye reverse of w^t I expected). His table ye most luxurious of any nobleman's in this Country—and his Chapel, where I attended him &c. last Sunday, at once so comfortable as well as superb, y^t it is perfect Luxury to say one's Prayers in it.

I have about 4 or 5 more of *these* visits to make, soon; after which I shall resign myself to Winter solitude; & to literary matters, *if my Health allows me.*—I wrote yesterday to Mr Rice Williams, availing myself of y^r remarks on ye Welch Ode he sent me; altho it stands much higher in *y^r* opinion y^n it really does in *mine*. The solemnity of ye writers invocation & transition thence to his Subject is well; but it abounds with infinite tautology; &, what is worse, deals so much in *general* terms y^t it has, with me Little poetical merit.

I sent y^r Book of old Poems to Mr Sketchley, & believe I *did* mark some few Pieces with a Pencil—Perhaps you may admit some of those y^t have first-rate marks; but I question whether you should go so low as second-rate, unless you have particular reasons for so doing.—Do not let y^r Volumes be too thick—nor y^r notes too verbose—& take great care what you admit.

Be so good as Let me hear from you as soon as you well can; and believe me to be, with constant affection,

Y^r most faithfull hum: Servt

W. SHENSTONE.

My best respects to Mrs Percy.

Sheridans Pamphlet^4 has some just remarks, which were new to me; but he is not always right in ye application of his Rules; & it is a cursed *quarto* of half a guinea.

'Ogilvies Poems,'^{5} ye same—that also ornamented with Cuts from ye authors own designs. The Specimens y^t appear in ye monthly review give me no Pleasure.

I believe I shall purchase ye 2 additional volumes of Dean Swift.^{6}

What think you of ye Reviewer's remarks upon ye New Liturgy, in y: Review for Novr last?^{7}

Could you any way contrive, for me to see ye Poems by Scotch Gentlemen?^{8}

There is I believe a mighty neat Edition of (John) Philips's Poems just published with Cuts.^{9}—Adieu—you see I've nothing to say—No Facts to communicate, & no Imagination to supply ye Place—wch is perhaps ye same Case with that of a Kingdom wch abounds neither in Cash, nor Paper-credit.

NOTES

^{1}Edmund Smith (1672–1710), wrote *Phaedra and Hippolytus*, an artificial tragedy modelled on Racine's *Phèdre*. It was produced in 1707, and was received with hostility. 'Would one think it was possible (at a Time when an Author lived that was able to write the *Phaedra and Hippolitus*) for a people to be so stupidly fond of the Italian Opera, as scarce to give a Third Days Hearing to that admirable Tragedy?' *Spectator*, 18. Addison was a friend of Edmund Smith, and wrote the prologue to his play.

^{2}*Spectator*, 70 & 74, contains Addison's well known appreciative criticism of *Chevy Chace*, for which he incurred much ridicule from the bad taste of the time. 'I have heard that the late Lord Dorset, who had the greatest Wit temper'd with the greatest Candour, and was one of the finest Criticks as well as the best Poets of his Age, had a numerous collection of old English Ballads, and took a particular Pleasure in the Reading of them. I can affirm the same of Mr. Dryden, and know several of the most refined Writers of our present Age who are of the same Humour.' *Spectator*, 85.

^{2a}Horace, *Serm.*, II, 2, 135.

^{3}Percy's note in MS.: 'Description of the Leasowes.'

^{4}Thomas Sheridan (1719–1788), father of Richard Brinsley Sheridan, published in

1762, *A Dissertation on Difficulties in Learning the English Tongue, with a Scheme for an English Grammar and Dictionary.*

[5]John Ogilvie (1733–1813) published *Poems on Several Subjects, with Essay on Lyric Poetry*, 1762.
See *The Monthly Review*, 1762, 239–254.

[6]July 27, 1762, Swift's *Miscellanies*, vols. 13 & 14 of his *Works*, were advertised.

[7]*The Monthly Review*, October, 1762, contained a laudatory review of the 'new liturgy.'

[8]*A Collection of Original Poems*, by the Rev. Mr. Blacklock, and other Scotch Gentlemen was criticized in *The Monthly Review*, 1761, 507–8. 'There are, however, many good things in this Collection; and we hope the intended additional Volumes will have the advantage of a more select choice. But after all, it is feared, this undertaking will never equal the elegant Collection, in 6 Volumes, made by Dodsley.' 'This apprehension' was realized when the additional volumes appeared. See also *Monthly Review*, 1762, 226–7.

[9]*Poems attempted in the Style of Milton. With a new Account of his Life and Writings*, were published by Tonson, 1762. See *The Monthly Review*, September 1762: 'The admirers of this Bard will be pleased to see so handsome an edition of his works.'

CCCI

Works III, 380.

To the [REV. R. GRAVES].

THE LEASOWES,
Nov. 20, 1762.

Dear Mr. Graves,

Do I really owe you an apology? you who are embarrassed with such a number of momentous concerns, as hardly allow a fair trial to letters of mere amusement? Alas! I cannot shelter my long silence under a supposition of this kind. I believe, I even *hope*, that you have disapproved my long neglect; as I can very faithfully assure you, I have repeatedly done, *myself*. There are certain times and seasons when I have not either the *power* or the *will* to write: as Hannibal said about attacking Rome, 'quandoque mentem non dari, quandoque potestatem.' This being an intellectual kind of *lethargy*, it would have been at least a friendly office, if you had *rouzed* me, as you *might* have done, by a supernumerary letter. I never receive a line from you, but I feel an almost irresistible propensity to answer it that very instant. Impediments sometimes occur; and, that instant being neglected, matter is accumulated for a longer letter than I am always resolute enough to undertake: at the same time, I can never content myself with uttering one half of what I have to say.—Pray is not that *good sort of man*, to whom you allude, a Mr. K——? Let him be ever so good a sort of man in the common estimation, I dare aver him to be neither an ingenious person nor a candid critic. There may be fifty or more preferable readings to what are received in this new Horace;[1] yet he will find a better *text* there, *upon the whole*, than in any one edition before extant. As to the *beauty* of *type* and *presswork*, it is too obvious to need vindication. The accuracy of the *latter* almost exceeds what was ever found in any other book. Then as to the *frontispiece*, it is, I think, much superior to such as *ordinarily* occur; the *subject* animated, and well-chosen; and the *execution* very commendable: at least, if we allow for the *nice* touches which it required, and the *uncommon difficulty* of getting any thing of this kind done to one's direction.

Mr. Walpole is a lively and ingenious writer; not always accurate in his determinations, and much less so in his language; too often led away by a desire of routing prejudices and destroying giants. And yet there is no province wherein he appears to more advantage, in *general*, than in throwing new light upon Characters in British History. I wish he would compose a regular work, making this his principal point. He has, with great labour, in his Book of Painters, recorded matters of little importance, relative to people that were of less. I have a right to be severe, for his volumes cost me above thirty shillings; yet, where he drops the *antiquarian* in them, his remarks are striking, and worth perusal.—I have sent for 'Gesner's Rural Poems,' and intend to see 'The Death of Abel;'[2] though I expect to find small pleasure in this *poetical prose*, unless exquisitely well-tuned.—Thank you for the anecdote of Lord Courteney: a thousand such sort of things, that engage the public attention, are never capable of penetrating the depth of my retirement.

Mr. Melmoth you will probably see often, as he intends to make Bath his place of residence. The *Omphale* you sent me is a most excellent figure, and I shall wish much to get a good cast of it; at least, when I am able to afford it.—When I write again, I will give you the best account I can of *my share* in Dodsley's new Fables; though it will be no easy matter to speak *separately* of it, with any precision.

And now, I think, I have spoke to most of the articles in your last letter.—Mr. Dodsley, who says he visited you, would acquaint you how we divided our time whilst he was here, into two *principal* parts, 'l'un à dormir, l'autre à ne rien faire.' Yet we paid our devoirs to a good deal of genteel company; of which this season has afforded me at *least* an equal share with any that went before. I will particularize a few; opening the list with no less personages than the Duke and Duchess of Richmond[3]—Mr. Walsh, Member for Worcester[4]—Earl of Bath, with Dr. Monson,[5] Mrs. Montague (who wrote the three last Dialogues printed with Lord Lyttelton's), and other company, from Hagley—Sir Richard Ashley—Mr. Mordaunt—Dr. Charlton with Mr. Knight—Earl and Countess of Northampton—Mr. Amyand—Lord Plymouth and Sir Harry Parker—Mr. and Mrs. Morrice of Percefield—Lord Mansfield[6] with Mr. Baron Smythe, Lord Dartmouth and Mr. Talbot—Marquis of Tavistock and Earl of Ossory—your nephew Mr. Graves, with Mr. Hopton and one of the senior Proctors of Oxford—Lord and Lady Dacre—Baron Plessen, Gentleman of the Bed-chamber to the King of Denmark, with Mr. Wendt his Tutor—Lord and Lady Vernon of Sudbury[7] with his children, Sir Charles and Lady Tynte, and Mr. Garrick's brother[8]—Mr. Melmoth and Mrs. Melmoth[9]—Colonel James—Lady Ward and Lady Uill, with Miss Wrottesley, Miss Pigott, &c.—Lord Lyttelton, Mr. Lyttelton, and Mr. Rust—Lord and Lady Dartmouth with Lord and Lady Willoughby de Broke[10]—Mr. Anson of Shuckburgh with Mr. Stuart the painter and publisher of 'Athenian Ruins'—Mr. Pepys and Sir W. Wheeler's son,[11] Mr. Pitt's nephew, &c.—Colonel Bamfylde, with Mr. Knight's Family, &c. &c.[12]—I did not imagine my list would have engrossed so much of my paper, and leave so little room to speak about the individuals.—Lord M[ansfield] appeared to me rather a *man of wit* than a *man of taste*: Baron Smythe, the reverse.—Mr. and Mrs. Morrice, extremely polite and agreeable people, invited me pressingly to their habitation; I could not help reflecting on the singular happiness of Mr. Morrice, to be possessed at once of a large fortune, one of the finest situations in England, and a wife whose taste for rural improvements appears even superior to his own; at least, if the *beauty* of her *person* did not impose upon my judgement. There are many others whom I would distinguish, if my time or paper would permit.—I suppose that you and Mr. Dodsley would be mighty unanimous with regard to the propriety of setting my subscription on foot— I do not dispute any of your arguments—they tally exactly with my own opinion; at least, allowing for the higher idea you have of my pieces than they deserve—the truth is, that I have deferred the publication too long *already*—till many of the compositions will not appear to the same advantage as before: and till I have not half the power that I had formerly to improve them. When I am low-spirited, I almost shudder at this tremendous contract with the publick; when my spirits are elevated, I see the necessity that you do, of not losing a moment's time—were you here a week, you would put the matter upon a footing that was unalterable—would to God you *were* here, or any one *like* you! however, it is probable you will *soon* hear from me again upon this very subject—I *know* this, that, *if* I print at *all*, the subscription is by no means to be neglected this present winter.—I have seen our friend Dr. Charlton many times this season; at The Leasowes; at Mr. Knight's; at his own house; and at my Lord Foley's. This visit to my Lord Foley's was performed about three weeks ago. I went with young Knight; and the company of the Doctor and Sir Francis Charleton took off all restraint, and made the visit perfectly agreeable. My Lord's behaviour was entirely free and hospitable; and his conversation lively and entertaining—I must confess, far beyond the idea which I have been taught to conceive of him—His table the most magnificent, I believe, of any Nobleman's for thirty miles round—His park, and Woobery-hill adjacent, afford views that are either extensive, wild, beautiful, or grand. The portico before his lodge deserves particular notice—his house large, and commodious, and well furnished; but scarce any of the rooms *high* enough to stand the test of modern criticism. But what strikes more than all the rest, is the magnificence of his Chapel—which however I cannot stay to describe; for I, this very *moment*, receive your letter.—After having written so much before, I can only touch upon some few particulars.—I believe, my scheme of publication will proceed in a little time, and that you will soon hear from me again.—If you can possibly excuse me to Mr. Davenport, and keep me well with him for a week or fortnight, I will not fail to write him a respectful letter.—I am truly ashamed of my neglect; but have written more letters within this week, than I have done for a quarter of a year before.— That there is a faction forming against Lord B[ute], I readily believe. The war may suit the *mercantile* world; and the City of London has generally the art to represent the *landed* and *trading* interest as *precisely* the same thing—But I think there is a very material difference; which it would be no way difficult to demonstrate—at least I am one that cry out,

'Nulla salus bello; pacem te poscimus omnes!'[13]

I am quite unacquainted with the affair relating to Colonel Wilkes and Lord Bute's son.—And now (though I mean to write again soon) I will release you from this unpleasing scrawl. —I beg however that you would not fail to write to me *directly*, if you can find leisure; being quite impatient to converse with you, after such a chasm in our correspondence; and being, with unvariable affection, my dear friend, for ever yours.—Pray my best respects to Mrs. Graves.

W. SHENSTONE.

My friend Dr. Grainger has written a Poem, in blank verse, which he calls 'The Sugar-Cane.'—It is divided into four books, and is capable of being *rendered* a good Poem. My friend Jago has written another Poem, in blank verse also, which he calls 'Edge-hill.'[14] It is descriptive chiefly of the prospect— but admits an account of *the fight* there, and many little *tales* and *episodes;* with compliments also to the gentry of War- wickshire.—It lies now upon my table.

NOTES

[1]Baskerville's *Horace*.

[2]Solomon Gesner (1730–1788), author of various pastoral poems. *Rural Poems. Translated from the original German*, belonged to 1762. *The Death of Abel*, 'an oratorio or Sacred Drama for Music,' was set to music by Dr. Arne and performed at the Theatre Royal. Drury Lane, 1761. An extract from *The Death of Abel* appeared in *The London Magazine*, January 1762

[3]Charles (Lennox), Duke of Richmond, married 1757 Mary, youngest daughter of Charles, Earl of Aylesbury. The Duchess was a famous beauty, many times painted by

Reynolds. H. Walpole wrote (*Letters*, Vol. III, p. 67), 'They are the prettiest couple in England except the father-in-law and mother.'

⁴John Walsh (1725?–1795), Secretary to Clive, 1761, M.P. for Worcester.

⁵Messenger Monsey (1720–1800), close friend of Mrs. Montagu.

⁶Lord Chief Justice of the Court of Common Pleas, frequently mentioned by Boswell, *Life of Johnson*.

⁷George Venables Vernon of Sudbury, Co. Derby and Kinderton, Co. Chester.

⁸David Garrick had three brothers—Peter, William, and George—the last being David's fellow pupil at Dr. Johnson's school at Edial.

⁹Melmoth's wife, Dorothy, daughter of William King (1685–1763), was the 'Cleona' of Sir Thomas Fitzosborne's *Letters on Several Subjects*, and the subject of the ode written for the third anniversary of their wedding and found in the *Letters*.

¹⁰Lord Willoughby, Jago's patron, married, October 1761, Louisa, first daughter of Francis (North), 1st Earl of Guilford.

¹¹Jago mentions in *Edge-Hill*, IV, 'Thy villa Leamington,' the seat of Sir William Wheeler.

¹²Many of the names in the foregoing list are those of people known to have been particularly interested in garden design.

¹³Virgil, *Aeneid* II, 362.

¹⁴*Edge-Hill or the Rural Prospect delineated & moralized* was not published till 1767.

CCCII

Hull, II, 1.

To [R. DODSLEY].

THE LEASOWES,

Nov. 20, 1762.

My dearest Friend,

It is a very *surprising* and a *cruel* Thing, that you will not suppose me to have been *out of Order*, after such a Neglect of writing, as can hardly be *excused* on any *other* Score. I cannot, indeed, lay Claim to what the Doctors call an *acute Disease*: but *Dizziness of Head*, and *Depression of Spirits* are at best no *trivial* Maladies, and great *Discouragements* to writing. There is a lethargic State of *Mind* that deserves your Pity, not your Anger; though it may require the *Hellebore* of sharp Reproof. Why then did you not apply this pungent Remedy, before the Disease was gone so far. But seriously, I pass too much of that Sort of Time, wherein I am neither *well* nor *ill;* and being unable to express myself at large, am averse to do so by Halves. From the strange Laconicism of your Letter, I am really in Doubt, whether you are not angry at me; and yet had rather this were owing to *Anger* that *may* subside, than to any persevering *Fondness* you may have for such unusual Brevity.

2 T

Should the latter become habitual, I shall see the Letters of a Genius dwindle to '*per first will advise the Needful.*' God forbid such a Transformation!

Your *former* Letter, to my great Confusion, was dated *Sept.* 18. Let me speak first to some few Parts of it—The Lampreys arrived safe, and were as good as I ever tasted; but every Time I tasted them, I wanted *you;* and you are mistaken, if you imagine, I can half relish such Cates *alone*: however, I return you Thanks.

You gave me no Account how far the *Bath* Waters, &c. were judged expedient for you. A *charitable* Action called you up to Town; and you, in the Benevolence of your Heart, presume, that this *accounts for* the Neglect of every Advantage that concerned *yourself.* Pray let me know whether the Bath was proper for you at the same Time inform me, whether you were able to serve Mrs. H———. I shall be sorry for *you,* as well as *her,* if you should miss the Gratification you would derive from the Success of such an Endeavour.

Were I rich, I would erect a Temple to *Simplicity* and *Grace;* or, as the latter Word would be *equivocal,* to *Simplicity* and *Elegance.* I am glad to hear that Mr. W——— has undertaken to deify the *former*: as he will produce better *Grounds* for such a *Consecration* than ever was done by Pagans, or by Papists, on any *such* Occasion. By the Way, I take that Goddess to be a remarkable Friend to Ease and Indolence. There is another well-deserving Personage, *Delicacy,* whose Cause has been strangely deserted, by either Mr. MELMOTH, or Dr. LANCASTER.

Will it make better for me, or worse, to say, I've not yet written to Mr. GRAVES? But I will positively write, within this Week, if it cost me a Dose of Salts to clear my Brain. As to what he says about my printing immediately, he *may* be *right,* and I am *sure* he is *friendly*: but more of this in a Little Time.

Since the Receipt of your last Letter, Mr. PERCY and his Wife came and spent a good Part of the Week here; and *he,* also, would needs write a Description of the *Leasowes.* During the latter Part of his Circuit, my Friend JAGO and I accompanied him; and what was produced on that Occasion, you will go near to know in a little Time. Mean while I am more and more convinced, that no Description of this Place can make any

Figure in Print, unless some *Strictures* upon *Gardening*, and *other* Embellishments be superadded. ,

Mr. JAGO has been with me twice, having written a Poem in blank Verse, which he leaves here for my Revisal. 'Tis a descriptive Poem, called *Edge-Hill*, and admits an Account of the Battle fought there, together with many legendary Tales and Episodes.

About a Week ago, I paid a Visit of two or three Days, which I had long promised, to Lord FOLEY. His Table, for a Constancy, is the most magnificent of any I ever saw: eighteen or twenty elegant Dishes; a continual Succession of Company; his Behaviour, perfectly hospitable, and his Conversation really entertaining. I most readily own myself to have been under a Mistake, with Regard to his *companionable* Character. My Reception was as agreeable as it could possibly be. As to the rest, he has a most admirable House and Furniture; but without any Room or Utensil that would stand the Test of *modern* Criticism. The Views around him, wild and great; and the Park capable of being rendered *fine*: *twice* as striking as it is at present, if he would fell some Oaks, under the Value of a Crown, and some Hawthorns, under the Value of a Half-penny: but 'tis possible, at his Time of Life, &c. nothing of this Sort will be undertaken. The two Things at present remarkable are, his *Lodge* and his *Chapel*. The Portico of the former, (designed by FLEETCROFT)[1] affords three different and striking Prospects. The Chapel is so very superb and elegant, that Mrs. GATAKER has nothing to do but send you and me *thither*, to say our Prayers in it. In reality, it is perfect Luxury; as I truly thought it, last *Sunday* Se'en-night; *his Pew* is a *Room* with an handsome Fire-place; the Ceiling carved, painted in Compartments, and the Remainder enriched with gilt Stucco-Ornaments; the Walls enriched in the same Manner; the best painted Windows I ever saw: the Monument to his Father, Mother, and Brothers, cost, he said, 2000*l.* the middle Aisle rendered comfortable by Iron Stoves, in the Shape of Urns; the Organ perfectly neat, and good, in Proportion to its Size: and to this Chapel you are led through a Gallery of Paintings seventy Feet long—And what would you more? You'll say, a good Sermon—I really think his Parson is able to preach one.

And now I come, lastly, to speak of your Letter I received on Monday. What an uncommon Man you are! to take so much Thought for *those* who never took *any* for themselves! —— I have enquired after Mr. WEDDERBURNE, and it seems he is a very clever and a very rising Lawyer;[2] to whom I am the more obliged for mentioning me, as I fear I have not the Honour of being the least known to him.

Pray write to me as soon as possible, and I will make you Amends (if *Writing* will make Amends) for the scandalous *Omissions* of which I have been guilty. I have somewhat to tell you of Lord L[yttelton['s usual *great Kindness*, when the Lords D[artmouth?] and W[ard?] were last at *Hagley*; but I have not Time, and must conclude, my dearest, worthiest Friend!

your ever obliged

W. SHENSTONE.

NOTES

[1]Henry Flitcroft (1697–1769). Walpole, *Anecdotes of Painting*, III, 62, mentions in an insignificant note, that Flitcroft was much in demand at this time and that the entire rebuilding of Woburn Abbey was from his designs.

[2]Alexander Wedderburn (1733–1805), afterwards Lord Chancellor of Edinburgh, was at this time at the beginning of his successful career, having been called to the Bar in 1757.

CCCIII

Works III, 388.

To MR. JAGO.

1762.

My dear friend,

A thousand thanks to you for the very obliging and humorous Poem which you are so kind to send me. I really think it very ingenious, and, upon the whole, extremely correct; although I have taken the liberty of proposing one or two hints for farther improvement. The relation that it bears to me and my place *may* tend to prejudice my *judgement*; but I cannot conceive that it requires aught beside *impartiality*, to relish the beauties of this Poem. I beg I may receive a fair copy in your own hand, as soon as possible; and I will consider, in the mean time, how to shew it to the publick in the most advantageous manner. It certainly does me *honour*: as things are at present circumstanced, it may *tend* to do me *good*; which I am very sure you would be glad to see. I am a little ashamed to be so much behind-hand with you, in favours of *this* and *other* kinds: but I live in hopes there may come a day, when I shall find occasion to express my gratitude. The pictures you sent arrived safe on Thursday; and have been since cleaned, and put up in their places. I cannot enter upon this subject now; finding it almost six o'clock at night, and having just received a letter from Mr. Dodsley which he requires me to answer by return of post. It relates to the *scheme* mentioned in his last, which is intended for my emolument; but which I must not expect to succeed, without considerable mortification. This *inter nos.*—You must by no means lay aside the thoughts of perfecting *Edge-hill*, at your leisure. It is possible that, in order to keep clear of flattery, I have said less in its favour than I really *ought*—but I never considered it otherwise than as a Poem which it was very adviseable for you to compleat and *finish*. I am now to desire my best respects to Mrs. Jago, and to bid you an affectionate adieu.

'Tu comes antiquus! tu primis junctus ab annis!'

I am, my dear friend! ever yours, with the truest esteem,

W. SHENSTONE.

Dec. 18, 1762.

CCCIV

Works III, 390.

To SHERRINGTON DAVENPORT, ESQ;

THE LEASOWES,
Jan. 4, 1763.

Dear Sir,

Mr. G[raves] tells me, that you have done me the honour to lay some stress upon receiving a letter from me. Alas! it must be owing purely to your benevolence, which makes you wish to hear of an absent friend, and not to any expectations you can reasonably form of entertainment from his pen. The long letter with which you favoured me was so very lively as well as ingenious, that I despaired of drawing from my fountains the vivacity you do from the Bath waters. But, be this as it will, the vein of friendship that runs through your letter demands my amplest acknowledgements; and if you will accept of *such* returns, I promise they will be as *hearty* as they are *insipid*.

I agree with you, that the first sallies of imagination will generally prove the most sprightly; and that they will often comprehend the principal features of a subject. They are of the nature of dead-colouring in a portrait; which one sometimes thinks more spirited than the same performance when finished. And yet a *good* painter will not *hurt* a portrait by the subsequent labour he bestows upon it, nor will a *good* writer injure his piece by the pains he takes to round and perfect it. It must be some defect in the taste of either that makes his diligence detrimental, or gives occasion for a stander by to cry out 'Manum de tabula.'[1] I believe it will appear upon examination, that works which cost most labour have generally been thought the easiest and pleased the *longest*. One cannot, however, deny that there is a sort of persons formed by nature for *shooting-flying* (which, by the way, I could never *do*), and that their sallies of imagination are what they can hardly improve by any future pains. These may be called men of wit and fire, but it is the union of taste with these that constitutes fine writing. True taste will never stiffen or over-charge any performance: it will rather be employed to smooth, simplify, and give that ease on which *grace* depends. One can as little deny that there are *kinds* of writing which have a better chance than others to succeed without much labour, which start forth mature at *first*, as Pallas did from the brain of Jupiter. Works of *humour* are often of this sort; and there are many instances in Butler's Hudibras. Yet I think the humour of *Swift* was greatly owing to a judicious *revisal*.—Pardon me, my dear friend, for this tedious discussion, which you little thought of bringing upon yourself by the obliging hint you gave concerning those verses upon Venus. I do acknowledge that an additional stanza there, containing a reflexion on Chinese architecture, were better laid aside. It seemed to me one of the 'splendida peccata.' that might be a little *popular* at this *time;* and has, therefore, for this season, appeared on a board by the side of the Venus. We, who cannot erect fresh temples, or even add a new garden-seat every spring, are obliged to make the most we can of a new and tolerable copy of verses, that cost us *thought* instead of *money;* and even at a pinch to piece out a dull scene with duller poetry: how else could I keep my place in countenance, so near the pompous piles of Hagley? And yet there are few *fashionable* visitants that do not shew an *affection* for the little Amoret, as much as they admire the stately Sacharissa—'plerumque gratæ *divitibus vices.*'² I have often considered why those possessed of palaces yet esteem a root-house or a cottage as a desirable object in their gardens.—Is it not from having experienced the imperfection of happiness in higher life, that they are led to *conceive* it more compleat beneath a roof of straw; where, perhaps, it may really be as defective as in the apartments of a King or a Minister?—A thousand thanks to you and Mrs. Davenport for the accommodations you so kindly offer me. Experience will no more suffer me to question the *cordiality* than the politeness of your reception. What an amusing picture have you given of Bath! pleasures carried to the utmost height, and opiates ready when one is cloyed with pleasures! And yet let me confess a truth, you have *lightly* touched upon those *very* articles which would prove to me the most *specifically* pleasing. For can any temptation be stronger, than to say that *you* reside there? and does not my friend G[raves] reside at Claverton, of whose genius and friendship I have had proofs these twenty years past? and have you not Mr. Webb, and now Mr. Melmoth, to make Bath *enviable* for the residence of literature? what a joy would it afford me to go on a party with you to Percefield, whither Mr. and Mrs. Morrice gave me the most pressing invitations!—These surely are pleasures of which—I *hope* one day to partake.

My health, generally bad in winter and spring, has hitherto been tolerable. The *influenza* of last spring continued to depress me half the summer. Would you think the verses I inclosed were written on that occasion by a young journeyman shoemaker; and one that lives at the village of Rowley, near me?

He considered my disorder in somewhat too *grave* a light, as I did not think my life endangered by it;[3] but, allowing for this, and the *partiality* he shews *me*, you will think the lines pretty extraordinary for one of *his occupation*.[4] They are not, however, the *only*, or perhaps, the *chief* specimens of his genius; and yet, before he came to me, his principal knowledge was drawn from *Magazines*. For these two or three years past, I have lent him Classics, and other books in English. You see, to *him*, I am a great Mæcenas; although you and my friend expect me to become an author by subscription.—On this head I will say no more at *present*, than that I am infinitely obliged by your extreme friendly offers. My friend G[raves], who knows my sentiments, has sometimes the honour of waiting upon you; I ought not, therefore, after this tedious epistle, to begin to trouble you with a written explanation of them. Believe me, dear Sir, with my most respectful compliments to Mrs. Davenport,

Your ever obliged

and most obedient servant,

W. SHENSTONE.

I will send you some other of Woodhouse's verses, when I can get him to transcribe them.

NOTES

[1]Proverb: Cic., *Fam.*, VII, 25, 1.

[2]Horace, *Odes*, III, 29, 13.

[3]James Woodhouse (1735–1820). Shenstone, *Works* II, 337. To *William Shenstone, Esq.; in his sickness. By Mr. Woodhouse.* 'Ye flow'ry plains, ye breezy woods.'

[4]Woodhouse was "a journeyman shoemaker." 'His encouragement of the ingenious Woodhouse, chiefly recommended him to that munificent patroness of indigent merit, Mrs. M-nt-gue, who placed him in a situation, where he had leisure to gratify his taste for literary pursuits.'—*Recollection*, 158.

CCCV

Works III, 395.

To MR. JAGO.

THE LEASOWES,

Jan. 4, 1763.

Dear Mr. Jago,

My last letter must have been confused, and the arrival of it, I fear, uncertain.

The hare and birds in one of the pictures which you sent me, I think, are well. The other parts of it indifferent. The greyhound worst of all. The portrait is by no means equal to its companion, either in beauty of the person, or skill of the painter; yet it matches so well with the other, that I find my parlour very much embellished by it. Pardon the freedom with which I criticise your present; and accept once more my very thankful acknowledgements.

I am truly glad to find so worthy a Nobleman, and so warm a friend of yours, as my Lord Willoughby is, made a Lord of the Bed-chamber.

I have heard nothing since I wrote last in regard to *my* affair; though I expect to do so every day. I have such a tribe of humours and peculiarities, that it is easier to make me rich than to make me happy; and ten to one that the favour will not be conferred without disgusting some of these said humours, &c. However, one must make the best of it; and reflect, that mortifications in one place may preclude mortifications in another.

I go to-morrow, by appointment, to Enville; where I may probably stay till Saturday. I have wished most heartily for a copy of your Fable to take with me; but Dodsley has not yet returned that I sent him. Pray consider my proposed alterations rather as hints than real improvements, and let me have a copy as soon as you can. I wrote my criticism over twice, and know not whether I sent the best or the worst copy; so I send the other, though perhaps much the same. I forgot to particularize many shining parts in your little Fable, that are either elegant or humourous: of the former sort, nothing could be happier than what you say about H[agley]; as it touches in the *gentlest* manner, on a possible truth, which, if expressed rather than implied, might not be altogether inoffensive. This beauty is produced by substituting H[agley] instead of L[yttelton], the place instead of the proprietor.

I have lately read 'The Death of Abel.' It is not void of merit; but might have been made much more pathetic by a more simple and prosaic style.

I desire my best respects to Mrs. Jago and your family.—
May not I see you here this Christmas? as I wish to do, be-

cause it is the season present; and not that I am not at all times and at all seasons most unfeignedly glad to wait upon you, and most affectionately your ever faithful servant:

'Tecum etenim longos memini consumere soles,
'Et tecum primas epulis decerpere noctes.
'Unum opus, & requiem pariter disponimus ambo, &c.'[1]

Your kind remembrance of me in your Edge-hill has brought these quotations into my head.[2] Adieu!

W. SHENSTONE.

NOTES

[1]Persius Flaccus, V, 43.
[2]Speaking of early school-days at Solihull, Jago writes, *Edge-Hill*, III:

'Nor can the Muse, while she these scenes surveys,
Forget her Shenstone, in the youthful toil
Associate; whose bright dawn of genius oft
Smooth'd my incondite verse; whose friendly voice
Call'd me from giddy sports to follow him
Intent on better themes—call'd me to taste
The charms of British song, etc.'

CCCVI

Works III, 397.

To the [REV. R. JAGO.]

Jan. 11, 1763.

My good friend,

I am suspicious that my letters (of which I have sent two) do not reach you by the way of Warwick. This is meant as an experiment whether they will arrive by way of Southam. It is meant withall to remind you of perfecting your little Fable, and dispatching it to me as soon as may be. I would fain transmit a copy to Lord S[tamford]'s, before the family separates, or leaves Enville; by whom, I am sure, it would be admired.

I am just returned from a visit which I made there, of four or five days passed very happily. At coming away, I shewed my Lord two or three of Mr. D[odsley]'s last letters, which laid open to him the scheme that was carrying on for me. I requested also, if there should be occasion (which there possibly might *not*) that he would allow me the honour of being known to him. He said, 'he was glad to find what was going forward; and had long wished to see something of that sort begun before: that he should be in town, I think, in February; and would do me any service in his power. He desired me also to acquaint Mr. D[odsley] (in allusion to the latter's uncertainty about my Lord's political connexions) that he thought it the duty of every honest man to support the present Government; and that he should continue his regard for the Minister, so long as he saw nothing in his measures that was prejudicial to his Country.'

I know that you will take a friendly part in any good that may befall me. Pray write, be it ever so carelessly; and believe me ever yours and Mrs. Jago's most affectionate and faithful

W.S.[1]

NOTE

[1]Dodsley adds the following note: 'The writer survived the date of this letter but a short time, his death happening on the eleventh of the following month, to the inexpressible grief of his more intimate friends, and the generous concern of those, who, too late acquainted with his merit, were indulging themselves in the pleasing thought of having provided for his future ease, and tranquil enjoyment of life.'

CCCVII

B.M. Add. MSS. 28221.
Hecht, 90.

[*To* THOMAS PERCY.]

Jan. 16, 1763.

Mr Shenstone's compts to Mr & Mrs Percy.—I received your Packet at Enville; and, if I pay my respects to Ld Ward before he go to London, it must be the Beginning of this week —So that I cannot possibly return an answer to yr Letter, just at present—When I can, I will—Mean time yr Books are arrived from Sketchley's; & I have just *dipt* into every *one* of them. The Frost is too severe for me to use Exercise, & I am quite pampered with Snipes & Fieldfare—At ye same time, my mind starves, & I hunger more for a sixpenny Pamphlet, yn I do for ye freshest Barrel of Oysters. The wit of ye times is to be found in Party-books; & I profess *no* Party, but *moderation*. This I take to be both Ld Bute's & the King's, and for this reason, if I am *warm* on any side, it is on *Their's*.[1]

  To
    Mr Percy.

NOTE

[1]Note in MS.: 'The excellent Writer of this letter died 11th February, following, Universally lamented.'

APPENDIX I

[Six unpublished letters from W.S. to Mr. James Prattinton, in the possession of the Society of Antiquaries.]

I

THE LEASOWES, *July* 1.

Dear Sir,

I have this Moment receiv'd
ligence of Miss Lea's marriage to Mr. Br[1]
which I sincerely give you Joy—Mrs. R.
extreme sollicitous that you should en
no Doubts of her Fidelity; &, as I am
perfectly convinc'd of it, I trust I
no difficulty in recommending her to y
Admiral Smith appears greatly incens'd,
an express refusal of his Consent to Bri
swore to Mrs. Rock that He never *should*
it. As to some other Persons concern'd
have long known my Opinion, & will now be
able to fix your own— It is a Pleasure to
me to reflect that both I and all my Friends
deavour'd to serve you, while your *Success*
desireable: And believe me it is *now* with
truth, that I congratulate you on your
as well as upon the singular Honour
sity with which you have behav'd
—whole affair—Mrs Southwill & Mrs.
desire Compliments, & I am with my
—spects to y[r] Father, Brother, & Mr. Cheek,
　　　　　　Sir,
　　　　　　　　Your most obedient Serv[t]
　　　　　　　　WILL: SHENSTONE.

NOTE

[1]Elizabeth Lea, sister of Lord Dudley, married, on July 14, 1759, the Rev. Benjamin Briscoe. There is in the Hagley collection a letter from Briscoe, dated July 19, 1759, to Sir George Lyttelton, who with Charles Lyttelton was co-guardian of Elizabeth Lea, asking for his approval of the marriage. Wyndham, II, 137.

II

I desire my hearty Thanks to Mr. Prattinton for his very obliging Present; and my best Respects to his Father, Brother, & Mr. Cheeke. I'm sure I've great Reason to think well of a Garden so liberal as that of my worthy Friend, & wish I had any thing in mine, that might induce him to favor me with his Company.

WILL; SHENSTONE.

The Leasowes,
    August ye 19, 1759.
To
    Mr. J. Prattinton,
        in Bewdley.

III

THE LEASOWES. *May* 22, 1760.

My best Compliments to Mr. Prattelton's Family, wth many thanks for their obliging Invitation; which, I fear, it will not be in my power to accept—I have agreed with Miss Wight to take half her white Lead & oil, wch I desire may be charg'd to me accordingly—I must also beg Mr. Prattelton to send me, by ye First Conveyance, a Quarter Vessel of ye same Raisin-Wine which he sent to Mr. Uylton; & Let me know, if at any time he sees a boat y^t he thinks would suit me, somewhat in y^e *Form* & ye Dimensions. I am much oblig'd to Mr. Prattelton sen^r for ye assistance he Lent me in regard to the Tiles; & shall be glad at all times to shew him at the Leasowes my sense of ye Civilities I receiv'd at Bewdley Pray my Service to Mr. Cheek—and also to Mr. Best.

WILL: SHENSTONE.

To Mr. Prattelton, Merchant,
    in Bewdley.

IV

Dr Sir

I have receiv'd from Mr. Best the obliging offer of any of his Curiosities I chuse to accept. Indeed I believe he has collected many, y^t few People could *relish* more than myself. But you know my slender *Pretensions* to any favors of this kind. It is to *you* I am indebted for my short Interview with that Gentleman; & it is *you* who must convey my acknowledgments, & also instruct me what I may, or may not, accept with Propriety.

I hope when my Pool is finish'd to pay my respects to you all, at Bewdley. Mean-time, I have your Picture at the Leasowes, ready to be sent wherever you order it. I have moreover ye pleasure of acquainting you, that it is one of the *best* y^t Alcock has done; The Drapery well fanc'd & well perform'd; & the Head, in a better *style* of Painting y^n what I have seen of his heretofore. I yesterday receiv'd a Head of Mr. Dodsley, by Reynolds; which cost him at least 10 Guineas, and is in point of colouring, much inferior. Be so good as make Compliments to y^r Family, & believe me to be very faithfully yours

WILL: SHENSTONE.

The Leasowes, *July* 20, 1760.

Could you (without offence) procure me any Little List of what Mr. Best chuses to part with?

To Mr. J. Prattenton,
  at Bewdley.

V

Monday, near 10.

The Compliments of to-day's Party wait on Mr. Prattenton. We purpos'd to have been at Bewdley, before *One*—But Lady's Tempers are a Little various, & sometimes wholly incomprehensible; as Mr. Prattenton well knoweth —— Some Difficulties from that Quarter have made it impossible for us to reach Bewdley before Four o'clock, when we shall arrive in two or three Post Chaises. &c:

W. SHENSTONE.

July 29, 1760.

VI

THE LEASOWES, *Aug.* 12, 1762.

I desire my best respects to Mr. Prattenton, and to his Father & Brother—I would beg the Favour of Mr. Prattenton to send me, by y^e *First* opportunity, half a Hundred of white-Lead ground, with a proper Quantity of Linseed oil to mix with it.

I was much out of order all ye time I made my visit to Mr. Knight's; or I should have been tempted to make an Excursion to Bewdley, as well as Kidderminster. Mr. Dodsley desires Compt^s to ye Mr. Prattentons, & to Mr. Cheek & good Mr. Best. Should Mr. Prattenton sen^r have it in his Power to favour me wth a Little Fruit, it would prove very acceptable.

W. SHENSTONE.

To Mr. James Prattenton,
            at Bewdley.

APPENDIX II

'Shenstone's Billets'

In the Harvard College Library (Percy MSS., Folder 273) there is a number of pages of manuscript, bearing on the outside the words, 'Shenstone's Billets.' This material consists of lists of ballads, sent by Shenstone to Percy, at the time when the latter was preparing to publish the *Reliques*, together with critical comments of considerable interest and characteristic marks of approbation for individual ballads. Undoubtedly, as Mr. Irving L. Churchill pointed out (P.M.L.A., 1937, p. 114), the 'billets' were originally 'an integral part of the Percy-Shenstone correspondence,' but, as they are undated, it is not easy to place them 'in their proper places in the sequence of letters that passed between the two men.' Nevertheless, the second missive was obviously sent to Percy in answer to his letter to Shenstone of May 22, 1761, Letter XXIV in Dr. Hans Hecht's edition. Billet 3, moreover, was sent before the letter to Percy, of July 5, 1761.

The lists are in eight groups, numbered 2 to 9, so it would seem that 1 is missing.

2. From the old Collection of Ballads in 3 vols., printed 1727, 1726, 1738.

Vol. I. #

Pag

18	Queen Eleanor.	108	Chevy-chase.
37	Moore of Moore-hall.	120	Dukes of Hereford & Norfolk.*

64 Robin Hood.
Robin Hood.
Robin Hood.
Robin Hood.

{ Many of R. Hood's ball: are in yᵉ true ballad-stile; and only deficient in their moral: which, however, is of a mixt nature.

221 Children in the Wood.
249 Lord Thomas & fair Eleanor.
53 First Part of yᵉ King & yᵉ Miller.

271 Gilderoy
275 Bonny Dundee

{ agreeable Ballads, particularly the Last, if their Moral do not exclude them.

Vol. II.

Pag

8 King Leir.*	182 Roger's Delight.
49 King John & the Abbot.	191 Spanish Lady.
173 Wife of Bath.	202 Blind Beggar.

*More historical y^n poetical.

Vol. III.

189 Time's Alteration.	233 Fiddle—perhaps too modern
178 The baffled Knight.	&c.
218 William and Margarett.	249 Slighted Nancy.
230 Broom of Cowdenknows.	

Vol. I. ‡

Pag

1 The unfortunate Concubine.	159 Andrew Barton.
23 St. George & the Dragon.	170 Johnny Armstrong.
28 Seven Champions.	199 London Prentice.
43 King Alfred.	211 Northern Ditty.
53 Second part of King &	227 Devonshire Nymph.
Miller. +	231 Bride's Burial.
130 Sir Richard Whittington.	244 Lady's Fall.
145 Jane Shore.	252 Patient Grissel.

Vol. II.

21 Launcelot—poor, but may-be curious.	152 The Black-moore. cold Narr: of a moving story.
34 Godina. flat narrative.	195 Margaritta—in Cowley's
39 Robin Hood & the Bishop.	works.
44 Allen a Dale.	212 Jolly Roger.
121 Robin Hood.	220 James & Susan.
125 A Wedding. perhaps too modern.	222 Sawney & Teague.
133 Swimming Lady. D^o	224 Dialogue.
137 Wife suckling her Father.	230 An old woman clothed &c.
145 Alphonso, very cold Narrative.	235 Crafty Lawyer.

Vol. III.

148 Sack.	243 Bessy, Bell & Mary Gray.
229 Ïo or the Metamorphosis.	247 Scornfu Nansy.
241 Lass of Peaties Mill.	253 Bush aboon Traquair.

I have made only two Distinctions of First (#) and second (#) Merit, tho' 'tis obvious yᵗ *each* Class would admit of farther Discrimination. I think yᵉ *former* may be safely admitted; and if you do not find a sufficient number of Ballads that are *preferable* to the Latter, I would have you select what you think the *best* of them. The remainder of this Collection, that appears in *neither* of these Classes, I am well convinced, ought to find no place in your intended publication. I am *rather* fearfull yᵗ. I have admitted too *many* into this class of second-rate Merit—But there are Many Ballads among these Last, that are *possest* of a kind of Fame which perhaps they Little *deserve*—And this notoriety will appear to some, a tolerable reason for their admission—For my *own* part, I think a dead song, I mean one yᵗ is not animated by the Least spark of Poetry, requires to be *buried*, as much as a dead Carcase. But if my opinion should be *singular*, you ought not to regard it.

⤶

Mere *Historical*, without *poetical* Merit, is not a sufficient recommendation. And there are many Pieces in this Collection that falsify history, almost in yᵉ same Degree that they discredit Poetry—written perhaps by the same rank of Men that produce our modern half-penny ballads— And for the writings of *Such*, even when they are most *true* to History, This old Collection I have been examining will be a suitable repository.

⤶

Robin Hood's Ballads (as *All* that we have concerning him are hardly worth insertion) perhaps were better divided, unless where they illustrate each other.

⤶

I think you have determined extremely right, as to rendering yᵉ Collection promiscuous, &c.

⤶

As to modern *Imitations* of old Ballads, I am also for ranging these promiscuously—I mean, *not* suffering them to follow Those of which they are Copies. I think this would have no good effect, whether you suppose them *better*, or *worse*, or *just as good*, as the originals.

⤶

I like 3 vols as well, or better than two, provided they can be furnished with *good* Materials—of which you cannot at *present* be well able to judge. Neither can you so well know what to *admit* till you know the Number of pieces yᵗ will offer——

⤶

I am glad you have agreed wᵗʰ Mʳ Dodsley.

⤶

As to a Glossary, if you admit very many of the Scotch Songs, you will find it either necessary to compose one, or to deface y^r Margin by numerous explanations; in which case, I should prefer y^e *former*. They have *many* ballads of *second* merit and *first* reputation—Perhaps you had better admit none whose language requires much explanation, except it be Those of *First*-rate merit. And indeed they have some truly Fine ones.

∽

I rather chuse to *prefix* what is requisite to make ye ballad *understood* or *interesting*, y^n to add it by way of Note at Bottom. But you should make Brevity, a Point here; and add no more y^n what Contributes to one or other of these Purposes.

∽

I think you right in admitting what I call *Songs*, as well as *Ballads*: And y^t it is not ye Chief Merit of either, Merely to record Facts, or gratify Curiosity.

∽

I cannot readily propose any thing for Frontispieces, y^t will not be trite. 2. Would not a few Top and Tail-pieces in each Vol. give the work a more elegant appearance—? Mottos also, should be new and striking, or had better be quite omitted. I will think farther on these Heads.

My best respects to Mr Johnson, whom I rather *wish* y^n *hope* to see here.

∽

I will select some more Ballads for your Insertion in a Little time, and direct them to you, as usual—Mean time I should be very glad if you would give me a Line before you leave ye Town.

W.S.

I perused this old Collection a 2^d time, since I rec^d y^r last Letters.

3. From the tea-table Miscellany, published by Allan Ramsay—Chiefly *Ballads*.

120	Lady Ann Bothwell	⧣	170	O Waly Waly		⧣
221	The Braes of Yarrow	⧣	56	My Jo Janet		+
267	Pretty Parrot say	⧣	58	Auld Rob Morrice		⧣
324	Sweet Williams Ghost	⧣	61	The young Laird		⧣
343	Barbara Allen	⧣	62	Mary Scott		⧣
409	Ld Henry & Catherine	⧣	65	Polwarth on the Green		⧣
38	A Lovely Lass to a Friar	⧣	70	Jockey said to Jenny		⧣
53	Bessy Bell	⧣	75	Patie & Peggy		⧣

78	Gaberlunzie Man .	‡
85	High-land Laddie .	‡
90	This is nae mine ain &c.	‡
97	The Malt Man . .	‡
100	The ault Wife . .	‡
105	Take your auld Cloak .	‡
125	John Ochiltree . .	+
166	Rob's Jock . .	‡
177	Jenny Nettles . .	+
230	All in yᵉ Downs .	‡‡
236	Of all the girls yᵗ are .	‡
237	Would ye have a .	‡
242	Desparing besides a .	‡‡
244	'Twas when yᵉ Seas were	‡‡
261	Since times are so bad .	‡
266	Of all Comforts &c. .	‡
278	When Cloë we ply .	‡
279	One long Whitsun holid:	‡
283	A trifling Song . .	‡
285	Some say Women are .	‡
289	Diogenes surly . .	‡‡
291	Down among yᵉ dead men . . .	‡
292	He yᵗ will not merry be	‡‡
297	Ill sail upon yᵉ Dog-star	‡
297	James & Susan . .	‡
304	Shall I wasting in &c. .	‡
303	Hark how yᵉ trumpet .	‡
321	Rare Willy drowned .	‡
322	The Miller . .	‡
326	As musing I ranged .	‡
327	Did ever Swain a Nymph	‡
229	By the side of &c. .	‡
333	Watty & Madge . .	‡

332	Come Neighbours now &c. . . .	‡
340	Bellaspelling . .	‡
349	Leinster famed for Maidens . . .	‡‡
354	All in yᵉ downs &c. .	‡
355	A Cobler there was .	‡
356	Ye highlands &c. .	‡
357	When I was a young man . . .	‡
360	When my Locks are &c.	‡
439	Nurse's Song . .	‡
441	The Mag-pie . .	‡
368	Sweet Nelly my &c. .	‡
370	Young Roger came .	‡
378	Tarry woo . .	‡
379	Young Roger of yᵉ M.	‡
384	Dear Chloe . .	‡
390	As tipling John . .	‡
393	The sweet rosy Morn: .	‡
402	What tho' they call &c.	‡
413	Let's drink &c. . .	‡
427	Johnny Faa . .	‡
428	Old Chiron . .	‡
431	As Dolly was . .	‡
432	What woman could do &c. . . .	‡
26	The Meal was dear .	‡
6	Let's be jovial . .	‡
40	Lass of Peatie's Mill .	‡
169	what tho' they call me &c.	‡
47	Ye shepherds & Nymphs	‡
54	I'll never leave thee .	‡
247	Alexis shund his . .	‡

I find myself liable to be prejudiced in favor of words by a remembrance of yᵉ tune annexed to 'em; which I presume may be yᵉ Case with others——

I have The Hive in 3 vols, and another Collection of Songs in two—I will examine them in yᵉ manner I've done the former, if Mʳ Percy think it will have any tendency towards regulating his Decisions, or shortening his Labour——

From the same; chiefly elegant Songs, but perhaps too modern, or found too often in other Collections; both of which are arguments for their exclusion, where not ballanced by their merit.

P.

4	Tweed-side	#	280	One April Morn	#
36	Tell me, tell me &c.	} #	282	Selinda sure's &c.	#
36	The reply		289	Blest as the imortal	#
110	Lochaber	#	392	My Goddess Lydia	#
32	Love inviting reason	#	305	Fair Amoret	#
102	My dear & only Love	#	300	Awake thou fairest &c.	#
119	It was the charming	#	314	We all to conquering &c.	#
124	If Love's a sweet Passion	#	365	Fluttering spread thy &c.	
139	The Sun was sunk beneath	#	448	My Love was fickle	#
144	Cowdenknows	#	370	When thy beauty app^{rs}	#
146	Now Spring	#	375	Little Syren of y^e	#
227	While I fondly view	#	392	The Nymph y^t undoes me	#
229	My Days have been so &c.	#	395	The sun was sunk	#
231	Sweet are the Charms	#	396	When Delia	#
235	Stella & Flavia	#	399	False tho she be	#
245	Remember Damon &c.	#	403	You meaner beauties	#
246	On a bank beside a &c.	#	415	Why will Florella &c.	#
254	I'll range around the &c.	#	416	If Phyllis deny me &c.	#
255	Tho' cruel you seem to	#	318	Birks of Indermay	#
256	Rosy bowers	#		By Mr Mallet [in Percy's handwriting]	
257	{ O Lead me to some	#	335	When the bright God of &c.	#
	{ See see she wakes	#			
270	O the charming month of	#	336	Were not my Heart	#
272	In this grove my	#	401	Dear Colin prevent	#
273	A Quire of bright &c.	#		The Answer	#
274	As I saw fair Chlora	#			
274	Ye Beaux	#			

The distinction here betwixt *songs* and *Ballads* is by no means accurate; but may serve to afford some sort of *Hint* to Mr Percy.

It may be proper to peruse ye same ballad &c. in different collections, in order to select ye best readings.

As I presume Mr Percy will call his, 'a Collection of old Ballads,' Those Songs or Ballads y^t have antiquity on their side, and that best answer y^e *Idea* of a *Ballad*, should, cæteris paribus, be prefer'd.

These being ye general rules there may be some deviations permitted in favor of superiour Merit.

The circumstance of being too *common* in *other* Collections should be an argument for their exclusion in Mr Percys; yet not so as to exclude Ballads of equal Merit to Chevy-Chase, and some few others.

I do not imagine Mr P. will admit a tenth part of what are marked here; Many will be rejected for their modernism, or appearing too oft in other Collections. yet there are some *very good* Modern ones, in the true old Ballad style, y^t will appear agreeably in his Collection. 'Leinster fam'd for.'

The Age of many, Mr P. will determine better yⁿ myself; who have *excluded* few or none upon y^t score. What I *have* excluded, will perhaps deserve little or no regard.

I shall be glad to see what Mr P. pitches upon before he sends them to ye Press; I shall be more glad to see him here, and to re-consider them in his Company.   W.S.

4.   The vocal Miscell: 2^d edit:, London 1734.
Page

Page				Page		
1	Sweet if you love	.	+	20	Cupid God of .	⧺
2	I'll tell you a story	.	+	20	Twas in ye Land of	⧺
3	Gently stir	.	⧺	27	When Fanny Blooming	⧺
4	Woud Fate to me	.	+	28	From good Liquor	+
4	With an honest .	.	⧺	28	In spite of Love .	+
5	As Celia near a .	.	+	30	My Goddess Celia	⧺
5	How pleasant a .	.	⧺	31	By ye side of a glim:	⧺
6	I am a jolly bowler	.	+	34	Once I lovd a Char^g	+
9	Phyllis as her wine	.	⧺	34	What care I for .	⧺
9	In Tyburn road .	.	⧺	36	Twas when ye seas	⧺
12	Jolly mortals	.	⧺	37	Hear me ye Nymphs	⧺
12	What tho Heir is	.	+	38	Whilst ye town's &c. .	⧺
14	Trade's weary &c.	.	+	39	Ghosts of every .	⧺
16	That all men are .	.	+	39	Sweet are ye Charms	⧺
18	Bacchus must now	.	+	41	By ye side of a great	⧺

End of Vol. yᵉ I.

5.   Vocal Mis: Vol 2^d

Pag

Pag

Mr. Percy will run a great risque of printing some of these twice over; as they occur so in ye same Collection, and even volume. He will however obtain a good text by comparing 'em together——

6.   The Hive vol. the First.

Page

Page

Vol. II.

Vol. III.

7.

N.B. Here are several good *Mad* Songs, in this Collection—quere whether you woud throw 'em together!

N.B. Several Songs are printed twice over here, in different manners —It will be incumbent on you, in general, to select yᵉ *best readings of common songs.*

N.B. *Ballads* in general suit my Idea of yʳ Collection, better than *Songs.*

8.   From a Miscell: sent me by Mʳˢ Duff, from Scotland.

Hardyknute . .	#		⌠obscure
A scotch editⁿ of		Banishment of Poverty +	⎪and of
Chevy chace .	#	Battle of Harlaw . +#	⎨second
Gill Morrice . .	#	Ballat of reid Squair . +	⎪merit at
Young Waters . .	#		⌡most.
Edom of Gordon .	#		

The Miscell: called yᵉ Ever-green consists of scotch Songs &c so obscure in point of Language & orthography yᵗ I cannot pretend to examine them so critically as to fix their merit. 'Christ's kirk on yᵉ green' is famous. but I guess there are scarce any yᵗ exceed yᵉ merit of second-rates; which is perhap's ballanced by their obscurity.

9.   I see no songs in Ben Johnson that have the least pretensions, except yᵉ following—which will admit of hesitation.

   ╫   Cynthias revells. P. 228.

Thou more yⁿ most sweet Glove, &c. N.B.—(The last verse should not be divided into two lines.)

   ╫   Fox 489.

Come my Celia let us prove &c

   ╫   Silent Woman 432

Still to be neat &c

   +   The Forest 9.

Follow a Shadow

   ╫

The Hagg's stanzas thrown together.

I should be glad, once more, to receive a Copy of Adam Carr—Iv'e a mind to try my Hand again, at the Alterations of yᵉ Last part.

INDEX TO CONTENTS

In the case of letters to the principal correspondents reference is made only to the first page of each letter.